HOMELANDS AND WATERWAYS

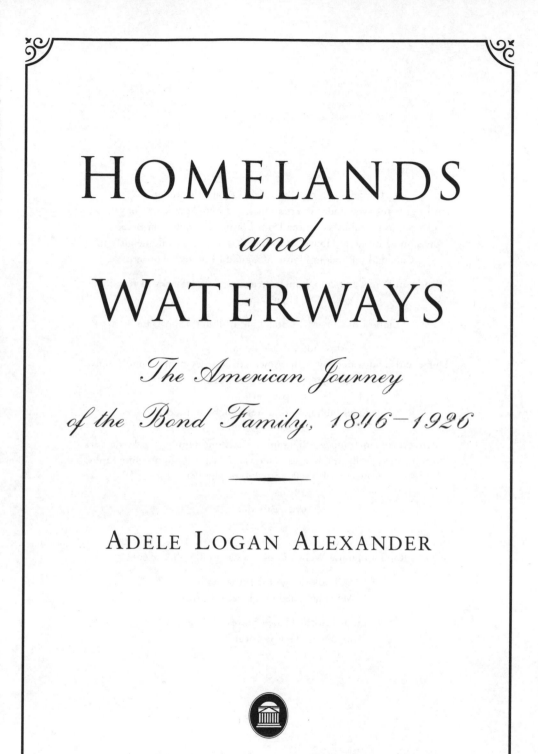

HOMELANDS
and
WATERWAYS

*The American Journey
of the Bond Family, 1846–1926*

ADELE LOGAN ALEXANDER

PANTHEON BOOKS · NEW YORK

Pantheon Books and colophon are registered trademarks of Random
House, Inc.

Library of Congress Cataloging-in-Publication Data

Alexander, Adele Logan, 1938–
Homelands and waterways : the American journey of the Bond family,
1846–1926 / Adele Logan Alexander.
p.   cm.
Includes bibliographical references and index.
ISBN 0-679-44228-6
1. Afro-American families—Biography.   2. Bond family.   3. Hyde Park
(Boston, Mass.)—Biography.   4. Tidewater (Va. : Region)—Biography.
5. Liverpool (England)—Biography.   I. Title.
E185.96.A47 1999
974.4'61—dc21
[B]   98-43775
CIP
Random House Web Address: www.randomhouse.com

Book design by Trina Stahl
Maps designed by Hazel Edwards

Printed in the United States of America
First Edition
2   4   6   8   9   7   5   3   1

For Jonah, Maya, and Solomon

ELIZA KELLY

(Liverpool, England) JOHN ROBERT BOND
1846 - 1905

JAMES BOND

JOHN CURRIE

(The Virginia Tidewater) EMMA THOMAS
1846 - 1926

-?- THOMAS
1826 - ?

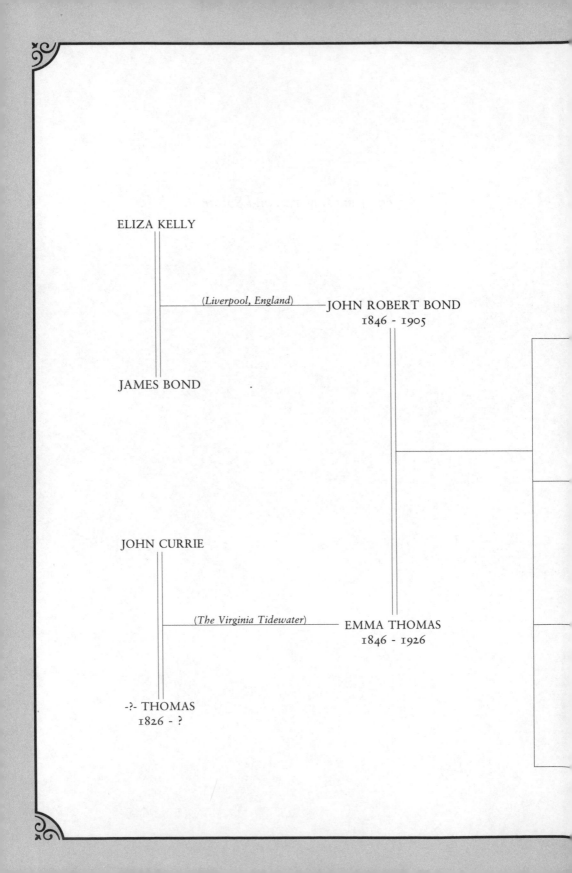

Family of EMMA THOMAS BOND *and* JOHN ROBERT BOND

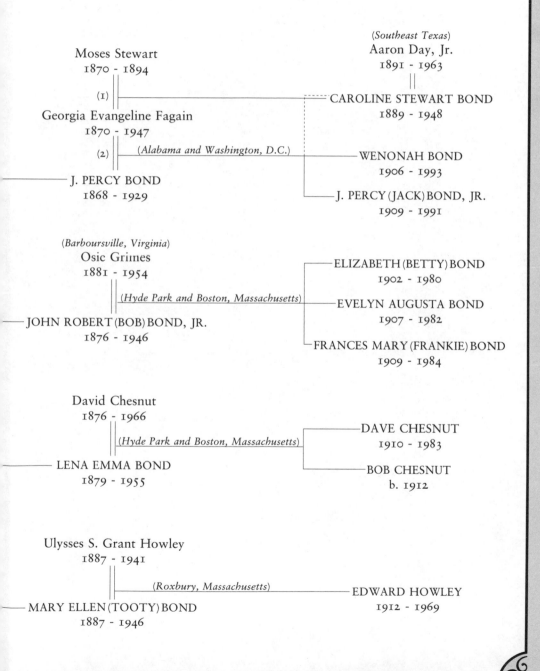

Moses Stewart
1870 - 1894

(1)

Georgia Evangeline Fagain
1870 - 1947

(2) *(Alabama and Washington, D.C.)*

J. PERCY BOND
1868 - 1929

(Southeast Texas)
Aaron Day, Jr.
1891 - 1963

CAROLINE STEWART BOND
1889 - 1948

WENONAH BOND
1906 - 1993

J. PERCY (JACK) BOND, JR.
1909 - 1991

(Barboursville, Virginia)
Osic Grimes
1881 - 1954

(Hyde Park and Boston, Massachusetts)

JOHN ROBERT (BOB) BOND, JR.
1876 - 1946

ELIZABETH (BETTY) BOND
1902 - 1980

EVELYN AUGUSTA BOND
1907 - 1982

FRANCES MARY (FRANKIE) BOND
1909 - 1984

David Chesnut
1876 - 1966

(Hyde Park and Boston, Massachusetts)

LENA EMMA BOND
1879 - 1955

DAVE CHESNUT
1910 - 1983

BOB CHESNUT
b. 1912

Ulysses S. Grant Howley
1887 - 1941

(Roxbury, Massachusetts)

MARY ELLEN (TOOTY) BOND
1887 - 1946

EDWARD HOWLEY
1912 - 1969

CONTENTS

———

Heritage: Groundwork and Waterscapes · 3

All the rivers run into the sea;
    yet the sea is not full:
unto the place from whence the rivers come,
    thither they return again.

ECCLESIASTES 1:7

HERITAGE: GROUNDWORK *and* WATERSCAPES

My mother reminisced often about her childhood, but for years I knew only four tales that pertained to John Robert Bond, my maternal great-grandfather. They concerned matters as diverse as his food preferences (potatoes, not rice), religious affiliation (staunch Episcopalian), and which newspaper he wanted to read (the *Guardian* of Boston).

The most significant story, however, seemed to explain, at least in part, how Bond became an American. He had been born and reared in England, the son of an Irishwoman and a man of African ancestry both of whom had arrived in the intriguing port of Liverpool by the mid-1800s. Because of his atypical parentage, Bond was an example of what might be considered a wholly improbable racial oxymoron. Virtually all of us have been taught, and therefore may take it as an immutable truism, that the British were (perhaps still are) by almost uncontested definition, Caucasians. But John was not one of those renowned, revered, and sometimes parodied "WASPs"—white Anglo-Saxon Protestants. Rather, as a rarely encountered and therefore hard-to-imagine *black* Anglo-Saxon Protestant, he inadvertently reconfigured that stereotype.[1]

My family's sketchy oral history maintained that as a youth, Liverpool's John Robert Bond crossed the Atlantic during the United States' Civil War, and the boat on which he sailed docked at a Massachusetts port. The unlikely British sailor then forsook his vessel and shipmates, and a few months later joined the Union navy. Despite white America's intermittent reluctance to allow Negroes into the military and enduring skepticism about their bravery, loyalty, and leadership capabilities, John served in the epic war to free the slaves. He saw battle and, ultimately, was severely wounded.[2]

Preconceived expectations and restricted categorical thinking, however, often overwhelm the most incontrovertible evidence to create their own reason-blind reality. And even as one of John Robert Bond's grandsons examined a snapshot of his ancestor's brown face—the photographic negative of a "true" English countenance—he insisted (despite visual proof to the contrary) that his British-born forebear had been a white man. The English, he knew, simply *were not Negroes.* Even his progenitor's dusky complexion in a very distinct portrait failed to convince the younger man that his Liverpool-born grandfather actually was (according to his landsmen's preferred spelling) "coloured."[3]

After the lucrative international slave trade that forcibly brought millions of Africans to the Americas had been outlawed in the early 1800s, but decades before Ellis Island became inundated with Europe's voluntary immigrants as the United States' major portal for the world's "homeless masses yearning to breathe free," John Robert Bond, like legions of white Europeans before and after him, hoped to embrace this nation as his own.[4] After the Civil War, he settled in Massachusetts, the state where he first had set foot on American soil, and in 1884 finally became a citizen by dint of his loyal service in the military forces of his chosen country and his longtime, law-abiding New England residency.

For the "average" male European at that time, acquiring his citizenship and becoming "Americanized" was not a very difficult proposition in a country that, for the most part, still cherished its immigrants. But legally, philosophically, socially and economically, it was a far more complex undertaking for a nonwhite person like Bond. Nonetheless, despite various complexities and barriers to his assimilation, he became a pillar of the community, voter, and juror in a town called Hyde Park, Massachusetts. For decades after the war, he periodically donned a uniform and led patriotic events sponsored by the Grand Army of the Republic, the organization of Civil War veterans who had fought to preserve the Union. Despite a serious battle injury, he worked as a janitor, constable, and lamp-lighter, but he never returned to England.

I grew up in New York City hearing abbreviated versions of those stories about my great-grandfather Bond, but until recently did not know that my favorite childhood song, *Keemo, Kimo,* a tongue-twisting nonsense ditty, also played a part in the many-dimensioned family legacy. Unlike the pop tunes, lullabies, Mother Goose and A. A. Milne verses that virtually every girl and boy of my age and era committed to memory, that song seemed uniquely mine. None of my colleagues (African American family friends and neighbors, or first-to-third-generation Jewish-European Americans at school) had heard it. I begged my mother to sing it with me, yet neither she nor I knew its origins.

When I finally asked her, my mother, who by then suffered from senile dementia, could not recall the first name of her Grand-mother Bond, whom she scarcely had known. Mother remembered only that in her own early years she had referred to her as "Grand-mother in Boston." I since have learned that she was born Emma Thomas, and also discovered that slaves in southeastern Virginia (and apparently there alone), where Emma had grown up, often sang *Keemo, Kimo.* She probably learned it in childhood and passed it on to her firstborn—my grandfather. Hence, it came to my mother, and then to me.[5]

My only photograph of Emma Thomas Bond shows her dressed in black, looking stern and withdrawn. But perhaps she had good reason to ration her smiles. She had been born in slavery, and by the time that snapshot was taken, she was an elderly Negro woman whose country barely granted her the full rights of citizenship.

Yet much like other migrants and immigrants of their own and other origins, Emma and John had uprooted themselves from their places of nativity and upbringing, and during the country's Reconstruction Era established significantly reordered lives in New England. I attempt here to resurrect them, to explain what their status as African American citizens meant for each of them: John Robert Bond, raised in England where men of his racial ancestry were few; Emma Thomas Bond, raised with many other slaves on a Lower Tidewater Virginia plantation.

Liverpool, John Robert Bond's place of birth, flourished in the eighteenth and nineteenth centuries, first as Europe's most important hub of the slave trade with the Western Hemisphere, then as its primary port of entry for America's plantation-grown cotton. But it also was a center for Britain's abolitionist activities, and the major point of debarkation for westward-bound emigrants from all of Europe. Concurrently with John's English upbringing, Emma Thomas's childhood on a Virginia plantation unfolded a few miles downriver from historic Jamestown, where, in 1619, the very first "negars" from Africa (involuntary immigrants, every one) had been put ashore in the British North American colonies.

More than two centuries later, during the Civil War, renegade blockade runners, mostly of British registry and greedy for profits, crisscrossed the Atlantic bound to and from southern ports. They carried illicit supplies that helped to sustain the secessionist Confederacy, desperately maintaining its citizens' right to own human chattel. And in 1864, John Robert Bond, serving with the Union navy, almost lost his life in an encounter with one of those hostile privateers.

The question rarely has been asked, but what might (or should) we make of the *voluntary* immigration and subsequent military service of a dark-complexioned British seafarer in the early 1860s when the vast majority of people of his race remained enslaved in the United States? Can a man such as John Robert Bond be granted any cultural legacy before he arrived here? If so, what sort of singular, contradictory, or skewed history would it have to be?[6] Certainly, when he came to these shores and for decades thereafter, most white Americans never doubted that John's "primitive blackness" (always identified with slaves and slavery) heavily outweighed, even negated, his otherwise "superior" English heritage.

This country's laws consistently reinforced the majority's attitudes about Negroes. Our first congresses passed statutes concerning naturalization that limited the privilege of becoming a citizen to free white men, but they *did not* exclude from that advantaged class the indigents, wastrels, convicts, and other unfortunate Caucasians who served indentures.[7] On the other hand, they *did* statutorily deny membership in the cherished body politic to Negroes (even those who had never been enslaved) like John Robert Bond, as well as to Native Americans, Asians, the world's "mixed races"—and women. The Supreme Court reinforced the inability of nonwhites to claim any rights of citizenship in 1857 with its infamous Dred Scott decision. Thus, in the United States, citizenship maintained a circumscribed, white racial identity. And into the 1900s, it remained a specifically male phenomenon as well. "Real" card-carrying Americans chose their country, but the country also, very selectively, chose them. Only after 1870 were men from Africa or others of African ancestry, like Bond, granted the right to become naturalized here. Meanwhile, most men of European descent habitually have stood together under the protection of the "free white" umbrella, and have continued to enjoy a historically grounded and privileged status—though anti-Semites, antipapists, and other similarly biased nativists sometimes have challenged (often effectively) that sense of entitlement.[8]

If the United States and its white male leaders granted John Bond and his slave-born wife Emma any recognizable, even multi-faceted, heritage of their own, it was one that had long been perceived by the majority as tainted, inferior, and less "civilized." Negroes (alternately "colored" people, blacks, or African Americans) have been seen as vital to white America in servile capacities, and have been lauded as entertainers—minstrels, clowns, and gladiators.[9] But what else, many still ask, that is positive and significant, have they contributed to the country? And, for this particular family, would those contributions have derived from its improbably oxymoronic "coloured" English progenitor, or from a black mother, who, because of her dark skin, authoritative mythology directs us to believe, could only have been "made in America"?—though in many ways she undeniably was as much an American as any native-born white person. These are disturbing questions, since where people of color are concerned, the shadowy past often has been kneaded into an undifferentiated mass, ignored and forgotten, deliberately obliterated or suppressed. There has been too little investigation, and scant respect for the myriad confluences of racial, ethnic, and cultural streams that have circled, flirted, and trifled with one another, disengaged, coalesced, then, sometimes uneasily, come together to constitute our country's heterogeneous twentieth-century population.

Although the United States' huge Negro minority never has been totally separate or polarized from the majority, it nonetheless incorporates a complex yet recognizable body of values and common culture. The great majority have thought, and continue to think, of themselves as Americans, and relatively few have professed (or acted on) a sustained desire to return permanently to their forebears' unfamiliar, transoceanic homelands.[10] And even prior to the Civil War, when those often dark-complexioned people were presumed to be chattel and had no acknowledged rights of citizenship, most of them already were no longer truly "Africans." They more accurately could be described as "black residents of the United States," but by reasonable standards had not yet become "African Americans," much less linguistically undifferentiated "Americans."[11]

This does not suggest that we diverse, multihued "black" people were or are monolithic or unshifting in our beliefs, in our demographic, social, economic, and genetic makeup, or in our use and sanction of the words with which we describe ourselves. Far from it. The nuances, stratifications, "colorations," differences of opinion, and ongoing metamorphoses within the African American community are central to our experience, and certainly to the Bonds' story.

Nonetheless, the disturbing reality that the lives, ideas, and contributions of powerful, affluent, educated white men inherently are deemed more significant and substantive, more worthy of recording than the experiences of anyone else, always remains close at hand. For me, this residual bias surfaced in reference to my great-grandmother, Emma Thomas Bond.

Only gradually did I come to see Emma as an intriguing woman who, though seemingly content with her life, was consistently denied the opportunities needed to reach her greatest potential. She had few financial assets and little authority outside her home. Emma never accomplished anything traditionally designated "of note," or worked with or for institutions that preserved records of her contributions. Winking slyly at Virginia's laws that denied slaves any education, her owners gave young Emma a rudimentary exposure to the ABCs. Still, she remained only minimally literate, and never kept a diary, composed sonnets, or even—when finally allowed to do so in 1920—voted. Yet she was not silent, though discovering and interpreting her muted voice has been difficult. She was a treasured wife, mother, grandmother, and comrade, as well as a fine seamstress, cook, and gardener. Emma Bond was also a memorable teller of stories, a singer of songs, an herbalist and medical practitioner lacking certification. But all too often, we have been persuaded that the lives of "invisible," "ordinary" women such as she are not meaningful or worthy of preservation and re-creation.

Toward the end of the American Civil War, John Robert Bond, a mulatto sailor from Liverpool serving with the Union navy, found himself looked upon as decreasingly English, increasingly black. In Virginia, he met and married a former slave named Emma Thomas. They migrated north, settled down, bought a home, and raised their children in a town that included few Negroes or southerners, but many long-time Yankees plus a plethora of European newcomers. John was propertyless when he and Emma met, and only recently a family of white Virginians had considered her their lawful property; but in Massachusetts the Bonds became property owners. By the banks of an old millstream they found no land of milk and honey, yet stitched and patched together a satisfactory new life for themselves and their kin.

No person crosses the same river twice, claims an old maxim, and the very real characters in this tale wade through many, changing streams. The Bonds' story moves from the mid-nineteenth century—via immigration and migration, slavery and emancipation; Reconstruction, reinvigorated white supremacy and segregation; the advent of telephones, automobiles, and motion pictures; by way of natural and man-made disasters; three wars; births, marriages, illness, and deaths—through eight decades. And a number of other families became intertwined in the intricate tapestry of this story that attempts to evoke, recall, and record some of the irregular-edged pieces in the days and years of John and Emma, their offspring and spouses, and finally, the early decades of those children's children's lives.

My mother's myriad tales of her youth included remembrances of a conservative Papa and an often exasperating Mama; sibling devotion and strife; the delights and obligations of friendship; attendance to weighty responsibilities contrasted with delicious frivolity; accommodations to and circumlocutions around the color line in a great and supposedly egalitarian country besmirched by intolerance and segregation. But concerning her grandparents John and Emma Bond, only a few incomplete anecdotes survived.

Nonetheless, this is the true story of an authentic American family. In all societies, families (regardless of how they are defined or structured) provide the elemental building blocks. Members often become alienated from one another, but then extend their arms to embrace newcomers. Networks of kin divide and multiply, shrivel and almost expire, reconsolidate and regenerate, then surge forward. Janus-faced, clans such as this simultaneously look to both past and future generations. By so doing, they honor, learn from, and care for the elderly; nourish and teach the young. At best, they provide each member with a safe harbor from life's tempests, a sense of personal worth as well as a complex identity: an understanding of who one is, whence one came, and where one might be headed.

All families have similarities, yet they differ in numerous respects. They rouse the tenderest, most protective, and also the most repugnant passions. While some forms of history may seem remote, family history also offers welcome access to an eagerly sought and usable past. It is common to us all, and families can provide ideal portholes through which to observe the critical and passing events of an era.

Herein lie some domestic parables about both singular and common experience, but this saga also challenges popular fictions concerning the destructive tangle of pathology and violence that presumably has been endemic among African American families. It portrays instead an occasionally quirky—even mean-spirited—yet largely stable, law-abiding, patriotic network of kinfolk.[12] With similar unfashionability, the narrative, though suffused with music and muscle, and shaped by faith and Scripture, focuses on no renowned athletes, entertainers, or preachers, as "our people" are wont to be pigeonholed when we achieve even moderate measures of success.[13] Yet at their best, race notwithstanding, families such as these supply human conduits for currents of culture and values to flow in and out of the mainstream, through the generations. And they provide sturdy bridges—bonds, perhaps—to institutions, neighborhoods, and nation.

Here is a quintessentially American story about legacies and traditions, gains and losses, blissful reveries and hair-raising nightmares, obligations, allegiances, devotion to and sacrifices for country, community, and family. It is a still-evolving chronicle assembled around and about the uneasy journey of the first citizens Bond.

. I .

JOHN

ODYSSEY OF AN ABLE-BODIED SEAMAN,

1846–1864

Reverse: John Robert Bond in his Grand Army of the Republic uniform, ca. 1900.

MONGREL LIVERPOOL, EMPIRE,
and the "NIGGER JACK"

*Beautiful blacks . . . up to the ears in pumpkins, and doleful
whites . . . without potatoes to eat; never till now, I think, did the sun
look down on such a jumble of human nonsenses.*

THOMAS CARLYLE, "*The Nigger Question*," 1849

SPRAWLED NEAR THE Irish Sea, on England's windswept River
Mersey, Liverpool—its population nearing 400,000 by the 1840s
and distended by masses of immigrants—became the island nation's
greatest port.[1] In earlier years, the Mersey had been little more than
a broad, shallow estuary where treacherous currents, silting, and
extreme tidal fluctuations hampered passage from the sea through
the narrow channel at the river's mouth. Predatory buccaneers once
had imperiled whatever ships dared to venture through that neck,
and for centuries Liverpool seemed destined to remain a drowsy
fishing village surrounded by Lancashire's feudal agricultural hinterlands. But the Royal Navy's increasingly effective controls, ambivalent transformations generated by the Industrial Revolution,
plus lucrative maritime commerce (including the transatlantic trade
in slaves) converted the river delta "from an obscure, ill-cultivated
swamp into a busy, lively region, multiplying its population tenfold
in eighty years," observed a young German Communist named
Friedrich Engels.[2]

Liverpool stretched six miles along the Mersey's east banks. Its mercantilists envisioned, and soon dredged, channels deep and wide enough, then carved out and constructed mazes of quays, slips, and wharves that were vast and sturdy enough, to provide access and secure havens for the legions of battered or elegant passenger liners, cargo ships, and fishing boats that found their way to, dropped anchor, and thus enriched Liverpool's increasingly busy port.

Though pervasively rank and replete with commonplace as well as atypical urban woes, to some observers Liverpool seemed madly romantic. The "forest of masts belonging to the vessels in dock" inspired one visitor. She marveled at "the glorious river along which white-sailed ships were gliding with the ensigns of all nations . . . [the] clouds of smoke from countless steamers . . . telling of the distant lands, spicy or frozen, that sent to that mighty mart for their comforts or their luxuries."[3]

With her cousin and husband Prince Albert at her side until his untimely death in 1861, Victoria, whose name and ethos characterized the entire age, was Defender of the Faith, queen of the United Kingdom of Great Britain and Ireland, the empire's monarch, mistress of all she surveyed—and much that extended far beyond her royal reach or vision.[4] She heeded the counsel of shrewd advisors (including the commanding, Liverpool-born Liberal Party leader William Gladstone, heir to a family fortune amassed in the slave trade), and her epic longevity and fortitude would keep her on the throne into the next century.[5] An awesome maritime network controlled Her Majesty's domain, which at its peak, embraced fully a quarter of the world's population and inhabited lands. Without doubt, Britannia ruled the waves.

As a linchpin in Victoria's realm, Liverpool became home, or a habitual point of arrival, transit, and debarkation, for a crazy quilt of the world's peoples. A majority of its residents, of course, were white and English, Irish, Welsh, or Scottish born. Nonetheless, ample numbers of Caribbean mariners and stowaways; able Kroo seamen from West Africa's Pepper Coast; Chinese "coolies"; Bombay, Madras, and Calcutta's turbaned, work-hungry laborers; plus Lascar sailors (often regarded by the indigenous British as a "species of wild animal") from Malaya and Burma, all began arriving by 1800.[6] "Coloureds" from many countries also ended up in

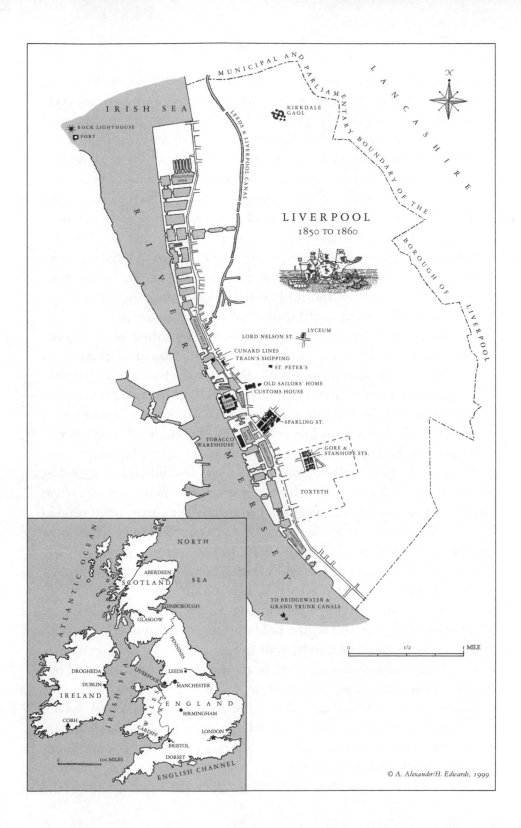

IRISH SEA

★ ROCK LIGHTHOUSE
◻ FORT

MUNICIPAL AND PARLIAMENTARY BOUNDARY OF THE BOROUGH OF LIVERPOOL

LANCASHIRE

KIRKDALE GAOL

LEEDS & LIVERPOOL CANAL

WELLINGTON DOCK

R I V E R

LIVERPOOL
1850 TO 1860

LORD NELSON ST.
LYCEUM
CUNARD LINES
TRAIN'S SHIPPING
ST. PETER'S
OLD SAILORS' HOME
CUSTOMS HOUSE

SPARLING ST.

TOBACCO
WAREHOUSE

GORE &
STANHOPE STS.

TOXTETH

M E R S E Y

TO BRIDGEWATER &
GRAND TRUNK CANALS

NORTH

SEA

ABERDEEN

SCOTLAND

ATLANTIC OCEAN

EDINBOROUGH

GLASGOW

PENNINES

DROGHEDA

DUBLIN

IRELAND

LIVERPOOL

LEEDS

MANCHESTER

IRISH SEA

COBH

CARDIFF

WALES

ENGLAND

BIRMINGHAM

LONDON

BRISTOL

DORSET

ENGLISH CHANNEL

100 MILES

0   1/2   1 MILE

© A. Alexander/H. Edwards, 1999

London's East End, Bristol, Manchester, Cardiff, even Aberdeen and Edinburgh, but the early surges of heterogeneous, darker-complexioned foreigners made Liverpool's nineteenth-century racial amalgam more diverse than that of other localities in Britain.[7] Elsewhere, the majority of black, brown, tan, and yellow refugees appeared more than a century later when immigrant job seekers and their families flooded to the metropole after colonial power withdrew from the scattered outposts of empire, often leaving behind a heritage of turmoil, poverty, and ignorance to fill the breach.[8] "Here was England," wrote a discerning Negro American some decades later, "with her flag draped around the world, ruling more black folk than white and leading the colored peoples of the world to Christian baptism, civilization, and eventual self-rule."[9]

Its poor were legion, but Liverpool and its entrepreneurs flourished during much of the nineteenth century. Rugged workers from throughout the empire swarmed about the wharves finding employment as porters, stevedores, rope- and sailmakers, caulkers, or shipwrights. A Negro carter named James Bond belonged to that multitude of anonymous laborers who toiled and lived near the waterfront in the 1840s. Judging from his Anglo-Saxon name (at some point in the past replacing an African one and possibly suggesting his forebears' status as bondsmen), rather than being a new arrival from Africa, Bond, and perhaps his antecedents, may have resided in England for quite some time. Alternatively, he could have come more recently from the British West Indies as an ex-slave who accompanied a homeward-bound master, but no records substantiate the circumstances of his arrival in Liverpool.[10]

James Bond and others in that city's multiethnic and multiracial laboring classes crammed the holds of outward-bound vessels with diverse manufactured goods, coal mined in Wales or the Pennines, cured meat or fish destined for ports anyplace on the globe. They also unloaded, among a variety of foodstuffs and raw materials, cumbersome, burlap-sheathed bales of slave-cultivated cotton. That *Gossypium hirsutum* was the prized, staple crop which, so long and so well, had kept mainland North America's slave empire financially afloat, even flourishing.

Flat-bottomed, cotton-laden barges plied the Leeds & Liverpool

Canal, the Bridgewater Canal that linked Liverpool and the River Mersey with Manchester, and the murky Grand Trunk, which headed southeast to grimy Birmingham. As early as 1810, those man-made waterways had become conduits for more than forty thousand tons per year of raw cotton that fed the droning mills of the country's sooty industrial hubs, and the tonnage increased through the next half century. Though intermittent oversatiation, secession, the Civil War's onset, and the ensuing Union naval blockade of southern ports periodically curtailed the transatlantic commerce in slave-grown cotton, perhaps more than with any other European city, human and mercantile interests tethered Liverpool to the eastern United States.

Despite their nation's indispensable maritime links with much of the world, many Englishmen thought that even the usually pale-complexioned (though still "foreign" and, almost unforgivably, Roman Catholic) local Irish "yahoos," as they were called, were "creature[s] manifestly between the gorilla and the negro." One of those "yahoos" who resided in Liverpool was a woman named Eliza Kelly.

Especially during the cataclysmic 1840s' famine—as the Emerald Isle's mysteriously plagued potato fields turned black and putrid with rot, forcing legions of its denizens to forage for roots and berries, even gnaw on tree bark—many of the Irish embarked for the Merseyside port. Almost two million emigrants (a quarter of the population) left Ireland between 1845 and 1855, while hunger-provoked deaths claimed well over another million. Unmarked grave sites littered the island's pastoral green slopes.

Destitute, dispossessed from their lands, laden with any transportable belongings, and weakened by debilitating bacteria, refugees like Eliza Kelly arrived on packed ships from Drogheda, Cobh, and Dublin, crossing the Irish Sea in a few hours and receiving far less care or concern than other, more valued cargo, such as swine. Nature's cruel vagaries fused with harsh economic and political misfortunes to wrench the rural poor from Erin's countryside and thrust them into daunting confrontation with the beastliness of urban industrialism. Throughout Lancashire, a caustic visitor commented, "abides [the Irishman] in his squalor and unreason, in his falsity and drunken violence, as the readymade nucleus of degradation and disorder." But at least in England those scorned exiles believed they would eat, though critics sighted whole families "sleeping upon the cold hearth-stone for weeks in succession, without adequate means of providing themselves with food or fuel . . . starving in a crowded garret or damp cellar, gradually sinking under the pressure of want and despair into a premature grave."[11]

During the famine years, the Negro abolitionist Frederick Douglass visited Ireland, where he compared the "wailing notes" of indigenous ballads there to American slavery's sorrow songs with their roots in distant Africa. And a traveling French aristocrat found among the Irish human misery even worse, he claimed, than that of the New World's enslaved Negroes.[12] Some of Liverpool's newcomers may even have been the fabled "black Irish," often thought to be descendants of local women who had borne daughters and sons of the African survivors of misdirected, wrecked slave ships.

England's myriad Hibernian aliens—Eliza and other Kellys, plus Healys, Murphys, Higginses, Callahans, and Fitzgeralds among them—were considered the Merseyside city's detritus, whom predatory Liverpudlians both loathed and habitually snookered.[13] Despite widespread elitist presumptions and chauvinistic antagonisms, however, not only the Irish, but a steady stream of the empire's other racially and religiously disparate subjects, as well as a great variety of raw materials and manufactured produce, coursed through that teeming port.[14]

But people of African ancestry arrived and stayed in Eliza Kelly's and James Bond's Liverpool under different circumstances. With motivations both pragmatic and idealistic, the courts had acted to end slavery in England during the 1700s' final decades, characterizing it as an "odious" institution, yet in truth, many Negroes remained long thereafter in an agonizing, intermediary state. Their circumstances usually fell somewhere between the Western Hemisphere's black chattel slavery and white English domestic servitude. As late as the 1820s, a few Africans still were being sold on the Mersey docks, though any such acts flew squarely in the face of established law. Nonetheless, those unfortunates brought with them intricate cosmologies, food preferences, music, and other manifestations of their African cultures.[15]

One observer argued that, because slavery officially had been abolished, "in Liverpool . . . the negro steps with a prouder pace and lifts his head like a man." Many English people concluded that the southern United States remained obstinately wrong-headed in its justification and retention of bondage, which they considered a besmirched badge of cultural and economic backwardness, as well as moral degeneracy. Nonetheless, darker-complexioned visitors knew that even in England there was continuing "prejudice against colour, [and] the leprosy of racial hatred affect[s] some on British soil, especially those who come into contact with American merchants and captains." When Douglass returned in 1859, he found increased intolerance in the streets of Liverpool, stimulated, he believed, by the deplorable influence of America's blackface "Ethiopian minstrels," though he still marveled that monarchical Britain assumed him to be a free man while his own republican homeland did not.[16]

By the time war broke out within the United States in 1861, in fact, the port of Liverpool—its commodities brokers and merchants ever ravenous for slave-grown cotton and tobacco—was known as "a hotbed of southern sympathy."[17] On the other hand, Prince Albert, not only Victoria's blood kin and consort but also one of her more enlightened counselors, had bestowed the monarchy's seal of approval on abolitionism by serving as titular head of the British and Foreign Anti-Slavery Society. The Royal Navy struggled to suppress the residual transatlantic slave trade, and Liverpool, like many other English cities, sometimes provided public platforms for men and women (home-grown or foreign, black, brown, and white) whose writings and rhetoric promoted a swift end to slavery in the American South.[18]

In 1859, the expatriate Negro American emigrationist Martin Delany expounded in the *Anglo-African Magazine:*

> *I heard old England plainly say,*
> *[That] we could all forsake*
> *Our native land of Slavery,*
> *And come across the lake.*[19]

William Andrew Jackson, "black as a Congo Negro," was another of Liverpool's antislavery advocates. Early in the U.S. Civil War he fled from bondage in Virginia, where he had served as coachman for Jefferson Davis, president of the renegade southern Confederacy.[20] "Coloured" rhetoricians from the United States such as Frederick Douglass, and Ellen and William Craft, a runaway-slave couple whose autobiography enjoyed great popularity in England, became fashionable though "exotic" notables who spoke out against the "peculiar institution" as they toured the country's lyceums. One such hall was located on Liverpool's Lord Nelson Street. There and in other forums, black performers, often under the direction of the entrepreneurial former bondsman William Wells Brown, found eager audiences for pageants depicting slavery's most lurid offenses—including realistically feigned flagellation and a "slave" who seemingly was burned alive—plus reenactments of hair-raising escapes. The presentations roused observers to outraged indignation, tumultuous ovations, even compassionate tears. They raised funds for black fugitives and heightened awareness of the abolitionist cause, but concurrently may have augmented stereotypical images of victimized Negroes.[21]

Strong indicators of reformist ideologies flourished in Liverpool. A decade prior to the United States' Civil War, a visitor there observed "a negro with tracts in his hand and a placard upon his breast, upon which was a wood-cut of a black man, kneeling, his wrists heavily chained, his arms held high in supplication, and around the picture . . . the words, 'Am I not a man and a brother?' "[22] That haunting plea long had been an abolitionist rallying cry worldwide.

One Negro American argued that "some Britishers . . . say that . . . niggers [are] as good as the whites, and that the whites did not look down on them and ill-treat them as they do in New York," yet fervent English orators often disparaged people of different races, ethnicities, and religions. Antipapists and anti-Semites stridently cried: "No Popes, no Jews, no Wooden Shoes!" as they advocated either the expulsion of Roman Catholics and Jews, or their forced conversion to the established Anglican Church. Some xenophobes called for the wholesale removal of all, broadly defined, "foreigners" and "infidels," though they tolerated a few distinguished exceptions, such as Liverpool's "Jew banker," Mr. Morley, who had been elected to the Town Council.[23]

The 1850s also brought on the advocacy and disseminatation of scientific racism, promoted by a faction within the Royal Anthropological Society who argued that people of African ancestry were a separate, intellectually and morally inferior species, more akin to apes than Caucasians, who needed the "civilizing" influence of "superior" Anglo-European culture. Some Englishmen who developed that finely honed sense of racial superiority favored the Confederate cause in the early 1860s.[24]

Contradictory crosscurrents of religious or racial liberality, ethnocentrism or tolerance, egalitarianism or paternalism, and pro- or antislavery sympathies intermingled in mid-nineteenth-century Liverpool.[25] Not only the elite, but members of the uneducated lower classes such as James Bond and Eliza Kelly would have heard those roiling debates. Yet despite widespread endorsements of abolitionism, plus the port's racial and ethnic hybridity, for more than a century it had prospered as Britain's hub for the commerce in African slaves, even after 1807 when the nefarious Atlantic trade, though diminished, simmered along covertly in defiance of both British and United States law.

Liverpool's first slave ships had sailed for the New World in 1709. One-third of its vessels engaged in the profitable business of buying, transporting, and selling men, women, and children though legally sanctioned slavery within Britain itself ended in 1772. At the start of the new century, it still controlled more than forty percent of the European-based commerce in African laborers.[26] The entrenched, transoceanic trade in Negroes, and increasingly in slave-produced coffee, sugar, tobacco, and especially cotton, meant that racial issues remained interwoven with Liverpool's economic life. Because of the port's dependency on slave trading, the tides of passion favoring its continuation ran high. A scrap of popular doggerel documented those emotions:

> *If our slave trade be gone, there's an end to our lives,*
> *Beggars all we must be, our children and wives:*

No ships from our ports their proud sails e'er would spread,
Our streets grown with grass where the cows might be fed.[27]

Even after slavery, as well as the obscene human trade, allegedly had been terminated throughout the empire, most Englishmen continued to consider Africans and their descendants little more than commodities, the lowest of servants, or subhuman producers of essential goods. In 1856, a London newspaper declared, "The one great service the world demands from the negro race is the production of cotton." Then as the United States Civil War began, Liverpool's elated William Gladstone proclaimed in the House of Commons: "Jeff Davis has created a nation!" Yet many of his colleagues and constituents feared that the Confederacy might pull bondsmen out of the fields, impress them into military service, and generate a cotton famine that could jeopardize the British economy.[28]

Cotton and African ancestry remained associated both with one another and with bondage, or at least inferiority, for James Bond and other members of that marginalized segment of England's population. For most people in the Anglo-Saxon mainstream, the combination of brown skin, broad features, and tightly curled hair—irrespective of wealth, education, or deportment—marked anyone with those physical attributes as a member of humankind's most subordinate order.[29]

Even self-declared progressives such as Engels argued that England's white laborers "are worse slaves than the Negroes in America, . . . and yet it is demanded of them that they shall live like human beings, shall think and feel like men!" The ineradicable stigmas that in Engels's (and many others') eyes seem to have totally excluded black people from the ranks of thinking, feeling men were physiological, cultural, and social. In contrast, a "true" English heritage and light complexion denoted a loftier status and were considered inseparable from human liberty. As the familiar anthem, *Rule, Britannia*, proclaimed: "Britons never, never, never shall be slaves."[30]

In the mid-nineteenth century, mongrel Liverpool also became Europe's main point of departure for multitudes of Scandinavian and German, English, Welsh, Scottish, but especially Irish people. For some time, the Irish born comprised ninety-five percent of the city's westward-bound emigrants. During those years, three-quarters of Europe's total transoceanic travelers—as many as a quarter million annually—departed from Liverpool bound for the United States.[31] Fleeing private, political, and religious woes, plus unemployment, poverty, even starvation in the lands of their birth, they left relatives, friends, and most worldly possessions behind. Desperation, combined with the wildly contagious epidemic of "America fever" (not to mention typhus, dysentery, and other pernicious diseases), profoundly afflicted them.[32] No Circe could have lured those sojourners more seductively than did the beguiling promises of the U.S.A.

Crossing Waterloo Road, Strand or Wapping Streets, they inundated the Merseyside piers—from the Wellington Docks on the north to Harrington's on the south—where James Bond labored. Streaming out of loathsome cellars or lodging houses, transients bound for the lands of their fondest illusions and presumed salvation engorged the sewage-filled alleys, besieged booking offices, mounted gangplanks, overflowed creaking decks, and jammed the turgid steerage quarters of ships that prepared to cross the Atlantic. Barring tempests, adverse winds, or death from accidents or the myriad diseases that in some years claimed one-sixth of all passengers, the dogged immigrants arrived four to six uncomfortable weeks later in Quebec, Boston, and New York (even southern ports such as Norfolk and Savannah), all of which had provided refuge and opportunities, as well as unanticipated perils, for many others who had preceded them.[33]

At the height of this exodus, Enoch Train's Massachusetts-based shipping line operated twenty-four vessels (the *Anglo-American* and the *George Washington* among them) "sailing from Boston semi-monthly, and from Liverpool every week," its broadsides promised. Competition for passengers became intense. For a few pence, a disconsolate Irishman could cross the channel to Liverpool, stay several days, weeks, or years, then purchase a one-way ticket to America for as little as three pounds.[34]

Another ship that shuttled between Liverpool and the northeastern states was the Cunard Line's HMS *Cambria*. However, Negro passengers—including celebrated ones such as Douglass and the Crafts who had funds and sponsors that should have assured them first-class cabins—sometimes found themselves denied suitable accommodations, restricted to the dingiest quarters, even menaced by "salt-water mobocrats." Nonetheless, that particular liner (its scarlet flag bearing the image of a golden lion cradling a globe in its paws), commanded by a captain who may have harbored nascent antislavery sentiments, became a preferred transatlantic carrier for a number of black American abolitionists.[35]

In May 1846, at the time of an overwhelming influx of potato famine refugees and coinciding with the Corn Laws' repeal that reduced the price of bread but depressed British agriculture, a child was born in Liverpool to Eliza Kelly, a white woman of Irish ancestry, and James Bond, the black dockhand who was her lover.[36] James and Eliza's only son did not become a Roman Catholic, as his mother (like most of the Irish) may have been. Rather, two months after his birth—as Prince Albert arrived in the city to open a vast dockside complex that bore his name and became home base for the lucrative East India and China trades, and the locally built paddle steamer *Ethiope* launched an ill-fated expedition to explore West Africa's River Niger—in the eyes and annals of the established Church of England, the boy became known as John Robert Bond.[37]

J. G. Baldham, the curate at St. Peter's Church, christened the baby, who was attended by both parents. In nineteenth-century Liverpool, very few Negro children received Christian baptisms, often because of poverty and social marginality, disinterest, or differing religious preferences, but other times as the result of intolerance among members of the clergy. Many of the white, native-born English (clerics included) assumed that any person of African ancestry or other dusky foreigner must be a Muslim or a "pagan . . . fond of and addicted to all sorts of superstition and witchcraft."[38] Yet for a "coloured" boy in a predominantly white world, the Anglican Church could provide some sense of belonging, order, and empowerment in a frequently hostile environment that otherwise deemed him an outsider. St. Peter's pastors shepherded a flock that included not only middle- and upper-class parishioners, but mariners, indigents, and single mothers as well. Young John Bond's parish even maintained a missionary affiliation with the borough's Kirkdale Gaol.[39]

John grew up an Anglican in the boisterous, untidy port replete with great ships and sagas about distant lands and far-flung empire that became at least a temporary home to a sizable body of transients and immigrants who spoke varied dialects and unfamiliar tongues. Liverpool claimed more than its share of England's dark-hued people, but in that gritty, water-dependent metropolis mostly populated by paler-skinned residents, the boy's intonations and glottal accent would have been local, and English was his native tongue. His deep caramel complexion, combined with minimally Negroid features, however, remained less common.

At the time of their boy's birth and christening, Eliza Kelly and James Bond lodged in a warren on Sparling Street—named for a local family that had made its fortune in the slave trade.[40] The couple apparently never married according to law or in a church (such conventionalities could have been beyond their financial means), nor do they seem to have had other children together. But like some others among Britain's diverse populace who entered into common-law conjugal arrangements or adapted rituals prevalent in lower-class Liverpool and throughout the black Atlantic world at that time, James and Eliza may have been united in a ceremony solemnized by jumping over a broomstick, then celebrated with chums, a fiddler, and brimming pitchers of beer or rum. After that, they would have "lived tally" or "over the brush," as common parlance characterized such nonsanctioned matrimonial alliances. However, even the establishment of only a less-than-formal marriage did not prevent them from facilitating their son's traditional and profoundly English affiliation with the Anglican Church.[41]

Most men among the Bonds' neighbors on Sparling Street worked on or near the docks, or at sea, while the women who stayed behind swigged tea and gin; cooked, stitched, scoured, and "moaned . . . over sailors and seaport towns, stormy weather and sleepless nights, and trousers all over tar and pitch."[42] Many of them (probably including Eliza Kelly) were called the "Liverpool

Irish." In the 1840s and 1850s, residents of that tawdry sector who hailed from Ireland or elsewhere in the British Isles, newcomers from continental Europe and Canada as well as seagirt outposts of the empire such as Malta, Gibraltar, and Antigua or St. Vincent's in the Caribbean, almost equaled the indigenous English.[43]

The Crosbie Street rail shipping station backed up to the crowded flats that lined the south side of Sparling. The Bonds' truncated thoroughfare was situated near the Old Sailors' Home, the King's, Queen's, and Salthouse Docks, Customs House, and Liverpool's quayside tobacco warehouse, Britain's greatest repository for that valuable, seductive Virginia- or Carolina-grown import. Rooming houses, pubs, even brothels occupied many nearby buildings. That clamorous district, lacking greenery or sanitation, was hardly an ideal place to raise a child.

Together or separately, the Bonds left Sparling Street soon after their son's birth and may have moved a short distance to Toxteth.[44] That wretched enclave in Liverpool's southernmost sector had been laid out around 1800 in response to demands for cheap housing near the wharves. One observer recalled its "mean narrow streets, filled with close, gloomy courts, into which . . . many dwellings were packed, irrespective of light and air," which became home to a disproportionate one-third of the city's paupers. Mingled odors of curry and ghee; chilies, cabbage, souse, and callaloo; coal or peat smoke; plus human and animal wastes, would have permeated the area around the intersection of Gore and Stanhope Streets, where Africans, East and West Indians, sea dogs, "street Arabs," drifters, and others among the baser classes clustered. It became infamous as the most squalid corner in one of England's most squalid cities, and a contemporary observer reported that while "the average longevity of [Liverpool's] upper classes, gentry, professional men, etc., was thirty-five years, . . . [that of] the serviceable class in general, [was] but fifteen."[45]

Some of those short-lived members of the city's multiracial community—poor and uneducated, usually tied to maritime activities, and including a generous handful with one or more African forebears, often by way of the Caribbean—could trace their antecedents' local residency back as far as the 1600s. Others were newcomers or transients. To demonstrate their status and affluence, slave traders or planters returning from New World colonies sometimes had brought dark-complexioned servants home to Liverpool.[46] "There was always a market for little black boys who, dressed up in trousers and turban, and girt with a scimitar were frequent attendants on ladies of fashion," a local pundit had commented, implying that those elegantly garbed youngsters might be treated as cosseted household pets.[47]

Toward the end of the eighteenth century, two of every five British slave vessels that plied the sea-lanes between Africa and the Americas had been built in Liverpool, and prior to abolition in England, black, enslaved laborers had constructed many of the city's docks and municipal buildings.[48] An inebriated yet empathetic white tragedian once berated an appalled audience of Liverpudlians with the bitter accusation that "every brick in your town is cemented with an African's blood."[49]

Iberian traders had conveyed the first Africans to England before the arrival of the New World's tobacco and potatoes, or even Will Shakespeare's birth.[50] For centuries thereafter, seafaring Englishmen remained integral participants in the lucrative Triangular Trade that carried guns and trinkets to the African littoral to exchange for black people, most of whom were transported as slaves to labor on plantations in the Americas. There they produced raw materials to satisfy the metropole's burgeoning industrial needs and seemingly insatiable yearnings for sweets, caffeine, and nicotine. Much slave-grown produce—and more than a few Negroes—inevitably ended up in England. Yet because English census records specified residents' places of birth but not race, estimates of their numbers in the eighteenth and nineteenth centuries are unreliable at best, and details of their lives remain hazy and dependent on scattered or anecdotal evidence.[51]

Some authorities argue that by the late 1700s, eighteen to twenty thousand blacks resided in London alone, while others insist that no more than ten thousand people with any measure of African ancestry lived throughout the entire country in 1801. As a result of interracial liaisons (such as that of Eliza Kelly and James Bond), a number of mulattoes began to be gradually, often grudgingly, assimilated into Britain's lower classes, where they formed varied kinship alliances and dwelt among or melded with other "quasi-British," darker-skinned minorities.[52]

Despite differing approximations of their numbers, continuing diffusion into the mainstream, and ongoing antagonism to the presence of Africans in England, commerce between the Mersey ports and much of the Guinea coast continued unabated.[53] As the human cargo destined for the Americas dwindled, other components of the Anglo-African trade expanded. The commercial traffic included calicoes, rifles, and cheap manufactured goods that were shipped south to be exchanged for ivory and hardwoods, spices and cocoa, as well as palm oil for soap, cooking, and lubricating the textile industry's massive machines. Liverpool's African Steamship Company operated a mail service down and around the west coast as far as the Bight of Biafra, and the intercontinental commerce remained so prodigious that a seaside village there was called "Black Liverpool."[54]

Britain had moved to eliminate bondage at home, officially banned the international slave trade, then terminated slavery in its West Indian colonies—all prior to 1840. But ships from the Western Hemisphere still transported the racially mixed offspring of planters and dark-complexioned Caribbean women, a few well-connected Negroes denied access to an education in the United States; desperate stowaways; plus an ample supply of black sailors to the city by the Mersey. A handful of the academy-bound sons of Africa's ruling families also arrived from the "Dark Continent."[55] "In Liverpool, . . . I saw under the shadow of the great dingy street-wall of Prince's Dock," reported the American writer Herman Melville, "a common sailor so intensely black that he must needs have been a native African . . . in his ears were big hoops of gold, and a Highland bonnet with a tartan band set off his shapely head." One parliamentary initiative required that bonds be posted to discourage further influxes of any such Negroes, who wary Englishmen feared might swell the ranks of the dependent poor. Other provisions designated compensation for captains who promised to deport the often unwelcome aliens. Nonetheless, many nonwhite newcomers inexorably gravitated to, then remained—more than anywhere else in Liverpool—in Toxteth. There, like James Bond and his son, they might at least have found neighbors who somewhat resembled them, and a meager haven of familiarity and acceptance in an often hostile land.[56]

Young John Robert Bond was a mulatto, the bastard son of a white mother and a father of African ancestry who worked on or near the docks.[57] While not commonplace, such interracial alliances were hardly unknown. Around 1830, a seaman from British Guiana named John Glasgow had debarked from a merchant ship that had moored in Liverpool. Despite the distaste for his dark complexion expressed by a number of the locals, he married a Lancashire farm lass who bore him two "fine brown babies." In time, however, Glasgow realized that he was a skilled sailor who knew a ship thoroughly "from her kelson to her signal halyards," but was entirely unsuited to agrarian life. He returned to sea (his autobiography recounted), and his "vessel left the Mersey with a favorable breeze, bearing him away," he mourned, "with a sadder heart than he ever had" known before.[58]

Unlike John Glasgow and James Bond, some of Liverpool's less able or fortunate black people turned to mendicancy. Others worked as servants, coal heavers, street vendors, ragpickers, minstrels, or artisans' apprentices. One mid-nineteenth-century Englishman observed, "It is only common fairness to say that negroes seldom if ever shirk work. Their only trouble is to obtain it," while another noted that "negroes in Liverpool . . . are hardworking, patient and too often underpaid."[59]

A few black Americans, toughened by bare-knuckled, owner-sponsored plantation bouts, became boxers in England. Jemmy Robinson, once a Virginia slave, and Bob Smith from the nation's capital were among those pugilists. Black entertainers performed in Liverpool's theaters during the 1850s as well. The Aberdeen-bound actor Ira Aldridge (who later had to appease the public by closing his classical performances with bawdy Negro music hall songs) arrived as a ship's steward. Other favorites from the United States included William Lane, whose rolling eyes, snapping fingers, and "single shuffle, double shuffle, cut and cross-cut" choreography dazzled his audiences. Adapting the popular but demeaning minstrel tradition, then adding elements from Irish clog dances, Lane evoked his somewhat remote African heritage when he appended the stage name "Master Juba" to enhance his exotic appeal. In 1843, Peter Ogden, a Negro seaman who had joined a Liverpool lodge of the fraternal Grand United Order of Oddfellows, convinced his multiracial, multinational English chapter to sponsor an affiliate in New York. It became the first anywhere in the United States to accept black men.[60] A decade later, an itinerant American youth named Michael Healy—one of eight children of an affluent southerner (Irish by birth) and his slave "wife"—was seduced by the sea and signed up as a cabin boy on a merchant ship headed to the Far East.[61] Commonplace yet tangled transatlantic ties such as those permeated Britain's diverse, transient, nineteenth-century "coloured" communities.

A few people of African ancestry became educated and even self-employed, managing—sometimes owning—modest shops, pubs, or lodging houses, but the majority, like Bond, Healy, and Ogden, affiliated themselves with England's maritime endeavors. In 1857, for instance, a vessel that had sailed from the United States with an all-white crew, was remanned in Liverpool with an all-Negro one. Hardy black seafarers hoisted billowing white sails all around and across the Atlantic's vast blue expanses. They labored on piers, served on merchant ships' "chequerboard crews," even joined the Royal Navy.[62] One Englishman commented that men of African ancestry "take easily to sea-life and become . . . excellent sailors."[63]

Within the linguistic context of their predominantly white, seagoing counterparts' designation as "Jack tars" (a term derived from the red-white-and-blue standard known worldwide as the Union Jack), the empire's dark-skinned sailors were called "black Jacks," sometimes "Nigger Jacks." Despite such appellations, Parliament confirmed those Negroes' equality in theory and in law, stipulating as early as 1823 that they were "as much British seamen as a white man." One observer characterized them as "woolly headed and ivory grindered," yet also noted that "where the Union Jack flies, Nigger Jack is well treated. English sailors do not disdain to drink with him, work with him and sing with him," as if that reported lack of "disdain" for darker shipmates nullified the epithets' bitter sting.[64]

John Robert Bond's Anglo-African or West Indian father and white mother, however, inverted the characteristic colonial pattern of gender and racial relations that prevailed wherever enslaved, or at least dependent, black women (often reluctantly) bore the children of lustful white men. Yet because most members of the dominant race, both in the New World and in England, considered women of African ancestry bestial, indiscriminate, and voracious in their carnal appetites, those sexual couplings, even when coerced or violent, rarely troubled the white majority.[65]

But on the Atlantic's European shores, white women (Eliza Kelly, for one) who struck up intimate relationships with Negro men (like James Bond) faced censure for their choice of partners. They were considered deviants, even trollops. One Briton condemned the formalization of interracial ties by any errant countrywoman who deigned "to accompany . . . [a black man] *to the altar,* to become his wife, to breed English mulattoes, to stamp the mark of Cain upon her family and her country."[66] Many white Englishmen loathed "mongrelization," deprecated brown-skinned youngsters, labeled them "half-castes," and became outraged when they observed "tawny children playing in the squares," describing them as "mischievous as monkeys, and infinitely more dangerous." Yet the heavy numerical imbalance (at least five to one) between black males and females in England's ports reinforced the tendency of men such as James to mingle with white women like Eliza. The potential for any sort of conjugal life almost required those alliances. In the words of one shrewd observer: "Frequently such a mate was the only possible choice."[67]

Interracial couplings, of course, led directly to the birth of those "mischievous monkeys." Critics issued dire warnings about "the rapid increase of a dark and contaminated breed," and griped that "the nation already begins to be embronzed with the African tint."[68] Though slavery in Britain had been banned seven decades before John Bond was born, many of his countrymen still believed that his deeply pigmented skin imbued him with simian qualities (amplified, perhaps, by his often similarly described Irish heritage), and denoted both baseness and perversity.

Some of Liverpool's Irish-born indigents, such as the Bonds' Sparling Street or Toxteth neighbors, facing pervasive bigotry themselves, resented the presence of black men in their midst, complaining that "not only were these ugly, tribal-scarred fellows from the West Coast of Africa accepted by white women as equals; many times they were considered the white man's superior." A number of Englishmen, regardless of social status, both mistrusted and demeaned outsiders. They compared alien cultures to their own, found them lacking, and judged all of the non-English inferior when they failed, or refused, to replicate the established, ethnocentric attributes of British life. Those judgments applied most consistently to dark-complexioned foreigners, collectively and pejoratively called "wogs."[69] Prejudicial assumptions about the disparaging supposed characteristics of their race stubbornly clung to Britain's Negroes, indeed, to any of its varied and marginalized "coloured" people, and curtailed their residential, social, occupational, and financial opportunities.

In Victoria's realm, and elsewhere that Europeans and white Americans journeyed and settled, men of African lineage like James and then John Bond were believed to be imbued with sexual traits and erotic propensities that inflamed white women's sensuality. Shakespearean images evoking the "gross clasps of a lascivious Moor," or a "black ram . . . tupping your white ewe," remained familiar cultural fare.[70] One misogynist, racist (and perhaps envious) Englishman alluded to Africans' reputedly oversized sex organs, snickered that "the lower class of women in England are remarkably fond of the blacks, for reasons too brutal to mention," then added: "They would connect themselves with horses and asses, if laws permitted."[71] Caricaturists fanned those treacherous flames and titillated the public with images depicting the presumably salacious nature of interracial sexual relations, and a few British artists had depicted the progeny of such unions as zebra-striped or dappled like leopards.[72] The ensuing paranoia and suspicions sometimes degenerated into loathing, though Britain, unlike the southern

United States, never passed demeaning laws statutorily prohibiting carnal congress or marriage between the races.

During his childhood in that often fractious milieu, the Anglican Church may have provided John Robert Bond with spiritual guidance, but he acquired no formal education, and, like many youngsters in a city replete with destitute, diverse transients, could neither read nor write. Sporadic parliamentary reform initiatives attempted to create wider access to elementary education, but the lower classes' economic marginality, reinforced by elitist cultural biases and practices, continued unabated. Most of Liverpool's disadvantaged "coloured" population, as well as many among the white majority, remained uneducated.[73]

Economic conditions in the west of England deteriorated in the early 1860s. Agriculture did not fully recover after the corn tariffs' repeal, and thousands of the wretchedly underpaid or unemployed, mostly women and children (discharged as more productive machines displaced them or mills shut down due to a dearth of blockaded Confederate cotton), inundated the already teeming streets and alleys of Manchester, Birmingham, and Liverpool. Homelessness and crime escalated, while sanitary conditions and health deteriorated. When they learned of those circumstances, some of Massachusetts's sympathetic and charitable citizens—often recent immigrants who remembered similar miseries of their own—collected $40,000 and donated shiploads of grain to help feed "the hungry working poor of Lancashire."[74]

In late summer 1862, John Bond stood at the threshold of manhood. Like other local boys who needed work, caught the briny scent borne on the prevailing westerlies, had tall ships and the beguiling ocean as ever beckoning neighbors, and used wharves for their playing fields, that "coloured" child of a woman of Irish origins and a black English dockworker (a cog in Liverpool's working-class community) turned seaward. He prepared to bid his economically depressed region farewell and recast his future.

As a pauper who set out to board an unfamiliar vessel during the second year of the United States' Civil War, John Robert Bond would have had little to carry other than the cultural baggage of his African-Irish-English heritage. The sturdy little steamer *Pactolus,* engaged in the salt codfish trade out of south England's Dorset County, seems to have borne him away from all that he had known, and cherished or loathed, for sixteen years. In fact, the commerce in ocean cod had been so widespread around the time of John's birth that Alexandre Dumas, *père,* the French-Afro-Caribbean *auteur de romans historiques,* had observed: "It has been calculated that if no accident prevented the hatching of the eggs and if each egg reached maturity, it would take only three years to fill the sea so that you could walk across the Atlantic dryshod on the backs of cod." At an undetermined, previous point in time, different ships altogether (conveyors of sundry ideas and information as well as human and inanimate cargoes), which were the transitory bridges linking remote outposts of a world washed by those cod-rich Atlantic tides, had brought each of John's parents, or their forebears, to Liverpool.[75]

In 1862, John Bond most likely signed onto the *Pactolus* as an apprentice who learned to tie common knots and hitches, and was directed to man the pumps, holystone the decks, load and unload cargo. As he disengaged himself from English roots to become a seagoing citizen of the world, he faced arduous weeks of omnipresent salt cod and salt pork, wormy biscuits, beans, rusty water or cheap rum, tiresome days and fearful nights slung in a mildewed hammock in the cramped, dank forecastle. John (seeking new stars to guide him) left Liverpool's congested harbor behind to head west across the ocean toward an enticing yet still unknown place called Massachusetts, much like another restless Lancashire lad who proclaimed about his own migratory intent: "I'm going to Boston, U.S., that's Uncle Sam."[76]

John Bond's chosen calling also could prove perilous. A ship from his home port recently had been wrecked with its entire crew lost, and many of England's Jack Tars feared the "frequent use of the knife by foreign sailors."[77] Yet as they hastened seaward chasing favorable winds and tides, many eager "packet rats" sang:

> *On the Liverpool docks at the break o' the day,*
> *I saw a fair packet bound west'ard away,*

She was bound to the west where the wild waters flow,
  She's a Liverpool packet. Oh, Lord, let 'er go.

An' now we are leavin' the sweet Salthouse Docks,
The boys an' the gals to the pierhead do flock;
The boys an' the gals are all shoutin' "hurro!"
  She's a Liverpool packet. Oh, Lord, let 'er go.

An' now we are waitin' in the Mersey so free,
Awaitin' the tugboat to tow us to sea;
An' we'll round the Rock Light where the salt tides do flow,
  She's a Liverpool packet. Oh, Lord, let 'er go.

An' now we are howlin' down the wild Irish Sea,
Our trav'lers are many, an' their hearts full of glee;
Our sailors like tigers, they walk to and fro,
  She's a Liverpool packet—Oh, Lord, let 'er go.[78]

An intrepid youth named Bond decided to join that bold and boisterous, all-male, water-bound universe. And in the eyes, minds, hearts, and words of his gold-earringed, queue-wearing, tattooed, rough-and-ready shipmates, John, the novice "half-caste" of bastard birth, became "Nigger Jack" incarnate.[79]

· 2 ·

NEW BEDFORD, *the CAMBRIDGE,* *and* "SEEING *the* ELEPHANT"

So rally, boys, rally, let us never mind the past;
We had a hard road to travel, but our day is coming fast,
For God is for the right, and we have no need to fear,—
The Union must be saved by the colored volunteer.

—O, give us a flag, all free without a slave,
We'll fight to defend it, as our Fathers did so brave.
The gallant Comp'ny "A" will make the rebels dance,
And we'll stand by the Union if we only have a chance.

Marching song by a private in the Fifty-fourth Massachusetts Regiment,
from the *Liberator*

WAVES OF MID-NINETEENTH-CENTURY Europeans steered their various courses west to major Atlantic ports such as Boston and New York where, as often as not, they hoped and planned to establish permanent residency and become citizens. But mariners from around the globe like Liverpool's "Nigger Jack," John Robert Bond, headed instead for New Bedford, Massachusetts, the world's greatest whaling center. The cargo ship *Dreadnought* and its crew completed the round-trip between New Bedford and Liverpool three times in 1862, but that September only one vessel from Bond's home port arrived at the bustling Massachusetts seaport.

The salt fish trader *Pactolus,* with the novice seaman Bond almost certainly aboard, navigated south of Cape Cod (its name celebrating the Atlantic's most prevalent harvest), which provided so many New England–bound sailors with a first glimpse of their avidly sought terra incognita. Skirting the cape, then entering Buzzards Bay, the *Pactolus* headed into the snug harbor to tie up along New Bedford's Acushnet River. Like more than a few other British mariners, Bond soon addressed the vivid Red Ensign (the standard flown by Her Majesty's merchant ships) one last time and bid his "limey" Jack Tar mates farewell as they put out to sea again, bound north for Quebec.[1]

The port where he disembarked was known for its diversity. Not only white New Englanders, Native Americans, and more than 1,500 Negro Americans, but *mestiço, crioulo*-speaking Cape Verdeans, Polynesians, Eskimos, Sandwich Islanders, and voyagers from all the world's seafaring territories comprised a sizable portion of the city's permanent population of 22,000.[2]

John Bond's 1862 odyssey to New Bedford, however, stood in stark contrast to the transatlantic journeys of other Negroes, most of whom had been brought to the Americas as slaves—their anguish heeded no more than salt tears in the sea. A majority of those captives had originated in West Africa, where they dwelt near the equatorial banks and mangrove-swamp deltas of the Gambia, Niger, and Congo Rivers, which poured their silted waters into the South Atlantic. Concerned with little but profits (and benefiting from the cooperation of more than a few Africans), European and American slave traders snatched their human bounty from families, stable communities, and entrenched traditions. They dragged the quarry to seaports where uncaring crews crammed the new cargo into the fetid underdecks of slave ships that soon set sail and headed west. The Atlantic leg of that coerced diaspora became known as the Middle Passage, and the whole sordid commerce, which persisted from the early sixteenth century through much of the nineteenth, reeked with the aura of moral destitution and death. Even Africans who survived the Middle Passage and preserved vestiges of their legends, languages, theologies, music, and cuisines, found themselves destined for a lifetime (often a short, brutal lifetime) in bondage. Most of the newly enslaved people wound up on labor-intensive sugar, rice, coffee, tobacco, and cotton plantations in Brazil, Jamaica and the Antilles, Cuba, Louisiana, the Carolinas, and Virginia.

Unlike those sub-Saharan black people who endured forced dislocations, John Robert Bond—a youngster of African and Irish ancestry with the ambition and temerity to grasp at opportunities that at first may have seemed much like those of his predominantly white countrymen—eagerly crossed the ocean from his native England. Perhaps he craved adventure, needed work, or left home seeking a new life in a new land. At the same time, however, he had loftier, though still hazily formulated, objectives as well.

Nonetheless, any "coloured" seaman such as Bond needed to take care lest he join the crew of a vessel headed for the southern United States, where he might be imprisoned or sold into slavery. That had been the fate of the Guiana-born John Glasgow, who, though "a freeman born, a British subject, and unoffending, was seized, handcuffed like a common felon, [and] conveyed to gaol" in Savannah under provisions of Georgia law concerning that reputedly treacherous class, free people of color—especially black seamen.[3]

When they landed in welcoming New Bedford, however, Negro sailors like John Bond often headed straight for hangouts like the "Subterrainian"—notorious for the raucous carousals of its interracial clientele. Bond remained in the port city nine months, probably working on fishing boats or the wharves, and, like Melville's Ishmael, gulping "chowder for breakfast, and chowder for dinner and chowder for supper till you began to look for fish-bones coming through your clothes." Ishmael had called New Bedford "the dearest place . . . in all New England." Though smaller by far than Liverpool, it had a similarly disparate population, a reputation for embracing that diversity, and on a couple of Atlantic vessels out of New Bedford, everyone, including the captains, was black. Nonetheless, fewer Negroes manned the port's whaling ships than had in previous decades. One sojourner observed that the city "was not entirely free from race and color prejudice," and several shipyards, another added, "did not give work to colored men."[4]

Unlike nearby Providence, Rhode Island, few of New Bedford's entrepreneurs had amassed their wealth in the slave trade, and many Negroes had lived there for generations, creating a solid, viable community. Late in the previous century, Paul Cuffe, a Quaker merchant and shipbuilder who was the son of an African-born former slave and a Wampanoag Indian mother, had challenged Massachusetts laws denying him and other black male taxpayers the franchise. Then in the early 1800s, deeply concerned about the future of his people in the United States, Cuffe advocated the voluntary colonization of free people of color in "Mother Africa" and sailed to and from the British colony of Sierra Leone where slavery was banned. The family's prosperity waned, however, and by the time John Bond arrived, Cuffe's granddaughter had to seek assistance from the local Overseers of the Poor.[5]

Before 1840, the abolitionists Nathan and Mary Page Johnson had befriended an escaped slave from Maryland. They opened their home and gave a new surname—Douglass, which he always used thereafter—to the vigorous young man who boarded with them for three years. Frederick Douglass observed that the Johnsons "took, paid for, and read more newspapers; better understood the moral, religious, and political character of the nation,—than nine-tenths of the slaveholders in Talbot County, Maryland," where he had been born. That was a formative period for Douglass, who soon championed the rights of women, his fellow black Americans, Chinese and Irish immigrants, even exploited British seamen.[6]

Joseph Wilson, George Teamoh, and Thomas Bayne, all fugitive slaves from Norfolk, Virginia, and future leaders there, also received warm welcomes in New Bedford, where Wilson and Teamoh became seafarers. Another, less fortunate sailor from Norfolk died in a New Bedford "house of ill-fame," but Teamoh nonetheless declared that he "held that municipality in highest admiration" because its residents "laid down as principle . . . the full and untrammelled possession of one's ownership of himself."[7]

New Bedford's diversity stimulated its townspeople. From his pulpit in December 1862, a local minister proclaimed, "We call different races white, yellow, red, . . . and black; but we find them so only in falsely colored pictures." "Strange that these proud United States should find their problem in a downtrodden race of men," he added. Every August, a local journal reported, an international contingent of black seamen joined "the colored people of New Bedford, with representatives of their friends from Boston, Providence, and elsewhere" to celebrate the anniversary of emancipation in the

British West Indies. In many venues and on many occasions, the city's disparate itinerants enhanced its eclectic creole culture.[8]

Whatever their race, wherever they originated, whaling most often drew people to New Bedford and employed perhaps ten thousand, despite the fact that its historic livelihood had begun to decline because of glutted oil markets and the recent discovery of Pennsylvania's petroleum deposits. Townsmen and transients of all ethnicities and colors went to sea, while others housed, fed, nursed, and prayed for the mariners. A panoply of laborers constructed, supplied, and repaired ships, cut, stitched, and patched topgallants, royals, spankers, mizzens, jibs, and other sails. Coopers shaped staves and welded iron hoops for countless thousands of oil barrels, rope makers braided mile after mile of hemp and cotton fibers, while others provided the varied accoutrements needed for all phases of the omnipresent whaling industry. In 1848, Lewis Temple, a New Bedford Negro, had developed and perfected a device he called the toggle harpoon, sometimes hailed as the single most significant technical innovation in New England's whaling history.[9]

New Bedford was home port to a fleet of more than three hundred square-rigged whalers that sailed the world's oceans for years at a time. One black seaman, in fact, spent only twenty-three months ashore during an eighteen-year stretch. The ships featured doubly reinforced hulls to smash through Arctic ice in pursuit of their mammoth, elusive prey, and Melville's Ishmael had surveyed the oleaginous payload they hauled home. "Hills and mountains of casks on casks were piled upon the wharves," he observed, "and side by side the world-wandering whale ships lay silent and safely moored at last." Local women paced widows' walks scanning the horizon anxiously awaiting the return of their seafaring loved ones—the latter-day progeny of Jonah.[10]

New Bedford's intrepid mariners routinely confronted the oceangoing perils of savage storms, ice floes, and truculent whales. But in addition, during the early Civil War years the brazen, barkentine-rigged Confederate raider *Alabama,* with a crew of Irish and English hooligans largely recruited from Liverpool's waterfront, tried to sabotage any successful manifestations of the North's maritime economy. Prior to its own climactic demise, the belligerent *Alabama* destroyed at least fifteen whaling ships.

Mariners returning to New Bedford reported on the progress of whalers they encountered, such as the bark *Roscius,* which in fourteen months at sea, with more to come, already had loaded on and processed five hundred barrels of oil. Another, the *Roman,* finally came home to a tumultuous welcome after three-and-a-half years navigating the world's most abundant whaling grounds. More than two thousand barrels of golden sperm oil (an important lubricant), a thousand of whale oil (valued for illumination and soap), plus six thousand pounds of baleen—the whales' elongated, filtering "teeth," destined to become the flexible stays in fashionable ladies' corsets—engorged its hold.[11]

Townspeople gossiped about the brazen young woman discovered aboard the whaler *America* who "had disguised herself and played her part so well as to live for months in the forecastle without detection." When the dumbfounded captain finally determined the imposter's sex, he discharged her, whereupon he learned that having been abandoned by a disgruntled husband, she already had served fifteen months (also garbed as a man) with the Union's army of the Potomac, and after her curt dismissal from military service had arrived in New Bedford ready and eager to go whaling. With few exceptions, however, women's presence on the high seas was limited to the objectified, wooden figureheads on the prows of sailing ships.[12]

While that town ceaselessly talked whales and whaling, the country had been at war with itself for more than a year when John Bond arrived in early fall 1862, but the killing fields remained hundreds of miles away. All of New England, however, seethed with both reliable information and wild speculation about the Civil War's progress. The rampant gossip and tabloid accounts pertaining to maritime affairs especially would have attracted the attention of Bond and his seafaring colleagues.

One prophetic incident concerned the fate of a Yankee ship named the *Emily* that Confederate forces ambushed in the Great Dismal Swamp Canal forty miles south of Norfolk. After seizing the *Emily,* one journal reported, "the rebels made our men work the boat in order to pass our gunboats without detection." The episode embarrassed the Union, which earlier had appropriated that same vessel from the Confederacy. The *Emily*'s peripatetic course soon found it under British registry, serving the Rebels again as it furtively shuttled back and forth across "the pond."[13]

Of further interest to a Liverpudlian like Bond would have been the identification of the steamers *Gladiator* and *Giraffe,* from his home port, as blockade runners. They were but two of many such British renegades, and Liverpool's shipyards were surreptitiously building or outfitting much of the Confederate navy. The *Gladiator* sailed from the River Mersey bound for a southern harbor (probably Wilmington, North Carolina, where it could pick up a payload of cotton to make the round trip doubly profitable) laden with "1500 barrels of bread and 1045 . . . of bacon." That venture, providing sustenance for the South, seemed to confirm "the great destitution of the rebels." Endeavors such as the *Gladiator*'s, as well as clandestine shipbuilding, called into question England's avowed neutrality in America's Civil War.[14]

New Bedford's citizens, in addition to debating all aspects of their major industry, concerned themselves with the war and their country's progress toward general emancipation. With flags waving and bands playing, they celebrated the departure for the South of a new military unit the week John Bond arrived. Their newspaper observed, however, that a number of white Union soldiers maintained a "malignant and cruel spirit towards the unfortunate [Negro] 'contrabands' with whom they come in contact." That same month, eager New Englanders offered their president the services of three projected "colored" regiments. Although a few Union officers already had deployed several bands of blacks on military forays in the South, the formal proposal to establish units of northern Negro soldiers was peremptorily "declined for the present," and the young men advised to "wait till such a course seemed to be a direct command of Providence."[15]

That September of 1862, many journals discussed the issuance of Abraham Lincoln's preliminary Emancipation Proclamation, offering the seceded states an opportunity to abandon their rebellion and rejoin the Union. "If this generation shall extinguish slavery," New Bedford's *Evening Standard* editorialized, "it may suffer to some extent, but all future generations shall call it blessed." Despite common knowledge that the presidential edict, ironically, was directed only at those jurisdictions that disavowed his authority, "the first of January," the newspaper asserted, marked "the downfall of the slave system in America—a date hereafter . . . celebrated as a high national anniversary." "At noon today," it pronounced immediately after the long-anticipated moment of deliverance, "the bells of the city were rung an hour, and one hundred guns fired," extolling the proclamation.[16]

Despite New England's brutal weather ("the ice-bound . . . city [shivered] with clouds along the skies like mountains of flint, while piercing winds from frozen oceans left no nook unsearched," the former Virginia slave George Teamoh complained), after January 1, 1863, the drumbeat summoning recruits into the military intensified.[17] "Colored citizens of New Bedford," one leader exhorted, "do your whole duty as men, and be not drawn away from the right path." William Wells Brown, well known in John Bond's Liverpool for his antislavery discourses, spoke about the Emancipation Proclamation at the North Christian Church, stating that his race had many preachers and poets, but needed heroes on the battlefield. "Colored Men, Attention!" advertisements proclaimed, "Your Country Calls!" The *Evening Standard* reprinted Frederick Douglass's "Call to the Negro to Arms" in which he stated that "liberty won by white men would leave half its lustre." "Massachusetts now welcomes you to arms," he continued, "the nucleus of this first organization is now in camp at Readville, a short distance from Boston."[18]

New Bedford raised its own company (which proposed to call itself the Toussaint Guards, honoring Haiti's black emancipator) for the new Negro regiment—the Fifty-fourth Massachusetts. Enlistees included the onetime Virginians Joseph T. Wilson and William Carney. Other recruits, representing all classes and walks of life, came from throughout Massachusetts, twenty-five states, the District of Columbia, even Africa. Before he joined the Fifty-fourth and the struggle to end slavery, a volunteer named Nicolas Saïd had been a Sudanese leader. He spoke eight languages, plus his own vernacular, Kanouri.[19]

Not only did New Bedford recruit black men for the Fifty-fourth, but many of its mariners joined the Union Navy. As early as October 1862, over two thousand sailors of all ethnicities and backgrounds had enlisted from that port alone.[20]

John Robert Bond, freshly arrived on an English salt cod trader, had crossed the ocean not only as a typically ambitious, economically driven European immigrant, but also as a youth with solid maritime skills and an emerging mission. He hardly could have forgotten the epithets ("wog," "half-caste," "monkey," and "Nigger Jack") that had been bandied about, characterizing him and other black or brown people during his childhood and his interval at sea. Relatives or colleagues of African ancestry also may have instilled in him a lasting sense of outrage at the injustices perpetrated against men and women of their race. Growing up in Liverpool, Bond would have known of, and possibly been motivated by, abolitionists such as Frederick Douglass and William Wells Brown whose rhetoric familiarized many of the British with the horrors of slave life. The mindless delirium of war also may have stirred his blood. But regardless of what other specifics stimulated him to act, Bond decided to volunteer for the Union Navy because, he later asserted, he wanted to help free the slaves—dark-complexioned people like himself, whose bondage he knew about but could only imagine.[21]

In the final week of May 1863, Bond sought out (or was solicited by) Thomas Fenney, a recruiting officer at the naval enlistment center located on a steep, cobbled street overlooking the harbor, hard by the Sailors' Bethel Church and Mariners' Home. Fenney assigned the young Englishman to the receiving ship ("or guardo as they are called," one sailor explained) *Ohio*. In the context of his personal experiences, an emerging race consciousness, desire for decently paid work at sea, and perhaps a hormonally spurred craving to assert his burgeoning manhood, all heightened by New Bedford's patriotic frenzy, Bond contracted to serve for one year with the navy of the United States.[22]

The fratricidal struggle for which he volunteered already had wrenched the country asunder for two years, and from its inception had raised daunting political, economic, ideological, even personal issues that legions of Americans remained uncertain how to answer. The contest pitted North against South, abolitionists against slavery's champions, federalists against states' rights advocates, but also, and most tragically, family and friends against one another.

Even before the war began, many Americans had wondered if the Constitution allowed states unilaterally to withdraw from the Union to form a new, sovereign Confederacy. In addition, the United States maintained among its most basic tenets the sanctity of property rights that the government pledged never to violate. And the property—the major assets—of many white southerners included more than four million of their fellow human beings. By the time the nation's all-male, almost all-white electorate chose Abraham Lincoln as president in late 1860, the country had reached a point when it became imperative to challenge the entrenched belief that race, as legally yet speciously defined, could determine whether darker-complexioned people deserved the privileges of citizenship that American men with lighter skins had come to assume were theirs by divine right, reinforced by government sanction. But how long could a country that declared itself "dedicated to the proposition that all men are created equal" (as its new president proclaimed) tolerate the moral scar that allowed some of its residents to hold others in slavery much as they might own swine or cattle?

Lincoln pledged to hold the fractious Union together and also resolved to prevent the extension of slavery westward. He vacillated on the central question of slavery itself, however, and had argued that for the races to remain together, "there must be the position of superior and inferior, and I as much as any other man am in favor of having the superior position assigned to the white race." But the president was becoming increasingly anxious to end the noxious, "peculiar institution" altogether. He envisioned emigration to Negro-populated territories in Africa or the Caribbean as one solution to the "problems" that he believed would be engendered by millions of newly emancipated black people in his own country.[23]

As those debates raged, in early 1861 most of the slave states followed South Carolina's lead and began seceding from the Union. They realigned themselves into a Confederacy, chose Mississippi's Senator Jefferson Davis as president, and adopted a constitution almost duplicating that of the United States, but dedicated to doctrines of states' rights and untrammeled personal liberties, the most sacred of which was its white citizens' curious "liberty" to enslave and own others. On April 12, challenging the presence of an unacceptable "foreign" installation within its presumptively sovereign territory, a contingent from the military arm of the new Confederate States of America besieged Charleston, South Carolina's Fort Sumter, forcing the surrender of Union troops stationed there. The Army of the Confederacy claimed that stronghold as its own, and war began.

Many white northerners proclaimed themselves willing, if not eager, to fight as a means of reuniting their bleeding country, defending it against all challengers, and maintaining internal order. Some of them bluntly made it known that "we don't want to fight side by side with the nigger," while others thought it imperative that black men join the armed forces.[24] A popular verse concocted in an affected Irish brogue expressed that position:

> Some say it is a burnin' shame
> To make the naygurs fight,
> An' that the thrade o' bein' kilt
> Belongs but to the white;
> But as for me, upon me sowl,
> So liberal are we here,
> I'll let Sambo be murthered in place o' meself
> On every day in the year. . . .
> Though Sambo's black as the ace o' spades
> His finger a thrigger can pull,
> An' his eye runs sthraight on the barrel sight
> From under its thatch o' wool.[25]

But would whites really fight to emancipate a massive band of what they considered woolly headed "Sambos" who might deluge the country with a primitive, alien darkness? Once freed, would those men and women demand to be treated as equals in both political and social arenas? And especially, would the former slaves then create a huge font of inexpensive labor that presumably would threaten the livelihoods that many Americans—native-born and immigrant—believed, by right, belonged to white men?

Those angry debates focusing on race, caste, and the country's future raged throughout the war, but navy receiving ships such as the one on which John Bond first served, a black sailor observed, carried "all kinds and all classes of men."[26] The 2,700-ton USS *Ohio* had been launched four decades earlier and, like other aging ships in the Union navy, no longer was a state-of-the-art vessel. It was, however, a distinguished, intricately rigged, three-masted wooden ship. The prow displayed a carved, lacquered depiction of a black-bearded Hercules (the snarling Nemean lion—the first conquest of that Greek hero—draped across his shoulders) as its daunting figurehead.

In an earlier era, as part of the fledgling United States Navy, the *Ohio* had crossed the Atlantic as a flagship of the Mediterranean Squadron, attempting to suppress the illegal yet still thriving intercontinental slave trade off Africa. During the Mexican War it participated in the siege of Vera Cruz, then patrolled the California Territory's coast in the early months of the Gold Rush. An officer who once served on it declared, "I never supposed such a ship could be built—a ship possessing in so great a degree all the qualifications of a perfect vessel." By 1863, however, that perfect vessel's adventuresome history was little more than memory. In May, one newspaper reported, "the *Ohio* was surveyed for the purpose of ascertaining whether . . . she could be made seaworthy. She was found to be very unsound above the present water line." Despite its daunting battery of seventy-four cannons, it had become noticeably decrepit, and was therefore assigned to perform tedious, but essential, harbor or near-shore wartime duties. Bond took "the oath of Allegiance to the Government of Uncle Samuel" and saluted the flag that he newly had sworn to defend. It had thirteen broad stripes of red and white, and thirty-one bright stars on a deep blue field.[27]

At the time of his rendezvous on the *Ohio* in May 1863, John Bond's height was five feet seven and three-quarters inches. He was slender, with curling black hair, a gently cleft chin, high cheekbones, and brown eyes. His visage reflected both an African and Gaelic parentage, and his proud bearing was that of a person never enslaved.[28] He claimed to be twenty-two but, in truth, was only seventeen, and may have falsified his age to shake off boyhood and make himself seem more a real man. He was clean-shaven—perhaps still unshaven—and, unlike many other mariners, had not a single tattoo.

Unknown circumstances had cost him his right index finger plus the first joint of the middle finger on that same hand. Bond's injury may have resulted from a routine mishap, but at least one New England newspaper reported the account of a sadistic British sea captain who, "offended at one of his crew . . . ordered the ship's carpenter to chop the poor fellow's fingers off."[29] The *Ohio*'s surgeon observed and noted Bond's minor amputation, and apparently concluded that it made him no less "able bodied" or impaired his ability to perform shipboard duties. Bond acquired the standard-issue uniform including a wool jacket, midnight-blue flared "trowsers," flannel overshirt, silk handkerchief and jaunty, ribbon-trimmed cap, plus other essentials, for which the navy would deduct a total of $31.27 from his future pay.[30]

Though most black men—many of them former slaves—who served in the Union Navy during the war were shunted into ratings such as "boy," coal heaver, or mess attendant, Bond's skills and experience at sea (plus, certainly, some timely prevarication about his age) earned him the more prestigious rank of "able seaman."[31] Compared to lower-ranked landsmen's twelve-dollar stipend, seamen earned eighteen dollars per month, and that rating supposedly required five years of prior maritime experience. To entice acquisitive young men into the navy, recruiters offered bounties for enlistment, and held out the tantalizing possibility of prize money that might be awarded for the capture of enemy ships and confiscation of their cargo.[32]

Sixteen sailors in New Bedford, John Robert Bond among them, boarded the *Ohio* in late May. They included three other Negroes:

a local man, one from Demerara (colonial British Guiana), and a Marylander. Another recruit from the "Isle of Guam" was described as "copper-collored." Six enlistees were foreigners, while the remainder were white Americans. Within a few days, the re-manned *Ohio* left New Bedford en route to Boston.[33]

Among the men who disembarked from the *Ohio* shortly after Bond arrived was a sailor named William Gould, rated a "boy." He was a North Carolina–born contraband—an escaped slave claimed and liberated by the Union's armed forces. But Gould soon had to leave the guardo, because, he explained, "the measels broke out from me and I was sent to the Hospital."[34] A decade later, their paths reconverged and they became fast friends, but in May 1863 neither man had any reason to expect to see the other again.

Long before either Bond or Gould was born, black sailors had served in the United States Navy with varying degrees of welcome and success. They continued to do so during the early war years when most patriotic men of their race still were refused entry into the land forces.[35] There was little organized resistance to their inclusion in the navy, however, and several interlocking reasons contributed to this relative absence of concern.

Five percent of the peacetime navy traditionally had been black. Although their presence did not lack controversy, Negroes had served in that seagoing branch of the military during the two conflicts with Britain: the War for Independence and the War of 1812.[36] And the navy routinely assigned most such men to the supposedly servile job categories deemed appropriate for people of their race and which whites often were loath to fill. Also, black sailors had been noncombatants in a commerce-oriented, peacetime maritime service when enlistees of diverse nationalities and races were vigorously recruited (and as often simply vanished) in ports around the world. They usually carried no firearms, and therefore were not considered as menacing as weapons-bearing "colored" soldiers. As long as they served at sea, sailors remained an ample distance from most civilians, especially white women. Finally, Secretary of the Navy Gideon Welles—called "Father Neptune" or "Rip Van Winkle," the first moniker suggesting his departmental affiliation and the latter his luxuriant silver beard—held antislavery convictions that helped to chart the relatively unbiased course along which he steered the branch of the armed services under his command.[37]

In October 1861, Welles had issued a directive concerning the potential military use of contrabands. He authorized recruitment officers "to enlist them in the naval service under the same rights and regulations as apply to other enlistments," although at first, those former slaves could hold no rating higher than "boy." By the following year, however, revised regulations let them be promoted to the rank of able seaman. With their virtual "invisibility" in the southern landscape and knowledge of shorelines, ports, and waterways, contraband sailors proved especially valuable in undercover intelligence efforts.[38]

Unlike the army, where not until after the Emancipation Proclamation's issuance did blacks officially serve in the segregated regiments that became known as the United States Colored Troops (USCT), Negro sailors lived and worked alongside white shipmates from the first months of the war. They included ex-slaves such as William Gould, free Negroes from the North, and a few dark-skinned foreigners like Bond.[39] Estimates of their numbers have varied, but ultimately they totaled about eighteen thousand, and comprised almost one-sixth of the Union navy. In addition, the mulatto seafarer Michael Healy, like unknown numbers of others, passed for white. He received a commission in the adjunct Revenue Cutter Service—later the Coast Guard.[40] Especially on ordnance and supply ships, black men advanced into the ranks of petty officers, but with only a single exception Negroes did not receive commissions. A number of blacks did become cooks and stewards, who, though serving in presumably less prestigious categories than seamen, earned higher pay.[41]

Some distinguished themselves at sea during the war. At least eight hundred were killed, captured, or wounded in battle while another two thousand drowned or died from disease. William Tillman's exploits on the *S. J. Waring,* Jacob Garrick's aboard the *Enchantress,* and especially Robert Smalls's dramatic capture of the Confederate steamer *Planter* nourished the lore about courageous maritime ventures by contrabands. The navy never decorated those men, but during the four-and-a-half years of hostilities, the Union awarded eight other black sailors (five landsmen, two seaman, and a cook) the Medal of Honor.[42]

Negroes such as Bond and his black shipmates signed up for varied reasons. Some were slaves fleeing bondage who sought refuge and hoped to help end the "peculiar institution." Others, like many white boys, sought decent work at decent wages, were patriotic, just wanted to leave home, and perhaps had an aptitude, affinity, or romantic yearning for life at sea. One observer argued that Negroes joined the navy because "Jack has never been squeamish"— suggesting that white mariners lacked prejudice, and therefore unreservedly welcomed "colored" colleagues—while another commented that "they mess with their colored shipmates . . . toil, suffer, rejoice, sing, and divide prizes together without showing the least difference."[43]

Those claims of universal tolerance, however, seem vastly overstated, and fail to recognize that Negro seamen often encountered harsh treatment and bitter, racially generated difficulties. Frequently, white sailors reflected society's racism, though the Navy Department usually enforced its military regulations that (at least on paper) allowed few race-based inequities. While recruiting blacks to join the armed forces, Frederick Douglass conceded that "colored men going into the army and navy must expect annoyance," adding, "they will be severely criticized and even insulted."[44] Despite such "expected" criticism and insults, throughout the war "colored" seamen served as loyally as any others. A few sailors of African ancestry, however, deserted (as did many men of all races and ethnicities) for a variety of reasons, sometimes as a result of white shipmates' taunting or even physical attacks, which, despite the Navy Department's comparatively nonracist policies and administration, were not unusual.

Race notwithstanding, Bond and other tan-, brown-, or black-skinned sailors received the same monthly stipends as whites of comparable rank. In contrast to the financially discriminatory standards that plagued the USCT, the navy scarcely challenged the propriety of equal compensation for people of different races who performed the same jobs.[45] Until mid-1864, on the other hand, blacks in the Union army fought frustrating battles to gain equal pay. Although it remained certain that most of them would stay clustered in the lower job classifications, Negroes aboard Yankee ships rarely lived in separate quarters or worked in segregated units as did men who joined the land forces. Pragmatic logistics and the exigencies of life aboard crowded vessels, at least as much as egalitarian ideology, however, may have prompted, even necessitated, the navy's policies and practices.[46]

In May 1863, while John Bond served on the USS *Ohio* in or near Boston's harbor, the men who comprised the new Fifty-fourth Massachusetts Infantry Regiment prepared to leave their Camp Meigs training grounds. That post, which for decades thereafter would bear great significance for black people (including Bond) who fought for the Union, was located in an area called Readville, soon to be incorporated into a new town named Hyde Park.[47]

Avid supporters of the Fifty-fourth and then the Fifty-fifth Regiments (after the first unit filled up, "it slopt over, so the spilt ones are now the germ of another regiment," a corporal explained) included the state's governor, John Andrew, a leader in the movement to mobilize Negro troops. Frederick Douglass, whose sons Lewis and Charles joined the Massachusetts regiments, and white abolitionists such as Theodore Weld and his wife, women's rights advocate Angelina Grimké Weld, visited the men, applauded their mission, and praised their dedication. The exhilaration generated by the North's first black troops spread well beyond Boston. New Bedford's patriots hastened to their local railroad depot—its mausoleumlike, Egyptian-inspired architecture led residents to call it "the Tombs"—and joined the festive excursion to Readville (a round-trip ticket cost $1.35) to bid their company farewell.[48]

Government policies combined with racial prejudices, including rampant assumptions about blacks' supposedly inferior leadership capabilities, however, meant that not only did the federal government intend to pay Negro soldiers less than whites, but for some time, all of the Massachusetts regiments' commissioned officers were Caucasians. The initially reluctant Robert Gould Shaw, the "blue-eyed child of God" (and a son of dedicated abolitionists) who had been reassigned from the Second Infantry, became their colonel, and ultimately his men's staunch advocate.[49]

In spheres of purely military significance (organization, strategy, deployment), the Union army fully incorporated the Massachusetts units. In other respects, as state militias, they remained under the Commonwealth's jurisdiction. The politically powerful Republican governor Andrew promised his "boys" the same pay as whites, and citizens raised bonus money to encourage and reward them. But the men who trained at Camp Meigs ultimately turned down Andrew's offer and decided that they would accept no pay at all rather than tolerate "that the Federal Government should throw mud on them" through the unequal remuneration of *any* black soldiers in the USCT. They likened equal pay to full manhood. Their boycott carried profound moral weight, and many of the unit's white officers eventually joined the protest.[50]

Serving in the armed forces became a powerful indicator of male esteem. "Let the black man get upon his person the brass letters, U.S.," Frederick Douglass asserted, "let him get an eagle on his buttons and a musket on his shoulder . . . and there is no power on earth which can deny that he has earned the right to citizenship." As his country's awesome internecine struggle heated up, the great abolitionist also had predicted that "the side which first summons the Negro to its aid will conquer." That side was the Union.[51]

On May 28, Boston held a parade—reviewed by men and women from every walk of life, politicians, and luminaries including the "cream of Massachusetts society"—to honor the proud fellows who comprised their departing regiment. The soldiers arrived from Readville that morning, traveling nine miles into town via the Boston & Providence Railroad. Tricolored bunting was displayed everywhere, and the Colored Ladies' Relief Society and other civic groups presented silk flags to their champions. Drums rolled, cornets and French horns blared out martial anthems, and boisterous curbside crowds "such as only the 4th of July or some rare event causes to assemble," stated one eyewitness, applauded and tossed confetti as the dark-skinned, blue-uniformed men marched smartly from Boston Common down Tremont, Court, and State Streets toward the docks. At four o'clock, amid cheers, tears, and tumult, the men of the Fifty-fourth Massachusetts boarded the USS *De Molay,* which then steamed slowly away from the navy yard's Battery Wharf. They were bound for both glory and tragedy on southern fields of battle.[52]

During the ensuing weeks, seaman John Bond remained on the *Ohio* as it sailed out of that same harbor, hugging the misted coast around Cape Cod, past the paired islands of Martha's Vineyard and Nantucket, back to New Bedford where more recruits signed on. Then it returned to Boston. In the first week of July, as the divided country celebrated yet another birthday, Bond and sixty-eight other sailors from the guardo *Ohio* transferred onto the USS *Cambridge,* which recently had come under the control of a new captain: Commander William F. Spicer.[53]

The *Cambridge* was younger, smaller, swifter, and more fit than the venerable *Ohio.* Just three years old, it had been constructed in a Boston shipyard and named for the renowned university town across the Charles River. With its coal-fueled engine below, plus canvas sails fashioned to harness the wind, it was a two-masted, square-rigged, single-cylinder screw steamer with one towering smokestack—illustrating how the age of sail was yielding to the age of steam. The *Cambridge* was made of white oak and weighed 850 tons. Its length was two hundred feet and the beam thirty-two across. When wholly loaded it drew more than thirteen feet, and under a full head of steam or catching a stiff breeze, cruised at ten knots. The armaments included howitzers, plus fixed Sawyer, Schenkle, and Parrott rifles, for a total of forty-two guns in the battery.[54]

By the time Bond went aboard, the *Cambridge* (assigned to the North Atlantic blockading squadron) had amassed a history of successful exploits. The navy had awarded its officers and crew eleven prizes for the seizure of enemy vessels and cargo. The previous year, in one brief week, the *Cambridge* helped to capture four blockade runners at sea—though several of its sailors were taken prisoner during one costly skirmish—and chased ashore and destroyed a fifth.[55]

Despite successes such as those through which the navy had eliminated numerous hostile vessels by the summer of 1863, the blockade of southern ports still created both diplomatic and practical problems for the Union. Just declaring a blockade gave credence to Confederate claims of sovereignty, a status that President Lincoln wanted, at any cost, to deny. A country should not, after all, have to blockade its own harbors, only those of a belligerent nation. To deal with an internal uprising, federal authority should simply need to reestablish control of any anarchic ports. Finally, in order to be recognized under international maritime law, a blockade had to prove itself effective. Many argued that this was only a "paper" blockade (leaky as a sieve), and therefore need not be respected by foreign powers that wanted to continue their commerce with the secessionists. *Punch,* the British humor magazine, published an impudent limerick deriding the sometimes futile efforts of the navy secretary:

> *There was an old fogy named Welles,*
> *Quite worthy of cap and of bells,*
> *For he tho't that a pirate*
> *Who steamed at a great rate,*
> *Would wait to be riddled by shells.*[56]

Despite such journalistic gibes, the blockade of almost two hundred ports, harbors, and navigable inlets along thirty-five hundred miles of the Confederacy's Atlantic and Gulf coastlines continued throughout the war. General Winfield Scott, "Old Fuss and Feathers," labeled this the "anaconda plan" (cynics called it "Scott's snake"), suggesting that the Union naval blockade coiled around its prey like a python, gradually tightening its grasp to squeeze the victim to death.[57] If it never completely strangled or isolated the rebels, it did cripple their ability to import crucial war matériel and consumer goods. It also curtailed most exports of cotton—so vital to the southern economy.

The Union navy's questionable merits, especially the dubious effectiveness of its blockade, evoked sharply barbed cartoons. One such representation singled out the ship on which John Bond served, depicting the *Cambridge* as a wooden washtub equipped with flimsy side paddles, a jerry-built smokestack, and one ineffectual cannon. Sailors busied themselves brewing tea as the unseaworthy vessel feebly pursued a sleek Confederate blockade runner.

"Ship ahoy! Heave ho, and surrender!!" the foppish, caricatured captain called to his quarry, "don't you see that the 'Department' has . . . fitted up this magnificent vessel on purpose to catch you?" "Give our compliments to the Secretary," the blockade runner's skipper taunted as his ship sped away, "and tell him he shall certainly hear from us by every Northern vessel that we meet."[58]

During the months that Bond remained on the ridiculed USS *Cambridge,* it carried a contingent of from 140 to 160 men. On a ship such as that, a war reporter observed, seamen "clung to the rigging like bees to a hive, in clusters as close as they could cling."[59] More than 50 of the high-climbing crew were foreigners. They hailed from a number of maritime nations and spoke Italian, Spanish, French, Portuguese, Swedish, Danish, Norwegian, German, and Russian. An officer on a comparably manned Union ship observed: "We had a motley . . . crew from all parts of the world."[60] Foreign-born staff officers made up seven percent, lower-ranked warrant officers fifteen percent, and enlisted men about one-third of the Union navy. Of those, the greatest number hailed from the British Isles as did John Robert Bond, men from that most "civilized" region of the world being considered the most worthy and assimilable of all foreigners.[61]

When Bond boarded the *Cambridge,* twelve of its crew were designated "Negro," "black," or "mulatto." More nonwhite sailors signed on later that year, and during his entire period on the ship, twenty-two Negroes joined him. Fourteen were southern born and reared, most of them contrabands, and five were northerners, two from Massachusetts. Three others were aliens, including a Jamaican and a Puerto Rican. Thomas Fowler, another mulatto "Nigger Jack" from Liverpool, had been transferred from the *Ohio* along with Bond. As to rank, only Bond and Fowler became able seamen. There was a black cook, while the rest were about equally divided between greenhorn "boys" and landsmen.[62] The *Cambridge*'s officers, on the other hand—as was the case throughout the navy with some exceptions in the ranks of petty officers—all were white.

In early 1864, one of the Union navy's rear admirals formally issued a directive statutorily linking nonwhites and foreigners. He directed his recruitment officers: "When opportunity offers, I wish you to enlist all the able-bodied men you can accommodate, without regard to nation or color, provided they will take an oath of allegiance to our flag." Despite that edict, Bond and his shipmate Fowler were among the navy's very few Englishmen of African ancestry.[63]

During July and much of August 1863, Boston remained its home port as the *Cambridge* patrolled New England's coast. It spotted several ships that appeared suspicious, but they either slipped away or identified themselves as nonhostile vessels pursuing legitimate business. On one expedition, Commander Spicer's ship ventured south off the Carolinas, where it crossed paths with the USS *Hendrick Hudson* bound north from Key West with many Confederate prisoners aboard, but during the summer of 1863 the *Cambridge* came no closer than that to any encounter with the enemy. Most ships in the North Atlantic blockade only sighted belligerent vessels somewhat more often than once a month, and confronted or intercepted them even less frequently. "Day after day," a world-weary officer lamented, ruing his similarly mundane routine, "we lay inactive, roll, roll."[64]

The summer of 1863, however, was more eventful for others. It saw the culmination of the siege of Vicksburg, Mississippi, where the Union navy played a major role, but the most portentous events surrounded conscription. A new federal fiat forced economically disadvantaged men into uniform, while permitting the affluent to buy their way out of military service. If he wished, three hundred dollars enabled a person with adequate financial resources to avoid serving by engaging a surrogate. Too often, the struggle became a rich man's war, but a poor man's fight.[65]

On July 14, 1863, as John Robert Bond remained in port aboard the *Cambridge,* Boston's draft riot began in the largely immigrant North End when a group of angry women assaulted two agents who had served conscription notices on several local lads. Idlers joined the fray and, armed with only fists and clubs, almost killed a constable who tried to restore order. The mayor mobilized militia companies and called in a contingent of United States troops garrisoned nearby. Crowds attacked the armory where they assembled, and authorities resorted to cannon fire to repulse the rioters.

Protesters surged out of their neighborhood seeking weapons, but the well-armed police and soldiers soon terminated the uprising. Father James Healy, an up-and-coming priest of Irish and African heritage—and a brother of the ambitious young U.S. Navy Cutter Service officer Michael Healy—issued a timely call for order that many of the local Catholic clergy read at Sunday masses to help quell the simmering unrest.[66] Despite the uproar, Boston defused its draft protests with far less loss of life and property than did New York City that same week.

Many of that larger port's immigrant dockworkers had gone on strike for higher wages, and some employers replaced them with lower-paid black men. By 1860, the Irish had come to perceive the waterfront as their occupational preserve, and New York's *Herald* sarcastically declared that the stevedores "must feel enraptured at the prospects of hordes of darkeys . . . working for half wages and thus ousting them from employment." Adding insult to injury, as idle and irate workers viewed it, they found themselves susceptible to conscription in a war of which most of them wanted no part. Many whites considered it an effort to emancipate (and then insinuate into America's mainstream) black people, some of whom already had supplanted them on the docks.[67]

On July 13, crowds of predominantly poor, often Irish-born residents—victims of harsh nativist bigotry themselves—began gathering in curbside knots, venting their fury at the perceived injustices they suffered.[68] The Democratic Party, representing that immigrant consituency, encouraged them. Many women shared the men's outrage at the draft law's economic discrimination, and joined in a four-day rampage of terror and destruction. Wielding clubs, throwing bricks (victims called them "Irish confetti"), even potatoes, they attacked draft offices. But blacks became the preferred targets, with "mobs chasing isolated negroes as hounds would chase a fox." They were hunted down, hanged from lampposts, battered and murdered in their ransacked residences. A white woman was beaten to death as she tried to rescue her mulatto child from cremation at the hands of the rabble, while drunken vandals incinerated the city's Colored Orphan Asylum. A few of the hoodlums reportedly even mutilated black corpses.[69]

More than a hundred people died in New York's disturbances, and many times that number were injured. Losses from theft, arson, and property destruction mounted into the millions. Union troops straight from a costly victory at Gettysburg had to be called in to quell the savagery. Most participants went unpunished, but authorities arrested, tried, convicted, and imprisoned some of the more heinous offenders. A Negro physician swore that his people would hold the city responsible for their losses, though any municipal action or reparations, he mourned, "cannot bring back our murdered dead [or] remove the insults we feel."[70]

Even on their ships, sailors such as Bond would have learned about those antiblack, antidraft riots. Yet despite widespread class and racial tensions, plus conflicts between older residents and immigrants epitomized by urban America's turmoil, a few days later, the Fifty-fourth Massachusetts, supported by the navy and joined by other army units, prepared to assault Battery Wagner. It was a key Confederate stronghold guarding Charleston's harbor, across from the notorious Fort Sumter. The evening prior to the battle, Harriet Tubman (an Underground Railroad leader, wartime nurse and scout who once led Union cavalrymen on a foray that freed dozens of slaves and destroyed valuable southern cotton) purportedly served Colonel Robert Gould Shaw his last supper.[71]

According to the New York *Tribune,* a cynical Union general declared, "I guess we'll . . . put those damned niggers from Massachusetts in the advance; we might as well get rid of them one time as another." Waves of "those damned niggers" beseiged the battery, but the southerners lay low. Suddenly, a cannon barrage deluged the Yankees, and, one participant observed, "a sheet of flame, followed by a running fire, like electric sparks, swept along the parapets." When his company's flag bearer fell, Norfolk and New Bedford's wounded Sergeant William Carney (who would become the first black soldier awarded a Congressional Medal of Honor) seized the Stars and Stripes and raised it aloft. "The old flag never touched the ground!" he cried.[72]

In that hard-fought struggle, the rebels ultimately repulsed the onslaught and maintained control over the citadel. Bloodied, often dismembered bodies, many of them African Americans, littered the harborside combat zone. "When we came to get in de crops," Harriet Tubman mourned, "it was dead men that we reaped." Nurse Clara Barton, the "angel of the battlefield," later recalled "the scarlet flow of blood as it rolled over the black limbs beneath my hands."[73] Though unsuccessful militarily, that Union effort, spearheaded by a new Negro regiment, at least briefly deflected many white Americans' doubts about black soldiers' courage or capabilities.

Numerous members of the Fifty-fourth Massachusetts lost their lives that July day, including its leader, Colonel Shaw. Confederates dumped Shaw's body into a pit, then heaped his dead black troops on top. The rebel commander Johnson Hagood supposedly announced: "We have buried him with his niggers."[74] Despite heavy casualties and the Yankee defeat at Battery Wagner, equal rights advocates considered the battle more an epiphany than an apocalypse. "This regiment has established its reputation as a fighting regiment," wrote Sergeant Lewis Douglass about his comrades-in-arms, "not a man flinched, though it was a trying time." "I wish we had a hundred thousand colored troops," he concluded, "we would put an end to this war." In fact, before the conflict ended, twice as many blacks as Douglass's proposed "hundred thousand" served with the Union forces. The avid abolitionist Angelina Grimké Weld, who soon thereafter moved to a home near the Fifty-fourth Massachusetts's training grounds, added, "I have no tears to shed over their graves, because I see that their heroism is working a great change in public opinion, forcing all . . . to see the sin & shame of enslaving such men."[75]

As part of the ongoing sea war during the troubled summer of 1863, the USS *Cambridge* was but a single link in the far-reaching chain of the North Atlantic blockading squadron. The disparate assemblage of ships assigned to the flotilla patrolling the coast north of South Carolina constantly sought out and tried to intercept, capture, or destroy, and generally to negate the effectiveness of, those privateers—predominantly of English, or at least British Empire registry—that remained intent on reinforcing the still resolute Confederacy. Blockade running in and out of the southern states' Atlantic and Gulf of Mexico harbors was a lucrative enterprise for bold adventurers who ceaselessly attempted to resupply the South with embargoed goods.

The blockade runners used a variety of low-slung vessels, painted slate gray to blend with the sea and the hazy horizon. They burned smokeless anthracite coal further to conceal their approach, and sped about or changed course with greater agility than their sluggish Yankee pursuers. Sometimes because of their pro-Confederate, proslavery ideology, other times stimulated by their ventures' inherent exhilaration, but always with an eye to ample profits, renegade skippers challenged the Union navy and chanced serious risk to liberty and lives, as well as confiscation or demolition of their seafaring property.[76]

With Seaman Bond plus well over a hundred others aboard, the *Cambridge* continued on blockade duty during July and August, but for several weeks it anchored off Newport, Rhode Island, to serve as a training facility for a contingent of midshipmen from Annapolis—all of them white American boys—on summer maneuvers, accompanied by the U.S. Naval Academy's superintendent.[77] Beyond that singular episode, however, those months passed with minimal diversion.

By early September, however, the *Cambridge* was on the high seas again, bound south to join that portion of the blockading squadron stationed off the Carolina coast. Other than pausing to discharge some ailing sailors at the waterside Union army hospital in Beaufort, North Carolina, and the fleeting embarrassment of running hard aground on a sandbar, little transpired during the first days of this new excursion.[78]

After a week, however, the vessel's steering became erratic and shipboard mechanics identified the problem as a cracked engine pin. The *Cambridge* limped back to Beaufort, but then had to be towed north along the Atlantic coast. It was guided landward and proceeded west past Virginia's Fortress Monroe (where many black people fleeing their owners first claimed freedom as contraband of war under the Union army's protection), traversed the treacherous straits at Hampton Roads, then continued to the naval supply depot at Newport News, located at the mouth of the James River, across from a rural county called Isle of Wight. Rebel militia had not yet been totally dislodged from that county, though Union forces had wrested from the Confederacy and resecured portions of nearby southeast Virginia, including the critical ports of Norfolk and Portsmouth. After weeks of delay, Spicer obtained the parts needed for repairs, and his ship then shuttled south across the channel to Portsmouth's Gosport shipyard situated alongside the Elizabeth River. There it would remain for several monotonous months.[79]

While the *Cambridge* was docked in Portsmouth, life for Bond and his mates was tedious. The war-ravaged shipyard was not off limits, but shore leaves beyond its confines were few, and the men usually were given wretched grub. A sailor from a comparable Union ship reported that early each morning the crew had a breakfast of coffee and hardtack. Pork and beans, potato soup, or "Cape Cod turkey" (salt codfish) might comprise their midday meals with little more than bread and coffee for late afternoon suppers. On some ships, intolerant white mariners, determined to maintain their presumed and accustomed positions of superiority, even forced black mates to consume the meager fare in separate facilities. The contraband sailor William Gould reported an incident on the *Cambridge* when some old salts "refused to let ["colored" recruits] eat out of the mess pans and called them all kinds of names." "In all," he concluded, black crewmen were "treated shamefully."[80]

The men slept in hammocks, cheek-by-jowl. Sailors such as Bond occasionally washed their bodies (though one admiral groused that blacks "are not naturally clean in their persons"), prayed, gambled, told endless yarns, and danced jigs or reels accompanied by their fiddles, mouth organs, or banjos. Theatrically inclined white mariners entertained their shipmates with minstrel shows. Aboard the USS *Brazileira,* one skit, replete with grinning, liver-lipped, bug-eyed portrayals of people of African ancestry, was titled *Niggers in a Daguerreotype Saloon,* and the *Nigger Serenade* became another popular musical refrain on Union ships.[81]

Bond and his mates assembled on deck twice daily. They were ordered to swab down the ship; scrape, then repaint masts, decks, and stacks; polish the brass; wash their uniforms; rinse and air sleeping hammocks; lower, clean, dry, then raise once more the heavy sails and awnings, and check out the dinghies and cutters in routine, unending maneuvers. Every couple of days they repeated those same, predictable and mundane cycles of work.

The *Cambridge* received essential stores—food, ammunition, and thousands of gallons of fresh water—once per week. Crew members reported to the infirmary complaining of laryngitis and headaches, constipation, diarrhea, flatulence, and aching joints. They sustained fractures, contracted rubeola and virtually incurable venereal infections. Sailors' complaints often reflected the excesses of shore leaves spent in taverns and brothels, as well as the wages of sin resulting from dissolute shipboard activities.[82] Dockside brawls erupted between secessionist civilians and Union sailors, and between white seamen and the contrabands who had deluged the region. One of the ship's wounded sailors had to be transferred to the massive naval hospital near the shipyards. The hardy John Robert Bond, however, was among the few seaman aboard the *Cambridge* who never fell victim to any reported malady or injury.

A sailor from a similar vessel wrote letters about his tedious shipboard experience, asking that his mother compare it to her life at home. "Go up to the roof," he suggested, "talk to a half-dozen degenerates, descend to the basement, drink tepid water full of iron rust, climb to the roof again." "Repeat the process . . . until fagged out," he concluded, "then go to bed."[83] A few years earlier, a young marine had been even more explicit about the "degenerates" whom he encountered. "There is no school of vice comparable to the Navy," he asserted. "Ninety per cent of the white boys," he added, "are, to an extent that would make you shudder, blasphemers and sodomites."[84]

The navy's "grog ration" had been rescinded in 1862 and distilled spirits officially were allowed on board for medicinal purposes only. Nonetheless, judging from the number of minor infractions—drunkenness, brawling, using insubordinate language or cursing, defacing property, sleeping on duty, and overextending shore liberty—that occurred during this period, these were months of great tedium and tension.[85] One old tar on the *Cambridge* was disciplined for filching a ham, a second for selling parts of his uniform, a third for cutting down a comrade's hammock. And shipboard high jinks sometimes took on more ominous implications.

The navy court-martialed another landsman following several assaults, combined with sundry lesser misdemeanors. Fully half of the men faced disciplinary measures during fall 1863 and the early winter of 1864, though black crew members were minimally better behaved and less frequently punished than others.[86]

For prescribed periods, miscreants were put in the brig. Either they were gagged, restrained in irons, restricted to bread and water, or confined in the sweat box. It was a metal-encased closet, no more than three feet in any dimension, which provided a ship's most dreaded form of correction. A decade earlier, the navy command had prohibited further floggings with the cat-o'-nine-tails, designating it an excessively brutal punishment. Then, during that summer of 1863, while inspecting his armada anchored at Hampton Roads, Abraham Lincoln expressed horror at the sweat box's barbarity. At his behest, the navy henceforth officially forbade any further use of that apparatus as an approved form of discipline, and sailors celebrated word of the prohibition.[87] Aboard the *Cambridge,* however, Commander William Spicer apparently tolerated little bureaucratic interference with his hegemonic authority. The captain (a grim-faced, bearded man who topped his uniform with a singular hat in the shape of a truncated cone, and was given to striking a haughty, Napoleonic pose) defied the presidential order, and continued to punish members of his crew in the infamous sweat box when and as he saw fit.[88]

Thanksgiving, Christmas, and New Year's Day came and went with the *Cambridge* still disabled at Gosport, while its men both relished and abused their shore leaves. The previous December, William Gould had pined for family as he recalled the welcoming "table at home." He and his colleagues, Gould reported, were "verry lonesom," and "all have the blues."[89] The uncelebrated 1863 holiday season aboard ship also kindled untoward incidents that prompted intensified discipline. Nostalgia, homesickness, or prevailing agitation notwithstanding, John Robert Bond conducted himself as a model seaman, because not once did his name appear among those of his ship's numerous transgressors.

For his first six months of service on the *Cambridge,* Bond and his mates never became directly involved in war-related hostilities.

During that autumn and early winter in Portsmouth, they observed billows of smoke and heard the thunder of distant cannons from across Hampton Roads and north and west along the James River, but beyond that, had little firsthand evidence of battle. Alternating spates of numbing boredom and feral barbarity always character-ized wartime operations, both on land and at sea, and as far as the men of the *Cambridge* could have ascertained, in late 1863 they had done nothing either to help free the slaves or to preserve the Union.

The primary hazards for the *Cambridge*'s crew since the previ-ous summer had been bronchial and bowel distress, outbursts of shipboard or dockside fisticuffs, and the ever present threat of swift punishment for dereliction of duty or other infractions. The most dangerous adversaries the ship and its men encountered were foul weather and tempers, virulent ennui, and mechanical breakdowns. In mid-January 1864, however, with their engine screw finally re-placed and repairs completed, the crew of the *Cambridge* leaving Portsmouth's shipyard cautiously shifted all guns to starboard to heel the ship. They stoked the furnace, revved the engine, weighed anchor, and at last, again set out to sea. The *Cambridge* steered east into open Atlantic waters, then south past the Hatteras light-house, bound for that expanse of "the pond" due east of Wilming-ton, North Carolina, one of the Confederacy's most rigorously protected ports. Much of this hazardous stretch of coastline re-mained in secessionist hands.

The renewed voyage of the *Cambridge* did not continue long without unanticipated incident as the accustomed and seductive rhythm of shipboard life ominously shifted during that first week back on the water. Within a few days, two shoreside Confederate batteries fired threatening volleys at the ship. Following those as-saults, the *Cambridge* sighted and chased away several hostile ves-sels that attempted to run the blockade. Then at three-thirty A.M. on February 6, the officer standing the overnight watch on the bridge spied a suspicious craft that had run aground on one of the unpopulated barrier islands near Masonboro Inlet, just off North Carolina's southernmost coast. It smoked and blazed as menacing tongues of flame probed the inky sky.

Dawn revealed the beached ship's markings, identifying it as the twin-propeller steamer *Dee* out of Bermuda, en route to Wilmington, near the mouth of the Cape Fear River. It was laden with lead (for Rebel munitions), spirits, bacon, and coffee, to help resupply the struggling Confederacy. That elusive craft was an especially welcome quarry because its captain, George Bier, a turncoat former United States Navy lieutenant, had maneuvered through the Union blockade on at least three prior occasions. But this time, the *Dee*'s previously uninterrupted string of good fortune ended. With escape routes cut off and facing almost certain capture, the crew had torched their vessel to avoid confiscation of the ship, cargo, and records.[90]

As the wreck burned that February morning, the intense heat ruptured whiskey barrels in the hold. The payload of lead "pigs" melted down, while aromatic coffee beans roasted and bacon fried to a crisp, creating a macabre breakfast pyre. Amid the smoke, fire, and disarray, the officers and most of the crew fled on dinghies up a shallow inlet to escape the approaching Yankee blockaders. Sailors from the *Cambridge* debarked from their ship in a small landing craft and tried in vain to extinguish the flames that ultimately incinerated the *Dee* almost to the water line. Unexpectedly, a band of enemy seamen who had concealed themselves in the underbrush fired several feeble volleys toward the approaching Union sailors, but wounded no one.[91]

The newly aroused landing party flushed out their attackers, capturing seven prisoners. None were officers—the *Dee*'s wily, traitorous Captain Bier slipped away—and, like Union Seaman John Robert Bond, all, save one, were subjects of Her Majesty, Queen Victoria. Sailors from the *Cambridge* boarded the wreck, seized what cargo and official logs they could salvage, and returned to their own ship without further incident. Then, mercilessly, they turned the big guns on their charred, hapless quarry and blasted away until they splintered the hull into tinder. The captives from the *Dee* were shackled, transferred to a Union cruiser, and delivered to the commander of the blockading squadron. During the Civil War, soldiers and sailors called the combat experience "seeing the elephant," and the crew of the *Cambridge* confidently encountered and mastered the fabled beast that winter day. Bond and his mates could celebrate their achievement, and they also each would receive a small but welcome purse of prize money for capturing the *Dee*.[92]

Four days later, the crew arose to observe a similar situation almost at the same location, this time sighting two stranded blockade runners, both "enveloped in flames." They soon were identified as the *Fanny and Jeanne,* out of Nassau, and the *Emily,* a privateer of English registry. The latter bark had a history of illicit slave running, and was the same vessel whose capture in the Great Dismal Swamp Canal and impressment into service with the Confederacy had been reported when Bond was in Massachusetts the previous spring.[93] Other Union blockading ships had pursued the *Emily* and run it aground on one of the coastal islands, while the *Fanny and Jeanne* lay burning nearby.

At dawn on February 10, the weather was "hazy and thick," the temperature unusually mild for midwinter. Clement breezes blew three to five knots out of the northeast. The *Cambridge* anchored and prepared to investigate the seemingly helpless and abandoned blockade runners. Just after nine that fog-shrouded morning, Captain Spicer dispatched a detachment of men, including John Robert Bond, under the command of two junior officers. They lowered a pair of dinghies over the side and rowed through the shallows toward the beach. But as they debarked from the landing boats and started down the misty shoal preparing to board and secure the *Emily,* a squad of armed privateers who had secreted themselves behind the dunes opened fire. Members of the ambushed Yankee search party scrambled toward their side boats, heading for the ship to obtain reinforcements. Before they reached safety, however, a well-aimed rifle ball fired by one of the shoreside snipers hit Seaman Bond, ripping through his right upper chest and shoulder, passing near the main arteries and vital organs.

The skirmish ended quickly. Bond's shipmates rowed their fallen comrade back to the *Cambridge,* carrying him to the ship's infirmary for medical attention. Then they returned to the sandy island, where they managed to salvage only one puny dinghy from the stranded barks. They failed to take a single prisoner or recover any cargo. The frustrated crew destroyed the *Fanny and Jeanne,* then sank the *Emily* with its once valuable, but now sodden, payload of salt, thereby closing out that infamous vessel's checkered career as an illicit slave carrier, a Union supply craft, and finally, a Confederate blockade runner of British registry. Shortly before six that evening, its mission complete and all men back on ship, the *Cambridge* charted a new course, stoked the engine, "weighed kedge and steered northward."

His race or foreign birth notwithstanding, a sailor in the military service of the United States had been grievously wounded. The retaliatory demolition of the *Emily* and the *Fanny and Jeanne,* therefore, could have provided Bond's predominantly white, American shipmates with a solid measure of satisfaction. To some extent, their destruction of those belligerent blockade runners that mild winter afternoon may have helped to avenge the dark-skinned Englishman's injury. On the other hand, despite one significant casualty, plus the competence and valor demonstrated by the intrepid sailors from the USS *Cambridge,* none of them received medals or prize money for that day's dangerous exploits. As for Seaman John Robert Bond, his climactic year before the mast of an American navy ship had ended and he was able-bodied no more. He had served in battle, he briefly but clearly had "seen the elephant," and at least on that one inauspicious February day in 1864, the treacherous behemoth of war prevailed.

3

AN ABLE-BODIED SEAMAN
NO MORE

Somebody's knockin' at the Gates o' Hell,
It's Bully John an' we knows him well.
Somebody's knockin' at the Gates o' Heaven,
There was eight little nigger boys, now there's seven.
Saint Peter's knockin' on the fo'c'sle door,
But I ain't ready for the Golden Shores.

Nineteenth-century sailors' song

IN MID-FEBRUARY 1864, Seaman John Robert Bond, chilled, sweating, and intermittently delirious, began a wretched ten days on a cramped, shipboard infirmary cot as the *Cambridge* navigated the leaden Atlantic waters off North Carolina's coast. Almost two-thirds of the combatants who suffered similar upper chest wounds during the Civil War did not survive, and for a time, Bond's life hung in the balance as well. In his medical log, S. C. Granger, the ship's surgeon, diagnosed, described, and duly recorded the gunshot injury as *"vulnus sclopiticum."*[1]

Unfortunately for Bond—and the entire crew—the mild weather soon became dangerously unsettled. Heavy winds, torrential squalls, with "hail . . . as large as pigeons eggs," accompanied by lightning and bone-jarring thunder, caused such furious pitching that sailors became seasick or injured as the tempest swept overboard several "brass rods and a handspike."[2] The *Cambridge*'s most defenseless passenger was miserable as his ship tossed in heavy Atlantic seas.

Not far south of that turbulent expanse where the *Cambridge* patrolled, the Union sustained a portentous loss the same week. After dark on February 17, the primitive, subsurface Confederate vessel *Hunley* maneuvered through Charleston's harbor. Making a stealthy underwater approach, the *Hunley*—little more than a cigar-shaped, converted iron boiler—rammed one hundred pounds of explosive powder affixed to a wooden spar into the hull of the Union sloop *Housatonic,* which was lying at anchor, participating in the siege of that critical port and adjoining Fort Sumter and Battery Wagner. Although its entire crew perished and the *Hunley* itself disintegrated and literally vanished following the powerful blast (justifying its designation as the "peripatetic coffin"), the deadly rendezvous ushered in a new age of warfare at sea. Never before had a submarine, one of naval technology's most innovative devices, destroyed an enemy ship in combat.[3]

For several days in the sick bay's tight quarters aboard the *Cambridge,* Bond ran a perilously high fever as he drifted in and out of consciousness. The rifle ball had struck and splintered his right clavicle. Tearing through flesh and bone, it pierced the lung's upper lobe and induced copious internal bleeding. Attendants cleaned the wound and bound the area to immobilize the shoulder joint, then applied localized pressure and cold compresses to stanch the hemorrhage and reduce his temperature.

Bond, however, fared better than many soldiers in army field hospitals. At least in the *Cambridge*'s infirmary, where he remained the single, gravely ill patient, infections did not pass unchecked from man to man by way of unwashed hands or instruments, virulent effluvia, shared swabs, or blood-soaked sponges and bedding. For several days Dr. Granger administered doses of whiskey—service physicians' favorite, all-purpose medication—and catheterized John Bond when he could not urinate. In all, Bond received decent medical care, though his former shipmate and future friend William Gould had reported the dismissal of one shipboard surgeon on grounds of egregious "maltreatment" of a seaman, which included "striking the man, producing sickness."[4] Bond also must have been in estimable physical condition, and his youthful restorative powers served him well following the near-fatal injury. There was considerable inflammation and a light, pussy discharge from the wound, but no serious problems arose. Within a short time, his condition stabilized, then gradually improved.

The third week in February, the *Cambridge,* with its still feeble English-born patient aboard, steamed from the storm-prone Atlantic into the more tranquil waters of North Carolina's Bogue Sound, where a local harbor pilot—probably a reluctant "secesh"— came aboard to help the ship negotiate the intricate currents, steering it toward a wooden pier.[5] At two in the afternoon on the twentieth of the month, Bond and a shipmate were transferred onto one of the *Cambridge*'s cutters. Orderlies met that craft, then transported the patients across an attenuated jetty to Beaufort, North Carolina's Hammond Hospital. It was a major Union army medical facility, where the *Cambridge* previously had dropped off several other patients and in the same safe harbor where it had sought repairs a few months earlier.

The port of Beaufort—belittled by a visiting Massachusetts woman as a shabby "fishing village, a decayed Marblehead"— which Yankee forces had resecured from the Confederacy in early 1862, had become a coaling station and resupply depot for Union ships.[6] In addition to its brief stopover to drop off the ailing men, the *Cambridge* received routine maintenance and conducted other vital business. But only three days later, with its fuel and supplies replenished, the ship raised anchor, refired the engine, unfurled its sails, and once more was underway toward open waters to rejoin the blockading squadron. John Robert Bond never again laid eyes on the USS *Cambridge*.

Prior to the outbreak of war, the building occupied by Hammond Hospital—named for William Alexander Hammond, the Union army's controversial surgeon general—had been the Atlantic Hotel, a fashionable resort with nearly five hundred rooms. Acclaimed for the delightful sea bathing and opportunities for shell collecting along the beachfront, the three-story edifice, completed in 1859, was situated on Beaufort's waterfront, across a causeway from the town, and constructed atop massive pilings. The building was elevated considerably above sea level, and waves rolled in beneath the first floor with a metronomic cadence, creating blissful zephyrs and ameliorating the often oppressive heat. Because of its strategic waterside location, the hostelry had been sacked by Yankee troops who splintered its costly furniture and pianos and shattered an abundance of fine china and crystal. Once those forces had secured the city, they declared the hotel contraband property and appropriated it from the Confederate owner for military use.[7]

Though Beaufort's immediate environs remained in Union hands after mid-1862, over the next several years battles between the Blue and the Gray sporadically raged across eastern North Carolina. As precautionary measures, Union troops dug trenches and constructed barricades around the facility where John Bond was hospitalized. From time to time, all of the men there (even convalescents) who were physically able to handle guns were armed—in case any bold Johnny Rebs ventured by. On one occasion, as fighting drew near, Yankee dependents had to be evacuated, and, a resident soldier reported, "the Doctors wife & all the other northern women" were sent across the channel to Fort Macon, the federal stronghold guarding the harbor's mouth.[8]

During the former hotel's initial months of service as a medical facility, conditions were so deplorable that the secretary of war, Edwin Stanton, persuaded New York City's Sisters of Mercy, a Catholic order dedicated to the urban sick and indigent, to dispatch a small contingent from their convent. Stanton hoped that the nuns might establish some order and help care for the many ill and injured soldiers and sailors.[9]

But not everyone was enthusiastic about that experiment. John Baxter Upham, "a man of middle age and commanding appearance," who became the hospital's first superintending physician, disapproved of "placing sick soldiers under the care of Sisters whom . . . he regarded merely as lady-nurses" and categorically disdained. The entire country had no nursing schools, scarcely recognized the profession, and many people rejected the very idea of having any women care for male patients.[10] During their stay, however, the nuns attended the most severely afflicted and acquired desperately needed equipment, medicines, and sundries. They proved stalwart workers who tackled, organized, and supervised the hospital's rehabilitation with such amiable efficiency that they earned Upham's grudging admiration. They arranged for walls to be replastered, floors scoured and polished, windows cleaned, and muck scraped from the cavernous kitchen. Pursuant to their explicit but tactfully expressed demands, previously scarce supplies became more than adequate with the arrival of "brooms, tubs, scrubbing brushes and cloths, mops, lamps and kerosene, matches . . . starch, kitchen utensils," even fine castile soap and "Aunt Klyne's cologne."[11]

In mid-1863, however, the secretary of war reassigned the dedicated sisters, leaving Beaufort's hospital again in the hands of the military, plus civilian medical personnel on temporary assignment with the army. J. W. M. Davis replaced Upham, then he was succeeded by F. P. Ainsworth, who had become supervisor by the time John Robert Bond arrived in February 1864. Doctors Wilson and Vaughn served as Ainsworth's key medical assistants.[12]

Most patients at Hammond Hospital were wounded army men who streamed in from bloody encounters to the west, but when they arrived by water, Union sailors such as Bond were borne on stretchers across the wind-whipped causeway. The choice rooms along the building's east facade had breezy ocean-front porches (called "piazzers") overlooking the channel where convalescents could survey those comings and goings from their waterside windows.

Bond remained at Beaufort's military facility during that winter of his discontent as gales continued to assault the coast, but bone-chilling cold rarely accompanied them. Wind-driven tides often ran high, lapping at the foundations of the seaside edifice. Oblivious to the proximity of mortal conflict, sea birds—terns and herring gulls—wheeled and mewed overhead, skimmed the water, then pierced the ruffled surface as they fiercely dove for fish. Egrets, geese, and tundra swans nested alongside uninhabited channel islands overlaid with undulating, emerald sea grasses. That season rarely brought snow to coastal Carolina, but often, one of the Sisters of Mercy observed, a "southern rainstorm poured down and gave an aspect of desolation to the landscape."[13] Fort Macon, the Union sentinel of defense for the harbor and hospital, was visible through the mists on a sandy spit across the watery neck of Bogue Sound.

In January 1864, just before Bond's arrival in Beaufort, the War Department acknowledged the utility of African American women in the conflict. It authorized U.S. General Hospitals to hire them as cooks and nurses, and to remunerate them at a rate of ten dollars per month, supplemented by a daily food ration. Their numbers ultimately swelled to about two thousand. Under those new provisos, a woman known as Aunt Clarissy served as Hammond's principal cook, and pork and beans was the repast she most frequently offered. Other meals included locally grown potatoes, onions, and squash, plus gallons of soup, perhaps even nurse Clara Barton's "bully broth," made from water and wine, thickened with cornmeal, and flavored with ginger.[14] Edward the baker—"an obliging young man"—kneaded and rolled out dough for buns, cookies, or fruit and custard pies on the denuded marble top of the former hotel's billiard table, but the humid air quickly bearded his bread with mold. Milk from a resident goat made the tea more palatable, yet the coffee never seemed strong enough, and in the absence of sugar it had to be sweetened with syrup. During their sojourn, the Sisters of Mercy had rescued some chickens destined for the stew pot, "contrived a sort of coop," and the venerable hens continued to provide the hospital with a few fresh eggs. A "colored" man called Uncle Dick supplied other dairy products—welcome additions to the cuisine.[15]

Seafood, however, was the most prevalent dietary supplement. The kitchen had a deliberately unrepaired hole in its floor that had been smashed through during the Yankees' appropriation of the hotel. Members of the staff swept the edible "relics" of patients' meals through that aperture down to the swirling waters below. Opportunistic fish and scavenger crabs festooned with seaweed garlands swarmed in to feast on those morsels, at which juncture they were netted by agile hirelings, eviscerated and cleaned, then baked, fried, or poached for subsequent meals.[16]

Aunt Clarissy labored alongside an army steward—a taciturn native of Maine named Kit Condon who eschewed any standard-issue uniform, went barefoot in the sultry southern heat, and wore a battered straw hat. Like many recruits, Condon, a woodsman before he was drafted, could not read or write. He stationed himself in a wheelbarrow by the kitchen door and kept keys to the supply pantries knotted on his apron strings.[17]

Tripp, the dour sous-chef, never had wanted to join the army, and only reluctantly prepared the convalescents' meals. Bob Sprawl, Charity, and the "imperturbably silent" Andrew assisted the senior kitchen personnel. They were local black youngsters who performed numerous menial chores, including scouring, toting supplies, plucking chickens, and fetching well water. "The only pure water in the town fitted for drinking by patients," reported Superintendent Ainsworth, "is found in the cistern attached to the premises," though he cautioned that all water "should be boiled before [being] used for drinking."[18]

Chloe, a "saucy" former slave, was one of the laundresses. A younger woman named Ellen, admired for her "sweeter face and softer manners," was another. They were hard-pressed to keep up with demands for clean bed sheets, towels, and nightclothes that they scrubbed—with questionable thoroughness—in the on-site laundry. "Poor escaped field slaves" wrung out, hung up to dry, and ironed the linens. Many of those black women who labored at the hospital "washing and so forth, slept in rooms over the kitchen," a nurse reported.[19]

Most orderlies and nurses at Hammond were low-ranking Union soldiers who arrived as patients, then remained as ward attendants during their recuperative weeks and months. One of them commented, "It does a sick soldier more good to have a lady visit him than all the medicine he can take," and some of the white Union officers' wives who had followed their husbands south believed it their patriotic and Christian duty to perform those services. Orderlies praised the abilities and dedication of the doctors for whom they worked. They were seen as "skillfull in both medicine & surgery. Pleasant & agreeable men . . . [who] take more interest with the sick men than they do with their office & pay." One nurse considered Hammond "as good a home as a soldier can ask for & as good officers to be under as the army or navy can boast of." To supplement the physicians' efforts, a medical student named Babbitt held sway at the pharmacy during Bond's respite. Thanks to the nuns' foresight and systemization, Babbitt's storeroom remained well stocked, even with its quickly depleted supplies of "medicinal" whiskey.[20]

The nearly unintelligible Hungarian priest who accompanied the sisters from New York converted several of the local women to Catholicism. But the Methodist preacher—his face almost hidden by a wild, russet beard reflecting his flamboyant personality—who arrived soon thereafter to serve as hospital chaplain, terrified the black girls whom he, in turn, considered unrepentant heathens. He importuned them to "experience religion" when they attended his fire-and-brimstone sermons. For the most part, however, the young women eluded his fundamentalist Christian clutches. Yet another clergyman, an Episcopalian ("next thing to a catholic," grumbled a Baptist orderly in a letter to his sweetheart), came to preach at the facility "once a fortnight, half a day at a time." "It suits the irishmen very well," he sarcastically added. Those liturgies, similar to the ones he had enjoyed in Liverpool's Anglican churches, also would have suited Seaman John Bond, Hammond Hospital's uniquely brown-skinned, English-Irish patient, very well indeed.[21]

As the men recuperated, they played cards and participated in vigorous ball games, as well as "greased pig. greased pole. Sack & foot races." For those, unlike Bond, who could read, the hospital had a small library, and convalescents also enjoyed musical diversions. One nurse (a former patient from New England named Lyman Chamberlin) at Hammond reported: "Amongst the . . . men that we have here are quite a number of good singers & musicians of all kinds such as violin. Guitar. Accordian. Claronet. Bugle. Flute. Fife. Bones & Drum." "Get them all together," he added, and "it will make some noise if not any music." A group of aides staged "a sort of negro performance." The men "blacked themselves up & played the negro to a charm," observed Chamberlin, "it was quite a laughable affair." Caricaturing "darkies" in an amateur minstrel show was considered excellent sport at Hammond Army Hospital. Dancing, however, generally was waived, since there was "no good place, [and] . . . no girls of any account here & what there is do not understand dancing very well." Chamberlin clearly did not consider the ubiquitous black girls acceptable partners, or "of any account." Despite the lack of social dancing, the universal mating dance continued unabated as white Yankee soldiers met, wooed, even married southern "ladies." "An instance of the sort happens every day or two," he further commented.[22]

The seaside army hospital had five wards plus semiprivate rooms where patients were assigned according to rank, possibly race, and the severity or contagion of their conditions. During its years as a medical facility, thousands of the sick and wounded—military and civilian—passed through. The main building accommodated four hundred patients, and even healthy Union soldiers occasionally were garrisoned there. Some seriously injured men arrived with "heads and faces wrapped in . . . coarse cloth which was so saturated with blood that it was painful to look at." A number suffered "broken legs, broken arms, and one unhappy victim," reported an observer, "had both hands shot off, another had the greater part of [his] chin and lower jaw shot away." One of the Sisters of Mercy recalled that "the foul condition of . . . these agonizing wounds was something terrible." Despite such horrors, conditions at Hammond were preferable to those at the army's perilous and makeshift field hospitals.[23]

Disease brought others to Hammond. In the fall of 1863, typhoid, one of the war's most lethal afflictions, accounted for more than a hundred admissions, and the next January a smallpox epidemic deluged the facility. By the time John Bond arrived in February, the situation had become so acute that the victims—more than fifty, most of them black civilians—had to be quarantined (or segregated) in a separate building. Many did not survive. During the months that Bond spent at Hammond Hospital, death was such a constant companion that one fatalistic young man commented, "I am so use to it that I hardly notice."[24]

On several occasions, former slaves, "trembling with fear, fatigue and excitement," fled their intransigent masters across the causeway leading to the hospital. Yankee patients and staff encouraged the runaways and threatened the pursuing "owners" with leveled rifles, promising to pitch them into the sea if they as much as "laid a finger" on the fugitives. A Confederate diehard complained about one such defector to the Union military command. "She is my gal, she was born on my place," he bellowed, demanding her return. Northern officers, however, rebuffed such claims, explaining that, like all Negroes who became contraband of war, the woman "was free from the moment she claimed the protection of the Army."[25] That determination had been authorized under provisions of the Union's wartime Confiscation Acts and complied with military policy first established at Virginia's Fortress Monroe. In addition, as of January 1, 1863, President Lincoln's Emancipation Proclamation declared free anyone still held in slavery in those portions of the Confederacy—all of North Carolina included—that remained in rebellion against the Union.

The region's generally temperate winter of 1864 slipped by while Bond recuperated at Hammond Hospital. As spring arrived, Lincoln appointed the contentious Ulysses S. Grant (whose intransigence toward the Rebels earned him the sobriquet "Unconditional Surrender" and made him an idol of many black Americans) as his new general-in-chief. Union forces seemed poised on the threshold of success, but ultimate victory eluded them as the Confederacy proved an unexpectedly tenacious foe. Apparent and much anticipated triumph dissolved into ongoing frustration, especially in Virginia's extended campaigns.

Nonetheless, spring burst forth early in the Carolinas, the vernal resurgence began, and by late March, one observer noted, "the fruit trees are all in bloom & garden vegetables up & peas blowed out." By mid-April, another commented, "the weather began to be very warm but the abundance of roses and other flowers more than compensated for any inconvenience." April also brought reinvigorated encounters with Confederates and a new influx of refugees—many of them white women and children who were Yankee soldiers' dependents or camp followers—"in a condition of extreme destitution." When they arrived at the hospital, most had few belongings other than the ragged clothes on their backs. The oldest person among that abject assembly was ninety-eight; the youngest was a baby born on the premises that very month.[26]

Disease took a tragic toll. "Mothers who came . . . with four & five children," reported an orderly, "left here alone." Youngsters died from measles, scarlet fever, and whooping cough. One Yankee soldier who attended the mostly white patients at Hammond had scant sympathy for the newly emancipated, often ill and destitute local blacks. He complained that "Uncle Sam . . . put these poor white people in tents & use them worse than dogs. While their husbands are in the army fighting for the union, & the niggers are laughing & grinning around the streets."[27]

As May arrived, more sultry weather settled in. An invasion of bedbugs, fleas, ticks (called "graybacks" by Union soldiers for their gray-uniformed Rebel adversaries), and especially mosquitoes inundated coastal Carolina. Those plagues brought threats of malaria and yellow fever, and tall tales as well. One anecdote concerned an unsuspecting Yankee soldier whose knapsack had been smeared with a viscous glob of tar. The fable contended that one humid evening an unusually robust mosquito landed on the sticky patch. Then, reportedly, the mosquito's "feet got stuck fast, . . . he just set sail, took knapsack & all & has not been heard of since." In addition to (and surely more welcome than) infestations by those legendary, muscular, and occasionally larcenous insects, it was the time of year when succulent berries began ripening throughout nearby fields and gardens.[28]

John Bond remained at Hammond Hospital recuperating under the army's authority from mid-February until mid-May 1864. Then, with his condition considerably improved, he received transfer orders at last. He left his fellow convalescents; Aunt Clarissy, Kit Condon, and Bob Sprawl in the kitchen; Chamberlin, the orderlies, and the novice apothecary; Doctors Ainsworth, Wilson, and Vaughn; Chloe and the obliging laundresses; the long-winded Episcopal minister and others, military and civilian, black and white, who had looked after him for three long months.

Bond and six other navy patients were transferred onto the ordnance storeship *Release*. That antiquated vessel, which in previous years had transported supplies throughout the Caribbean, around South America, even as far afield as Gibraltar and Morocco, navigated up the Neuse River to a Union medical facility in the town of New Bern. From there, the men were transported farther north by way of Pamlico Sound, past the barrier islands of Ocracoke, Hatteras, Roanoke, and Nags Head, then up the Pasquotank River at the mouth of Albemarle Sound.[29]

Despite threats of Confederate ambushes, the small ship entered the Great Dismal Swamp Canal, its surface a polished onyx ribbon. Muted wet slaps against the wooden hull, frogs' chirps, the monotonous buzz of insects, and intermittent bird cries barely intruded on the waterway's heavy silence. Even at midday, the corridor remained dark as dusk. Feeble sunbeams pierced the dense growth of shaggy cypress that canopied the inky canal. Lianas trailed in, and were mirrored by the glassy water. In 1831, Nat Turner, who had led Virginia's most memorable slave uprising in Southampton County, left that bloody venue. Some reports claimed that he crossed through Isle of Wight into Nansemond County, where he hid out among the secluded maroon slave colonies in the swamp's protective gloom for weeks before he was captured.[30] Stories about the mysterious marsh's purported resident specters reverberated through local legend. The boat carrying John Robert Bond out of North Carolina cautiously traversed the fabled channel to its terminus at the flyspeck village of Deep Creek, Virginia, located on the southern branch of the Elizabeth River.

After a day and a half of travel through those tenuously secured waterways, John Robert Bond was put ashore several miles farther north at Portsmouth's naval hospital. That fortresslike building, with its columned, neoclassic granite facade, had been opened in the 1830s. The Confederacy appropriated the hospital in 1861, near the beginning of the war, but Union forces resecured it the next year along with the urban centers and shipyards of the strategically vital Hampton Roads area—one of the world's foremost natural harbors.[31]

The massive structure surrounded a courtyard, with two ward wings enclosing the quadrangle's longer sides. Situated on a landscaped promontory of more than one hundred acres, featuring specimen trees—oak, hollies, and vibrant crape myrtle—and *grandes allées,* the hospital overlooked the tidal Elizabeth River just above the Gosport Navy Yard, and faced the city of Norfolk across the channel to the northeast. The quarters of Dr. Solomon Sharp, the commanding officer, graced the gardens. A low seawall surrounded its point of land and a lighthouse stood sentinel at the water's edge. That complex (the navy's largest of its kind, built to accommodate two hundred patients) included a laundry, bakery, apothecary, stables, greenhouse, quarantine quarters, and employees' lodgings, while makeshift shacks assembled by contrabands cluttered the grounds. At high tide the property was subject to flooding, then at ebb tide an odor of raw sewage permeated the site.[32] From the uppermost porches, patients could look north toward desolate Craney Island, where thousands of black refugees had been interned, and beyond, almost to the Hampton Roads site of the 1862 battle of the ironclads between the Union's *Monitor* and the Confederacy's *Virginia,* still known in some circles as the *Merrimac.*

John Robert Bond was admitted to that facility on May 20, 1864, and assigned to the third ward on the south wing's first level. He was one of forty to fifty men domiciled there. Though most patients were white, there was no evidence of racial segregation. Each floor had a sizable smoking room, but only two toilets located "in the newels of the stairways," with water flowing from a rooftop tank. "The abundant supply of water," reassured a contemporaneous examiner, "allows frequent flushing." The wards consisted of a series of vaultlike alcoves with small windows. The awkward layout forced every bed into a dark corner that enjoyed only a minimal circulation of air. "In general," a critic concluded, "the wards have the appearance of cells."[33]

Nature's healing powers and further rest comprised Bond's only treatment during his convalescence—no medical procedures or prescriptions, not even the familiar tot of brandy—and the overextended surgeons made their rounds to check on him, and most others, no more than twice a week. Robley Evans, another despondent invalid at the hospital, remarked, "No doubt the medical officers did the best they could with the tools they had to work with, but the tools were awfully bad."[34]

Norfolk's 1855 yellow fever epidemic had severely taxed the institution, but the Civil War's demands surpassed that earlier crisis. A number of recuperating patients served as orderlies, as they had at Hammond, though Evans also observed that at least one such man, though "strong as an ox and scrupulously honest . . . knew nothing about nursing." Everyone on Bond's ward was designated "noncritical," yet a sailor assigned to a nearby cot unexpectedly hemorrhaged, then died. Such occurrences led Evans to observe, "The wonder is that any of us got well." Ailing Confederate prisoners were shackled, and occasionally received medical attention, in the subterranean "dungeon." The dire straits in respect to medical treatment resulted, at least in part, from understaffing and overcrowding. Evans also sourly commented: "No language of man can convey any idea of the quantity and variety of vermin in that hospital."[35]

In that rodent- and bug-infested, broadly deficient facility, some men relied on the help of an orderly who at dawn each morning brewed "a pot of strong coffee, and each patient would have a cup of it with enough whiskey . . . to make it bite." "Then we would smoke a cigar or two," a grateful inmate added, "and be ready for what breakfast we could get."[36] Breakfast, indeed, all the food prepared in the basement kitchen, was barely adequate. The grounds included a vegetable garden that should have provided ample fresh produce, but Robley Evans commented that any palliative "hospital diet was unknown," though he acknowledged that for weeks he had consumed whatever was offered, "until bacon and cabbage knocked me out." Most liquor and all tobacco products were not officially prescribed, yet sometimes seemed preferable to the pork-laden cuisine, and the daybreak jolts of nicotine, alcohol, and caffeine buoyed the men's spirits and apparently made some of them feel much better.

Coincidentally, Commander William Spicer, Bond's captain from the *Cambridge,* was a patient at Portsmouth during those same weeks. He was ensconced on Ward Seven (reserved for officers), while he recovered from opisthotonos, a virulent form of tetanus. It would have caused painful contractions of the dorsal muscles and arched his body into a grotesque backbend as invasive toxins attacked the central nervous system.

Just as at Beaufort's Hammond Hospital, the wives and daughters of naval officers stationed in Portsmouth helped however they could. One patient believed that "had it not been for their kindness and care I should undoubtedly have died."[37] Some local black people, usually contrabands, worked as orderlies, cooks, and laundresses, and volunteered their services as well, or brought food and sundries to the hospital to assist and encourage the sailors who, as they saw it, had been wounded in the valiant struggle to end slavery.[38]

White clergymen offered patients solace as their health improved or, as often, declined. One clerical visitor, recalled Robley Evans, "never hesitated to tell me that I was dying, and also just where I was going to bring up after I was dead."[39] Ferries traversed the Elizabeth River in only minutes, and a mulatto minister named Lewis Tucker also may have crossed over from his Norfolk church—Bute Street Baptist—to address the spiritual needs of the facility's few "colored" patients.[40]

John Robert Bond remained for several weeks at that hospital where assistant surgeons William Whelan and William Johnson, Jr., observed and evaluated his condition. The two Williams plus Solomon Sharp, the senior medical officer, reported on June 2, 1864, that, in their estimation, Bond should be discharged from the hospital and the navy, and considered permanently disabled. They described his injury as a gunshot wound in which the bullet had entered the thorax through the right collarbone. The shattered clavicle, the doctors agreed, never knit properly. The rifle ball had so severely damaged the nerves, muscles, and tendons leading to Bond's right arm that he had—and, the doctors anticipated, would continue to have—little use of it. Their patient could barely lift his arm or rotate the wrist. The limb fatigued quickly, and often became painful or numb.[41]

The three surgeons advised that John Bond should receive a pension based on what they predicted would be his irreversible disability resulting from an injury received in the line of duty. The navy gave Bond his "big ticket" (an honorable discharge), and released him in Portsmouth, Virginia, little more than a year after the immigrant Englishman had enlisted in New Bedford, Massachusetts. Higher authorities accepted the medical evaluations, approved the pension, and in mid-1864, Bond began receiving a stipend of eight dollars per month from the United States government.[42] Neither his foreign citizenship nor his race seems to have played any role in determining his eligibility or remuneration.

Care at Portsmouth's naval hospital almost always was wanting due to faulty architectural design, insufficient supplies and poor nourishment, too many patients, undertrained and overworked personnel, and generally, the unparalleled exigencies of war. It therefore was imperative for a man such as John Bond to find and make friends who might assist with his various needs. Another patient observed that a male nurse frequently ferried over to Norfolk to "buy things for us, generally sugar and coffee and whiskey."[43] Bond had crossed paths with black shipmates, some of them contrabands like William Gould, on both the *Ohio* and the *Cambridge*. He also had encountered nonmilitary Negroes, often former slaves, in Beaufort and then at the Portsmouth hospital. Culturally, Bond was an Anglo-African; genetically, he was a mulatto—no more black than white—but African Americans were the ones who seemed willing to support him and to whom he turned as he prepared to leave the navy. Because of his debilitating injury, he needed much more than supplemental coffee, sugar, and whiskey to expedite his progress through the ensuing months.

One person who may have met Bond and offered him camaraderie and aid was an orderly named Isaac Thomas, a man of fifty whom the hospital intermittently employed in menial positions. Before the war's circumstances facilitated his liberation and brought him to Portsmouth, Isaac had been enslaved in nearby Isle of Wight County. An eighteen-year-old named Emma Thomas, perhaps a relative, had lived in that county as well. Emma, also once a slave, might have hailed from the same plantation as Isaac, since they shared a former master's surname.[44] Like many others, she had come to the Norfolk-Portsmouth area as a contraband, and she attended the Reverend Lewis Tucker's Bute Street Baptist Church.

Decades later, Emma Thomas told her descendants that during the Civil War she had taken fruit to Union sailors on ships in the harbor and to hospital patients. While John remained at that facility, Emma not only brought and sold her fresh produce, but also befriended the young Negro from Liverpool. She helped care for him, and when the navy released him in early June 1864, still weak, with no family nearby, and in need of help with even basic functions such as dressing, bathing, and feeding himself, Emma probably took him to stay with some of her people in the overcrowded, war-beseiged port city of Norfolk.[45]

Scarcely more than a year after he had entered the service of the United States Navy in New Bedford, ablaze with youthful zeal and hoping to do his part to help end slavery, John Robert Bond no longer was a "half-caste" member of that dark-complexioned band of British seafarers sometimes called Nigger Jacks. Nor was he still an able-bodied seaman, or the untested lad he had been in May 1863. African and Irish-English by ancestry, birth, and upbringing, he had sustained his life-threatening injury while fighting for the Union in a skirmish with a renegade blockade runner of British registry (most likely crewed by his own countrymen) that was engaged in a clandestine endeavor intended to support slavery and sustain the Confederacy. In those months, Bond's tenuous patriotic allegiance began shifting from Victoria's England to Lincoln's United States. He was only one of a half-million similarly disposed, foreign-born men who saluted the Stars and Stripes and served with the Union Navy and Army, sometimes even forming their own ethnically distinct companies.[46] An ill-starred, off-shore encounter, however, injured Bond to a degree that prevented him from returning to the shipboard life that was the only vocation he had ever known or expected to follow.

At eighteen, he also had crossed the threshold dividing callow youth from more serious adulthood. Though he had left home and kin in England not long before, the war's carnage and the agonizing death of comrades that he observed so close at hand would have quickly sobered and matured him. Bond unquestionably, and too soon for one of his few short years, had to confront the almost paralyzing possibility of his own mortality as well.

During thirteen months in the navy, he had met many whites, but also had encountered, come to know, and probably had begun to care for, contraband slaves and other darker-skinned people like himself, both civilian and military, who spoke the same language, but with decidedly different, more liquid intonations and accents. Most of them, too, had been denied the opportunity to acquire an education, and most were lifelong residents, though not yet citizens, of the United States of America.

On the other hand, like thousands of others—the majority of them white Europeans—with similar origins, Bond was a foreigner:

a disabled, brown-complexioned immigrant who had left England behind but had not yet been granted his chosen country's full rights or privileges. Federal laws barred nonwhites from becoming naturalized citizens, but many idealistic and patriotic Americans, bolstered by changing circumstances argued that, despite race or nation of birth, fighting to preserve the Union should insure citizenship and egalitarian treatment (in the abolitionists' compelling language) as "a man and a brother."[47]

Bond had grown almost to manhood in predominantly white England, an ocean away from Virginia's battle-plagued shores. He never had been enslaved, but he began to cast his fate with men and women of his own (his father's) race, many of whom, recently emancipated, had spent their lives in bondage. John Bond was a grievously injured, honorably discharged veteran of the ongoing Civil War, who, by mid-1864, enthusiastically or deliberately, optimistically or perhaps haltingly, was moving along the road toward becoming a "colored" American.

Even before he enlisted, his right hand, as a result of unknown circumstances, lacked most of one finger and the first joint of another. His recent battle-related injury rendered that arm nearly useless. On June 6, 1864—the official date of his release from the navy—Bond, who barely could read or write, affixed an X (probably using his undamaged left hand) to the hospital ticket listing the belongings that had been retained since his transfer four months earlier from the USS *Cambridge* to Hammond Hospital. The navy was returning those few possessions.

Bond left Portsmouth's hospital and the United States Navy that day with several blankets, a hammock and mattress pallet, but no pillow, towel, or sheets. He had four standard-issue shirts (three of wool flannel), bell-bottoms, underdrawers, one "frock," two pairs of shoes, a pair of socks, his seaman's cap, neckerchief, and a compact ditty bag. No other assets whatever had John Robert Bond—neither gaiters, watch, books, musket, nor cash. Not even a canvas knapsack.[48]

. II .

EMMA

OLD BONDS, NEW BONDS,

1846–1870

Reverse: Emma Thomas Bond, ca. 1905.

4

"TURKEY BUZZARD LAY ME":
A CHILDHOOD
in TIDEWATER COUNTRY

Keemo, Kimo, dar you are,
Hey, ho, rum to pum-a-diddle,
Set back penny wink,
Come Tom Nippie Cat,
Sing song Kitty
Can't you carry me home?

Traditional slave song from southeast Virginia

Keemo, Kimo, dar-ee-yo,
Mee-yi, mee-yo,
Mee rum-tum paddy whack,
Blue-eyed pussy cat,
Sing a song of kitty
And away we go.

Song from one of Emma Thomas's grandchildren

THE ISLE OF WIGHT County town of Smithfield has always been associated with the savory hams cured from its mean-and-lean razorback hogs. It lies alongside shallow Pagan Creek, which feeds into the lower James River not far north and west of the hospital where John Bond received his navy discharge and met Emma Thomas during the Civil War. As it appears on maps, Isle of Wight actually resembles one of those famous hams, with its porcine haunch slumped along the lower James, where the river broadens to five miles. To the north, Lawne's Creek divides Surry County from Isle of Wight. It then narrows to an attenuated shanklike western end with that boundary marked by the twining Blackwater River, which separates it from Southampton County, site of Nat Turner's slave rebellion. On the southeast, Isle of Wight abuts Nansemond County, now Suffolk, and Nansemond in turn, adjoins the paired ports of Portsmouth and Norfolk. Traveling by water, those two cities are somewhat closer to Smithfield, and far more accessible, than is Isle of Wight's remote westernmost tip. The county stretches more than thirty miles from east to west and about fifteen along its greatest north-south axis. Characterized by its proximity to the windswept channel where the James flows into Chesapeake Bay, Isle of Wight belongs to the water-logged, water-dependent region known as Hampton Roads.

As the visiting northerner Frederick Law Olmsted observed in 1853 while en route by steamboat southeast from Petersburg to Norfolk, "the shores of the James River are low and level—the scenery uninteresting; but frequent planters' mansions, often of considerable size and some elegance, stand upon the bank."[1] Verdant or loamy embankments, coves, marshy islands, and bounteous oyster beds characterized Isle of Wight's coastal fringe, but most of the county west of the broad river was farmland. Shadowing oaks, hedgerows, split-rail fences, and rutted wagon routes demarcated that low-lying acreage. Sinuous streams honeycombed planters' fields that were interspersed with bogs, including Beaverdam, Cattail, and Rattlesnake Swamps. The best known was Champion Swamp. Its name either derived from a family who owned property nearby, or evoked macabre memories of an eighteenth-century duel that reportedly had occurred there. According to legend, the vengeful victor severed his adversary's head, mounted up, then vanished into the impenetrable foliage and miasmas. But years later, trembling passersby still reported sighting a pair of spectral riders gliding through the murky marsh. One, they swore, was the "champion"; the other was headless.[2]

In 1608 (the same winter of famine when a demented Jamestown settler slew, then began to devour, his wife; although, commented Captain John Smith, "whether shee was better roasted, boyled, or carbonado'd, I know not"), the first Englishmen had come to the territory that soon became known as Isle of Wight. It was one of the Virginia colony's eight original shires.[3] At first, however, the newcomers called it Warrosquoyacke, meaning "point of land," from the indigenous people's tribal name. But as they fought and traded with, then killed, or forced the original Ameri-

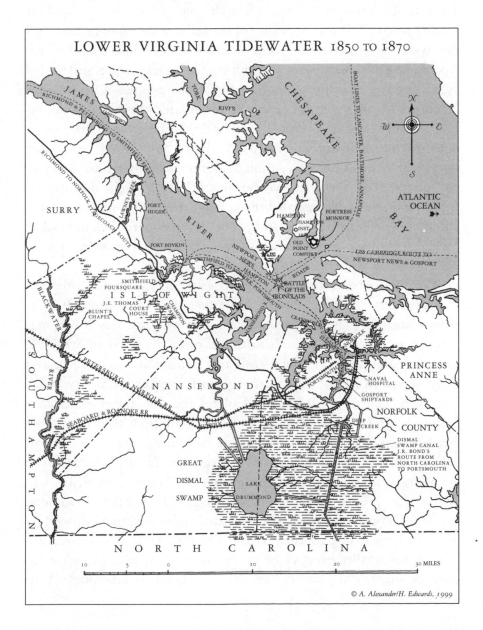

LOWER VIRGINIA TIDEWATER 1850 TO 1870

© A. Alexander/H. Edwards, 1999

cans inland from their ancestral homes, some of the settlers, finding the original appellation difficult to pronounce and far harder to spell, renamed it to honor their own south-of-England origins.

Isle of Wight sits across the James, downstream, and around a river bend from that earliest permanent English settlement at Jamestown Island, with its welcoming deep-water harbor, where, John Rolfe wrote in 1619, "a dutch man of warre ... sold us twenty negars." Those Africans (of initially indeterminate legal status) were the first of their race to arrive in colonial mainland North America.[4] Only four years thereafter, the nearby shire still called Warrosquoyacke acquired its first few black people. Within half a century Virginia's statutes clearly differentiated the rapidly increasing, forcibly imported dark-skinned population from its predominantly white indentured servants. Colonial laws soon designated people of African ancestry, though never any others, as slaves in perpetuity. Over the next two centuries, Isle of Wight did not develop plantations that equaled the cotton, rice, and sugar-producing enterprises of the Deep South, but its prosperous landholders owned from two or three, up to fifty, and even as many as a hundred, slaves.

For the first 175 years of English settlement, Orinoco tobacco, the infamous "stinking weed," remained the major crop. In Virginia's ideal habitat, that aromatic, addictive plant developed mature leaves as long as a man's arm and more than a span across. It became highly valued in both local and transoceanic commerce and often served in lieu of hard currency until the Revolutionary War.[5] But avaricious tobacco quickly depletes the soil. Bitter experience taught Virginia's new farmers of English ancestry that they must fertilize heavily, periodically let fields lie fallow, rotate their crops, turn to alternatives, or ultimately move on to farm elsewhere.

White settlers also adapted methods the Native Americans had shared for preserving meat. They enclosed traditional wooden frames and open-fire pits and designated them as smokehouses.[6] As early as 1779, a hog breeder named Mallory Todd had started exporting the quality product he prepared (trading with the West Indies for sugar, rum, and coffee, even shipping to Liverpool), thus establishing the international reputation of Isle of Wight's pork.[7] A unique method of butchering the swine also made Smithfield hams unusually lean. Todd and those who emulated his techniques soaked the pork in brine, smoked it over hardwood coals, peppered, then aged and dried it at least throughout a full summer. The cured meat remained not only edible, but delicious, for years. According to one slave's boastful account, "We sends our Virginny hams . . . acrosst de water ter Queen Victorious . . . an she say dey de bes' she ever tas'e."[8]

In 1846, the year that Liverpool's Eliza Kelly gave birth to the boy she named John Robert Bond, Emma Thomas—her coffee-colored skin, broad features, and tightly curled hair suggesting an unmixed African heritage—was born into slavery in southeast Virginia. Her owners, Jonathan Eldred Thomas and his wife Martha, had a daughter of their own, born ten years earlier, whom they had called Emma. A decade later, in characteristically proprietary fashion, the white family apparently bestowed the same name on the baby of a favored slave. Like her Caucasian namesake, the younger, darker-complexioned girl grew up on the Thomas estate not far from fabled Champion Swamp and the town of Smithfield.[9]

"When I wuz eight years old," another former slave like Emma from that Lower Tidewater region recalled, "I started working in de field wif two paddles to keep de crows from eatin' up de crops." By the late antebellum years, the local people still cultivated some tobacco, but corn had become their primary crop and it nourished the ubiquitous pigs and chickens as well as both black and white residents. "One for the worm, one for the crow, one for the beetle, and one to grow," became the timeworn formula that slaves and white farmers alike intoned as they ritually embedded four kernels into each mound of newly turned earth to insure that at least one would reach maturity.[10]

Slaves of both sexes and all ages not only sowed, tended, then harvested the silk-tasseled ears, but supplied the vast majority of labor for area plantations. Often before the age of six, barefoot boys and girls like Emma Thomas had to stand so long at watchful attention that their joints stiffened or they became numb with hunger. But they faced harsh punishment if they failed to chase away the voracious crows or could not keep the bumbling cattle and swine from trampling through the fields. In the bucolic region along the broad James River across from the Newport News shipyards, even very young slaves labored at least six-day workweeks positioned as sentinels, to protect the corn, wheat, potatoes, carrots, lettuce, and field peas. They also weeded, plucked caterpillars or grubs, gathered kindling, formed trash brigades, and tended to the white children's every whim.[11]

Plantation "pickaninnies" such as Emma could be very useful. Even as toddlers they didn't simply consume the meager rations their masters doled out without providing compensatory services. Black youngsters, dressed only in scratchy osnaburg shifts, were expected to earn their keep.[12] Parents tried but could do little to save their young ones from hard labor or otherwise shelter them. "During slavery," a local woman asserted decades later, "it seemed lak yo' chillun b'long to ev'ybody but you." Arduous work dictated by indifferent or callous owners, combined with easily disrupted family relationships, eliminated virtually all possibilities for a secure or carefree childhood.[13]

The county where Emma would grow up in slavery had become quite well settled by the end of the eighteenth century. During the first six decades of the nineteenth, its total population fluctuated little, increasing from 9,300 in 1800 to a high of 10,500 in 1830, then leveling off at just under 10,000 by 1860. The slave count declined from 4,000 to 3,600, while the number of whites rose from 4,700 to 5,000, and free people of color more than doubled from fewer than 600 at the turn of the century to almost 1,400 just before the Civil War.[14] Though somewhat isolated from the state's urban centers, Smithfield, with almost 1,000 inhabitants by 1840, was situated along the heavily trafficked waterside stagecoach route from Richmond to Norfolk.

Like most of the Lower Tidewater during the late antebellum period, Isle of Wight had five, rarely overlapping, classes of residents. Families of the great planters and slaveholders occupied the top rank, and men from this class monopolized politics. Heredity,

fine estates on ample acreage, plus the ownership of slaves designated members of that elite circle as leaders of local society. The
group included Jordans, Todds, Carrolls, and others, such as the
large, extended Thomas family.

Just below them were lesser, but nonetheless well-established
white farmers who were about on a par in Virginia's social firmament with physicians, lawyers, and a variety of successful merchants. Those people, too, often owned a few "servants," as they
euphemistically referred to the slaves.

The bottommost category of whites consisted of the landless
poor—farmworkers, watermen, and drifters—many of them descended from the colony's original indentures. The sense of unity
and identity among members of this often illiterate, ill-nourished,
too-poor-to-own-dirt segment of the population, and one of their
few satisfactions, evolved from their belief that due to the South's
bipolar racial and social construct, no matter how impoverished or
disempowered they might be, they were inherently superior to all
black people. Though economic interests occasionally aligned them
with free blacks, for the most part, having others to despise and
look down on helped Virginia's lowest-class whites forget that they
had empty pockets, rags on their backs, and holes in their shoes.[15]

And as Virginia's solons defined the distinct, debased legal status of Negroes, they included anyone with the slightest trace of
African ancestry. Any whiff of "mongrelization" or "amalgamation" (designated a crime before 1700) would brand someone a
Negro, who therefore was inferior in every way.[16] The status of Native Americans, sometimes seen as "noble savages," remained debatable, but an evocative 1797 document exemplified the prevailing
sentiment toward persons with any "black blood." It affirmed that
one particular (perhaps swarthy) Isle of Wight man "is of English
and Indian descent and is not a negroe nor a mulatto as by some
falsely and malitiously stated."[17] Even to be accused "malitiously"
of being a "negroe" could result in grievous consequences, and
every presumably unsullied Caucasian understood that that demeaned station must be scrupulously avoided. Isle of Wight's nonwhites, slave or free, who made up half the county's antebellum

population, never fell within the same legal or societal universe as Anglo-Americans, even those who comprised white society's least admirable segments.

First among this separate and debased racial stratum were the free, or quasi-free, Negroes who (though they cared for their families, worked diligently as domestic servants, farm laborers, and watermen, and sometimes owned land, houses, or livestock) were made to understand that they must accept their irreversibly inferior social position, retain their subservient manner, and scrupulously obey the law. They enjoyed few privileges or protections of citizenship, tread on uncertain, shifting ground, and rarely could better themselves to any substantive degree.[18] Kinship and mutual interests often linked free people of color with the slave community, but they also frequently were dependent on—even blood kin to—local whites. At least, however, they were not property. Although anxieties about the possibility of illicit (re)enslavement might haunt them, they rarely lived in fear of having immediate family members wrenched away. In addition, they could choose (or sometimes had) to leave Isle of Wight and the state without undue concerns that they might be tracked down like animals by owners or slave catchers any place in the country, with the full authority of federal law behind them.[19]

Relegated to the bottommost rung of Tidewater society were the slaves, such as the Negroes owned by Jonathan and Martha Thomas. Shortly before war broke out, the populous Old Dominion was home to nearly half a million slaves, more than any other state. Viewed by whites as childlike, irresponsible, emotional, loyal, bestial, clownish, and devious, they were chattel—transportable property—who toiled throughout their lives with little comfort, little reward, and little hope of bettering their own condition or their children's. The forebears of much of Isle of Wight's white population had voluntarily, even eagerly, immigrated from England, but most of the ancestors of its "Guinea niggers," both enslaved and nonenslaved, had been forcibly removed from West Africa prior to the international slave trade's legal termination in 1807.[20]

Both races and all classes in that hierarchical milieu nonetheless lived and worked in close proximity to one another as they moved about Isle of Wight's countryside and villages. Smithfield had been laid out during the late colonial era by Jordan Thomas (a forebear of Emma's master Jonathan), who had served as the town's first surveyor. Before the mid-nineteenth century, the thriving little river port had ten stores, several warehouses, three churches and a masonic lodge, separate academies for young ladies and young men, plus another small school attended by both boys and girls. Isle of Wight even made intermittent efforts to provide a rudimentary education for some of its indigent youths, but of course, excluded all nonwhites.[21]

Members of the black Thomas family, like Emma and her mother who lived not far from Smithfield, were descended from America's most significant assembly of unwilling immigrants. Her father, however, a man named John Currie who also was born and had grown up a Virginia slave, was not a local fellow. He hailed from Lancaster County, where a village named Mollusk reflected the region's dependence on the yield of its myriad estuaries. The portion of Virginia's Upper Tidewater where Currie passed most of his years is called the Northern Neck. He probably came to Isle of Wight by boat, either with his master or with another white person who hired him as a waterman, sailing down the Rappahannock, into the open waters of Chesapeake Bay, southward, then west again, past Hampton Roads and up the James to moor at Smithfield's wharves. On maps, the Chesapeake's five great western tributaries—from north to south, the Patuxent, then the Potomac, Rappahannock, York, and finally the James—seem almost like skeletal fingers. They meander hundreds of miles southeast toward the vast tidal bay from their origins in the Appalachian highlands. By watercraft, the favored means of travel and transport throughout the Tidewater, the trip from Lancaster County to Smithfield was easy. During the mid-1840s, John Currie lingered at the Thomas plantation long enough to impregnate Emma's nineteen-year-old mother and establish his presence as a lasting memory in her life and that of their daughter, but there is no indication that he ever returned.[22]

In the southern states, slaves could not legally marry, but jumping the broom was a traditional though nonbinding matrimonial ritual (known throughout the Atlantic world) that a number of Negroes eagerly embraced.[23] Many masters in the Old Dominion accepted the ceremony's validity as well. In the interests of plantation productivity and stability, and reflecting, to some extent, their own Christian ethics they sometimes even encouraged the practice. A former slave from that region remembered how her onetime owner "called up all de slaves . . . an' he'd make 'em line up." Then a black man who was "wid his master when dis linin' up is gwine on . . . pulls de gal to him he wants." After that, she added, "de master make dem both jump over a broomstick an' dey is pronounced man an' wife."[24] But John Currie and the Thomases' slave with whom he became sexually intimate couldn't even jump over a broom, because he already had a "wife" and child back home in Lancaster County.

Between the proprietary demands of some black men and, far more significantly, their masters' omnipotence, bondswomen would seem to have had little voice in choosing partners. But a number of them fiercely resisted the conjugal arrangements that whites tried to impose. Another slave told how her mother's owner beat her "nekkid 'til de blood run down her back to her heels." She had asked the older woman "wot she done fer 'em to beat her so." "Nothin'," her mother had replied, "other than she refused to be wife to dis man."[25] Though few Virginia masters resorted to such draconian measures if a slave rejected an arranged "marriage," regulating their "servants'" conjugal and reproductive lives was an effective way to maintain hegemonic control. That state also became a breeding ground for Negroes who often were sold off farther south, where the demand for an enslaved workforce increased during the late antebellum period.

Resistance on the part of black women as well as retaliation by whites assumed many forms. "That Nigger Mahala has broke another china plate and saucer," griped one petulant Norfolk County plantation mistress.[26] And a Tidewater woman recalled that while her enslaved mother was pregnant, she (intentionally, perhaps) burned some biscuits. "Missus . . . order her to the granary, make her take off all her clothes," the outraged black woman asserted, and when she was "naked [Missus] beat mother wid . . . a nigger whip."[27]

Emma Thomas's mother may have been compliant, or she, too, may have been insubordinate. She may or may not have smashed dishes, scorched bread, or otherwise defied Jonathan or Martha and thus imperiled her safety when she took up with John Currie. But, with deliberate intent or not, in the mid-1840s she and the amorous sojourner from Lancaster County became Emma's parents. When girls and boys on the farm where Emma grew up asked, "Who's yuh pappy?" she could have responded, as did some other black children in the region, "Turkey buzzard lay me an' de sun hatch me," and gone about her business. Emma Thomas used her onetime owner's surname until she married, but she would always remember the long-departed John Currie.[28]

That and similar circumstances dividing slave families may have been more the rule than the exception. Black people tried to keep their kinfolk united and cared for, but often those goals were unattainable. One heartbroken Norfolk mother reported that her owners sold every one of her twenty children, including a girl who "was sold to buy Missus' daughter a piano." Wracked with anguish, the woman imagined that "I heard my child crying out that *it was bought with her blood*." And a Portsmouth slave recalled, "Jes' before the war, my mistress sold [two brothers] an' a niece of mother's . . . like all the other white folks wuz doin', to keep em from runnin' away." By 1860, both the owner-generated separation of black families, as well as running away (self-generated departures, sometimes aided by Underground Railroad "conductors") became common throughout Virginia.[29]

In that period, shortly before the southern states fired on Fort Sumter, seceded from the Union, and precipitated the Civil War, Jonathan Thomas's plantation in Isle of Wight County—near the courthouse, Boykin's Tavern, and the new Petersburg & Norfolk Railroad line—had forty-six slaves: eighteen female and twenty-eight male. According to the often inept federal census takers, all were "black." Emma Thomas shared a cabin there with her mother and, in time, with several other children.[30]

Most dank, mud-floored Virginia slave quarters were cramped, windowless, gloomy fire traps.[31] But if the nearby facilities owned by Jonathan Thomas's nephew Julius are any indication, Jonathan and Martha's "Guinea niggers" may have been better housed than many others. The quarters surrounding Julius Thomas's stately residence called Four Square (built in 1807 and in fine condition almost two centuries later) were two-family frame cottages, probably whitewashed to enhance their appearance. Those units shared a center dividing wall and a double-faced brick fireplace with the ample hearths providing winter warmth and serving as year-round cooking centers. The wooden floor was elevated above the damp earth, and each side had its own door and a small window or two. At the rear corner, ladderlike steps led to a sleeping loft. From there, the pitched, shingled roof rose to a peak of about eight feet so that air could circulate freely and a person might stand erect except at the perimeters of the upper chamber.[32]

Other outbuildings at Four Square, such as the laundry and the dairy, incorporated similar atticlike sleeping areas for the "servants" who toiled there by day. Like many of his neighbors, Julius Thomas had a brine tank in the basement, a smokehouse and kitchen out back, and his plantation included other so-called dependencies: a gristmill, stable, dovecote, granary, forge, and barn. The daughter of a nearby planter revealed that during her childhood she had envisioned "the world [as] one vast plantation bounded by negro quarters." That family domain circumscribed her universe. In much the same way, the fenced compound called Four Square, stated one observer, seemed much like "a busy village."[33]

Each week, masters provided the "servants" with a meager "'larrence" (allowance) of cornmeal, molasses, "a small junk of meat" (salt pork), and perhaps a few dried herring. Some southeast Virginia plantations had communal kitchens, but most slaves prepared and ate their meals out in the quarters. That probably would have been the case at both Four Square and at Jonathan Thomas's nearby estate. "Mammy used ter bake ash cakes," recalled a former area bondswoman, from "meal wid a little salt and mixed wid water." Black women formed moistened cornmeal into patties that they baked on their hearthstones. Midway through the cooking process, they buried the bread in ashes. "Wen dey wuz nice an' brown," they were removed from the embers, dusted off, and declared ready to eat.[34]

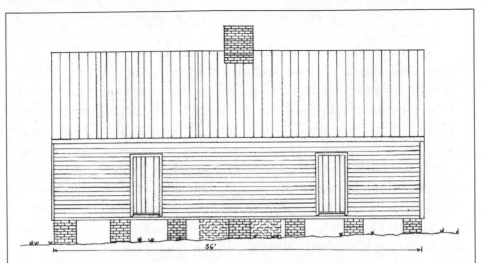

ELEVATION

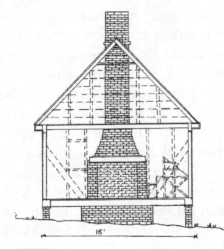

SECTION

SLAVE QUARTERS AT
FOUR SQUARE
ESTATE OF JULIUS THOMAS
ISLE OF WIGHT, VIRGINIA

ADAPTED FROM PLANS DRAWN
BY WILLIE GRAHAM, 1982, FOR
THE ARCHITECT'S OFFICE
THE COLONIAL
WILLIAMSBURG FOUNDATION

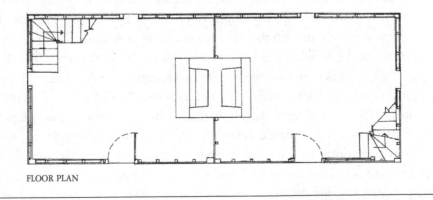

FLOOR PLAN

In their infrequent spare hours, some slaves cultivated garden plots and raised poultry.[35] Others trapped game, or trawled in nearby streams and rivers. Bean, corn, even crab soup (all devised from plentiful local produce and seasoned with fatback) might supplement the basic fare. As rare treats, "horse cakes" made from lard, flour, molasses, and ginger, and cut in the shape of galloping steeds were baked in the owner's kitchen, where black women maintained an ample degree of control, then taken to the quarters by those with "toting privileges." Slaves such as Emma's mother nourished their children as best they could, but necessity taught them to make do with relatively little food, autonomy, time, or energy to address their families' needs.[36]

Life was quite different for the privileged white people who lived in Isle of Wight's "big houses." Just after 1800, Martha Stringfield and her future husband, Jonathan E. Thomas, were born in the county where their antecedents had resided for more than a century. In 1828, the Reverend John Blunt married the young couple in his nearby Methodist chapel, and they remained in Isle of Wight more than forty years thereafter. They had four children, three older girls (Mary, followed by the white Emma, then Senora) and later a boy. Shortly before the Civil War, two of Martha and Jonathan's offspring resided with them: their teenager, James K. Polk Thomas—his name proclaiming Jonathan's veneration of the expansion-minded president who led the country at the time of his only son's birth—plus their recently widowed eldest daughter, Mary Thomas Stott, and her two youngsters.[37]

Mary Stott's spouse may have died in Hampton Roads' yellow fever outbreak during the summer of 1855. Following that awful epidemic, which annihilated thousands of area residents and caused Norfolk to be labeled the City of Pestilence, local Negroes asserted that "white folks treated the niggers so mean that God made up his mind to punish them, killin' off the cruelest." "On a lot o' plantations," stated an elderly woman decades later, "every . . . white person died, but not a single slave."[38] Although she exaggerated, that statement contained a solid kernel of truth. Many black people, slave and free, did contract yellow fever—the virus transmitted via the *Aëdes aegypti* mosquito (the name suggesting its presumed origins)—but they succumbed far less often than whites, due to inborn immunities acquired from their forebears' long-term exposure to the disease in tropical climates.[39]

Martha Stringfield Thomas and her daughters were at least minimally literate, though formal education for young ladies remained widely disparaged. Nonetheless, a New England woman had established the county's first girls' academy in 1826. Some white patriarchs argued that whatever schooling their female offspring might receive should be limited to that "obtained around the family hearth." Reading "novelettes or other light literature," one Smithfield man cautioned, resulted in "the neglect of . . . domestic duties and no preparation for household affairs."[40] Isle of Wight, however, was home to a number of Quakers who held beliefs that often placed them at odds with neighbors. Although the local Friends seem not to have worked covertly with the Underground Railroad as did others of their persuasion in the Upper South, many had moral reservations about slavery and also believed in some manifestations of women's equality, especially in schooling girls as well as boys. That commitment could well have tempered the area's latent hostility toward education for women.[41]

In addition to Martha and Jonathan (or John) E. Thomas, other white families bearing that surname also lived—and owned slaves—in Isle of Wight County during the late antebellum years. Judging from an almost obsessive dedication to men's given names beginning with *J*, they were, with little doubt, somehow related to one another. The heads of households were the aforementioned Julius, plus John C. and John P., James, Jesse, Jordan, Joshua, Josiah, and William J. Thomas. They had wives, sons, daughters, and many additional, sundry relatives.[42]

For those local presumptive patricians and others of similar station, the cyclical rhythms of weather and seasons, incessant demands of crops and livestock, plus the management of slaves, regulated life on Tidewater plantations. A friend (and Thomas in-law), Charles Driver Jordan, wrote often in his diary about the "servants" on his farm.[43] Jordan periodically went into Smithfield where he "bot. clothes for negroes." He chronicled a comfortable existence greatly consumed with overseeing the dark-skinned people whom he owned. Jordan supervised the work of the black folks who cultivated his corn, cabbages, turnips, "cukes," strawberries, peaches, melons, pumpkins, even asparagus. From the slaves' understandably dissimilar perspective, a scornful Norfolk County woman described how almost daily during her childhood she had observed her master "strutting down the field like a big turkey gobbler to see how the work was going on."[44]

Under the watchful eyes of owners or overseers, Negroes dug yams and Irish potatoes; set out, then pruned back, apple and pear trees; hauled straw mulch and manure to compost; and built fences, henhouses, and shelters for the hogs and cattle. The labor force required for those activities sometimes spread across a number of plantations and required cooperative efforts. Jordan reported that, on occasion, some of the "Thomas servants" worked for him.[45] Any large Virginia plantation—one with more than twenty slaves—would have had, or shared with neighbors or kin, a blacksmith, shoemaker, weaver, cook, and seamstress.

Nor was life all work and no play for planters such as Charles Driver Jordan, or Julius and Jonathan Thomas. The gentry—as well as whites of inferior station and blacks—fished in the Blackwater, or crabbed and dug oysters along the saline lower James River. Negroes were customarily (and by law) denied access to firearms, but white men shot squirrels, rabbits, partridge, and pigeons. For the exhilaration of pure blood sport, members of the county's upper echelon went fox hunting. Julius Thomas's annual revel at Four Square, for which he served as master of the hounds, was renowned throughout the region and relished by his booted and spurred, armed and mounted colleagues and kin. "In the early morning hours," reported an avid participant, "all of Smithfield was awakened by the sound of the horn and deep voice of the hounds." "Fox hunting," blissfully proclaimed Julius's brother, "has ever been the sport of kings, . . . of those of aristocratic blood and gentlemanly leisure."[46] Nearby Boykin's Tavern adjoining the county courthouse, however, remained a rowdy watering hole for white men of all classes.

In that courthouse, locals observed the trials of both errant whites and slaves, presided over by Isle of Wight's "gentlemen justices," among whom was John P. Thomas, who served as justice of the peace, then sheriff. Both the whippings administered to black offenders on plantations and the public judgments swiftly handed down by the courts served as blunt warnings to other bondsmen and deterrents to further misconduct.

Occasionally, white women were permitted to attend political assemblies, and sometimes brought their viewpoints into play at public dialogues. Usually, however, such endeavors were deemed strictly within the white male province.[47] The men's activities included functions such as a local rally highlighted by the ringing address delivered by Stephen Douglas, the New England–born presidential candidate (and race-baiting slavery apologist) during the 1860 campaign. Protesting his Republican opponent Abraham Lincoln's supposedly egalitarian racial ideologies, Douglas's supporters sometimes accompanied his speeches with menacing chants of: "White men, white men!"[48]

Both business and pleasure took Isle of Wight planters such as Jonathan Thomas and Charles Driver Jordan on ferries from Smithfield's docks, east along the lower James to Norfolk and Portsmouth.[49] Steam packets also carried passengers upriver to Petersburg and Richmond, and even ventured out into the Chesapeake and north as far as Annapolis and Baltimore.

Christmas, other holidays, and barbecues—featuring a whole hog, spitted and grilled over hickory embers until the meat fell from the bones—crab feasts, as well as oyster roasts (with coal-roasted, stewed, fried, even pickled oysters), offered opportunities for gala social assemblies among white families. Brunswick stew, made from squirrel or rabbit, limas, onions, corn, tomatoes, and potatoes, all seasoned with bacon, was another preferred dish. Pastry-encrusted hog's head became familiar fare, and ham biscuits were one of the most popular delicacies. In plantation kitchens, slaves, such as the women and girls of the black Thomas family, supplied the creative genius as they fricasseed game birds with parsnips to sweeten the meat, then courteously served their own "white peoples" and guests in the "big house" dining rooms. Corn bread or hush puppies, especially those enriched with eggs and flavored with "cracklin's," graced the tables presided over by members of the more fortunate segments of local society. Favorite desserts included milk custard—luscious, as well as supposedly possessing remarkable curative properties—topped with sweetened lemon and sherry "so-good" sauce, plus a traditional "1-2-3-4 cake," made with a cup of butter, two of sugar, three of flour, four eggs, and iced with a frosting that was caramelized by adding a splash of vinegar.[50]

James River plantation kitchens generated a sophisticated, eclectic cuisine to which artful slave cooks contributed an indispensable African influence with their familiar yams, okra, collards and kale, peppers, field peas, and benne (sesame seeds), first transported across the Atlantic hidden in the tangled hair of black captives. The Tidewater's affluent people enjoyed dishes prepared from locally cultivated foods, but as early as the 1820s they were also acquainted with pastas, curries "after the East Indian manner," "gumbo—a West Indian dish," Spanish "ropa vieja" and "gaspacho," plus recipes of French derivation.[51]

They drank honeyed tea (hot or chilled), homemade cider, peach, plum, grape, and cherry brandies and wines. For some time, Isle of Wight had more distilleries than any other Virginia county, suggesting the alcoholic beverages' rampant popularity.[52] For fritters, trifles, tarts and cobblers, jellies and preserves, as well as distilled spirits, fruit came from the county's bountiful orchards.

Primarily because of economic rather than ideological reasons (though some southerners did oppose the "peculiar institution" on moral grounds), slavery was on the decline in much of Virginia and throughout the Upper South. By the 1850s, only fifteen percent of white Virginians held slaves, and a substantial portion of the region's "colored" population no longer was enslaved.[53] Isle of Wight, where well over a thousand quasi-free but still subordinated people of color lived just before the outbreak of war, was no exception. Hiring nonenslaved black laborers to work daily, seasonally, or annually had become a viable option for the local gentry. It often was cheaper than owning slaves outright and being obligated for their sustenance, including care and feeding of the infirm, and the nonproductive very young or very old. The white Thomases retained many slaves, but also had released some of their "servants" from bondage.

Even after their previous owners had either manumitted them

or allowed them to purchase their freedom, a number of that family's onetime slaves remained nearby.[54] They included Betsy, Lany, David and Becky, Lucy and (yet another *J*, perhaps imposed at birth by a former master) Judah Thomas, most of whom were agricultural laborers. Two such people lived and worked alongside the bondsmen on Jonathan Thomas's plantation.[55] Several free people of color, Betsy, Lany, and Lucy Thomas among them, even held slaves of their own—probably family members—whom state laws made it extremely difficult for them to emancipate. Some of Isle of Wight County's free Negroes became artisans. Though few possessed substantial acreage, one woman had extensive orchards and fermented greatly admired wines.[56]

Although Virginia's restrictive Negro Codes often were ignored or circumvented, the former bondsmen were supposed to keep track of their records of manumission, known as freedom papers, that confirmed their nonslave status. During several intervals in the early-to-mid-1800s—especially in the wake of Nat Turner's 1831 rebellion, which many white people believed implicated *all* blacks—hastily enacted statutes required them to leave the state within a year. The nonenslaved men and women of color who managed (and for whatever reasons chose) to remain in Isle of Wight through the rest of the antebellum period were required to register at the county courthouse every three years.[57]

A short distance from that courthouse, Jonathan and Martha Thomas's establishment consisted of the white family, slaves, and farm animals, living on as many as 2,400 acres. In 1860, their plantation was valued at $15,000. Jonathan was also a partner in Smithfield's successful commercial enterprise known as Thomas & Adams, purveyors of alcoholic spirits, ammunition and weaponry, plus a variety of sundry provisions. Like several other families among the region's wealthier citizens, the Thomases had a second residence and a few bondswomen in nearby Norfolk—accessible by ferry, stagecoach, or rail.[58] Because of the threat of epidemics that flourished during summers in the city, they probably used their house in town intermittently during the cooler months when the plantation's agricultural demands were less onerous and Norfolk's elite enjoyed a vibrant social and cultural life.[59]

By 1860, Jonathan Eldred Thomas had become one of the most affluent men in the area. His slaves (the estate's disempowered majority) had increased from twelve, to thirty-three, to forty-six over the preceding twenty years. In addition to his acreage and "big house" in Isle of Wight, the "servants" plus other personal and real property brought Jonathan's accumulated wealth to more than $66,000. Just prior to the Civil War, black laborers on the vast farm where Emma Thomas and her kin were enslaved annually sowed, cultivated, and harvested 30 tons of hay, 600 bushels of wheat, 300 of oats, almost 4,000 of corn, 350 of field peas, 40 of white potatoes, plus 300 of yams. The livestock included three horses, eleven mules, ten cows, five oxen and ten other cattle, forty-five sheep, two hundred mud-slopping pigs, and almost certainly a wide variety of poultry.[60]

Martha and Jonathan Thomas's slaves milked cows and annually churned about one hundred pounds of butter. They sheared sheep ("chillums would pick de burrs out of the wool"), slaughtered hogs (dazed them with a blow to the head, slit their throats, and "hang him up by his back feet [to] starve the blood out of him so the meat will be clear," one Virginia woman reported), then cured the pork. They tended swarming hives from which they collected twenty pounds of honey, and satisfied the domestic demands of the "big house" as well. In his early childhood, Jonathan Thomas had been promised his first four slaves through provisions of his grandfather's will. By the late antebellum years, he and his family would have had little reason to imagine a life without their "servants," and, like many slaveholders, probably convinced themselves that a state of benevolent bondage was both economically essential and the most beneficial condition for the black people, whom they perceived as perpetual children.[61]

In addition to their arduous field labor, female slaves such as Emma Thomas's mother had other duties. Their work "began at sun rise and lasted 'till sun down." The women carded, then spun the wool into yarn, and, a former Norfolk slave remembered, eased the tedium of labor (like preindustrial workers throughout the world) as they would "pat dey feet an' sing":

Wind de ball, wind de ball,
Wind de ball, lady, wind de ball,
Ding, ding, ding,—wind de ball,
Wind de ball, lady, wind de ball.[62]

When they had spun out the raw fiber, "all of de cloth . . . was made on de loom," a Portsmouth woman explained. "We had to knit all our stockings an' gloves," she revealed, and "we'd plait blades of wheat to make up bonnets." Spinning, sewing, even fashioning braided straw bonnets, baking, and preserving fruits and vegetables were domestic skills that girls such as Emma Thomas on southeast Virginia's plantations learned in childhood from grandmothers, mothers, a network of "sisters," and white mistresses.[63] Female slaves worked long and hard for the "white folks" and, when they finished those chores, for their own black kin as well. Another area woman remembered sewing bees that became intimate, all-female gatherings: "Evenings we would spin, quilt, make clothes, talk, tell jokes." As a rule, she concluded (and her experiences probably resembled those of the Thomas family's slaves), "we growed everything we et, an' we'd make everything we'd wear."[64]

Insofar as health care was concerned, conflicts sometimes arose between masters and the male physicians they retained, on one hand, and slaves, on the other, who were convinced that they best knew how, and with what methods and medicines, to treat their own ailments. Whites prescribed patent nostrums or "a dose of garlic and rue" as a tonic formulated to make young slaves "grow likely for market," while the "Guinea niggers" dug roots, gathered grasses, berries, and flowers, and stripped bark from familiar trees to make medications. They used this vegetation in ways that often derived from West African botanical traditions. Blacks in Isle of Wight drank a potion distilled from flagroot to enhance their general well-being. Quinine, vinegar, and herbal infusions helped to control fevers, poultices soothed insect bites, while senna was a standard springtime purgative. Steeped burdock, round holly, and "cedar balls" served as blood builders, and cherry bark tea supposedly cured whooping cough. Emma Thomas absorbed such medical lore, and still used it decades later. A number of Virginia slaves became doctors and nurses for their people, and "grannies" functioned as midwives, guiding mothers through labor, "catching" babies, cleaning them with lard and swaddling them in flannel—often for whites as well as women of their own race. Isle of Wight's gentry esteemed Lizzie Purdue for her inestimable work, "especially among ladies" (white "ladies") during pregnancy and "accouchement."[65]

Some of the late antebellum period's most memorable tales surrounded the phenomenon known as Cox's Snow. With drifts up to twenty feet and cold so numbing that people could walk "all the way down the Hampton Roads on the ice," it was the most brutal blizzard ever to assault the Old Dominion. "It snowed all day Friday, all night Friday," continued through the weekend, one black woman recalled, "an' didn't stop Tuesday 'til 'bout five o'clock." "Here's how dat come to be called Cox's Snow," she explained. "Ole Doc Phillip Cox . . . was a great drinkin' man," she continued; "he went out into dat snow, though his folks tole him he hadn't ought to." "Dey found him arter de snow was over settin' in his buggy . . . holdin' his reins like he was drivin', frez to death." More in conformance with African than white European conventions, blacks in America often pinpointed their ages not according to the calendar, but in the context of such memorable events. In later years, therefore, many of southeast Virginia's former slaves recalled exactly how old they were that harsh winter when Dr. Cox "frez to death." The great storm hit early in February 1857, when Emma Thomas was eleven.[66]

Not all memories from that period were dismal or climactic for black people in the Virginia Tidewater. A former Southampton County slave remembered "candy pulls from cooked molasses," and singing "in the moonlight by the tune of an old banjo picker." Songs conveyed from one generation to the next included hymns of English origin such as *Rock of Ages,* but also *Keemo, Kimo,* a tongue-twister and nonsense ditty of obscure derivation that black girls (Emma Thomas among them, because she passed it along to her children) sang repetitively to needle their elders.[67]

Another woman evoked old plantation festivities that featured a fiddler acclaimed for "callin' de figgers." "Gals would put on dey spare dress ef dey had one," she recalled, and "fix up fo' partyin', even ef dey ain't got nothin' but a piece of ribbon to tie in dey hair." Their work boots, however, were cumbersome: "Couldn't do no steppin' in dem field shoes." Slaves like Emma, therefore, twirled and promenaded in bare or stockinged feet when they joined the number called "cuttin' de pigeon wings." It included "flippin' yo' arms an' legs roun' an' holdin' yo' neck stiff like a bird." A fiddler might take a "charred corn-cob an' draw a circle on de flo', den call one arter de odder up an' dance in de circle." That was the cake-walk, with a tasty award presented to "de one dat did de mos' steps." It derived from West African celebrations, and black people in the New World emulated the motions of "swinging a scythe, tossing a pitchfork of hay . . . rolling a hogshead of tobacco, saw-ing wood, hoeing corn"—familiar tasks in southeast Virginia. Slaves relished those frolics, and "danced 'spectable, . . . shiftin' round from one partner to 'nother." Those "'spectable" dances mingled traditional African with old British patterns of gesture and rhythm to create uniquely syncretic diversions on the region's antebellum plantations. Following the Civil War, former slaves brought along their dances and music when they migrated north.[68]

Despite those occasional recreational activities, some black peo-ple labored seven days a week. But others, because of scrupulously negotiated work conditions plus owners' religious convictions, could preserve Sunday as a day of rest. "The master and the preacher both say that was the Lord's day and you warn't 'spose to work," one former slave reported. "We went to church," she added, "and stayed the biggest portion of the day."[69]

As best they could, however, masters regulated religious prac-tices and beliefs on their plantations, and laws reinforced their ef-forts. "Yer better never let mastah catch yer wif a book or paper, and yer couldn't praise God so he could hear you," a black man re-called. "If yer done dem things, he sho' would beat you." During the Civil War's early months, one slave preacher stepped far out of line—according to the Rebels' prescribed guidelines—and a Portsmouth woman recalled his demise after he "carr[ied] news to the Yankees." In retribution, local whites "made him dig his own grave an' preach his own funeral." Finally, she grimly concluded, "dey hung him to a tree 'xactly over de pit he done dug. . . . When he was dead, dey let his body fall right in de grave." But another intrepid slave shared with friends "what God had told him in a vision, dat dis freedom would come." The white Thomas family and "servants" such as Emma (relegated to the back of the building or assembled for separate services) attended Blunt's Methodist Church, where the minister undoubtedly would have espoused a consistent proslavery philosophy. In later years, one Negro man recalled that at Sunday school the younger slaves always were taught: "Be nice to Marsa and Missus . . . be obedient, an' wuk hard."[70]

Some of the Lower Tidewater's most often repeated stories concerned Nat Turner, and epitomized the empowering yet potentially unsettling significance of Christianity among the black population. Turner had been a literate, charismatic slave preacher called the Prophet, who was, one Portsmouth man remembered, given to "holding dark communion with familiar spirits." He hailed from Southampton County (carved out of Isle of Wight in the late 1700s and adjoining it to the west), and his apocalyptic revelations and radical interpretation of the Bible as a source of strength and resistance had influenced him to lead a rebellion against the institution of slavery, as personified by his owners and other local white people. A mystic vision of "white spirits and black spirits engaged in battle" and a darkened midday sun—a solar eclipse—had appeared to Turner as compelling portents summoning him to action. In August 1831, he and his cohorts demonstrated their pent-up fury by killing fifty whites near the town of Jerusalem, only eight miles from Isle of Wight.[71]

Federal troops stationed at Fortress Monroe plus militias from nearby counties swiftly quelled that uprising, but Turner and some disciples, tracked by baying hounds, were rumored to have forded the Blackwater River and passed through Isle of Wight's southwestern reaches. The visionary leader himself was eventually captured right in Southampton County, tried, found guilty, and hanged. In the incident's bloody wake, vengeful citizens murdered more than a hundred black people who were unapologetically slain, reported a stunned white man, "without trial and under circumstances of great barbarity." Many victims of those reprisals had been totally uninvolved in the affair, although whites claimed that slaves throughout the region knew of the event well in advance and planned to "rise on that notable day and assert their right to freedom by slashing their way through human flesh." Decades later, people of both races preserved vivid memories of the preacher Nat Turner's awe-inspiring revolt.[72]

During the late antebellum years, whites feared further rebellions, and one Negro asserted, "De preaching us got 'twont nothing much." The "ole white preacher" whom he remembered well "was telling us slaves to be good to our marsters." As best they could, whites around the lower Chesapeake (and throughout the South) insisted that slaves' Christian practices must reflect and project a message of strict obedience. "Obey your masters," slave owners consistently argued that the Scriptures directed. According to their interpretation of the infamous Old Testament curse that supposedly had been visited on the dark-skinned descendants of Ham, every Negro was destined always to remain the "scrvant of servants."[73] Christianity, claimed members of the dominating race, never was meant to provide a message of either defiance or deliverance.

The eloquent George Teamoh, a former slave of Norfolk's Josiah and Jane Thomas (probably distant relations of Emma Thomas's owners), argued in his diary that masters interpreted the Turner rebellion to mean that "all who bore in any degree marks of having descended from the African race were not to be taught, or allowed to read God's holy word."[74] Whites also believed, paradoxically, that black people, innately, were too dim-witted to benefit from a formal education. One Virginia slaveholder further rationalized that to "enlighten them is to make them unhappy at their condition."[75] There, and in all other southern states, teaching Negroes to read, write, and cipher was forbidden by law, and usually withheld in practice as well.

Emma Thomas certainly was not exempt from the impact of such regulations. During her youth, however, her master or mistress may have recognized that a slave with at least a minimal education (stringent laws notwithstanding) could be more useful, efficient, and therefore more valuable than a totally illiterate one. Or, perhaps believing it their Christian duty, as did some other slave owners, they helped Emma learn to read—but just a little. Quite a few slaves, often with surreptitious help from literate black friends or unsuspecting white children with whom they memorized "the alphabet in song," learned to read and write. Teamoh also observed that because masters enjoyed hearing their "servants" sing, "no one had any . . . objection to a slave learning . . . music."[76] Negroes, however, well understood the symbiotic relationship between education and empowerment.

In spring 1861, the Commonwealth of Virginia, along with Arkansas, Tennessee, and North Carolina, followed the lead of South Carolina (then Mississippi, Florida, Alabama, Georgia, Louisiana, and Texas) and decided in the wake of the election of an apparently hostile, antislavery Republican president to secede from the Union and join the breakaway Confederate States of America.[77] Of Virginia's 200,000 voters (all of them white men), only about 35,000 were slaveholders, and some members of Isle of Wight's small electorate maintained reservations about secession. But when the time came to settle the issue, they made clear their determination to abandon the Union that their antecedents had done so much to establish. In Isle of Wight, casting a ballot endorsing secession (as every local voter did) probably was more a declaration of loyalty to race and class, combined with the sacred principles of states' rights, than a representation of any deep conviction that withdrawal would resolve the prickly questions surrounding slavery, or the fearfully anticipated calamities that the new president (despised throughout the white South) might precipitate.[78] The Civil War soon affected the whole state of Virginia and transformed the lives of everyone in Isle of Wight County.

Not long after the onset of war, portions of the Union fleet lay at anchor by the nearby Yankee stronghold and shipyards at Newport News. By the next year, all along the lower James River, a former slave reported, Union "gunboats would fire on the towns and plantations." Favored targets included Fort Boykin's riverside ramparts near Smithfield, and Fort Huger atop the palisades a bit farther north.[79] Despite their strategic locations, those Isle of Wight bastions, tenuously held by the Confederacy, could not long defend that stretch of the James when confronted with the power of the Yankees' shipboard cannons. County residents also looked east across the water and observed the Union's hot-air surveillance balloons floating above Hampton's fortifications. In May 1862, they heard the muted thunder of powerful explosions and saw a dull red glow in the southeastern night sky as retreating Confederate troops torched Portsmouth's shipyards. At the same time, the first Yankee ground troops under the command of Captain Drake McKay marched into Smithfield and demanded its surrender. Local elders complied, eliciting the captain's promise that he would respect citizens' rights.[80]

A brief but bitter armed encounter took place later that year at a town on the Blackwater River, with another skirmish along the nearby Nansemond. The following spring, local people debated the travails of Miss Hozier, a white woman from nearby Suffolk, whom Yankee scouts intercepted, arrested, and searched. They found documents pertaining to a projected Confederate recapture of Norfolk tightly rolled in the handle of her parasol, and accused her of trying to transport them to a secessionist general positioned somewhere on the Blackwater.[81]

Despite the county's surrender, whites remained resistant to their truculent yet negligent occupiers. In 1864, the genuinely trifling "battle of Smithfield" provided a moment of exhilaration and fleeting sense of empowerment for local Confederates when their men seized a small Yankee boat that had run aground at the mouth of Pagan Creek. They managed, briefly, to deter the Union sailors who arrived to salvage their property. As white citizens and some of the few remaining slaves huddled in cellars, ragtag militiamen wrenched the gilded American eagle from the vessel's pilothouse, then confiscated its cargo and elegant appointments, including crystal goblets, plus varied scarce and prized comestibles. The ground shuddered and windows all over town shattered when local defenders blew up the intrusive boat, and a number of fortunate folks in Smithfield enjoyed a rare treat of steaming Yankee coffee that evening.[82] No significant military engagements, however, decimated Isle of Wight.

Although Union troops did not fully pacify the county for some time, several regiments camped near Smithfield for months. Bands of soldiers made forays around the countryside forging strategic yet transient alliances with black people, harassing local whites, scavenging food and equipment, even torching homes, barns, and crops. Nearby Yankee authorities received complaints about "marauding and piratical parties composed of fugitive slaves, free negroes and white men under cover of the U.S. flag, [who] destroyed furniture, [took] to their own use jewelry, fowling pieces, ornaments, . . . stock, etc., breaking open houses, etc., making no exceptions in the cases of widows and orphans." According to Thomas family legend, northern cavalrymen spared the residence, but provocatively rode their horses straight through Four Square's handsome vestibule.[83]

Virtually all of the county's able-bodied white men, including members of the Thomas family and their in-laws, the Stringfields, served with Rebel units. J. H. Thomas volunteered for the James River Heavy Artillery. Algernon Thomas enlisted in the Smithfield Light Artillery Blues, then transferred to the Isle of Wight Grays. He was killed in 1864. Two other Thomases joined the Sixth Virginia Infantry. J. E. Stringfield was captured while fighting with the Twenty-fifth Virginia Cavalry, and several cousins died with the Third Virginia Regiment.[84]

Other Isle of Wight boys and men lost their lives during the war (from disease, medical maltreatment, or neglect exacerbated by the appalling "hog and hominy" diet more than from battle-related injury), despite the fact that their county was spared serious armed encounters. But the Civil War's concomitant deprivations and disruptions were very real indeed for slaves, free people of color, and whites of all classes—the aged and infirm, women and children—who remained at home. Mail and railway services were disrupted, Confederate currency became almost worthless, and there was little to eat or buy even if one had cash. Emma's master Jonathan Thomas and his business partner loaned their county two thousand dollars to provide supplies for the militia.[85]

Because of the absence of able-bodied white men and the wholesale departures of slaves, plantation production ground to a virtual standstill and domestic order deteriorated. In mid-1863, whites in

Isle of Wight complained to an occupying Union general that farm work could not be adequately performed because so many bondsmen had left, and a militia officer asserted that "bands of lawless freebooters, composed of runaway negroes and worthless white men have recently begun to . . . pillage in the counties of Isle of Wight and Surry." The navy blockade sharply curtailed imports of consumer goods. Food, especially sugar and salt, was in short supply, as was cloth of any sort, plus many other necessities and niceties of life. In May 1864, a smallpox outbreak ravaged the county, reinforcing the aura of despair.[86]

Long after the conflict ended, however, white people in Isle of Wight reverently retold the story of Randall Booth's wartime endeavors. Booth had been a slave who belonged to the clerk of the court, and late in 1862 he hid his owner's county records from the Yankees who circulated at will throughout the area. Local authorities rewarded him for his loyalty and appointed him courthouse caretaker—or janitor. But that isolated case of unquestioning fealty was very much the exception.[87]

Although one couple stayed on at Four Square with the Julius Thomases and served as the white family's household retainers for years thereafter, even residing in the old slave quarters, like most others of her race and caste, Emma Thomas felt no need to remain faithful to her owners. She and other "unruly negro girls" were disinclined to linger in bondage while the country was in turmoil and a fresh scent of freedom permeated the air.[88] Shortly after war broke out, east around the river bend at Old Point Comfort, thousands of black people from up and down the peninsula, across Hampton Roads and the James River, began to inundate the Yankee stronghold at Fortress Monroe, which they called the "freedom fort." They embraced their precarious status—legitimized and made possible by the Union military—as contrabands, exerted their newly attained liberation, and dedicated themselves to help end slavery.

Although the forced separation of families, in particular, was intolerable, the concerns that had made slaves' circumstances most unbearable were not so much physical abuse, wretched living and working conditions, or even hatred for their owners specifically or white people in general. The emotional burdens of having their psychic, legal, social, and economic inferiority continually reinforced, however, were overwhelming. At the same time, despite their servile status, most believed that their longtime country of residence had been established on the principles of liberty, justice, and equality. It was supposed to be the land of opportunity, no matter how lowly one's birth. "God made man, man made the slave," asserted Portsmouth's George Teamoh, suggesting that those unjust and temporal man-made circumstances could and would be reversed, and natural rights restored. Like America Sparrow, a patriotically and optimistically named free woman of color in Isle of Wight, the vast majority of blacks wanted to work for themselves or for decent wages, worship and marry as they pleased, protect and educate their children, own a plot of land, and forge a proud new affiliation with their nation. They wanted to be citizens of the United States.[89]

Black people knew that they deserved to reap the benefits of their country's democratic premises and its inherent and potential wealth. Few wished to emigrate and resettle in Haiti, the Republic of Liberia, or elsewhere in Africa as a number of white people such as President Lincoln (as well as some sincere and dedicated, but disillusioned members of their own race) proposed as a "solution" to the escalating "problem" of free Negroes. Instead, as the Civil War brought an increasingly palpable sense of approaching liberation, most blacks wanted and expected to share in the promise of America. Looking toward the future, they hoped and planned to restructure their lives and control their destinies in the only homeland they had ever known.

Because of their obsessive but well-justified concerns about the slaves' accelerating departures, white people in Isle of Wight destroyed, disabled, or confiscated many of the oyster skiffs, dinghies, and skipjacks that lay moored in the shallows and inlets along the James River, where they offered a beguiling, accessible means of deliverance. No black Virginian could board a train unless a white person had purchased his or her ticket, but throughout the early war years a swelling stream of fugitives nonetheless left Smithfield by land and water, as they similarly abandoned other areas around the Confederacy's periphery—deserting masters, mistresses, and work, and concurrently providing critical support to the Yankees. A number of slaves, along with free people of color, rowed across the river to contraband camps at Newport News or Jamestown Island, where some joined the Union navy. "Not only wuz dere men slaves dat run to de Yankees," a Portsmouth man reported, but "de women slaves . . . help by washing and cooking." In neighboring Surry County, a band of runaways killed three white people who tried to thwart their escape efforts. The covert black exodus began as a trickle but burgeoned into a cresting flood. By mid-1863, almost the entire enslaved population had forsaken Isle of Wight.[90]

Emma Thomas (still a girl, but compelled by destiny quickly to become a woman) joined that surging migration. In the wake of the wartime Confiscation Acts and issuance of the Emancipation Proclamation—alone or with companions and kin, traveling by raft, mule, or oxcart, even, perhaps, on foot—she left the plantation where she reluctantly had spent her early years. Like multitudes of others, Emma headed off to find and claim her freedom in the teeming, challenging city of Norfolk.

5

WARTIME NORFOLK, LIBERTY,
and a LEGITIMIZED MARRIAGE

Mammy, don't yo' cook no mo',
Yo' ar' free, yo' ar' free.
Rooster, don't yo' crow no mo',
Yo' ar' free, yo' ar' free.
Ol' hen, don't yo' lay no mo' eggs,
Now yo' free, yo' free.

Traditional verse of black women in southeast Virginia

NORFOLK WAS THE modest port, crouched along the Elizabeth River near Hampton Roads' south shore where, like thousands of contrabands, Emma Thomas arrived during the Civil War. She had successfully shed her enslaved childhood in Isle of Wight County.

The city that Emma sought out in the early 1860s often had been perceived in contradictory ways by outsiders as well as its residents. In 1854, just prior to Norfolk's lethal yellow fever epidemic, the visiting Frederick Law Olmsted had described it as "a dirty, low, ill-arranged town, nearly divided by a morass." One of his colleagues, however, countered that the marshy port was ideally positioned "to have commanded the business of the Atlantic seaboard." "There is no harbour from the St. John's to the Rio Grande," he declared, "that has the same facilities of ingress and egress at all times and in all weathers." "It has the double advantage of an inner and an outer harbour," and, he concluded, "the inner harbour is as smooth as any mill-pond."[1]

The Great Dismal Swamp Canal led from the Elizabeth River south into North Carolina. It provided passable access for conveying raw materials to both Norfolk and Portsmouth (its subordinate sister, coupled by similar interests and constant ferry traffic) that lay southwest across the river's narrow saltwater neck. But those fortuitously situated ports could not achieve their economic potential until they gained improved access to the interior and its agricultural produce. To some extent, the operations of the Petersburg & Norfolk and the Seaboard & Roanoke Railroads (their silvery rails threaded through Isle of Wight's cornfields and hamlets) had accomplished that by the late 1850s. Nonetheless, despite the region's ocean commerce and its shipyards' proficiency, as the Civil War began, Norfolk remained an inferior satellite to the country's northern Atlantic seaports, and smaller and less prosperous even than industrial Richmond, Virginia's upriver capital.

Norfolk County's population totaled over 32,000 and was about one-third Negro. Compared to Richmond's nearly 38,000 people, just prior to the war the city of Norfolk (thirty-six percent Negro, both slave and free) barely topped 14,000. Portsmouth numbered almost 9,500 and was fifteen percent black. Except for those slaves who slept "under the stairs" or in shabby quarters adjoining their masters' homes, most black people lived on Norfolk's north side in slums such as Hen-house Lane and the dismal Cow Bay, graphically depicted as "a hive . . . bordered on all sides with . . . filthy houses."[2]

While complaining that Norfolk possessed "all the immoral and disagreeable characteristics of a large seaport, with few of the advantages," Olmsted conceded that the presence of naval officers and their families contributed to the town's "agreeable, refined, and cultivated" society. It also had antebellum Virginia's only publicly supported schools (albeit for white children only), a nascent program of relief for needy residents, and—because of the fear of recurrent epidemics—moderately effective means of disease control. The city boasted ten newspapers, numerous restaurants, public music halls, and private libraries. Some outsiders complained that Norfolk's populace was unrefined and interested only in commerce, yet others praised the elegant homes and panoramic vistas of Craney Island and Hampton Roads from the sparkling harbor that seemed "ever alive with sail-boats and steam-boats." "The live-oak, branching like an apple-tree with leaves like a berry, is one of the glories of this region," commented an admiring newcomer.[3]

The Jonathan Thomases, on whose Isle of Wight plantation Emma spent her early years, maintained a residence in Norfolk. That second home was substantial as well, with a domestic staff comprised of several black women, from forty to seventy years of age.[4] Those "servants" would have known, and might have been related to, Emma Thomas. Even as a child, at her owners' behest, Emma may have shuttled between the farm near Smithfield and Norfolk, and thereby become thoroughly acquainted with the city.

Many slaves as well as free people of color in Hampton Roads' waterside hub led less restrictive lives than their country cousins. They often were better able to develop their innate capabilities—to learn how to read, write, and handle money. City trades more than agricultural work demanded such skills. In contrast to most black people in the hinterlands, they more openly asserted their independence to cope with the complex world in which they found themselves.[5]

As residents of a significant, if underutilized Atlantic seaport, they caught glimpses of a universe spared the curse of slavery. The northern states, Canada, even England—the adopted home of former Virginia bondsmen such as Jefferson Davis's onetime coachman William Andrew Jackson and the boxer Jemmy Robinson—seemed not far removed or unduly inaccessible, thanks to the constant arrivals and departures of sailors and other transients headed from or to many ports worldwide. Although their numbers declined during the late antebellum period, "colored" crewmen from nearby as well as far-flung, seafaring territories passed through Hampton Roads. Their recurrent presence personified the possibility of a new and different, free life.[6]

The American Colonization Society (ACS), an organization largely comprised of affluent whites who perceived removal to Africa as a practical solution to the vexing "problem" of free Negroes in the United States, had chartered a Norfolk branch as early as 1821. For varied reasons, some black people—following the lead of New Bedford's Paul Cuffe and others—also supported African colonization and helped raise funds for those of their race who wanted to emigrate. But despite the onerous economic, legal, and social hardships they faced, by the late antebellum years most Negroes in Norfolk, as elsewhere in the country, considered themselves Americans, not displaced Africans.

Nonetheless, they often retained (but continually transformed as well) manifestations of their West African cultures. Personal possessions and seashells, for example, adorned grave sites in a Norfolk slave cemetery to facilitate passage of the deceased spirits across the ocean to Africa, bound for the eternal realm of the ancestors.[7] Virginia's black people also fervently hoped for an end to slavery and relief from the pervasive racial discrimination they faced even if they were not enslaved. Yet most of them fully expected to remain in their country of birth, where, they believed, true democracy some day might reign, and, at least in theory, all were created equal.

The city's Joseph Jenkins Roberts (a light-skinned fellow of mixed racial ancestry whom the militant emigrationist Martin Delany disparaged as "a white man's Negro") was an exception. He was among the region's few people who emigrated to the ACS-sponsored settlement in West Africa where, ironically, his pale face would have stood out like a pearl in a sea of ink. There, Roberts became a successful "new African" merchant. The former Norfolk resident was elected president of the fledgling Liberian republic from 1847 to 1855, then again from 1871 to 1876. He was the first in a long progression of Americo-Liberians who maintained rigid political controls over the indigenous people for more than a century.[8]

In addition, and in contrast to ACS efforts to remove free people of color to Africa, even before the war a number of Virginia slaves took matters into their own hands. Often assisted by Norfolk and Portsmouth's Negro seamen and quasi-free dockworkers, they falsified papers and secreted themselves to steal away by ship, usually headed for Boston, New Bedford, or other New England ports. George Teamoh, Thomas Bayne, William Carney, Joseph T. Wilson, and Shadrach Minkins made their separate ways to those havens in Massachusetts during the late antebellum years.[9]

Teamoh had worked at Portsmouth's shipyards, married (although that union would not have been officially sanctioned), fathered four children, and endured the agony of having his family sold away, before concluding that slave life was intolerable. In the 1850s, with help from a sympathetic owner who had contracted out his services, Teamoh boarded a merchant vessel bound for Massachusetts. "To be carried on the 'high seas,' " he argued, was "tantamount to giving the slave his freedom." Thomas Bayne and William Carney both ended up in New Bedford as well, where Bayne, who had received some training from a former master, worked as a dentist. Carney later became a hero while fighting with the Fifty-fourth Massachusetts Infantry. In 1851, Shadrach Minkins had fled to Boston, but was captured and temporarily returned to his Virginia owner under newly stiffened provisions of the federal Fugitive Slave Act.[10]

Four years later, the white abolitionist Captain Fountain loaded both wheat and a shipment of black runaways into the hold of his schooner docked in Norfolk's harbor, but a search by local authorities failed to uncover the well-concealed human cargo. After considerable harassment and delay, the captain sailed for Quaker-dominated Philadelphia, where many escapees gained refuge. Hopeful fugitives often sang:

> *About our future destiny,*
> *There need be no debate—*
> *Whilst we ride, on the tide,*
> *With our Captain and his mate.*[11]

Two free women of color ran a "benevolence society" that was really a front for the Underground Railroad, while Henry Lewey, known as Bluebeard (the pirate), was recognized as one of the Railroad's "most dextrous managers." With their assistance, many "passengers" sighted *Polaris* as their astral beacon and followed it north to freedom. In all, well before the Civil War, black people (free and enslaved, sometimes aided by sympathetic whites) in Norfolk and Portsmouth had created a restive and often subversive subculture that sought to undermine the institution of slavery.[12] Unusual mobility, some access to education, plus a knowledge of and yearning for freedom in a wider world where opportunities exceeded those known by most rural blacks, characterized their urban society. Proximity to the ocean, contacts with free men and women of color, northerners, northern states, and the whole Atlantic world stimulated and inspired many Negroes in Hampton Roads.

A number of free people of color in the Norfolk region, such as the family of the Reverend Lewis Tucker (who became Emma Thomas's minister), owned property. Just prior to the war, the Tuckers reportedly held real estate worth $5,000, plus $2,000 in personal property. Those would have been sizable assets for white Virginians, and were amounts almost unparalleled in the Negro community.[13] But despite his family's antebellum success, God and his church called Tucker even more insistently.

One hundred and sixty black people appeared on Norfolk County's tax rolls in 1860. But property ownership for nonwhites carried perils unlike any assumed by whites. Because they were delinquent, or refused to pay taxes when they enjoyed no civil rights, about one hundred of Portsmouth's free persons of color were sold into slavery that year, an unconscionably punitive sentence that, nonetheless, was specified in the city charter.[14]

Though state laws denied all blacks an education, quite a few of the region's free "colored" people, and even some slaves, did learn to read and write. In the late antebellum years, a white woman who recently had moved to Norfolk openly conducted classes for black children. Local authorities, however, would not tolerate her defiance of tradition and statute, and in 1852 they fined and briefly imprisoned her. After that, such illicit efforts did not cease, but largely burrowed underground.[15]

An incident from 1860 exemplified the perception of another "inappropriate" liberty that had been allowed Norfolk's Negroes. In Petersburg, not far upriver, authorities arrested a free man of color for smoking in public. A local newspaper then protested that Norfolk was the South's only city "that gives this valuable privilege to the negro." But even that seemingly trivial "privilege" did not survive. In March 1861, following the example of other localities, Norfolk's council passed new legislation denying black people the right to smoke. If convicted, they could be fined or whipped. After 1862, however, that city began to undergo a significant social revolution. Its Negroes, already imbued with a pent-up yet viable insurrectionary temper, welcomed the arrival of more explicit means of salvation in the provisions of unprecedented federal regulations and the persons of occupying Union troops.[16]

The twin ports' late antebellum population included not only enslaved and nonenslaved blacks plus indigenous whites, but also a number of European immigrants—many born in Ireland. They often lived in squalid shacks or tenements near free Negroes and bondsmen. It was among those people in the Irish Row neighborhood, "overcrowded with inhabitants, and filthy in the extreme," that the 1855 yellow fever epidemic had erupted.[17]

That same dreadful summer, a Norfolk newspaper reported an anecdote titled "The Irish Negro." An immigrant freshly arrived from Ireland, the item asserted, was assisted on the docks by "a negro who spoke to Patrick in Irish." The newcomer recognized the "black fellow [as] one of his own countrymen, and asked how long he had been in America." "About four months," the dark-skinned man responded. Turning to his wife in amazement, "the chop-fallen Irishman . . . exclaimed: 'But four months in this country and [already] almost as black as jet!' "[18]

In addition to the Irish-born, Gaelic-speaking newcomer's consternation about a contagious melanin transference, he and his "black fellow . . . countryman" faced different futures in Norfolk, and the United States in its entirety, despite their similar origins and perhaps common aspirations. That city, like a number of others, had experienced virulent anti-Irish, anti-Catholic bigotry in recent years. Newspapers characterized such immigrants as "the scum of other countries who would rather beg than work, and rather steal than beg" and a visitor commented that "the Irish living there are almost in as degraded a state as they are in the half-starved districts of Ireland." In the eyes of many Americans, the sons and daughters of Erin, though hardly black, belonged to a wretched, transitional "race" situated somewhere between Negroes and true Caucasians. Yet the white newcomer, like most Europeans, would have had greater economic opportunities, and could have looked forward to becoming an American citizen, while the "Irish Negro," and the navy's Anglo-African John Bond, could not, since federal statutes restricted naturalization in the Promised Land to "free, white men."[19]

Apprehensive authorities, however, always feared potentially threatening alliances between recalcitrant slaves and seditious whites. In one case, an Irish-born servant in Norfolk had helped her slave sweetheart escape to Canada. And the 1859 Harper's Ferry raid in northern Virginia, instigated by the white abolitionist John Brown and supported by his interracial crew, reinforced whites' inherent misgivings. The next autumn, Norfolk County patrols, heeding rumors of an incipient slave insurrection, shot and killed an Irish laborer who had been a purported ringleader in the imagined conspiracy. For several weeks thereafter, local officials rounded up and imprisoned many "suspicious" Negroes.[20]

By late 1860, most white people in the slaveholding regions found themselves agonizing over Abraham Lincoln's election and what they perceived as his irrational determination to end slavery and disregard states' rights. The next winter, irate southerners who had begun to withdraw from the Union formed a secessionist Confederacy. In spring 1861 (despite the reluctance of quite a few pragmatic, nonideological Norfolk residents), Virginia seceded from the United States, and rebels lowered the Stars and Stripes and boldly raised the Stars and Bars over Craney Island in Norfolk's harbor.

As the internecine conflict boiled up and the Confederacy enjoyed an early surge of empowerment, Yankee troops made ready to evacuate Norfolk and Portsmouth. They hastily abandoned facilities such as Portsmouth's naval hospital, considered "the best . . . of its kind in America."[21] The chaotic, retreating forces also prepared to destroy the shipyards and the country's greatest ordnance supply, stockpiled in one of the South's most strategic harbors. Shortly before dawn one night in late April, they burned their bridges and other installations behind them in an inferno, "grand and terrific beyond description." It could be seen for thirty miles around, from Emma Thomas's home in Isle of Wight to the northwest, to the Hampton peninsula directly north, and the Norfolk-Portsmouth metropolis and hinterlands along Hampton Roads' south shore.²² Among the abandoned Union ships that were badly scorched but not destroyed during the embattled exodus was a large steam frigate called the USS *Merrimac.*

Although the Union naval blockade deprived Virginia's twin ports of much of their livelihood, they stumbled along in a frail approximation of normalcy. In December 1861, Norfolk's "colored" firefighters even took part in a major civic demonstration. "The sable firemen enjoyed their holiday parade," a local journal reported, "they had music, too, and marched along in evident consciousness of the importance and usefulness of their position."²³ Confederate laborers—black and white—began rehabilitating the sabotaged marine industries and prepared to meet new wartime challenges, while men at the Gosport Navy Yard covertly started to fashion an innovative ironclad ram on the salvaged hull of the USS *Merrimac,* renamed the CSS *Virginia.*

The Union army and navy, however, did not abandon the entire region. Fortress Monroe, north across Hampton Roads, never fell into Confederate hands, and after a brief hiatus of secessionist control, the Yankees resecured adjoining Newport News, with its docks and naval repair facilities. General Benjamin Butler (who hailed from Boston, and soon would be labeled "the Beast" because of his somewhat grotesque appearance and his severity toward the Rebels) was Fortress Monroe's commander the following spring when three Norfolk slaves rowed across the channel to the Union citadel. Butler refused to return the runaways to their outraged owner, arguing that as human property that might assist the enemy, they were legitimate contraband of war.²⁴

Some abolitionists complained that "the word 'Contrabands' is not a proper term to be applied to human beings," and added, "they are not exactly slaves and to the disgrace of our Government, they are not exactly freedmen." "Let them be called Colored Refugees," the protesters argued, "until we can obtain for them a recognized freedom and citizenship." Despite such righteous pleas, "contrabands" became the popular term used to describe the South's "colored refugees," and by July, nine hundred black fugitives—men, women, children—were ensconced at the "freedom fort" under the auspices of the Union army.²⁵

A secret society in Norfolk, called the Grand Enterprising Sons and believed to be affiliated with the Underground Railroad, aided aspiring escapees. But all of those who attempted to flee did not meet with success. Twenty-five slaves paid a white man $1,500 in gold to deliver them across the channel. Their Judas, however, betrayed them. He kept the money, but returned the Negroes to slavery.[26]

A number of slaveholders warned their "servants" that if they "run away to de Yankees dey'd bore holes in our arms an' put wagon staves through de holes an' make us pull de wagons like hosses," a former slave recalled. Those ghoulish fabrications deterred some, but hardly kept most black people (such as Emma Thomas) from leaving bondage as soon as they had an opportunity. Despite President Lincoln's equivocating racial policies, they considered him their Moses, and likened their own exodus to that of the children of Israel who fled Pharaoh's Egypt. "Dem niggers who left wid de Yankees," remembered a black man, "were sot free, but, poor things, dey had no place to go."[27]

By late 1861, thousands of ragged Negroes from throughout the region had abandoned their primarily agricultural work and reached the freedom fort. The contrabands lived there in makeshift tents or barracks and gathered on Sundays beneath Hampton's "emancipation oak" to sing hymns and anthems of liberation. They began to build shacks, plant gardens, and support themselves by selling fish, fruit, and other produce to Union soldiers and sailors. Often, army clergymen married couples who previously could only "take up together by mutual agreement."[28] But many Yankees, and almost all blacks, agreed that one primary task was to teach them, especially the children, to read and write.

Mary Kelsey Peake, the frail daughter of an English father and a nonenslaved Negro mother, had been born in Norfolk. As an adult, educating young people became her mission. She illicitly instructed a number of black children when she joined Norfolk's Bute Street Baptist Church, where the "colored" clerk, Lewis Tucker, had already started leading worship services under his white minister's supervision. By the fall of 1861, Mary Peake was operating a school for contraband boys and girls at Fortress Monroe. Early the following year, however, the overly conscientious woman succumbed to tuberculosis.[29]

Peake's abbreviated endeavor was hardly the sole wartime attempt to educate contrabands in Virginia's Lower Tidewater. The winter she died, the American Missionary Association started a school for the freedpeople, as did a former slave of ex-President John Tyler who opened his facility in the abandoned Tyler mansion located a few miles upriver on the James.[30]

While the Yankees occupied most of the lower Hampton peninsula, rebel troops controlled Portsmouth and Norfolk through early 1862. Free people of color and slaves who had provided so much of the region's labor force had little choice but to work for the Confederacy, reinforcing defenses, repairing naval installations, and in support of other wartime efforts. Those often coerced activities reinforced the Union's judgment that any runaways must be treated as contraband of war.

Resistance ran rampant in the black community. Mary Louveste, a slave seamstress with Union sympathies who was owned by a chandler whose shop was situated near Portsmouth's Gosport shipyard, surreptitiously crossed Confederate lines as she journeyed north through Virginia carrying a valuable packet. In a private meeting once she reached Washington, she gave Secretary of the Navy Gideon Welles crucial papers about the former *Merrimac*'s ongoing conversion into an ironclad. Louveste had copied stolen plans and documents concerning the reconfigured vessel and had ascertained its condition, capabilities, and date of completion. The old ship had been badly damaged, but its new two-inch-thick, iron-plate shell, plus ten powerful guns enclosed in a revolving armored turret, promised to make the *Virginia* almost invincible when the Confederate Navy relaunched it. When his informant applied for a federal pension some years later, Welles wrote on her behalf: "Mrs. Louveste encountered no small risk in bringing this information. . . . I am aware of none more meritorious than this poor colored woman whose zeal and fidelity I remember and acknowledge with gratitude."[31] The renamed, rebuilt CSS *Virginia*, about which Secretary Welles learned critical particulars from Mary Louveste, soon would play a major role in the war's progress, and in naval history.

During the winter of 1862, the Union navy and its ground troops occupied Fortress Monroe, Hampton, and Newport News, while the Confederates controlled Portsmouth, Norfolk, and Hampton Roads' south shore as the *Virginia* was being readied to depart from the local navy yard. Spearheaded by that powerful vessel, manned by almost three hundred sailors, the Rebel armada planned to establish full command over Hampton Roads and the lower James River.[32]

The first week of March 1862, the USS *Arrago,* one of many Union vessels anchored at Newport News, prepared to tackle the hazardous assignment of trying to sink the unseen, untested, but reputedly fearsome CSS *Virginia.* When they learned of their daunting mission, however, the *Arrago*'s predominantly white crew deserted. The quartermaster in charge of contraband laborers at Fortress Monroe requested and promptly obtained seven times the number of black volunteers needed to replace the defectors. The replacements signed on as seamen, but their designated task was never fulfilled due to the next few days' unprecedented events.[33]

On the morning of March 8, silenced crowds watched from both banks as the innovative ironside *Virginia* steamed slowly out of port, north along the sheltered Elizabeth River, past Craney Island, into Hampton Roads. As on many other Confederate ships, a few slaves served on board in menial positions. The massive, homely vessel rode low in the water, reminding some observers of a "half-submerged crocodile." It was clumsy and difficult to maneuver, needing an hour to negotiate a full turn, but was nonetheless a menacing presence.[34]

It built up a head of steam, moved into attack position, then fired on the powerful USS *Cumberland* and the fifty-gun frigate *Congress.* Mauled and crippled by the *Virginia*'s assaults, those Union ships and several smaller vessels became "scene[s] of carnage unparalleled in the war," an observer reported. The *Cumberland*'s decks were "covered with dead and wounded and awash with blood," and it was rammed repeatedly before plunging beneath the surface. The gory detritus of mutilated bodies, timbers, and jagged metal littered Hampton Roads' choppy waters. During those fateful hours, the apparently unstoppable *Virginia* caused the deaths of

250 Union seamen, wounded many more, and grounded, but did not destroy, the once mighty *Minnesota*. That ship included among its crew a mulatto youngster (tattooed with the figure of a woman perched atop an anchor) from New England named James Wolff, plus fourteen other Negroes manning the afterguns. "No gun in the fleet was more steady than theirs," boasted the accolades about those men's pluck and expertise. Over the course of that daunting day's exploits just off Norfolk, however, the *Virginia* proved itself as invincible as Confederates had hoped and Yankees feared.[35]

The Union armada's diverse ships valiantly counterattacked the Rebel ironside. Cannon fire suffused the air with acrid smoke and a deafening clamor, but barrages from the Yankees' most powerful guns barely dented the CSS *Virginia*'s armor. By afternoon, though its commander was grievously wounded, the *Virginia* had scored a remarkable success and, surrounded by sundry support vessels, stood ready to dominate Hampton Roads. Following that battle, whites throughout the South applauded their acclaimed ship and laudatory messages hummed through the region's telegraph wires. In contrast, distraught accounts carried via the slaves' ever active "grapevine telegraph" rued the day.[36]

What jubilant Confederates aboard the *Virginia* did not know as they anchored and retired for the evening, was that a similarly outfitted Union ship, the USS *Monitor,* had been dispatched from New York City. It steamed south along the Atlantic coast toward the mouth of the Chesapeake, and after dusk slipped into Hampton Roads.[37] Though 170 feet in length, the *Monitor,* an awkward-looking vessel disparagingly referred to as the "cheese box on a raft," was much smaller than the *Virginia*. It was equipped with comparable armor plate plus potent cannons, and was far more maneuverable than its southern counterpart.[38]

The next morning, scarcely the hallowed Sunday it might have been, the struggle recommenced. But as the *Monitor,* with its Dahlgren guns blazing, emerged from behind the firmly grounded USS *Minnesota,* the balance of power shifted and the participation of other ships became immaterial. In the confrontation that followed, one glancing blow by the heavier Rebel vessel—by then commanded by Alabama's Commander Catesby Jones—spun its

Union counterpart like a crazed gyroscope but inflicted little harm. The ironclads battled on without cease for more than four hours, "backing, filling and jockeying for position," directing thunderous cannonades at one another.[39]

Finally, low on ammunition and hindered by the ebbing tide, the *Virginia* swerved slowly toward port. Both ironclads suffered trivial damage plus minimal injuries and loss of life among their crews, but survived the ordeal well. The day ended, not with a bang but a depleted whimper, as the *Monitor* redirected its attention toward one of its major goals—rescuing the stranded, battered *Minnesota*. Although the USS *Monitor* did not destroy or even disable the CSS *Virginia* in the world's first encounter between armored vessels, it cleared the way for the Union navy to control the whole mouth of the Chesapeake.[40]

Those ships had bombarded each other and fought to a standoff in history's most widely observed naval confrontation. Slaves and contrabands (Emma Thomas perhaps among them) all around Hampton Roads' periphery abandoned work in fields, homes, and shipyards and thronged shoreward to watch that terrifying yet exhilarating contest. Few had been formally educated, but they understood that the war's progress and outcome—perhaps Hampton Roads' recent brawl especially—would significantly affect their lives. "I never found one at Hampton or Monroe," wrote a correspondent from the New York *World*, "who did not perfectly understand the issues of the war." Negroes closely followed military developments, and for them, the battle of attrition "off Newport News Point" remained a memorable event.[41]

As one woman recalled, "we was all standin' on de sho' watchin'." Her mother raised her "up in her arms so dat I could see." She heard the "awful noise dem guns was makin'," and remembered that "lots of men got kilt." Another man, vividly recollecting that milestone of his earliest years, reported that "the shores was lined thick with people watching that strange fight [but] all I could see was the flash of the guns."[42]

Although absolute maritime supremacy remained unresolved, Hampton Roads had been kept open to Yankee gunboats. Between the Union navy's enhanced efforts, the presence of the Army of the

Potomac on the Hampton peninsula, plus the forces headed up from North Carolina led by the intriguingly bewhiskered General Ambrose Burnside, the South's optimistic interlude was drawing to a close.[43] Nonetheless, many Rebels, for whom averting a loss seemed almost as great an accomplishment as victory, acted as if they had won, not only the naval stalemate but the war itself.

Southerners celebrated the CSS *Virginia*'s debatable success. One booster reported that "gratulatory words are passing from one to another as people meet in the streets . . . and thanksgiving is made in the churches."[44] Though neither side definitively established its preeminence that March day, the confrontation conclusively demonstrated that steam-powered iron vessels represented the maritime face of the future, and the era of the graceful wooden sailing ships' supremacy was grinding to a close.

In addition, new legislative developments soon would affect many of the country's black people. A federal mandate terminated slavery in the District of Columbia and the western territories in April 1862. Congress decreed that persons such as Emma Thomas who fled their Confederate owners would be free, and authorized some funds for former slaves—whom it did *not* anticipate granting the benefits of citizenship in the foreseeable future—to emigrate to one of the world's regions populated by black people. "The retention of the Negro among us with half privileges," the provision pontificated, "is but a bitter mockery to him, . . . our duty is to find him a congenial home and country."[45]

While the Union failed to control Norfolk immediately after the battle of the ironclads, within several months civilian leaders in the besieged port agreed to surrender rather than face further loss of life and property. As Rebel troops made ready to abandon the city, President Lincoln sailed down the Potomac and Chesapeake Bay into Hampton Roads, where he ordered an amphibious military landing. By mid-May, six thousand Union soldiers from Fortress Monroe under General John Wool's command prepared to cross the channel. Confederates at Gosport's shipyard burned that facility for the second time in a year, making a more thorough job of it than had the retreating Yankees in 1861. They soaked the CSS *Virginia* with kerosene, towed it into the harbor, and ignited a spectacular pyre. People throughout the region saw, heard, and felt the blast as the fabled ship sank into a flaming, watery grave. The midnight sky was ablaze, and "the noise made by the explosion," reported one source, "was perfectly terrible, shaking everything, even the very ground, apparently to its centre."[46]

Norfolk's mayor, bearing a flag of truce, surrendered his city. Most white people took the Union's oath of loyalty, but their coerced allegiance was barely skin-deep and some of their anxieties about the future were not ungrounded. One ex-slave recalled how a number of unruly blue-coated soldiers "went in all de white folks house, take dey silver, an' inything dey big 'nough [to] carry out." "When de Yankees came into dis town," another Norfolk man stated decades later, "dey broke in stores, an' told all de niggers to go in an' git anything dey wanted."[47]

General Wool encouraged a gala ceremony to welcome his troops. Most whites retreated behind closed doors or left town, but five thousand local blacks "in their most smiling holiday attire" greeted the liberators. That same month, the white pastor, like many others of his race, departed, and the Reverend Lewis Tucker took over the Bute Street Baptist Church, becoming Norfolk's first fully authorized Negro minister.[48]

No matter how daunting their new lives, many black people were no longer enslaved, and attending their own churches inspired them. "We wanted to sing, pray and serve God in our own way," asserted one man. "'Ligion needs a little motion," he added, "specially if you gwine feel de spirrit." But some of the contrabands' "horrible and startling" expressions of religiosity stunned wartime Norfolk's missionaries from the North. One straitlaced Quaker complained that the Negroes would "jump and spin, throw their arms into the air, embrace those near them . . . screech words of . . . rapture, and give an occasional staccato howl." "Their religious feeling is primarily emotional," that woman protested, "and of no practical utility." Emma Thomas and others, however, eagerly joined Tucker's church. Worshiping there, instead of at Isle of Wight's white-controlled Blunt's Chapel, she could serve God in her own way, as she and many others began to "feel de spirrit." They always had looked to a merciful Lord as a "horn of salvation" who "hast girded [them] with strength unto the battle: hast subdued those that rose up against [them]," and who would deliver them from all enemies.[49] Emma and thousands of similarly inclined rural blacks believed that the entire water-dominated, Yankee-controlled region—Fortress Monroe and Newport News on the channel's north side, Norfolk and Portsmouth to the south—was their sanctuary and safe harbor.

The "pest house," Norfolk's quarantine facility, and the jail, became points of entry for Negro fugitives from the hinterlands and sites of joyous reunions for their long-separated families. Churches such as Bute Street Baptist that served the black community provided refuge for contrabands who flooded the port cities. In 1862, thousands of displaced black people like Emma Thomas had no choice but to appropriate abandoned buildings or live in tents and shacks. When they had nothing to eat, the church on Bute Street somehow found loaves and fishes to feed them. Plantation life was brutal and enslavement agonizing, but owners had provided food, clothing, and shelter for the slaves, no matter how minimal those benefits. On her own during the war, one hardworking woman in Norfolk cooked "all week fer two an' three dollars" to support her family. She asked: "How kin you live off it . . . how kin yo'?"[50]

To support themselves and the war effort, black people took on whatever tasks they might pick up in and around Hampton Roads' Union enclaves and campsites. The Yankees impressed them to perform military support services, but often failed (or refused) to provide either pay or rations. Women labored as laundresses, cooks, and hawkers, youngsters were "water boys," and adults became stevedores or guards at the shipyards and docks along the James and Elizabeth Rivers. One former slave reported that her father had been a teamster at the Norfolk Navy Yard, while other newly emancipated men, many of whom had worked on or around boats for much of their lives, joined the Union navy. Though parents strove to hold fast to their children and women attempted to accompany spouses, all too often "whole heaps of families lost sight of each other."[51]

With the trigger-happy presence of legions of Union soldiers in town, the period was hardly tranquil. Some former slaves retained fond memories of the generosity of Yankee soldiers who offered famished black youngsters hardtack biscuits or brown sugar, but despite such random acts of kindness and the city's docile surrender, "dem were scared times," another woman noted, "cause you looked to be kilt any minute by stray bullets."[52]

On July 4, 1863, the country's anniversary—the first to reflect the independence of many Negroes in Norfolk—a white woman destroyed an American flag that had been carried by a black boy celebrating the occasion. That defilement of their standard was something that Union troops would not overlook, and they arrested the Rebel. Another white resident who asserted "I'd poison a Yankee in a minute, if I could get a chance," reflected the views of many others of her race. In an attempt to pacify the town and gain control over its often truculent Caucasian citizens, Union commanders instituted martial law.[53]

Norfolk ultimately became a temporary home for the greatest concentration of ex-slaves in all of Virginia. Though many whites departed during those stressful years, Emma Thomas joined about 26,000 contrabands who inundated the urban hub. As had already been the case at the freedom fort, educating black youngsters in Norfolk became a top priority. The American Missionary Association (AMA) first established schools there in 1862. At Emma's church, the Bute Street Baptist, more than 600 children and adults studied day and night, with almost equal numbers at several other houses of worship. Many people, desperate for the "book learning" that they long had been denied, trudged into the city from miles around. Grandmothers and grandfathers, aunts, uncles, older siblings, even fictive kin took responsibility for younger children; but because so many black youngsters had lost parents due to antebellum and wartime separations or premature deaths, the AMA also operated a much needed orphanage.[54]

General Butler initiated mandatory schooling for Norfolk's black children, dividing the city into three districts, each with ten teachers. Most were white, but the free-born, Oberlin-educated Sara Stanley (though she experienced shameful racial affronts at the hands of her white missionary hosts) became one of Norfolk's first Negro instructors. Another teacher boasted that his students progressed as well or better than whites, while a third cheerfully reported: "I have a class of twenty little boys and girls . . . coming to school for the first time; and some of them are so full of fun and frolic that it is difficult for them to sit still long at a time." Even young people like Emma Thomas who (apparently) did not attend school took pride in the achievements of others and the roles their churches played in the educational revolution. Stimulated by a hostile cognizance of those unaccustomed opportunities for former slaves, however, a number of spiteful white youngsters, egged on by embittered adults, taunted and even assaulted black children on their way to and from their cherished classes.[55]

In the fall of 1862, soon after Yankee troops completed their Norfolk-Portsmouth takeover, Lincoln issued his preliminary Emancipation Proclamation, leading Frederick Douglass to comment: "It has thrown a moral bombshell in the Confederacy." The pivotal Proclamation, crafted to encourage wavering Confederates to return to the Union fold, was scheduled to take effect one hundred days later, and as slaves throughout the South learned of the approaching presidential benediction, Douglass continued, they "flock[ed] in thousands to the lines of our army."[56]

Much of that burgeoning flood of contrabands was wretchedly sheltered throughout the Norfolk area's military enclaves, with the greatest number at Craney Island where the Friends of Worcester, Massachusetts, dispatched Sarah and Lucy Chase. Those white women found two thousand hungry people at the desolate location they described as "Gaza—this wilderness . . . this sandy bleak island cut off from the world."[57] Resourceful ex-slaves trapped, and even cooked and ate, the huge rats (which "taste like chickens," they asserted) that swarmed around the barracks, as Worcester's Quakers sent barrels of serviceable old clothing, and the Chase sisters started a school. They linked education with familiar chores, and students learned to "pick up the b-o-x, box, play with c-a-t and d-o-g, and fill their baskets with a multitude of words." Teachers assigned by the Educational Committee of Boston soon joined them, hoping "to improve the industrial, social, intellectual, moral, and religious" conduct of the freedpeople, and instruct them in the new responsibilities of freedom. That fall, additional refugees transferred from Fortress Monroe to Craney Island, further expanding the area's largest refugee encampment.[58]

In December, blacks received welcome news from Washington. Just prior to the issuance of the Emancipation Proclamation, the U.S. attorney general offered the president his judgment on the constitutionality of Negro citizenship. "I give it my opinion," he asserted, challenging the Supreme Court's noxious 1857 Dred Scott decision, "that the free man of color . . . if born in the United States, is a citizen of the United States."[59]

On January 1, 1863, on the heels of that finding, Abraham Lincoln issued the long-awaited Proclamation, with its forceful, moral imperative. It achieved the intended consequences of solidifying abolitionists' support, shoring up England's resolve to remain neutral in the war, and further undermining the Confederacy's enslaved workforce, but it had little practical enforceability. Officially, it affected only those regions that claimed allegiance to the Confederacy, which considered itself another country entirely, beyond Lincoln's jurisdiction. The Proclamation's provisions excluded the border slave states that had not seceded, where the president needed continuing military and political support, plus Norfolk and other slaveholding areas that had surrendered and reluctantly declared themselves loyal to the Union. The carefully worded pronouncement technically freed only those "persons held as slaves within any State, or designated part of the State, the people whereof shall be in rebellion against the United States." They, and they alone, it concluded, "shall be then, thenceforward, and forever free."[60]

This placed Norfolk-area blacks in somewhat contradictory circumstances. Theoretically, contrabands who fled their masters in parts of Virginia still in rebellion were free, while Norfolk-owned slaves were not. But that was not the reality. Virtually all of the urban region's Negroes soon enthusiastically exercised their liberated status. Many whites tried to bury their heads in the sand, but in most cases reluctantly had to acknowledge that the long-abiding institution of slavery was in its final, agonizing paroxysms.

By early December, there already had been chilling harbingers of the winter's oncoming harshness, yet as Christmas approached, members of Norfolk and Portsmouth's diverse African American community received a permit from the occupying military forces to hold a New Year's Day parade to commemorate the Proclamation's long-awaited issuance.[61] That celebratory event in Emma Thomas's new city of residence was one of the largest and most exuberant expressions of freedom in the country. The *New York Times* described the "procession of at least 4,000 negroes of all kinds and colors, headed by a band of music (drums and fifes), [that] paraded through the streets of the city." Two Negro women "trampled" some of the few remaining publicly displayed Confederate standards, while United States flags flew boldly in "colored" neighborhoods and along the city's most prominent thoroughfares as black people and Yankee soldiers cheered "the downfall of African slavery." Five hundred black men who were preparing to join their country's armed forces marched in the parade, and at the fairgrounds, celebrants burned in effigy the Confederacy's President Jefferson Davis.[62]

Anxious Rebels, on the other hand, "considered the Emancipation Proclamation a license to drown them in a sea of black rage," turned their backs on the festivities, and in the privacy of their homes (with fading bravado) implacably intoned:

> *Jeff Davis rides a fine bay mare,*
> *While Lincoln rides a mule.*
> *Jeff Davis is a gentleman,*
> *But Lincoln is a fool.*

A white Norfolk resident categorized the Proclamation's provisions as "abolition by fire and sword, raising the negro above the white man, and in so doing exterminating the whites of the South," while others predicted that January 1, 1863, would mark the "start of the long-feared general slave uprising."[63]

But die-hard secessionists were not the only ones who resented these changes in the racial status quo. Many Yankee soldiers, weary of ongoing responsibilities for the contrabands, wanted them sent anywhere else, while a white Union sailor stationed in Norfolk professed that while he liked and supported the navy, he abhorred Lincoln and his Proclamation.[64]

The ensuing months proved arduous, and residents of both races lacked income, fuel, food, and protection from the elements. In large part, Norfolk became a city of sailors and soldiers, refugees and paupers, who lived on and traipsed through streets that were filthy, unlit, and dangerous. One desperate black woman went "'roun' Norfolk sellin' milk." She begged "f'om door to door," and remembered well the "house o' bad women . . . called 'Free an' Easy,' " where she sold her produce to prostitutes who provided sexual services for sailors from the ships in port. Sometimes it snowed so hard "you couldn' see a foot ahead yourse'f." "I was so cold," she recalled, "I coun't git my han' off de bucket handle, and dey had ter pry it off."[65]

In April, after winter had unclenched its icy hold on the harbor, 450 blacks, seeking a new life among people of their own race, sailed from Fortress Monroe under the federal government's auspices, headed for resettlement in Haiti. But when they reached their destination, hostile Haitian authorities, ever burdened by devastating internal troubles, confronted them. Smallpox and starvation ravaged their party. Within a few months many had died, and the disheartened survivors returned to Hampton Roads in early 1864. Following that tragedy, the United States Congress declined to fund any further colonization plans.[66]

In June 1863, civilian rule had been tentatively reinstated in Norfolk, and Lincoln named Ben Butler, back from an assignment farther south, as commander of the Army of the James. Recruitment stations had been established in both Norfolk and Portsmouth, and self-confident black soldiers became increasingly common.[67] The assured demeanor of those recruits often outraged white people who had long accustomed themselves to traditional relationships between the races in which Negroes, whatever their status, were always expected to act subservient.

But a number of long-held traditions in Emma Thomas's new hometown were shifting, and the events that unfolded around Dr. David Wright reflected those realignments. Wright was widely considered "an upright, amiable and peaceful citizen," and his humanitarian efforts during Norfolk's 1855 yellow fever epidemic had made him a local hero. In the summer of 1863, however, that supposed model of probity behaved in a manner that even his staunchest supporters considered imprudent, and his actions ignited one of the city's most controversial and divisive wartime incidents.[68]

Wright contended that black troops had been brought into the city to torment its white citizens, and he hurled an ugly racial epithet at a contingent of Negro soldiers who marched through his neighborhood one July morning. Their officer, Second Lieutenant Alanson Sanborn, leapt to his men's defense. Dr. Wright also had sworn that he was prepared to "shoot the first [white] man whom he encountered with black troops." He emitted an "exclamation of disgust" and called the lieutenant a coward. When Sanborn tried to arrest the irascible physician, a fateful scuffle ensued. Wright drew his pistol, shot, and killed the young officer.

Appalled black soldiers who observed the attack threatened to bayonet the doctor to avenge their fallen leader, but cooler heads prevailed, and military police seized and jailed David Wright. A legal dispute arose over whether civilian or army courts should claim jurisdiction, but the occupying Union authorities prevailed. The trial extended through the summer as Wright protested in his own defense that he feared a recurrence of what he called the "Southampton menace"—the Nat Turner uprising. An unsympathetic Union military tribunal, however, quickly convicted him of murder and sentenced him to death.[69]

Most local whites labeled the killing justifiable, while black people and military men called for swift enforcement of the sentence. In an attempt to save the physician's life, his attorneys raised claims of insanity, and that appeal went all the way to an unyielding President Lincoln. Experts in matters of emotional instability interrogated Wright but found no evidence of any mental dysfunction, and the army prepared to execute him. In a bizarre but unsuccessful twist, the doctor's daughter visited and exchanged clothes with her father in a fruitless attempt to disguise him as a woman and facilitate his escape. Late in October, one of Norfolk's most divisive wartime episodes concluded when David Wright's death sentence was publicly carried out on the gallows.

During the stress-filled final weeks of that affair, the crippled USS *Cambridge,* a link in the North Atlantic blockading squadron, with seaman John Bond aboard, was towed to Newport News, then south across the channel for repairs at Portsmouth's Gosport shipyard. It remained there for two months, and Bond may have encountered Emma Thomas and made other local friends during that tedious period of land-based inactivity. A few sailors from the *Cambridge,* however, seem to have overindulged in the local hospitality. Bond avoided trouble, but three black shipmates were punished in the ship's dreaded sweat box for overextending their shore leaves. In addition, several underoccupied and probably inebriated white sailors became embroiled in bruising dockside brawls, while any or all of them may have frequented bordellos such as the "Free an' Easy."[70]

Negro sailors streamed through Hampton Roads, and during the ensuing year, five "colored" army regiments—the Second Cavalry, and the Tenth, Twenty-third, Thirty-sixth, Thirty-seventh, and Thirty-eighth Infantry Regiments—were organized in Norfolk, Portsmouth, and across the channel at Fortress Monroe. Black men from all over the Upper South who joined those units had been recruited or voluntarily poured into the area's conscription offices and soon played decisive roles in battles throughout Virginia. Two members of the Thirty-sixth and four from the Thirty-eighth would receive Congressional Medals of Honor. In late 1863 while both Emma Thomas and John Bond were in Norfolk, the city became temporary headquarters for the Fifty-fifth Massachusetts Infantry. It included one black, English-born seafarer, plus soldiers from throughout the North, especially large New England towns like Worcester and New Bedford. Its home base was Camp Meigs in the Readville community where James Trotter, who became one of that unit's (and the entire army's) first and few commissioned Negro officers, and several of his men later settled.[71]

On the Emancipation Proclamation's first anniversary, soldiers from those regiments paraded in Norfolk while ecstatic crowds comprised of people like Emma Thomas and Seaman John Bond observed. Uniformed Negroes marched through the streets, and Union generals at a festively arrayed reviewing stand lauded their deportment. The New Year's celebration concluded with patriotic speeches, martial music, barbecues, plus ceremonies conducted by black Prince Hall Masons, among others. A few weeks later, with its repairs finally completed, the *Cambridge* left the Gosport Navy Yard, steamed east out of Hampton Roads, then turned south toward a hazardous new assignment off the Carolina coast.[72]

Conditions among the contrabands remained dire that spring. "Boys wearing only rags crowded Norfolk's streets . . . [and] fill the air with curses," a dismayed observer complained. The refugees "huddled together in old Houses, in unhealthy Lanes and Alleys . . . where all kinds of sickness and disease exist," a federal official added. Illness plagued the South throughout the war, and Norfolk's smallpox victims of both races received treatment (together) at the city's dismal "pest house."[73]

Following his near-fatal injury during the *Cambridge*'s February encounter with a blockade runner near Wilmington, then months of recuperation in North Carolina, John Bond returned in May under circumstances that differed greatly from those that had accompanied his confident departure. He was ensconced as a patient at Portsmouth's naval hospital. Blacks, such as the former Isle of Wight slave Isaac Thomas, worked at that medical facility, while others hammered together shacks to camp on the grounds. Bond might have met Emma Thomas the previous fall, but certainly the two young people became acquainted during his convalescence, when she hawked her produce to many of the ailing men and especially befriended the mulatto Englishman.

Emma Thomas did her part in the war effort and supported herself as well, taking fruit to sailors on ships, at the dockyards, and in the hospital. Other entrepreneurial contrabands initiated similar business ventures. The resourceful hucksters also prepared and sold cakes, sweet or savory pies, and seafood. Some purchased, leased, borrowed, or pilfered what they called bumboats and paddled the dinghies out to Union vessels in the harbor. Seamen, ever hungry for fresh or homemade food, often paid five times as much for these simple treats as they would have in peacetime.[74]

One white Yankee sailor stationed in Portsmouth wrote home describing how Virginia's "pears, apples, and strawberries" delighted him, but they were not the only succulent "commodities" he lusted for. "About the niger women," he lewdly added, "I was out the other knight and see some good big lusty ones but did not derst to tush them for fere I should get my old thing crocked."[75] In his weakened state, Seaman John Robert Bond devoured Emma Thomas's fruit, but probably was not yet in shape for any erotic activity that might "get [his] old thing crocked." In addition, despite the wartime turmoil, Emma well may have subscribed to the slaves' tenets of sexual propriety that cautioned young women to "protect their principle."[76]

In early June, though still frail, Bond was dismissed from Portsmouth's hospital, then honorably discharged from the United States Navy. Emma Thomas helped to nurse him back to health, and their courtship intensified as the war continued.[77]

Rebels despised the uncompromising General Ben "Beast" Butler, but he won a place in the hearts of Negroes in the military and contrabands such as Emma. In September 1864, deeply impressed with the bravery and patriotism of black soldiers and sailors, Butler vowed that "they and their race should be cared for and protected by me to the extent of my power as long as I live."[78] He provided his novice "colored" troops with opportunities that sometimes proved highly provocative. A riot broke out on Portsmouth's waterfront between some of Butler's newly empowered black military police guards and belligerent white Union sailors.

But throughout Virginia and elsewhere, the divisive, costly conflict was winding down by late 1864 as Union forces grimly plodded onward. General William Tecumsuh Sherman's troops slashed across Georgia, then north through the Carolinas. From late October until Christmas, the Yankee navy plus black and white army divisions undertook a combined expedition to liberate Fort Fisher, guardian of Wilmington, North Carolina's vital harbor—on the same stretch of Carolina coastline where John Robert Bond had been wounded the previous February. Those assaults weakened that citadel, but it did not fall.

On January 1, 1865, the Emancipation Proclamation's anniversary, with victory's sweet fragrance in the air, Norfolk's blacks held yet another demonstration, including "colored" cavalrymen and local benevolent societies. That month also saw a second, this time successful, assault on Fort Fisher. The Yankees prevailed, but the battle resulted in the war's greatest naval losses. Three hundred Union sailors died, more even than had been killed during Hampton Roads' battle of the ironclads. But Wilmington had been the final open port for supplies needed to support the deteriorating Confederacy. Its capture fulfilled the blockade's "anaconda" strategy, resulting in the South's enislement and strangulation, and that achievement successfully concluded the Union navy's crucial role in the Civil War.

And in Washington, D.C., a new congressional resolution was introduced on the last day of January proposing a thirteenth amendment to the Constitution. "Neither slavery nor involuntary servitude," it iterated, "except as punishment for crime whereof the party shall have been duly convicted, shall exist within the United States." Virginia's provisional (Union-sponsored) government ratified that amendment in February, and black people in Norfolk, anticipating their altered and liberated status, held their first public political meeting in the city's Mechanics Hall.[79]

The federal government established the Bureau of Refugees, Freedmen, and Abandoned Lands (the Freedmen's Bureau)—Reconstruction's multifaceted vanguard, intended to centralize and standardize the diverse efforts to assist the South's former slaves. Nonetheless, the war dragged on, and an all-white, civilian state government functioned in those parts of Virginia under Union control.

By the beginning of April 1865, the Yankees were fully on the march throughout the state. Black troops from Norfolk had played crucial roles in battles to control the town of Petersburg. Nearby Richmond succumbed the day after Petersburg, and many of the same soldiers, on horseback and foot, spearheaded the deliverance of the Confederacy's hallowed capital. As their columns marched through central Virginia singing *John Brown's Body,* admirers caroled in response: "Slavery chain done broke at las'." Newly freed slaves applauded their liberators, embracing "Marse Lincum's black boys." "Negro cavalrymen rose high in their stirrups and waved their swords," one man observed, and "the cheers were deafening."

When they learned about the fall of Richmond, often referred to as Babylon, children at the freedpeople's schools in Norfolk sang *Glory, Hallelujah,* but became almost inconsolable when they learned that Jeff Davis had not actually been hung "from a sour apple tree."[80]

Soon thereafter, President Lincoln and his wife, accompanied, among others, by her Negro dressmaker and confidante, Elizabeth Keckley, steamed through Hampton Roads and up the James aboard the *River Queen,* to observe sites of the war's triumphant consummation. "Here stretched fair fields, emblematic of peace," Keckley wrote about her voyage west and north past Newport News, Isle of Wight County, Jamestown, and various "deserted camps and frowning forts, speaking of the stern vicissitudes of war." In Richmond, their party visited the Confederacy's senate chamber, where Keckley, a former slave and native of that city, brazenly seated herself in the chair once occupied by Jefferson Davis. As her president prepared to reboard his boat to head back downriver, a prescient black woman called out a warning: "Don't drown, Massa Abe, for God's sake."[81]

On April 9, Confederate forces surrendered at Virginia's Appomattox Courthouse. Several days later (despite ongoing complaints by some white officers concerning the conduct of black troops), Abraham Lincoln eloquently declared: "I would myself prefer that suffrage were now conferred . . . on those who served our cause as soldiers." "These people [who] have so heroically vindicated their manhood on the battlefield . . . in assisting to save the life of the Republic," he continued, "have demonstrated in blood their right to the ballot, which is but the humane protection of the flag they have so fearlessly defended."[82] Yet only days after that endorsement of at least limited black male suffrage, most Americans, especially the freedpeople who considered him their savior, plunged into profound mourning in response to their president's tragic death.

A mediocre, demented thespian and Confederate sympathizer named John Wilkes Booth, the American-born son of an Englishman, fired a bullet into Lincoln's head as he attended the British play *Our American Cousin* on the evening of April 14 at Ford's Theatre. Booth cried out, "*Sic semper tyrannis*" ("Thus, always to tyrants"), and broke a leg as he leapt from a balcony. The injured assassin fled from Washington, through southern Maryland, into Virginia, where he was hunted down. Sharp-eyed black men identified the felon and pinpointed his hiding place, and Booth's pursuers shot and killed him in the town of Port Royal along the Rappahannock River.[83]

Their deceased leader's final message concerning suffrage was not wasted on Norfolk's black people, who well understood the interdependency of citizenship and the vote. The city's Colored Monitor Union Club, led by the former slave Thomas Bayne, who had spent years in Massachusetts, issued a resolution (printed in New Bedford) supporting the franchise for Negro men. Soon thereafter, blacks held a mass meeting to debate the issues at Emma Thomas's Bute Street Baptist Church. John Robert Bond, the transplanted Englishman, easily could have attended and observed that incipient yet still thwarted expression of American democracy among Virginia's disfranchised people of his own race.

Despite state laws and entrenched practices denying them the franchise, a thousand or more black men in Norfolk registered at their churches and defiantly cast ballots that spring. The gesture was powerful, but their votes were not tallied, and former secessionists easily won the first postwar election.[84]

Norfolk, the entire Lower Tidewater, indeed much of the United States, wore two contrasting faces in the weeks following the war and Lincoln's assassination. On one hand, the Union had triumphed and few Americans of either race seriously doubted that the hydra-headed monster of slavery had been vanquished. On the other, deaths on both sides had been legion, animosities remained high, and the country had lost its towering though controversial leader under appalling circumstances.

Troubling events punctuated the newly achieved peace. At Fortress Monroe in May, a unit of Negro cavalrymen briefly mutinied to protest orders that ultimately dispatched them on a thankless mission to pacify clusters of recalcitrant Confederate troops in distant and still rebellious Texas. The following day, however, soldiers from the "colored" Fifth Massachusetts Cavalry passed through Hampton Roads, boarded the ships, and embarked on a disease-plagued final tour with the Union Army.[85] And in the civilian sector, many people realistically feared that, although they were no longer enslaved, former masters and other whites of their ilk were poised on the brink of establishing repressive new legal and political strategems and other means and methods of intimidation.

For many Negroes, the ignominious capture of the Confederacy's fleeing President Jefferson Davis that same month, the joyous reunions of long-separated families, including a flood of weddings between black men and women who officially had been denied that privilege during the slave years, combined to epitomize the era's more optimistic countenance. Nonetheless, while Virginia's all-white legislature quickly confirmed the legality of preexisting "customary" slave marriages, the law would not officially recognize *new* marriages among its "colored" residents until a full year later.[86]

On June 21, 1865, the year's longest day (the mythic summer solstice when the sun appears to pause in the heavens and the planets portend peace and renewal), Emma Thomas and John Robert Bond joined that band of celebrants as the Reverend Lewis Tucker married them at the Bute Street Baptist Church. Although Tucker was an ordained minister and community leader and his church had one of the city's most established congregations, the state, as was often the case in those stressful times, followed the letter of the law and preserved no record of Emma and John's union.[87]

Early in 1859—despite the Christmas Eve fire that delayed its dedication and prophesied similar arson attacks on Negroes' houses of worship—an articulated, arch-fronted brick edifice had replaced the church's original "Old Salt Box."[88] Even before Tucker succeeded its white pastor in 1862, Bute Street Baptist's once racially mixed congregation had become virtually all black. As the war ended, many other Negro congregations rid themselves of proslavery ministers, but white Episcopalians (some of whose clerics once piously had preached that "the house of bondage is a prison . . . however ornamented its architecture") opposed the presence of emboldened black people in their congregations.[89] Though his parents had never officially married, a chilly reception by the modified,

New World, Virginia branch of the church in which he was christened may have deeply wounded the still English, but incipient Negro American, John Robert Bond.

When he assumed formal leadership of Bute Street Baptist, Lewis Tucker, his wife Elizabeth, a former slave, and their children moved from their outlying residence into Norfolk proper, where they lived near the church. To make ends meet, the minister, whose kin (like so many white Virginians), lost much of their assets during the war, also worked as a day laborer, while Elizabeth Tucker became a "washerwoman." Martha and John Blye were another couple who resided nearby and belonged to Tucker's congregation. Martha stayed at home, "keeping house," while John Blye, whose nonenslaved family had worshiped at Bute Street Baptist for many years, became a "corn measurer."[90]

Two other interlinked families who befriended John Bond and Emma lived on Portsmouth's South Street. They were Frank Whiting, his wife Silena, his parents and several siblings, plus a recently married couple named Isaac and Mary Mullen—Whiting's brother-in-law and sister. The New England–born Isaac Mullen had served in the Union Navy and, like Bond, had been a patient at Portsmouth's naval hospital. For several years thereafter, the Gosport shipyard employed both Whiting and Mullen. Whiting acted as John Bond's best man, while Isaac Mullen and Martha Blye officially witnessed the marriage ceremony.[91]

When Emma Thomas met and married her mulatto Englishman, urban legends such as that of the "Irish Negro" confirmed that the presence of brown-skinned men with origins in the British Isles was unusual but not unknown in East Coast seaports. Even before the war, Norfolk had become home to a number of Irish-born people, though with few exceptions those newcomers were white. John Bond, however, did not become part of an immigrant community when he left the hospital, married, and remained in the region. Caucasian aliens faced daunting challenges of their own, and in the United States, they learned, a dark-skinned person, regardless of status or national origin, was usually considered "just another nigger" who should be avoided.[92] Rather, John's closest new associates—those who most readily embraced him—belonged to the city's diverse Negro community, comprised of former slaves (like Emma Thomas and Elizabeth Tucker), local free people of color (Lewis Tucker, the Blyes, the Whitings), and once and future New Englanders and sailors such as Isaac Mullen.

There is no telling whether Emma's mother, John Currie—her father in the Upper Tidewater's Lancaster County—even her former owners, Jonathan and Martha Thomas, or any of their one-time slaves, came to her wedding. Of course, any kin that John Bond may have left behind in Liverpool remained an ocean away, but members of Emma's family, such as the hospital lackey, Isaac Thomas, his wife, and their children could have observed the celebration. Other blacks (possibly relatives) with ties to Isle of Wight who lived and worked around Norfolk after the war included Samuel Thomas, a cook named Fannie Thomas, and her granddaughter.[93] But whoever may have attended the ceremony, the sacred event itself imbued John and Emma's lives together with an ordained legitimacy that law, racial bias, economics, and custom had conspired to deny their parents.

Unfortunately, the planets' supposedly optimistic configuration during that first postwar solstice badly misconstrued Norfolk's circumstances. John and Emma's nuptials may have been blessed, but the times were not tranquil. Many of the occupying Union troops resented the freedpeople almost as much as did the obdurate Confederates. Consumed by racist beliefs, stimulated by alcohol, and emboldened by handy weaponry, some Yankees rioted the next day, raiding a tavern where Negroes celebrated the rebels' demise, rampaging through black neighborhoods, firing at random, throwing bricks and shouting, "We'll kill every nigger, or drive 'em all out of town." Worcester's missionary Lucy Chase reported that several "colored men were found hanging dead upon trees."[94]

Such hostile acts, not only on the part of former rebels, but also by those whom they had considered protectors and friends, outraged African Americans. "We are a nation that loves the white people, and we would never attack them, but if we are driven to exasperation," a Norfolk man warned, "we know our duty." Profoundly provoked, they armed themselves to respond in kind. Several Negroes assaulted a white Union soldier, and uniformed troops retaliated. Undisciplined members of the army of occupation fired on blacks near the fairgrounds, then marched downtown, attacking various ill-fated, dark-skinned people.[95]

But blacks would not be intimidated into acquiescence or passivity, and their quest for the ballot became one of the most provocative aspects of their burgeoning postwar assertiveness. Several days after Emma and John's wedding, their church was the site of another mass meeting concerning suffrage, which, combined with earlier efforts, resulted in a commanding resolution about the significance of citizenship and the vote.

Signed by Thomas Bayne, Joseph T. Wilson (a nascent journalist who had served with the Fifty-fourth Massachusetts), and a number of other African Americans, the statement asserted that "personal servitude having been abolished in Virginia, it behooves us . . . to speak and act as freemen, . . . to claim and insist upon equality before the law, and equal rights of suffrage at the ballot box." The petitioners "insisted" on acquiring the "elective franchise . . . as a right, not tamely submitting to its deprivation." "The safety of all," they boldly concluded, "requires that all loyal men, black or white, should have equal political and civil rights."[96] Even in the wake of those forceful declarations, Lucy Chase warned, "I am confident that the Negro will suffer more in the coming year of Peace, than he has during the War: [Nothing] can shield him from all the injustice he will be exposed to from the vengeful *Southrons.*" And in that contentious climate, Emma and John Bond, both only nineteen years old, embarked on married life.[97]

Several intermingling currents characterized the lives of such young people as the war-divided country began its painful Reconstruction. Negroes at Hampton Roads and throughout the South pressed for citizenship rights. Churches played central roles in those embryonic efforts at political organization and empowerment. The Bonds' church and others also became primary locations where freedpeople received their schooling. And black families, separated by uncaring owners during the antebellum era or by more recent wartime crises and misfortunes, struggled to reunite, while both longtime and newly affiliated couples hastened to legitimize their conjugal unions.

In most instances, Virginia's black people were resolutely self-reliant, but their most trustworthy white supporters, from Governor John Andrew, to General Benjamin Butler, to Boston's AMA teachers, to Worcester's Chase sisters ("God bless Miss Chase!" a former slave in Norfolk cried out when those Quaker missionaries finally prepared to return north, "I shall love you as long as I live"), hailed from Massachusetts.[98] It also was where dozens of Hampton Roads' bondsmen had fled prior to the war, and was home to several celebrated black military units—Massachusetts's Fifth Cavalry, the Fifty-fourth Infantry Regiment, and the Fifty-fifth, which for many months was garrisoned in Norfolk.

Those were sturdy linkages, and when some of Virginia's Negroes began to consider leaving the South, they thought of going to Massachusetts. As early as the summer of 1865, those fruitful seeds may have been sown for the former Isle of Wight slave Emma Thomas and her new husband, England's John Bond.

6

FIRE, ASHES,
and the HOBBLED PHOENIX

Yielding up the other cheek,
Dropping humbly on the knees;
Closing lips when dared to speak,
Will not do in times like these.

True Southerner, Norfolk, 1866

LIKE THE REST of the South during the late 1860s, Tidewater Virginia's twin ports, where John and Emma Bond first made their home as a married couple, were emerging from the country's most cataclysmic half decade. The Bonds and other Negroes vigorously applauded slavery's demise. They may, however, have believed that in what they hoped would become a utopian, postemancipation world, the "peculiar institution's" perpetrators would be rebuked and black people rewarded for their years of deprivation, abuse, and uncompensated labor. As many optimistic African Americans asserted: "Bottom rail on top now." But much of the fence—the racially bifurcated, slave-dependent configuration of antebellum society—had been demolished, and a fierce struggle ensued over what new structures might replace it.

According to a preacher in Nansemond, adjoining Norfolk County on the west, the freedpeople's postwar mantra became "Buy some land, build a home, get some education." Yet lacking tangible assets and confronted by defiant whites, those goals would be hard to achieve. The dream of owning, rather than being, property had been raised by pie-in-the-sky promises from several Union officers that plantations would be taken from their onetime Rebel owners and every freedman given forty acres and a mule.[1] But black people like Willis Hodges of neighboring Princess Anne County knew that Virginia's bloodied but unbowed majority never would agree to any confiscation of their land. In addition, Hodges protested, white people "have denied [Negroes] the right to live upon the soil for which we . . . bled." "I say this with pride," he continued, "for . . . my grandfather fought in the cause of independence under George Washington."[2]

Carl Schurz, a German-born Union general, took a similarly dim view as he observed the shifting tides in postwar Virginia. "Before the war," he wrote, lamenting the antebellum plight of non-enslaved "colored" people such as Hodges and the Reverend Lewis Tucker, whites "did not want a free Negro about at all." To the distress of many former Rebels, Schurz concluded, after the war, "all have become free Negroes."[3] Some white Virginians hoped that the plethora of newly emancipated men and women like Emma Thomas Bond might just vanish, possibly as a result of mass emigration to Africa or the Caribbean. Failing that, a number of southerners insisted, the lives of their "racially inferior" former slaves would have to be strictly regulated by whatever means possible.

Yet at first it hardly seemed that the cards would become so dauntingly stacked against Negroes. In the early postbellum months, the Freedmen's Bureau assisted with education and medical care, and handled certain judicial matters. When it became apparent that Virginia's court system would not deliver equal justice, the bureau temporarily assumed that responsibility and adjudicated African Americans' legal affairs in autonomous Freedmen's Courts. But it soon disbanded those arrangements when the legislature reluctantly amended state laws to allow "Negro testimony" and occasionally even permitted black men's inclusion on juries. The Freedmen's Savings & Loan Company opened a Norfolk branch, and for its network throughout the South, that quasi-public institution installed a board of directors largely comprised of the country's leading white financiers to oversee its operations. A number of Emma Thomas Bond's relatives and friends entrusted their hard-earned dollars to the care of that bank's all-white clerks.[4]

By mid-1866, the still empathetic United States Congress passed civil rights legislation (overriding President Andrew Johnson's vetoes after several failed attempts) that voided many of the southern states' repressive, postwar Black Codes. During the latter half of the decade, the requisite number of states also ratified three critical amendments to the Constitution. Approval of the Thirteenth and Fourteenth Amendments by states of the former Confederacy became requirements for reentry into the Union and partial indicators of their satisfactory "reconstruction." As conceived, those provisions not only ended slavery but assured the civil rights and citizenship of most persons born in the United States—including African Americans, but excluding the country's indigenous people. Starting in 1870, the Fifteenth Amendment purportedly reinforced black men's right to vote. Yet otherwise the federal government neither addressed the knotty dilemmas of intransigent racism nor provided relief for Negroes' entrenched economic disadvantages. Even most former abolitionists and Radical Republicans, supposed allies of the country's African Americans, believed that Negroes belonged to an inferior race in its early phases of evolution. Slavery's ugly moral scar had been removed from the world's most admired democracy, but racial equality scarcely appeared on white America's hectic postwar agenda.

The Norfolk-Portsmouth region faced daunting rebuilding difficulties, though it was better equipped to deal with postbellum problems than areas of the South that had been more profoundly ravaged by the war. As the Norfolk *Post* reported, "everywhere there is bustle and noise and the pleasing sound of labor." Sailors, shipwrights, and dockhands of both races toiled on the Elizabeth River's busy wharves, piled high with outbound shipments of lumber and turpentine, tobacco, smoked pork, and gunnysacks of peanuts. To stimulate Hampton Roads' latent international trade potential, local entrepreneurs contracted with owners of the Liverpool-based freighter *Ephesus*. In early 1866, that ship from John Robert Bond's home port steamed out of Norfolk's harbor en route to England laden with its first cargo of Virginia's produce. The ill-fated vessel, however, soon sank off Nova Scotia, scuttling hopes for the city's emergence as a significant participant in transatlantic commerce. But the Seaboard & Petersburg Railroad (disabled by Union troops during the war) had been resurrected, and it supplied the harbor with raw materials and agricultural produce from the hinterlands that then could be shipped off to various North Atlantic ports.[5]

In the wake of their region's embryonic revitalization, many of Norfolk and Portsmouth's more successful residents began to participate in diversions such as horse racing, cockfighting, and yacht regattas from Craney Island's lighthouse across the windswept channel to the mainland. The cities' first semipro baseball teams also became wildly popular. "For oysters, beautiful girls, and French brandy," bragged one booster, "we stake Norfolk against the Union."[6] Nonelite southerners and newly arrived white northerners alike took advantage of the synergistic postwar ferment and inserted themselves into a rejuvenated, yet almost exclusively Caucasian, power structure.

Virginia's former slaveholders were anxious to reestablish their hegemony over the state's political and economic life and its blacks. To facilitate such reempowerment, government-imposed bans on office holding by former Confederates often were either removed or ignored with President Johnson's acquiescence and blessings.[7] Just after the war, the all-white legislature passed repressive Black Codes (replacing the old Slave Codes) that situated the Commonwealth's freedpeople, one critic claimed, "in a condition of post-emancipation serfdom," demonstrating that "the fruits of victory so recently gained were in danger of slipping away." Another Virginian protested that the government "left us entirely at the mercy of these subjugated but unconverted rebels, in *everything* save the privilege of bringing us, our wives and little ones, to the auction block." Harsh apprenticeship provisions allowed former owners forcibly to retain custody of black children and skewed labor and vagrancy regulations against the Negroes' interests. "Among those declared to be vagrants," the revised statutes concerning African Americans iterated, "are all persons who, not having the wherewith to support their families, live idly . . . and refuse to work for the usual and common wages." During this period, many Negroes (no longer enslaved and determined never again to reside alongside former owners) established new, predominantly black enclaves such as the Eureka settlement on Norfolk's waterfront.[8]

In 1865, delegates to Virginia's first black political assembly proclaimed their patriotism, decorated the podium with the Stars and Stripes, and burst into gusty renditions of songs such as *Rally 'Round the Flag, Boys,* while some of them received daunting, anonymous warnings. "Negroes will die before the autumn leaves fall," one stated, "You are never to be on an equality with the whites, and many of you will die soon if this Freedmen's Convention continues. . . . So beware!" "The south must and shall be avenged!" a malevolent letter threatened: "The black man, like the Indian, will . . . pass from this land."[9]

During that tense period, the Norfolk *Virginian,* a journalistic voice of the city's disgruntled white populace, covered, and presented predominantly negative images of, the Negro community. The newspaper warned whites about potential insurrections by African Americans and chronicled instances of suspect behavior. "A fight took place between a number of the Daughters of Ham," the paper reprovingly reported in late 1865, and "the sable belligerents were taken off to the lock up."[10]

On New Year's Day 1866, the third anniversary of the Emancipation Proclamation, the *Virginian* observed the annual parade, featuring black people attired in their "best Sunday go-to-meeting clothes," accompanied, the article added with disdain for the Negroes' presumed pretensions, by "marshals . . . on horseback with scarves after the mode and manner of white men." Members of the Yankee army of occupation joined the festivities, as the celebratory march snaked through the city and terminated in a rally at the Bute Street Baptist Church, where Emma Thomas and John Bond recently had married. Always quick to expound on the scarcely cloaked antagonisms between the city's whites and African Americans, the *Virginian* noted that, following the celebration, a black man was stabbed by a white person whom an angry band of Negroes then stoned. The editors concluded that emancipation had unleashed a surge of anarchy and brought about a flood of dire consequences. Blacks' attempts to achieve what the paper considered inappropriate racial parity, epitomized by their sometimes elegant dress and public demonstrations, incensed the region's whites. Echoing the beliefs of many people around Hampton Roads, the Richmond *Dispatch* cautioned: "It is idle for the negro to suppose that there is to be any social equality here."[11]

Despite the bubbling prosperity, one bitter observer criticized the area's ambience, characterized by "recklessness of dissipation and openness of vice" among Norfolk's lower classes—especially, but not exclusively, most white residents believed, its Negro citizens. Every evening, another man commented with barely veiled lechery, the "*purlieus* of vice are thronged with the falling and fallen indulging in open revelry."[12]

In that milieu, the *True Southerner* became Hampton Roads' only Negro journal. It reported in late 1865 that "without any cause" a white mob in nearby Isle of Wight County almost killed several black people. "One of the colored men was dangerously wounded with a pistol shot," it added, "and the other was badly beaten." Clerks at Thomas & Adams, the town's general store owned by Emma's former master, refused to sell ammunition to African Americans, citing Virginia's Black Codes that denied freed-people such rights. "This is but one of hundreds of instances," the *True Southerner* editorialized, "by which the [white] people of this State show their determination to keep the same relation they sustained with the colored people before the war." Emma Bond's former life in Isle of Wight could not have seemed far removed from her current one in Portsmouth, as the solid grasp of white power around Smithfield remained intact.[13]

The *True Southerner* was a unique publication. It was sponsored by the Union League, the political organization including carpetbaggers and scalawags that prodded black men to vote Republican. A white Union officer supportive of African Americans brought out the first issues in the town of Hampton. Joseph T. Wilson became a frequent contributor, then took over the journal and moved the offices and Franklin-style hand press south across the channel to Norfolk. Wilson had once been a Virginia slave, but had escaped to New Bedford (where, like so many sons of that port, he became a whaler) before the Civil War. In 1863—the same year, in the same town, and with motivations no doubt similar to those of

John Robert Bond—Wilson joined the military. After the war, he was honorably discharged from the army, where he had served with the Second Louisiana Native Guard, then the Fifty-fourth Massachusetts Infantry.[14]

"We hold these truths to be self-evident: that all men are created equal," the country's revolutionary and patriotic credo, appeared on the *True Southerner*'s masthead. The paper provided a powerful voice for Hampton Roads' black people, and tales of both abuse and heroism filled its pages. It detailed accounts of freedpeople's efforts to attain justice in all aspects of their lives. The *True Southerner* quoted prominent Yankees such as the wartime Secretary of the Navy Gideon Welles. "I favor intelligence, not color as the qualification for suffrage," Welles asserted. It also became a community bulletin board for information of all sorts, including announcements of marriages, births, and deaths; relatives sought or found; church and school activities; local, state, or federal government initiatives; advice on obtaining military pensions, as well as a variety of goods and services provided for or by the region's blacks.[15]

The paper directed itself to female as well as male readers. For people such as Emma Thomas Bond, "Anna," a benevolent white lady, contributed a column titled "To the Freed Women." Even Emma and other former slaves who could barely read had relatives or friends who would share and interpret such information. "Anna" sympathized with the women who so recently had been enslaved, arguing that sexual abuse ("the blackest of sins") and the forced separation of families had made bondage even worse for members of their sex than for men. But she also contended that the black women's new, nonenslaved lives resembled white women's more than the lives of black men resembled those of white men. Regardless of race, no woman had the right to vote. Both black and white females, "Anna" concluded, remained subject to substantial inequities on account of their sex.[16]

The Fourteenth Amendment did seem to promise American-born black women like Emma Thomas Bond some legal protections and rights of citizenship. But she had married an English immigrant and, at least in theory, relinquished those rights and derivatively assumed his residual national identity, because any wife's nationality essentially was subsumed into that of her husband. In the myopic eyes of the law, Emma, who had never left the state of Virginia, became Queen Victoria's subject.[17] When she and John Bond wed, becoming a naturalized United States citizen remained a privilege limited to "free, white men."

"Anna" probably was unaware of such legalistic absurdities as she urged readers to exercise "the strictest economy in all your expenses" and save a little money every month to facilitate their later years. She encouraged making or buying those items "which will wear longest, and at the same time look well." "Never purchase gaudy clothing," she warned, reinforcing the stereotype of African Americans' presumably genetic propensity for garish attire, "for there are but very few who look well in bright colors." But she also lauded her followers on their "good taste and judgment," because, she insisted, few other groups with such onerous burdens to overcome had ever coped so well, so quickly.

Concerning child rearing, "Anna" touted consistent school attendance, contending that neither girls nor boys should be "allowed to play any length of time in the streets," where they might "learn all manner of vice." The clarion tones of the *True Southerner*'s columnist in many ways echoed white middle-class ideals of "true womanhood" and reinforced messages espoused by other well-meaning members of her race. A missionary from the North who visited Emma Thomas Bond's Bute Street Baptist Church also found herself "deeply impressed with [the women's] moral wants," and established weekly meetings to advise them "about their household matters." During Reconstruction's early years "Anna" and other whites, such as Sarah and Lucy Chase, believed that they bore a responsibility to indoctrinate young women like Emma with basic precepts concerning modesty and virtue, practical homemaking, economy, and education.[18]

The *True Southerner* became an empowering voice for Hampton Roads' African Americans. It encouraged them to assert their legal rights, strive to obtain the franchise, vote and elect to office men of their race, and it even, though subtly, protested women's politically inferior status. But as often has happened with effective instruments of a free press, a publication such as that threatened the status quo. In this case, it was Norfolk's white-dominated, all-male power structure that feared the diminution of its war-interrupted but endemic and carefully nurtured systems of racial supremacy. Virginia's legislators did not defy the U.S. Constitution to consider any proposed law "abridging the freedom . . . of the press," but as 1866 drew toward an end, a mob of white hooligans torched the offices and destroyed the presses of the city's crusading black-run newspaper. No one, however, was charged with the crime.[19]

A few months earlier, Norfolk's African Americans, led by a citizen named Edward Long, had organized a demonstration to celebrate the congressional override of President Andrew Johnson's veto and the subsequent enactment of the country's new civil rights legislation. On a rain-drenched afternoon, the Rising Sons of Freedom and other civic groups carried banners through wet city streets heralding that "Day of Jubilee," and touting "The Ballot Box for All."[20]

William Moseley, an inebriated, off-duty white policeman, however, tried to prevent the celebration committee from publicly reading the landmark bill. He attempted to arrest a Negro who noisily fired off several blanks, but only succeeded in mauling the fellow. That assault on one of their own inflamed the assembled black people. An armed youth named Robert Whitehurst—a Confederate veteran and Moseley's cohort—entered the fray and began shooting into the crowd that was pummeling the drunken constable. Parade marshals led by Edward Long took Whitehurst into protective custody and attempted to prevent retaliation at the hands of the throng, but an unidentified Negro shot and killed the abusive white man. A riot ensued, and that evening a horde of whites murdered an African American man and a child. Some ruffians, provocatively uniformed in Confederate gray, fired on the Union troops who were trying to restore order. The army swiftly imposed martial law throughout Norfolk County.[21]

One report that was sympathetic to the Negroes' cause argued that the soldiers had prevented a more "serious riot between the roughs and [the] colored population" and confirmed that, for the most part, black people had behaved "in an orderly manner." But the local (all-white) police force, it concluded, was "bad in quality and wholly insufficient in numbers," and city officials furthermore "exhibited great inefficiency . . . dealing with the rioters."[22]

Despite the municipal authorities' inadequacies, within three days they arrested, arraigned, and charged seven black men with Whitehurst's murder. After a trial climaxed by emotional testimony from the deceased man's father, six of the accused were freed, but the court convicted and sentenced the parade's well-intentioned marshal Edward Long to eighteen years in jail.[23]

Norfolk's race-baiting *Day Book* posed the question: "Does the negro suppose that freedom means to butcher indiscriminately white men, women and children whenever they may choose to have a procession?" The newspaper railed at what it labeled the trend toward black "superiority" and queried whether that goal prompted "drunken carnivals of the blood of white people." It called African Americans a "semi-barbarous" people aroused by the "wild teachings of fanatical instructors"—presumably the Union army, the Union League, and Yankee carpetbaggers. The 1866 disturbances in the Bonds' jittery hometown reflected not only Norfolk's racial tensions but more widespread postwar unrest as well. Additional riots followed soon thereafter in other southern cities.[24]

Though the Ku Klux Klan never established a strong presence in Virginia, biased law enforcement, attacks on black people in nearby Isle of Wight, and the *True Southerner*'s wanton destruction were but a few instances of the terrors and injustices endured by Hampton Roads' African Americans. In Norfolk, a school for Negro children burned to the ground, with arson a near certainty, and white marauders destroyed a black-owned tavern, smashing doors, furniture, bottles, and glasses.[25]

In that same period, black Virginians like Emma Thomas Bond wanted and needed to create reconfigured, reconstructed lives for themselves, yet many also hoped to remain where they had grown up, near former homes, families, and churches. Emancipation, however, did offer a welcome new freedom of mobility, and some of them began migrating north in search of education, better jobs, and an escape from the state's Reconstruction-era turmoil and hostility toward members of their race. The solicitous Freedmen's Bureau arranged for thousands of "really worthy" men and women to relocate to the Boston area, where it promised them work as domestic servants, because "no region [is] more desirable as a home for the negro . . . where colored help is in great demand and where such sympathy is felt for their race."[26]

Others reversed that incipient trend and came south instead. Joseph T. Wilson, George Teamoh, and Dr. Thomas Bayne were former slaves who returned to the Norfolk-Portsmouth area to seek economic opportunities, help their people, and reunite with loved ones. John and Emma Bond's friend Isaac Mullen, who had lived in Boston before joining the navy, also believed that he could find employment and other satisfactions around Hampton Roads. And the country's first licensed black female physician, Rebecca Lee, who had recently graduated from Boston's New England Female Medical College, moved to Richmond not long after the war to address the freedpeople's pressing medical needs. Yet despite her contributions, dedication, and solid credentials, some critics scoffed that her "M.D." stood for "mule doctor."[27]

England's newlywed sailor John Robert Bond, a resident alien who was quite an anomaly in postwar Virginia, received his hardwon monthly pension as a disabled navy veteran. As his physical condition improved, he probably found menial work of some sort on the waterfront, while Emma Thomas Bond may have continued hawking her fresh produce to supplement their income.

Norfolk County, however, soon instituted stiff fees and taxes that threatened to put many such small-scale black vendors out of business, but the power of local authorities did not faze a cadre of outraged female hucksters like Emma once they resolved to act. They directed their complaints to General O. O. Howard, who headed the Freedmen's Bureau. "Our old masters . . . say our Freedom shan't do us any good," their 1866 petition began. Most of the women did not have the money needed to pay the recently imposed tariffs, but, they asserted: "Let them . . . put me in jail or do what they please . . . I am done serving them." They argued that newly installed municipal officials had supplanted "officers favorably disposed to the colored people." "Throughout . . . a four years' war," the protesters added, "the government have found [us] true as steel to the country, its soldiers and sailors collectively and individually." They had "often given their little alls to comfort a Union soldier distressed, with bleeding wounds and dying groans."[28]

Women such as Emma Thomas Bond—"true as steel" to her country and one such wounded sailor—had huckstered for a living during the Civil War. She and many others had done their patriotic duty by supporting themselves and succoring members of the liberating Yankee navy and army with fresh fruits and vegetables, seafood and baked goods. A number also had "laid their children, some their only child upon the altar of the country." Those women's husbands, hard-working African Americans, "though called upon to pay a head tax . . . have no voice in making city, State or national government."[29]

The *True Southerner* had forecast such protests. "The question now arises," it had speculated, "whether this people who have no voice in government, who have no representation in the government which has been saved in part at least by their blood, shall pay taxes to a rebel state." Linking blacks' current struggles to their country's independence efforts, editor Joseph T. Wilson had asked: "Has the moral code so changed that what was a virtue in '76 has become a vice in '66. . . . Have not the colored people the same right of self-Government . . . our forefathers had?"[30]

Like Emma Bond, most of the protesting hucksters could barely read or write, and George Teamoh became their amanuensis and spokesman. He had returned from his Massachusetts exile to Virginia, where his roots were planted as deeply as those of any white man. He wanted to reunite with family, take advantage of perceived economic opportunities, and become involved (as he did) in the region's evolving political scene.[31]

But the nation's political climate was shifting, and the former Confederate President Jefferson Davis's fate reflected those changes. In 1865, mobs in northern cities had burned Davis in effigy, but little surpassed the vivid (spiteful, bizarre, distorted, but concurrently hilarious) accounts of his capture.

In the weeks following Robert E. Lee's surrender at Appomattox Courthouse, Davis had been tracked to a rural Georgia hideout where he apparently had disguised himself in female attire. Describing the final, late May dénouement, a New York newspaper reported that "the appearance of a Colt's revolver drove all [Davis's] courage out of his heart and reminded him that he was only a poor, lone woman." "He dropped his skirts," the account continued, "and blushingly proclaimed, in falsetto tones, his indignation at being so energetically pursued." A Boston journal ran a malevolent verse that evoked howls of laughter and reflected many northerners' gloating mood:

> *Jeff Davis was a warrior bold,*
> *Who vowed the Yanks should fall;*
> *He jumped into his pantaloons*
> *And swore he'd rule them all.*
> *But when he saw the Yankees come*
> *To hang him if they could,*
> *He jumped into a petticoat*
> *And started for the wood.*

Satirical accounts and wicked caricatures suggested that the capture of the fugitive Jeff Davis garbed in women's clothing (much like Norfolk's fated Dr. David Wright in his last-ditch attempt to avoid execution) epitomized the successful and warranted demasculinization of the recently defeated South.[32]

Davis was imprisoned for two years at Fortress Monroe—just across from John and Emma's Portsmouth home—where only recently many of the people whose enslavement he zealously had tried to preserve first claimed their freedom. Then he was brought before a rare Virginia jury consisting of twelve white and twelve black men.

But by 1867, most Yankees had lost their vengeful appetites. A group of northerners, including the formerly dedicated antislavery publisher Horace Greeley, who by then urged political compromise and forgiveness for secessionist leaders, posted the ailing Jeff Davis's bail. The onetime Confederate president was never tried, and returned as a free man to Mississippi's sultry Gulf Coast, where many white southerners revered him, and he and his wife

Varina coauthored an apologia for the Rebel regime and the entire secessionist effort.[33]

Even before the war, conquests, treaties, and the country's manifest destiny agenda had established what many Americans considered a biblically ordained "dominion . . . from sea to sea," running roughshod over the indigenous people and the legitimate claims of the Mexican republic and its mostly nonwhite citizens. Then in 1867, the year that Davis gained his freedom, Secretary of State William Seward arranged to purchase the Alaska territory—labeled "Seward's Folly" by skeptics—from Russia for seven million dollars. It was the first expansion beyond that of the established, continental United States and presaged the country's turn-of-the-century imperialist efforts.

The following June, shortly after the United States House of Representatives had impeached, but the Senate had barely failed to convict, the increasingly unpopular President Andrew Johnson, twenty-two-year-old Emma Thomas Bond put her huckstering days aside when she gave birth to a child named John Percy, but called simply Percy. He was a pudgy, dark brown-skinned boy partially named after his father, but the image of his mother. From Emma, little Percy "inherited a slight degree of alveolar prognathism" (a heavy jaw) and a "pendulous, everted lower lip" (the full mouth that often characterized people of African ancestry). "His hair," continued that verbose description, "was frizzly, . . . coarse and wiry rather than soft."[34]

Though the Virginia Commonwealth preserved no record of Percy's birth, state laws enacted in 1866 had finally authorized marriages such as Emma and John's, and promised the Bonds and other Negroes that "their children shall be deemed legitimate."[35] By contrast, both of Percy's parents were the products of nonsanctioned conjugal unions and could well have been labeled bastards. Emma amused her "legitimate," frizzly-haired baby with southeast Virginia ditties such as *Keemo, Kimo,* while John Robert Bond, a onetime sailor who always retained his distinctive Liverpudlian intonations, also may have crooned to his firstborn son. A generation later Percy, in turn, sang the same nautical lullaby to his own children, then they to theirs:

Baby's fishing for a dream,
Fishing near and far,
For his rod a moonbeam has,
For bait a silver star.
Sail, baby, sail, out across the sea,
But don't forget when morning's here,
Come back again to me.[36]

During the months surrounding Percy Bond's unheralded birth, Norfolk's leading white newspaper continued its carping about the "lewd" and "disorderly" behavior of its black citizens. In early July, the *Virginian* warned that "idle and vicious negroes are on the lookout for the nation's birthday." On Independence Day, that journal complained, "a black pall hung over the city—it was negroes everywhere." Many whites left town, but some of those who remained taunted African Americans with a banner emblazoned, " 'A. Lincoln' . . . under which was a portrait of the Great Emancipator and National Joker." Roused to analogous vitriol, a black orator swore that "he hated any colored man with white blood in his veins."[37] People of mixed racial ancestry provided visible evidence that bitterly reminded many Negroes of their former masters' uncurbed sexual access to black women.

In the context of that era's teachings by scientists such as Louis Agassiz, as well as ribald cartoons in tabloid magazines, the mulatto John Robert Bond presumably carried a half-portion of "white blood." John, however, eschewed any racially grounded enmity. Judging from Percy's deportment in later life, his parents imbued him with tolerance, the respect for family and elders prevalent in West African cultures, a rigid code of ethics, and standards for exemplary deportment. Those lessons derived from John and Emma's training, experiences, character, and convictions, but also may have reflected the dictates of white women like "Anna," the *True Southerner*'s pedantic columnist. "Teach [your children] to shun the company of all who are quarrelsome or vulgar . . . who lie or swear, and all who are impolite in their manner," she counseled, because "good breeding will manifest itself every where."[38]

Months after his near removal from office and crippled by increasing unpopularity, Andrew Johnson did not receive his party's renomination for president that year when Percy Bond was born. The Civil War's intrepid General U. S. Grant replaced Johnson as Republican standard-bearer. In November, the nation's largely white electorate, supplemented by a growing number of Negro men (especially in the North) who asserted their citizenship rights, confirmed Grant as their choice to lead the nation.

Many of Norfolk's indigenous white people, however, had liked having a conciliatory southerner in the White House and admired Johnson's presidential course. They archly reshaped President Grant's name, Ulysses, into "Useless," and portrayed him as the devil incarnate—a symbol of the Confederacy's defeat and dishonor. They concurrently disparaged, diminished, and tried to thwart African Americans' efforts to participate politically, even to acquire any potentially empowering education. An unapologetic white Virginian had recently testified before the United States Congress that blacks "are not disposed to educate themselves." Nonetheless, ten schools for Negro children thrived in Norfolk under the aegis of the AMA and the Freedmen's Bureau, but they received no state or local funds. Though apparently neither John nor Emma Bond availed themselves of the educational opportunities at hand, several adjunct adult night schools flourished as well.[39]

Despite pockets of prosperity, the labor situation facing African Americans—and some whites—in postwar Hampton Roads left much to be desired. For decades, the area's shipyards (where noble ships such as the newly decommissioned USS *Lancaster* were placed in drydock) had been major employers of Negroes, both slave and free, and a mainstay of the water-dependent economy. In January 1867, a combined effort of blacks and whites, including John Bond's friends Frank Whiting and Isaac Mullen, protested the Gosport Navy Yard's threatened closing. Their interracial union, some of whose members had served in the navy, directed its petition to the United States Congress. The men—many of them relocated Yankees—recounted their efforts on behalf of the Union during the recent war. The signatories argued that if the shipyard closed, "they and their families and numerous others . . . will be left in a most precarious condition . . . which will place them in a state of starvation." The facility ultimately did not shut down, but despite some evidence of short-term cooperation, friction between the races remained critical. In one instance, a band of Negro seamen at the yards was "set upon and badly beaten."[40]

Isaac Mullen joined in and pressed the plea brought by dockworkers of both races, but he also wrote personally to General Howard at the Freedmen's Bureau, detailing other problems that uniquely beset African Americans. Mullen explained that he was an honorably discharged navy veteran who had labored for three years at the shipyard but had been denied any promotions "from the fact of my being a Colored Man and of being a Republican." He constantly encountered white people, he continued, "who have been so prejudiced against my color."[41]

Mullen also urged Howard to address the blatant employment discrimination at the local branch of the Freedmen's Savings & Loan Company. Negroes were its most important (almost its sole) customers, depositing a reported $12,000 during the first weeks of operation alone, but the bank refused even to hire them as clerks. Mullen articulated a strong appeal, arguing that men and women of his race were ready and eager to show "that we are capable of . . . positions either of honor, profit, or trust."[42]

Yet such arguments fell on deaf ears. One Norfolk newspaper editorialized that white Virginians "should concert measures without delay to fill the State with white laborers from the North and from Europe. *They must crowd the Negro out.*" "They must rid the State of an element that will hinder its prosperity," the diatribe continued, "an element that . . . would tax the property of others to relieve themselves of [the] obligation to educate their children and care for their paupers."[43] Many Caucasians complained that the recently emancipated population was lazy and irresponsible, but the black activist Thomas Bayne countered, "Colored people will not work because the employers do not pay them." At a time when John Robert Bond received his monthly, eight-dollar navy pension, Bayne insisted, "six dollars a month will not pay a man and feed and clothe his wife and children."[44]

Isaac Mullen's skills and assertiveness, almost certainly combined with solid ties to white Republican politicians, earned him a position as a customs inspector. After the shipyard laid off the Bonds' friend Frank Whiting (along with many others), he worked as a cobbler. Whiting's shop was modest, but a few blacks nominally shared in the postwar upswing. Several brick masons, butchers, and barbers were among the metropolitan area's propertied "colored" men. African American watermen launched the Oyster Association, and the hardy Negro community also supported social, benevolent, and fraternal organizations such as the Elks, Prince Hall Masons, and Odd Fellows.[45]

In addition, during the late 1860s the few but dogged black male voters and legislators successfully negotiated the right of passage on nonsegregated railroad facilities in Virginia for members of their race. Norfolk and Portsmouth's African Americans garnered the privilege of dining in a number of local restaurants, and could attend some theaters and other places of amusement, yet the Bonds and most others rarely could afford such diversions.[46]

And from the time when they had first convened at the Bute Street Baptist Church in 1865 to demand the franchise, the region's black people resolved that they would play active roles in Reconstruction's political life. George Teamoh, Thomas Bayne, and Joseph T. Wilson (all of whom, like John Robert Bond, had spent formative periods in New Bedford) and others such as Dr. J. D. Harris became some of Hampton Roads' most outspoken leaders.

Many of them attended the state's postwar "Black and Tan" convention, then worked with the Union League to elect Republican candidates. Former rebels who had temporarily been denied the right to vote were usually Democrats, but Negroes comprised a slim majority of Virginia's Republicans.[47] At an 1866 state party caucus, Dr. Thomas Bayne asserted his presence, proclaiming, "I got the floor, and I'm going to keep it; I'm never tedious or troublesome, and I don't see why you shouldn't want me to have my say." Bayne further protested that the white press exacerbated negative images and ridiculed the speech of black men by printing words such as "dis" and "dat" when quoting Negro delegates. They should remember, he insisted, that "t-h-a-t didn't spell 'dat.' "[48]

At the same meeting, Joseph T. Wilson introduced a platform

"of human rights—equality, confiscation and impeachment." He sought reparations to compensate for centuries of slavery. "If we don't support that we are no better than rebels," he added. The Richmond *Dispatch,* which resented those delegates who were northern carpetbaggers or home-grown scalawags even more than it disliked Negroes, grudgingly asserted that one debate "showed the colored men infinitely superior to their white conferees." The journal singled out Bayne and Wilson as "remarkable for their sharpness and fluency," concluding, "there were more brains in the colored leaders than in the white riff-raff."[49]

A number of politicians argued that the "disgrace" of Negro suffrage should not be "inflicted" on their state, then formed an exclusionary White Men's Party. Yet in late 1867, Bayne and Teamoh were among twenty-five Negroes chosen as delegates to the state Constitutional Convention. Much of the white press seethed over the significant black representation, and labeled that gathering the "mongrel" or "Black Crook" convention, but George Teamoh, for one, was proud to have the opportunity to help frame a progressive new state constitution.[50]

Observers considered Thomas Bayne—impeccably garbed in his formal cutaway suit with white cravat, immaculate cuffs and collar, and flawlessly polished shoes—one of the best-dressed men at the assembly. The elegant, eloquent Dr. Bayne maintained his vision of a color-blind society, explaining, "I pledged the good people of my section that I should endeavor to aid in making a convention that should not have the word black or white anywhere in it." "I wanted," he continued, "a constitution which our children fifteen years hence might read and not see slavery, even as a shadow, remaining in it."[51]

Bayne proposed a measure to place children of both races in the same schools, but the convention's white majority vanquished that provision. The new constitution ultimately did mandate free public education, though not unsegregated—or equal—schools, for all children. As a result of those developments, the Freedmen's Bureau prepared to withdraw.[52] Under pressure from men like Joseph T. Wilson, who remained active in Norfolk affairs even after the destruction of the *True Southerner*'s offices, the city council agreed to fund schools for blacks, but supported them far less generously than those for whites. The pending removal of the Freedmen's Bureau funds and personnel seemed justified in July 1869 when the new constitution took effect. Local regulations, but not Virginia's constitution, required that educational facilities be segregated, and the first state-mandated public schools opened in 1870, the year when little Percy Bond turned two.[53]

But for Thomas Bayne, insuring the vote for men of his race was the key issue facing the Constitutional Convention. Speaking in support of a proposal to enfranchise all adult males in the state, he bluntly asked a leader of the opposition: "Does the gentleman mean that black men are not to have rights in this country? Does he mean to set us free today and in fifty or sixty years to come . . . give us the right of suffrage?" Dr. Bayne "considered the right of suffrage inherent, God-given, commencing with [the] existence of man." "There is no power on earth or in hell," he concluded, "that can deprive the black man of his right to vote." The majority-white assembly, anticipating the demands of authorities in Washington and passage of the Fifteenth Amendment, reluctantly adopted provisions that allowed for the enfranchisement of all male citizens over twenty-one. Meanwhile, one of Bayne's colleagues observed, sarcastic white delegates "placarded" him as the " 'bane' of the convention."[54]

His militancy made Thomas Bayne highly controversial. In the summer of 1868, the Norfolk *Virginian* characterized him as "treacherous and deceitful and not to be trusted." After he lost his bid for reelection to the House of Delegates, white thugs beat him up, but that did not deter the black people who convened in a community church, condemned the appointments of numerous "Rebels" to public office, and reendorsed Bayne for office.[55]

Despite Emma and John's apparent happiness with their sweet Percy, life around Hampton Roads may have seemed unremittingly stressful. Assaults on black people and their property became common. Norfolk's newspapers routinely disparaged members of the darker race, and the city's only journal for Negroes had been destroyed. Ruffians attacked "colored" sailors, insulted men and women who celebrated their country's independence, and even shot children. Frederick Douglass aptly articulated the postwar circumstances that frustrated the Bonds and so many others in the South. "We have been turned out of the house of bondage," he contended, "but we have not yet been fully admitted to the glorious temple of American liberty." Douglass summarized the situation most Negroes faced: "We are still in a transition state and the future is shrouded in doubt and danger."[56]

Courts railroaded black leaders, and potential voters were intimidated, yet a few Negroes did serve in Virginia's House of Delegates, State Senate, and city councils. Nonetheless, the real power of government lay in the hands of men who believed in and enforced the entrenched traditions of white supremacy. The Freedmen's Bureau, which had helped its constituents obtain education, health, and legal aid, was on its last legs. A plague of fires, intended to undermine the "colored" community's most empowering institutions, destroyed schools and churches in the Norfolk region and throughout the South.[57]

Protests by the city's black hucksters as well as the grievous situations at local shipyards and the Freedmen's Bank reflected the pervasive denial of economic and occupational opportunities. When John Bond found few white Episcopalians who would welcome him into their church, it may have heightened his malaise. John and Emma's growing resolve to leave the South also reflected the overall racial hostility—the sour ashes of generations of slavery and oppression—that might be avoided in the North's more accommodating social, economic, and political climate.

During the summer of 1869, natural forces conspired against Norfolk County and the area faced a serious drought. Pump water became too brackish to drink and supplies had to be shipped down from Washington. The region's parched black populace had doubled during the war years, though a few residents recently had ventured northward. Emma and John Bond's Portsmouth was home to ten thousand people, while Norfolk had a population of more than nineteen thousand, including nine thousand blacks, most of whom were clustered (as a harbinger of hard-line Jim Crow segregation still to come) in the city's shabbiest wards.[58]

By that time, Virginia's Republican Party had split into a Radical wing and a Conservative faction. During the 1869 gubernatorial campaign, Hampton's Dr. J. D. Harris became the Radicals' candidate for lieutenant governor. White critics who loathed the thought of unity and equality between the races, mistrusted foreigners (nonwhite aliens like John Bond even more than others), and hated miscegenation triply disparaged Harris as "a Negro, a native of Jamaica, reported to be married to a white wife." White men abhorred relationships between black males and white females, and state laws prohibited interracial unions. At a rally, Harris's supporters raised a banner showing a white person and a Negro shaking hands, with the credo "United We Stand, Divided We Fall." But as the partisans unfurled their prophetic standard, the overloaded bridge on which they had assembled creaked, yielded, then plunged into the stream below, carrying several men to watery deaths and injuring many others.[59]

That tragedy easily could have been viewed by Hampton Roads residents as an omen of misfortunes to come. In a close vote, Conservative Republicans won the primary. They defeated Dr. Harris and many of his Radical colleagues and celebrated their victory over those "vampires and harpies." But in the general election, Virginia's voters nonetheless sent twenty-one Negroes, one Norfolk man among them, to the lower house. Six others, including Portsmouth's George Teamoh, went to the state senate, yet able politicians—Harris and Teamoh among them—faced pervasive resistance from the majority community. As one indicator of that unpopularity, only a meager twenty white men voted for Teamoh, although he (like Harris) conscientiously tried to nurture and build interracial alliances.[60]

When its legislature approved the Fourteenth Amendment and adopted a new constitution that was acceptable to officials in the nation's capital, Virginia qualified to be readmitted to the Union and have its unrestricted federal representation restored. After extended controversy and compromise, state legislators had adopted that constitution which, by and large (at least on paper), was an equitable instrument for Negroes. But the pivotal issue became how it would be interpreted and how faithfully it would be adhered to in the hands of a conservative governor, predominantly white legislature, local councils, and unsympathetic courts.

President Grant declared Virginia's Reconstruction complete in early 1870, removed federal troops, and recommended the Commonwealth's readmission to the Union, which would quickly facilitate the return to power of "white men with white men's principles." Norfolk's majority citizens hoped and assumed that Virginia's restoration to unfettered membership in the family of states would result in a government that, they claimed, was "redeemed, regenerated and disenthralled," but Negroes like Emma and John Bond had good reason to feel apprehensive.[61]

Despite African Americans' ebbing influence in those "redeemed" and "disenthralled" halls of power, a traveling Englishman noted that the House of Delegates included "three or four colored men, one of whom was a pure Negro, . . . while another, who seemed to have some white blood in his veins, was a quite masculine-looking person." "There were two colored Senators," the visitor further observed, almost certainly sighting George Teamoh, "quite black, but senatorial enough, and like men who in Africa, would probably have been chiefs."[62]

Perhaps more than any other day in 1870, April 27 became a landmark in Virginia's Reconstruction, but the tranquil spring morning bore no portent of the unimaginable occurrences soon to follow. In Richmond's capitol building, the State Supreme Court of Appeals had started hearing a case that could turn over city government to conservative whites who might be expected to institute racially discriminatory regulations. State and local officials, plus several hundred ordinary citizens of both races who awaited the decision, crammed into the upper court chamber.

The proceedings had just started when the crowd heard two ominous cracks that sounded like pistol shots. Without further warning, the overloaded floor buckled, then gave way altogether. Splintered wood, glass shards, mortar and bricks, along with scores of terrified, shrieking men, plummeted down to the building's lower level. Plaster dust billowed from the capitol's shattered windows as echoes reverberated throughout downtown Richmond.

Sixty to seventy people died on impact or were buried under the rubble, including the Negro senator J. W. D. Bland, whom George Teamoh described as "the most perfect specimen of human mould it has ever been my pleasure to look upon."[63]

That catastrophe, unparalleled in Virginia's history, injured more than a hundred others and perhaps also forecast Reconstruction's demise and the downfall of blacks' long-held aspirations in the Old Dominion. At the very moment "when freedom for the negro was about to be launched into being," mourned Senator Teamoh, evoking the imagery of the day, "the dark and thunderous clouds of persecution were breaking around us."[64]

Southern blacks could point to both positive and negative harbingers of the future in 1870. Early that year, the still "unreconstructed" state of Mississippi, where few former Rebels could vote, sent the African Methodist Episcopal minister and educator Hiram Revels to Washington as the first Negro member of the United States Senate. Somewhat ironically, he filled the seat once held by the eminent (some said infamous) Jefferson Davis. Revels quickly became a celebrity. He lectured throughout the country and was especially popular with New England audiences.[65]

Emma Thomas Bond had borne her son in Norfolk County during those troubled yet still hopeful early postwar years, and Hampton Roads had been her home in slavery and freedom. But many African Americans feared that—like Virginia's devastated capitol building and the bridge that had collapsed under the weight of J. D. Harris's interracial band of supporters—at least in the South, much of their exquisite postemancipation vision of racial equality in a democratic America was crumbling.

Black people in and around Norfolk maintained strong ties to New Bedford, Boston, and Worcester. Less than a decade earlier, John Bond, for one, had spent a year along the Massachusetts coast. Many Yankees whom African Americans admired—General Ben Butler, Colonel Thomas Wentworth Higginson (leader of an esteemed black regiment), and the Fifty-fourth Massachusetts's deceased Colonel Robert Gould Shaw—hailed from that state. And a Norfolk woman named Elizabeth Wilson, plus other former contrabands, eagerly accompanied the Quaker missionaries Lucy and

Sarah Chase back to Worcester. The reputations of white people such as those, and the nascent exodus of black colleagues, convinced the Bonds that New England might offer them better opportunities in a less hostile environment.

Percy Bond never knew his English grandparents, Eliza Kelly and James Bond, and by leaving Tidewater Virginia and any Thomas kinfolk in 1870, Emma and John effectively disengaged their new nuclear family from all other forebears and the wisdom and experience of their elders. At the tender ages of twenty-four, they became an unemcumbered but unguided senior generation.

John and Emma Bond also left friends and colleagues such as Frank Whiting and his family, the Mullens, Blyes, and the Reverend Lewis Tucker. They would have packed a few belongings, scooped up little Percy, and much like the freedom-seeking slaves who for many years had followed the North Star, left Hampton Roads to create fresh lives in the Commonwealth of Massachusetts, self-ordained and widely acclaimed as "freedom's birthplace."

.III.

NORTHERN EXPOSURES,

1870–1905

Reverse: (left to right) Emma, Lena, and Mary (Tooty) Bond, ca. 1905.

7

NO ROOM *at the* INN

———

May the prejudice of the past still
lingering in the hearts of some of our
distinguished men [pass away]. . . . It
remains to see how it will all come out;
I think it will come out pretty rough &
tuff; A bitter Pill to Swallow.

AMOS WEBBER, Worcester, 1874

WORCESTER'S BAY STATE HOUSE, its name spelled in prominent gilt letters across the granite facade and self-proclaimed as "one of the best and most popular [hotels] in New England," was where John Robert Bond, newly arrived from Virginia, obtained a job in 1870. He found work as a fireman in the boiler room.[1]

The five-story Bay State House was situated at the well-trafficked intersection of Main and Exchange Streets, a prime location where it first had opened in 1856. The hotel advertised itself as the only edifice in Worcester equipped with "all modern improvements" for the convenience and comfort of its guests, most remarkably, the innovative apparatus called an elevator. Its handsome dining room and saloon ranked among the city's most esteemed facilities. The cost of furnishings had been estimated at $15,000, and construction of the adjoining stables set the sponsors back $5,000—princely sums at that time—but those expenses were more a source of pride than consternation, because the hotel became a glittering jewel in the city's modest crown.[2]

Just yards from Bond's workplace inferno, liveried hansom

drivers, whips arched over their horses' curried haunches, picked up and delivered the Bay State House's fashionable guests and spirited them through Worcester's cobbled, gaslit streets to and from restaurants, music and lecture halls, or railroad depots. Most hotel patrons hailed from other New England cities—chiefly Boston—plus New York and Albany, but a few had traveled from as far away as Mexico, Germany, France, England, even Japan.[3] John labored in close proximity to those well-heeled guests, but as an uneducated, brown-skinned immigrant, he could not forget that economics, class, and invariably race separated their world from his.

By 1870, George Thrall had become the hotel's proprietor. Though John Bond and other essential employees had to make cramped quarters at the Bay State House their primary residence, Thrall provided no room at the inn for Emma and little Percy.[4] Rather, John's dependents lived out in Worcester's Sixth Ward.

To reach that neighborhood on his infrequent days off, John would have hitched a wagon ride, taken the streetcar (which started operating in 1873), or trudged down Southbridge Street, which forked left off Main below the town center. The total distance was not prohibitive, but over the ensuing dreary mile and a half, three sets of railway tracks (the Boston & Albany, Norwich & Worcester, then the Providence & Worcester) crossed the thoroughfare. Southbridge skirted the city's looming gasworks and Adriatic Mills on its way toward Gouldingsville, a working-class South Worcester enclave where several families crowded into and tenanted each of the stark, triple-decker residences haphazardly jumbled along muddy alleys.[5]

During their years in Worcester, the Bonds shared one of those frame buildings with others, including John and Ann Brown. John Brown had always lived in the Bay State, but like Emma Bond, Ann was a Virginia-born African American. Julius and Nancy Jackson—he black and she white, bound by a marriage that Virginia's antimiscegenation laws forbade—also were neighbors. They all resided in an area where, amid a few foreigners and many working-class Yankees, eight Negro families congregated, squeezed in among the city's noisy and perilous railroad lines.[6]

Worcester's low-income Sixth Ward, with 6,240 residents, had

92 Negroes—a proportional fragment of the city's total black population that in 1870 barely topped 500. By contrast, the adjoining Fifth Ward, with its largely immigrant population (often hostile to Negroes, with whom they competed for menial jobs) of more than 6,700, was home to only 19 African Americans. Altogether the city totaled about 41,000 residents, with more than one-quarter of them, like John Robert Bond, foreign-born.[7]

Industrial Worcester, in east-central Massachusetts, was the state's second-largest city. Despite its lack of a port, raw materials, or significant waterpower, by the mid-nineteenth century it nonetheless had become one of New England's major manufacturing hubs.[8] But Worcester—forty miles from the Atlantic and in many ways more akin to gritty, inland Manchester or Birmingham, England, than to John Bond's seaside Liverpool or Emma Thomas's Norfolk—still remained a pale moon in Boston's powerful orbit. Nonetheless, paths to and from the state capital were well trod. Hotel guests, including businessmen, or visiting lecturers and performers, frequently made that trip, and during the recent war, black and white New Englanders often had traipsed through Worcester on their way to enlist in the army at Camp Meigs, in Boston's suburb of Readville.

Working-class enclaves distinguished by humble, rented dwellings dominated Worcester's eastern half. The elevated slopes of the western sector, on the other hand, contained most of the city's affluent old Yankees gracious single-family homes, and, excluding the prototypical common, where cows and sheep recently had grazed, its only public park.[9] As was often the case in new, urban America, Worcester had a "right" and a "wrong" side of the tracks—in this case, the parallel rail lines that divided the city into antithetical hemispheres of "haves" and "have nots." The Bonds had little choice but to reside east of the city's economic and class divide.

The stubborn winter that was barely yielding as John, Emma, and Percy Bond arrived in Massachusetts had been unusually grim. John had endured one such season in New Bedford, but Emma had not yet faced the North's climatic assaults. Late March, already springtime in Virginia, saw deep snow still blanketing the ground, and although the region normally expected months of numbing cold, blizzards, and leaden skies, many activities in Worcester had to be curtailed in early 1870.[10] Hordes of residents, domiciles, and humming factories saturated the city, but farms sprawled across the frozen hinterlands, and as the frigid weather grudgingly eased, rocky eruptions heaved up from New England's fields as more prolific and dependable crops than fruits or vegetables.

As Emma Bond's initial Massachusetts spring finally routed winter's chill that cruel April, the city's visitors—of express interest to its Negro residents—included Mississippi's Hiram Revels, the country's first African American senator, whom Worcester's *Evening Gazette* touted as "the colored successor of Jeff. Davis." Senator Revels spoke at Mechanics Hall (two blocks from the Bay State House) on the rather ill-defined topic "The Tendency of Our Age."[11] Yet more than Revels's message for Worcester's citizenry, John Bond's first Decoration—later Memorial—Day in New England demonstrated the recently enhanced civic status of a few of the city's darker-skinned minority and may have been an unforgettable event for the English-born veteran, who was incrementally acquiring a new American identity.[12]

The Grand Army of the Republic's (GAR) George W. Ward Post 10 organized those late May activities. Its solemn parade wound through downtown, near the Bay State House and the town hall, then passed out toward Gouldingsville, pausing at cemeteries along the route to lay floral tributes on the graves of patriots who had given their lives in service to the nation. The GAR, founded in 1866 and comprised exclusively of Civil War veterans, was well on its way toward becoming the country's most influential political lobby. In what became characteristically effective fashion, the local organization persuaded the city to offer its members (out of respect for their noble defense of the Union) preferential treatment when they sought municipal employment.

Statewide, the GAR numbered its posts according to their order of incorporation and charter. As Post 10, Worcester's unit, therefore, was one of Massachusetts's first, and ultimately became the largest in the entire United States. As a numerical indicator of the local GAR's dominance, by 1870 it already had a thousand members, more than ten percent of the city's adult men.[13] In Worcester, as elsewhere in the state and nation, belonging to that organization was rapidly becoming an indisputable badge of patriotism, respectability, and male honor.

Ultimately, Post 10 complied with its parent group's presumptively color-blind guidelines and inducted quite a few black veterans, but their admission did not come without profound struggle. The unit's minutes from its mid-1870 sessions, shortly after the Bonds arrived, reflected the ongoing bitterness.

Bassill C. Barker, a barber, reportedly had served as a sergeant with the all-Negro Fifth Massachusetts Cavalry. In May, he applied for admittance to the GAR, but a secret polling of the membership turned him down. "The question being raised," queried the unit's secretary, "why was he rejected?" No one openly challenged Barker's eligibility—though a slim possibility exists that he distorted his military credentials. Some members, however, had no doubt as to the reason for the blackball: "One comrade vouchsafed the reply that it was because he was a *nigger*." To comply with national GAR policies, Post 10 passed a resolution stating that its sole membership requirements were that an applicant be of "good character," have served in the army or navy during the war, and been honorably discharged. "With these qualifications," it continued, "no inquiry as to race, color, or nationality of any applicant should, or by right ought to be made." Barker twice resubmitted his application, but covert "nays" from one or more unidentified members still denied him entry, prompting the angry resignation of three white post officers.[14]

Certainly, Barker was not the only applicant whom the GAR rejected. Black veterans in other towns protested that they, too, had been turned down because of race, and an outraged white man claimed that a post in Pennsylvania denied him entry because he was a Democrat. The national organization usually declined to intervene in such cases, and in 1872 its judge advocate general somewhat equivocally ruled that "no comrade ought to be influenced by personal dislike or malice, but should decide in every case upon his honest convictions."[15]

In light of the nasty controversy surrounding Barker's application, it might be assumed that GAR Post 10 included no Negroes. But that was not so. It had already inducted a few black men, most notably Amos Webber, who worked as a messenger at the Washburn & Moen wireworks. In contrast to his post's handful of righteous white officers, however, Webber, who like Barker had been a sergeant with Massachusetts's "colored" cavalry, did not resign when the GAR denied his comrade admission. Their unit had seen action in combat following its formation in 1863, and at the war's end its men (like thousands of other black soldiers and sailors) passed through Hampton Roads, near John and Emma Bond's former home.[16]

Several factors might have contributed to the discrepancy between the GAR's treatment of Webber and Barker. Barker was marginally self-employed, while Webber's workplace associations with white colleagues—even in a low-level position—may have given him forceful advocates and made him familiar and therefore more acceptable to other post members. Or perhaps Worcester's white veterans reasoned that two or three black members could be tokens of their group's nonracist practices and philosophy, while more might portend or precipitate a menacing flood of darkness. Despite fears or enmity lurking in the hearts of some of Post 10's members, soon after the ugly Barker incident, the malevolent mood ebbed, or chagrin overwhelmed the bigoted minority, and the post admitted other Negroes—but never Bassill Barker. Over the ensuing decades, its membership rolls expanded to include nearly forty African American veterans who, much like white men, sought an organizational affiliation that had influence and prestige in the community, reflected their patriotism, and recalled common sacrifices for country.[17]

Amos Webber played a role in the GAR's late May parade and wreath-laying ceremonies in 1870, as did he and an increasing number of black colleagues in the ensuing years.[18] Like Webber and Barker, most of Worcester's African American veterans had trained at Readville's Camp Meigs, thirty-five miles east, and had joined either the state's "colored" Fifth Cavalry, or the better-known Fifty-fourth and Fifty-fifth Massachusetts Infantry Regiments. John and Emma Bond may even have encountered some of those Worcesterites when the Fifty-fifth passed through Norfolk in 1865. And like John, several of the city's black men had served in the Union navy. For Negro as well as other veterans, the bonds formed during the war continued to frame many of their postbellum experiences, practices, and attitudes.

At that time, many onetime soldiers and sailors, swayed by wartime relationships, were leaving their antebellum places of residence. When a veteran moved to a new town, others (of any race) who had shared the formative military experience often became mentors during his transition. Their support might include finding him work, making other family members welcome, and introducing newcomers to the community's organizational life, including its schools, churches, and fraternal associations.[19]

Not only Decoration Day but also the traditionally "glorious" Fourth of July were times when Worcester's veterans, plus others of all races, religions, and places of origin, displayed their devotion to country. They set off firecrackers, played baseball, picnicked, wagered on trotting races, heard patriotic speeches, and waved flags as brass bands blared rousing anthems. Nonetheless, Independence Day also had become the occasion when working-class men in particular got "gloriously," stinking drunk. Many laborers considered that particular date—one of their very few holidays—a compelling opportunity for flagrant carousal. The expected yet dreaded intemperance included not only excessive alcohol consumption, but brawling and raucous revelry of all sorts. The annual commemorative day of liberty embodied an explosive rejection of the routinized discipline, monotony, and workplace hierarchy that the men otherwise endured year-round.[20]

Ironically, that quintessential all-American jamboree also became a deeply divided event when the city's Swedes, Irish, and French Canadians, as well as Germans and even Negroes gave voice to, not common liberation from oppression, but rather, preexisting ethnic (or racial) ties and customs.[21] Immigrants wanted to take advantage of the United States' freedoms and economic opportunities, but remained reluctant to shed old loyalties and languages or to abandon their indigenous celebratory rites. Worcester's diverse minorities experienced the classic anguish of so many others who struggled to clarify their often conflicted status as hyphenated Americans.

Every January 1 since 1863, black people in Emma Thomas Bond's Norfolk, Virginia, had celebrated the Emancipation Proclamation's anniversary, and claimed that as their own day of independence. Occasions such as July 4, on the other hand, may have starkly reminded John Robert Bond that officially he remained a foreigner. Yet when a census taker that decennial summer of 1870 asked if he was eligible to vote, John declared himself a United States citizen, though in truth he had not yet attained that favored status.²² Perhaps John's innocent but duplicitous assertion revealed his heartfelt desires. Or it may have reflected an awareness that in New England, despite some instances of manifest bigotry, a man of his unusual Anglo-African ancestry might more readily participate in the country's democratic rituals than he could in Virginia's confrontational climate, with its deep-seated legacies of slavery.

Understandably, before and during the Civil War very few alien Negroes had opted to come to a nation that still fervently embraced slavery; and the United States did not amend its first immigration law to allow Africans, or men of African ancestry from elsewhere, to become naturalized until the year John Bond went to Worcester and claimed to be an American citizen.²³ That spring, the new Fifteenth Amendment also promised that "the right of citizens to vote shall not be denied or abridged . . . on account of race, color or previous condition of servitude." But sex was *not* eliminated as a deterrent to exercising the franchise, and women's citizenship remained a derivative privilege that largely accrued to them through the status of fathers or husbands.²⁴

For some years, Worcester had been home to a small group of reformers who supported both slavery's abolition and women's rights. For many women, their deliberate exclusion from the Fifteenth Amendment became and remained an inflaming issue. But in a community largely comprised of immigrants like himself where proof of citizenship often was not demanded of a man prior to casting his vote, even a noncitizen such as John Bond just might have paid Massachusetts's poll tax, grappled with the state literacy test, and become part of Worcester's ethnically diverse—though predominantly white—all-male electorate without undue interrogation or other interference from authorities.[25]

Residents of that city had been the country's first Negroes to serve on juries, yet they lacked the necessary numbers to influence city politics significantly. Still, a fair number of Worcester's African American men voted.[26] Massachusetts, in toto, had a small but vigorous black electorate that dated back to the late eighteenth century, when New Bedford's Cuffe family successfully challenged laws denying the franchise to men of their race. Several black Bostonians recently had been elected to the legislature, but Massachusetts retained its poll tax until the 1890s, and that economic barrier, supplemented by erratically enforced literacy requirements, continued to keep a number of economically marginal "colored" people—as well as poor whites, who often were uneducated or non-English-speaking immigrants—from voting.

Worcester's post–Civil War electorate, bolstered by its small assembly of African Americans, usually maintained a narrow Republican majority despite inroads made by more newly arrived ethnic groups. Not until 1873 when the *Democratic Journal* started publication did the local press reflect the increasing political strength of the city's immigrants. As in other urban centers, most foreign-born, recently naturalized citizens voted Democratic and often viewed not only indigenous Yankees, but also (perhaps especially) black people, as their antagonists.[27]

When their town's mainstream party organization denied them membership in 1868, Worcester's Negro Republicans had formed the Colored Grant and Colfax Club.[28] During that campaign, those men had marched in the city's torchlight parade as an autonomous uniformed assembly led by white officers. But many among the opposition disliked Republicans generally and expressly resented the African Americans who participated in that display of political activism. Their bold affirmation of citizenship rights had challenged the presumably appropriate bounds of black inferiority and humility that many white Americans, in the North as well as the South, took for granted. Gunfire rang out and hostile crowds stoned the Negro marchers, but the blacks repelled their mostly immigrant assailants. Ultimately, with no one killed, but minor injuries aplenty, the outraged yet triumphant black Republicans completed the procession's predetermined route.[29]

Around the time when John and Emma Bond moved to Worcester, shortly after passage of the Fifteenth Amendment, the city's Negroes sent a marching ensemble to Boston to celebrate what many people considered Reconstruction's crowning accomplishment. With their band trumpeting *Glory, Hallelujah,* the celebrants (some of them Civil War veterans) paraded to the depot. The group—men and women—filled four railroad cars for the journey east. Ironically, that patriotic rally virtually coincided with the GAR's racially grounded rejection of Sergeant Bassill Barker.[30]

Like Barker, Webber, and others, John Bond, who arrived that same spring, was a Union veteran, but he, too, became just one more anonymous member of the city's poorly paid working class. Laboring as a coal heaver at the Bay State House was arduous, especially for a man who lacked several fingers and suffered from a war injury that left him with restricted use of his right arm. Yet at that central location, Bond nonetheless was situated near Pearl Street's All Saints' Episcopal Church, the town hall, the characteristic New England common facing the imposing Mechanics Hall, plus other lyceums frequented by civic organizations including the GAR, Masons, and Odd Fellows. Had social conventions and economic circumstances permitted, downtown Worcester would have provided ample opportunities and activities to fill John's limited idle hours. But because the furnaces that warmed the rooms and supplied hot water for the city's foremost hotel had to be stoked around the clock, he undoubtedly toiled and sweated through a sixty-hour, six-day workweek.[31]

In addition to Bond's lack of financial resources or free time, and despite Worcester's deserved reputation as a home of social reformers and stronghold for liberal ideologies, disturbing and seemingly paradoxical events akin to the stoning of its black political demonstrators would have kept him from unconstrained participation in the city's public life. There were activities that explicitly excluded Negroes, places they did not go, organizations they could not join.

Even before the Bonds arrived, a number of saloons had been

established that catered to one or another of the city's major ethnic groups: German, Swedish, Irish, or French Canadian. But Worcester's Negro population (unlike Norfolk's) was too small to sustain its own pubs. In some ways, those designated white working-class "social clubs" epitomized America's patchy egalitarianism and became centers for many male laborers' recreational lives. They emphasized solidarity within a circumscribed group, and drinking privileges were not granted on the basis of wealth or elite status; but each tavern only accommodated imbibers of the "right" sex, ethnicity, occupation, and certainly race. Owners, their employees, or patrons resolutely, even forcibly, ejected alien intruders. Similarly, many old-time Yankees wanted nothing to do with *any* of the city's motley newcomers, and especially deplored their sometimes unrestrained drinking habits. A locally popular, chauvinistic ditty brashly asserted:

> The Irish and the Dutch; they don't amount to much,
> For the Micks have their whiskey,
>   and the Germans guzzle beer,
> And all we Americans wish they had never come here.[32]

In Worcester as in other cities, the American Colonization Society (ACS) recruited and claimed a related but differently focused nativist following. That predominantly white organization's "solution" to the country's postwar racial situation continued to promote the resettlement of Negro Americans in Africa. "Colored people are made more energetic by the climate," testified the ACS's Reverend D. C. Haynes to a rapt local audience. He insisted that blacks had "the right qualities for missionaries," and urged "all of those who have African blood in their veins" to emigrate.[33] Along similar lines, President U. S. Grant recently had suggested annexing Santo Domingo because, he argued, that Caribbean island colony of Spain was capable of "supporting the entire colored population of the United States." The proposal died largely because its opponents successfully argued that as an "Anglo-Saxon Republic" the United States should not append any territory where the "black race was predominant."[34]

Most Negroes—whose antecedents had lived in the United States far longer than most ethnics—who even thought about those emigrationist schemes, did not want to leave their country. But at the same time, Worcester's African Americans, like others elsewhere, sometimes fell victim to racially motivated abuse on city streets, as well as exclusion from places of public accommodation and a variety of civic, fraternal, and reform groups. The local branch of a leading temperance organization rejected one man who applied for membership, asserting that it "would make trouble . . . to bring a nigger in." That rebuff prompted another of Worcester's black antiliquor advocates eloquently, though fruitlessly, to protest: "God will ask then, where is thy brother Ethiopian, you see in the gutter drunk, and never lift thy hands to raise them[?] They are my Children too."[35]

At least once during Emma and John Bond's years in the city, a restaurant staffed by "Irish girls" refused to serve a party of Negroes who belonged to the Grand United Order of Odd Fellows' local North Star Lodge. Those aspiring diners, the *Evening Gazette* reported, epitomized the city's "most respectable and influential colored men." That uncivil act did not represent the eating establishment's official policy, and the surly immigrant waitresses were dismissed, but only after the familiar message of racial insult had been effectively delivered.[36] The Bay State House's dining room was not the place that denied service to Worcester's "most respectable" Negroes, yet John Robert Bond surely never was a patron there, and probably had the opportunity to leave his stygian workplace at the opulent hotel only one day per week to visit his wife Emma and son Percy in Gouldingsville.[37]

A number of Emma Bond's female neighbors worked as domestic servants in the city's more affluent residences, but they were white women—usually of Irish or Swedish heritage. To an unusual extent in urban, nineteenth-century Massachusetts, Worcester's industrial labor force remained an all-male domain, and blue-collar employment of all sorts occupied the majority of the neighborhood's primary (white male) breadwinners. The city was noted for its wide range of industries, and its workers made carpets, belts, boots and shoes, fabrics and finished garments, paper goods, and all sorts of tools and machine parts.[38] By 1870, the local Washburn & Moen wireworks had merged with one of the country's largest manufacturers, and it employed more than six hundred at its primary Worcester facility alone.

The city's foundries and other industrial enterprises fouled the air with acrid fumes and spewed noxious wastes into ponds splattered throughout southeast Worcester and near the Blackstone River. There, at the headwaters, the Blackstone was a minor stream, but then plunged exuberantly through the Massachusetts hills, down hundreds of feet toward sea level, providing power for grimy mill towns bunched along its banks. The Blackstone River Valley had long been called the "Birthplace of the American Industrial Revolution." In 1828, Worcester's nascent entrepreneurs had underwritten construction of a canal that linked their scarcely navigable river with Rhode Island's Narragansett Bay and, ultimately, the Atlantic Ocean. That man-made waterway, followed and then largely supplanted by rail lines that improved access to ocean shipping ports and world markets, generated a mid-nineteenth-century explosion in the city's commercial and manufacturing capabilities.[39]

Despite its diverse workforce, John Bond's new hometown was a nonunion stronghold characterized by management's paternalism, and punctuated by hard-nosed, antilabor tactics. Many workers maintained chauvinistic passions about their indigenous cultures and countries of origin. They lacked class solidarity because they were so alienated from one another by differences of ethnicity, religion, and race. Recent immigrants and African Americans had the least bargaining power of all. Canny employers perceived that with easy access to such a fragmented labor pool, they could hire eager, cheaper, newer arrivals to replace their disgruntled, sometimes troublemaking, longtime employees.[40]

Shortly before John Robert Bond went to work at the Bay State House, its restaurant's black waiters had called a carefully timed job action one evening just prior to the dinner hour. They sought a raise of five dollars per month—only two cents an hour. Respectfully, they stood shoulder to shoulder and refused to put on the pristine linen aprons that symbolized their occupation and servile status. But not for a moment did the hotel's many white employees

back their Negro colleagues. The manager disparaged the protesters' demands and threatened to replace them if they did not immediately resume work. Wages earned by members of the Negro
community were lower and their jobs less secure than those of the
native born, or even most immigrants. Such service employment
was needed, respected, and relatively well paid in the black community, and the men quickly perceived that, despite an embarrassment to management and the inconvenience caused a group of
ravenous diners, they had little bargaining power. "After a moment's reflection," a Worcester newspaper reported, the thwarted
waiters relented and "silently donned their aprons."[41]

Although the hotel that hired John Robert Bond in 1870 faced
no other significant labor protests during that period, on several occasions workers at Washburn & Moen, Worcester's largest employer, walked out to protest hazardous conditions, long hours,
and wage reductions. They had little success. One confrontation
turned violent when strikers assaulted a contingent of replacement
scabs with bricks and iron bars. Management met with individual
protesters, but refused to recognize any formal labor "associations." The owners threatened to shut down the wireworks altogether "until they could ascertain that the great majority of their
employees were ready to conform to existing regulations." They
easily outmaneuvered the unhappy but disunited predominantly
Irish-born strikers and replaced them with native-born Americans
or German aliens.[42]

As in many nineteenth-century American cities, a mosaic of
those and others of the working class comprised the major portion
of Worcester's population, and the Bonds' Gouldingsville neighborhood was no exception. It hunkered down in a barren hollow near
the city's shabby fringes before the hills soared skyward to the south.
Dirty, clamorous industrial facilities dominated South Worcester,
and in springtime, as melting snows oversaturated the ground, the
area became a toxic, fetid flood plain hemmed in by crisscrossed
railroad tracks, the looping Blackstone River, and its tangential,
polluted canal.[43]

Despite the gasworks' proximity, neither gaslight nor town
water supplied Gouldingsville. Yet above that dingy community,

atop Mount St. James (Worcester's most elevated escarpment) by the city's southern boundary, rose the spires of Fenwick Hall, testament to the celestial splendor of the Catholic Church and its metaphorical proximity to God. It was one of only two buildings which then comprised the College of the Holy Cross.

Instructors at that seminary (founded in 1843 as New England's first Catholic college) belonged to the Jesuit order. A majority of the several hundred students who attended Holy Cross in the early 1870s hailed from out of town, out of state, even out of the country. Despite their dominant Protestantism, Worcester's elites as well as its working-class Catholics welcomed and supported an institution of escalating reputation and scholarship in their unpretentious, mid-Massachusetts city.

From the time of its inception, Holy Cross welcomed Catholic boys from around the country and the world. Its first valedictorian, James Healy, was the son of an Irish-born planter and the Georgia slave who became his companion. John Bond had been born to an Irish mother and a black father, but (except for the significant gender reversal and his lighter skin) James Healy's ethnic and racial heritage resembled that of the English-born former sailor. Other children from the Healy family also attended Holy Cross before dedicating themselves to the church or, in one instance, a life at sea. When the school's first building burned in 1852, the affluent Healys contributed to its reconstruction.[44]

The Healy boys' ambiguous appearance meant that they might not be readily recognizable as "colored," but they seem to have made no deliberate attempts to conceal their racial heritage when they were Holy Cross students and then instructors. Rather, they identified themselves as Catholics, neither Negro nor white, and even participated in classmates' antiblack high jinks. They were handsome fellows and gifted clerical scholars, further endowed with ingratiating personalities. James Healy had served his church in Boston during the Civil War when he helped to defuse the city's ugly draft riots, and ultimately became bishop of Portland, Maine—the first of his (unacknowledged) race to achieve that exalted rank in America's Roman Catholic Church.[45]

A younger sibling, Patrick F. Healy, also a Holy Cross graduate, similarly rose through the church's hierarchy. Around the time that John and Emma Bond lived in Worcester, Georgetown University (which had no recognizably Negro students or other faculty until the mid-twentieth century) in the nation's capital installed the deracinated Father Patrick Healy, S.J., as its president. Because of his ivory complexion, wavy hair, and unrevealing features, people who knew the race and enslaved status of Patrick's deceased mother strategically ignored that disquieting fact—as did the Healys themselves. Throughout the United States, even during the reform-oriented Reconstruction era, any light-skinned mulatto officially would have been considered a Negro who might be subjected to the degrading treatment generally accorded all members of the darker race.[46] Yet despite such harsh realities and ludicrous racial paradoxes, the Catholic Church (at least in Washington, D.C., Maine, and Worcester), though often imbued with the same bigotry that infected so many white Americans and their institutions, winked at the country's prevalent and enduring biases when it served its interests to do so.

Like most members of their socially and legally defined race, however, the Bonds could not assimilate and pass for white, nor were they Catholics. Geographic proximity linked them to Holy Cross, but their religious preferences lay elsewhere. Some Negroes joined Worcester's predominantly white Protestant congregations, but the black community had established a small African Methodist Episcopal Zion (AMEZ) congregation long before 1870, and more recently had organized the Methodist Bethel Society.[47] Yet neither Negro church fulfilled Emma Bond's expectations as had Norfolk's Bute Street Baptist.

The Anglican Church–raised John Robert Bond, on the other hand (accompanied on occasional Sundays by Emma and little Percy along with a very few others among the city's Negroes), attended All Saints' Episcopal, which was situated near the Bay State House. It was most notably, however, the parish of preference for hundreds of Worcester's most respected and affluent white citizens, many of whom lived in the west side's surrounding highlands. Luminous stained glass windows and a striking procession of Gothic arches adorned the graceful wooden church, and its elegant carillon tower thrust upward toward the heavens.[48]

In 1869, All Saints' parishioners had held a successful Christmas bazaar to raise money for a proposed new mission in town. Two years later, members of the Episcopal clergy conducted the inaugural ceremonies, climaxed by a traditional rendition of *Gloria in Excelsis* on St. Matthew's Day, to consecrate the recently completed chapel that would bear that name. But unlike downtown Worcester's stately All Saints, St. Matthew's occupied a modest frame building that seemed little more than a cozy cottage topped by a small bell tower and surrounded by a picket fence. The new church was located in South Worcester, in close proximity to the Whittall carpet mills and John Robert Bond's residence. The fortuitously selected name of St. Matthew's may also have honored its major benefactor, the local factory owner Matthew J. Whittall.

Most of Whittall's employees were that paternalistic industrialist's fellow countrymen—white Englishmen, of course, not mulattoes. He had arranged to transport them from Kidderminster (his own place of birth and a major town in England's Worcester County, not far southeast of John Bond's Liverpool), to Worcester, Massachusetts, to work at his facility and live nearby. Like Bond, many of those British-born millworkers also wanted, and expected, to affiliate themselves with a *New* England church that would resemble their ancestral Anglican denomination. St. Matthew's social and comunity activities soon included, not lemonade socials or baseball games, but strawberry festivals, tea parties, cricket matches, and especially Mothering Day. That was the traditional English celebration (ultimately adopted in the United States) when domestic servants who had to work for their employers' families on Easter Sunday could attend services and celebrate with their own kinfolk on a designated, late springtime Sabbath. All Saints was Worcester's upper-class "American" Episcopal church, but St. Matthew's, where John Robert Bond often worshiped after 1871, became its working-class "English" counterpart.[49]

While many of Worcester's townspeople, such as Whittall and his British millworkers had immigrated from Europe, most of its

Negroes had arrived only recently from the American South. A few men (like John Bond) could have relocated there as a result of brief, yet significant, military associations, but Isaac Mason, an escaped slave who had tracked the North Star to freedom, had come prior to the Civil War. Colonel Thomas Wentworth Higginson, a Worcester minister, had led one of the country's first black regiments, and some of his soldiers also followed him home. Elizabeth Wilson and her husband (perhaps even Emma Thomas Bond), had been protégés of Worcester's Sarah and Lucy Chase during the Quaker sisters' long Norfolk sojourn and, with other former slaves, accompanied the Chases north. The Wilsons even named their new daughter Sarah to honor their mentor.[50] Those southern migrants settled in Worcester with full faith in the city's reputation as a secure and welcoming harbor for people of their race.

Just over one percent of Worcester's population was African American in 1870. Most members of that darker-skinned minority, unable to afford better neighborhoods and also restricted in their choice of housing because of bias, clustered in lower-class, racially and ethnically mixed enclaves. Though few in number and of modest means, Worcester's Negroes nonetheless created a community notable for its fervent though appropriately skeptical patriotism, political activism, and religious and fraternal associations. It was a small, well-organized circle that in certain ways avoided dependence on or subservience to Worcester's white power structure. Some black people worked for the city's major employers, but others were self-employed, as carpenters, seamstresses, upholsterers, or barbers.[51]

A handful of Worcester's African Americans had even moved out of the financially marginal classes. For several years, the *Evening Gazette* acknowledged the activities of a group called the Neptune Yacht Club. Its membership, the journal explained, was limited to "those who can afford to spend the sultry days of August in briny recreations along the shore." The spot where that clique gathered was probably Newport, Rhode Island, which for more than a decade had been the site of a small summer colony of economically comfortable Negroes. Some of those water lovers also may have belonged to Newport's well-established Ugly Fishing Club, which combined leisure and frolic with serious civic endeavors.[52]

On January 2, 1872, the Neptune Yacht Club held its annual winter soirée at Worcester's Horticultural Hall. A "brilliant attendance of the elite of the colored society of Worcester and other cities" went to the event, reported the *Gazette,* adding, "none but the favored few are admitted." In addition to local attendees, guests arrived from New Bedford, Cambridge, and Boston, Massachusetts; Newport and Providence, Rhode Island; and Bristol, Connecticut. To prepare for the ball, the "jovial tars" (the newspaper's repetition of that slur, so widely used to demean Negroes, may have suggested either a sly affront or a tacit acceptance of the word's pejorative implications) discarded their "pea jackets, their sou'westers, their telescopes . . . and appeared in the swallow tail of the period." The women dressed in stylish gowns of velvet, tulle, satin, and lace, which featured sweeping trains and voluptuous décolletages variously adorned with "sprays of orange blossoms [or] bouquets of roses."[53]

"The Gallant Tars and Their Partners" danced the night away, exhibiting the "same zeal with which under the summer solstice, they . . . [honor] the god of the billows and the whales." A "full quadrille band" performed a mélange of twenty-eight numbers as celebrants dined on fine cuisine, then twirled to the season's most fashionable melodies, including the "polka, redowa, and varsovienne." One favorite tune was aptly titled *Who Caught the Big Fish?*[54] But southern black people's traditional dances, such as the cakewalk or "cuttin' de pigeon's wings," were far removed from the scene at the Neptune Yacht Club's upper-class hoedown.

That event, from which Emma and John Bond surely were excluded, might have provided them with their first glimpse of New England's small but stratified, and geographically scattered, Negro "high society." Yet despite the *Evening Gazette*'s report, most white Americans ignored or dismissed class structure in the African American community, seeing Negroes generally as a troublesome, undifferentiated mass of "others."[55] Members of the Neptune Yacht Club, however, probably considered their group to be as exclusive as any that limited its membership to the old Yankee gentry. In some ways, members tried to emulate the white upper class (though they never approached economic parity), but kept largely to themselves and established their own traditions at occasions and in places where they knew that their families would not be exposed to offensive and hurtful racial insults. And the white community undoubtedly was relieved that the "colored elite" did maintain a respectful distance. But Worcester at least acknowledged their existence, and its major newspaper covered the annual celebration much as it did the activities of many local white organizations.

The Neptune Yacht Club was a group that, because of its members' nautical pastimes and obsessions with boating, fishing, and other water-focused activities, might have seemed to suggest a natural affiliation for a seaman (a genuine "tar") such as John Robert Bond. Unlike Bond, however, the yacht club's members never worked at their maritime avocations. They were leisure-time sailors only, who earned adequate incomes toiling as pharmacists, caterers, clerks, musicians, and tailors.

Like John Bond, many were mulattoes, and lighter skin—seen as something of an asset in their limited circle—may have been most prevalent among the group's women. Occupation and money, but more significantly, education, "family heritage," "manners," and "breeding" separated that New England–wide coterie of the "colored aristocracy" from men and women such as John and Emma.[56] The Bonds' social universe in Worcester would have been almost as far removed from that of the Neptune Yacht Club and the Ugly Fishing Club as it was from the rarefied world of affluent Caucasians who patronized the Bay State House.

By the early 1870s, New England's Negro population was hardly a monolithic entity and had developed a structured society, articulated within itself, distinct from the region's immigrants, and decidedly distanced from "Old Worcester's" revered white families. Members of the Anglo-Saxon upper stratum such as Lucy and Sarah Chase were not, however, immune from familial tragedies resembling those that often afflicted the lower classes of all ethnicities and races.

Their cousin Alice Chase had married Thomas Earle, who belonged to another respected Worcester clan. During the Civil War,

Thomas became a Union officer. While he was gone, Alice was suspected of marital infidelity. When her husband returned, Alice Chase Earle could not assuage his wrath and moved away with their children. The couple divorced, and despite a jury ruling that awarded Alice custody, Thomas stalked, found, and then "stole away" his sons. When authorities jailed him for attacking an officer who came to retrieve the boys, his inexplicably compassionate father-in-law bailed him out. But the court concluded that Thomas Earle was a menace to his family. He was judged insane and sequestered at Worcester's "Lunatic Asylum," where he soon died. Amos Webber, an empathetic observer, recounted the wretched story in detail, then somberly commented, "Therefore the Rich must suffer as well as the poor."[57]

Sorrows beset Worcester's most esteemed families, but especially its humblest. Accounts of dementia, suicides, and savage episodes permeated Webber's diary and the newspapers. People drowned in the Blackstone River or froze in snowdrifts, and a raging kerosene fire burned to death a young Irish servant. "Buried in the New World; sad," lamented Webber. Industrial accidents killed a number of the city's workingmen, while railroad trains maimed their children. A brawl at a boardinghouse near the Bonds' residence resulted in half a dozen "broken heads." That melee left the site "littered with broken bottles and crockery, gouts of blood and hair, and fragments of clothing." In late 1870, while Mayor James Blake was inspecting the gasworks in that neighborhood, a thunderous explosion almost demolished the facility, injured a number of employees, shattered windows for blocks around, and terrified nearby residents. Just days before Christmas, Mayor Blake died of his injuries.[58]

Nor was the Bond family spared a profound loss during those years. Emma Thomas Bond—who lived in an enclave plagued by significant industrial toxicity, near the perilous gasworks, in lodgings that lacked heat and indoor plumbing—became pregnant in late 1871. But her second boy, born prematurely the following May, survived only two days.[59] That surely would have been John and Emma's most agonizing time in their new Massachusetts home.

At the Republican presidential convention the following fall,

James Lynch, a mulatto minister and political activist from unreconstructed Mississippi, addressed his party. He touted the United States' aspirations for international expansion—a hope at that time still primarily espoused by white southerners. Of greater significance, Lynch declared to cheers from the mostly white assembly that "colored men were born of the Republican party and by it they stand." "They are bound to Grant by cords that can never be separated," he added, emphasizing the debts that Negroes believed they owed the memory of Abraham Lincoln.[60] Throughout the country that November, recently enfranchised black male voters ardently supported the Republican ticket.

John Bond might have considered making an illicit attempt to cast his first ballot for president as Worcester's black men paraded about the city carrying banners bearing the slogan "We Vote in '72 as We Fought in '62." They vigorously encouraged male members of their community, especially veterans, to hasten to the polls and support Ulysses S. Grant and Henry Wilson.[61]

In some way, however, the fates may have frowned on Grant's reelection, because soon thereafter an unusual number of American cities, including both Worcester and Boston, endured devastating fires. And the Massachusetts winter of 1872–73 was characterized by temperatures that plummeted and remained well below zero, reinforced by thirty-nine major snowfalls, resulting in a total of "105 days of good sleighing," reported Amos Webber. Despite drifts that still measured more than three feet, Webber gleefully commented on April 7, "To-day the street cars commence."[62]

The following autumn, Worcester hosted the state's Republican gubernatorial convention. General Benjamin Butler, a hero to Virginia's black people during the war, became a contender for the nomination. But in the shifting light of Reconstruction's altered racial landscape, Butler had begun to reevaluate his former earnest efforts on behalf of Negro Americans. With clear pleasure, therefore, Amos Webber stated, "a majority of the votes of the Convention . . . favor Gov. Washburn." Butler withdrew from consideration for the time being, and the party renominated William B. Washburn by acclamation. To the great satisfaction of the city's black Republicans, he was reelected in November.[63]

Through the early 1870s, John Robert Bond continued his grueling work at Worcester's finest hotel. He also lost a child whom he never had a chance to know, but may have developed a somewhat fulfilling life in the city, or at least one that roughly forecast his future. He attended either of two Episcopal churches, not unlike the Anglican establishments of his youth. Downtown Worcester featured the predominantly white GAR (that grudgingly admitted men of his race) and, like Norfolk, had an "African Lodge" of Prince Hall Masons and the Grand United Order of Odd Fellows (GUOOF). Such associations, for blacks or whites, conducted their activities in postbellum peacetime, but the GAR's rituals were grounded in the shared masculine ordeal of war. Though John did not join the GAR or either all-black lodge at that time, their members, often Union veterans, probably became his companions. The all-white orders of Masons and Odd Fellows in the United States both had resolutely refused to accept black men, or even grant them charters to start their own groups, but John surely knew, or learned, that the autonomous African American fraternal orders had their roots in, and owed their existence to, the country—in one case the city—of his birth.

On August 1, 1871 (and that same date in subsequent years), black Worcesterites watched and cheered as members of the GUOOF's North Star Lodge paraded in full regalia through the city streets. The lodge's name recalled the celestial guide that had summoned escaping bondsmen through the darkest nights toward freedom, and August 1 commemorated the anniversary of slavery's abolition in the British West Indies, a date that would have reverberated in the consciousness of a "coloured" Englishman such as John Bond. The 1871 festivities culminated in a picnic for members and their guests by Lake Quinsigamond (well known throughout New England for its thrilling new amusement park) just southeast of the city and very near John and Emma's residence.

Robert Jones, the GUOOF's national grand master, came to Worcester on that occasion. His keynote speech explained how the symbolic chain on its members' insignia represented links between "Friendship, Love, and Charity." Negro Odd Fellows, he declared, "inculcated charity and brotherly love" throughout the community, and promoted ever-improving relations "of man toward himself, his family, his country and his God." Religious beliefs, along with devotion and responsibility to family, community, and country became indivisible precepts. In contrast to white Odd Fellows, who not only denied membership to Negroes but often demeaned the entire race, Robert Jones reiterated, his "colored" order applied the tenets of brotherhood to "all men, of every clime and condition." He further asserted that "the descendants of Jacob, the followers of Mahomet, and the worshippers of Christ, commingle together with fraternal greetings." Those principles, stressing racial and religious tolerance, Jones insisted, bound members of the GUOOF to their English "brothers" ("who gave us our charter and honored us as men"), and distinguished their group from the all-Caucasian branch (the International Order of Odd Fellows, IOOF) in the United States.[64]

The GUOOF in John Bond's new country of residence had been founded three decades earlier as a result of the black American seaman Peter Ogden's affiliation with a supportive, multiracial lodge in Liverpool where John had grown up.[65] Worcester's lodge, indeed all of African American Odd Fellowship, celebrated its origins in that transoceanic brotherhood. Clear comparisons also could be drawn between the GUOOF's moral precepts and the unfulfilled democratic ideals to which black people so eagerly aspired. Such a telling (though ironic) message scarcely would have been lost on a man of John Bond's heritage. Grand Master Robert Jones exposed the exclusionary flaw—the pivotal contradiction—that marred the otherwise admirable, supposedly egalitarian creation and exercise of American democracy.

Activities of their political clubs, black Odd Fellows and Masons, the AMEZ church and the Bethel Society, were not the only endeavors that attracted and occupied Worcester's Negro residents. Every year at one of the city's largest auditoriums, the Colored Drum Corps presented a popular "winter evening entertainment," including music, dancing, and dramatic skits, featuring a reenactment of Norfolk's memorable battle at sea between the *Monitor* and the *Merrimac* (the CSS *Virginia*).[66]

And in 1872 (en route to a European tour during which they

sang for Queen Victoria and were feted by England's Liverpool-born prime minister, William Gladstone), the Fisk Jubilee Singers performed before throngs of Worcesterites. The group selected its songs to satisfy the expectations of the predominantly white audiences who supported their school. The *Evening Gazette*'s account emphasized the seemingly primitive culture that the black students introduced to Massachusetts. "The music of Southern negroes at their prayer meetings" typified those programs. For curious, often benevolent white New Englanders, that assemblage of young people who had been born in slavery performed what appeared to be "essentially the music of another race"—a lower and still-evolving one.[67]

Though they all may have welcomed these infrequent yet acclaimed presentations, there was common ground but also some distance between black people who had lived in New England for decades (even generations) and Worcester's newcomers, primarily southerners and former slaves who came to the city during the post–Civil War years. Though few people in either group had substantive financial assets, Worcester's better-established African Americans were more economically secure and generally had some formal education. By contrast, many recent arrivals like Emma Thomas Bond were understandably, almost predictably, illiterate. They also were suffused with manifestations of a vigorous creole culture, epitomized to some degree by the Jubilee Singers, that had survived slavery's worst outrages. A number of them were habituated and devoted to emotional forms and expressions of religiosity (evoking the African roots of their faith and practices) that many longtime Negro New Englanders, emulating their often undemonstrative yet disapproving white neighbors, viewed with suspicion and disdain.

Despite internal variants, even conflicts, among Worcester's black people, they all had to conduct themselves as members of a small, impotent minority community living in a society that frequently oppressed them. As Amos Webber cogently observed, it was "pretty rough & tuff; a bitter Pill to Swallow." In Norfolk, Virginia, despite the overt hostility of many white people, African Americans comprised a substantial portion of the city's population, but that was not the case in Worcester.[68]

Emma Thomas Bond was a newcomer, scarcely a decade removed from slavery, who lacked any formal education, yet her sunny disposition (warmer than that of the English, and rather aloof, John) could have endeared her to their Gouldingsville neighbors.[69] But in many ways, her life during those years must have seemed quite isolated. She was far from her old church, family, and companions in Isle of Wight and Norfolk Counties. In the rundown neighborhood where she resided with Percy, Emma could not see her hardworking husband for days at a time. Opportunities in the North were presumed to be better for black people and the South's menacing bitterness had been left behind, but the friendly, darker faces that always had surrounded her were far fewer. And for both Emma and John, landlocked and often malodorous Worcester lacked the Atlantic's ameliorating, briny offshore breezes and fragrance they had known throughout their lives, which could help to dispel the repugnance of even the dingiest surroundings.

Yet the Bonds muddled through several years there. In April 1871, Father Nugent, a prison chaplain from Liverpool, England, came to speak at a public forum about his hometown's overwhelming woes. He lamented the prevalence of unruly ragamuffins whom he called "nobody's children." "In 1868," Nugent asserted, "48,782 children in Liverpool between the ages of five and fifteen . . . attended no school, and 25,000 of the number were the street Arabs of that city." Without relief, he predicted, only anguish and delinquency awaited those hordes of unsupervised, uneducated, homeless youths. Nugent pleaded with New Englanders to sponsor some of those "starving boys and girls" and help them immigrate. Such piteous descriptions hardly could have failed to recall for John Bond dismal aspects of his own childhood and remind him of the often obscured blessings of his (and his son's) current life.[70]

Then in late 1873, an itinerant journalist named Edward Jenkins lectured Worcesterites about "The England of Today." He compared and contrasted John Bond's motherland with the United States. Jenkins praised what (with his finite perspective) he considered the two countries' "common race, their common language, their common literature," but also argued that local government in England, unlike Massachusetts, was "the very motley of Bumbledum." "Ignorance and knavery," he intoned, "had a peculiar tendency to crystalize in its institutions." He cautioned his audience about the outrages that could be perpetuated by a state-sponsored church, specifically the queen's established Anglican Church.[71] Jenkins's overblown and biased account graphically (almost frighteningly) illuminated the flaws that to some degree characterized the island nation that John Bond voluntarily had left behind more than a decade before.

On April 5 the following spring, Worcester's All Saints' Episcopal Church celebrated Christ's resurrection with choral renditions of the traditional *Te Deum* and *Jubilate* to pealing bells and the resonant accompaniment of the mighty organ. Verdant foliage and "crosses, wreaths and bouquets" of white lilies and roses blanketed the pulpit, nave, and arches that joyous Easter Sunday. But only two nights later, nearby residents smelled smoke, then spotted the first threatening licks of flame. Fire wagons hurtled through the dark to Pearl Street. "Portions of the roof were falling into the center of the floor," reported the *Evening Gazette,* "and the hiss of the water, the crashing of hooks and axes, and the shouts of the firemen outside made the whole effect terrific in the extreme." "Tongues of fire [issued] from the circle where the illuminated window had been over the door," the account continued. "An immense crowd," possibly including the faithful Anglican-Episcopalian parishioner John Robert Bond who worked nearby at the Bay State House, "collected about the burning building" and remained throughout the night, but the old wooden church could not be saved and only a few bronze organ pipes survived the unholy conflagration.[72]

The 1873 depression had battered Worcester much as it did the rest of the country. Financial scandals rocked the nation and banking institutions that had made rash investments during the postwar boom collapsed. Several years earlier, the Bonds' friend Isaac Mullen had protested the discriminatory hiring practices at the Freedmen's Savings & Trust Company branch in Norfolk, and that national bank, which held the life savings of many of Emma's relatives and friends in Virginia, also "went down in the maelstrom of national corruption."[73] The fire at his church may have seemed a sinister portent to John as well, because in 1874 he and Emma determined that Worcester should no longer be their home.

During his stint in the Union navy, and after, John Bond encountered and befriended many black men who had fought for their flag. He was proud of his own participation in the recent war, and had begun to think of his still relatively new, flawed, but remarkable country of residence as his own. And a recently incorporated township that carried enormous symbolic significance for Negro Civil War veterans was Hyde Park, Massachusetts, because it was the site of the Readville sector's Camp Mcigs, where the country's most renowned black army units had trained.

Lieutenant James M. Trotter, a "colored" officer with the Fifty-fifth Massachusetts who had been stationed there in 1863, returned to live in Hyde Park. And Readville bordered on Dedham, where William Gould, briefly John Bond's shipmate aboard the USS *Ohio*, resided and worked as a stonemason. Hyde Park also was home to the renowned white abolitionists Theodore and Angelina Grimké Weld. As members of Massachusetts's network of social reformers, the Welds and Worcester's Chase sisters were longtime friends.[74] Hyde Park (its name celebrating the spirit of the London landmark and epitomizing the common Anglo-American traditions of free speech), its Readville enclave, and adjoining Dedham stretched along Boston's southwest city line. And that noblest of New England ports may have recalled for the Bonds John's Liverpool and Emma's Norfolk.

Four years after they had arrived in Worcester, John, Emma, and six-year-old Percy bid farewell to colleagues at the Bay State House, Episcopal coparishioners, and neighbors and friends in hazardous South Worcester where Emma had borne, then lost a newborn child. They put that unsatisfactory interlude behind, boarded the Boston & Albany Railroad (day and night the sooty trains had clattered by within earshot of the Bonds' shabby residence), and headed east to establish new lives in Hyde Park.

8

CITIZENSHIP, FRATERNITY,
and a DUTIFUL SON

And if a stranger sojourn with thee in
your land, ye shall not vex him. But
the stranger that dwelleth with you
shall be unto you as one born among you,
and thou shalt love him as thyself.

Leviticus 19:33–34

FIVE YEARS BEFORE the Civil War, a band of hardy Yankees, seeking more elbow room for their families in congested coastal Massachusetts, had come across a surprisingly undeveloped tract of land just nine miles south and west of central Boston. They negotiated its purchase, surveyed, constructed houses, launched their settlement, and then in 1868 incorporated the town they named for London's Hyde Park. Unlike most nearby communities that traced their origins back to the seventeenth and eighteenth centuries, it was carved from Dorchester, Dedham, and Milton's sparsely populated corners occupied by only a few preexisting homes, farms, and mills. But new residents came quickly, and when John and Emma Bond arrived six years later with their son Percy to put down roots in the working-class neighborhood called Readville, Hyde Park's population had reached six thousand.

Among that number were other Negro veterans of the Civil War, lured there by personal memories and the enduring legends of wartime Readville. A decade earlier, Readville's Camp Meigs had reverberated with bugle calls, drumrolls, and the cadenced thunder of pounding feet, as black men trained in segregated companies, but at the same cantonment as whites as they all prepared to join the struggle to end slavery and save the Union. Ironically, the acreage that served as the North's foremost encampment for Negro soldiers once had belonged to the Sprague family, who were the last people in the entire state of Massachusetts to emancipate their slaves.[1]

Thanks, perhaps, to an unschooled, unlicensed, but capable medical practitioner named Mehitable Sunderland, who, unlike many reluctant whites, would lease or sometimes sell her properties to black people, the Bonds found a residence in Readville. Because of its history as the home of Massachusetts's black Civil War regiments plus the gathering of African Americans who settled there during Reconstruction, a number of Hyde Park's white residents called that modest enclave "Nigger Village."[2]

In 1874, the Bonds moved into a small, two-story frame house with an increasingly fruitful waterside garden beside a narrow dirt road (laid out as early as 1661) somewhat grandly named River Street. Major excavations soon widened it to fifty feet, yet it remained unpaved, badly rutted, and without streetlights, which generated great dismay because of the frequent nighttime carriage accidents.[3]

In John and Emma's neighborhood, their "river" was really Mother Brook, the country's oldest industrial canal, constructed in 1639. It connected the famed Charles River, which coursed to the north past Harvard University, with the lesser—and lesser-known—Neponset River. Those canal-linked waterways flowed eastward into Massachusetts Bay and literally enisled the city of Boston.

Just behind the Bonds' home, Mother Brook broadened into an appealing but sometimes treacherous millpond edged by cattailed marshes with locks and churning falls nearby. Fish, frogs, and raucous waterfowl populated Mother Brook as it dropped more than fifty feet in three-and-a-half miles. The canal and river also attracted substantial aquatic traffic, including "the scull, the wherry, the flat-bottom, and the birch canoe," known as "the navy of the Neponset."[4] The Bonds hammered together a small wooden pier in the shallows at the back of their garden, enjoyed the water's prox-

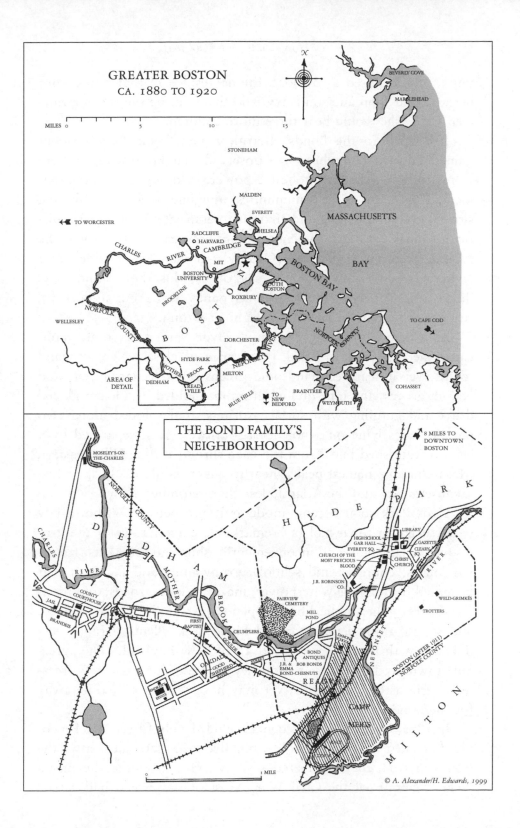

GREATER BOSTON
CA. 1880 TO 1920

MILES 0   5   10   15

BEVERLY COVE

MARBLEHEAD

STONEHAM

MALDEN

EVERETT

MASSACHUSETTS

CHELSEA

RADCLIFFE
HARVARD
CAMBRIDGE
MIT

TO WORCESTER

CHARLES   RIVER

BOSTON
UNIVERSITY

BOSTON BAY

BAY

BROOKLINE

SOUTH
BOSTON

ROXBURY

NORFOLK   COUNTY

TO CAPE COD

NORFOLK COUNTY

WELLESLEY

B O S T O N

DORCHESTER

DEDHAM

NEPONSET   RIVER

AREA OF
DETAIL

HYDE PARK

MOTHER
BROOK

MILTON

TREAD
VILLE

BLUE HILLS

BRAINTREE

COHASSET

TO
NEW
BEDFORD

WEYMOUTH

THE BOND FAMILY'S
NEIGHBORHOOD

8 MILES TO
DOWNTOWN
BOSTON

MOSELEY'S-ON
THE-CHARLES

NORFOLK   COUNTY

H Y D E

P A R K

D

E

D

H

A

M

LIBRARY

HIGH SCHOOL
GAR HALL
EVERETT SQ.

GAZETTE

CHARLES

RIVER

CHURCH OF THE
MOST PRECIOUS
BLOOD

CHRIST
CHURCH

CLEARY
SQ.

MOTHER

J.R. ROBINSON
CO.

RIVER

COUNTY
COURTHOUSE

B

R

O

O

K

WELD-GRIMKÉS

JAIL

BRANDEIS

FAIRVIEW
CEMETERY

MILL
POND

TROTTERS

FIRST
BAPTIST

CRUMPLERS

BOND
ANTIQUES

NEPONSET

BOSTON (AFTER 1911)
NORFOLK COUNTY

AVONDALE

GOOD
SHEPHERD

J.R. &
EMMA
BOND-CHESNUTS

BOB BONDS

R E A D

M I L T O N

CAMP
MEIGS

0   1 MILE

© A. Alexander/H. Edwards, 1999

imity, and acquired a rowboat. Emma resided in that house with her husband John and son Percy, and there during the ensuing thirteen years, she would bear three more children.

Just prior to the Bonds' arrival, a new Hyde Park resident named Edward Humphrey had observed that his town's "society seems to have very little cohesive power, made up as it is of fragments from many older communities, mingling freely, but adhering slowly, everyone willing and anxious to associate, yet finding it difficult to make new attachments." Humphrey argued that it was the "spunkiest town in Norfolk [County's] domain" and added that "whatever out-of-towners may say of us, this they cannot say: 'lukewarm'. . . . No halfway, hanky-panky style, but a positive, straight-out advocacy of what is right or wrong."[5]

As a new community, "spunky" Hyde Park never quite replicated the prim, self-satisfied appearance of classic New England towns, yet it featured handsome greenswards, cedar, birch, and walnut groves, and pine-quilted drumlins molded by ancient glacial drifts and gurgling with surface springs. It developed along two parallel vales lying on a northeast-southwest axis, separated by a central watershed line. From the haze-shrouded Blue Hills (eastern Massachusetts' highest peaks) nearby, hikers could easily spy Massachusetts Bay and the Atlantic less than ten miles away.

Hyde Park soon became moderately prosperous. Within a few years, it had a town hall (a "remarkable combination of the grotesque, ornamental, and inconvenient"), shops and markets, fraternal lodges, churches and schools, grimy mills and factories that benefited from ample waterpower, mazes of lanes, roads, and modest squares. The public library opened just as the Bonds arrived, and several train depots serviced Hyde Park. Plentiful rail access linked it with Boston proper and all of New England.[6] The agreeable town lay just an hour's journey by train due east of Worcester's perilous Gouldingsville, yet may have seemed a lifetime away for the Bonds.

In 1870, Hyde Park's residents included only fifteen black people domiciled in six households, but five years later, just after the Bonds arrived, they numbered seventy-eight, including the proud Negro veterans of the Civil War. Most of those men had served with the units that had trained at Readville, but like Bond, one other black man had been a sailor. Cornelius Weeden, a corporal from the Fifty-fourth Massachusetts Infantry who sprang from a family of Boston abolitionists, and the Canadian-born Robert Jackson became John Bond's neighbors and special friends.[7] Another local veteran was James M. Trotter, a writer, musician, realtor, and onetime lieutenant with the Fifty-fifth, who worked as a post office supervisor in Boston—a significant position for a man of his race. Some Euro-American detractors, however, scornful of the Mississippi-born Trotter's adopted Massachusetts identity, disparaged him, and by extension any African American in the Boston area ("home of the bean and the cod") as a "bean-eating nigger." People such as Trotter never could become what some called "birthright New Englanders."[8] Many foreign- and native-born white men who had fought for the Union also dwelt in Hyde Park, as did Theodore and Angelina Weld and their mulatto kin. Angelina's sister, Sarah Grimké, had passed away in 1873.

Three decades earlier, following his wife's death, Angelina and Sarah Grimké's brother Henry (unbeknownst to his abolitionist and feminist siblings who had relocated to New England) had fathered several sons by a slave woman on the Grimké family's South Carolina plantation. Henry Grimké himself died in the early 1850s without emancipating his children, but Archibald and Francis, two of the boys in that "shadow family," attracted their previously unknown aunts' attention when their names appeared as top scholars at Lincoln University, a Pennsylvania school for Negroes. The white and tan branches of the family corresponded, and the Grimké sisters and Theodore Weld soon incorporated the "colored" youngsters into their household and vowed to support their continuing education. Francis became a minister, while Archie went to Harvard Law School and for years thereafter usually made Hyde Park his home.[9]

Since decades before the Civil War, the educator Theodore Dwight Weld had been a respected, feisty, and sometimes maligned reformer, and he had moved to the embryonic town in 1864, where he continued his iconoclastic ways. In March 1870, a group of women, encouraged by Theodore and led by his wife and sister-in-law (the radical Grimké sisters), plus the "doctress" Mehitable Sunderland, had tramped through a blizzard to a Hyde Park town meeting where the women had cast unauthorized ballots. The Fifteenth Amendment, supposedly guaranteeing the franchise to Negro men, but no women, recently had been ratified, and the suffragists' motivation and tactics that day of rebellion greatly resembled the actions of Norfolk, Virginia's disfranchised black men in 1865. By law, local officials, who did not deter or arrest the protesters, could not tally those votes, but theirs was the first such woman suffrage demonstration anywhere in the United States.[10]

Such brooding political unrest, however, did not disrupt the effective functioning of local government. During John Bond's earliest years of residence, Hyde Park's Overseers of the Poor provided the wounded, immigrant veteran—and more than a hundred others—with a few dollars in emergency welfare funds.[11] But despite John's disabled arm, he always worked, albeit at menial jobs, and the family's economically dependent status was short lived.

Among the Bonds' other neighbors, William Gould—briefly John's shipmate on the *Ohio*—had settled with his growing family in adjoining East Dedham. As a mason, he helped to construct a number of his town's buildings and soon became a member of the working-class Episcopal Church of the Good Shepherd (its dark, half-timbered bulk bespeaking solid Christian rectitude), located in an area called Oakdale Village near the Dedham–Hyde Park town line. Good Shepherd was closer to Readville than Hyde Park's Episcopal church, requiring only a half-mile walk up the River Street hill, and in keeping with John's Anglican resolve, faith, and upbringing, he and his family joined that parish in 1875.[12]

For the most part, John, Emma, and Percy Bond's lives during their early period in Hyde Park seem to have been uneventful, but that same year a highly touted concert presented by the "Hampton Colored Students," the county's *Gazette* newspaper reported, drew the largest audience in the town's brief history. Among the local residents, James M. Trotter almost certainly went, since he was researching a book that he would title *Music and Some Highly Musical People*. It extolled the talents of men and women of his race, and performers such as the Hampton singers inspired and delighted him.[13] The Bonds also may have wanted to hear them, since Hampton Institute, the famous new school for Negroes, lay just across the James River from Isle of Wight County, Virginia, and equally near Norfolk, the couple's former home.

Hyde Park's predominantly Anglo-American concertgoers relished the group's "primitive" spirituals, exquisite voices, and passionate renditions, but the conspicuous appearance among the black choristers of a lanky "white" youth named Warren Logan, who sang with and managed the otherwise dark-complexioned ensemble, may have puzzled them. Such difficult-to-categorize people of color challenged the stereotypical images of Negroes retained by the majority, and also evoked and personified the disconcerting specter of miscegenation. His comrades in song, however, gleefully caroled: "Sound the slogan / Wake up Logan / With his merry band / To delight our land."[14] They knew him as an enthusiastic young "colored" man who became an integral part of their musical fund-raising endeavors. One of Warren Logan's closest friends, an ambitious fellow named Booker Taliaferro Washington, graduated from Hampton Institute the same spring that its traveling chorus enthralled Hyde Park's residents.

During that period, John submitted to repeated medical examinations (his residual infirmity confirmed by Cornelius Weeden, his friend, neighbor, and fellow Negro veteran) as he attempted to convince the U.S. Navy to increase his pension.[15] John's initial failure in those well-justified efforts during the mid-to-late 1870s may have made him think further about seeking to join the Grand Army of the Republic (GAR), which was noted for its successful arm-twisting efforts on behalf of members who sought to secure or ameliorate their government compensation.

After years of observing and evaluating the GAR's influence in Worcester and then in Hyde Park, John finally became a member in 1879.[16] His new hometown's GAR Post 121 had been organized in 1870. The next year, Massachusetts in its entirety boasted the largest membership of any state in the country, yet by 1878 the numbers had dwindled almost by half. After that, however, vigorous recruiting efforts and veterans' increasing desires to commemorate their common experience, combined with an awareness of the organization's political clout, expanded the membership considerably. A decade later, Massachusetts had been restored to its former position among the leading states in the ranks of Grand Army participation, with 191 posts and more than twenty thousand members.[17] Among the Negro veterans known to John Bond who became involved with the Massachusetts GAR were Worcester's Amos Webber, Hyde Park's Cornelius Weeden and James Trotter, Dedham's William Gould, and in Boston, Archie Grimké's law associate James Wolff, plus John's old friend from Norfolk, Isaac Mullen—the last three men all former sailors.

Also in 1879, many of John and Emma Bond's neighbors crowded in to see, hear, and greet " 'Uncle Tom' at the Congregational Church." He was the ninety-year-old black man who had served as the model for the cabin-dwelling protagonist of Harriet Beecher Stowe's momentous antebellum novel that epitomized the ignominy of slavery but concurrently reinforced many stereotypical and demeaning images of Negroes. Hyde Park residents flocked to that event because of their residual abolitionist sympathies, and also because the popular antislavery opus, *Slavery As It Is,* compiled more than a quarter century before by the town's venerable icon, Theodore Weld, had provided much of the background for *Uncle Tom's Cabin.*[18]

Those years also became notable ones for the (all-white) pennant-winning Boston Red Stockings baseball team. The team's recent excursion to Liverpool had failed to convert the British to the quintessential American sport, but its stateside successes transfixed the entire Boston region. Tommy Bond, the Red Stockings' Irish-born star pitcher, with his trademark underhand cannonballs and parabolic sidearm curves, became a popular celebrity as he flummoxed opposing batters and from 1877 to 1879 achieved a never-to-be-equaled record of three consecutive seasons with forty or more victories. That revered athlete shared John Bond's surname and similarly had an Irish mother, but surely claimed no "demeaning" African paternity.[19]

By 1880, 144 Negroes (including the Bonds, Weedens, Grimkés, and Trotters) had settled into 37 residences in Hyde Park, with a number living right in Readville. Many, including 28 former Virginians, were southern born, 20 others were New Englanders by birth, while 10 (John Bond's friend Robert Jackson among them) hailed from Canada and half a dozen from the West Indies. Twenty-three of the women worked as domestic servants, several were seamstresses, but even more, like Emma Bond, emulated the patterns aspired to in middle-class white families and considered "keeping house" their primary occupation. Six of the men owned or worked in barbershops, with the same number in some manner tending to horses. There also was a picture frame gilder, while others had become masons, machinists, grocery clerks, carpenters, or—like John Bond—common laborers.[20]

Still, African Americans remained a tiny minority in the town. Old-time Yankees predominated, and in its earliest years, a majority of the recently arrived aliens were, like Bond, British-born Protestants. But increasingly, the newcomers were Catholics (Irish, Germans, and then Italians), who in 1885 would indelibly stamp the community with their presence, contributing time, brawn, faith, and pennies to complete its most dominating edifice, the Church of the Most Precious Blood.

The Bonds' economic situation had noticeably improved by 1880. John aquired a steady job as janitor at the nearby Damon Grammar School. He earned $150 per month for his day work, an additional $30 for cleaning up after night school sessions, and received $20 more in newly increased disability payments from the navy. By the following year, the Bonds (only recently welfare recipients) had become self-supporting taxpayers. Their contributions to the town's coffers grew consistently thereafter, and in 1889 their property—the small house on a quarter-acre lot alongside Mother Brook—was valued at $1,100.[21]

Hyde Park's Archibald Grimké practiced law for a while with his Harvard classmate (and Civil War sailor) James Wolff. Archie had also married a white woman, despite her family's opposition, and in 1880 the couple had a child, whom they named—to honor her recently deceased great-aunt—Angelina Weld Grimké. Archie and his wife soon separated; the mother spirited Angelina away, but decided after several years that she was incapable of raising her "colored" daughter in a racist world. She returned the girl to Archie and to the care of the widowed Theodore Weld.[22]

From 1883 until 1885, Archie Grimké edited and published *The Hub,* a newspaper for New Englanders (especially, but not exclusively, Negroes), dedicated "to elevate their citizenship . . . [and] contend for equal rights and exact justice to all, regardless of race and sex." But by that time, he was spending much of his time in Boston proper, so his daughter passed most of her childhood living and àttending school in Hyde Park under her grand-uncle Theodore's guardianship and tutelage.[23]

John Bond increasingly immersed himself in local GAR activities. For some time, that organization had petitioned the state government to have May 30 designated as an official (instead of just an ad hoc) holiday, "set apart for the decoration of graves of deceased soldiers and sailors." Those efforts had borne fruit in 1881, and John joined post members and other Hyde Park residents who celebrated the event.[24] "The grandest result of the war," the GAR's speaker proclaimed to an audience that probably included Emma Thomas Bond and a handful of other former slaves, "was the wiping out of American slavery." The GAR also organized and led annual Fourth of July celebrations climaxed by cycling displays, bonfires, fireworks, and parades down River Street, where local residents (the Bonds among them) "decorated with flags and bunting . . . many houses along [the] line of march." On many occasions, the local newspaper observed that "meetings of the Post are fully attended, and a lively interest is taken by the members."[25] Despite his foreign birth, immigrant status, and brown skin, John Robert Bond's involvement with the GAR wove him securely into the fabric of Hyde Park life, and stamped him with a worthy identity as a patriot and respected member of his town's most significant civic organization.

The membership of Timothy Ingraham GAR Post 121 peaked at over three hundred, but (from choice or possibly selective blackballs, as had been the case with Worcester's Bassill Barker), only four of the town's fifteen Negro veterans belonged. Foreign birth, however, was not an impediment to membership. By 1890, the post included forty non-American-born members, but except for John Robert Bond, all were white. Twenty-nine men had been sailors, one of whom, like Bond, even served on the USS *Ohio*.[26]

In its entirety and all its parts, the GAR dedicated itself to creating a crystalline vision that depicted the Civil War as the defining event in the country's history. Men who had fought together envisioned and portrayed themselves as noble saviors of the Union. Evolving GAR ideology claimed that during the war, the country's soldiers and sailors had participated in a cosmic phenomenon, imbued with a moral import that transcended individual experience. The Civil War had provided, and the GAR reinforced, the personal and collective bonds of a lifetime.[27]

The GAR established a female auxiliary, and in the Boston area wives or widows of several black soldiers and sailors participated, even gaining leadership roles in the Women's Relief Corps (WRC). Susie King Taylor had been a teacher and nurse (or, according to the accounts of white men, a "regimental laundress") during the Civil War, serving near the front lines and endangering her own life. She was also the widow of a Negro soldier. Taylor worked with the GAR's adjunct WRC and became an officer in a Boston post. She qualified, however, not due to her own valor and patriotism, but because of her brief marriage to a onetime sergeant with a black infantry unit who had died in the service of his country. Mercy Wolff was another WRC member, and her persistent prodding finally convinced her husband, Archie Grimké's law associate James Wolff, that he should become more active in the GAR's virtually all-white Brighton post.[28] No records, however, indicate whether Emma Bond, Virginia Trotter, or the other wives of Hyde Park's few "colored" GAR members similarly took part in WRC activities.

For the rest of his life, John Bond dedicated himself to the GAR and its patriotic endeavors, but he needed, above all, to earn a living and support his growing family. Worcester's GAR had lobbied for and won preferential hiring advantages for veterans who had put their lives on the line to defend the Union, and Hyde Park's Post 121 may have helped to obtain similar positions for loyal members like John Bond.

The Damon School, where he found long-term employment, was situated just a few blocks from his Readville home. In addition to his work, John also could have taken advantage of the school's new adult education programs that addressed the needs of a town replete with non-English-speaking immigrants who wanted to become American citizens. During the day, John and Emma's children, along with more than two hundred others, the vast majority of them white, would attend the Damon Grammar School. At night (when he was in his late thirties), John probably studied the U.S. Constitution, and—at Damon or elsewhere—he certainly learned to read and write.[29]

By that time, he had long since forsworn any residual loyalty to Britain. In 1884 (bolstered by his recent education and sponsored by Hobart Cable, a civic leader in Hyde Park, and Joseph Burton from neighboring Milton, both of whom were upstanding white citizens who vowed that John was "a man of good moral character, attached to the principles of the Constitution"), John Robert Bond applied to become an American citizen. His naturalization, however, was almost uniquely saddled with a complex history.[30]

More than a century earlier, a radical new vision had redefined the world's traditional concepts of governance and citizenship. North America's eighteenth-century patriots or their forebears had traversed the Atlantic to settle an unknown continent, but following their revolutionary break from Britain, those new "Americans" needed to establish new national identities to define their entry into the body politic. Neither religion (the Founding Fathers preferred Protestantism, but constitutionally separated church from state) nor class, they soon decided, would deny, restrict, or guarantee citizenship in the United States.[31] The predominantly English settlers also brought women with them, who became wives, mothers, and workers, but never full-fledged citizens, as their civic rights and privileges continued to be derived mainly from fathers or spouses.[32]

Those English Americans also contended that the indigenous people whom they encountered had not served as competent guardians of the splendid lands, and had impeded the inevitable and appropriate progress of civilization. So they forced the "savages" westward and gradually isolated them in remote tribal reserves.

They considered them pagans, undeserving of citizenship in a nation suitably being molded by white Christians.

Most Native Americans also refused to work for the interlopers, yet the vast expanses seemed to require more laborers than voluntary settlers would supply, or could be culled from among the criminals or debtors out of Scotland, England, and Ireland. Africa, however, seemed ripe to provide unlimited numbers of workers, so white sea captains crossed the Atlantic on slave ships crowded with black captives destined to fill the Western Hemisphere's labor vacuums. From the early 1600s onward, physiognomy, and then laws that confirmed their rarely excepted condition of bondage, differentiated and separated those bondsmen and their North American descendants both from the Indians and from the destitute white indentured servants who acquired their untethered freedom after a few years. Here, no Caucasians (untarnished even by the faintest stroke of a tarbrush) ever were enslaved.

Chattel slavery flourished in the South, and also for almost two centuries maintained a secure hold in the North, where seafaring entrepreneurs profited from their participation in the transatlantic slave trade. Most members of the majority race—even in New England where the Revolution's supposedly egalitarian precepts claimed their most devoted following—did not contest the widespread belief that bondage was the appropriate status for the dark, "barbaric" Africans and their New World descendants.

When the new country's legislators enacted the Naturalization Act of 1790, only three years after creating their remarkable Constitution, it reflected the overall temper and conditions of the times and allowed only "free white men" to become citizens. The era's liberationist rhetoric proclaimed that "all men are created equal," but the phrase did not connote "mankind" or "men and women." The law excluded Native Americans, Negroes (enslaved or not), even the smattering of Asians—and women. Those who could become citizens and receive the new country's full benefits and protections would have to be free, *and* white, *and* male. Some years later, a perceptive American visionary, born in bondage, who cast aside a slave name and identity to reinvent herself as Sojourner Truth, reportedly observed: "I hears talkin' 'bout de Constitution and de rights of man. I come up and takes holt of dis Constitution. It looks mighty big, and I feels for my rights, but dere ain't any."[33]

In the decades following the American Revolution, the New England states (plus most in the Mid-Atlantic and parts of the new western territories) abolished slavery. Debates arose over prerequisites for naturalized citizenship as several congressmen introduced proposals to define which rights and privileges might ensue at what particular point in time. One abolitionist charged that no slave owner was worthy of being a citizen, while another idealist proposed renouncing his own citizenship to protest the country's tolerance of slavery and maltreatment of its indigenous people. But for eight decades, nothing substantively altered the stringent provisions that limited naturalization to "free white men." The Supreme Court reinforced the status quo by ruling in its 1857 *Dred Scott v. Sandford* decision that Negroes had no rights as citizens that white men were bound to honor, and denied even nonenslaved, native-born black men the prerogative of claiming that privilege.[34]

During the Civil War, an emergency provision determined that after only two (instead of five) years' residency, foreigners who served in the Union military and received honorable discharges could apply for citizenship. That provided an enticement for them to join the army or navy, yet assumed that such men would be white Europeans.[35] And most, but far from all of them, were. It did not apply to the West Indians, Africans, and black Canadians who fought as bravely as any Irish, Germans, or Frenchmen, or to a Negro English sailor like John Bond.

Only amid Reconstruction's fleeting, egalitarian spirit did legislators substantively amend the existing statutes. An 1870 rider to the original Naturalization Act excluded "aliens of African nativity and . . . persons of African descent" from the Caucasians-only stipulation. But it did not remove the restrictions with respect to women, Native Americans, or the Asians who were providing so much of the labor associated with building transcontinental railroads through the West. The nativist anathema toward those hardworking immigrants reached full flower in the 1882 Chinese Exclusion Act.[36]

Voluntary black immigration remained minimal even after slavery's abolition. In 1870, the United States' foreign-born "colored" population, "exclusive of Chinese, Japanese, and civilized Indians," stood at less than ten thousand—and most of those people were elderly former slaves. The number of non-native-born Negroes increased to about fourteen thousand by the next census, but this group still comprised under two percent of the nation's immigrants. Of the new arrivals, twenty-eight percent came from Canada, twenty-one percent from the African continent, sixteen percent from the Caribbean, with the remainder from Portugal, Spain, and Mexico. Men like John Bond who had immigrated from the British Isles were so few that they were not even statistically identifiable. The prevalent stereotypes of Negroes as debased people, perceived to be lacking roots, culture, or history, seemed to exclude them totally from the traditional American idea and image of "real" immigrants.[37]

Despite the revisionary 1870 legislation pertaining to Negroes, John Bond, for reasons lost in time, did not apply for United States citizenship until 1884. That delay, however, probably had little effect on his or his family's daily lives (rights and privileges provided by state and local jurisdictions often were more pertinent and significant than those granted by the federal government), and the town of Hyde Park did not discriminate against the hardworking, brown-skinned Civil War pensioner because he was not yet an American citizen. Union veterans, especially GAR members, were highly respected, and many other Hyde Park residents similarly were foreign born.

John Bond finally made his citizenship application twenty-two years after he had arrived in New Bedford from Liverpool, fourteen years after the country permitted men of African ancestry to be naturalized, and a decade after he, his wife, and their firstborn settled in Hyde Park. But the government form that would confirm his new status still prominently featured that demeaning, qualifying word: "white." John Stetson, a clerk at Boston's federal circuit court, who was clearly informed about the law's current status, dutifully scratched out "white" and substituted "colored." Stetson, however, must have been flabbergasted to find himself face-to-face with a rarely (if ever) seen Negro Englishman. Because he was

British born and raised, John, despite his biracial parentage and humble birth, had to swear on that noteworthy fall day that he never had "borne any hereditary title, or been of any of the orders of the nobility." He also unreservedly promised to "renounce and abjure all allegiance and fidelity to every foreign Prince, Potentate, State or Sovereignty whatsoever; and particularly to **Victoria,** Queen of the United Kingdom of Great Britain and Ireland."[38]

John, Emma, and their children would have celebrated his new citizenship in their sweet land of liberty. Concurrently, the U.S. Congress acted to make the country a complicit partner in a forcible division of the African continent, which relegated the massive mineral-rich territory that henceforth would be called the Belgian Congo to the control of King Leopold. That colonial scheme purportedly also would provide a place to which thousands of African Americans might be deported. It was the same year that the Italian sculptor Frédéric-Auguste Bartholdi, in concert with a French engineer named Eiffel, completed the statue of a regal, torch-bearing woman called Liberty, ultimately to be situated on an island overlooking the shipping channels in New York City's harbor. On July 4, 1884, its cornerstone was laid, and the people of France formally presented Miss Liberty as a gift to the people of the United States. She became the eternal symbol of welcome for millions of European and many other new immigrants.

Yet in many instances, even in Massachusetts, African Americans remained unwelcome in their country. Personal slights abounded, labor unions routinely excluded black men and thus limited their economic opportunities, and that summer Archibald Grimké's newspaper, *The Hub,* reported that "in certain portions of this city colored people cannot rent houses which are readily let to the Irish in no better circumstances." The month that John Bond became a citizen, it added: "The colored people of Cambridge have put on their war paint and feathers and are after the scalp of a skating rink manager who refuses to allow them to skate on account of color."[39]

Shortly after his naturalization, John Bond began paying a two-dollar poll tax. That made him, like more than six thousand other Negro men (Grimké, James M. Trotter, James Wolff, and others among them actively involved in politics), a Massachusetts voter.

Most European immigrants became Democrats, but black people (though not Grimké or Trotter) almost always voted Republican. In the Bay State, they eagerly exercised the franchise, and elected a few "colored" men to the legislature throughout the late nineteenth century.[40]

The Civil War's General Benjamin Butler occupied the Massachusetts governor's chair in 1884. He expediently had abandoned the Republicans, along with his commitments to black Americans, and joined the Democrats, who represented the state's new urban working-class electoral majority. That fall, the renegade Greenback Party selected Butler (who had no chance of winning) as its presidential candidate. Because of his Negro, rather than immigrant, identity, John Robert Bond almost certainly joined the party of Lincoln and became a James Blaine supporter that year when he first truly became eligible to cast a presidential ballot. But during that wretched campaign, with its scandalous charges that the Democratic candidate Grover Cleveland had fathered an illegitimate child, the newly labeled "Grand Old Party" deeply offended and subsequently mobilized many Catholic voters when it labeled Democrats the party of "Rum, Romanism, and Rebellion." The Mugwumps, a reformist contingent (the party of Hyde Park's Archibald Grimké, who unsuccessfully ran from his hometown for a seat in the Massachusetts legislature), also backed Cleveland, further splintering the GOP vote, and for the first time since 1856, the country elected a Democrat to the presidency.

Though he always voted, and served as a county juror, John Bond had little time to expend on politics, and he soon obtained improved employment. He served as a town constable and lamplighter, working from dusk until daybreak, igniting and then extinguishing Hyde Park's streetlamps, which first were fueled by volatile naphtha, then by gas. That work, however, ended around 1890, when Hyde Park fully "electrified" the illumination of its sidewalks, streets, and roads. Soon thereafter, John began laboring—again as a janitor—for his hometown's leading bank.[41]

Many black Civil War veterans like John Robert Bond joined the majority-white GAR (although a few, even in the North, established all-black posts), but most of them also maintained strong ties to former soldiers and sailors of their own race. In December 1884, a small group met in Washington, D.C., to formalize those relationships. The first recorded meeting of the Massachusetts Colored Veterans Assembly convened at Worcester's GAR Hall in late May 1886, coinciding with Decoration Day, which commemorated the country's *second* major war for liberty. James Trotter, plus a number of Boston area men, traveled to the city where John and Emma had lived during the early 1870s to attend that convocation with others of those "brave boys who for the first time stood face to face since twenty-[one] years ago." The gathering evoked vivid memories of valor, shared experience, sacrifice, and pain. "Tears trickled down the cheeks of the men," reported the Boston *Advocate,* a newspaper serving New England's Negro community. The veterans resolved to "form a permanent organization of all colored soldiers and sailors of this state."[42] John almost certainly became part of that group, in addition to the GAR.

During the century's final decades, John Bond still cherished the worthy but traumatic memories of his brief stint as an English-born Negro who had worn the blue uniform of the United States Navy. He worked hard for his family in a mostly white, yet mostly tolerant hometown, while Emma managed her household on River Street and their oldest child approached manhood.

Around the time that his father became a citizen, and after finishing Damon Grammar School plus two years at Hyde Park High School, Percy Bond and several other local young people began boarding the train at Readville's depot (forty-five trains per day shuttled commuters in and out of town) and traveling into central Boston to attend the Hub City's preeminent institute of accounting and business. Bryant & Stratton, "The Largest and Most Successful Commercial School in America," had been founded in 1860. With an enrollment of more than four hundred students, it vowed to "teach your boys that which they will practice when they become men." The meticulous J. Percy Bond quickly mastered accounting, bookkeeping, and stenography at Bryant & Stratton, and learned to use the school's ingenious new typewriting machines (manufactured by the Remington Company only within the last decade) with exceptional competency.[43]

In 1885, when the town's population passed 8,500, Hyde Park's largest commercial enterprises were Bleakie's woolen mills, Tileston & Hollingsworth paper makers, and American Tool & Machine. Prominent in its second tier were the J. T. Robinson paper-cutting machinery shop that employed forty men, and the Clifton Manufacturing Company (administered by one of the country's only female executives), which made rubberized "gossamers" (raincoats). Dowd's Sewing Machine Company, one of numerous smaller businesses, hired young Percy Bond as a clerk.[44] While Dowd's employed him, he may have bought his mother the sewing machine that became central to her life. Percy also served as a subscription agent for the "colored" Boston *Advocate,* and when he reached his majority in 1889, joined his father as a Hyde Park voter.[45]

A decade later, the country gleefully grasped at imperial power (an ambition that only a few years earlier had been largely limited to white southerners), and more sophisticated diversions than "Uncle Tom" and the Hampton singers entertained Hyde Park residents. The Waverly Opera House Minstrels, "one of the best of the burnt cork shows ever," performed regularly, and regaled local audiences with riotous numbers such as *Mammy's Little Pumpkin Colored Coon* and *Laugh You Little Niggers.*[46]

Although he was over thirty in 1900, Percy still lived at home with his parents. Hyde Park friends and relatives may have believed him to be a confirmed bachelor, but that was when he met the widowed Georgia Evangeline Fagain Stewart.[47] Georgia and her eleven-year-old daughter Caroline (called Carrie) boarded with Samuel Courtney, a distinguished physician and Boston school board member who was Harvard Medical School's second Negro graduate. Patients of the elegant, light-skinned Dr. Courtney included a substantial number of whites. He had privileges at several of Boston's best hospitals and resided on a block that included no other Negro households, yet he never denied or abandoned his racial heritage.[48]

Courtney also was one of the chief northern cohorts of the increasingly renowned Booker T. Washington. Washington first had taught Sam in their mutual hometown in West Virginia, steered the able youngster to Hampton Institute, then enlisted him for a brief tour of duty at Alabama's Tuskegee Institute, founded in 1881.[49]

Before the turn of the century, Courtney had become ensconced as a member of Boston's diligent Negro elite and, at his home during the summer of 1900, convened the first organizational session for the National Negro Business League (NNBL), which would become one of Booker T. Washington's most significant and enduring ventures. The ambitious, hardworking Percy Bond, who by that time had become an accountant and stenographer for the Boston & Maine Railroad (unusual and highly respected employment for a black man in Boston), joined that organization.[50]

Percy might have qualified for inclusion as a member of Boston's more privileged class of Negroes because of his education and (modest but nonetheless) white-collar job; manners, dress, and precise verbal syntax; affiliation with organizations like the NNBL; acquaintance with people such as the Courtneys, Grimkés, and Trotters; and probably his father's rare, yet well-perceived nativity and military service as well. His mother's former enslavement, her illiteracy and rural southern background, John's menial employment, the whole family's fairly recent arrival in the Boston area and absence of recognizably distinguished forebears, plus Percy's own dark skin, however, all could have presented barriers to whatever social aspirations he may have had.[51]

Longtime New England residency, nonenslaved ancestry, education, the assumption of civic responsibilities, appropriate church affiliations, decorum and dress, cultural achievements, pride in and contributions to the advancement of the race, and in some (but not all) instances light skin characterized Boston's Negro upper class around the turn of the century. Josephine Ruffin, a club woman, suffragist, and the widow of a Harvard Law School graduate who had served as Massachusetts' first black judge, was the circle's doyenne. In response to recent slurs demeaning the virtue of all Negro women, Ruffin became a prime mover in founding a reform network to help "uplift" her race and sex under the aegis of the National Association of Colored Women's Clubs. But she also was a respected rarity who had been accepted as a member by several local white women's clubs.[52]

Hyde Park's Trotters and Grimkés, Archie's law partner James Wolff, and the Courtneys were included in that "elite" group as well. They were well-educated and well-mannered, hardworking professionals, tradespeople, and community or church volunteers who vehemently maintained their right to participate in and maintain access to all of the area's events and facilities, race notwithstanding. They also planned and attended elegant, exclusive social events. Members of that circle engaged an orchestra of white musicians to play for one such party. "At the finish of the ball, which was a beautiful affair," reported an enthusiastic attendee, "the leader said he was amazed . . . he never knew there were such colored people." Boston's mayor, William Reed, observed: "I never saw such well-behaved, beautifully gowned women or such well-dressed men anywhere in all my life."[53]

Although that crowd's social arbiters routinely inquired about newcomers: "Who are her (or his) people?" a few outsiders, such as Atlanta University's affluent, creamy-complexioned elocutionist Adrienne Herndon (a serious student of drama who strategically concealed her full racial heritage when she circulated in the white world and performed in Boston), for one, possessed the proper credentials. And Georgia Stewart, another sojourning southerner who became acquainted with Herndon, Josephine Ruffin, and others among "colored" Boston's "better" set during this period, also might have qualified as at least a provisional member of that group as a result of her appearance, breeding and background, and links to the well-established Courtneys.[54]

Georgia, Sam Courtney's pretty southern-born boarder, a woman of grace and charm, immediately enchanted the stodgy bachelor Percy Bond, and his infatuation never waned. Her white male progenitors (whose relationships with her darker-skinned female antecedents can only be surmised) had bequeathed her their pale complexions, hazel eyes, and auburn hair. Only a telltale "frizzle" at the nape of the neck revealed her minimal African ancestry.[55] Intricate legal, social, and economic forces, however, conspired to reinforce the South's prevailing "one drop" standards. Despite her "white" appearance, both law and practice categorized Georgia Fagain Stewart as a Negro. She therefore would have been subject to all the indignities, inequities, and perils of growing up a "black" girl in Jim Crow Alabama, unless, like some others of similarly ambiguous appearance, she opted to abandon family and friends in order to pass surreptitiously into the Anglo-American community.

Because of the country's history of slavery and continuing racism, the white majority not only remained obsessed with race and color, but so thoroughly appropriated and manipulated the standards that evaluated and measured a woman's appeal that it became difficult for Negroes to attribute positive merit to the variant physical characteristics prevalent within their own community. White people, who retained virtually all power, plus economic and social advantages, reinforced a demeaning network of interwoven messages relating to aesthetic (as well as moral) values. Those messages maintained that the behavior of women who belonged to the dominant race and upper classes was "pure," "ladylike," and therefore desirable. Straight hair was "good," tightly curled hair was "bad," as if the sentient follicles themselves somehow incorporated genetic determinants of virtue or vice. Small features and pale skin were considered more attractive than any alternatives. The word "fair" itself connoted not only "light," but "pretty." Many American Negroes, especially, perhaps, those who were more upwardly mobile, deplored the patriarchal history of often enforced coitus between white men and black women that had generated numerous mulattoes, quadroons, and octoroons. Nonetheless, with few alternative positive images available, and recognizing the advantages that often accrued to the paler complexioned among them, a number of Negroes bought into Caucasian aesthetic standards. They often valued light-skinned women more than their darker sisters. Even if the world was not his oyster, Percy Bond believed that he had discovered a pearl beyond compare in Georgia Fagain Stewart.[56]

Georgia had been born around 1870, the second child of a sizable family in Montgomery, Alabama, where the Confederate flag, celebrating a venerated tradition of slavery and secession, flew boldly over the state capitol.[57] Her parents, James (a builder of modest success) and Caroline Fagain, were literate, and their nominal finances circumscribed their lives, but never their aspirations. Their second daughter, christened Georgia Evangeline (either James or Caroline may have been a devotee of the poet Henry Wadsworth Longfellow), read extensively, dabbled in writing, and played the piano. She mastered the art of engaging conversation, became adept at fashionable amusements, was proficient in crocheting—single and double chains, netting, rose and shell patterns—and embroidery, including quilted satin stitches and "lazy daisies" punctuated by tidy French knots.[58] On the other hand, Georgia acquired few basic (cooking, cleaning, laundering) household skills. Her parents apparently believed that their winsome daughter, with her unblemished Caucasian appearance, should be raised as much like a privileged white girl as possible.

Home training committed her to a traditional "one hundred strokes of the brush" every evening to burnish her exuberant reddish hair. She religiously smoothed her hands with glycerine, emoried her nails into perfect ovals, then buffed them to glowing pink shells with luminous half moons at the base. Meticulous grooming seemed essential, and the Fagains considered manners, carriage, diction, grammar and elocution, plus a well-modulated voice, central to a lady's persona.[59] But in contrast to the vast majority of Negro girls of her generation, domestic labor never intruded on the fair Miss Georgia Fagain's agenda.

In 1885, recognizing the import of formal education and anxious to maintain a tenuous hold on the family's somewhat shabby gentility, James and Caroline Fagain prepared to send their princess to Nashville's Fisk University. Her academic training in the capable hands of dedicated white northern teachers might at least insure that she would never have to become a laundress, cook, or maid in some white person's house, or worse, end up sharecropping or tenant farming—almost the only occupations available to uneducated Negro women. Benevolent white family members who sporadically acknowledged their "colored" kin, presented their pretty cousin Georgia with elegant, seldom-worn clothes (much as some slave owners once bestowed cast-off finery on favored household servants), and may have contributed to the expenses of her education as well.[60]

At Fisk—one of the very few "colored" institutions offering an academic program comparable to that of many northern "white" preparatory schools and colleges—most of Georgia's colleagues were Nashville residents. Others came from throughout Tennessee and the rest of the South, a smattering from the North and Midwest, even one from Africa. A dozen schoolmates hailed from Montgomery, as did a recent graduate named Venus Hardaway, who had returned to teach in her hometown and may have encouraged girls like Georgia to follow in her footsteps.[61]

Georgia Fagain entered Fisk's Common English Department (with its equivalent of a rigorous high school curriculum) at fifteen, but abandoned that discipline after a year. She remained at Fisk but transferred to a less challenging program. Many Americans, even in the pragmatic, education-starved, postemancipation Negro community, subscribed to traditional gender conventions defining the "proper" role of women in society, and agreed that more than serious book learning, even "colored" girls needed "finishing" to prepare them for courtship, marriage, and motherhood.

Fisk, however, had serious educational opportunities aplenty for girls and boys who wished to partake of them. A young man from western Massachusetts named Willie (William Edward Burghardt) Du Bois, who soon became one of his country's leading scholars and political activists, was a contemporary and acquaintance of Georgia at Fisk. Another was a resolute Mississippian, older by several years, named Margaret Murray. If she knew anything of Miss Murray's origins, however (Margaret was a washerwoman's illegitimate child who worked her way through school), Georgia Fagain might have considered her decidedly lower class. Despite such possible snobbery among some of her slightly more privileged schoolmates, when Margaret graduated in 1888, she so profoundly impressed one of Fisk's trustees, the man who had founded and become principal of Tuskegee Institute, that she negotiated a job for herself at his Alabama school. Within a few years, the intrepid Margaret Murray also would become the twice-widowed Booker T. Washington's third wife and a significant power at Tuskegee.

But if Willie Du Bois (who delighted in Fisk's "delicious girls—'colored' girls" as much as its academics), Margaret Murray, and many students were conscientious, Georgia was not. She was hardly a scholar, but had modest literary and artistic talents, and she slid gracefully into the Music Department—widely known due to the successes of the Jubilee Singers—where she studied piano and "voice culture."[62]

After three years, she abandoned her schooling entirely and slipped out of Fisk into the waiting arms of Moses Stewart, Jr. He was a handsome, dark-skinned Nashville youth with Cherokee and African antecedents, the fourth of Elizabeth and Moses Stewart, Sr.'s children. Both of his parents had grown up under slavery's yoke and had been denied any formal education, but they saw to it that their Reconstruction-era offspring all attended school.[63]

Georgia Fagain left Fisk in 1888 and married when she and Moses Stewart were only eighteen. He somehow managed to purchase a wide eighteen-karat gold band that he had inscribed "Moses to Georgia." In a year, the naive pair became the parents of a daughter whom they named (for Georgia's mother) Caroline Lucile and called Carrie. Carrie, a captivating yet oddly monochromatic sprite with beige skin, frizzly tan hair, and Georgia's tawny eyes, soon exhibited a probing curiosity about her world's myriad riddles. But the Stewarts' idyllic interlude as lovers and parents was short-lived. Moses worked as a bridge builder. He died in 1894, possibly as the result of a fall, leaving his only child and a grieving widow with few financial assets and little notion of how she might support herself and her daughter.[64]

Georgia, however, acquired considerable inner steel in those years. Soon after Moses' death, she wrote her sister Lilla on the occasion of her marriage, expressing hopes that Lilla would "appreciate even 'the widow's mite'" Georgia offered. "Live to be a true and noble woman," she advised, and "above all, be careful whom [you] confide in." The letter concluded with a cautionary poem:

> *What is friendship but a name,*
> *A charm that lulls to sleep;*
> *A shade that follows wealth and fame,*
> *And leaves the wretch to weep.*[65]

Georgia had been an indifferent student, but vowed that her fatherless child would have a good education, and Boston, she believed, was the place that offered African Americans the best schooling in the country. Before the turn of the century, for example, Maria Baldwin, a suffragist, teacher, and renowned disciplinarian, had become Massachusetts's first Negro principal. She headed the Agassiz Grammar School in Cambridge, where people such as Georgia Stewart from throughout the region endeavored to enroll their daughters and sons.[66] W. Monroe Trotter, son of Hyde Park's James M. Trotter, became the first Negro member of Phi Beta Kappa, and in 1895 Georgia's Fisk schoolmate W. E. B. Du Bois received the first doctorate awarded to a person of his race at Harvard University. That famous school was always a presence and an inspiration for blacks. Radcliffe—Harvard's bluestocking adjunct for women—the Massachusetts Institute of Technology, Boston University, and similar schools also admitted very limited numbers of "respectable" and gifted African Americans. Booker T. Washington's children (progeny of his first two wives) attended other nearby institutions.

As to Georgia's residence in Boston, she or family members in Montgomery, Alabama, surely knew, or knew of, Samuel Courtney through the nationwide, middle-class "colored" community's well-nurtured grapevine, and possibly from his earlier stint at nearby Tuskegee. So before the turn of the century, Georgia and young Carrie had come to board in Courtney's combined home and medical offices on a fashionable block of West Springfield Street.[67]

In 1900, the Courtneys' extended family-in-residence was sizable. It included Sam and his wife Lila, both of whom were thirty-four, and their three stair-step babies. Sam's mother, two brothers (who may have known Percy Bond through their common employment with the railroad), a niece, an office nurse, plus the lodgers, Georgia and Carrie Stewart, completed the household.[68]

Booker T. Washington often visited Sam Courtney during his travels to Boston. He had received an honorary degree from Harvard University in 1896, then participated in ceremonies dedicating a monument honoring Robert Gould Shaw and the Fifty-fourth Massachusetts Regiment the next year. He also took annual vacation trips to his cottage in nearby Weymouth, and made many fund-raising, speechmaking junkets as well. On such occasions, the very proper (but destitute) widow, Georgia Stewart, had opportunities to become acquainted with the country's most influential man of his race, who coincidentally had married her Fisk schoolmate, Margaret Murray. Washington greatly admired attractive women, and hardly would have been blind to Georgia's charms.

By early 1901, Georgia Stewart and her daughter had moved out of the Courtneys' household into a modest apartment on Shawmut Avenue, where she obtained employment of sorts. She became weekend guardian and landlady for Booker T. Washington's handsome but sometimes recalcitrant teenaged son Baker, who was a five-day boarder at a nearby preparatory school. Baker's half sister Portia, whom he often visited, studied at Wellesley College. Margaret Murray Washington also sojourned briefly at the Stewarts' flat, and on one such occasion Georgia wrote: "We are . . . pleased to have Mrs. Washington with us." Georgia's flurry of letters in spring 1901 suggests that a very friendly relationship developed between her and Booker Washington. One of her coy notes read, "If you will drop me a line on receiving this, I shall be pleased to call and see you." Another stated, "I write to know when you expect to be in Boston," and concluded with a semipetulant, "I sent you a letter several days ago, but have had no reply." Georgia closed her chatty missives with "Carrie sends love."[69]

The *Colored American,* a Boston-based magazine sponsored by Booker T. Washington (Georgia's brother James Fagain, Jr., served as one of its southern distributors and sales agents), published Georgia F. Stewart's egregious short story "The Wooing of Rev. Cummings" in 1901. She awkwardly employed a Negro dialect, emulating the genre often used by the noted poet Paul Laurence Dunbar, that magazine's prolific literary editor Pauline Hopkins, and its gifted contributor Charles W. Chesnutt—but Georgia totally lacked their artistry. What the *Colored American*'s willingness to publish her wretched tale and those cozy letters might imply is open to speculation, but certainly the official nature and content of Georgia's friendship with Booker T. Washington focused on young Baker.[70]

Georgia Stewart fed the willful boy, sent out his dirty laundry, had his boots resoled, oversaw his homework, dragged him to Boston's Trinity Church, and was remunerated for her expenses and ministrations by his famous father. Her vouchers included meticulous annotations for the cost of theater tickets, shoe repairs, room and board, utilities, and laundry. "Baker is well and seems to appreciate more and more the importance of improving his time while in Boston," Georgia wrote "Dear Mr. Washington" in April 1901, adding, "I shall visit him in school tomorrow."[71]

Georgia's income from that role in loco parentis for Baker Washington, however, scarcely covered her expenses, and she may have found herself yearning for her Alabama family and the South. Boston's once-rosy promise waned as employment at Tuskegee Institute (less than forty miles east of her kin in Montgomery) became an increasing necessity and a possibility due to her associations with the Washingtons. "I wish to talk with you in reference to your kind offer," Georgia wrote the school's principal in 1901, adding, "I should enjoy nothing more than to be associated with you and your work in Tuskegee." "Whatever your offer may be," she somewhat coquettishly concluded, "I should like to give the subject attention."[72] But either Booker T. Washington delayed a firm employment proposal, or the widow Stewart chose to remain a bit longer in the North, because it was autumn 1902 before she prepared to move back to Alabama.

That same spring, Washington had recruited the ambitious Roscoe Conkling Bruce, a new Harvard graduate, to come to Tuskegee as director of the institute's academic department, though Bruce temporarily would have to leave behind at Radcliffe College his fiancée Clara Burrill.[73] The Alabama school's reputation, combined with Washington's standing as the country's most powerful Negro (following the death of Frederick Douglass in 1895), attracted many such dedicated and well-educated African Americans to his oasis in Alabama. As an additional enticement, Roscoe's mother Josephine—widow of one of Reconstruction's foremost politicians, Mississippi's Senator Blanche K. Bruce—already had moved from the nation's capital to Tuskegee, where she served as the institute's lady principal.[74]

As part of his employment package, the precocious, well-connected Roscoe Bruce stressed to Washington his need for a capable administrative assistant. In Boston, he found just the man: the Bryant & Stratton–trained stenographer, accountant, and clerk-of-all-trades Percy Bond, whom he may have met at Dr. Courtney's home or through his friends the Glovers, who became one of Hyde Park's few Negro families.[75] For Percy, this must have seemed a fortuitous development. The love of his life had ties to the Booker T. Washingtons and wanted to return to Alabama. He recently had experienced a rift with his younger brother, and also, even in his middle thirties, as long as he walked in his father's shadow and dwelt in his parents' home, he was destined always to remain their child.

In 1902, residents of Percy's hometown chattered excitedly about the unprecedented visit to Readville by the fashionable "Miss Alice Roosevelt of Washington, D.C.," while sophisticated Negro Bostonians savored the critical and popular success of the new operetta *In Dahomey*, with its lyrics by Paul Laurence Dunbar and compelling music by Will Marion Cook.[76]

Roscoe Conkling Bruce moved to Alabama soon after his Harvard graduation, and several months later informed his betrothed, Clara Burrill, that he had "telegraphed Percy Bond a proposition to come to Tuskegee to be my clerk at $30 & room & board." Percy accepted that modest offer, to the obvious pleasure of Roscoe Bruce, who enthusiastically added: "I am glad that Percy is coming here. I can rely absolutely on his loyalty. You may be sure that I shall stand by him."[77]

Not only was Samuel Courtney one of Booker T. Washington's closest friends, but he also had become a key player in the highly political, increasingly powerful "Tuskegee Machine." Like Roscoe Bruce, Dr. Courtney would have vouched for Percy Bond's loyalty and respectability. Percy remained a devout Episcopalian who had solid professional training and credentials, and surely was courting Georgia Stewart with appropriate decorum. With Sam Courtney's blessing, and under Roscoe Bruce's aegis, in September 1902, Percy, along with Georgia Stewart and her daughter Carrie, set forth to establish new lives for themselves at the Wizard of Tuskegee's remote empire in the "Hither Isles" of sweltering, segregated Black Belt Alabama. They left behind in Massachusetts associates and neighbors such as the Courtneys, Trotters, and Grimkés, Percy's parents and younger sisters, plus his sometimes vexing, often unfathomable brother Bob, whose life had veered off in an altogether different direction.[78]

· 9 ·

WAKE *of the* LANCASTER:
LITTLE BROWN BROTHER
and the NAVY BLUES

I did not volunteer to . . . be called a brave kid; but because I thought
it my duty to defend the stars and stripes of my country, although it
may cost me my life. . . . If such sad misfortune should happen to me,
when I fall, I intend to draw my last breath for the old flag under
which I was born, which bears the colors, red, white and blue,
better known as "Old Glory."

PRIVATE SIMON BROWN, Twenty-third Kansas Infantry,
U.S. Volunteers, 1898

EMMA THOMAS BOND had been thirty years old with a pregnancy
rapidly coming to term the month that the United States observed
the hundredth anniversary of its separation from her husband's native land. Telegraph wires also hummed with chilling news of Captain George Custer's massacre in the Montana Territory at the
hands of angry Cheyenne and Sioux, but Hyde Park's preparations
for the gala centenary continued uninterrupted and paralleled those
in other locales throughout the country. The zealous town planted
a thousand new trees that summer, and a glittering display, the
local newspaper reported, spelled out the words "Hyde Park . . . in
fiery letters" alongside the dates, 1776–1876. Only a thunderous explosion of fireworks that injured several residents marred that noteworthy commemoration of the Glorious Fourth.[1]

Emma and John Bond's second son, John Robert Bond, Jr.,
called Bob, missed the historic Independence Day by several weeks,
but was born later that July. The Reverend William Cheney, from

neighboring Dedham's Church of the Good Shepherd, christened the baby, and William Gould, John Senior's onetime shipmate and fellow parishioner, became the child's godfather.[2]

It soon became obvious that young Bob Bond would be different from his older sibling. Lighter-skinned like his father, more slightly built and handsomer than Percy (and a bit of a scamp, though he got into no serious trouble and remained a churchgoing Episcopalian), Bob followed in his brother's footsteps at the Damon School. He must have pleased his teachers, because at his June 1890 commencement, as "the Damons . . . kept the old flag in sight" and sang the *Star-Spangled Banner,* thirteen-year-old Bob, perhaps inspired by parental accounts of exploits in the Civil War navy and deliverance from slavery, presented an original recitation titled "The War in the South."[3]

John Bond shaped his sons into men as he taught them the importance of patriotism and self-discipline, which, intertwined with New England's Puritan ethic, nurtured the fused attributes of manliness and good citizenship so esteemed in late-nineteenth-century America.[4] But like a majority of youngsters throughout the country for whom further education seemed an indulgence or folly, Bob did not finish high school. Racial bigotry rarely made lethal assaults on Boston-area Negroes as it did on southerners of the race, yet prevalent biases disproportionately stifled their career opportunities despite education, successful urbanization, rectitude, and refinement. Hyde Park's schools, however, respected their small cadre of Negro students and, steeped in the heritage of their town's acclaimed Civil War regiments and a legacy of Grimké-Weld abolitionist doctrine, also exhibited a marginal interest in black history. One graduation program even included an address lauding the Haitian patriot and revolutionary, Toussaint L'Ouverture.[5]

Like many men of his race, Bob Bond was working as a porter six years later when Hyde Park experienced one of the most distressing incidents in its brief, and mostly tranquil, history. The local newspaper, the Norfolk County *Gazette,* carried the grim headline "Sexual Assault on a Child." On Bob's twentieth birthday, July 27, 1896, a "vicious looking negro male" recently released from prison attacked a Readville girl. The "villain" constrained "the child . . .

long enough in [his] clutches," the paper claimed, "to accomplish his dastardly purpose." That hideous crime occurred within a stone's throw of the Bonds' house, and the suspect fled into the dense marsh foliage alongside Mother Brook. With obvious relief, the *Gazette* reported the following week that the "negro jailbird" had been captured and identified as a resident of neighboring Dedham named George Henry, "a.k.a. George White, although he is very black."[6]

Despite prevailing outrage following the "sexual assault," no one tried to lynch the "very black" Mr. White. There was no hysteria, no generic anti-Negro response.[7] Unlike many Americans elsewhere, Hyde Park's majority residents did not seem to fear, suspect, or loathe without distinction other young Negroes such as the Bond brothers, or consider them potential rapists.

During the post-Reconstruction era, however, much of the country, especially the South, had developed a virulent yet inconsistent collective psychosis which did just that. Many Caucasians judged all Negroes to be uncivilized, subhuman, and therefore "unmanly," yet at the same time, saw them as highly sexual beings whose potent maleness imperiled the virtue of white (but only white) women and girls. Most members of the majority did not characterize as rape any sexual assaults on black females, because they were considered so inherently lascivious that such eventualities seemed impossible. "I sometimes hear of a virtuous negro woman," a white southerner sneered, "but the idea is absolutely inconceivable to me." Yet even a presumed threat of rape became the excuse for some white Americans to take the law into their own hands and lynch supposedly bestial black men. More often than not, those men and boys were uninvolved, unconvicted, or stood accused of offenses as diverse as cattle stealing, burglary, "reckless eyeballing," miscegenation (meaning consensual but illegal—throughout the South—sex between a white woman and a black man), "frightening [a] child by shooting at rabbits," "unpopularity," or simply being "saucy to white folks."[8]

One hundred or more lynchings (with black males comprising the vast majority of victims) occurred each year in the United States during the 1890s and reached a "high-water mark" of 241 in 1892.

Supposedly law-abiding whites instigated violent abductions that erupted into pagan community rituals. Women and children watched and goaded on husbands, fathers, and town elders who pistol-whipped, hanged, burned, and castrated or disemboweled Negroes, thereby both eliminating the brutes and nullifying their sexuality. Some participants and observers claimed as souvenirs shreds of clothing, teeth or nails, fingers, toes, even scraps of genitalia.[9] Lynchings were meant to terrorize and dishearten a broad spectrum of black people who otherwise might not "know their place." Relatively few whites took part in such brutish sport, but many others tacitly approved the acts, viewed them with detached bemusement, and remained silent or silenced as savage mobs trashed the constitutional rights of a significant segment of the population. Fundamental elements of Anglo-American culture may have subtly encouraged that sort of aberrant behavior by stimulating middle-class white men to assert their intertwined race, gender, and class dominance. "Brave men or women," a Negro journalist named Ida B. Wells furiously protested, should not "stand by and see such things done without compunction of conscience, nor read of them without protest," but she was one of very few Americans who so boldly spoke out.[10]

In the 1890s, Wells mounted vigorous attacks against those outrages, but realized that she needed potent allies to support her "crusade for justice" and sought them in innovative places. In that "Progressive" Era pervaded by reformist ideologies and neo-Darwinist theories about survival of the fittest, "civilization" (evolving from and supplanting "savagery" and "barbarism") had acquired distinct racial attributes. Most white Americans maintained that Anglo-Saxon culture, whence their own presumably sprang, was uniquely masculine and self-disciplined, and therefore they considered the British their intellectual and moral lodestars. Recognizing that "America cannot and will not ignore the voice of a nation that is her superior in civilization," the canny Ida B. Wells turned to England to plead her case.[11]

In 1892, and again two years later, she sailed to Liverpool, John Robert Bond's birthplace, where her fiery yet clear-headed lectures inverted the standard prolynching argument. Wells had amassed statistics that proved just how tenuous were the links between lynching and rape. She created a radical, alternative dialogue assigning uncivilized behavior and a lack of manliness not to "debased" Negroes but to whites who participated in, trivialized, or ignored lynching. She also secured influential backers such as the archbishop of Canterbury, as the Liverpool *Post* contended that America's lynchings "horrif[ied] the whole civilized world." That newspaper urged Britain to stop "sending missions to the South Sea Islands, . . . leave the heathen alone, [and] send the gospel of common humanity across the Atlantic."[12] Wells's English initiatives embarrassed some timorous white residents of the United States and helped to convince at least a few that lynching and anarchy were unacceptable responses to the "Negro problem" and the "Negro crime." That certainly was the case in Massachusetts, where such behavior never took hold.[13]

Two years after Hyde Park's own race-tinged but judiciously resolved rape, many United States citizens first became aware of Spain's brutal colonial governance in Cuba and began to sympathize with the island's independence movement, which was inspired by their own revolution more than a century before.[14] Flexing his country's ample military muscle, President William McKinley, under the self-assumed authority long licensed by the unilaterally initiated Monroe Doctrine, dispatched the battleship *Maine* to Havana. He vowed to reestablish order and protect lives and American financial interests that the escalating struggle between Cuban guerillas (many of them "born of a mongrel spawn of Europe, crossed upon the fetiches of darkest Africa and aboriginal America," one white man professed) and their Spanish overseers might endanger.[15]

McKinley's interference in what Spain considered an internal family squabble, however, outraged most Spaniards. But at that volatile juncture, on the night of February 15, 1898, the USS *Maine* exploded and sank in Havana's harbor. Thirty-three blacks were among the 266 men who died. "In the Spanish-American war," a knowledgeable sailor stated several years later, "the Negro was given an opportunity to display his bravery . . . on the high seas, . . . to his credit be it said he proved himself worthy of the nation's trust." "When the floating forts lined up before Santiago, either to give or take life for the honor of a nation and the uplifting of an abused people," the paean to Negro seamen queried, "Who displayed the heroism characteristic of a struggling race? Who perished with the ill-fated *Maine?*"[16]

The United States' majority population cared little about those black casualties, but blamed Spain's hostile administration in Cuba for the tragedy that preliminary inquiries attributed to an explosive device planted alongside the *Maine*'s keel. Later investigations suggested that an on-board blast more likely was the cause, but whatever its true origin, in the winter of 1898 the die was cast. Spurred on by cries of "Remember the *Maine*, to Hell with Spain!" in early June the outraged United States Congress unilaterally proclaimed Cuba's independence, authorized the president to send troops and ships to neutralize or drive out the colonial malefactors, and declared war.

Yet even before that declaration, the United States had gone on the offensive in the Philippine Islands, a Spanish colony in the Pacific where many of the oppressed, indigenous people had also rebelled. In his superior's brief absence that March, Assistant Secretary of the Navy Theodore Roosevelt ordered Admiral George Dewey to Manila. A black gunner's mate fired the first shots in the brief yet decisive foray as Dewey's USS *Olympia*, flagship of the Asiatic Squadron, plunged into action.[17] Within half a day, all ten vessels that comprised the paltry Spanish-Philippine armada lay at the bottom of usually serene Manila Bay.

American troops arrived by August to reinforce the navy's victory and engaged in brief skirmishes that crushed Spain's army of occupation, but it soon became apparent that the United States would not honor the homegrown liberation efforts. Early in 1899, a resolute Filipino named Emilio Aguinaldo announced the establishment of an independent Philippine republic and began a protracted struggle against the acquisitive new interlopers.

In their benevolent moments, white United States soldiers called the Filipinos "little brown brothers." More often, they labeled them "gugus," or just "niggers." As African American comrades-in-arms began arriving, *I Don't Like a Nigger Nohow* became a popular song among the white servicemen, one of whom asserted: "All

Commander William Spicer, captain of the USS *Lancaster*, and the U.S. Navy Hospital in Portsmouth, Virginia, where he, like John Robert Bond, recuperated in 1864. (*U.S. Naval Historical Center and U.S. Naval Medical Center, Portsmouth*)

Left: Docks, whaling ships, and barrels of whale oil in the port of New Bedford, Massachusetts, sometime in the 1860s, around the time that John Robert Bond arrived there from Liverpool and joined the Union navy. (*Spinner Publications, Inc., New Bedford*)

America's most renowned photographer, Matthew Brady, took this picture of black and white sailors who served together during the Civil War on a U.S. Navy ship much like the *Lancaster*. (*National Archives*)

Left: Starting in 1861, slaves from Tidewater, Virginia, deluged Fortress Monroe, where they were granted their freedom during the Civil War. *(From* Harper's Weekly, *August 1861. Image of the Black in Western Art Project, Harvard University)*

Right: Yankee soldiers burned the Portsmouth Navy Yard as they abandoned the facility to Confederate forces in 1861. *(Portsmouth Public Library)* *Bottom left:* Overloaded by the weight of myriad observers, one floor of the state capitol in Richmond collapsed in early 1870, killing seventy people. That tragedy symbolized the downfall of Reconstruction in Virginia and coincided with the Bonds' departure for Massachusetts. *(Virginia State Archives)*

Above: George Teamoh, who fled slavery in Virginia for New Bedford, Massachusetts, then returned to Portsmouth as a civic and political leader during Reconstruction. *(Library of Congress)*

Right: The Bay State House in Worcester, Massachusetts, where John Robert Bond worked and lived from 1870 to 1874. (*Worcester Historical Society*)

Left: Carrie Stewart, 1891. (*Collection of Elizabeth Alexander*)
Above: Georgia Fagain Stewart in 1900, at the time she first met J. Percy Bond in Boston. (*Collection of the author*)

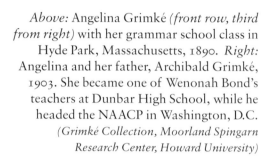

Above: Angelina Grimké *(front row, third from right)* with her grammar school class in Hyde Park, Massachusetts, 1890. *Right:* Angelina and her father, Archibald Grimké, 1903. She became one of Wenonah Bond's teachers at Dunbar High School, while he headed the NAACP in Washington, D.C. *(Grimké Collection, Moorland Spingarn Research Center, Howard University)*

Bottom left: Memorial honoring Colonel Robert Gould Shaw and the Fifty-fourth Massachusetts Infantry Regiment that trained in Readville and fought in the Civil War. Booker T. Washington delivered the keynote address when this monument was dedicated on Boston Common in 1897. *(Hickey & Robertson, Houston, Texas. Image of the Black in Western Art Project, Harvard University)*
Bottom right: This cartoon about citizenship compared the predicament of Native Americans, Chinese immigrants, and blacks. *(From* Harper's Weekly, *February 1879. Image of the Black in Western Art Project, Harvard University)*

Top left: W. Monroe Trotter, who grew up in Hyde Park, Massachusetts, owned and edited the *Guardian* newspaper in Boston. He was a thorn in the side of both Booker T. Washington and President Woodrow Wilson. *(Trustees of the Boston Public Library)* *Top right:* Frederick Douglass, the towering abolitionist who visited Liverpool, England, during John Robert Bond's childhood. He championed the rights of African Americans and, in 1896, his family established the vacation community at Highland Beach, Maryland. *(Moorland Spingarn Research Center, Howard University)*

James Wolff served in the U.S. Navy during the Civil War, attended Harvard Law School, became a civic leader in Boston, and headed the 20,000-member Massachusetts Grand Army of the Republic in 1905. *(State Library of Massachusetts)*

Sailors dancing together and being tattooed aboard the USS *Olympia* in 1899, at the time when Bob Bond served in the U.S. Navy. *(Frances Benjamin Johnston Collection, Library of Congress)*

This memorial to Civil War heroes was dedicated in 1911 at Fairview Cemetery in Hyde Park, Massachusetts. John Robert Bond's gravesite is visible at the bottom and is enlarged as an inset above. *(Photographs by Mary E. Pitts)*

Left: This photograph of Booker T. Washington was given to Georgia and Carrie Stewart (later Bond) around 1901 in Boston. *(Day Collection, Peabody Museum, Harvard University)* *Below:* Executive Committee, Tuskegee Institute, 1902. *Front row, left to right:* Margaret Washington, Robert Taylor, Emmett Scott, Booker T. Washington, Jane Clark, Warren Logan. *Back row:* George Washington Carver *(far left),* Josephine Bruce *(third from left),* Roscoe Bruce *(far right).* Carver was shot at by white Alabamians when he escorted the photographer Frances Benjamin Johnston (a white woman) around the Tuskegee area. *(Johnston Collection, Library of Congress)*

Right: The Logan family of Tuskegee Institute, Alabama, 1913. Adella Hunt Logan *(back row, second from left)* was a suffragist and Georgia Stewart's mentor; Warren Logan *(back row, center)* was the institute's treasurer; Ruth Logan (later Roberts) *(back row second from right)* was Carrie Stewart Bond's good friend. Arthur Logan *(front row, center)* married Wenonah Bond in 1936, and Myra Logan *(front row, right)* became Wenonah's best friend at Atlanta University. *(Photograph by Arthur Bedou, collection of the author)*

Right: J. Percy Bond at Tuskegee Institute, 1904. *(Collection of J. Percy Bond, III)*

Left: Advertisement (an ink blotter) for Bond & Company, featuring a photograph of J. Percy and Georgia Bond's daughter, Wenonah, 1907. *(Collection of the author)*

Right: Downtown Birmingham in 1912, showing bicycles, automobiles, trolleys, horse droppings, and the steel skeleton for one of the city's new "skyscrapers." Bond & Company was on this block. *(Birmingham Public Library)*

coons look alike to me."[18] Nonetheless, the outgunned but determined "gugus" proved themselves more able foes than the Spanish, and the mighty U.S. military needed almost three years to suppress the independence movement, pacify the islands, and lay the groundwork for its own occupational rule.

The United States had acquired the Samoan island of Pago Pago in 1897, deposed Hawaii's Queen Liliuokalani and annexed her paradisial archipelago early the next year, then set its sights on other Pacific territories. Those acquisitions were pieces of a tactically, philosophically, and geographically disparate strategy to gain access to the raw materials and markets of the Far East, and also to furnish the world's benighted darker races with the blessings of civilization, democracy, and Christianity. Bringing such territories under the United States' sphere of influence was meant to provide new navy coaling stations and enhance national security. Such was the covetous spirit of the age near the dawn of the "American Century" when much of the Pacific became another proprietary United States bathtub.

Closer to home, the War Department, convinced that its black soldiers were unusually well suited to serve in the Caribbean, sent south many Negro regular army units (the "black immunes") that had been stationed throughout the country in preparation for deployment to Cuba. Like most white regiments, they were seriously undermanned, and due to hasty preparation and inadequate supplies, soldiers of both races were poorly armed and ill equipped for the tropics. That April of 1898, the Bonds' state of Massachusetts was one of the few jurisdictions that responded promptly to President McKinley's call for volunteers, and it even formed a "colored" company in Boston.[19]

Negro Americans faced endemic political, social, and economic problems at home. The great majority, however, expected to defend their country and the policies of the time-warped party of Lincoln to which they still maintained an allegiance. They refused to abandon the counsel of the recently deceased Frederick Douglass, who had proclaimed, "The Republican party is the ship—all else is the sea." But unlike the situation during the Civil War when blacks almost unanimously had supported the Union, the Spanish-American

War and Philippine Insurrection roused conflicted loyalties within the African American community.[20]

Some Negroes, including Booker T. Washington, bruited the benefits that the nation's imperialism could bring. They were as patriotic as any other Americans, and a manly defense of country, they believed, would enhance their status in the eyes of Caucasians, while exposure to different "colored" cultures might widen the horizons and diminish the bigotry of prejudiced whites. A small but resolute number of black citizens also hoped that federally sponsored emigration ventures and economic opportunities would materialize in the underdeveloped former Spanish colonies already populated by various other dark-skinned people.[21]

Yet anti-imperialists also spoke out, Boston's Archibald Grimké and the up-and-coming activist W. E. B. Du Bois among them. They acknowledged Spain's despotism, but correctly asserted that it never imposed a system of racial discrimination in its colonies like that which was becoming entrenched in the South. Grimké contended that McKinley's "absolute supineness" in respect to lynching made Negroes "shudder for other peoples who may come under the yoke." His open letter to the president claimed that

> to win the support of the South to his policy of "criminal aggression" in the Far East, [McKinley] was ready and willing to shut his eyes, ears, and lips to the "criminal aggression" of that section against the Constitution and the laws of the land wherein they guarantee civil rights and citizenship to the negro.[22]

Proponents of Grimké's views argued that the country's overseas initiatives amounted to a Jim Crow war leading toward a colonial, Jim Crow empire in which "colored" Americans, as well as dark-skinned people in the Philippines, Cuba, and Puerto Rico would end up more oppressed than ever. Only if their government granted Negroes the full benefits and protections of democracy at home would black anti-imperialists support efforts to liberate the Spanish colonies or, in the case of the Philippines, placate the recalcitrant natives, who, due to their "primitive" natures, could not understand that America's conquering heroes had crossed the world's greatest ocean to save them from themselves.

A young imperialist named Winston Churchill (the son of an Englishman and an American woman) argued that Spain ought to maintain control of Cuba because "two-fifths of the insurgents in the field are negroes." If the indigenous forces won, he said, they would "demand a predominant share in the government of the country." Churchill, and many others, feared that such an eventuality would result in "another black republic."[23]

Cuba did become independent—though the United States maintained a naval base and a strong military presence there, but few people thought that nonwhite Filipinos or Puerto Ricans (former colonial subjects of Spain) should be granted the full privileges of U.S. citizenship. Would citizenship, as the language of the times suggested, "follow the flag" throughout what soon would be called "America's Negro empire"? "It is a sorry, though true, fact that wherever this government controls, injustice to the dark race prevails," argued Frederick Douglass's son Lewis, adding, "The people of Cuba, Porto Rico, Hawaii and Manila know it as well as do the wronged Indian and outraged black man in the United States." But with an alternative, markedly nativist slant of his own, one black journalist asserted that "the bushman of today cannot be the legislator of tomorrow."[24]

Negro Americans had ambivalent feelings, but most considered military service an obligation of citizenship that they would fulfill as honorably and capably as white men. They always hoped that such proof of patriotism would dissipate the country's virulent racism. Still, many harbored serious misgivings about the new imbroglios perpetrated by their nation. The United States had committed itself to Anglo-Saxon supremacy at home, but concurrently, and paradoxically, declared its intent to uplift the "little brown brother" wherever he might be found abroad.

African Americans often felt an affinity with other repressed dark-complexioned people. "I am ready to die upon the battlefield defending our country, 'Grand America,' and the poor Cubans as well, because I am convinced that these people are of our Negro race," a soldier wrote home. Responses to the Spanish-American War and Philippine Insurrection among blacks in the military (as well as civilians) reflected varying degrees of chauvinism, common racial identity, self-interest, or altruism. They were patriotic, yet it seemed ludicrous to take up the "white man's burden" on behalf of a nation that treated them as unmanly or uncivilized and denied them equal rights at home. The Bonds surely found themselves as perplexed as other African Americans, like the frustrated volunteer who asserted: "We black men here are so much between the Devil and the Deep Blue."[25]

One journalist proposed and promoted a provocative boycott: "No officers, no soldiers," as Negro leaders called for black commissioned officers to lead black units. Most whites, however, opposed such initiatives. Putting African Americans in uniform at all gave them a sense of equality, empowerment, and manliness. Making black men officers, whites feared, would further encourage them to "forget their place." The Supreme Court had sanctioned institutional racism—which was becoming enshrined in practice and encoded in state and local statutes—with its 1896 *Plessy v. Ferguson* decision, and few Negroes in the army could overcome the odds to acquire or keep commissions. White officers, therefore, commanded most black American troops in both Cuba and the Philippines.[26]

In Cuba, African Americans shored up and fought alongside the Rough Riders, a unit incongruously composed of cowboys and eastern college dudes led by the zealous Colonel Theodore Roosevelt, who had resigned his civilian Navy Department post to accept a commission and don a uniform. Colonel John "Black Jack" Pershing, who earned his sobriquet that summer of 1898 while commanding the "colored" Tenth Cavalry, argued that his experienced men saved the hides of Roosevelt's white novices. A few months later, however, the self-promoting "T.R.," whose very conspicuous march up San Juan Hill marked his first strides toward the White House, complained that the Negroes had been "peculiarly dependent upon their white officers" and prone to panic under pressure. To prevent their withdrawal, he boasted, "I jumped up . . . drew my revolver, [and] halted the retreating soldiers." When taken to task for such distortions, he blurred his commentary by attributing the alleged cowardice to "the superstition and fear of the darkey, natural in those . . . but a few generations removed from the wildest savagery."[27]

The beleaguered Spanish colonials, however, labeled the intrepid Negro troops "Smoked Yankees," and in a blunt summation a white American war correspondent exclaimed: "God bless the nigger!" Five men from the much-debated Tenth Cavalry received Medals of Honor, while the navy awarded a black fireman named Robert Penn its comparable decoration for valorous service.[28]

The United States Navy wielded almost unopposed power in the Caribbean, and on July 3, 1898, handily crushed the Spanish fleet guarding Santiago's harbor. Despite copious blunders, by midmonth the army surrounded that city and vanquished Spain's land forces, although mishaps, food poisoning, and yellow fever proved more daunting foes than Spanish bullets and killed fifteen times as many Americans. In keeping with the pervasive belief that the "black immunes" could not contract yellow fever, a unit of Negro soldiers was detailed to staff the central military hospital. Those African Americans (with more than three generations of United States residency in temperate climes behind them) may have retained a minimal inherited resistance to the mosquito-borne tropical virus, but nearly half of the Negro soldiers who reported for hospital duty contracted the disease, and a number died.[29]

United States military might, however, more than outweighed its ineptitude, and the Cuban struggle came and went so quickly that the Bonds' Hyde Park, like much of the country, scarcely had time to respond. Many lads had joined up, but by September the *Gazette* already was welcoming "Home from the War" soldiers and sailors who had traipsed off scarcely two months earlier. Still, the town was not without casualties and soon would rename its central square in honor of John Cleary, a local boy who had died a hero in Cuba. A number of New Englanders remained aboard navy ships that autumn, and one of Bob Bond's contemporaries reported his observations in "A Hyde Park Boy in Honolulu," an open letter to the folks at home. In words far less disparaging than those of most other white Americans, he described Hawaii's "native race" as "a peculiar cross between the Negro and the Malay, splendid physically but very homely."[30]

Hyde Park's newspaper also featured a lengthy "Rastus" story that opened with a stereotypical portrayal of a "Buffalo, . . . eyes and teeth gleaming, and breath coming in laborious gasps between thick lips."[31] Long before they went to Cuba, members of the Tenth Cavalry had become known as Buffalo Soldiers, because Native Americans on the vanishing western frontier asserted that the black men's hair resembled buffalo pelts. Their regimental badges, therefore, bore silhouettes of the country's most representative, indigenous quadruped.

Despite the cartoonish depiction introducing the *Gazette*'s article, it continued more positively, reminding its readers that "under the flag [Negro soldiers] are today free men." It congratulated the Tenth Cavalry on its contributions in the Cuban encounter, because "a braver charge was never made; there [was] no color line on that bloody day." As the African American hero breathed his last, "white and black alike stooped over Rastus," the sentimental saga concluded, "and with gleaming eyes watched the life of the brave black man go out beneath the flag he had honored."[32] Other reports about the country's war-related ventures appeared on the pages of his local paper in late 1898, yet Bob Bond still hesitated at home.

Around Thanksgiving, however, he decided to act. Bob surely knew something about Negro sailors' current achievements, and tales recounting their Civil War exploits would have filled his childhood. Following in his father's footsteps, those of his godfather William Gould, and other former sailors such as John's old friend Isaac Mullen, the patriotic (and menially employed) twenty-two-year-old Bob Bond joined the navy.[33] He volunteered to serve for three years, expecting to take part in the country's efforts to suppress the embryonic Philippine Insurrection.

His nation's acquisitive and patronizing endeavors among the darker races who inhabited the world's tropical latitudes both reflected and fulfilled a fundamental, turn-of-the-century Anglo-Saxon precept. Bob signed on with a rapidly changing United States Navy charged by the country with assuming the "white man's burden" to uplift the barely civilized "little brown brother."[34]

Percy Bond's brown-skinned younger brother Bob had a limited education, yet he read and wrote well enough and had a good head for numbers. He had no prior maritime experience but had developed into a capable river rat growing up by Mother Brook. Bob could swim, handle small boats well, and he knew Boston's wharves and shipyards. He smoked and drank but was a practicing Christian with no police record, alcohol problem, physical infirmities, or contagious diseases. His qualifications for service surely equaled those of the white farm boys whom the navy most wanted to entice into its somewhat depleted ranks. Lieutenant Commander William Randall swore in Bob Bond early in December, rated him a landsman, and assigned him to the receiving ship *Wabash*.[35]

With little doubt, Bob looked forward to a stimulating life in the navy, and two weeks later, on a typically cold and snowy, gloomy New England winter morning, he transferred onto the USS *Lancaster* to begin his initial tour of duty at sea. As a reader of the scriptures, Bob could have anticipated that the more than a thousand days of his navy contract would speed by "as the swift ships: as the eagle that hasteth to the prey."[36]

The three-masted steam sloop *Lancaster* that Bob Bond boarded that holiday season had been commissioned in 1859, and four decades later was creaky, leaky, and outmoded. Its galley was begrimed, and the heads—too old and too few—reeked of excrement and disinfectant. "She is simply the old wooden gun-decked man-of-war," one of its surgeons wrote, "with auxiliary steam power, a modern battery, [and] electrical lights." Weighing 2,400 tons, it was 236 feet long, 46 across the beam, and cruised at up to ten knots. The *Lancaster*'s most compelling feature was the wooden likeness of an American eagle adorning the prow, with its feathers, unblinking yellow eyes, and hooked beak all distinctly carved. The shrieking raptor had been captured in mid-flight, wicked talons and wings extended, poised to ravage any unsuspecting prey.[37] No predator ever cleaved air or sea more boldly than that virile, national bird.

Throughout the Civil War, the USS *Lancaster* had served as a flagship of the Pacific Squadron, but soon thereafter was placed in drydock at the Norfolk Navy Yard, where several of John Bond's friends were employed.[38] Recommissioned in 1869, it sailed with the Atlantic Squadron until 1875. Following six more years on decommissioned status, it became a flagship of the European Squadron, and navy dignitaries journeyed on the *Lancaster* to Tsar Alexander III's coronation. It shuttled between Africa and South America in 1888, was decommissioned in 1889, then recommissioned two years later for deployment to the Pacific. The vacillating U.S. Navy decommissioned the ship in 1894, recommissioned it again the next year, re-retired it in 1897, then pulled it out of mothballs as tensions escalated in the Caribbean. To prepare for the Spanish-American War, the *Lancaster* set sail in spring 1898 as a gunnery training facility. In early 1899, it departed from Portsmouth, New Hampshire, to patrol the East Coast, bearing an experienced crew, plus Landsman Bob Bond and nine other novices. Commander Thomas Perry, a patrician, silver-haired Naval Academy graduate from the class of 1865, but a pale flame, nonetheless, in the country's luminous dynasty of seagoing Perrys, recently had become captain. The *Lancaster,* though authorized to carry 400 or more men, at that time bore a minimal complement of only 247, including 50 petty officers and almost 100 apprentices—youngsters who expected to make the navy their life's work.[39]

In addition to Bob Bond's manifest patriotism and the influence of a paternal seafaring legacy, he probably joined the navy for reasons, and with dreams and ambitions, much like those of other young Americans. It promised hard work but broad vocational horizons, decent pay, and a chance to sever the moorings of a lifetime and sail the seven seas unencumbered by apron strings or other ties to home. Restless youths who forsook gray New England's granite coast and ice-choked harbors envisioned star-spangled nights, pellucid aquamarine-to-lapis Caribbean or South Pacific waters, and sugary, sun-washed beaches. With any luck, their ships would be populated by gentlemanly officers and hearty, supportive mates, and their ports of call graced with heavy-handed barkeeps and lubricious wenches.

When Bob Bond embarked on the *Lancaster,* he was five feet eight and a half inches tall and weighed 158 pounds, had brown eyes, curly black hair, and a deep sepia complexion that a navy officer generically described as "mulatto." He had no tattoos, but bore two old, livid scars on his left forearm and thigh.[40] Possessed of physical grace, dimples, and an impish grin, Bob was a young man whom forthright observers might even have described as pretty. He had a volatile personality and could be either gregarious, generous, and wildly funny, or an abrupt and malicious tease.[41]

By the late 1890s, however, the service that Bob joined mirrored the country's burgeoning dedication to Jim Crow, and with few exceptions assigned its black sailors to menial positions and classifications. Only he and one other Negro on the *Lancaster* were rated as landsmen, and a disheartened sailor from another vessel disparaged even that rating as "the service designation for domestics."[42] The ship to which Bond was assigned carried not one black of seaman's rank, and the navy was loath to recruit any African Americans who might want to make it a career, preferring to enlist only those who could be briefly deployed as seagoing servants. That branch of the military had been far less racially biased during the Civil War when John Robert Bond, père, became and remained an able-bodied seaman.

Besides the two landsmen, just twelve blacks served on the *Lancaster,* as coal stokers, stewards, and mess attendants.[43] An experienced Negro sailor named Nicholas Campbell confirmed in the *Colored American* magazine that "the majority of the colored men in the navy are servants—cooks, stewards, attendants, firemen and coal-passers." He added, however, that naval service afforded men of his race "the opportunity of studying the relations existing between himself and representatives of almost every other race . . . from the pea-eyed Chinaman of Hong Kong to the detestable 'cracker' of Louisiana." Campbell laid out the conditions that youngsters such as Bob Bond should anticipate.[44]

"Filled with true patriotism for the country and the flag," he added, the black seaman "is a hero in time of war, and in peace suffers a caste prejudice more deadly than the poisonous fangs of the Fer-de-lance." "I am convinced," Campbell said of his often thwarted colleagues, that "the Negro sailor . . . is capable of enduring hardships and overcoming obstacles that would drive a Caucasian to despair." A typical African American in the navy, he counseled, "comes in contact with the prejudiced and the unprejudiced, is undisturbed by the hatred and malice of the one and encouraged by the friendship of the other, while he sustains an unswerving loyalty to the flag."[45]

Campbell had lived and worked at sea for years, but only recently had he observed "colored sailors seated at a separate table." Imposition of such conventions mirrored the rising tide of segregation throughout the United States that became a deluge in the wake of the Supreme Court's 1896 sanction of "separate but equal" public facilities. The navy increasingly relegated Negroes to shipboard assignments that led to racially segregated messing and berthing, because sailors ate and slept in the company of others who performed similar duties.[46]

Some white sailors, however, "know full well that they are not superior to their dark-skinned messmates in any respect, and realize that to labor under a delusion of superiority would be arrant foolishness," Campbell continued. "Visitors to different ships," he added, "have departed with entirely different ideas of the relations existing between the two races. Some have had the pleasure of seeing them affiliating happily without a trace of prejudice . . . others, unfortunately, have viewed the dark side of the picture."[47]

"The chance of advancement for the colored sailor is very poor," Campbell warned, since "promotion to higher rates depends entirely upon the recommendation of officers" all of whom were believed to be white, with the vast majority racially prejudiced. Michael Healy, a veteran of the U.S. Navy's adjunct Revenue Cutter Service, remained an anomaly. That son of an Irish-American father and an enslaved mother knew that the navy denied Negroes almost any prospect of advancement, so the ambitious, light-skinned Healy embraced his father's national and racial identity but dismissed his mother's to pass for white. He rose to captain's rank in the 1890s and sailed through Arctic waters, where he categorized and divided those who populated his seagoing cosmos into lowly "natives" (Inuits and Aleuts) and superior "white men"—of whom he clearly considered himself one. Healy was a harsh taskmaster whom some of his crew cursed as a "God damned Irishman."[48]

Most "white" officers (Healy among them) embraced common

ethnic and racial stereotypes and "acquired [the habit] of judging a man by the color of his skin rather than by his moral qualities," Campbell protested. "To them," he continued, "a Negro genius is the most astonishing thing under the sun." Discovering the rare, "good officers," he further lamented, "is the old tale of hunting the needle in the hay-stack."[49]

Many African American seamen, however, maintained their own prejudices. Some Negro sailors, Nicholas Campbell confirmed, believed that "Japanese and Chinese servants [in the navy] are unclean in their habits, but conceal this fact with Oriental duplicity," and stood in the way of blacks' advancement. In this period, numerous white United States citizens (many of whom were onetime aliens themselves) also increasingly resented the newer waves of immigrants, and the percentages of non-Americans in the navy had decreased considerably from the time when John Robert Bond, Sr., served in the military with several hundred thousand other worthy foreigners during the Civil War.[50]

By the late 1890s, a growing consensus maintained that Asian seamen's smaller size per se made them preferable to African Americans, even in the navy's "servile" classifications. White officers had started complaining that the generally taller, bulkier Negroes had an "unmilitary appearance," would not assume an appropriately obsequious demeanor, and consumed too much grub. To retain their good standing, said Campbell, black sailors always "must be polite and submissive" (also, one might suspect, abstemious), "while the lack of these qualities in the scum of foreign dens is overlooked." "West Indiamen," he added, while "energetic and ambitious," achieved some success because they were "conspicuously submissive and respectful to Caucasians."[51]

The forthright Nicholas Campbell also volunteered details about rifts within the ranks of African American sailors. "[One] class of Negroes is composed of those who enlist to escape the responsibilities of civilian life," he admitted, who, "upon discovering that service [in the navy] is . . . strenuous, drift back into their customary state of careless negligence." Those laggards, he argued, became a "source of delight" to "crackers" who always looked for "degeneracy in our people. . . . It tickles their self-esteem to delude themselves with the thought of their own superiority." "On the other hand," Campbell continued, "there are numbers of colored men . . . whose good breeding and intelligence are far above that of their white shipmates." "Many positions held by the whites," he added, "could be promptly filled by the superior Negro."[52]

Despite "disappointments and humiliations, [the] colored sailor . . . remains the happy optimist," Campbell reported. Off duty, "he allows no one to suffer from the blues [and] plunges his listeners into spasms of laughter by the comical telling of one of his thrice-told yarns for which Jack Tar is noted." Bob Bond was a raconteur cast from such a mold, and photographs of black sailors sharing stories and playing their guitars, horns, or harmonicas accompanied Campbell's article. They trumpeted, strummed, and warbled the newest tunes, and the bawdy *There'll Be a Hot Time in the Old Town Tonight* became the military's most popular refrain during the Spanish-American War era.[53]

Such diversions notwithstanding, Campbell warned, "the navy is no place for the ambitious colored youth of today. He pants to achieve, but finds 'the door of hope, of opportunity' is barred." Youngsters such as Bob Bond personified those aspiring Negro sailors. It was well understood but not codified, Campbell further asserted (the data mostly accurate but his views sullied by familiar nativism), "that the honors of the naval academy shall not be bestowed upon a black man, although the anarchistic immigrant; the very scum of darkest Europe is welcomed, and the choicest honors heaped upon him by Uncle Sam."[54]

The ebbing presence of black men in the navy after the Civil War reflected America's rising racist tide. From nearly twenty percent in the 1860s, they had declined to a still dwindling ten percent by 1890. Only one recognizably "colored" man had *ever* been commissioned, and after the latter year, none was even listed as a first class petty officer.[55] Faced with endemic repression, many black people viewed the navy, the nation's far-flung aggressions, plus its ongoing acquisition of a colonial empire, within the context of their own declining status. As the bumptious, confident United States strode toward the new century, it became difficult to distinguish between the potentially ugly realities of its imperialist endeavors and the ringing rhetoric of patriotism.

The foul climate generated by deteriorating, racially grounded conditions on the home front prompted serious ramifications aboard the *Lancaster,* where even Bob Bond's middling rating as a landsman failed to survive. Within a month, officers changed his classification and demoted him, not because he thieved, brawled, drank to excess, shirked responsibilities, or was mutinous, but because one night early in 1899 he was charged with being "noisy after taps."[56]

Other than that single, seemingly trivial transgression, Bob Bond compiled an undistinguished though unblemished record, yet his punishment was much harsher than the discipline imposed on white sailors for far more egregious infractions. For minor offenses, they might have rations withheld, be briefly confined to quarters, lose leave time, or receive extra duties. It is difficult to believe that the decision to alter Bob's classification and lower his rank was not singularly grounded in racial bias. One officer on the *Lancaster* bluntly charged that Bob was "better suited" for a new assignment as "mess boy."[57]

Two years after the *Lancaster*'s brass changed Bob's rank, the U.S. Navy officially acknowledged that it did "not consider negroes desirable persons for landsmen," but with few exceptions, it already had deemed black men unsuited to serve as "real" sailors, and acted accordingly. They had become as unwelcome as convicts, derelicts, or carriers of contagious disease in the increasingly "professional" navy, which in its human composition as well as the dazzling paint on its new ships, was on the way to becoming the Great White Fleet.[58] In the context of this widespread degradation of blacks, the *Lancaster*'s officers ("through whose veins," Nicholas Campbell warned, "runs the poisonous blood of Negrophobia") reduced Bob Bond's rating as soon as they had an excuse to do so. But even more severe consequences of that episode when he was punished for being "noisy after taps" plagued Bob for decades thereafter.

On January 31, 1899, very soon after that problematic incident, the navy pensioner John Robert Bond, Sr. (in a surprisingly graceful, well-trained hand), wrote Commander Thomas Perry while the USS *Lancaster* was docked at Port Royal, South Carolina. He asked that his younger boy be transferred from Perry's ship, cruising in peaceful Atlantic waters, to the "Asiatic Squadron now in Manila," where the United States' most critical maritime endeavors were unfolding. John Bond must have believed that this request on behalf of his son was urgent, because he further demanded of Perry: "Is it necessary to write to Washington, or will you be kind enough to transfer him?" Despite that resolute parental epistle, Perry coolly responded: "I have to inform you that it would not be practicable to transfer him." Whether or not the senior Mr. Bond sent any follow-up correspondence "to Washington" remains a mystery, but the navy did *not* reassign the younger man to the Philippines.[59]

The brief exchange yields no further clues (though the fact that the family preserved the correspondence at all suggests its import), but it must have been a previous entreaty from Bob that prompted John Bond's letter. Both father and son, however, also may have been influenced by views espoused in the *Colored American,* arguing that many Americans, race notwithstanding, expected that Negroes' "racial sympathies would naturally be with the Filipinos." Those guerillas were "fighting manfully for what they conceive to be their best interests," but, the article concluded, "we cannot for the sake of sentiment turn our back upon our own country."[60] Bob Bond may have hoped to serve his nation in the Far East, yet he also wanted to get off the USS *Lancaster* as quickly as possible, by any means possible, for reasons that transcended even an understandable resentment of his harsh discipline, revised classification, and reduced rating.

Interpreting the events surrounding Bob Bond's misfortunes on the *Lancaster* poses difficult challenges, but ultimately, only one ugly scenario makes sense of all the diverse evidence. At the least, several matters that at a casual glance might seem trivial or unrelated were very much amiss. First, the *Lancaster* had three captains (Thomas Perry, Theodore Jewell, then Charles M. Thomas) in three months.[61] Such a rapid turnover was not unparalleled, but it seems possible that the navy secretary shuffled those officers around because, in one way or another, each failed to maintain mastery of his ship, especially the respect and loyalty of the crew. In that same brief period, a trio of medical officers, also without explanation, rotated in and out as well.

In addition, eighteen sailors from the USS *Lancaster* were "invalided" in 1898, meaning they were granted transfers for reasons of health. That was by far the greatest number of such relocations from any of the Atlantic Squadron's ninety-eight ships. After those eighteen transfers from the *Lancaster,* the vessel with the second-highest number had only seven. Most ships, even those with much larger crews, lost only one or two seamen per year under those circumstances.[62] Neither the ship's logs nor the navy command provided any explanation for that suspiciously aberrant and troubling statistic. Short of an unprecedented catastrophe or epidemic, what could explain such a highly disproportionate exodus? And, like so many white sailors on the *Lancaster,* might Bob Bond have had reason to seek (though fail to obtain) a medically warranted reassignment?

The awesome prevalence of venereal diseases—the fabled but all-too-real afflictions of Venus—must be swirled into the witch's brew. The *Lancaster* carried about 250 men, and from December 1898 through the following summer, 47 of them reported to the medical officer for treatment of various sexually transmitted diseases.[63] Shipboard surgeons, however, readily admitted that they rarely saw or treated syphilis, in particular, until it reached the debilitating secondary or tertiary stages.

The medical corps asserted that most seamen contracted such diseases in "the usual manner"—through heterosexual activity—yet some did not. One of the *Lancaster*'s surgeons cautioned sailors to "refrain from *tattooing* others, or from allowing their pipes, partly used cigars, cigarettes, or chewing tobacco to be used by another or from using those of others."[64] Tattooing by shipmates who might use contaminated needles, or sharing illicit drugs, tobacco products, or surgical supplies (though the navy tried to remove sailors with venereal infections from assignments as medics), were among the less common ways that such diseases might be transmitted. Yet the risk of infection probably seemed insignificant compared to the heady benefits of ritual initiation into the sacred fraternity of seafarers by acquiring, and thereafter boldly displaying, replicas of the country's most patriotic symbols. Like a number of his shipmates, Bob Bond therefore received a ceremonial emblem of manhood and joined the brotherhood of illustrated seamen when he had an American flag tattooed on his right deltoid while he was on the *Lancaster*.[65]

Homosexual encounters, however, were more likely avenues by which syphilis could be passed on, but the navy brass shied away from even mentioning such activities, and shipboard punishments, courts-martial, or discharges for sodomy or homosexual assault were nonexistent at that time. One navy physician, nonetheless, cryptically asserted that "the danger of infection . . . does not deter, and . . . a large proportion of . . . men do not endeavor to repress their sexual cravings."[66] Not even the acknowledged health hazards, however, prevented an unspecified number of the *Lancaster*'s libidinous seamen from satisfying their varied "sexual cravings" while at sea, any more than did sailors on other ships.

Those combined factors suggest the presence of a pathogenic, disordered, yet in some ways typical shipboard culture on the USS *Lancaster* that swept Bob into its vortex. Concerning the overall straits in which Bob Bond found himself, one officer reported that no novice sailor was "allowed liberty, and . . . therefore practically finds himself in prison" during his first months of duty at sea. As best can be surmised, on a night in mid-January 1899, the virtually captive, impotent newcomer Bob Bond and a black friend raised an unholy ruckus while one or more shipmates forced Bob into a closet or bent him over a rail to engage him in a homosexual act. Rather than dealing with the ruthless perpetrator(s) and the incident itself, if they knew of it or cared, the *Lancaster*'s officers instead punished Bob, and the buddy who tried to assist him, for their vociferous protests.[67]

That could or could not have been an isolated occurrence, but it had lasting consequences because Bob Bond, like a number of his shipmates, contracted syphilis. One ailing sailor on the *Lancaster* suggestively protested that he too had been "worried by harassing," and physicians medicated more than twenty percent of the ship's enlisted men for sexually transmitted afflictions during Bob's months at sea. To treat syphilis specifically, the *Lancaster's* surgeons (P. A. Lovering, J. D. Gatewood, and then E. M. Shipp) drained pus-filled chancres, administered belladonna, and rubbed lead, mercury, or bismuth ointments laced with opium or morphine onto the genitals. Enlarged lymph glands and an "indented sore on [his] prepuce," a shipboard physician noted, characterized one sailor's "syphilis primitiva," while "syphilitic eruptions" covered another's body. That seaman became so incapacitated that he and several similarly afflicted shipmates were transferred to navy hospitals. Others, like Bob (who reported to the infirmary only twice for minor respiratory distress and never lost a day of duty to illness or injury), probably were infected, yet failed to receive any treatment.[68]

With venereal infections so rampant, serving on that ship of knaves and fools could have imperiled the well-being of everyone on board. That would have been especially true if a promiscuous, unrestrained syphilitic bully (seeking the raptures of the deep) raped one or more vulnerable greenhorns. Whatever their origins or means of transmission, the odious family of venereal diseases took a heavy toll. More than twenty percent of the navy's total incapacity due to illness resulted from such infections.[69]

While prevalent worldwide irrespective of ethnicity or race, syphilis also had acquired more specifically focused racial connotations. The supposed menace of nonwhite and primitive "syphilization" seemed to threaten the "civilization" of Caucasian voyagers, while a navy doctor preached that Negro prostitutes, "among the lowest classes in some of the West Indian ports, . . . [are] capable of infecting in a day or two more than ten per cent. of a crew."[70] Shipboard surgeons advocated rigorous prophylactic procedures for sailors who copulated with women in tropical ports, but never recommended any methods of disease prevention for men who might engage in the homosexual acts that remained officially unmentionable. One civilian physician at the time explained that the phrase "'racial characteristics' . . . means a 'syphilitic history' when referring to colored people." Others condemned Negroes as a "syphilis-soaked race" addicted to sexual gratification, and contended that the disease represented a just reward for their barbaric, sinful, and racially determined erotic behavior.[71] Navy officers often censured blacks as potential carriers who therefore would make unacceptable sailors, but turned a blind eye to problems created by homosexual transmission of venereal ailments where race played little or no role.

Perhaps Bob Bond truly did not know (or want to admit or believe) that he had acquired syphilis as the result of a homosexual assault aboard the *Lancaster* and fell into the category of presumably naive Bostonians lampooned by a contemporaneous limerick:

> *There was a young man from Back Bay*
> *Who thought syphilis just went away.*
> *He believed that a chancre*
> *Was only a canker*
> *That healed in a week and a day.*[72]

More likely, however, he felt humiliated, feared retribution from shipmates or officers in that authoritarian milieu, and was reluctant to report his homosexual encounter(s) or seek treatment. He probably experienced but ignored mild primary symptoms such as a slow-healing but fairly painless chancre or bubo in his battered rectum, followed by a slight fever and unexplained rash, perhaps most vividly apparent on his palms.

The years when physicians administered purgatives such as jalap and calomel had passed. However, the standard but imprecise and often ineffective treatment for syphilis used around the turn of the century, involving arsenic, mercury, or other metal salts and ointments, was such that dosages strong enough to annihilate the almost indiscernible, corkscrew-shaped *Treponema pallidum* spirochetes might impair or even kill the patient. Soon thereafter, Wassermann tests definitively diagnosed the disease and salvarsan compounds offered improved therapy, but an effective nontoxic remedy with penicillin was still four decades ahead. Seafarers' lore included somber tales of melancholy, syphilitic sailors who congregated on deck and hunkered down in circles to massage each others' naked backs with mercury salves.[73]

Although the navy refused to acknowledge any links between syphilis and homosexual shipboard acts, they nonetheless were real.

At the same time, military service was an important route by which American boys established themselves as valued citizens and expected to become men. The army and navy vowed to attain that goal in a society which so highly prized manliness. Shortly before his death in 1895, the aging patriot Frederick Douglass had similarly stated, "We are men and our aim is perfect manhood, to be men among men," underscoring that attribute's express significance for members of his often emasculated community.[74]

In that era of aggressive, imperialist expansion when the word "masculinity" first surged into common use, Theodore Roosevelt, America's quintessentially virile white hunter, made popular a traditional West African proverb: "Speak softly and carry a big stick." Roosevelt was becoming a major Republican political star, and his bold, priapic imagery defining that national (and nationalistic) assertion of manhood came to shape and characterize much of United States foreign policy.[75] Ironically, when opportunities arose, some sailors who saw themselves as the war gods' chosen emissaries of a chosen country that espoused such a "masculine" course may have brandished their personal "big sticks" at anyone nearby who might seem conquerable—especially an appealing, and perhaps vulnerable, "little brown brother" (his race perceived as preempting the full realization of manliness) like Bob Bond.

Many people in the United States associated patriotism and their country's expansionist initiatives with collective and individual manhood. But removing young men from kin, familiar neighborhoods, and traditional (usually) Christian mores and placing them in a remote and hierarchical single-sex environment often increased the chances that they would encounter homosexuals. Novice seamen worked and lived in close proximity to experienced shipmates who sometimes partook of and relished previously unfamiliar or forbidden sexual practices. The newcomers then were able to—sometimes forced to—explore variant erotic possibilities as some of the old-timers, one sailor revealed, instructed them "in the details of a nameless vice." "I never met one until I came in the Navy," another youth admitted about the "perverts" he encountered, but he, too, soon engaged in (con)sensual acts that only weeks earlier seemed unthinkable.[76]

Homosexuality has never been an unfamiliar or time-specific phenomenon at sea or observed any barriers of rank. In the early 1800s, the revered Admiral Stephen Decatur reportedly always wore the initialed gold ring bestowed on him by his male lover. Later in the century, Philip Van Buskirk, who rose from drummer boy to captain, catalogued copious details about a panoply of homoerotic activities aboard U.S. Navy ships.[77] In recent years, the most popular song (throbbing to a heavy, insistent beat) by a troop of exotically costumed performers who gear their act to gay audiences leaves little doubt about the raunchy escapades that "new recruits" might hope or fear to experience *In the Navy*.[78]

The boundaries between homosocial and homosexual conduct among men who remain at sea for long months in a confined, all-male universe always have been difficult to determine. Embracing, kissing, and holding hands were unconcealed collegial practices aboard many vessels around the turn of the century, while some off-duty seamen artfully made up their faces and dressed in drag while pursuing their erotic pleasures in various ports. One black sailor observed his shipmates waltzing in the arms of favored partners during leisure hours at sea, and a noted photographer's candid camera captured men aboard Admiral Dewey's flagship USS *Olympia* openly enjoying similar diversions. Beyond such social routines and interactions, solitary or collaborative masturbation as well as oral and anal copulation were expected and prevalent (though usually clandestine) shipboard activities.[79]

Many homosexual encounters were voluntary and enthusiastic. Sometimes they reflected intimate desires, passion, and affection between longtime couples or casual acquaintances. Other such acts provided sexual release with no commitment made or rewards conferred, while some seamen bartered erotic favors for bribes, privileges, or gifts. Homosexual shipboard exploits, however, could be nonconsensual. Physical coercion, threats, or promises might convince a sailor to oblige unwelcome demands, and the navy included many (heterosexual more than homosexual, although those terms were scarcely familiar at the time) brawlers and thugs. Bullies or criminals who might have abused children of either sex or women on land assaulted vulnerable young men at sea, snaring them in a dangerous undertow, knowing they could take their pleasure with little fear of reprisal. The navy rarely took official notice of such malfeasance, and did not (at that time) protest or claim that sailors' sporadic liaisons with "queers" created shipboard problems or compromised their intrinsically masculine nature. Few in the chain of command even acknowledged such activities—consensual or otherwise.[80]

Epithets such as "sissy" and "pussyfooter" recently had crept into the American vernacular, but by 1900, homosexuals—in civilian life, jails, and at sea—also had developed a largely covert subculture with its own arcane lingo to describe themselves and their favored acts.[81] "Pogues" were men who enjoyed, or agreed to, "browning," or anal penetration. "They were willing partners who offered themselves in the same manner which women do," confided one participant. "A punk's a boy that'll give himself to a man," another added, and copulation between predatory "wolves" and those receptive "punks" became common among prisoners, hoboes, and seafarers, all of whom were similarly disengaged from traditional, judgmental surroundings that monitored normative sexuality. As to when or whether a man who "play[ed] the woman's part" should be labeled a "queer," emergent sentiment contended that a man's sexual designation might best be determined by the gender role he assumed rather than the extent of his homosexual activity, especially in a transitory, isolated environment distinguished and characterized by the absence of women. In addition, the navy and society at large still differentiated, to some extent, between act and identity. Bob Bond, however, saw himself as very much "a man's man" (despite that phrase's bizarre and pertinent ambiguities), so the possibility of being called or considered a "punk," "sissy," "pogue," or "queer" surely would have appalled him.[82]

The turn of the century, observers argued, witnessed the "invention of the homosexual." Some Americans adopted and sanctioned a medical model that labeled homoeroticism as "sexual inversion." Seafarers participating in such behavior might be called "deviants," who differed in nature from other men, but they were not necessarily condemned as sinners or criminals. That sort of quasi-scientific evaluation, however, played little role in shaping the behavior itself, or promoting its acceptance in the navy and among the working classes generally. When mentioned at all, such activities carried an odor of disapproval, yet many sailors who first became acquainted with a homoerotic culture at sea continued to be regarded and to regard themselves as "normal." Sexual connections with "queers" usually were ignored or condoned as long as the men involved eschewed effeminate behavior or dress and established no romantic ties with their partners.[83]

Despite divergent ways that the scientific community, the navy brass, and his colleagues viewed such acts, the emotional and physical injuries that Bob Bond incurred in 1899 must have been painful. He had grown up a devout Episcopalian and, recalling time-honored biblical teachings, might have believed that, voluntarily or not, he and his shipmates "leaving the natural use of the woman, burned in their lust one toward another, men with men working that which is unseemly, and receiving in themselves that recompense of their error." Bob only could anticipate with trepidation the scripturally predicted retributions for his "shameless acts."[84]

Compounding his bodily afflictions, Bob Bond's rating had been changed and reduced. He must have known that serving as a mess boy offered little training, prestige, honor, or hope of promotion.[85] Unlike his father, Bob would have no chance to serve his country on an active front, since the navy's wartime forays in the Caribbean had ended with the Cuban conflict's swift conclusion and even John Senior's intervention could not stimulate a transfer to the Philippines. Unless these explanations are far off target, Bob Bond had become an angry, frustrated young man as the USS *Lancaster* cruised the unchallenged Atlantic coast.

The black seaman Nicholas Campbell articulated a thought that could well have applied at that critical time when desertion might have seemed Bob's only escape. "We are often asked," Campbell wrote, "why the percentage of Negro deserters is so small." "To this there is but one answer," he concluded: the African American sailor "places a high value upon his citizenship."[86] Bob also had John Bond, Sr.'s estimable example in the Civil War navy to live up to. If he abandoned the service, would his own father (whose name he bore and in whose wake he sailed) judge him a failure?

When the USS *Lancaster* was docked in Boston on July 1, 1899, Bob Bond petitioned Captain Charles Thomas, the ship's new commanding officer. "I respectfully request that I may be granted leave of absence from this vessel for five days," he wrote, "for purposes of visiting my home at Hyde Park, Mass."[87] Bob promptly received Thomas's permission to go home for the Fourth of July.

A family conference of sorts no doubt convened as the Bonds and their town celebrated the country's independence. Bitter and frustrated by the discrimination he encountered, thwarted in his attempts to transfer to the Asiatic Squadron, and shamed, terrorized, even revolted by the possibility of further sexual assaults that threatened his manhood and his health, Bob must have thought that another two-and-a-half years in the navy would serve no useful purpose. If they knew the full extent of his travails, wouldn't John and Emma have agreed that their son had endured enough? But how awkward, embarrassing, even agonizing it would have been for Bob to admit the worst of what happened aboard the *Lancaster*! "I would not care for my folks to learn anything about this," confessed another anxiety-wracked sailor about his homosexual shipboard acts, "because I want them to know me as they think I am. This is something that I never did until I came in the Navy." The Bible's Proverbs, Bob might have recalled, warned that "a foolish son is a grief to his father, and bitterness to her that bore him." Nonetheless, if they were to bail him out, Bob almost certainly would have had to tell much of his wretched story to those nearest him, at least his father and older brother, whose moderately successful employment earned him a major say in crucial family decisions, especially those concerning allocation of financial resources.[88]

The Bonds, despite their modest circumstances, apparently pooled their minimal assets to buy out the remainder of the three-year contract for which Bob had enlisted. His "purchase discharge" after eight months (precisely 255 days) was an honorable one, and the Prodigal Son returned home in August 1899.[89] Thereafter, Bob remained close to his mother and sisters, but his fraternal relationship with the straitlaced Percy seems to have deteriorated.

Bob Bond ultimately revealed to his doctors that he had contracted syphilis "at the time I was in the navy." Whether he ever shared suspicions as to how he acquired it cannot be determined. Shipboard physicians, however, neither diagnosed nor dealt with his disease in 1899. Bob bore no telltale marks from lesions on or near his penis and testes that might have remained had he acquired syphilitic chancres as the result of a heterosexual encounter, but he did suffer contusions, tearing, and scarring of his rectum. Around the turn of the century, a revolted doctor reported about one of his male patients: "The state of the rectum left no doubt of the abominable practices to which this individual had been addicted." Those words characterized Bob Bond's condition as well. His own, less judgmental physician described Bob's anus as "a mass of scar tissue," rife with oozing fistulas and "external hemorrhoids." Bob Bond complained that he became "totally disabled as to control of my rectum," prone to "break wind or pass foul air."[90] It is possible, of course, that he contracted syphilis in what navy surgeons called "the usual manner" (heterosexual intercourse), or from a septic needle when he was tattooed, but rough, anal penetration occurring aboard ship early in 1899 seems a far more likely diagnosis.

This account of Bob's seafaring misadventures singularly explains his urgent desire, first to transfer off the *Lancaster,* and when those efforts failed, to leave the service entirely. He loved the navy, despite his altered classification and reduced rank. He wanted—and tried—to continue serving his country, but his demeaning demotion combined with the coerced shipboard pederasty convinced him and his family that remaining in such a malevolent environment was inadvisable, if not inconceivable. The apparent assaults that tore Bob's rectum and bestowed on him the dubious gifts of the wily and amoral, pallid syphilis spirochetes, plus his unwarranted official discipline—a consequence of the navy's disdain for his dark skin—combined to make unbearable his continued presence on that despised ark of mismated humanity.

Bob Bond, however, was a plucky fellow who would not allow a little buggery, then a chancrous eruption followed by a rash and fever, seriously to disrupt his life. He returned to Boston, acquired a landlubber's job, and courted Osie Grimes, an attractive young dressmaker who lived in the city with two of her sisters and a brother-in-law, all of whom hailed from deep in rural Virginia. Like Percy Bond's love, Georgia Stewart, Osie, too, had light enough skin to pass for white. More urbane "colored" Bostonians might have considered her a country bumpkin, but her genteel vocation, combined with a peaches-and-cream complexion, may have helped to establish her as a marginal member of Boston's often exclusionary middle-class Negro community.

In 1901, the world mourned the demise of revered Queen Victoria and the era bearing her name. The United States imposed civilian rule in the Philippines and prepared to enforce its territorial status, then lost its imperialistic leader, William McKinley ("shot down by a dastard's hand, without motive, without provocation," reported a leader of the Massachusetts GAR to a grieving audience that included John Robert Bond, Sr.), to an alien, psychotic assassin's bullet. Theodore Roosevelt inherited the presidency, his "bully pulpit," and, with a gesture that set tongues wagging all across the race-obsessed nation, invited Booker T. Washington to dine at the White House that October, thus essentially crowning him "king of a captive people."[91]

The Hyde Park *Gazette* also reported in its social notes that "Miss Osie Grimes, daughter of Mr. and Mrs. Daniel F. Grimes of Barboursville, Va. and Mr. John R. Bond [Jr.] of Hyde Park were married Christmas morning at the home of the bride's sister." "The ceremony was performed," it continued, "in the presence of a large number of relatives and friends by Rev. Leroy T. Montague of the Ebenezer Baptist Church, Boston." Percy, significantly perhaps, did not serve as his only brother's best man, or even an usher. Some people would have considered the Bonds' majority-white Episcopal church in Dedham more "high toned." Nonetheless, West Springfield Street's imposing Ebenezer Baptist, established in 1871 by former slaves from Virginia, with (its founding minister explained) "habits and customs [that] were their heritage from slavery," was one of Boston's largest and most respected black congregations.[92]

The modiste, Osie Grimes Bond, almost certainly created her own outfits, and the *Gazette* admired her stylish "traveling costume of grey crepe de chine with steel trimmings and hat to match." Following the ceremony, it continued, "the newly married couple started on a tour to Chicago." "Upon their return," it predicted, "they will live at 696 Huntington Avenue," the home of Osie's older sister. Following a short interlude in Boston proper, however, Osie and Bob Bond came back to reside near his family in suburban Hyde Park.[93]

Despite Bob's wretched experiences during his brief military stint, he remained a loyal citizen who, in the fall of 1902, might have appreciated his hometown newspaper's featured article, "The New American Navy." It declared that "victory over the foe of 1898 must be attributed to the patriots who foresaw their country's need and . . . took measures which enabled her to meet it."[94] He displayed the Stars and Stripes (tattooed on his shoulder and hanging by his door), always celebrated national holidays, and ultimately joined the Veterans of Foreign Wars.

The *Treponema pallidum,* however, continued to circulate through Bob's body. Perhaps he believed that residual distress from the attacks on his rectum did not portend further problems, but in truth, the treacherous, reclusive spirochetes were only swimming unseen and unnoticed, as they typically did. When Bob and Osie had sexual intercourse, the bacteria seem to have entered her body through permeable mucous membranes, wriggled into her lymph capillaries and infiltrated the nodes, moved on to incubate in a nourishing amniotic bath, then penetrated the placental barrier to caress a vulnerable developing fetus. To characterize such all-too-common transmissions, turn-of-the-century social hygienists coined the telling phrase "syphilis of the innocent."[95]

Nothing, however, suggests that Bob Bond even imagined such hazards in 1902. He concerned himself with earning a living, plus the more apparent manifestations of his wife's pregnancy and imminent delivery. The couple's seemingly healthy daughter, Osie Elizabeth, called Betty, was born in September, with Dr. Samuel Courtney (Georgia Stewart's former landlord and Booker T. Washington's favorite Bostonian) in attendance.[96]

Bob worked diligently for his new family and squirreled away his savings to make purchases of real estate for the businesses he ultimately would own and operate in Hyde Park, as Percy (no longer his troubled and troublesome brother's keeper) left Boston for Alabama. Their father, John Robert Bond, continued his own work and his church and GAR activities, while Emma doted on a first grandchild and tended to her two growing daughters and her home.

· 10 ·

WALKING *in* EMMA'S FOOTSTEPS: TIME *and* TIDES *along* MOTHER BROOK

Parents should hold on to their children, and children should stand by their parents until the last strand of the silken cord is broken.

REBECCA LEE CRUMPLER, M.D., 1883

IN 1902, BOB BOND, his wife Osie, and their little Betty came back to live just east of his parents' Edenic garden and cottage on River Street where Bob had spent most of his life. His sisters, meanwhile, remained at home with Emma and John in the family house almost next door. Those younger girls, however, had been born and had grown up under somewhat different circumstances than had Percy and Bob.

In 1879, Emma Bond had found herself gravid once again. That same year, a somewhat older couple, Arthur (a porter) and Rebecca Crumpler, settled into a cottage near the Bonds, on a truncated lane in Readville leading from River Street down to Mother Brook. Hyde Park had a handful of other southern-born Negro women among its residents, but Dr. Rebecca Davis Lee Crumpler's proximity, plus her association with the healing arts, must have endeared her to Emma Bond, who had acquired in her own youth, and still used, a substantive body of knowledge about herbal medicine.[1] Crumpler recalled similar African American folk remedies, combined them with hands-on nursing experience, a full course of professional training, and more than a decade of medical practice.

In its early phases, Rebecca's path to her profession seemed commonplace, but it grew increasingly unique. In 1831, she was born in Delaware to Absolum and Matilda Davis. Given that state's demographics, the possibility of her having been born into slavery was slightly greater than having been born free.[2] As a teenager, she somehow made her way to Boston, worked as a nurse through the 1850s, and married a man named Lee. In a few years, however, Rebecca again was single—almost certainly widowed.

"I early conceived a liking for and sought every opportunity to be in a position to relieve the suffering of others," she explained, reflecting black women's long involvement with healing and expressing emotions similar to those of many family health-care providers like Emma Bond. The country still had no nursing schools, but Elizabeth Blackwell, the first licensed female doctor in the United States, had completed her formal medical training in 1849. Yet by 1860, no more than 300 women had joined the nation's ranks of 54,000 male physicians. Rebecca Lee's sponsors, recognizing her gifts and dedication, encouraged her to pursue that reluctantly opening profession and steered her to Boston's decade-old New England Female Medical College.[3]

Rebecca matriculated there with the assistance of a scholarship, having satisfied the entrance requirements with a record that included a spotless "moral character." She garnered hands-on experience in the school's clinic for needy women and children, then undertook "three years of medical studies under the direction of a respectable practitioner of medicine." She passed the final examinations, presented "a Thesis written in her own hand," and remitted her commencement fees. In March 1864, Rebecca Lee graduated along with two white women, and became the school's only Negro alumna.

She did not, however, complete the course of studies without controversy. Several of the medical college's professors (four of whom were female) "hesitated very seriously in recommending her certification," but agreed to do so "out of deference to what we understand to be the wishes of the Trustees & the present state of public feeling." That professed "public feeling" may have reflected many Bostonians' abolitionist sentiments. During the Civil War, "Rebecca Lee, (colored)," thus became a licensed "Doctress of Medicine," the first female physician of her race in the nation.[4] Though more than a few African American women became accredited medical doctors during the ensuing decades, no others attended New England Female Medical College, probably at least in part because the faculty in some way disapproved of Rebecca Lee— their single, dark-skinned "experiment."

After a brief interval when Rebecca practiced medicine in Boston and traveled through Canada, she went to Richmond, where she attended to the health needs of the newly liberated people. She married a Virginia man, Arthur Crumpler, and the couple returned to Massachusetts in the late 1870s.[5] They may have moved to Hyde Park to enjoy the rural ambience of a town near familiar Boston. "A cheerful home . . . in the country, with wholesome food and water," declared Dr. Crumpler, "is worth more to preserve health and life, than a house in a crowded city with luxuries and twenty rooms to let."[6] That aptly characterized the Crumplers' frame cottage by Mother Brook, but perhaps Readville's historic military significance for Negroes also attracted Arthur and Rebecca, just as it lured a number of others, like John Bond, who had lived through the Civil War.

Down the street from the Bonds, Rebecca Crumpler, "tall and straight, with light brown skin" and graying hair, wrote her *Book of Medical Discourses,* dedicating it to "Mothers, Nurses, and all who may desire to mitigate the afflications of the human race."[7] It resembled some but differed from many other such texts in its personal tone and content, commonsense approach, and reliance on traditional healing. "I desire that my book shall be as a primary reader in the hands of every woman," she wrote, "yet none the less suited to any who may be conversant with all branches of medical science." *Medical Discourses* focused on gynecology, obstetrics, and pediatrics because of Crumpler's interests and experience, but for other reasons as well. "Women doctors, or, more properly speaking doctresses of medicine," she added, with clear disdain for any male-imposed strictures on her professional life, typically were "treated with less courtesy by doctors," and also "considered to be in their proper sphere in the confinement-room and nursery."[8]

Crumpler, regarded as "a very pleasant and intellectual woman," utilized the knowledge and skills imparted by the white physicians who had instructed her at New England Female Medical College, but she also incorporated methods and medications much like those used by black people during her own and Emma Thomas Bond's childhoods, and often derived from traditional West African pharmacology. Almost next door, Emma cultivated her own garden with its array of flowers, shrubs, and fruits, many of which possessed tried-and-true curative properties. Emma also combed nearby fields, woods, and waterways, seeking grasses, roots, and leaves like senna—her springtime purgative—to use as preventive or ameliorative treatments for family and friends.[9] Rebecca Crumpler similarly touted the values of readily available herbage, and prescribed decoctions derived from peaches, blackberries (both fruit and foliage), heliotrope and crocus, red oak and cherry bark, watercress, and burdock.

In southern communities, many grandmothers and midwives retained such ancestral botanical lore and shouldered the responsibilities of overseeing childbirth, but such women and their nurturing care had been left behind when Emma Bond went north. When Emma's new child was expected in 1879, Rebecca Crumpler, who resided and practiced medicine just around the corner, probably assisted her through labor and the delivery of her first daughter. The Bonds named the baby Lena—almost certainly for the family's old Portsmouth friend Silena Whiting, who had relocated to Boston.[10] Crumpler believed that "it is just as important that a doctor should be in attendance before the birth of a poor woman's child as . . . before the birth of the child of wealth." She also observed with clear contempt that "the male physician, unlike the woman physician, does not always remain long enough to see this important duty properly performed."[11]

As the labor contractions intensified, Crumpler would demand warm water and an "all wool blanket" for women like Emma, adding, "as soon as the babe is freed from the mother, it should be wrapped in the blanket and laid aside in a comfortable place." She used "lamp wicking or several strands of white spool cotton" to tie off the umbilicus, then would "slip the cord, fold it closely, but flat and smooth, and lay it over to the left side of the belly, that it may not intercept the circulation of the liver." She sashed the baby's torso with an "all-wool flannel band," then swabbed it with "pieces of soft linen or cotton about as large as your hand" saturated in "fresh hog's lard or sweet oil." After bathing and swaddling the newborn, "the head," she advised, "should be thoroughly greased and cleaned, taking care not to press the bones in the least." She sponged away scalp "scurf" that appeared during a child's early weeks with cloths soaked in a brew made from red oak bark or burdock root. Crumpler insisted, however, that "no Bay Rum, perfume, puff powders or other unnatural substances should be tolerated," and warned against a new mother's undue jocularity, because "suppressed laughter soon after delivery . . . before the womb has had time to get in place" might cause "internal convulsions."[12]

To induce lactation in women such as Emma Bond, Crumpler—as Negro "granny women" so often had done—would "besmear the hands with warm goose . . . oil, and anoint the breasts slowly and evenly from under the arms down to the nipple, until the glands soften and the milk begins to flow." Should the "milk veins become knotty and painful," she recommended hot tea, both to drink and bathe in, derived from Indian posy or life-everlasting herb, and argued that for most babies "the first milk from the breast is the only medicine needed." If problems arose with nursing, she suggested temporarily bottle-feeding the infant while treating the mother's breasts with "a poultice made of bruised burdock root and elm flour." When a baby such as Lena Bond developed "rattling or wheezing in its throat," Crumpler stroked a dampened feather across the back of the tongue, because "the tickling excites a coughing or gagging, which dislodges the phlegm, so that it can be hooked out with the finger." But she firmly rejected out-of-date remedies such as catnip, castor oil, laudanum, or even "a little weak toddy."[13]

Rebecca Crumpler also counseled "that a few dollars paid to a physician for a half-dozen extra visits during the first weeks of confinement, might prevent months and years of gloom," yet she still "received children in [her Hyde Park] house for treatment; regardless . . . of remuneration." And she was neither unduly directive nor aloof with her patients. She believed that sound maternal and child care required open interaction between mother and physician. "Surely if women ask no questions of the doctors, no answers can be given," she contended.[14]

When Lena began teething, the childless yet caring Rebecca Crumpler may have issued one especially dire warning, pronouncing it "possible to trace the cause of insanity to the pernicious custom of rubbing the gums of infants." She preferred leaving a baby to teethe in its own good time, but in a stubborn case, she added, "the least touch with the lancet will part the skin and assist [a new tooth] through." For teething-associated diarrhea, she administered "a decoction of blackberry or raspberry," and as a recipe for nutritious biscuits to soothe the gums of fretful babies recommended "two teacupfuls each of wheat and Graham or Indian meal; one-half cup of brown sugar or molasses; half teaspoonful of salt; mix with warm milk, knead well, cut into medium size cracker form, and bake quickly."[15]

Beyond obstetric and pediatric care, Rebecca Lee Crumpler offered advice for ameliorating problems associated with cholera ("peaches boiled in milk"), menstrual cramps (poultices made with "soothing herbs," hops, and vinegar), and menopause ("avoid . . . stimulants, and secure cheerful exercise for the mind, with an abundance of outdoor scenery"). Her other remedies included molasses for burns, tea made from "seneca snake root or valerian" for rheumatism, and "inhalations of tar, pine bark, or roasted coffee" to relieve bronchitis.[16]

She added a formula for "Doctress Crumpler's vegetable alternative," touted as an all-purpose cathartic to relieve "bloating, worms, cough, . . . morbid craving for tobacco, alcoholic beverages or other blood poisoning idols." It called for "Indian posy and water pepper herbs, . . . white pine bark, [and] horehound . . . simmer[ed] in two quarts of water . . . four or five hours." After straining the bitter elixir, she continued, "add two and one-half pounds of loaf sugar," boil down to a thick syrup, then stir in "one teaspoonful of pulverized mandrake root"—a plant of African origins with legendary powers, equated in the United States to the common May apple.[17]

Crumpler also provided formulas for a holistic approach to life that she shared with readers and friends as freely as she dispersed medical advice. She lauded her country's merits, and stressed hard work and frugality, stating: "This is a land of opportunities; in it the laborer gets, or should get, his hire." "It therefore becomes his privilege to aid by prudence, industry and economy, in elevating his family to the discouragement of pauperism and willful neglect of the laws of health," Crumpler continued. "I would suggest," she added in words presaging the dogma that Booker T. Washington soon would espouse, "that an extra ten cent piece be deposited in safe keeping each day as a surety for a baby's comforts for the first six months; which should afterward be increased to twenty cents a day, and thus continued during his childhood." Further revealing her conservative values, Crumpler asserted, "Pauperism, like familiarity, 'breeds contempt'; therefore persons should try with all their mind and might to avoid its conditions."[18]

Rebecca Crumpler, "an indefatigable church woman," also held strong opinions about education. "Heaven bless our schools, for they are invaluable," she cheered, almost certainly observing and evaluating institutions such as the nearby Damon School that all of Emma Bond's children ultimately would attend. She cautioned, however: "In school at four and a half, and in the grave at five; or in school at five, and in some State Reform School at seven or eight! just when the mind is beginning to be formed."[19]

Crumpler directly addressed the well-being of girls such as Lena Bond who had no shrewd and caring Irish-English or black Virginia grandmothers to counsel and guide them. "We find, when comparing the statistical reports of the death-rates of children under one year," she further wrote, "that they are largest in those cities where the influx of immigration is constant, and the women, either from choice or necessity . . . do not take care of their young." Those views reflected not only her own, but widespread concerns about the rapidly increasing and impoverished foreign-born population in cities such as Boston.[20]

On the male and female behavior she observed in African American families, Crumpler bluntly stated: "The laboring men of my race, generally speaking, take much better care of the horses intrusted to their care than they do of their own health." Women like Emma Bond, for whom cooking, cleaning, laundering, and sewing must have seemed interminable, Crumpler added, "work under heavy disadvantages; if the family is small, they are never through with their work; if it is large, there is a double excuse for having no time to rest."[21]

In addition to her focus on the family, Crumpler held adamant political views. "By real earnest, devoted measures," she argued, walking in the ideological shoes of Negro women like Sojourner Truth and Boston's reformer Josephine Ruffin, and Hyde Park suffragists such as the nonaccredited Dr. Mehitable Sunderland and the Grimké sisters, "women may be enabled, within the next decade . . . to exercise the right of franchise, and fill positions of honor outside of the domestic circle."[22]

Finally, she lashed out against racism, violence, and especially the detrimental impact of one particular, widely acclaimed manifestation of popular culture. "Do . . . the little children who witness the farce of 'Punch and Judy' on Boston Common every summer, gain a moral, or feel that it is wrong to imitate beating a wife, killing a baby, or hanging a black man?" she asked about the alfresco entertainment that attracted legions of children like Percy, Bob, and Lena Bond from throughout the metropolitan area. "The popular adage, 'No nigger, no fun,' " Crumpler scolded, "is why such [programs] are tolerated in our Public Parks." "May not such shameful scenes prove to be the primary lessons in pugilism, murder, and suicide?" she queried. "They best serve to prolong the barbarous system of flogging, whether it be by lashing to a post and applying the cat-o'-nine-tails, or otherwise." Dr. Rebecca Crumpler concluded: "Will it not pay to endeavor to cultivate inborn morals early in life, thereby shutting out a desire for vulgar and debasing sports?"[23]

Throughout Lena Bond's first seven years, the hardworking, principled, and alternately fierce and gentle Doctress Crumpler and her husband Arthur lived near the Bond family alongside Mother Brook. "God willing and the creek don't rise," an old adage contends, but not only did Hyde Park's major waterway claim novice boaters, froggers, skaters, and swimmers as drowning victims over the years, but rise it ultimately did, and the great flood of 1886 nearly washed them all away.[24]

Mother Brook, Hyde Park's usually serene canal, branches off the Charles River, snakes in from the west, and feeds into the Neponset near the heart of town. In the 1880s, only three railroad crossings and a couple of footbridges spanned those linked waterways that even now cascade through locks and over falls on a predetermined course toward Massachusetts Bay.

Icy, drenching, blustery nor'easters characterized January 1886, and the Neponset River and Mother Brook, a contemporaneous account attested, were "swollen by the melting of a winter's snow and an almost unprecedented fall of rain." By mid-February, a wary resident observed, the streams' "ice-encrusted and frozen surface[s] were raging torrents, overflowing their banks in every direction, and carrying destruction before them." The Neponset rose nine feet above its usual level and "Mother Brook was the highest ever known." Flood-borne debris pummeled struts and trestles, wrenching away one precarious bridge over the profoundly troubled waters. Frigid torrents deluged basements, streets, and gardens, carrying sludge, trees, dead fish, amphibians, and an ugly array of detritus.[25] The Bonds and their neighbors Arthur and Rececca Crumpler, who lived so near the rampaging canal, surely were among the eighty families "obliged to vacate their homes." Finally, however, as Genesis had foretold, "the waters . . . abated from off the earth," and the Bonds cleared out muck, dried their sodden furniture, rugs, and treasured possessions, and returned to rehabilitate their home of more than a decade. But the Crumplers abandoned Hyde Park for the high-and-dry security of Boston's established African American community often referred to as "Nigger Hill," located just behind the state capitol.[26]

The next year, but perhaps without the departed Dr. Crumpler's assistance, Emma Bond gave birth to a second daughter. Mary, always called "Tooty," was born when Emma (who must have thought that bearing and raising babies was behind her) was forty-one, and Percy, her oldest child, was almost twenty.

During the century's next-to-last decade, Hyde Park's immigrant population, as well as the Bond family, increased. In 1885, Readville had been the scene of a festive "Hotel de Italy," where longtime residents "watched with much interest the foreign element preparing their meals." The next year, a packed gathering of the Irish National League met "for the purpose of giving moral and financial aid to Ireland," and according to the Norfolk County *Gazette,* Sam Kee, "the Chinese Laundryman," celebrated Thanksgiving much like his native-born customers. He reportedly declared, "Chinese fixings necessary for the Mongolian happiness," adding, "gleat day, no washee, all eatie."[27]

Around that time, many Boston-area residents also followed a vigorous journalistic debate about the relative qualifications for American citizenship of Negroes and Chinese. Concerning the "average mental ability of these two races," the *Herald* contended, "the Chinese won, hands down." "The Negro, apart from the influence of the white man, has never shown the ability to lift himself above the level of the barbarians," that polemic continued. "We do not say that American citizenship should be given to either," it rationalized, but if one had to be chosen, "the argument is altogether in favor of the Chinese."[28]

The Boston *Journal,* however, took exception, claiming that "the colored man has the same stake in America as the white man." "In spite of all obstacles, and the most obstinate and perverse prejudices, he will yet have a fair chance, if not for social equality, for equality under the laws . . . which the founders of this nation declared to be inalienable." The *Courant* supported those arguments. "Is the Negro opposed to Christianity? Is he un-American in any particular whatever? No indeed!" it declared. "See who rejoices most on the Fourth of July, and at Christmas. The Negro, even in his illiteracy, comprehends the deep meaning of all these." "The Negro's blood alone," it boldly concluded, "remains untainted by foreign associations."[29]

As those debates on race, ethnicity, and citizenship raged, in addition to its intermittently ridiculed "foreign element," Angelina

Grimké, grandniece of the venerable Theodore Weld, was one of the few Negroes living close by who was of Percy, Bob, Lena, and Tooty Bond's generation. The Bonds' great friend William Gould, his wife, and their six boys resided equally near in East Dedham, while W. Monroe Trotter and his younger sisters Maude and Bessie, children of the Civil War veteran James Trotter and his wife Virginia, also grew up in Hyde Park. When James Trotter died in 1892, the whole town mourned and lauded him as "the most notable colored politician in the country." GAR Post 121's entire membership, in uniform, led the funeral services.[30]

The Bonds, Grimkés, Trotters, and Goulds faced subtle racial slights more than overt discrimination in their ethnically diverse home communities during the late nineteenth century. But the Boston area in its entirety, which once had committed itself to abolitionism and interracial amity as much as or more than any other place in the nation, did not escape noteworthy instances of prejudice and discrimination against Negroes. Its economy wavered, immigration burgeoned, and the South's subversive Jim Crow mentality infiltrated even the country's onetime bastions of racial tolerance.[31]

In her waterside garden, Emma sowed, weeded, hoed, trimmed and cut flowers, and gathered fruits from her fecund grapevines and pear, plum, and apple trees that were not unlike those that had been so plentiful during her childhood in Tidewater Virginia. She preserved fruits, made pies, jellies, and jams, while her husband John sometimes sold her produce and wares around town.[32] Though Rebecca Crumpler no longer lived in Readville, Emma befriended other, mostly white neighbors—Murphys, Higginses, Callahans, and other Irish immigrants prevalent among them—exchanged recipes and local gossip, and cared for her home and younger children.

Despite eight years' difference in age, Lena and Tooty were very close to one another, and to their mother. But as dutiful daughters, both acquiesced to their father's religious preference and attended the Episcopal Church of the Good Shepherd, where the Reverend William Cheney infused his sermons with guidelines for righteous family life as well as reminiscences of his annual summer sojourns in England. The church's carved ash chancel arch featured the classic text limned in gold leaf with Old English letters: "Holiness Becometh Thine House, O Lord, Forever."[33]

Archie Grimké's Boston-based newspaper, *The Hub,* also laid out guidelines that many Negro families such as the Bonds observed in raising their female children. They knew that the stereotypes portraying women of their race as sexually promiscuous must be vigorously countered, and acted accordingly. "Wildness is a thing girls cannot afford. Delicacy . . . cannot be lost and found," *The Hub* counseled. "It is the first duty of a woman to be a lady," it continued. "Good breeding is good morality. . . . A lady is always inalienably worthy of respect." Similarly, Rebecca Crumpler had advised that every "girl should be subject to the advice and protection of her mother or guardian, till sufficiently able to care for herself," and added, "poverty, with chastity . . . is an enviable condition."[34]

As Lena and Mary grew up under their parents' watchful care, Percy Bond, in his early but dependable manhood, "always kept an eye out for the welfare of his younger sisters." He saw to it that they learned to play the piano, a skill proclaiming middle-class status and ladylike refinement, ably practiced by his beloved friend Georgia Stewart. In addition to many, often stultifying behavioral lessons, Emma tutored her daughters in the domestic skills she had learned in childhood, and slave girls in southeast Virginia had not only cooked, cleaned, and sewed, but also had braided and woven wheat straw to make their bonnets.[35]

When Lena finished her education at Hyde Park High School, therefore, Percy steered her into an apprenticeship in a millinery shop on Boston's Newbury Street. She moved on to become an assistant buyer in the Pitts-Kimball department store, where salesmen from New York City familiarized her with the newest and most fashionable chapeaus. A position like that in a first-rate Boston emporium was rare and respected work for a "colored" woman. Using the sophisticated, contemporary expertise she absorbed on Newbury Street, and combining it with her own innate taste and artistic bent plus her mother's home training, Lena Bond (who dressed with tailored but stylish flair) became a skilled milliner.[36]

During the 1890s, Hyde Park's newspaper initiated a column devoted to women's fashions, with illustrated commentaries on the "straw toques" and elegant "birds and birds' wings" used by chic "Paris milliners." It lauded the newest headware "follies," such as those with "yellow lace over white mousseline de soie" or a "soft green straw with a crown of Tuscan straw gauze."[37] The Boston-based *Colored American* featured Madame Runford's "Prevailing Styles for Early Summer," and Julia Coston's *Afro-American Journal of Fashion* may have stimulated Lena's interests as well. The latter magazine focused on couture, and also benefited from the contributions of women such as Washington, D.C.'s social leader and reformer, Mary Church Terrell. Journalist Victoria Earle Matthews called it "so pure, so womanly—positively agreeable in every feature."[38] Elizabeth Keckley had become Mary Todd Lincoln's confidante and modiste in the 1860s, and dressmaking and millinery were always respectable occupations for gifted Negro women who needed to support themselves and had few other remunerative outlets for their creativity. After 1900, Lena's interest in fashion may have been further spurred by the influence of her brother Bob's wife Osie, a skilled dressmaker, and by Percy's clothes-conscious and tastefully dressed friend, Georgia Stewart.

But as Emma and her girls stitched away, they also may have recalled Rebecca Crumpler's warnings about certain unexpected perils. "The operator sits too far from the [sewing] machine," Crumpler had protested, "thereby causing a motion of the whole body, while she leans too much forward; second, operates too fast; thirdly, works too long at a time; fourthly, allows herself but little time to eat or sleep." "What is more," she concluded, the woman "frequently gets angry with the machine, unstrings it, and gets it in as bad condition as she has her own nerves."[39]

The Crumplers' departure from Hyde Park in 1886 (though they briefly returned) would have seemed a personal misfortune for the Bonds, but the whole town's major loss occurred almost a decade later with the death of its moral lodestar, Theodore Weld. It was the same year that Rebecca Crumpler died and, like Weld, was buried in Hyde Park's Fairview Cemetery. In keeping with the town's patriotic traditions, one of the first poems by Weld's grandniece Angelina Grimké and published in the *Gazette* had been a Memorial Day tribute, "The Grave in the Corner," commemorating an anonymous Civil War soldier. For his ninetieth birthday, Angelina also had written a paean to Weld, the venerable abolitionist who served for years as her guardian.[40] In many ways, Theodore Weld's death (and that of Frederick Douglass) in 1895, symbolized the end of the whole country's idealistic era of racial reform. The Supreme Court's legitimization of Jim Crow in the case of *Plessy v. Ferguson* the next year epitomized that retreat.

To observe Decoration Day in 1897, John Bond and members of his family probably joined the many Hyde Park residents, plus African American Civil War veterans from around the country, who traveled to Boston for the dedication of a monument honoring Colonel Robert Gould Shaw, the white leader of the black Fifty-fourth Massachusetts Infantry. Booker T. Washington was among the notables who proffered laurels to Shaw and his famed Negro troops that day. Yet he tempered his praise by refusing to hold white Americans (who lionized him) in any way responsible for the country's racial problems, and placing the blame for their recent woes on the shoulders of Negroes themselves. "The full measure of . . . all that this monument stands for," Washington declared, "will not be realized until every man covered by black skin shall, by patience and natural effort, grow to the height in industry, property, intelligence and moral responsibility."[41]

Hyde Park residents of both races sustained an ongoing interest in those black Civil War soldiers who had trained in their town. And John Robert Bond, with his singular Liverpool accent, became widely acclaimed as an inspirational speaker who delivered patriotic orations at nearby schools every Decoration Day. He worked and negotiated his way up to become a ranking officer in the local GAR post. Not only that organization but the whole town took the rights and privileges of American citizenship very seriously. Its newspaper boasted that Hyde Park "is taking no one's dust in the matter of flag raisings, and the enthusiasm seems to increase with each one."[42]

John also represented Hyde Park's Timothy Ingraham Post 121 at Massachusetts-wide annual encampments of the GAR in the years around 1900. John's friends and colleagues Isaac Mullen and William Gould similarly became delegates to those winter events, and the graying veterans who attended the 1904 Boston gathering heard spirited accounts about the previous summer's reunion of old "colored" soldiers (joined by some of their white officers) that convened under the auspices of the alumni association for the three Negro regiments that had trained in Readville in the early 1860s.[43]

But of further interest and pride to "colored" navy veterans such as Bond, Mullen, and Gould was the unprecedented progress of the former sailor and lawyer James Wolff, a notable representative of his race, through the ranks of Grand Army hierarchy. Wolff was his department's (Massachusetts's) judge advocate in 1900, was detailed to the national organization in Washington, ascended to the state's junior vice-commandership in 1903, became senior vice-commander the next year, then in 1905 presided over the entire, predominantly white, politically powerful organization when its statewide membership topped twenty thousand.

With John Robert Bond and almost a thousand other spellbound delegates in attendance, Wolff pleaded in an emotional address: "Mothers, take your children upon your knee—whisper into their ears the story of the sacrifices of their fathers and the blessings of freedom." "Liberty," he added, "has always been the theme of the nation, from the time the Pilgrims planted their feet upon that eternal rock, and it will continue to be from now until the end of time." "America shall be the home of liberty, freedom, justice and equal rights for all," he concluded to resounding cheers from the assembled men, "it matters not what combination of forces may intervene."[44]

When James Wolff assumed command of the state organization, his white predecessor declared: "Don't ask anything, don't try to be anything, because of race and color." "Put it on the score of manhood," he continued, "and let us forget the color."[45] Black people in Massachusetts, however, could scarcely "forget the color." Although they faced less daunting obstacles than their counterparts in the South, they routinely encountered discrimination in hiring and promotions, housing, and public accommodations. Personal slights and gross insults were routine.

Despite James Wolff's unprecedented rise to power, white GAR members never disregarded race either. In 1905, Boston's popular mayor, John Fitzgerald, declared to their assembly: "It means a great deal for this city, this state, and this country, to have such a body of men have a black man at its head." "I say God bless the Commonwealth of Massachusetts and the Grand Army of the Republic for giving such an example of comradeship," Fitzgerald concluded to a roar of approval.[46]

John Bond worked diligently with the local GAR, which not only sent him as its delegate to those statewide assemblies but ultimately elevated him to the rank of junior vice-commander for the large Hyde Park post. He also, however, involved himself for a time in the black brotherhoods of both Prince Hall Masons and the Grand United Order of Odd Fellows.

In 1775, an army lodge of British Freemasons stationed in Cambridge had initiated fifteen Negroes into their order. Prince Hall, who had been born in Barbados to a white Englishman and a free "colored" woman, led those black men.[47] Hall had immigrated to Massachusetts, where he became a minister and antislavery advocate. He had felt some residual kinship with the British, and may or may not have fought with the patriots during the Revolution, but a few years later he unsuccessfully sought permission from white American Masons to organize a separate masonic chapter for Negroes. In 1784, however, England's Grand Mother Lodge promptly granted the black men a charter, and Prince Hall established in Boston the country's first "African" lodge. He soon became grand master of the rapidly growing independent order of African American Masons, which thereafter bore his name.

Over the ensuing decades, Prince Hall and his followers became known for their godliness, their patriotism combined with outspoken condemnations of slavery, and advocacy of full rights of citizenship for all men, race notwithstanding. His philosophy combined idealism with realism and provided guidance for the African lodges—and for every Negro in Massachusetts. "There is here a great number of worthy good men and good citizens," he had contended in 1795 about some white people in his state, "that are not ashamed to take an African by the hand; but yet there are to be seen the weeds of pride, envy, tyranny, and scorn, in this garden of peace, liberty and equality." Ever aware of that crucial ambiguity, Prince Hall died in 1807, and his grave site became a shrine for Negro Masons. Almost nine decades after he first had taken the vows that initiated him into the sacred Masonic brotherhood, a military Prince Hall lodge was attached to Readville's Fifty-fourth Infantry Regiment during the Civil War.[48]

Despite limited areas of cooperation and the majority order's supposed credo of universal fraternity, many white Masons disparaged Negroes, and the rhetoric intensified after the Civil War. In 1866, Lewis Hayden, a onetime leader among Boston's black abolitionists who later became an elected state official, wrote a pamphlet condemning the white organization's racism. Confirming Hayden's critique, five years later a white Mason published a treatise titled *Niggerdom in Regalia* denouncing the legitimacy of Prince Hall Masonry and the "leprosy of negro association." Soon thereafter, a member from Ohio proclaimed: "I took my obligation to white men, not to negroes. When I have to accept negroes as *brothers* or leave Masonry, I shall leave it." By 1890, most southern lodges adopted policies of total "non-intercourse" with African American Masons, but some white northerners at least acknowledged a limited Masonic kinship exemplified by the separate Negro units.[49]

In the context of that contentious history, in the mid-1890s John Bond affiliated himself with the Mt. Moriah Masonic Prince Hall Lodge in Cambridge (neither Hyde Park nor neighboring Dedham had enough Negro residents to sustain separate lodges, and the mainstream chapters were all white) that met on the third Tuesday of each month. The Cambridge group had twenty-six members, and in addition to Bond, among them were Hyde Park's John Brooks, and Dedham's William Gould, Bond's friend from the navy and their common Episcopal church. Mt. Moriah's members maintained their lodge "in a harmonious and thrifty condition," and attended annual gatherings when units from around the state paraded through Boston in full regalia (black suits adorned with diagonal white satin sashes, plumed hats, swords, and military decorations) to pay respects at the grave of their revered founder.[50]

"The Masons [and] Odd Fellows . . . organize purposefully to keep him out, but the Negro turns up the next day wearing the[ir] badges . . . and in possession of all their secrets," the *Colored American* reported. "When you will not admit him to the lodge," that article chastised the white brotherhoods, "he will imitate you, set up for himself, and with the true spirit of universal love and fraternity, he will invite you in." Masonic records substantiate John Bond's membership in the Prince Hall lodge in Cambridge, but only his obituary confirms that he also "helped found a lodge of Odd Fellows in the same city." Certainly, however, the Harvard Lodge in "Cambridgeport" did get started around the time that the Bonds moved to Hyde Park. The origins of Negro Odd Fellowship in the United States dated back to the black seaman Peter Ogden's affiliation with a Liverpool chapter just prior to John Bond's birth in that English port. With its celebrations of abolition's anniversary in the British West Indies and pronouncements that "the distant Australian, the wild Arabian, or the American Negro will embrace a Briton," the all-Negro Grand United Order of Odd Fellows seemed to provide a natural affiliation for John Bond.[51]

Odd Fellowship, like Masonry, held a temporary appeal for John Robert Bond, but he and Hyde Park's John Brooks both severed their Masonic connections by 1900. Perhaps two monthly treks from Hyde Park over to Cambridge demanded more time and effort than Bond could commit. Or perhaps those fraternal orders' pomp and circumstance, arcane rituals, elaborate regalia, even Prince Hall Masonry's "African" identity simply was not the Americanized Englishman's cup of tea. John Bond may have preferred the GAR's limited interracial fellowship to the Masons' accepted separate (or segregated) dichotomy. Whatever the reasons, his attachment to those groups never equaled his affection for and dedication to the GAR or the Episcopal Church that evoked the religious traditions and rituals of his English childhood.

Although the number of Negroes in Hyde Park had increased rapidly during the 1870s when the Bonds arrived, that segment of its population stopped expanding before the turn of the century. The immediacy of the town's Civil War significance for many black people almost certainly waned as the veterans aged. Shortly after James M. Trotter died, his widow and three children moved into

Boston proper, as did Archibald Grimké. Following Theodore Weld's death, Archie's daughter Angelina, a close friend of Maude Trotter, went away to school, and frequently resided during the ensuing years with her uncle, the Reverend Francis Grimké, in Washington, D.C.[52]

By 1900, when Hyde Park's overall population hovered around 11,000, no more than 150 Negroes lived there. They included a number of the same old-timers, such as the venerable picture framer who had been a resident at least since 1870. Arthur Crumpler and his wife Rebecca had returned to the cottage by Mother Brook shortly before she died in 1895, and he remained thereafter. Fewer of the town's black women worked as servants by the turn of the century, and in addition to Lena Bond, who was a milliner, two Negroes had entered the dressmaking trade.[53]

As some of the town's African Americans left, newcomers took their places. At the beginning of the twentieth century, twenty-two black men worked with horses, reflecting increased employment opportunities associated with Readville's splendid new racetrack, located on the site of the old military camp and touted as "the most attractive and beautiful trotting park in the country."[54] Three Negro women cooked for the many smiths and grooms (black and white) who boarded at or around the stables.

One track worker was a blacksmith named John Brady, who was as unique as John Robert Bond. Although Brady had become an American citizen twenty years earlier (even before Bond), both he and his wife were Irish-born Negroes.[55] In Hyde Park, which included so many people of Irish nativity or ancestry and so few blacks, it was surprising to find not only Bond, but also John and Helen Brady who, like millions of white immigrants, had come to America in search of economic oportunities and political freedom, leaving mothers and other kin behind. And would John Bond and the Bradys have been welcome to join so many others among the Boston area's sons and daughters of Ireland who vociferously celebrated their ties to the Old Sod on St. Patrick's Day? Or would their darker skin, and variant features and hair formation have excluded them from such established observances of common cultural heritage?

Among Hyde Park's other immigrants, six Negroes had been born in Canada, one in Africa, and several in the Caribbean. The Boston area as a whole had started attracting a number of West Indians by the turn of the century. Most of the native-born African Americans hailed from New England or the South, but in their entirety (and despite Readville's clinging appellation, "Nigger Village"), blacks never comprised as much as two percent of the town's population, which by 1900 included seven Chinese laundrymen as the only other non-Caucasian residents.[56]

In 1901, the Hyde Park–raised Monroe Trotter and his partner, with assistance from Monroe's new wife and his sister Maude, started editing and publishing the *Guardian,* a newspaper for black New Englanders. "To real Bostonians," observed a proud Negro resident, "it is the biggest little paper in the country [and] the voice of long-suffering colored America."[57] The journal became regular reading in the Bond household, even as its editorials and reportage grew increasingly critical of Booker Washington's accommodationist policies, with which the Bonds also identified because of Percy's new post at Tuskegee Institute.

Monroe Trotter was becoming Washington's major nemesis, but that hardly deterred the Bonds from subscribing to the *Guardian.* The late James Trotter and John Bond had strong ties because of their common wartime service, and had been comembers and officers of Hyde Park's GAR post. The Bond children had grown up with Monroe and his younger sisters, Maude (Bob Bond's exact age) and Bessie, born in 1883. For twenty years, the two families had been among the small cadre of black people in their town. "Black," however, was an egregious misnomer when applied to the second generation of Trotters, especially the light-complexioned girls, whom rude Hyde Park schoolmates taunted by calling "white niggers."[58]

In the *Guardian,* Monroe Trotter protested that President Theodore Roosevelt had invited to the White House in 1901 a man (Booker T. Washington) who wrongly "advised his race to keep out of politics." Trotter criticized Roosevelt for his woeful record of black governmental appointments, and Washington for his sycophantic support of the president. Washington's manipulative cadre of followers, the Tuskegee Machine, quickly struck back at such heresy. Before he went south to Tuskegee Institute accompanied by Percy Bond, Roscoe Conkling Bruce had tried to undercut Monroe Trotter by threatening his partner's employment, and Bookerites missed few opportunities to criticize him.

The simmering schism between Trotter and Booker Washington climaxed in July 1903 as a result of the ugly event that became known as the Boston Riot. The Boston branch of the National Negro Business League under the leadership, among others, of Dr. Samuel Courtney, had invited Washington to address a meeting to be held at the huge Columbus Avenue AME Zion Church. Trotter, outraged over what he perceived as his habitual abuse by Washington and his cohorts, deliberately orchestrated a confrontation with the man known as the Wizard of Tuskegee.

Two thousand Bostonians crowded into the church that sweltering evening. The attendees may well have included members of the Bond family, who had ties to the Washington faction through Percy's employment at Tuskegee and his personal acquaintanceship with Sam Courtney. They also had a professional connection with Courtney, who was Osie Bond's physician. Washington's supporters and his opponents were girded for a fight, and the packed crowd and stifling weather contributed to the volatile atmosphere. Many of Boston's leading (as well as its anonymous) citizens of both races had gone to the church to gather whatever pearls of wisdom the great man might cast before the multitudes.[59]

Monroe Trotter and members of his feisty oppositional contingent immediately challenged the Wizard's presence. They shouted to be recognized, loudly hissed Washington ("If there are any geese in the audience they are privileged to retire," scolded the master of ceremonies), jammed the aisles, then surged toward the dais. Archibald Grimké and his daughter Angelina had arrived early, but he prudently spirited her away as tensions escalated. Trotter climbed onto a pew demanding to be recognized, and posed the evening's most insolent question: "Is the rope and the torch all the race is going to get under your leadership?"

The police soon arrived to restore order, but someone had sprinkled cayenne powder on the rostrum and paroxysms of sneezing overwhelmed several dais guests. As the featured speaker was introduced, fistfights erupted, onlookers screamed, and several participants were ejected, with Trotterites shouting protests such as: "We don't want to hear you, Booker Washington," and, "Your views and aims are not . . . best for our race." In response, the usually dignified Samuel Courtney shouted, "Throw Trotter out the window!" The country's most renowned Negro leader sat dumbfounded as his daughter Portia, who attended school nearby, watched in horror. When minimal order was finally reestablished so that Washington could begin his address, he had little to offer that might have reestablished his moral authority. He claimed that only a few ill-mannered individuals who opposed free speech protested his appearance, and then, in drably pedestrian fashion, lauded "the gospel of thrift," "the dignity and beauty of labor," and "the disgrace of idleness."

Portia Washington wanted to pummel Trotter who, in addition to raining on her father's Boston parade, recently had printed in the *Guardian* a humiliating (and true, but churlish) report that she had flunked out of Wellesley College.[60] Members of the Washington faction refused to admit that their leader's badly behaved but genuinely frustrated critics (whom they labeled "vulgar" and "insane . . . hoodlums") had solid points to make and myriad—though often covert or silenced—followers.

Authorities arrested both Monroe Trotter and his sister Maude, who reportedly stabbed a policeman with her hatpin during the fracas. Washington and his cohorts pressed charges against Monroe, who refused to back down or apologize, and he was tried and sentenced to a month in jail. A zealous Bookerite crowed: "From Harvard College to the gaol—the distance is great; but Trotter has travelled it in short order." Washington also excoriated Archibald Grimké, singling him out as one of the attendees "who were not so brave as those who were arrested, but in the most cowardly manner stood in the dark, urging them on, without showing their own hands." The Wizard of Tuskegee remained vindictive in response to Monroe Trotter's conviction and later wrote to a friend, gloating that "Trotter, . . . Grimké, and two or three others, have by their actions completely killed themselves among all classes, both white and colored."[61] In the wake of the Boston Riot, Washington's antagonism toward those whom he perceived as his sworn enemies in the African American community festered and then solidified.

To members of Booker Washington's thin-skinned inner circle, anyone associated with the Trotters, even peripherally or by implication, might be suspect. The Bonds' conservatism resembled that of Samuel Courtney and Washington, but they consistently read the controversial newspaper published and edited by Monroe Trotter. Despite his affiliation with Courtney and his employment at Tuskegee Institute, leery members of the Washington machine may have wondered whether Percy Bond might be an empathetic Boston radical. Or perhaps they began to distrust him as they did the irrepressible Hyde Park independent, Archibald Grimké.

Percy's beloved Georgia Fagain Stewart had known W. E. B. Du Bois from almost three decades past, and found herself attracted to his progressive views and policies. Washington also soon became convinced that Du Bois, who spent the summer of 1903 as Trotter's houseguest, not only supported his host's actions but had participated in a Machiavellian Boston conspiracy.[62] In fact, the confrontation was only an early skirmish in the escalating war between Du Bois and Booker T. Washington over control of the hearts, minds, and destinies of the country's African Americans.

The heat within the African American community took months to cool in the wake of the infamous Boston Riot, and it never totally disappeared because that incident epitomized such basic, and often conflicting, principles concerning the future of the race. The Bonds' involvement was peripheral, but like many others, they maintained significant links and sympathies with both of the sparring camps. As Du Bois later wrote, "The fight cut deep: it went into social relations; it divided friends, it made bitter enemies."[63]

It was probably sometime during the following year that John Robert Bond began noticing blood in his stool, but in the absence of serious discomfort may have disregarded the problem for months. In due time, however, a physician could have felt an indurated mass in his lower colon, and from its texture or a biopsy, diagnosed John's rectal cancer. As the tumor grew and metastasized, he would have developed symptoms such as sharp pain, blockage of the rectum, nausea, weakness, and weight loss. Surgery was both rare and risky, and other than analgesics like morphine, little treatment was available. Emma may have supplemented her own herbal remedies with "Doctress Crumpler's vegetable alternative," but John ultimately turned to Readville's homeopathic doctor, Charles Sturtevant, a former Civil War navy surgeon, (white) Mason, and GAR colleague. Sturtevant could have prescribed small doses of a substance such as calomel in a futile effort to purge the carcinoma gently. Lena and her younger sister Tooty (who finished Hyde Park High School's general course that spring of 1905) prepared their father's tea when he could tolerate little else, and took walks with him during his final ordeal. In his adopted country, early in June when he was fifty-nine, and just weeks before his fortieth wedding anniversary, John died.[64]

A few years earlier, Dr. Charles Sturtevant's poem had specifically eulogized another member of GAR Post 121, but his words could have applied equally to his patient John Robert Bond.

> *Born in a home far over the sea,*
> *Seeking a home 'neath the flag of the free,*
> *Loyal he proved to the land of his choice,*
> *Trace to his interest with heart, hand and voice.*[65]

When John Bond died, the *Gazette* identified him as "a well-known colored resident of this town," and lauded him as a man "in whom to place implicit confidence." The obituary mentioned John's birth in Liverpool, immigration, navy service in the Civil War, honorable discharge "by reason of a gun shot wound in the right shoulder," and work as a janitor for the Hyde Park Savings Bank. It listed his activities and office holding with the GAR, Odd Fellows, and Masons, and membership in Dedham's Church of the Good Shepherd, "where he was greatly loved by his rector." The funeral was not held at Good Shepherd, however, but at Hyde Park's own, more elegant Christ Church (Episcopal), which was adorned for the occasion with "numerous floral contributions." A six-man honor guard of Bond's colleagues served as pallbearers. They included his brother in Prince Hall Masonry John Brooks, his coparishioner and old navy shipmate William Gould, and the black, Canadian-born Robert Jackson, who had marched off to war in 1863 with the Fifty-fifth Massachusetts Infantry. The full membership of GAR Post 121, where John Robert Bond had been an esteemed member for more than a quarter century, "attended in a body, and did escort duty to Fairview Cemetery."[66]

After her father's death and solemn burial, the competent, twenty-six-year-old Lena attended to her mother's correspondence and negotiated her widow's benefits, because (unlike John) the slave-born Emma never learned to read or write with any degree of proficiency. After 1890, a significant piece of federal legislation spearheaded by the GAR promised pensions to all honorably discharged Civil War veterans of at least ninety days' service who suffered from a physical disability, regardless of its source or their financial circumstances. Any such pensions thereafter might accrue to their worthy widows, as needed. With her own determination, letters of support from some of Hyde Park's most esteemed leaders, plus affidavits from the Bonds' old friends Isaac Mullen and Frank Whiting, who swore to their attendance at John and Emma's undocumented marriage in Norfolk, Lena Bond finally secured a continuing pension for her mother.[67]

The industrious Lena carried on her work at a Boston department store. She also began teaching piano in the Bonds' parlor, where she and her sister Tooty—both of whom remained at home with Emma—"put their sign out" and initiated a modest, in-house enterprise in custom millinery. Bob Bond, Osie, and their daughter Betty lived just a few houses down River Street, while Percy returned to his autonomous life in Alabama.[68]

With dignity and perseverance, but no acclaim, John Bond had done the best he could with the hand that life dealt him. For forty years, he loved, and retained the affections of a devoted wife, worked diligently, helped raise four children, and saw a granddaughter born. Without exaggeration, his minister could have declared about that family of devoted parishioners that John's wife

Emma had been "as a fruitful vine by the sides of thine house: thy children like olive plants about thy table."[69]

John Bond had become an American citizen who earned his community's respect. But who can guess what he might have accomplished had he been a white, Irish-English American (without his shoulder maimed in a noble cause) like the Red Stockings' star pitcher Tommy Bond? What would have transpired had his African-Irish parentage and the Catholic Church enabled him (and he had chosen) to pass for white and secure a first-rate Jesuit education as did the remarkable Healy brothers with their similar ancestry? Or suppose, like the parents of Boston's new political luminary, John F. Fitzgerald, John Bond's Irish-born mother Eliza Kelly had found her way to Massachusetts during the Great Famine instead of remaining in Liverpool to bear a Negro dockworker's bastard child? If his Caucasian rather than his genetical and cultural African heritage had predominated to stamp his features and structure his life, would John Robert Bond, like most other European immigrants, have been scarcely remembered, or a man of noble achievements and acclaim?

The town's new Fairview Cemetery was situated on a forested site just across the canal from the Bonds' home. Six years after John's death, the GAR relocated his remains to a prominent clearing atop one of that cemetery's hills. His headstone stands in a line of similarly unpretentious granite markers recognizing twenty of Hyde Park's Civil War heroes. Those grave sites face an iron cannon, a small pyramid of cannonballs, and the statue of an anonymous armed and marching Union soldier. The 1911 reinterment ceremony attracted "more than 3000 persons, including the town's Civil War veterans and members of other soldier and auxiliary organizations." The cult of the fallen soldier loomed large in the new century, and such rituals rekindled the conflict's fading legacy. Schoolchildren sang *The Soldiers' Farewell,* and Dr. Charles Sturtevant recited a patriotic poem as the Bonds (and probably John's old navy friends like Isaac Mullen and William Gould) and many others looked on. Hyde Park's selectmen then "gave the monument into the care of the [GAR's Timothy] Ingraham Post." There, in his final resting place, "Jno. R. Bond, U.S. Navy" is not classified as foreign born, a "colored" man, or a janitor. He is just an American patriot, buried among a few other such guardians and saviors of the Union. The memorial overlooks the town, Mother Brook, the mill pond, and the River Street home and garden where John had lived with his family for thirty years.[70]

.IV.

PERCY'S TRIBE,

1902–1926

Reverse: Percy, Georgia, Wenonah, and Jack Bond, and Georgia's mother, Caroline Fagain, ca. 1913.

WIZARDRY, *and* JIM CROW'S ALABAMA TRILOGY

*This is a white man's country. I am opposed to negro education
because it is an established fact that an "educated negro"
is as a rule a worthless imp.*

A candidate for the Alabama legislature, 1906

"THE OBJECT OF the Tuskegee Institute," its verbose catalogue
stated in 1902,

> is to furnish to young colored men and women an opportunity to
> acquire through moral, literary and industrial training, an educa-
> tion, so that when they go out from Tuskegee, by putting into ex-
> ecution the practical ideas learned here, they may become the real
> leaders of their communities, and thus bring about healthier moral
> and material conditions.

That was the year when J. Percy Bond first saw Alabama, and his
love, Georgia Fagain Stewart, returned to the state of her birth.[1]

Booker T. Washington, a consummate pragmatist, had become
the nation's most admired Negro, and his institute—really just a
sprawling country school, but designated "capital of the Negro nation" by no less a critic than W. E. B. Du Bois—was widely emulated. It included 62 buildings situated on 2,631 acres, with more
than 1,100 head of livestock and 60 wagons, carriages, and other

vehicles. "The scenery about it is not surpassed, if equalled, in the whole South," the descriptive passages continued, adding, "the climate is salubrious and unsurpassed for healthfulness."[2]

For the 1,365 students from throughout the United States and the Indian Territories, Africa, the Caribbean, and Central America who attended during the school year 1902–3, tuition was free, room and board eight dollars per month, with books an added five to seven dollars a year. Yet even those amounts were scarcely affordable for many Negroes who wanted to acquire some academic instruction along with their vocational training. In compliance with Alabama's prohibition on interracial education, none of the students or faculty were white, and the institute attracted sharp criticism when a group of Cuban and Puerto Rican youngsters were categorized as such. Some more fortunate black people could and did benefit from rigorous academics, but others remained so entangled in poverty, ignorance, the legacy of slavery, and similar burdens of a racist society that they first had to acquire the most basic skills. That was the mission to which Tuskegee Institute primarily devoted itself.

Booker T.'s wife Margaret often griped about girls and boys "mingling together," and the school established a rigid behavioral code and doled out demerits that could lead to dismissal even for minor transgressions. Social dancing, card playing, alcoholic beverages, tobacco, and firearms all were "strictly forbidden." "Low or profane language subject[ed] student[s] to severe discipline," and they could not "take part in any political mass-meeting or convention." Also, the catalogue iterated, both the "wardrobes and rooms of students are subject to inspection and regulation." Young people were "required to bathe at stated periods, . . . letter writing is subject to regulation, [and] all mail and packages are inspected and contents noted."[3] Any remaining rights might be readily suspended, and Washington administered his school like the omnipotent overlord of an immense plantation. He delegated some authority, but more often maintained personal control over even the most trivial matters.

Aspiring Tuskegeeans soon learned that the education they hoped to obtain was serious business and attending the institute a selectively granted privilege. The campus operated as an authoritarian island of security surrounded by the hostile sea of Jim Crow Alabama. Washington created an environment where dedicated faculty and compliant students alike usually could insulate themselves from the degradations of the outside world. The missionary Tuskegee staff impressed on young people that they were not just striving for personal success, but must behave admirably to achieve for the entire Negro community.

Virginia-born Percy Bond, despite his long residence in Massachusetts, may have been a southerner at heart. He savored the "salubrious" climate, and accommodated himself to Tuskegee's regime, Booker Washington's expectations, and the demands of Roscoe C. Bruce, his supervisor in the Academic Department. "Percy Bond is as irrepressible as ever," Bruce wrote his fiancée Clara Burrill back at Radcliffe College, "He is thoroughly loyal to me, . . . and he aids me very importantly in my work."[4]

Percy Bond performed both personal and promotional duties for Roscoe Bruce that clearly exceeded his job description. As Roscoe's marriage to Clara drew near in spring 1903, he assured her that their wedding list would receive the closest attention, because "I'll have Percy print it on his typewriter, and then I can send mother a copy." "Mother" could have referred either to Josephine Bruce, Tuskegee Institute's lady principal, or to Clara Burrill's mother in Washington, D.C., but certainly, many particulars for the nuptials passed through Percy Bond's capable hands. As Clara's arrival in Alabama approached, Roscoe assured her that "at Chehaw [the nearest railroad depot] Mr. Bond will meet us with a carriage and we'll drive the seven miles to Tuskegee."[5]

"I read the article in the Congregational Week on the life of a certain young man I know," the discerning Clara Burrill teasingly wrote her fiancé shortly before their marriage. "It was supposed to have been written by Prof. J. P. Bond," she added, "but he didn't write it." "You wrote it," she concluded. "There are certain phrases that . . . always appear in whatever you write."[6] Clara clearly believed that Roscoe had drafted a self-exalting profile about himself for his loyal assistant to submit for publication in the church journal.

The semester following Clara Burrill and Roscoe Bruce's wedding, the institute's Executive Council determined that the school needed "a new division . . . that of Buildings and Grounds," and appointed "Mr. J. P. Bond, until recently stenographer in Mr. Bruce's office" to the position of director. The fine "results he . . . achieved in the direction of keeping the buildings and grounds in more satisfactory shape" delighted institute officials. A photograph of Percy Bond taken in August 1904, when he served as the school's "Acting Commissariat" during the vacation period, shows a slightly pudgy brown-skinned man crossing the verdant quadrangle. He wore poorly cut but immaculate clothes and seemed greatly pleased with his augmented authority. "Snap shot on lawn at Tuskegee," reads the cheerful inscription, "New academic building in rear. Sun shiny day."[7]

For the most part, the Alabama-raised Georgia Stewart (by then at least informally engaged to Percy) had appreciated her Massachusetts years. She believed that Boston offered people of her race fine educational opportunities in a relatively egalitarian environment, but also knew that a supportive network of kin awaited her in nearby Montgomery, while within Tuskegee's sheltered confines, her daughter Carrie would face little racial discrimination and could acquire decent academic skills at minimal cost. Georgia and Carrie, therefore, though perhaps reluctantly, had left Boston with Percy Bond.

But Georgia was unprepared for what she would encounter at Tuskegee Institute. In Boston, she had served for a while as a surrogate parent for young Baker Washington, yet may not have been fully aware of the awesome power that his stepmother and Georgia's former Fisk schoolmate, Margaret Murray Washington, wielded and the manipulative ways that she asserted her hegemony. Even before Georgia arrived, some of Tuskegee Institute's most influential women had conspired to determine her fate.

In a note to Booker T. Washington, Josephine Bruce stated that "Mrs. Washington" had instructed her that "it would be better for Mrs. Stewart not to go into the housekeeping division." "Housekeeping" suggested a dignified matron's position in a girls' dormitory. Jane Clark, the librarian, similarly wrote the principal that

"Mrs. Stewart would hardly be the one for the work" that became available within her literary domain.[8] There seems little doubt that Margaret Washington orchestrated those dead ends in her husband's well-intentioned search for an appropriate position at his school for Georgia Stewart, who had cared for his older son in Boston.

Margaret was a clever and handsome woman, but at about forty years her looks were fading and the stubborn fleshiness of middle age upholstered her stocky body. Though she was a mulatto, she was darker skinned (and sensitive about the fact) than the shapelier and slightly younger Georgia, whom Booker T. had visited in Massachusetts and with whom he carried on a spirited correspondence—most, but not all of it, concerning his son.

That association may have irked the wife of Tuskegee's principal. Although the overworked Booker T. Washington had little time for sexual dalliance, he did admire comely women, and occasional rumors circulated at Tuskegee about his flirtations with some of the attractive teachers and faculty wives, such as Jane Clark, and even Adella Hunt Logan, the wife of Tuskegee's treasurer (Washington's loyal second-in-command) Warren Logan.[9] Margaret Washington may have suspected that the widow Stewart had developed a relationship with her husband that surpassed the official bounds of familial necessity.

In addition, from their sojourn together at Fisk nearly twenty years earlier, Margaret Murray (soon-to-be Washington) could have remembered that Georgia Fagain (soon-to-be Stewart) came from a "better" family than her own. Mr. Fagain had been a modestly successful Montgomery builder, while Margaret may not have known her white father at all, and her mother worked as a laundress. Those class distinctions, combined with Georgia's manifest elitism, could have rankled the principal's wife for years. When Georgia, with her pale skin and meticulously manicured nails, arrived in Tuskegee, widowed and a bit humbled by adverse circumstances, Margaret Washington assigned her neither to a "ladylike" matron's job, nor to a nominal position in the library, but to her own department: Industries for Girls.

That division held its classes, euphemistically called "domestic sciences," in a new two-story brick building known as Dorothy

Hall. The iron-willed Margaret Washington oversaw a staff comprised of ten women (with more soon to come) who instructed female students in cooking, sewing, and upholstery. She also assigned three members of her faculty, including Georgia Stewart, to the unenviable task of teaching laundering.

In the one-year course that instructors carried out in three basement rooms, "one for washing, one for drying, and one for soapmaking . . . young women are taught the art of washing and ironing according to approved methods, including scientific analysis of blueing, soap, starch, etc." The catalogue also noted with pride "specialties in laundering laces and silks, hand and machine washing," and it praised the new equipment, including "four washers, two extractors, a mangle, starchers, and a collar and cuff ironer . . . added to lighten the drudgery."[10] Because of the institute's commitment to self-sufficiency, Georgia's program dealt with a constantly replenished mountain of soiled uniforms, plus bed, bath, kitchen, and table linens that the school continually generated. Tuskegee Institute's Industries for Girls division trained young Negro women to excel in the areas of work for which white America considered them most ideally suited.

Georgia Stewart's assignments required her to work elbow-deep in soapy water, bleach, blueing, and starch for hours at a time. The havoc that such labor wreaked on her previously well-cared-for hands can be easily imagined. Georgia's untested back and shoulders must have throbbed as she demonstrated preferred methods of washing, rinsing, mangling, and ironing clothes—work from which her own family had deliberately shielded her. Her unfinished education at Fisk might not have qualified her for an academic position, but there would have been hardly any job at the institute for which Georgia was less well prepared than that of an instructor in laundering. Nonetheless, she learned to respect (but despise) the reality of many black women's work lives from which she theretofore had been assiduously protected.

In short order, Georgia Stewart realized that the influential Margaret Murray Washington was not her ally. In later years, Georgia usually held her tongue, but on occasion, characterized Booker T.'s wife as "a very difficult woman."[11]

Margaret Washington did not, however, attempt to keep Georgia out of the Tuskegee Woman's Club. That organization comprised a key portion of Margaret's multilayered fiefdom, and she served as its perennial president. Her power network also included not only her "first lady" and division-head positions at the institute, but ongoing leadership roles with the Alabama Federation of Colored Women's Clubs and the National Association of Colored Women (NACW). Membership in her local group was open to (even required of) all of the institute's female teachers and wives of male faculty members or administrators, but no one else.[12]

Recognizing the opposition she faced from Tuskegee's Queen Margaret and its lady principal, Josephine Bruce, the resourceful Georgia Stewart looked elsewhere for support, and cultivated a powerful, though controversial ally. Tuskegee Institute's "second lady," Adella Hunt Logan, had been a good friend of Georgia's former landlord Dr. Samuel Courtney from his early years at Tuskegee. Adella's husband Warren Logan and Emmett Jay Scott, Washington's executive secretary, dominated the second tier in the institute's official hierarchy. Logan held the school's purse strings, as well as the overall reins of power during Booker T. Washington's frequent absences. Vigorous, mustached, a bit portly, and (many people observed) quite a Teddy Roosevelt look-alike, Warren Logan was the same pale-complexioned fellow who had traveled to Hyde Park, Massachusetts, with the Hampton Institute student singers almost three decades earlier.[13]

Georgia Stewart's new friend, Adella Hunt Logan, came from a family whose female members had been free people of color—a tiny minority in the state of Georgia's slave-heavy plantation belt. Because of her predominantly Caucasian ancestry, Adella (ivory skinned, straight haired, and narrow featured), looked like a white woman. Adella Hunt's mother had been illiterate, but fiercely encouraged her children's education. Her white father had fought with the Confederacy, yet also "talked politics" with his opinionated and high-strung daughter, who had been born during the Civil War, though not, she maintained, "a slave, nor in a log cabin."[14]

She started teaching at sixteen, then finished her schooling at Atlanta University. Booker Washington founded Tuskegee Institute in 1881, his Hampton Institute pal Warren Logan arrived the next year, and Adella Hunt followed in 1883. Five years later, she and Warren married, and by 1902 when she met Georgia Stewart, she had five children, had seen two others die, yet had scarcely interrupted her teaching. Her second child, Ruth, was a year younger than Carrie Stewart, and the girls became fast friends.[15]

In addition to Adella Hunt Logan's family and her ongoing commitment to education, her chief passion became the struggle for woman suffrage—at a place and time when most Americans considered her undeserving of the franchise because she was both not white and not male. Booker T. and Margaret Washington tepidly endorsed the principle of votes for women, but it never ranked high among their priorities. Mostly, Tuskegee's principal wanted to avoid that hornets' nest, and Margaret once stated that women's lack of the franchise "has never kept me awake at night."[16] Adella Logan also had raised eyebrows at Tuskegee when, in contrast to Booker Washington's outspoken support for the McKinley administration's imperialist ventures during the Spanish-American War, she aligned herself with anti-imperialists such as Archibald Grimké and W. E. B. Du Bois.[17]

Margaret Washington may have slept in peace, but woman suffrage triggered Adella Hunt Logan's insomnia, and she found an ally in Georgia Stewart, who needed a mentor. Many of their mutual activities, including community outreach and cultural affairs, took place under the aegis of the Woman's Club. Club members also served as Margaret Washington's captive cadre of hostesses when guests such as Josephine Ruffin, whom Georgia knew from Boston, and Washington, D.C.'s elegant Mary Church Terrell visited Tuskegee. Though she and Mrs. Washington clashed over both ideology and leadership of the NACW, Terrell (a 1903 graduation speaker at the institute) was a tireless reformer and educator, and, like Logan and Ruffin, an advocate of woman suffrage.[18] For others of the club's efforts, Georgia Stewart served on the charitable works committee, solicited books for the reading room in the Sojourner Truth Club of her old hometown (Montgomery), portrayed Queen Elizabeth on an evening devoted to notable women in history, and made the most of her musical training at Fisk when she performed politely applauded "vocal solos."[19] But Georgia and Adella ventured onto more perilous waters as well.

Adella recently had become a life member—the entire state of Alabama's *only* life member—in the country's most significant organization advocating votes for women, the National American Woman Suffrage Association (NAWSA), and she contributed anonymously to its *Woman's Journal*.[20] She also led debates on suffrage issues at monthly meetings of the Tuskegee Woman's Club.

White colleagues in the suffrage movement who recognized Logan's ardor and eloquence had recommended her to the NAWSA's venerable leader Susan B. Anthony as a convention speaker. But Anthony—who was reluctant to offend Caucasian supporters by featuring an unrenowned "colored" woman—demurred, protesting that the articulate and educated Adella Logan should "wait until she is more cultured and can be more of a credit to her race." Logan, however, remained undeterred by such slights. She maintained a blind admiration for Anthony and continued to work on behalf of woman suffrage.[21]

Shortly before Georgia Stewart arrived in Tuskegee, Adella Logan had surreptitiously attended a suffrage conference in Atlanta, which, in deference to the state's Jim Crow laws and practices and in keeping with the NAWSA's unwillingness to antagonize its southern hosts, was meant to be an all-white gathering. Women such as Logan, however, easily could, and sometimes did, "pass" on selected occasions.

During that late-1901 convention, Logan arranged a private appointment with the NAWSA's new president, Carrie Chapman Catt, but then, she sarcastically confided to a northern colleague, "could not resist the temptation to stay in the meeting a while observing how the superior sister does things." "I attended this lecture in company with a friend," she wrote, adding, "we were the only two colored women in the room." "Yet if they [the white suffragists] had known me" (had known that she was not, by their definition, really white), Logan's letter to her ally concluded, "I would have been ordered out in no very gracious manner."[22]

Adella Logan made it her practice to attend certain suffrage conferences incognita. When Georgia Stewart arrived in Tuskegee,

Adella found an equally "white" enthusiast to accompany her to such meetings (because no "lady" would travel alone).[23]

Becoming a full participant in the United States' flawed democracy was central to Logan's beliefs and activities. She especially espoused the importance of the franchise for "colored" women, and shared information, theories, and tactics she had gathered at "all white" conferences with her Tuskegee colleagues and women associated with both the Negro Alabama Federation and the NACW.

Adella also must have talked with Georgia Stewart about the article, "Woman Suffrage," that she was preparing for the *Colored American,* the national journal sponsored by Booker T. Washington that had published Georgia's own short story several years earlier. "Government of the people, for the people, and by the people is but partially realized so long as woman has no vote," Logan declared in that essay. "If white American women with all their natural and acquired advantages need the ballot, that right protective of all other rights," she asked, "how much more do black Americans, male and female, need the strong defense of a vote to secure their right to life, liberty, and the pursuit of happiness?" Concerning the anguish provoked by their political impotence, and various other agonies that so many women (of both races) endured, Logan wrote, "She meanwhile stays at home to cry, to swear or to suicide—as she chooses."[24]

The fair-skinned Adella Logan and Georgia Stewart may have anonymously attended the NAWSA's 1903 convention in New Orleans despite the fact that all of the official delegates were Caucasians. Following that meeting, and persuaded by a reformer who was a Tuskegee Institute supporter, a group of white suffragists visited the campus. Among them were Carrie Catt, Susan B. Anthony, and, the *Tuskegee Student* stated, "perhaps ten others." Fifteen hundred people, including the Washingtons, Logans, Georgia and Carrie Stewart, Percy Bond, "officers, teachers, families, and the entire student body," welcomed the visitors by waving "a sea of white handkerchiefs." After a lengthy program, all of the female students "passed in review before Miss Anthony and received each a hearty hand shake." Weeks after that memorable ceremony, and revealing how much her perceptions about appropriate education for black people resembled those of most white Americans, Anthony sent the school a contribution earmarked for a new program being developed under the auspices of Margaret Washington's Industries for Girls division. That course of study would teach young African American women how to make brooms.[25]

Suffrage proponents like Anthony, and Negro Reconstruction leaders such as Louisiana's former governor P. B. S. Pinchback, often visited the school, but its regulations forbade students from taking part in political activities.[26] Residents of the white-controlled town of Tuskegee, a mile from the campus, welcomed the renown, famous visitors, and income that the Wizard attracted to their isolated burg, but they hardly tolerated student activism. Adella Logan, nonetheless, sometimes imposed on her well-grounded relationship with Washington. She acquired his special dispensation for her classes to hold debates, mock elections, political rallies and marches to familiarize students with the principles and workings of democracy. As a member of Tuskegee's inner circle, Adella was a formidable friend for a newcomer such as Georgia Stewart, but any association with her sometimes radical ideas and activities also was tinged with controversy, though her husband Warren remained Washington's oldest friend, most faithful subordinate, and frequent surrogate.[27]

The same winter that Anthony and her associates visited the institute, Warren Logan announced a $600,000 donation from the Scottish-born steel magnate and philanthropist Andrew Carnegie. That gift, which like many of Carnegie's donations was partially earmarked for library construction, brought with it, however, at least one unanticipated development. In the context of its prohibitions against "mingling," the school provided no place for girls and boys to be alone together. But one student couple did manage to find some privacy. When the young woman conceived and gave birth, the pair (though promptly expelled) reportedly named their child "Carnegie" in fond remembrance of Tuskegee's library, where they had consummated their relationship. Such fabled incidents, of course, horrified the Washingtons, Bruces, Warren Logan, Emmett Scott, and others who clamped down on transgressors with single-minded fervor. The institute's viability (and their own well-being) depended on avoiding even a whiff of impropriety.[28]

At least as much as rampant adolescent heterosexuality, any hint of homosexuality, with its odor of perversion, appalled members of Tuskegee's establishment. Such rumors, however, circulated around George Washington Carver, one of the institute's most gifted teachers and its resident genius in agricultural sciences. An admirer once charged: "You are the most seductive being I know, capable of making yourself loved by all the world when you choose."[29] Often, however, the "seductive" but periodically irascible Carver did not so choose.

Carver's work with cowpeas, sugar beets, sweet potatoes, and most of all, peanuts, earned the institute acclaim. His efforts also provided Alabama's poor farmers of both races with the wherewithal to increase productivity and help overcome the South's scourge of malnourishment. The school's benefactors and trustees usually winked at questions about Carver's personal life because they appreciated his continuing contributions to the school's reputation, and his achievements in practical, scientific agriculture did not seem to challenge what white America perceived as society's appropriate racial and intellectual hierarchy.[30]

Nonetheless, Carver's cantankerousness, combined with the slovenly maintenance of his minor domain in agronomy and animal husbandry (especially his disreputable chicken yard), brought him into conflict with the fastidious Percy Bond's Buildings and Grounds Division, and ultimately with Booker T. Washington. Of greater significance, however, Carver was one of the few Tuskegeeans who habitually challenged the Wizard's authority.[31]

Rumors about his relationships with some of the students disturbed many adults at Tuskegee, but he truly inspired young people. At the core of Carver's differences with the school he loved was that his entire persona deviated sharply from the straitlaced Tuskegee norm, and he displayed emotions and concerns that much of American society viewed as chimerical, and even feminine. Carver was sensitive, spiritual, nurturing, and he enjoyed painting, needlework, and cooking, attributes and interests that stereotypically were labeled "womanly."

Despite their dichotomous attitudes toward Carver, the school community united soon after Percy Bond's arrival when the potential perils of Jim Crow Alabama struck home. Carver had escorted Frances Benjamin Johnston, a well-known white photographer, around Tuskegee's environs, but a distance from the secure confines of the institute itself. Late one night, some local whites greeted with gunfire Carver's unarmed party of two black men traveling with a white woman in defiance of the South's established racial protocols. On that terrifying occasion, Carver realistically believed that "it was a very serious question indeed as to whether I would return to Tuskegee alive."[32]

Despite his "nonmasculine" qualities, many Tuskegeeans, like Adella Hunt Logan, remained close to Carver. Adella encouraged his artistic endeavors and her sister Sarah, a teacher in the English Department, was the woman whom, in 1905, Carver seriously considered marrying. Carver explained the courtship's ultimate termination on the grounds that he and Sarah Hunt had divergent goals in life, but some people credited the split to his questionable sexuality.[33] Still others, however, argued that members of her family did not want the light-skinned Sarah to marry someone as dark as Carver. That perspective, while patently offensive and evoking the specter of intraracial schisms, could have been partially grounded in legitimate anxieties arising from incidents such as that in which gun-toting white Alabamians attacked Carver and Frances Benjamin Johnston. Such potential dangers may have raised serious concerns for couples like Georgia Stewart and Percy Bond as well. Trigger-happy southerners who saw them together might shoot first and ask questions later when faced with the provocative image of a black man accompanying a "white" woman in clear defiance of "legitimate" racial, social, and sexual relations in the South.[34]

The Wizard had to walk on eggs in Jim Crow Alabama, which made life so perilous and demeaning for its Negro residents, but his contributions to his adopted town were not unappreciated and resulted in tenuously maintained benefits. Alabama's revised constitution of 1901 had disqualified a vast majority of the state's black voters, and a Birmingham politician exultantly proclaimed, "We have disfranchised the African in the past by doubtful methods; but in the future we will disfranchise . . . [him] by law."[35] Yet Washington's school remained a unique preserve where a number of people of the darker race (but only well-educated, institute-associated, morally irreproachable, gainfully employed male taxpayers) could and did vote, thanks to the grudging acquiescence of local white politicians. In those years, Booker Washington also, cautiously and covertly, supported several legal challenges to his state's constitutionally justified abuses of Negroes.[36] For a northerner such as Percy Bond who cherished his citizenship rights, voting must have been a strong attraction that lured him to Tuskegee, rather than anywhere else in the state, though residency provisions required him to live in Alabama for two years before he could qualify for the franchise.

Percy was respected and successful in his work at the institute, though miserably underpaid. Nonetheless, the paranoia following the 1903 Boston Riot (the school newspaper briefly reported that "[Monroe] Trotter and several puppets" disrupted a National Negro Business League convention being addressed by Washington), combined with W. E. B. Du Bois's scathing appraisal of the Wizard in *The Souls of Black Folk* the same year, made some of Tuskegee's insiders question and try to undercut the authority of any and all outsiders. Percy was a Hyde Park, Massachusetts, man who, despite his conservatism, had long associations with the feisty Trotter and the often suspect Archibald Grimké, with whom he intermittently corresponded. His original supervisor, Roscoe Bruce, like many northern-born, -raised, or -educated men, was becoming somewhat frustrated at the institute because of Washington's perpetual downplaying of academics, as was the Columbia University–trained architect Wallace Rayfield, another valued teacher who was vexed by the Wizard's tight fist and iron hand. And like her mentor Adella Logan, Georgia Stewart admired her Fisk schoolmate Du Bois (whom some irreverent Tuskegeeans began calling "Doctor Dubious"). Though untouchable as the treasurer's wife, Adella herself also was recognized as an iconoclast and a "problem" at the school.[37]

What Georgia Stewart perceived as her demeaning employment, however, was something that she could not tolerate indefinitely, though she briefly obtained what she considered more appropriate work at the nearby Cotton Valley School, one of the institute's satellite extension projects. She taught younger children there, and daily buggied back and forth to Tuskegee with her confidante and fellow teacher, Caroline Smith.[38]

The institute's rigid standards defining and limiting socialization between the sexes applied to faculty members—who were expected to set an impeccable example and moral tone—as much as to students. Georgia had to reside with other unmarried faculty (like her housemate Julia Walton) at the school's Model Cottage, where female students acquired domestic skills such as how to groom themselves, set a table, and properly make a bed. That residential arrangement made courtship difficult, and especially would have rankled a mature woman such as Georgia, who had lived on her own for years and was unaccustomed to being treated like a wayward adolescent. But "respectable" Negroes knew that they must behave with unchallengeable prudence, restraint, and decorum. The white majority always suspected them of endemic promiscuity and lewdness, and remained ready to castigate the entire race for the indiscretions of a few.

Georgia Stewart also appreciated the educational opportunities available to her daughter, and Carrie thrived at Tuskegee. A number of faculty members (Booker T. Washington, Josephine Bruce, Adella Logan, and Emmett Scott among them), who—at least covertly—considered themselves part of what Du Bois had labeled the Talented Tenth, sought greater academic advantages for members of their own families, even as they continued their efforts in industrial, agricultural, technical, and mechanical training for the race's less-advantaged "masses." One scholarly institute graduate (and phenomenal baseball player as well) named William Clarence Matthews, for example, had gone on to Phillips Andover Academy and then to Harvard. When Carrie Stewart finished Tuskegee Institute's preparatory program, with her mother's and Percy Bond's blessings and support, she moved on to the more intellectually challenging program at Atlanta University.[39]

Carrie's graduation ended Georgia's dependency on Tuskegee. On September 5, 1905, three months after that occasion and the concurrent death of John Robert Bond in Hyde Park, the Reverend John Brooks officiated at the wedding of J. Percy Bond and

Georgia Stewart at the Presbyterian Church of the Good Shepherd (bearing the same name as Percy's old Massachusetts parish) in Montgomery, Alabama.[40] Percy's sisters and mother—still in mourning—may not have traveled all the way from Massachusetts, but Georgia's hometown clan and local friends surely attended. A few close Tuskegee colleagues (like Caroline Smith, Julia Walton, and Adella Logan, who presented the newlyweds with an elegant sterling silver bonbon dish) also joined the festivities.[41]

Percy adopted Georgia's fifteen-year-old daughter, who appended his surname, becoming Caroline Stewart Bond. That seemed appropriate, since Carrie scarcely could remember her biological father and Percy had been part of her life for many years.[42] Because Negro families so often have been subject to disruptions of all sorts, such formal or informal adoptions have been more prevalent in the African American community than in the white. As Carrie headed to Atlanta, Percy and Georgia Bond abandoned the Wizard's domain for the "Magic City" of Birmingham.

If Tuskegee Institute was Booker T. Washington's kingdom, Birmingham was Vulcan's forge. A fifty-five-foot statue of that deformed Roman god of fire and metalwork cast from Alabama iron had been returned from the 1904 World's Fair in St. Louis, where it had won a grand prize and proudly exemplified Birmingham's industrial prowess. Except for New York City's famed national hostess, Lady Liberty, Vulcan was the largest such figure in the entire country. Its looming, awkward presence at Birmingham's fairgrounds, near where Percy and Georgia relocated in 1905, was emblematic of the city.[43]

From its unsung incorporation thirty-four years earlier, when it was considered just a "new boom town in an old corn field," Birmingham, Alabama, named for England's industrial municipality and situated near the intersections of several rail lines, had exploded to epitomize the best and worst of the New South. By 1900, Birmingham had burst through its established city limits three times, and would do so soon again. A decade later, its mushrooming population would top 130,000. It quickly had become the former Confederacy's third-largest city.[44]

Birmingham was unlike any other metropolis in the region, and more akin to smoky Appalachian cities such as Pittsburgh than anything in the South. Red ore lavishly streaked its encircling ranges, while coal extracted from nearby deposits stoked the furnaces that transformed the ore into iron and steel products. Some people called the stench of sulphur gas (a by-product of the smelting processes) the industrialists' perfume, and workers streamed in to labor at the clamorous, reeking mills and mines.

Most of Birmingham's African Americans hailed from nearby agricultural districts where their parents once had been slaves, then worked as tenant farmers or sharecroppers, always uncertain of their income, dependent on and indebted to white landlords. As he arrived, one country boy remembered that "the Terminal Station was lit up like a big mansion or something." "I pointed and told them 'Pretty lights! Pretty lights!' " he continued. "It looked like heaven to me." The city became a way station for blacks who left rural roots behind, but were not yet ready to move north—or even farther. A few Americans continued to tout black emigration, but a typical white Alabamian recently had declared: "The Negro loves the sacred soil, the old home, the climate, and his surroundings. He has no more idea of going to Africa than the Southern Jew of going into business in Jerusalem."[45]

Birmingham soon included more Negro residents than any Deep South city, and a higher concentration of them (thirty-nine percent) than any other major urban center in the country. And unlike the situation throughout most of the region where white people, predominantly of English or Scotch-Irish heritage, had lived for generations, diverse newcomers ("every nationality—Italian, Greeks, Yugoslavians, Hungarians, Bulgarians—all of them was up in there," a white, native-born collier recalled) characterized the Magic City, and the foreign born comprised thirteen percent of its population when the Bonds arrived.[46]

Birmingham's industrialists resisted unionization even more ruthlessly than did similar moguls in the North and Midwest, and concurrently superimposed many of the South's most repressive segregationist traditions and practices. In 1908, aided by vigilantes and the state militia, they ruthlessly broke the backs of aspiring unions. Nascent cross-racial organizational efforts foundered when the governor played on white workers' fears that unions might seek to erase differentials between the races, and declared himself "outraged at the attempts to establish social equality between black and white miners." At work, at home, and at leisure, color divided the city more decisively than class.[47]

Accidents maimed and killed men of both races, but for the most part, Negroes who toiled in Birmingham's extractive and related industries performed the miserable "nigger work" that white people believed was appropriate for members of the inferior race. They considered a rigid labor hierarchy essential to maintaining the required social order, and the shared, though unequally configured, workplace rarely transcended race. Blacks remained the mudsills of the local economy, but their labor in and around the mines was better remunerated than most other employment. Men who became gardeners, butlers, or chauffeurs for wealthy whites received lower pay but had greater status, more job security, and performed less onerous work than mill hands who could be subject to illness and injury, or layoffs during strikes or recessions.

Although Birmingham's leaders, like those in the region as a whole, remained committed to white supremacy, theirs was not a sleepy southern town but a burgeoning modern city, clamorous with activity and construction, and gritty from the mining and smelting operations that functioned around the clock, seven days a week. The industrialists who controlled Birmingham had few links to the antebellum South. Most were former northerners who believed that they could bully, cajole, and haul their adopted city into national economic and industrial prominence. In 1905, Percy Bond and Georgia arrived in the Magic City with every intention of coping with its evident liabilities but making the most of its opportunities.[48]

Percy opened a haberdashery store ("Shoes, Shirts, Neckwear, Hats, Umbrellas, Gloves, Hosiery, Suspenders, Handkerchiefs, Underwear and Everything in Men's Wear") on North Eighteenth Street in the central business district, next to the Alabama Penny Savings Bank, the country's largest black-owned financial institution. It enjoyed unprecedented success, largely because it made loans to African Americans when white-owned banks would not. Its founder, the Reverend William R. Pettiford, a Baptist minister-turned-entrepreneur known as "the father of black banking," was the city's most influential Negro. He preached that "money is power, and labor is capital," and urged members of his race to "have banks under our control in all cities large enough to maintain them."[49]

Pettiford maintained a primary loyalty to his own "colored" middle-class community, and often emulated the messages of Booker Washington as he prodded black laborers to become more efficient and reliable in their work and personal habits if they aspired to better themselves. Many of Birmingham's whites, one of whom argued that "it was more or less natural for a negro to be shiftless and lack ambition," echoed those views. With similarly Washingtonian rhetoric, another white man insisted that Negroes should be urged to move along a "parallel channel" to Caucasians, as long as it "never touch[ed] the latter's social side."[50]

Much of the supposedly enchanted city where Pettiford established his bank and reaped his success was squalid. Tuberculosis and other contagious diseases ran rampant. Reckless urban development had created myriad rat-infested, undrained construction sites, while livestock grazed in Birmingham's open garbage dumps, and housing in many parts of town was wretchedly substandard. "It is impossible to emphasize too strongly the danger to both whites and blacks crouched in these ill-ventilated, dark, over-crowded living conditions," the anguished director of the city's Associated Charities complained.[51]

But Birmingham had a brighter facade as well. By 1900, its residents had seen a first ten-story, steel-girdered "skyscraper" rise, with many more soon to come, while the city "assum[ed] an importance architecturally in keeping with the progressive spirit of its citizens," a national journal observed. Electric streetlights abounded, and Birmingham had laid more steel trolley tracks (one hundred miles) than any other American metropolis, save one. Glistening olive-green cars with cream and gold trim and slick rattan seats clattered their staccato music along downtown streets, providing up-to-date public transportation—but black people always had to sit in the back.[52]

Those trolley riders, the few Negroes who owned buggies or automobiles, bicyclists, and pedestrians—all had easy access to Percy
Bond's shop. It was well situated near the central post office, the
People's Home Telephone Company, and around the corner from
the city's largest department store. With "Bond & Co." spelled out
in bold gilt letters, a plate-glass display window, striped roll-down
awning, and even a telephone, Percy's motto was "Wear Our
Made-to-Order Garments and You Will Wear a Perpetual Smile."
He became a hardworking, ambitious Birmingham merchant whose
personal appearance had improved considerably from the rumpled
look he affected at Tuskegee. From his immaculate starched collar
and striped four-in-hand or polka-dot bow tie, to his favorite white
summer flannels or three-piece vested suit draped with a gold
watch fob, down to the toes of his polished ebony wingtips, J.
Percy Bond served as a walking sartorial advertisement for his modest emporium.[53]

Stores such as Bond & Company supplied Birmingham's black
residents with clothing and nourished their dignity as well. The
Birmingham *Age-Herald* maintained that "the real mission of the
negro in business was not so much to make money, as it was to de-
serve the patronage of the people." White clerks at white-owned
stores treated black customers discourteously, accepted their money,
but did not allow them to try on clothes and shoes before purchase, or return or exchange damaged goods and items that did
not fit.[54]

In addition to the Alabama Penny Savings Bank adjoining Bond
& Company, black Birmingham supported many other businesses
and boasted a sizable middle-class "colored" community, which
embraced Percy and Georgia Bond. Their circle included an architect, physicians, lawyers, builders, teachers, ministers, and several
undertakers—whose success came about in large part because whites
refused to handle Negro corpses. Percy became a member and then
a leader of the local branch of the National Negro Business League,
and surely was invited by his colleagues to join one or more of their
established clubs.[55]

After the venerated Reverend Pettiford, T. C. Windham may
have been Birmingham's most influential African American in the

early 1900s. He was a builder whose advertisements boldly proclaimed "no contracts too large or too complicated." Windham Brothers Construction Company built Pettiford's Sixteenth Street Baptist Church ("which cost upwards of $60,000," reported a reliable source), the Masonic Temple, and "T.C.'s" own home, known as "The Mansion," in the Smithfield neighborhood where the Bonds also settled. In 1908, the *Colored American* marveled that so many of the city's Negroes "own their own homes, some residences costing as much as $6,000." Windham's abode became the site of memorable social events, as he provided his family with the accoutrements of wealth, including elegant dress and home furnishings, a chauffeured automobile, and liveried servants. When he moved to Birmingham, the architect Wallace Rayfield (one of Georgia and Percy's disgruntled former associates from Tuskegee) designed many of the houses that graced Smithfield.[56]

The Bonds settled into a six-room frame cottage on North Sixteenth Street near many of the city's other Negro businessmen and professionals, and three years later they moved to a more comfortable house right around the corner. Their residential neighborhood, known as Smithfield, lay just west of downtown Birmingham, and at that time was a soon-to-be-annexed suburb.

Georgia almost certainly joined one of the local women's organizations, such as the Twentieth Century Club or the Climbers, along with her neighbors and coparishioners Juliette Bradford, Sadie Hadnott, and Jennie Rayfield. The mission of the Climbers, an association comprised of female teachers, was more than social, and in 1913 their bazaar raised $3,000 to retire the mortgage on the city's Home for Aged and Destitute Negroes. Despite Georgia's ongoing interest in woman suffrage, however, and though she easily could pass for white away from home, the chance of exposure, humiliation, and expulsion would have made it hazardous for her and her Tuskegee friend, Adella Logan, to defy Jim Crow traditions and join the small cadre of elite white women who met in Birmingham to create Alabama's ironically titled Equal Suffrage Association.[57]

But a majority of Birmingham residents—black and white, female and male—disregarded, downplayed, or disapproved of any such evidence of women's struggles for political equality. Most southern Negroes embraced orthodox values in the public and private domains, and tried to emulate the patterns established in idealized white families, where a man's status in his community largely derived from his ability to provide for and regulate the activities of his dependents. As Birmingham's affluent white population expanded, however, demands for domestic workers increased, and economic needs often transcended the possibility of maintaining a traditional family structure. Many lower- and working-class Negro families included women who had no choice but to leave their homes to labor as laundresses, cooks, and maids. To help make ends meet, their children often had to drop out of school to take on whatever menial work might be available.[58]

Although residential segregation characterized the city, like many of their Smithfield neighbors, the Bonds had little social contact with those less fortunate African Americans, but attended church and fraternized mostly with their "own kind." Georgia did not have to work, and she and Percy hoped for children whom they diligently would keep in school.

Georgia's second and Percy's first biological child was born in December 1906. Carrie Stewart Bond had immersed herself in her studies—especially Longfellow's poetry—at Atlanta University's Preparatory Division, and when she came home that Christmas, Georgia and Percy gave her the honor of naming the baby. She bestowed on her new sister (who did look much like a papoose) the name Wenonah, for the fictional Hiawatha's ill-fated mother. Reinforcing her choice, Adrienne Herndon, an acquaintance from Boston as well as Carrie's school mentor in Atlanta, had recently written a play in which a lead character bore that name.[59] The naming ritual may have served to bond the half sisters to one another, because Carrie, a favored only child for seventeen years, and Wenonah became each other's closest allies.

Percy worked assiduously, and the Bonds usually remained in Birmingham or went to see Georgia's family in Montgomery, but in late fall 1908, Percy himself, and at least Carrie and two-year-old Wenonah, visited the Bonds in Hyde Park. With his girls in tow, swaddled in fur-trimmed coats, muffs, and plumed hats to combat the unaccustomed cold, Percy attended his sister Lena's wedding, and Emma Bond (whom Wenonah would remember only as her "grandmother in Boston") met her first son's first child.[60]

Soon thereafter, Georgia gave birth to another (and her final) baby, J. Percy Bond, Jr., always called Jack. Wenonah had amber skin and wavy jet-black hair. She was lighter-complexioned than her father, but Percy could see his Thomas-Bond genes imprinted on Wenonah's face, and he featured photographs of her on his Bond & Company advertisements. The new boy, by contrast, was as pale as Georgia, and blessed (or cursed) with golden curls. Family and friends soon recognized that Georgia's youngest, her fairest, her only son, always would be her favorite. When privacy allowed, Percy called his adored Georgia "Darling," and as soon as Jack could lisp his first words, he tried to replicate his father's term of endearment. To her son, Georgia became and remained, never "Mother" or "Mama" but always "Darly."[61]

Class notwithstanding, Negroes in Birmingham (as elsewhere in the South) were restricted in their options for recreational activities. The city had no public parks they could use, the new "Movietorium" admitted only whites, and not until 1915 did a first cinema open "for colored people."[62] But churches served multiple purposes. They satisfied congregants' spiritual needs, helped them endure hard times, provided an extended, supportive "family," and often became a focus of leisure-time activities. Some of the city's major industrial employers, recognizing and appreciating—to a degree—the multifaceted significance of the black church, built Baptist or African Methodist Episcopal (AME) churches for their workers, but the origins of the congregation that the Bonds joined were quite different.[63]

Birmingham's churches were notable as much for their racial and caste distinctions as any other elements of city life, and the Bonds became communicants at St. Mark's Episcopal Church, a bastion of Birmingham's Negro upper class. At that church, Percy and Georgia Bond joined a number of Smithfield neighbors and several former Tuskegeeans, like the Wallace Rayfields. "The colored men of the Episcopal Church are as loyal . . . to her historic continuity as any of her [white] sons," proudly declared a Negro cleric about his denomination, concluding: "They would no more be guilty of setting up a schism than of sacrificing their manhood."[64]

St. Mark's was located on the south side of town in a building it first occupied in 1892. It was acclaimed not only for its austere, brick-fronted propriety and well-established parishioners, but also because it had opened (and would operate until 1940) Birmingham's first secondary school for Negroes. The minister, the Reverend Charles W. Brooks, a man of African and Scottish ancestry who had moved to the city in 1898, prided himself on the fact that his "father, while born a slave, was freed while quite a young man and enlisted in the United States Army." Reverend Brooks christened Wenonah and Jack at St. Mark's early in 1907 and 1910, respectively. Their neighbors, the Bradfords and the Hadnotts, plus Georgia's brother James Fagain and her friend Caroline Smith from Tuskegee, became the Bond children's sponsors and godparents.[65]

Their rectitude, relative prosperity, and solid standing in the Negro community characterized Reverend Brooks's parishioners, many of whom, like Georgia Bond, were also noted for their very light complexions. An apocryphal story contends that when the impeccably dressed, well-mannered delegates from that parish went to a statewide diocesan conference, entered the hall, and moved to seat themselves in a cordoned-off section, a white usher discreetly admonished them: "You can't sit here, these seats are reserved for the niggers from St. Mark's." With great hauteur, the pale-skinned, supposed interlopers courteously responded to the gaping aide: "Sir, we *are* the niggers from St. Mark's."[66]

St. Mark's, Birmingham's "black" Episcopal church, one of only three in the state, was located across town from Smithfield. The huge Sixteenth Street Baptist Church, however, with its mushroom-capped turrets, stained-glass windows, and imposing ceremonial staircase gracing the facade, had been designed by Wallace Rayfield and completed in 1911, just around the corner but on the same block as both houses in which the Bonds resided during their Birmingham years. Half a century later, at that church, the import of the civil rights movement became tragically personified for millions of Americans when a rabid segregationist's firebomb killed four little girls as they were headed to choir practice.

The most concerted challenges to the South's segregated status quo, however, still lay decades in the future, but despite endemic race discrimination, for an ample handful of Birmingham's Negroes, the years between 1905 and 1913, when the Bonds lived there, seemed promising ones. Percy Bond's involvement with the National Negro Business League (NNBL) peaked during that period. In 1909 and 1910, he served as president of the sizable civic-minded local chapter, while Georgia's brother James Fagain headed the Montgomery branch.[67] Birmingham's *Age-Herald* explained that the NNBL "has been the real stimulus to much of the progress among the negroes in business enterprises, in awakening in them the desire to enter commercial life, and opening their eyes to the vast opportunities before them in the south."[68] With little question, Percy's most climactic days with the Business League occurred on a trip north early in 1910 when that national organization convened in New York City.

In keeping with the philosophy of Booker T. Washington—the NNBL's founder and perennial president—one speaker proclaimed on that occasion, "You men are doing more to please God and bring justice to our race than any set of public men have done since we first were given the rights of citizenship." "This is a wonderful age," he declared about that Jim Crow era when few men (and no women) of his race could vote in the South and hundreds of others were lynched or otherwise intimidated, "it is full of life and motion, full of business activity, mental energy, and characterized by great scientific achievement." "Truly," he rhapsodized, "it might be called an Edisonic, photographical, electro-telegraphic, telephonic and aeroplanic age."[69]

During the same session, it also became evident that Percy Bond had become caught up in a squabble with the venerable Rev. W. R. Pettiford, former minister of the Sixteenth Street Baptist Church and president of the Alabama Penny Savings Bank. "I would like to speak concerning a recently organized banking institution of our race in Birmingham," Percy asserted during a testy exchange at the New York convention, "that Dr. Pettiford does not know much about, and of which I happen to be a director." Almost certainly, Pettiford did know but chose not to acknowledge the new Prudential Savings Bank, a competitive upstart enterprise that had opened up right in his own back yard. "Our deposits on the first day, . . . were $4,000," Percy continued, and "they are already doing a good business."[70] The NNBL's (indeed the whole nation's) entrepreneurial spirit had captured him, but his run-in with the influential Pettiford may have come at a cost, because members of the Birmingham chapter did not reelect Percy Bond as their president, though he remained on the state organization's board of directors for several years.[71]

Following that civilized spat and other more vacuous paeans, mingled with intervals of serious business, an address by "Col." (and former president) Theodore Roosevelt provided the conference's climax. Roosevelt, one of Booker T. Washington's boosters and a Tuskegee trustee, lauded the NNBL because, he argued, "it teaches you not to whine or cry about privileges you have not got, but to turn your attention to making the best of opportunities that are at your doors." "An ounce of performance of the work of good citizenship is worth a ton of complaint," he pontificated to the Negro businessmen who surely dared not cry, whine, or complain.[72]

"A colored man who lives a life . . . of idleness or the life of a ne'er-do-well," Roosevelt continued, "is not only doing badly for himself, but he is doing badly for all of his people." "Let him know . . . that we will force him, not only for his own sake, but for the sake of his people to conduct himself as a good citizen," Roosevelt added to "hearty applause." He failed to acknowledge, however, either that white people never were judged by the weakest among them, or that the country's usurpation of citizenship rights afflicted not only Negro "ne-er-do-wells" but all of his diligent, rapt, and enthusiastic audience.[73]

"I believe in this League, as I wrote them five years ago when I was President," Roosevelt continued to "tumultuous applause" at the mention of his once, and hopefully future, reign in the White House. "It is a League that is out of politics" (that zinger evoked robust laughter), "and you devote yourselves to stimulating among colored people the spirit of business enterprise." Clearly, Roosevelt believed that even modest economic achievements for African Americans far surpassed in importance their right to vote, be treated with dignity and receive equal treatment under law, live where and with whom they wanted, get the best health care, attend schools of their choice, ride public transportation in comfort, go to movie shows, or stay at the better hotels.

Formal education for Negroes (but not the industrial or vocational sort that Booker Washington advocated) received short shrift from Roosevelt. "I don't care how well educated a farmer is," he interjected, "if he can't farm his land he is going to be a failure, and the greatest amount of learning in the possession of a woman who can't cook won't make her food taste well."[74] That orthodox gratuity may have struck home for Percy Bond, whose dear Georgia, with all her airs and refinement, could not cook.

The former president wound up his rambling stem-winder with sentiments that might well have been articulated by Booker Washington. "When you succeed in getting the ordinary white man of the country to realize that the ordinary colored man is a good citizen, you have a friend," Roosevelt asserted with bravado, "and that white man benefitted so greatly, that there is only one person who receives a greater benefit, and that is the colored man himself." NNBL delegates greeted those concluding pronouncements with "prolonged applause, cheering, and the waving of the flags," and surely returned to their homes across the country sated, elated, and with stories to last a lifetime.[75]

Within three years of that memorable event, however, the Bonds (who bemoaned Roosevelt's failed attempt to regain the presidency in 1912 and the victory of the suspect southern Democrat Woodrow Wilson) prepared to leave Birmingham. Percy's contretemps with Pettiford in New York may have had unpleasant repercussions that prompted him to seek other options. Wenonah Bond also was ready to enter the first grade, and her parents would have deplored the fact that although Birmingham had St. Mark's Academy and an industrial high school for Negroes, public schools for blacks operated in wretched facilities, crammed to more than two-and-a-half times' capacity. The city spent seven times the amount on education for its white as for its Negro children.[76]

Perhaps Georgia also wanted to be nearer her family in Montgomery, and the Magic City's grime and brash demeanor may have distressed her as well. A local newspaper conceded that the blast furnaces cast "a dirty splotch upon the fair face of Birmingham. They daily and nightly spew their noisome smoke and poisonous gases into the air." In addition, four lynchings had occurred in the area during the Bonds' residency there: one in 1909, two in 1912, and the following year that of a mentally retarded lad charged with "frightening women and children."[77] Birmingham was showing chinks in its fabled armor, with the massive statue of Vulcan rusted, tarnished, and cracking. The one-time magic may have begun to seem little more than acrid smoke and cracked mirrors for the Bonds. New opportunities concurrently opened up in a supposedly more genteel town where Percy thought he might become a larger fish in a smaller, less treacherous pond.

Whatever their compound reasons, the Bonds left Birmingham for Selma, "Queen City of the Black Belt."[78] In November 1913, Georgia and Percy contracted with the owners of Selma's largest department store to purchase a residential lot on Washington Street. The Bonds soon settled into their new home, though Wenonah, who much preferred macadamed streets and trolleys to dirt roads and grass, was not pleased with the move.[79]

Selma was a traditional southern town, and as different from Birmingham as could be imagined. It had been established in 1820, just after the state was admitted to the Union, and had always based its economy on cotton raised in the agricultural hinterlands and shipped off via the Alabama River as far as Liverpool and other European ports. Neoclassic mansions graced portions of the city and its environs, while the pervasive legacy of slavery, traditions of antebellum life, and residual Confederate passions combined to characterize the community.

In 1853, one of the Queen City's most acclaimed men, William Rufus King, had briefly and forgettably been the country's vice president (he was sworn in, but died before assuming office) during the almost equally unmemorable presidency of Franklin Pierce. Among white Selmans' other idols were Catesby Jones, who had captained the CSS *Virginia* in battle against the USS *Monitor* during the Civil War's best-remembered sea battle, and Edmund Winston Pettus, brigadier general in the Confederate Army and then U.S. senator, for whom Alabama's most notorious bridge was later named. Fifty years after the Bonds lived in Selma, Americans of all persuasions watched their television screens in horror as white state troopers mercilessly assaulted civil rights demonstrators who tried to traverse that span, which arched across the Alabama River, during their Selma-to-Montgomery march.

Scarcely recalled by the white community, but a hero to black Selmians, was Benjamin Turner, elected to the U.S. House of Representatives during Reconstruction on a conciliatory platform of "universal suffrage and universal amnesty." Dazzling Jeremiah Haralson ("cotton-stealing Jere") succeeded Turner, but his controversial flamboyance, internal schisms among Republicans, and especially the convenient disposal of Negroes' untallied ballots cut short his time in office.[80] It would be a century before Black Belt Alabama's majority citizens managed to send another African American representative to Congress.

In the surrounding countryside, most black people worked as tenant farmers and sharecroppers, but Selma's middle-class Negro community grudgingly adapted to the insults, dangers, and deprivations of segregation and dedicated itself to retail trade, religion, and education. To compensate for the voids in public education for Negroes, church leaders started schools for "colored" children such as the Presbyterian Knox Academy, with its racially integrated faculty in 1874, Baptist Selma University in 1886, and the AME Payne Institute soon thereafter.[81] In 1904, Payne moved into its new quarters on the corner of Washington and Franklin Streets.

The Bonds' compact, two-story frame house almost nestled into the shadow of that school, and they could look a mile down their street to the Alabama River. They had a porch graced with lush asparagus ferns and accessed their pretty garden through a vine-tangled archway. Georgia relished her traditional spousal role. She furnished her new home with taste, dressed and groomed herself and her children with care (meticulously pomading and braiding Wenonah's long, thick hair), probably joined one of Selma's preferred "colored" women's clubs, and almost certainly attended the

1915 gathering—greeting longtime Montgomery, Tuskegee, and Birmingham colleagues—of the Alabama Federation of Colored Women's Clubs that convened in Selma.[82]

Percy kept the tools of commerce—a telephone and a typewriter—near at hand, and bought his children a puppy and bicycles. At only six years of age, Jack, a chip off the old entrepreneurial block, pedaled around his neighborhood selling *Crisis,* the monthly magazine of the National Association for the Advancement of Colored People (NAACP), edited by his mother's Fisk schoolmate W. E. B. Du Bois. Wenonah played in her swing while Charles Melton, the yardman, cared for the garden and (reflecting Georgia's distaste for such drudgery reinforced by her hated employment under Margaret Washington's aegis at Tuskegee) his wife laundered the Bonds' clothes in her outdoor tub.[83]

Georgia did not work outside the home—and very little in it. She embroidered, crocheted, and painted opalescent gold-rimmed china teacups. Sometimes she quilted, using hoarded scraps of satin and lace, brocade and lustrous velvet randomly pieced together with brilliant silk thread and goose-foot stitchery. Her few, resplendent creations scarcely resembled the utilitarian, geometric-patterned "American" coverlets that many women, black and white, created from sturdy cottons and wools.[84]

Georgia was inept in the kitchen, however, and others did most of the family's cooking. She was delighted when her mother, "Mamma Dear," and occasionally her benevolent white relatives as well, came over from Montgomery. "Mrs. Caroline Fagain who had been visiting her daughter, Mrs. G. F. Bond in Selma, is home again looking very much improved as a result of her trip," the *Colored Alabamian* reported in April 1915. Wenonah and Jack basked in their grandmother's nurturing food, care, and presence. Percy's favorite biblical quotation that he often (and fittingly) applied to his adored, pale blossom of a wife was: "Consider the lilies . . . they toil not, they spin not; and yet . . . Solomon in all his glory was not arrayed like one of these."[85]

Payne Institute's president and his wife lived next door to the Bond family, while two of that school's deans and several of Selma's few Negro physicians (in 1914, only 4 of 113 applicants for state medical licenses were black), pharmacists, and restaurant owners also resided on the block. African American neighbors such as the Meltons (the Bonds' gardener and laundress), however, did not belong to that "colored" middle class.[86]

Caucasians lived nearby as well, but the father of one of Wenonah's white contemporaries sternly cautioned his daughter that the two girls must never exchange home visits. Wenonah's safe refuge from such affronts became her own father's nostalgic tales of his Boston childhood, books, and always school. Given their parents' relative financial comfort and dedication to education, instead of going to Selma's woeful "colored" public schools, Wenonah and her brother Jack probably attended nearby Knox Academy, whose teachers (in disparate circles) were either praised or condemned for their conspicuous "Yankee ways."[87]

J. Percy Bond wore several hats in Selma. He established himself on Franklin Street in the town's preferred black business district, next door (as he had been in Birmingham) to a branch of the Alabama Penny Savings Bank. He soon took over office space—where he invested in and served as southern Alabama's representative for the new Atlanta-based Standard Life Insurance Company—from a gentleman named H. B. Kenan. Kenan had been an insurance agent on Franklin Street, and a "merchant tailor" a few blocks away in an area occupied mainly by white businesses. Bond and Kenan also apparently joined forces in a haberdashery store. Drs. L. L. Burwell and R. B. Hudson, Negro leaders in Selma, had attended the formative Boston meeting of the NNBL in 1900, and they surely became colleagues of Percy Bond as well.[88] Percy's drive and dedication would have gratified the editor of the black-owned Selma *Advocate,* who stated in 1915: "Each Negro who successfully carries on a business of his own, helps the race as well as himself, for no Negro can rise without reflecting honor upon other Negroes." With his concurrent ventures, Percy would have satisfied his own personal and biblically mandated industriousness, too, in that he was never "slothful in business; [but] fervent in spirit, serving the Lord."[89]

Despite Alabama's increasingly unyielding segregation, and the valid observation that eleven o'clock Sunday morning was the country's most segregated hour, Percy, Georgia, and their children joined St. Paul's Parish, Selma's white (and its only) Episcopal church. Their church had been welcomed into the Alabama diocese in 1838, and in 1875 held the first services in what remains its home even now. The resplendent brick building was intended to reflect the glory of both God and its affluent parishioners.[90] Its ceiling had been painted azure with gold stars, and profuse trefoil tracery symbolized the Trinity. A shimmering mosaic featuring a Greek cross, twining ivy (the classic symbol of affection), lilies, and an Easter angel totally sheathed the altar, and the New York studios of Louis Comfort Tiffany designed the regal, jewel-like procession of stained-glass nave windows.[91]

Father Edward Watts Gamble, more a humanitarian than an orator, had been installed at the church in 1903. As Jim Crow restrictions throughout the South began to crest, a Negro journalist protested, "The Episcopal Church South has drawn its social and ecclesiastical skirt and robe about it with a mighty scorn lest they so much as touch the colored man and brother." In that spirit, St. Paul's pastor and its other parishioners (all pillars of the community) were white. But the lifelong Episcopalian Percy Bond, true to his father's English heritage and devoted to his religion, attended St. Paul's, made weekly donations, and even became a lay reader. In addition, and in thoroughgoing defiance of accepted southern protocol, all of the Bonds often sat down around the dining room table to share midday Sunday meals with the Reverend Edward Gamble and his family at their spacious nearby home.[92]

The broad-minded Gambles must have considered Percy Bond a gentleman and Georgia a lady, race notwithstanding. In that singular instance, class rather than caste seems to have prevailed. Years later, Percy and Georgia's daughter argued that, even in the face of Alabama's obdurate segregation, some Episcopalians' inbred elitism made them shrink from forsaking any members of their flock to the supposedly inferior ministrations of the "lower" denominations. Negroes outnumbered whites in Selma's Dallas County by four to one, but the vast majority were Baptists or AMEs. A few of St. Paul's white parishioners were also supporters of woman suffrage, and that "progressive" coterie included the well-heeled folks who owned the Selma *Times*. "Colored" Episcopalians were so few in Alabama that having one family, such as the Bonds, join the upper-class white community's parish of choice could hardly be expected to—and definitely did not—precipitate a flood of darkness on St. Paul's.[93]

Percy Bond also challenged Selma's racial hierarchy in another arena. As soon as he became eligible to vote, he paid his poll tax and (probably supported by a character reference from Reverend Gamble) became one of the city's very few Negro voters.[94] Any prospective voter had to have lived in Alabama for two years, his county of residence for one, and his electoral ward for three months. He needed to pay a retroactive poll tax, own property valued at three hundred dollars or more, be engaged in a "reputable" business, and never have been convicted of any crime, no matter how trivial the offense. He could also be required to read or write passages from the Constitution to the satisfaction of local registrars. Poor whites could be "grandfathered" onto voting rolls, but black men had virtually no chance to qualify. In 1901, Dallas County had almost ten thousand Negro voters, but a white Selmian boasted that the revised state constitution that year had but one purpose, "to kill snakes," by which he meant removal of all "colored" voters. In that respect, the legislature had been highly efficient. Only fifty-two Negroes appeared on the county rolls after the new Alabama constitution went into effect, and the nation's Supreme Court, piloted by the renowned Bostonian, Justice Oliver Wendell Holmes, upheld that racial exclusion.[95]

"We, the Southern people, entertain no prejudice toward the ignorant, per se, inoffensive Negro," a white Alabaman stated at that time, "but our blood boils when the educated Negro asserts himself politically." "We regard each assertion as an unfriendly encroachment upon our native superior rights, and a dare-devil menace to our control of the affairs of the state," he concluded. That was the political climate which J. Percy Bond confronted and to some extent overcame in Selma.[96]

But Percy's life was more than just family, work, church, and struggles to exercise the franchise. Baseball was his favorite means of relaxation and he served as manager of a team made up of others among Selma's Negro businessmen and professionals. "Dr. J. J. Daniels distributes the bandages while Duncan Irby makes wagons to haul home the lame players," explained a jovial account in the *Advocate*. "Wait for a good one," a reporter wrote about that game, "knock it hard, and zip . . . it will go." "Make for the bases, keep going, take a chance and steal second, don't go gay, and you can steal third," the lively article continued; "up will come a good hitter, and you will slide into home."[97]

The *Journal,* one of Selma's white-owned newspapers, devoted most of its attention to cotton, Alabama politics, lurid accounts of Negro vice and crime, and the escalating conflict in Europe, but it also followed major league baseball. In October 1914, it noted, "thirty-thousand fans are watching the [Boston] Braves and Athletics in the third game of the world series." Percy would have been delighted to read that his old hometown team, the "Miracle Braves" (resuscitated by their laconic catcher "Hankus Pankus" Gowdy), who had occupied the league's cellar in mid-July, won that game "5 to 4 in the twelfth inning," then finished off the vaunted Philadelphia Athletics in the first four-game sweep in World Series history. The next year, the *Journal* featured an article headlined "Negroes Seek to Suppress Film," concerning the NAACP's attempts to prevent showings of the new race-baiting blockbuster movie *The Birth of a Nation* in Boston and other northern cities.[98]

The *Journal* also followed the downfall of the black-owned Selma *Advocate*. The *Advocate*'s editor, D. P. Craig, supposedly had distributed circulars to white households claiming that the poor health and unsanitary living conditions of the city's black laundresses, cooks, and nursemaids endangered white women and children. Craig's purported economic motivation for those warnings was that he planned to start his own employment bureau that would certify the health of such workers before sending them out to the homes of affluent Selmians. Those charges outraged many black people, who considered them grossly insulting to their women. Craig denied authorship of the flyers and claimed that unknown persons had appropriated his stationery and framed him. "Negro Editor Assaulted," reported the *Journal* when unidentified men attacked Craig, who had received menacing death threats. The

Journal maintained that the whole brouhaha "raised a rumpus among the negroes the likes of which has not been seen in Selma in many a day." Fearing for his life, Craig hightailed it out of town, the *Advocate* folded, and the black newspaper's furniture, presses, and other accoutrements mysteriously vanished.[99] The journalistic voice of Selma's Negro community had been silenced.

With the racially driven logic that motivated much of their behavior, many white Alabamans called Percy Bond "Professor." He once, after all, had been associated with Tuskegee Institute. His respectable community standing discouraged them from saying "uncle," "boy," or using a first name, but addressing him as "Mr. Bond" seemed unthinkable. "I admire Booker Washington," a white southerner similarly confirmed, "yet I couldn't call him Mr. Washington." "We were in a quandary until a doctor's degree was given him," he added. "It saved our lives! We all call him 'Dr.' Washington now." "They are ready to call a Negro 'Professor' or 'Bishop' or 'The Reverend,' " a visitor from the North observed, "but never 'Mr.' "[100] To do so would have signaled a degree of social equality that blatantly flaunted accepted racial practice, so to deflect any disparaging personal nomenclature, black men (and some women) in the South routinely used only their initials, such as J. J. Daniels, D. P. Craig, and, of course, J. P. Bond.

Along the same lines, one white Selmian explained that he greeted Negro acquaintances with: " 'Hello Arthur, Hello George, how are you this morning?' They would reply 'how are you Mr. Grayson?' " "If I had said 'Good morning Mr. Cochran, or Mr. Merryman,' " he blithely continued, "they would think that I had gone crazy." Grayson professed fondness for "little black Sam at the post office, smiling and polite," and judged all black people "happy-go-lucky, take no thought of tomorrow." But he warned his dark-skinned acquaintances to "keep your blood pure, don't mix it with other races—if you know what I mean."[101] Negroes did know what he meant, because such warnings specifically referred to forbidden sexual relations between black men and white women.

Those demeaning protocols and racial inequities continued unabated, but Booker T. Washington's death late in 1915 stunned whites and Negroes alike. African Americans lost their most revered leader and white America lost the man who represented for them the best of an inferior race, whose respectful demeanor and accommodationist stances had allowed him to serve as a symbol of appropriate Negro success, and an interlocutor and mediator in a country torn by racial inequities and conflicts. Despite some long-standing tensions, Washington's death fell as a heavy blow on the Bonds, who had known the whole family professionally and personally for many years. Soon thereafter, the untimely demise of Adella Hunt Logan, their Tuskegee friend and Georgia's mentor in the cause of woman suffrage, compounded the tragedy.

After the Bonds left Tuskegee Institute, Adella had been plagued by chronic poor health. She had a kidney surgically removed, yet still bore two more children—the last when she was forty-six. Reinforcing her anguish, an older son was diagnosed with tuberculosis, a lingering but certain death sentence.

On the political front, Adella became disillusioned when the legislature defeated a bill that summer that would have required a statewide referendum on woman suffrage, yet she continued her passionate but fruitless advocacy of the cause. An anonymous pamphlet, circulated by a Selma cabal, had sounded the proposal's death knell. "Women's suffrage," it began, "is the most dangerous blow aimed at the peace and happiness of the people of Alabama and white supremacy since the Civil War," and the Selma *Journal* described Negro women as more dangerous than their men. Those inflammatory arguments had dissuaded wavering legislators from supporting any radical motion that might "strike a blow at the cleanest, highest and most beautiful civilization on earth."[102]

Adella was having marital difficulties as well. She became noticeably disagreeable, increasingly irrational, and her emotional deterioration no longer could be ignored when she ignited a fire one night in her husband's office. In October, the family sent her away for a "rest cure" at a Michigan clinic where, yielding to Booker T. Washington's pointed instructions, she agreed to masquerade as a white woman. After a less-than-adequate one month of treatment, a telegram containing word of Washington's rapidly declining health summoned her back to Tuskegee, where she encountered rumors that her spouse had become embroiled in a romance.[103] Of at least equal importance, the entire institute, indeed the African American community as a whole, was overwhelmed with grief when Booker Washington, the Logans' next-door neighbor and dear friend of more than thirty years, died just hours after Adella's return.

A month later, the institute welcomed humble admirers along with renowned and wealthy mourners to a ceremony memorializing Washington. Politicians and philanthropists from around the country and the school's trustees, including Theodore Roosevelt, who had to choose a successor (Tuskegee's Emmett Scott and Warren Logan, and Hampton's R. R. Moton were top contenders), to the man whom everyone considered unsucceedable—all had come to Tuskegee for the weekend. But the Sunday afternoon services had a pall cast over them by that morning's funeral for the school's long-time educator and resident firebrand, Adella Logan.

Two days earlier, Julia Walton—who had lived with Georgia at the institute's Model Cottage—encountered the thoroughly deranged Adella as she was preparing to fling herself from a top-floor window in the academic building. Julia grasped the frantic woman, trying to hold her back. She clutched so tightly that the muscles in her hands cramped up and she could not unclench them for days. Julia could not, however, restrain Adella Hunt Logan who jumped to her death as administrators, teachers, visitors, and many young people (including, most lamentably, two of her own children) watched in horror. A decade earlier, Logan prophetically had written that a woman's compound frustrations could lead her "to cry, to swear, or to suicide."[104]

Soon thereafter, the disconsolate George Washington Carver painted two murals in his quarters: one honoring Booker T. Washington, the other memorializing his friend Adella Logan.[105] Julia Walton went to stay with the Bonds in Selma while she recovered from the trauma of the tragedy she had tried so hard to avert. Julia and Georgia had been close friends at Tuskegee, and Wenonah often traveled over to the institute by train to visit her "Aunt Julia." Julia's brother worked for Percy in Selma as well, and members of the middle-class Negro community understood that they must support one another in any way possible during that grievous period. Percy also delivered a eulogy for Booker T. Washington, not at the white Episcopal St. Mark's, but at one of Selma's largest Negro churches, the AME Brown's Chapel.[106]

For several years, the Bonds and a select few other Negro families had succeeded moderately well in Selma. The boll weevil's unwelcome arrival, however, undercut the already precarious economic foundation of Alabama's black (and other marginal) farmers. By 1917, Dallas County's cotton production would drop to only twenty-two percent of what it had been just three years earlier. Gruesome lynchings of Negroes went unpunished, and rumors circulated that black children were being kidnapped from the countryside and confined in peonage.[107]

The Reverend W. R. Pettiford had died at the end of 1914. Soon thereafter, his Alabama Penny Savings Bank merged with the Prudential Savings Bank—the institution over which he and J. Percy Bond had tangled in 1910. That partnership represented an attempt to salvage both institutions in stringent economic times. The merged Birmingham-based bank with branches in Selma and Montgomery, however, failed in late 1915, costing many Negroes (possibly including the Bonds) their savings. In the summer of 1916, the Alabama River flooded Selma's environs. Hundreds of Negro farmers lost whatever minimal assets they still had, and those misfortunes generated a pernicious ripple effect on black businesses.[108] Wenonah also remembered hearing that her father's white competitors and the men from whom he leased his haberdashery store resented his success and raised the rent until they forced him out of business. The bank ultimately foreclosed on and auctioned off the Bonds' home.[109]

Despite his financial setbacks and the exigencies of the times, J. Percy Bond was an excellent insurance salesman and manager. He had worked for Standard Life in Selma, and the opportunity arose to launch a new branch in Washington, D.C., as his expansion-minded company spread out from the Deep South.[110]

Alabama ranked dead last in education among the states, and for black people the situation was far worse than for whites. The public school year for African American children was only seventy-six days. Birmingham made minimal expenditures on behalf of its Negro students, but Selma (Dallas County), which spent twenty times as much per pupil on whites as it did on blacks, was worse. The state legislature even debated new legislation that would ban whites from teaching in institutions for Negroes, such as Knox Academy. Church-sponsored schools like Payne Institute and Selma University (which had to stop paying its faculty for a while) stood at the brink of collapse and reflected the African American community's dire economic straits.[111]

With Howard University, Paul Laurence Dunbar High School, and the country's best (though segregated) schools for Negroes at all levels, educational opportunities seemed to abound for the Bond children in Washington. Georgia also welcomed the fact that the capital city was known for its diverse cultural resources and the supposedly elegant social life of the "colored" upper-class set that she fully expected to join.

To the distress of whites who feared the loss of their accustomed cheap labor, the field-to-factory migration of black people from the rural Deep South to supposedly welcoming cities of the Midwest and the North was gaining momentum, and the Bonds' southern family base eroded when Georgia's mother Caroline Fagain died in Montgomery.[112] Georgia's older daughter Carrie had graduated from Atlanta University, moved to New Jersey and then on to Cambridge, Massachusetts. She had matured into an independent young woman (vastly different from, though devoted to, her mother) who was determined to make her own way in the world.

Percy left Selma for the nation's capital in mid-1916, and Georgia and the younger children soon followed him as their country geared up to enter the Great War to save democracy. A visiting white northerner had spoken with an African American southerner who complained: "It's getting to be too dangerous for a coloured man down here, . . . I think I shall go to Washington." "Why Washington?" the white man asked. "Well, you see," the Negro patriot explained, "I want to be as near the flag as I can."[113]

· 12 ·

CARRIE:
THEORIES *of* EVOLUTION
and the COMPANY *of* WOMEN

---

*Your connection with the history of this country is as important as my
own. . . . I object to your alluding to Africa as your home, and to calling
yourselves Africans. . . . If you are African, I am European, and we are
both aliens, and the Red Man is the only true American. This is our
country, and its rights and immunities are ours together.*

EDGAR H. WEBSTER, professor of physical sciences,
Atlanta University, 1887–1929

FROM THE TIME she left Massachusetts for Alabama in 1902,
Carrie Stewart tried to strategize a return. Like her entire family,
she had been born in the South and there she would pass most of
her years, but Boston remained the home of her heart.

At least for a while, however, she could not avoid Alabama.
Her mother Georgia put in three years teaching laundering techniques at Tuskegee Institute so that Carrie might acquire a decent
education. She and all other students there had to supply themselves with a Bible, plus "good shoes, a pair of rubber overshoes
and a water-proof coat, . . . warm and comfortable underclothing,
wool if possible." In keeping with its commitment to conformity,
the institute also required female students to wear a "navy blue,
sailor uniform dress and a plain sailor hat." Carrie complied with
those demands.[1]

Georgia Stewart hated her work, but Carrie, though she
yearned for New England, nonetheless flourished at Tuskegee. She

mastered a body of traditional materials in the classroom but also absorbed progressive ideologies, including the prosuffrage messages expounded by her mother's friend Adella Logan and illustrious visitors such as Susan B. Anthony. And in 1903, just prior to the Boston Riot and the bombshell created by W. E. B. Du Bois's scathing essay "Of Mr. Booker T. Washington and Others," Carrie would have heard that increasingly controversial scholar's lecture at Tuskegee Institute: "The History of Negro Education in America."[2]

Carrie appreciated much that Tuskegee had to offer, and the school reciprocated. With her solid academic preparation in Boston, she became one of the institute's most lauded students. At the end of her first year, the *Tuskegee Student* printed her entire prize-winning essay "The Story of Three Indian Baskets."

Carrie wrote about an Indian girl, Chotowaik, and her "American" companion who together attended "a school not unlike our own." When the time came for Chotowaik to return to the reservation, as a parting gift she taught her friend how to fashion the intricate baskets that were a tradition among the women of her tribe. In Carrie's story, the "American" girl obtained a lasting memento of her beloved Chotowaik's indigenous heritage, and also mastered the exacting craft so well that she developed her own cottage industry and soon was selling the coveted "Indian" baskets for handsome sums. "This simple art," Carrie concluded, "was not only pleasurable, but profitable."[3]

Carrie Stewart's first published literary endeavor combined several elements that became recurrent motifs in her life. It featured a spunky "American" heroine bound to another young woman in an ardent friendship. The essay also foretold Carrie's love of writing, revealed a nascent preoccupation with anthropology, and epitomized Booker T. Washington's guiding principles of hard work, self-help, and modest entrepreneurship. With little doubt, that latter theme (even more than its skillful presentation) delighted both Washington and the editors of his school's paper.

Carrie Stewart participated in dramatic productions as well, though she later recalled being convulsed by uncontrollable giggles during a Greek "tragedy [that] became a comedy" when the curtain rose and footlights on the tiny stage revealed "a bust of Booker T.

Washington pedestalled on the one side, and on the other, one of Beethoven." In 1905, she won the institute's senior rhetorical competition. "This is the first instance in which either the first or second prize has been taken by a woman," the school newspaper announced as she broke that long-standing gender barrier. Carrie was the only girl who spoke at commencement, when she received the "Trinity Church Boston Prize," donated by parishioners of that revered Episcopal establishment where she and her mother had taken young Baker Washington to attend Sunday services a few years earlier.[4]

For graduation, the *Tuskegee Student* noted, "ten full coaches came from Montgomery," with Georgia and Carrie's doting relatives almost certainly aboard one of them. "The commencement sermon this year was presented by a Jew, Rabbi A. J. Messing, Jr. of Montgomery," the newspaper further reported. In his address, Rabbi Messing drew comparisons between the struggles of Jews and Negroes, and asserted that he, like Booker T. Washington, "represented a people who had risen out of slavery."[5]

Carrie had gleaned all that Tuskegee had to offer. She passed through Montgomery for her mother's marriage to Percy Bond that fall. Then, minimally enriched by the graduation award as a reminder of her beloved Boston, possessed of a new father and girded with his annexed surname, Caroline Stewart Bond headed off to the college preparatory division at Atlanta University.

Compared to Tuskegee's fifteen hundred students, her class in Atlanta (though the city's black population topped forty thousand) was quite small, with only sixty-eight members. The curriculum, however, was more challenging, and Atlanta University had a white president and faculty of both races. The Yale men and other Yankees who had founded the school after the Civil War aspired, as much as possible, to provide a few southern Negroes with educational opportunities that replicated those they once had experienced themselves in New England's halls of academe.[6]

At the end of Carrie's first school year at Atlanta, she won the top award (fifteen dollars) "for excellence in declamation," and Adrienne Herndon served as her mentor for the contest. Carrie and Georgia Bond no doubt had known the exquisite Herndon from their concurrent sojourns in Boston when Herndon had studied theatrical arts. Herndon, however, had returned with regularity to her son, her husband Alonzo (he owned and operated the city's most elite barbering emporia—catering exclusively to a white clientele—then started Atlanta Mutual Life Insurance Company), and to the school where she taught elocution and drama.[7]

In 1906, Columbia University's German-born Professor Franz Boas, the country's most progressive anthropologist, spoke at Atlanta University's graduation exercises. Boas (a kindred spirit of W. E. B. Du Bois, who taught in the College Division and had invited the New York–based scholar to Georgia), almost alone in his academic field, was using his methodology, skills, and writings to challenge the "scientifically grounded" racist assumptions promoted by most members of his discipline.

Much as their African and Caribbean counterparts correctly perceived white anthropologists as champions of paternalistic and repressive colonial ideologies, a small group of Negro American scholars (Du Bois prominent among them) viewed those scientists as a hostile cabal who bruited the precepts of black racial inferiority. Many anthropologists had attempted to prove the cultural necessity of slavery, white supremacy, and segregation, and their intellectual legacy from as far back as Europe's Middle Ages had slotted men and women of African ancestry along the Great Chain of Being in a position "closest to the ape in the evolutionary tree." A concurrent exhibition at New York City's Bronx Zoological Park reinforced those demeaning but prevalent beliefs. Ota Benga, a Mbuti pygmy "rescued" from Africa's Congo Free State, temporarily resided there in "one of the best rooms in the primate house." "The Bushman and the orang-outang frolicked together . . . locked in each other's arms" and titillated huge crowds of curious visitors, the *New York Times* reported.[8]

In the United States, early-twentieth-century anthropology and ethnology had evolved from entrenched intellectual traditions that had sanctioned not only the importation of slaves from Africa, but also the conquest, displacement, and even annihilation of Native Americans. Building on a reinvigorated, reinterpreted adherence to Darwinism, many anthropologists reinforced the widely held assumptions that Negroes (like the captive Ota Benga) were the world's most primitive people, and Caucasians its most advanced. Such ideologies maintained that all black people suffered from in-born moral insufficiencies, bestial sexual proclivities, and genetic propensities to sloth. In addition, the closely linked eugenics move-ment spread alarm about spiraling infusions into the United States of "inferior stock" from southern and eastern Europe. Early-twentieth-century eugenicists contended that all of the "deficient" alien "races" were prone to unchecked procreation and threatened to swamp the country's earlier waves of "superior" Anglo-Saxon immigrants.

Many white "authorities" argued that if the country would only stop coddling its "colored" people, they eventually (hopefully) would die out, and they viewed "mongrelization" as a more insidious threat than implausible fears of black domination. Most anthropol-ogists considered mulattoes intellectually superior to "full-blooded" Negroes because of their "white blood," but also characterized them as troublemakers and devious malcontents who often inher-ited the worst traits of both races. Around the turn of the century a number of influential scholars maintained that the United States' majority population must rigorously hold the line against any pol-luting infusions of "black blood."[9]

As an academic discipline, anthropology had emerged in mid-nineteenth-century Europe in an attempt to explain cultural and anatomical variants among the Family of Man, and the few Amer-ican Negroes who thought about it at all in the early 1900s rightly considered it a hostile science. Nonetheless, that intriguing and relatively new field also contained fertile intellectual seeds which ultimately might demonstrate that education, history, and environ-ment, far more than race, determined human behavior and achieve-ment. Anthropology, a few progressive thinkers like Du Bois and Boas believed (and hoped), had the potential to overcome a pre-vailing adherence to the racist tenets of genetic determinism, and Boas and his followers at Columbia University were trying to up-grade and update their science into what they characterized as a substantively reconfigured "American School."[10]

Boas thereby proved an exception to generalities about his

profession's mulish devotion to anthropological racism. He was developing alternative ideologies, and would become best known through *The Mind of Primitive Man,* published in 1911. When he spoke at Atlanta University in 1906, Boas stated, "An unbiased estimate of the anthropological evidence so far brought forward does not permit us to countenance the belief in racial inferiority which would unfit an individual of the Negro race to take a part in modern civilization."[11]

He did not claim that all races possessed equal abilities, but insisted that scientists in his discipline had never proved that the world's black, brown, red, yellow, or "mixed races" were inherently inferior, and he challenged the assumption that Anglo-European culture was immutably "better" than others. Even if Caucasians were in any way "superior," Boas contended, it was due to "circumstances of their historic development rather than to inherent capacities." With limited success, Boas, an immigrant, Jewish outsider, called on his academic colleagues to employ objective methodology to challenge the prevalent depreciation of "primitive" people, including American Negroes, and he expounded on those beliefs at his commencement address in Atlanta.[12]

The progressive, interracial amity generated that June day at Atlanta University was short-lived, however. Perhaps the city's Negroes should have more closely heeded the summer storm warnings as hatemongers who revered slavery's legacies and had internalized the dogmas of quasi-scientific racism began whipping white residents into a frenzy toward its black citizens. One newspaper column called for a revival of the Ku Klux Klan, while another proposed rewards for a successful "lynching bee." Those scurrilous writings heightened the already widespread negativity toward Negroes, while Georgia's politicians continued to disfranchise the state's already dwindling numbers of black male voters.[13]

As the autumnal equinox neared and the city's institutions for Negroes opened for the fall semester, with little judgment or justification, race-baiting journals reported lurid tales of sexual assaults on white women by black men. But nothing prepared Negro Atlantans for the melees that erupted on September 22 as wrathful whites began attacking them. "Negroes were quite unsuspecting that their white 'friends' had planned to destroy them," recalled Lugenia Hope, a community leader and the wife of Atlanta Baptist College's president. Rumors proliferated that African Americans were being slaughtered en masse. They deluged the campuses of Atlanta University, Atlanta Baptist, and Clark College seeking safe refuge, while a white policeman pistol-whipped the principal of another of the city's esteemed "colored" schools. Police tried to round up any armed Negroes, then shot haphazardly into an anxious throng. The blacks returned fire, killing one officer and wounding another. Following that provocative episode, white mobs cast aside any remaining semblance of civilized behavior and set out on a savage binge, looting and burning black people's homes and businesses. "The finest shop in the whole country had the glass front smashed because the owner was colored," an article reported about Alonzo Herndon's establishment, adding that several "barbers . . . were shot and a bootblack was kicked to death." Rioters slew at least four "colored" men and injured many others. Workplaces shut down all over town, and public transportation ceased operating when whites would "stop the street cars [and] pull the Negroes out to beat them."[14]

The primary fury spent itself after several days, and a few white residents admitted partial responsibility and mildly chastised the miscreants. They formed the all-white Atlanta Civic League in a feeble attempt to ameliorate contributory social conditions and prevent future disorders. Civic authorities, however, did little to discover or prosecute the offenders. In his "Litany at Atlanta," W. E. B. Du Bois wrote, "A city lay in travail . . . and from her loins sprang twin Murder and Black Hate," and Carrie Bond recited that entire passionate treatise at a school assembly. "White people knew how they had treated the Negro all the while, now they feared retribution," added Lugenia Hope, while Adrienne Herndon wrote Booker T. Washington: "Some times I doubt if there is any spot in the country where one with Negro blood can plant a home free from prejudice, scorn & molestation." The climate gradually improved, but Negro leaders such as the YMCA's Alphaeus Hunton and his wife Addie (a clubwoman, suffragist, and Clark College's bursar) moved north, vowing never again to dwell "in the midst of great racial conflict."[15] The pall cast by the September 1906 riots would hang over the city for years, and Carrie and others among Atlanta University's students and interracial faculty resumed their routines that fall in the shadows of heightened fears, antagonisms, and vigilance.

The next autumn, after she finished the preparatory program, Carrie enrolled with only twenty others in the freshman class of Atlanta University's four-year College Division. It was one of the country's most prestigious institutions of higher learning for Negroes. Adrienne Herndon, who taught "vocal expression, voice training and pantomime," continued as a major influence on Carrie. "One of her students, Miss Caroline S. Bond," the school's dean and first historian recalled, "caught a similar inspiration" and excelled in Herndon's renowned Shakespearean productions.[16]

While Carrie was devoted to Herndon, W. E. B. Du Bois became her primary intellectual mentor and stimulated her interest in the social sciences. Du Bois taught sociology and history, and incorporated segments about African civilizations and the "condition of the Negro" into his courses. In 1908, under his tutelage, students including Carrie collected data, snapped photographs, and drew up meticulous floor plans of houses for inclusion in their professor's conference and publication on the Negro family. Between 1896 and 1910, Du Bois organized and conducted those colloquia annually, and he compiled and published a series of groundbreaking studies about the social, political, educational, and economic attributes of African American life.[17]

In 1909, Du Bois also brought Harvard University's president Charles Eliot to speak in Atlanta, familiarized students with his own years as a Harvard graduate student in the 1890s, and touted the education—though not the social ambience—available at the country's most renowned institution of higher learning. By that time, forty-one Negroes had earned Harvard degrees (three young men from Atlanta University had matriculated in recent years), but Radcliffe, its women's adjunct, had graduated only four.[18]

Though Carrie Bond served as president of the women's Athena (literary and debating) Society and honed her oratorical skills, she compiled an erratic academic record. A dean later complained that she had needed from 1907 to 1912 to complete the standard four-year curriculum that included two years each of the classics and mathematics, physical sciences with Edgar Webster, one of the school's esteemed white professors, English with George Towns (another Harvard graduate), and courses with Du Bois.[19]

Reasons besides uncharacteristic sloth, unpreparedness, or intellectual mediocrity, however, would have to explain Carrie's transient lapses. At some time in her youth, possibly during those years, she endured three operations and developed a rheumatic heart condition that later precluded childbearing and periodically debilitated her.[20] Abundant extracurricular activities also might cast light on Carrie's scholastic inconsistencies. She composed songs, played the organ, immersed herself in the Young Women's Christian Association (YWCA), and attended its conferences.

Early in 1910, a classmate asked, "Now what possible reason could Miss C. S. B. have found for beating such a hasty retreat from the last sociable?"[21] For some reason, Carrie Stewart Bond chose to shun her school's coeducational social activities, and also may have been upset at that juncture by the rapid physical decline of her teacher and dramatics coach, Adrienne Herndon. Only weeks after Carrie fled from the "sociable," Herndon died at the age of forty after a brief bout with an incurable liver disease. Carrie probably had developed a schoolgirl crush on Herndon, felt her loss deeply, and experienced a period of profound mourning.[22] She would have been further distressed when W. E. B. Du Bois, her other favorite professor, left Atlanta University within a few months of Herndon's death and headed for New York City to edit the new NAACP's magazine, *Crisis*.

Despite her precarious health and those personal trials, Carrie dug in her heels and accepted the cheerful jibes of classmates who teased her in 1910 about having composed the year's most popular song, *A Perfect Day*—actually the work of Carrie *Jacobs* Bond.[23] She ultimately completed Atlanta University's college course and graduated on May 29, 1912.

Carrie's family came from Birmingham for her commencement. It should have been a joyous occasion, but a photograph taken that day shows her five-year-old sister dressed in a party frock with a sumptuous satin bow in her hair looking quite sulky. Wenonah clasped her beloved big sister's hand and a nosegay of pansies as she perched on a valise between Carrie and a pretty classmate. As Carrie matured, her tan hair darkened and her face acquired a mien of restrained cordiality, but her eyes that afternoon looked sorrowful. The two college friends, wearing virginal white cotton-lisle dresses, gracefully seated near one another in matched postures of intimate camaraderie, seemed to share an exquisite, adult secret, but their faces revealed little concern with Wenonah's apparent petulance.[24]

With her diploma in hand, Carrie Stewart Bond set forth for Montgomery, her mother's hometown, where she spent a year with her grandmother Caroline Fagain, and taught at Alabama Agricultural, Mechanical, and Normal College—later Alabama State. With support from the American Missionary Association, it had opened in 1866 in the town of Marion but soon relocated to Montgomery. William Burns Paterson became principal in the late 1870s, but his leadership was so inspired that everyone thought of him as the school's "father," and its first masonry building, Tullibody Hall, had been named for the Scottish town of Paterson's birth. By 1912, the institution had established a teacher training program and model school, and except for the durable Paterson, all of the instructors were black. Having a benevolent white principal supervise an all-Negro faculty was common in the South's "colored" schools.[25] For educated women like Carrie, positions at such institutions were prized, and teaching remained one of their few professional options. Many considered such work a calling rather than just a job, and only in the African American community did significant numbers of women have opportunities to teach in coeducational (but only all-black) colleges. Carrie Bond's stint in Alabama, however, lasted only a year, because her YWCA affiliations from Atlanta University opened up a challenging opportunity in New Jersey. That pending relocation also offered a way for her graciously to break the intimate but confining bonds of kinship and escape the well-meaning, but perhaps oppressive, domestic cosmos that her mother and grandmother so comfortably inhabited in the South.

Montclair, New Jersey's YWCA "For Colored Women and Girls" was unique. It was almost the only such operation that had been established first, and on its own (affiliated directly with the national organization), not as a black "branch," subordinated to a white "central" facility.[26] That YW, where Carrie worked and lived for three years, was located on Forest Street, near trolley lines, the town's busiest commercial strip, and the recently completed Lackawanna Railroad station that local boosters lauded as the handsomest edifice of its sort and size in the country.

A couple of years prior to Carrie's arrival, seventeen of Montclair's established Negro women had seen the need to provide a safe harbor for the southern girls who were flocking to their town. Most came to work in the architecturally eclectic mansions on Upper, North, and South Mountain Avenues, and throughout the posh Estate District. Their collective odyssey was part of the whole country's burgeoning rural-to-urban black migration. Those cooks, housekeepers, and nursemaids often lived in their employers' homes, but needed a place where they could secure their few possessions, find a bit of much-needed privacy, establish friendships, and "improve" themselves.[27]

Alice Hooey Foster, a college-educated Negro whose family published the Montclair *Monitor,* became the YWCA's guiding light when a formative group gathered at her home in 1911. Laura Tate, Foster's close friend and a dedicated churchwoman, was another local YWCA pioneer. The founders also included several men who had started the "colored" YMCA (recently honored by a visit from Booker T. Washington) just a few years earlier.[28]

"The influx of the colored people in Montclair . . . was the result of an effort to solve the servant question," a white resident had written as early as 1894. At first, that influx was sluggish, but it began to accelerate early in the twentieth century. Most of the new black people came from Virginia to the verdant, well-established town that was situated along the eastern slopes of a modest range called the Watchung Mountains, directly west of New York City and only twelve miles from the majestic Hudson River with its towering Jersey palisades.

The population was nearing 22,000 as Carrie Bond arrived in

1913, and included more than 2,000 black people. A few "colored" families remained from Montclair's earliest decades, when even the northern states had embraced slavery, but far more were recent arrivals, some of whom already had relatives in town who found jobs with white homeowners for the work-hungry newcomers. Some employers expressed a benevolent interest in the Negroes' well-being and encouraged their educational ambitions, and many domestic servants labored by day and attended school at night. "As a class," a white town leader maintained, he and his ilk considered the African American household and grounds workers, who often married one another, built or bought houses, and started families, "quiet, industrious and well behaved."[29]

Under Carrie's direction, the YWCA, "housed in a seven-room building with two club rooms, kitchen and bedrooms," developed after-school and weekend programs for members' children in a secure venue, and brought together groups from the community's African American churches. In keeping with the YW's symbol, the younger women called themselves "True Blue Triangle Girls."

Visiting lecturers, including former Atlantan Addie Hunton, the YWCA's new "colored advisory secretary" to its National Board, and Eva Bowles, national coordinator of Negro activities, addressed black women in Montclair about social, spiritual, and cultural issues. Another fine speaker snared by Carrie Bond was Alice Moore Dunbar, a teacher, journalist, poet in her own right, and widow of the extraordinary Paul Laurence Dunbar. Carrie also organized YW conferences to secure the support of Montclair's combined charities organization, and she surely would have joined the town's newly organized NAACP branch.[30]

Carrie's work as the Montclair YWCA's first professional director, however, was only part of her ongoing affiliation with the national association. She soon became allied with a larger circle of YW women. Like Chicago's renowned settlement house founder Jane Addams, her female companions, and a number of other crusading white women, Carrie dedicated herself to social uplift and associated with a nurturing clique of hardworking, educated Negro women who had similar commitments and interests. Those all-female relationships within and beyond the YW satisfied many personal needs and fostered their pioneering activities. The neighbor-hood house and women's club movements, including the country's upsurge in social welfare work (like that undertaken by the YWCA), were inextricably enmeshed in the United States' Age of Reform.[31]

Carrie's circle of dedicated social workers and friends spread throughout the greater New York region. When finances and time allowed, those women (most of them unmarried) went to the the-ater and museums together, shared books, apartments, and vaca-tions, as well as personal triumphs and tragedies. They became surrogate family for one another, while a number of them shunned marriage, which they considered antithetical to their professional and personal development. Married life in those years, with few ex-ceptions, still brought realistic expectations of a subordinate wifely role, securely tethered to uncontrolled childbearing. Political lead-ers such as former president Theodore Roosevelt had accused edu-cated women, as a class, of neglecting their "responsibility" to bear and raise children—but the demands of husbands, pregnancies, and babies often seemed incompatible with these women's reformist missions. Some of them (Negro and white) also considered female friendships truly noble associations that admirably blended domes-tic intimacy, sisterhood, and independence. They sought alterna-tives to matrimony (singing the praises of "single blessedness") that might safeguard them from social isolation and economic hard-ship.[32] Like-minded female comrades provided many of the emo-tional satisfactions of family, plus personal support systems that helped them address societal problems as they worked diligently to shape a better future for women, and, in the case of Carrie and her circle, for "the race."

"Suffrageless as women are," the iconoclastic white anthropol-ogist Elsie Clews Parsons argued, "the fate of democracy depends more on them than on men." Carrie Bond and her colleagues tried to shoulder the burdens of democracy, but might not have readily applied to themselves a label such as "feminist," although that word was becoming prevalent in New York's intellectual circles. Nonetheless, it would have aptly described them. They were better educated than their mothers, had shucked off many restrictive gen-der conventions with which they had been raised, embraced a panoply of departures from the old order of women's lives, and earnestly believed in their right to vote. Perhaps, like Elsie Parsons, members of Carrie's crowd sought the "declassification of women as women, [and] the recognition of women as human beings."[33]

A number of those Negro reformers dedicated themselves to the YWCA, as evidenced by a photograph taken in Brooklyn around 1915. It included Carrie Bond, Eva Bowles, Addie Hunton, and many of the organization's other formidable leaders and workers in the New York area. Carrie also served as a YWCA delegate to the 1913 World Student Christian Federation conference. The Federation's multiracial, multinational party sailed up the Hudson to West Point, where the all-white, all-male cadet corps treated them to a parade at which the president's daughter, Jessie Wilson (another conference delegate), was the honored guest. From West Point, their assembly traveled on by train to an "earthly paradise" at Lake Mohonk, where they "rested, played, reasoned, and prayed together." The "colored" Americans in attendance included R. R. Moton, commandant at Hampton Institute, Alphaeus and Addie Hunton, plus a singing quartet from Atlanta University, young men whom Carrie almost certainly had known from her alma mater.[34]

Even within the embrace of her supportive network, Carrie Bond did not believe that she had fulfilled her potential. She was an intelligent, ambitious woman who wanted to create a place for herself in a larger and more challenging world than that of Montclair, New Jersey. Influenced by W. E. B. Du Bois and George Towns, her former professors who were "Harvard men," Carrie decided to apply to Radcliffe. It was Harvard University's affiliate and the country's most challenging women's college. Clara Bruce, the wife of Roscoe Conkling Bruce (yet another Harvard graduate, who had been Carrie's stepfather's supervisor at Tuskegee Institute), had attended Radcliffe, and she, too, may have encouraged Carrie to go there.

Nor was Carrie the only "colored" woman from Montclair who prepared to head off for one of the renowned but controversial Seven Sisters schools at that time. William Grigsby worked as a groundsman for the family of a white woman who was an early graduate of Smith College, where a few "colored" girls had matriculated since 1900. Grigsby vowed that his own daughters also would attend that scholastically elite institution, which he knew to be one of the country's finest, and two of them did, starting in 1915.[35]

Despite the fact that women's higher education was gaining increasing acceptance, many Americans still maintained an endemic hostility to it. They protested that colleges such as Smith and Radcliffe dislodged impressionable young women from the protective influences of hearth, home, and church, and thereby jeopardized their femininity. They even argued that rigorous academics could ruin a girl's health and impair her childbearing capacities by drawing blood to the brain and away from the womb.[36] Women such as Carrie, however, brushed aside such specious contentions.

Nonetheless, her attempt to secure admission to Radcliffe began in September 1914 and became a convoluted process that continued through spring 1916. Although she already had acquired a bachelor's degree from Atlanta University, Carrie knew that if she hoped ultimately to fulfill her ambition of pursuing graduate study in a major northern university, she would have to acquire a second diploma, and that from a prestigious "white" college.

Diverse circumstances, however, postponed Carrie's return to Boston. Atlanta University's dean delayed in sending Radcliffe her transcript, then gave her only a tepid endorsement, reportedly because of minor academic shortcomings. But the dean's letter also may have reflected his nebulous concerns that some obscure aspect of Carrie's conduct or character might emerge to reflect poorly on his school. There also was a question as to the "unclassified" standing she sought, since she already held an undergraduate degree. In addition, she had to earn and save enough money to cover her tuition and living expenses in Massachusetts. Her health was uncertain as well, and there was always the lurking "problem" that she was "colored." Not that Radcliffe did not accept Negro girls. It did. But only a very select one to three per class—and that not every year.

Radcliffe's admissions office discreetly annotated a couple of Carrie Bond's letters with the word "colored" penciled on one corner. In May 1916, once Carrie had been formally admitted, she wrote "Miss Buckingham," the college's executive secretary, requesting "information concerning dormitory accommodations." The circumspect Harriet Buckingham, a Radcliffe graduate herself, avoided directly responding to that apparently innocuous query, but instead circuitously replied that "students who do not live in our halls of residence are assisted by the Dean in finding suitable boarding places," as if it already were understood by all parties that as a Negro, Carrie would not (absolutely could not) reside in a dormitory. Miss Buckingham suggested that "My dear Miss Bond" might want to live at the Cambridge YWCA, "as you are connected with that association in New Jersey."[37]

Carrie Bond could go to classes and participate in school activities, but could not share a room—even a dormitory—with Radcliffe's white students. An irate contemporary expressed her amazement "that a place like Radcliffe would not allow Negroes in dorms." Geneva Jackson, who attended at the same time, was a Boston resident, like many of the school's white students, and she commuted. Washington, D.C.'s Mary Gibson encountered a Radcliffe dean (whom another student called "very prejudiced") who became "the fly in the ointment." She "demanded that I work as a domestic if I ever hoped to get her recommendation for a scholarship," Gibson griped. Gibson, who majored in French, liked to call herself an "*Américaine de couleur*" and proudly claimed Martha Custis Washington among her progenitors. Despite her grievances, she later asserted that at Radcliffe "I was just another one of the girls. . . . I was invited to parties in Boston where they wouldn't even receive the Irish." Mary Gibson moved to Cambridge with her mother, who worked there so that she could oversee the off-campus apartment where her daughter had to live. Carrie resolved her own encounter with institutional discrimination by crossing the Charles River from Cambridge and lodging directly across the street from where she and her mother had boarded in Boston with Dr. Samuel Courtney around 1900.[38]

Carrie did not let Radcliffe's racial snub deter her. She was delighted to be back in Boston, in academia, in a world replete with intellectual young ladies and challenging professors. In addition to Carrie, Mary Gibson, and Geneva Jackson, the college's African

American scholars in 1916 were Eva B. Dykes (already a 1914 summa cum laude graduate of Howard University), Charlotte Smith, Helen Fairchild, Nadine White, Ophelia Coates, and Frances Grant. A few other deceptively light-skinned Negroes occasionally attended the school but carefully concealed their full racial heritage. One such girl lived in Cambridge, employed a white maid, but did not associate with students who openly identified themselves as "colored."[39]

Carrie took English, fine arts, Slavic, and an introductory anthropology course that further focused her academic interests. Building on the foundation established during her previous Boston sojourn, she suppressed any vestigial southern drawl, cultivated a proper New England accent (with characteristically broad *a*'s), and resumed her academic life as an "unclassified" undergraduate shortly before her twenty-seventh birthday.[40]

For the most part, Radcliffe's white students at that time came from upper- or middle-class families in the Northeast. Elizabeth Brandeis, daughter of a new associate justice of the Supreme Court, for one, hailed from nearby Dedham. Few of those girls' mothers had been in the workforce, nor (in contrast to their Negro classmates) did most of them envision remunerative jobs in their own futures. They uniformly, however, had intense academic yearnings, and many—like Estelle Frankfurter, who followed her brother Felix—went to Harvard's "ladies'" affiliate because a male relative had preceded them. At least one understood that she was "supposed to go to Radcliffe from the time [she] was born." But with few exceptions and regardless of race, they were "women who considered studying important," and, Mary Gibson added, "competition was keen and assignments were long, but the quest for learning was thrilling. . . . We would always be able to find the truth and think for ourselves."[41]

White Radcliffe women commuted from family homes nearby, or resided in dormitories if they hailed from out of town. Some thought that the few westerners among them were looked down on, but others believed that the "townies" were lower class. They missed out on dorm dwellers' collective intimate activities like practicing the latest dance steps, confessing giddy crushes and romances, folding cotton Lister towels for menstrual protection, and, of course, studying together. Most Radcliffe women majored in the humanities ("Ladies do not take math!" one girl's father directed), but despite parental aversion to the sciences, a number of them enrolled in anthropology courses with Harvard's professor Earnest Hooton, whom one of Carrie's contemporaries described as "grumpy and sassy," but possessed of a "fine mind."[42]

Some white Radcliffe attendees were unaware that any Negroes attended their college, while others recalled spirited after-class discussions about race. One student from Carrie's years always had feared black people because a "colored girl" once had slapped her, but she also retained pleasant memories of Geneva Jackson, as did another about Frances Grant. Mary Lee (a Caucasian), from the class of 1917, claimed that she "championed the negroes, [and] used to ask them to sit with her at lunch."[43]

Issues surrounding the acquisition of votes for women became a "big thing," about which Radcliffe students "yelled a lot." The Suffrage Club was a popular school organization (there was a smaller antisuffrage group as well), and one young woman whose mother was a longtime activist wrote a prize-winning essay about the urgency of granting women the right to vote.[44] Most of them cheered Jeannette Rankin's 1916 election to the House of Representatives as the country's first female "congressman" two years after her home state of Montana boldly enfranchised women.

In addition to debating domestic politics, for several years Radcliffe girls, like people throughout the country, had observed the worsening storms over Europe. Many Euro-Americans had conflicting passions about the war because sturdy ties linked them to their forebears' homelands. The United States included millions of citizens of German and Irish ancestry, some of whom held exceedingly hostile feelings toward the English. The vast majority, however (even most German- and Irish-Americans), swayed by Anglo-American bonds of language, history, and culture, hoped for the victory of England and the combined allied forces.

Others, however, maintained strong pacifist views or isolationist aversions to any U.S. entanglements in European affairs. But the Allies, with the British press leading the ideological propaganda attacks, churned up latent prejudices by disseminating grossly exaggerated stories about atrocities by German "barbarians" who, despite those distortions, were rampaging through Europe. Germany further substantiated those indictments when early in 1915 it declared the whole North Atlantic a war zone and threatened that its submarines would torpedo any supposedly hostile vessels. Americans' worst fears came to pass when a German U-boat sank the liner *Lusitania* en route to Liverpool, killing twelve hundred people, including women, children, and many United States citizens.

The torpedoing of the *Lusitania* generated a furious response in the States. The impetuous and chauvinistic former president Theodore Roosevelt exhorted his successor (once removed) to declare war. President Woodrow Wilson, however, claimed that the United States occupied a unique position as the world's peacemaker. He maintained his country's officially neutral posture even in the face of Europe's raging Armageddon. After his 1916 reelection, Wilson continued to contend that "civilized" men of goodwill should resolve their differences peacefully, and made concerted attempts to negotiate between Europe's adversaries, but talks proved fruitless as Germany further intensified its naval attacks. The failure of diplomatic dialogue to resolve the crisis troubled the president, but he ultimately convinced himself and most other Americans that unless the United States entered the fray, Anglo-European civilization might crumble. In April 1917, during Carrie Bond's second semester at Radcliffe, the United States Congress (with Jeannette Rankin one of fifty unyielding members in opposition) approved Wilson's petition to declare war on Germany.[45]

Harvard transformed its main quadrangle into a training facility, and even the all-white Hasty Pudding Club canceled its Easter performances as members returned to drill in "the Yard." Harvard men (most of them white boys, with a tiny handful of blacks) marched in formation and prepared to volunteer as officers with the American Expeditionary Forces—the AEF. With few exceptions, a Radcliffe student recalled, the university also dismissed its German-born faculty members out of real or fancied concerns over national security. Similar anti-German acts materialized across the country as "racial" (more accurately "ethnic") determinations increasingly defined cultural intolerance. The newly bellicose and nationalistic Wilson condemned the entire pacifist movement and triggered bitter antialien repercussions as well.[46]

The scholar Elsie Parsons, for one, reasoned that the inherited and interrelated cultural biases of American life helped to rouse the country into its militaristic frenzy in 1917. She considered antidemocratic acts such as the disfranchisement, segregation, and lynching of Negroes, as well as bigotry against Jews and the recent waves of southern European immigrants, to be immutably intertwined. She also expressed concerns about the current hypocrisy of familiar patriotic catchwords such as "liberty" and "equality."[47] But President Wilson successfully capitalized on the gung-ho temper of the times as he wrapped himself in the flag and steered his ship of state into war.

American men of all ethnicities and races volunteered or were drafted to fight for their country, but women had to make more complex and nonconventional choices about what they should and could do in the face of the national crisis. Carrie's organization, the YWCA, stepped into the vanguard and distributed posters featuring the slogan "Back Our Girls Over There."[48]

Young women of that generation had been born and raised in the late-Victorian era and were expected to conduct their lives according to "ladylike" gender traditions, but the war's revised exigencies shredded that threadbare fabric. Their country needed its female "manpower," and motivated by patriotism and a blazing spirit of adventure, they tossed timeworn expectations to the winds. More than 25,000 volunteered overseas, and many times that number served on the home front. There were numerous exceptions, but for the most part, they were unmarried, middle-to-upper-class, educated urban women in their mid-to-late twenties, with feminist leanings, whom some people described as "honest-to-God American girls." A few volunteered to follow a beau into the breach, others departed with female partners, and most claimed that their motivations for service fell along the lines of "duty, honor, country."[49]

Radcliffe's Ruth Holder (who called herself a "man of all work") headed off to the Russian front, Mary Lee ran a YMCA canteen for the AEF, while a number of the school's white students sold war bonds, planted victory gardens, or worked with the Red Cross. Describing her initial encounter with the chaos of wartime, one Cantabrigian observed that railroad cars were "packed like a Harvard-Yale game, but not so polite a crowd," while another believed that she did her part for the war effort when she attended dances for servicemen and let a sailor kiss her. A Radcliffe report claimed "that the girls take the war seriously, give to it liberally . . . and work for it hard." "No matter how untrained we are, there is not one of us who cannot help in some way to win this war," the *Radcliffe Magazine* editorialized. Among the school's African Americans, Charlotte Smith dedicated herself to domestic Red Cross work, while Frances Grant "taught Negro soldiers to read and write" at a segregated YMCA near Fort Dix, New Jersey.[50]

Meanwhile, there were contributions from others of the all-female Seven Sisters schools. Vassar alumna Julia Stimson oversaw all army nurses with the AEF. Wellesley found itself deeply divided between proponents of the College War Council, which coordinated the efforts of students, graduates, and faculty who volunteered for service in France, and a pacifist contingent (accused in some quarters of being pro-German) led by Professor Emily Greene Balch. A Barnard woman led a division of "Hello Girls" with the Signal Corps, and scores joined the legendary Smith College Relief Unit to assist the Army Nurse Corps in French military hospitals.[51]

The circumstances also engendered spirited debates over what female volunteers would wear, with a number of them reporting that they loved dressing like men. "Pants, [or] should we have a long skirt," one brazenly asked, "or something that revealed more leg?" Posters urging women to "do their part" featured the slogan "Gee, I Wish I Were a Man!! I'd Join the Navy." Those who joined the small new women's corps of that branch of the armed forces became known as "yeomanettes." They filled essential noncombat jobs as "chauffeuses," switchboard operators, stewards, telegraphers, torpedo assemblers, and camouflage designers.[52]

W. E. B. Du Bois, Carrie Bond's onetime Atlanta University professor, editorialized in the *Crisis* that men and women of his race should "Close Ranks" behind their country in its time of need, despite the racism they could expect to encounter. Most Negro women, like their white counterparts, wanted to support the United States, but for them (even more than for white women or men of either race), that goal was difficult to achieve.

More than 5,000 female nurses went to France with the AEF to care for ailing or wounded Yankee soldiers. "Rumor, more or less authentic," Carrie's associate, the newly remarried Alice Dunbar-Nelson, argued, "states that over 300 colored nurses were on the battlefields, though their [pale] complexion disguised their racial identity." Nonetheless, 1,800 other fully trained and eager health-care professionals volunteered, but were denied requests for overseas service solely because they were Negroes. The Navy Nurse Corps would not talk with them, and the army said, "No thanks." They turned to the Red Cross (presumably representing humanitarianism in its purest form), which enjoyed a quasi-governmental status. That organization claimed that the central "problem" was "the question of separate quarters," and relegated "colored" female volunteers to its reserve corps. Tuskegee Institute's new principal, R. R. Moton, wrote the War Department's special assistant for colored affairs, Emmett Scott, expressing concern that the "exclusion of colored nurses . . . results in a certain sort of indifference on the part of colored people which ought not to be when the country needs every ounce of effort along every available line." "Dr. W. E. B. Du Bois, Maj. R. R. Moton, and Mr. Emmett Scott strongly endorsed the sending over of colored women," reported Addie Hunton, one of the few "colored" women even tangentially affiliated with the AEF.[53]

Only in mid-1918 were plans begun to send any black nurses to military posts within the United States which, one of them commented, "had large numbers of colored troops." Their activation would not take place for some time, though the army desperately needed additional nurses during the war's final months. Officially, the first few Negro women were called up for service on the home front only after the November 1918 armistice, so none received military benefits or pensions.[54]

Addie Hunton, one of Carrie Bond's YWCA colleagues, became a key spokesperson who reported the activities of African American nurses and others who hoped to serve in some way as their country went to war. In mid-1918, a YMCA official in Paris finally cabled his organization's United States headquarters: "Send us six fine colored women at once." "If hundreds of other women had answered the call to serve the armies of the Allies, surely among the thousands of colored troops already in France . . . there would be some place of service for six colored women," Hunton somewhat sarcastically commented. As she and a handful of others of her race and sex prepared to sail from New York for France, she observed a puzzled army sentry who "could not quite grasp the fact that colored women were really going to join the American Expeditionary Forces," but, she insisted, "we were crusaders on a quest for Democracy."[55]

Often, however, they found a very imperfect democracy with the AEF in Europe. One noncommissioned officer recalled that after a long trek, "muddy to the waist, cold and starving," he tried to buy food at a YMCA canteen, "but they refused to sell it to him under the plea that they did not serve Negroes."[56]

Addie Hunton and her few "colored" colleagues prepared hot lemonade or cocoa for weary soldiers, and penned their letters. "The chief educational work to be done among the colored troops overseas was that of teaching them to read and write," she added. "Sometimes," she commented, soldiers "shed tears at their first sight of a colored woman in France." More than anything, they "talked first and talked last of their women back home, [and] we learned to know that colored men loved their own women as they could love no other women in all the world." In contrast to the situation at "white" canteens, Hunton's crew helped any of the Yanks. "These are not colored boys," she said about the white servicemen who sometimes patronized her facilities, "but what matters that—they are soldiers all, and every lad of them a mother's son." "The French people brought flowers," she added, "the Red Cross and Y secretaries sang, the band played 'America,' the trumpeter sounded 'Taps,' [and] guns rang out for the dead."[57]

Another woman who spoke out on behalf of "colored" women in the Great War was the recently remarried Alice Dunbar-Nelson, whom Carrie Bond had wooed to Montclair a few years earlier, and with whom she carried on a sporadic correspondence. Dunbar-Nelson was a self-described "tall, broad-shouldered Juno," who, despite her middle-class and outwardly conventional personal life, enjoyed a series of lovers, both male (the War Department's top Negro appointee Emmett Scott current among them) and female.[58]

Dunbar-Nelson had failed in her own attempts to go overseas, but from her home-front perspective she maintained that when the United States was "filled with direful possibilities for the nation, . . . there was but one desire in the hearts of all the women of the country—to do their utmost for the men who were about to go forth to battle for an ideal." "For the first time in the history of the world," she added in her paramour Emmett Scott's *Official History of the American Negro in the World War:*

> a nation at war recognized its women as a definite asset in the conduct of the war, [and] called upon [them] to do definite and constructive work, . . . not only to make bandages for the stricken soldiers, but provide ambulances and even drive them; to fan into a flame the sparks of patriotism in the breasts of those whom the country denied the privilege of bearing arms.[59]

"Into this maelstrom of war activity the women of the Negro race hurled themselves joyously," Dunbar-Nelson continued. "They asked no odds, remembered no grudges, solicited no favors, pleaded for no privileges," she went on. "It was enough for them that their country was at war; . . . a race record of patriotism and loyalty had imbued them inherently with the flaming desire to do their part in the struggle." "The need for them was acute; their willingness to go was complete; the only thing that was wanted was authoritative sanction," she insisted. "Was [the black woman] to do her work independently of the women of the other race or was she to merge herself into their organizations?" Dunbar-Nelson mused: "There were separate regiments of Negro soldiers; should there be separate organizations for relief work among Negro women?" "Colored women since the inception of the war had felt keenly their exclusion from overseas service," she added. Supporting Addie Hunton's assertions, Dunbar-Nelson continued: "In every instance where organizations of colored women have been formed for War Relief there is a definite policy of 'No Color Line.' "[60]

Atlanta's Lugenia Hope moved north to Camp Upton on Long Island, where she assumed charge of volunteers and served as the YWCA's special war work secretary. Carrie Bond's mentor Eva Bowles coordinated that organization's "war work among colored women," and stimulated a gift of $4,000, contributed by President Theodore Roosevelt from his 1906 Nobel Peace Prize money, to continue those efforts. Said Roosevelt: "I have asked that Miss Eva Bowles be consulted in the disbursement of this item . . . [and] very much stand by [her] work."[61]

Overseas and on the home front, however, discrimination abounded against African American women who tried to serve their country. A'Lelia Walker Robinson (daughter of the country's first self-made female millionaire, Madam C. J. Walker, who had amassed her fortune developing hair-care products formulated to meet the needs of black women) wanted "to organize a Colored Women's Motor Corps" in New York City's Harlem. When Robinson, who previously had limited herself to mail, wire, or telephone inquiries, showed up in person at the driving school, its officials made an abrupt about-face and informed her that "they were filled up." A friend then initiated a test case by sending in a white woman—who promptly was accepted for training. The outraged Robinson first threatened to bring suit, but instead she enrolled (after token opposition) at a "YMCA Motor School for Women," and ultimately did drive an ambulance during the war.[62]

For her part, Carrie Bond took a year off from Radcliffe and headed for New York City. She had been recruited to work with the Circle for Negro War Relief that was being organized under the aegis of men and women of both races, including W. E. B. Du Bois and other NAACP leaders, one of New York state's former governors, Tuskegee Institute's R. R. Moton, and the U.S. Army's highest-ranking (but involuntarily deactivated) Negro officer, Colonel Charles Young. "The best minds of the country, white and colored" cooperated in that organization, Alice Dunbar-Nelson asserted. The Circle emphasized self-help and racial solidarity. It mobilized African American women and harnessed their skills and energies to circumvent the Army and Navy Nurse Corps's intransigence and the Red Cross's more subtle sabotage.[63]

The Circle for Negro War Relief was "an incorporated body under the laws of the State of New York," the *Crisis* explained, "and is working in co-operation with the Red Cross and other governmental agencies." Its aims were: "To help the colored soldier before he goes to the front; / To help the colored soldier at the front; / To help the family which the colored soldier leaves behind." "It will co-operate with all existing agencies to bring immediate relief, and," those statements (probably composed by Carrie Bond) continued, "will inaugurate new agencies where existing ones are insufficient." The announcements further exhorted *Crisis* readers: "You'll find it easy to start a Unit for the CIRCLE FOR NEGRO WAR RELIEF. . . . Your society will be officially affiliated at the National Headquarters, and you will receive a Charter from the Board of Directors."[64]

That language tactfully circumvented the unpleasant reality that such a conglomerate was necessary only because the military and most "white" support organizations (at home and abroad) excluded Negro women, and denied, or offered inferior services, to black soldiers and their families. The Circle represented a united "effort on the part of colored people to do something themselves to improve conditions among colored soldiers," its reports maintained. "Some help was secured from white people," they continued, but "this was inappreciable when compared with the service given and the money raised and donated . . . by the colored members and friends of the organization."[65]

The Circle for Negro War Relief "radiated its influence from New York City," wrote Dunbar-Nelson, who launched a Circle chapter in Wilmington, Delaware. Early in 1918, on its letterhead and in *Crisis* advertisements, Caroline S. Bond, "executive secretary," appeared as the only employee. Ruth Logan Roberts, Carrie's friend from their Tuskegee days, and her new husband Dr. E. P. Roberts soon joined the advisory board, as did A'Lelia Walker Robinson, who had met such resistance in her efforts to become an ambulance driver. The Circle adopted as its credo:

We have a record to defend, but no treason, thank God, to atone or explain. No negro has ever insulted the flag. No negro has ever struck down a President of these United States. . . . No negro ever ran under fire or lost an opportunity to serve, to fight, to bleed, or to die for the Republic's cause. We have but one country and one flag—the flag that set us free.[66]

Its annual report noted that the Circle's "activities ranged from the furnishing of sweets . . . and smokes, to the giving of a $2,000 ambulance . . . sent overseas for the use of the 'Buffaloes' "—the country's African American soldiers, all of whom served with segregated units. Volunteers ran canteens, knitted, supplied "Christmas boxes to the soldiers in France, and . . . real Southern hospitality to homesick boys in Georgia." Women with the Hoboken, New Jersey, unit bid farewell and then greeted packed troop ships on their way to and from France. When wounded Negro soldiers were brought back from Europe, eager for the comfort offered by "colored" women, "the Circle was the only organization of its kind privileged to have in the various base hospitals ward-workers whose happy duty it was to help make life easier for the boys." Members aided the orphaned children of African Americans who had died for their country, and furnished transportation for indigent mothers who yearned to see their wounded sons. Some chapters supplied nurses and provided "free professional services to all soldiers and their families." "Many a homesick boy, unused to the ways of the South," a report wryly observed, "received cheer and hospitality," while another group established "a railroad centre [where] there were no adequate accommodations for colored soldiers passing through" one of the many locales where Jim Crow reigned supreme.[67]

Those efforts grew out of longtime traditions of black women's church or club activities and social service work. The reason they were so effective, Alice Dunbar-Nelson insisted, could "be found in the fact that the colored woman had a heritage of 300 years of work back of her. . . . 'Come out of the kitchen, Mary' became the slogan of the colored woman in war time." She also sadly (but accurately) predicted that "when pre-war conditions return . . . she [will be] displaced by men and forced . . . back into domestic service." Nonetheless, she added, the newly confident Negro woman "emerges from the war . . . more responsible, with a higher opinion of her own economic importance; with [an] aim and ambition to devote her life to the furthering of the cause for which her men died." "She has . . . formed a second line of defense at home, when disaffection threatened, she fostered patriotism and overcame propaganda with simple splendid loyalty," and, Dunbar-Nelson concluded, "shut her eyes to past wrongs, present discomforts, and future uncertainties."[68]

The Circle coordinated the work of sixty-two units during the Great War. New York City alone established twelve; nearby New Jersey (where Carrie Bond maintained contacts from her years in Montclair) had eleven. Boston activated two chapters, one headed by the well-known Cambridge educator Maria Baldwin. Others operated as far west as Arizona, and as far south as Florida, where the indomitable Mary McLeod Bethune oversaw a vital group.[69] The nation's capital started one that functioned under the aegis of the poet Georgia Douglas Johnson, who wrote about African American soldiers during that time of strife:

The hour is big with sooth and sign, with errant men at war.
While blood of alien, friend and foe, imbues the land afar,
And we with sable faces pent, move with the vanguard line,
Shod with a faith that springtime keeps, and all the stars opine.[70]

While Carrie worked with Circle affiliates nationwide, she resided in Brooklyn, among a group of "colored" women whom she had come to know and care for through the YWCA. From autumn 1917 through mid-1918, she also traveled to distant places such as Camp Funston in Kansas, as well as nearby Camp Upton, Long Island, where most black (and white) soldiers passed through before being shipped overseas from the war-augmented port at Hoboken, New Jersey. She met, offered comfort and advice, and wrote to "colored" soldiers and officers. Her new acquaintances and correspondents included Aaron Day, Jr., a captain from Texas who had trained at the "colored" officers camp at Fort Des Moines, Iowa, took command of his company at Camp Funston, then proceeded via Camp Upton and Hoboken en route to France in June 1918.[71]

Carrie Bond put in a year at her challenging task on behalf of her country and its black soldiers, but that September, with an Allied victory and armistice on the horizon, she returned to Cambridge to complete the courses she needed to graduate from Radcliffe. During her previous semesters, Carrie had accumulated enough credits to achieve senior status, but with dormitories closed to her, she needed somewhere to live. A small clutch of white women at Boston's Franklin Square House had tried to evict the Negro educator (and wartime volunteer) Maria Baldwin, but Carrie ignored such lurking hindrances and staunchly took up residence there, as had her favorite Atlanta University teacher Adrienne Herndon while she had studied drama at the turn of the century.[72]

The Great War had politicized many American women and altered the country's perceptions of them. President Wilson (who showed little concern over the widespread disfranchisement of black men) declared: "Unless we enfranchise women, we shall have fought to safeguard a democracy which, to that extent, we have never bothered to create." One suffrage leader, evoking imagery from the recent war, asserted, "American women have begun to go over the top. They are going up the scaling ladder and out into All Man's Land." Certainly, the significant roles that women played during the war favorably influenced the 1919 passage of the Nineteenth Amendment to the Constitution that gave them, nationwide, the right to vote.[73] Even many diehards conceded that the "weaker sex" had earned the franchise, and a student in Cambridge, Massachusetts, wrote:

> *Do you see the girl with the saucy frown;*
> *Wears her raven locks as a queen her crown?*
> *The most rampant suffragette in town—*
>   *She's a girl from Radcliffe.*[74]

The Great War had affected American women's lives in other ways as well. In only two years, hemlines rose from the ankle almost to the knee, epitomizing how women hoped and planned to stride toward their reconfigured, less constricted futures. On a more mundane plane, "New Women" had learned from French nurses that cellulose provided more absorbent menstrual protection than cotton, and the Kimberly-Clark company responded to their demands for disposable pads.[75]

The spirit of the postwar era affected Cambridge girls much as it did women elsewhere. Amid a countrywide explosion of new demands, their request to charter a Radcliffe Association read, "The purpose of the organization is to obtain from Harvard University a proper recognition of the equal rights of Radcliffe women to all privileges held by Harvard men." Those "rights" included "admission to all classes, teams, [and] dining halls on an equal basis." In 1919, Radcliffe students threatened to push through their radical agenda at meetings, through boycotts, even by "breaking windows . . . and so forth."[76] In many ways—from demanding equal privileges with Harvard men, to going off to war, smoking, drinking (though Prohibition largely forced that practice underground), driving automobiles as they had driven ambulances, working outside the home, voting, bobbing their hair, even wearing trousers— a lot of American women wanted to contest and blur the lines of traditional and restrictive gender-based behavior.

During the year that Carrie had been away from Radcliffe, Eva B. Dykes had graduated magna cum laude, but continued at the school, working toward a Ph.D. Nadine White, Frances Grant (a Phi Beta Kappa), and Mary Gibson, who soon would join Dykes as a teacher at Washington, D.C.'s exceptional Dunbar High School, had all left Cambridge, while Geneva Jackson and four other veteran "colored" undergraduates remained. Eleanor Bowen (a Hyde Park, Massachusetts, girl), Eolyn Klugh, Louise Cook (who had to live far from campus, where she boarded with Dykes), and a gifted writer named Marita Bonner were the school's recently arrived African Americans. Not for another half century, however, would the number of "colored" women at Radcliffe College increase to any noticeable degree. Carrie reinforced her relationships with a devoted band of "sisters" when she joined the newly formed Boston chapter—started by Bonner—of the Negro sorority Delta Sigma Theta. A few blocks away, Alain Locke received his Ph.D. Harvard's few other African Americans included a scholar-athlete named Edward Gourdin and the medical school hired a single black instructor.[77]

Carrie Bond took more English and fine arts courses during the 1918–19 school year, but determined to immerse herself in anthropology. She probably was the country's first Negro to select that as an undergraduate major, and certainly, none had ever done any graduate work.[78] Nonetheless, W. E. B. Du Bois, Carrie's intellectual lodestar, said concerning that discipline's potential: "That there are differences between the white and black races is certain, but just what those differences are is known to none with an approach to accuracy." "Yet here in America," he continued, "is the most remarkable opportunity ever offered of studying these differences . . . and particularly of studying the effect of amalgamating two of the most diverse races in the world—another subject which rests under a cloud of ignorance."[79] Carrie prepared to pick up that intellectual gauntlet concerning racial "amalgamation" thrown down by Du Bois, and her academic work in anthropology unquestionably both influenced and reflected the future course of her life.

Concerning what he remembered as his initial encounter with Carrie Bond, Harvard University's foremost professor of anthropology, Earnest Hooton, recalled meeting a student "who had a real interest in, and an undoubted gift for, some kind of scientific research." "She turned up in one of my anthropology courses," he claimed, "an intelligent and attractive young woman with about half of Negro and Indian blood in her veins"—the unnamed half, of course, was white. "She was not only clever and intellectual, but frank and outspoken," Professor Hooton stated about his protégée. "You could talk plainly to her and receive straight, unguarded answers."[80] He was both enthusiastic and curious about Miss Caroline Stewart Bond and the "colored" upper class to which she belonged.

At that time, Hooton's discipline was almost as all-male as it was all-white. Elsie Parsons, a white woman who held a Ph.D. in education (considered an "appropriate" field for an aspiring female intellectual), had only sidled into anthropology after 1910. Shortly before Carrie went to Radcliffe in 1916, Parsons had initiated an innovative series of ethnological field trips to study Native American life. Like Franz Boas, Parsons—who knew W. E. B. Du Bois, consulted the work of black scholars at Hampton Institute, and gathered folklore and data about Negroes' cultural heritage—challenged conventional notions concerning the supposedly innate inferiority of nonwhite societies. She was attempting to carve out an expanded role for women in her academic field as well.

One of Parsons's colleagues recently had argued, "It is absurd to seek the origin of civilization in any particular region or to trace it to a single nation." That contention challenged traditional Eurocentric anthropological thought and bolstered the work that Carrie Bond was undertaking with Earnest Hooton. Elsie Parsons served as a singular model for what a resolute woman might hope to achieve, specifically in the unwelcoming field of anthropology, and generally in the predominantly male—and white—professorial world, where (even Parsons's supporters agreed) "a young woman, because of the likelihood of her marriage, is an unreliable element to build into the foundation of a staff structure."[81]

Concerning his ambitions for further research in physical (more than cultural) anthropology, and echoing Du Bois's message, Hooton announced, "An inquiry into the results of Negro-white mixture in the United States was imperative." Those Americans called mulattoes, quadroons, and octoroons intrigued him—perhaps in part because of his own racially ambiguous appearance. "To what extent had such crossings modified the physical, mental, and economic status of the population rated as 'Negro'?" he wondered. "Were these people of mixed origin," he mused, "destined to march with our colored compatriots side by side, distinguished only in physical features, or were they being absorbed, gradually and imperceptibly, into the 'white' majority?" In fact, most Negroes could have assured Hooton that unless such light-complexioned individuals successfully "passed," and thereby abandoned friends and family, Euro-Americans had no intention of letting them be "absorbed" into the " 'white' majority."[82]

"Nobody knew anything much about the anthropological results of race mixtures between Negroes and whites," Hooton admitted, and "the sociological results of such crossings were shrouded in equal darkness." "There were current in scientific circles a lot of old wives' tales about the sterility of the mulatto, his participation in all of the vices and none of the virtues of both races," he added about his field's biases and shortcomings.[83]

One reason "for the prevalent ignorance concerning the biological and economic status of the Negro-white section of our population," Hooton believed, "was the . . . self-respecting pride of the more educated members of that class." During the ensuing years, he occasionally addressed white audiences concerning that faction of "colored society." "These colored Americans suspected the motives of the white investigator and were not only reluctant, but entirely unwilling, to submit themselves and their family history to his scrutiny," he concluded: "[They] have been the victims of a terrible social injustice and . . . have grown to expect the worst."[84]

"It had long been my opinion that access to this class for . . . anthropological study," Hooton wrote, "could be gained only through the utilization of an investigator of the first quality who, himself, by virtue of Negro blood, could command that confidence in his motives without which no information of value could be obtained." Carrie Bond, *herself,* made much the same point, when a few years later she compared her work to that of Melville Herskovits, who passed through Harvard and then became a colleague of Professor Franz Boas at Columbia. "I have secured a more highly selected group of people than the average white worker could get in touch with," she accurately boasted.[85] But even as Hooton praised his own "quality investigator"—a woman—he had internalized the widespread assumptions about any scientist's automatically presumed maleness. "This colored investigator had to be a person not only of scientific gifts and outstanding tact, but also of such unquestioned honesty and impartiality as to guarantee the validity of his findings," he continued. Those findings, "to be acceptable, should be checked rigorously by a disinterested white scientist," Hooton added, confirming his own convictions (perhaps subconscious, but nonetheless in conformity with those of most other academics) that any reputable and competent scholar would have to be both male and white. Carrie gave further evidence of that prevalent bias when she confided to a friend that a group of academics "wanted a . . . white man" to continue some scientific work based on her original research, wryly adding that "men are still not entirely sold on women doing things."[86]

Nonetheless, Carrie Bond roused Hooton's zeal, and she did not let gender or racial barriers discourage her. "When I . . . became acquainted with her history, her abilities, her admirable strength and uprightness of character, it became apparent that she was the long-sought student of Negro-white crosses in the United States," Hooton wrote. "Her mother was a woman of culture and refinement," he added about Georgia Stewart Bond, and Carrie, he accurately observed, "was personally acquainted with most of the educated and prominent persons of Negro descent." Hooton was incurably nosy, but those, indeed, were the people whom Carrie Bond herself most wanted to study. She characterized them as "our crowd," and "our group of Negro intelligentsia."[87]

"In connection with a research course taken under me when she was a senior at Radcliffe," Hooton proudly reported, Bond "collect[ed] data pertaining to mulatto families." "[She] began with her own family," he added "and the families of her friends—measuring all available individuals, getting hair samples, collecting photographs of them and all of their descendants and ascendants." In the same vein, Langston Hughes, a luminary of the Harlem Renaissance, complained that Zora Neale Hurston, who began her studies at Barnard College with Franz Boas just a few years later, "always looked like she was out to measure someone's head for an anthropological treatise." Drs. Charles Davenport and Albert Love had obtained similar anthropometric data for a government study from six thousand Negro draftees (who could not exempt themselves from participation) during the recent war.[88]

Carrie Bond "was particularly careful . . . to determine with all possible accuracy the exact proportions of white, Negro, and Indian blood of each individual, going back to the primary crossings between ancestral pairs," Hooton wrote about his twenty-nine-year-old undergraduate student. "Thus," Hooton added, "she was able to reconstruct family pedigrees, going back four or five generations to the earliest cross." The "earliest" or "primary crosses" to which Earnest Hooton referred were those between a presumably "pure" Negro, Caucasian, or Native American with a person of another equally "unadulterated" race. "In many cases [Bond] secured photographs of individuals representing four generations," Hooton added, and "these, with the accompanying hair samples, were affixed to genealogical charts, and the exact blood proportions of each individual were calculated."[89]

"The amount of genealogical material obtainable from these educated colored Americans is astounding," Professor Hooton enthused. "Naturally," he for some unexplained reason presumed, "they are more interested in their ancestry and in the physical characters of their progenitors than are most pure-white people, because their entire family history is inevitably filled with the tragic consequences of their anomalous racial descent."[90] Whether any or all of Carrie's "anomalous" subjects considered themselves "tragic," however, remains open to speculation.

Carrie Bond, Hooton continued, "gathered information concerning the number and sex of the children born to each Negro-white family . . . the occupations and educational achievements of each person, their recreations and 'outside' interests." "In the case of contemporary families she found out a good deal about economic status; value of home, number of rooms, furnishings, presence or absence of lodgers, etc.," wrote Hooton, adding, "In many cases she took photographs of these homes." Carrie tackled her anthropological research under Earnest Hooton's tutelage at Harvard, but her methodology, she correctly insisted, was "similar to that which Dr. Du Bois used to do in connection with his conferences" at Atlanta University a decade earlier.[91]

A few years later, Carrie wrote W. E. B. Du Bois's wife Nina, explaining that Earnest Hooton had "taught a course in African Ethnography at Harvard for many years," and assured Nina that he understood the "value of certain African characteristics and qualities."[92] By 1919, Hooton reported, Carrie Bond began collecting data about her own family, as well as those of Du Bois; William Hunt, a U.S. consul in France; Colonel Charles Young, the army's ranking Negro officer; poet Georgia Douglas Johnson; Warren and the late Adella Logan, personal friends and educators at Tuskegee Institute; and a number of others. Most cooperated, but some of those acquaintances discouraged her, with one writing: "Oh, Carrie dear, raking out those horrid ancestral skeletons is so painful. I tried to bury them long ago." Another feared the exposure of a relative who was passing. "My brother . . . is strictly w—— in Boston," she wrote, adding, "You understand." Nonetheless, those families, with their complex racial ancestry, would comprise the core of Carrie's anthropological subjects for the next decade.[93]

"In college, I think we find a miniature world of opportunity and experimentation, a laboratory where we may try out our untrained powers with impunity, and gain skill for future days" another Radcliffe student wrote in 1919.[94] That June, Carrie Bond completed her undergraduate studies in anthropology at that revered institutional "laboratory" and aspired to continue her scientific research as soon as possible. Despite her uncharacteristic academic lapse at Atlanta University, she compiled a solid record at the country's most demanding college for women. More notably, she initiated the first anthropological investigations undertaken by a Negro about the physiological and cultural complexities of her people in the United States.[95]

Georgia, Percy, Wenonah, and Jack Bond traveled from their home in Washington, D.C., to Cambridge for Carrie's graduation on June 18, 1919, and probably took the opportunity to visit Percy's elderly mother in nearby Hyde Park as well. The Reverend Charles Edwards Park delivered the commencement address, and a small orchestra played *O, Beautiful for Spacious Skies* and *Radcliffe, Now We Rise to Greet Thee*. One hundred young ladies received Bachelor of Arts degrees, nineteen others were granted Masters of Arts, and two earned the ultimate Doctor of Philosophy. A pair of Chinese and one Englishwoman were Radcliffe's only non-American graduates, while Geneva Jackson (who earned distinction in Romance languages) and Caroline Bond were the sole Negroes. Years later, another class member succinctly summed up her experiences: "We rode trains and ships; . . . did as we were told by our elders, more or less; . . . and a woman who had her hair colored was probably living a life of shame."[96]

Carrie Bond "more or less" obeyed her elders, never colored her drab brown hair, or lived a life of shame. She did not have the financial resources needed to sail on ocean liners or to embark on further anthropological studies at that time, nor did Earnest Hooton have university funds to support her work. That summer, W. E. B. Du Bois accepted one of her stories for publication in *Crisis*, and with a second degree (one from a "white" college) in hand, Carrie left the country's most prestigious university, her favorite city, and a circle of academic women, to rejoin another sisterhood at the YWCA training school in New York City, where she started work as a "student secretary" with that familiar, and sometimes nurturing, national women's organization.[97]

CAPTAINS' TALES, BEFORE
and BEYOND *the* GREAT WARS

*With . . . thousands of others, I decided to offer my life upon
our Nation's altar as a sacrifice, that Democracy might reign and
Autocracy be forever crushed.*

LIEUTENANT WILLIAM HOLMES DYER, Company B, 317th Ammunition Train,
92nd Division, American Expeditionary Forces

MEASURED IN MORE ways than miles, it was a long way from
Boston and New York City to Dayton, Texas. Nonetheless, Carrie
Bond met an African American captain from that backwater town
while she worked with the Circle for Negro War Relief, and he was
either stationed stateside or headed off to France with the American Expeditionary Forces—the AEF. Carrie's urban world of women,
however, seemed so profoundly different from Captain Aaron Day,
Jr.'s frontier upbringing that at first glance an enduring relationship
between them might have appeared unlikely.

Aaron had grown up in Dayton, thirty-five miles northeast of
Houston and a spit-and-a-holler away from Liberty, the county
seat. Ferries that black men poled across the Trinity River linked
Dayton (for years called West Liberty) to its larger sister town. The
Trinity coiled through Texas like a great cottonmouth moccasin,
originating beyond Fort Worth and Dallas far to the northwest. It
was the country's longest river lying entirely within one state, and
drained a mammoth watershed of eighteen thousand square miles.[1]
Passing Liberty and Dayton, it snaked southward, trafficked by a

motley armada of shallow-draft cargo boats carrying hides, grain, fruit, and cotton loaded at upriver landings. That vital artery roughly bisected Liberty County and—except in the dry season—provided the hinterlands with ready access to coastal markets. As the crow flies, it was only forty miles (but one hundred via the twining waterway) from Dayton down to the delta where the lethargic Trinity slithered into the gaping maw of Galveston Bay on the Gulf of Mexico.[2]

In the decades when Dayton was known as West Liberty, it was just a subordinate quarter of Liberty itself, founded in 1831, and the huge, centuries-old municipality of Santissima Trinidad de la Libertad once had included both settlements and much more. Anglos had redesignated the Rio Trinidad the Trinity River, while the county and county seat (like sixteen others around the freedom-obsessed United States) were both called Liberty. Long before succeeding waves of Euro-Americans dispossessed them, the region had been home to a tribe of Orcoquiza Indians, who had lived near where Liberty and Dayton later sprang up. The indigenous people had felt safe when they camped by the riverside because they believed that tornadoes would not cross the broad water.[3]

In protean Texas, the Old South met the western frontier and was further molded by economic, political, and cultural *alianzas* with Mexico. Texas had wrenched itself from Mexico in 1836, became an independent republic, adopted the Lone Star flag, and attained statehood in 1845. Ample virgin timber, the Trinity River's alluvial bottom lands, and adjacent prairie "second bottoms" lured homesteaders west to inhabit that part of the New South. Their dispatches read "G.T.T.": "Gone to Texas." Seeking to preserve white southerners' right to own black people, the state seceded from the Union in 1861 to join the Confederacy. But as early as the 1850s, longhorn Spanish cattle already outnumbered settlers by seventeen to one, and Liberty County's slaves, who comprised thirty percent of the population, often worked as stock drovers right alongside free white men. Prior to the Civil War, most blacks lived in quarters that "was log houses buil' outer li'l pine poles pile' one 'pon de other," a one-time slave reported.[4]

The early settlement at West Liberty was redesignated Day's

Station, then Dayton Station—a flag stop for the Texas & New Orleans Railroad.[5] After Reconstruction, it became simply Dayton, in honor of Isaiah Day, who had been one of the county's wealthiest landowners and slaveholders. By 1890, the village bearing Isaiah's name had two small schools (one for blacks, the other for whites), three churches, and 239 residents. The region's African Americans prayed that a county which so boldly designated itself "Liberty" would treat them fair and square. They comprised nearly half of the population in 1880, dropped back to forty percent by 1890, then dwindled to only thirty percent a decade later.[6]

Dayton survived a major fire in 1892, and in September 1900 barely escaped the impact of a devastating hurricane. The Gulf of Mexico—nourished by savage gales and sopping, mountainous thunderheads that had matured off Africa's west coast and rampaged across the Atlantic—roared inland past Galveston, swamping the island and transforming the coastal plain into a putrid open-air graveyard as it demolished homes and drowned or washed away livestock and more than six thousand Texans. Measured in human loss, that lethal storm was the greatest natural disaster in United States history.[7]

The Liberty *Vindicator* reported the presence of two sawmills (where many black men labored) "at Dayton, which furnish all the lumber that is needed." Lumbering, fruit and cane cultivation, vegetable and cotton farming, as well as cattle raising, dominated the local economy until the late 1800s, when newly developed irrigation systems stimulated profitable rice cultivation. Added to corn, it became the major cash crop and began displacing cotton, which succumbed to the ravenous boll weevil during the twentieth century's early years.[8] By that time, a number of local men also traveled a few miles east to work the gushers at Spindletop—Texas's first major oil strike.

Within his circumscribed domain, Liberty County's sandy-haired, cobalt-eyed Isaiah Day (although a short man) had been a presence of noteworthy dimensions. His slaves raised cotton, sugarcane, and "lots of sheep an' hogs an' cattle" on the huge plantation. Those people, who knew far more about him than he might have thought or wished, had called him "Papa Day," one remembered, "'cause he won't 'low none he cullud folks to call him master." He preached the Gospel, prayed, shouted, and sang *Amazing Grace* with the Negroes, and liberally populated the town that bore his name. As the Lord purportedly had proclaimed through Isaiah's biblical namesake: "I will pour my Spirit upon thy seed, and my blessing upon thine offspring: And they shall spring up . . . as willows by the watercourses."[9]

Isaiah Day had married twice, siring four children by his first wife in the 1840s and three by his second in the 1850s. A Dayton woman referred to his latter spouse as "quite a fountain," most likely because of her ample wealth. In their early years together, in fact, the value of Isaiah's property spurted from $212 up to $80,000. It decreased considerably by 1870 due to losses incurred during the Civil War, when he fought for the Confederacy as a captain with the Second Texas Brigade, but also, perhaps, as a result of heavy expenditures on behalf of his many offspring.[10]

During both of his marriages, Isaiah also maintained a proprietary relationship with a slave named Amanda Cribbs, who bore nine of his children. "Colored" people called her Amanda Day and considered her Isaiah's wife, though antimiscegenation laws never would have allowed them to marry. One descendant heard her described as a "small woman of a light shade of brown . . . with a narrow, pointed face and rather bushy, frizzly hair." The appearances of that miscegenous couple's offspring ranged from Aaron Day, Sr., who looked "white, with perfectly straight hair" and light eyes, to several younger siblings who had amber skin, "heavier features and curly hair and brown eyes."[11]

Isaiah Day had been a contradictory and complex patriarch. Before the Civil War, he supposedly had harbored bondsmen who had run away from brutal owners, and one of his slaves recalled that he often "say us is born free as he is . . . our souls is jes' as white, . . . [and] we is human bein's an' not beasts." Despite his intermittent ferocity, Isaiah and Amanda's children also remembered "instances of his protection and generosity."[12]

When their sons and daughters were mostly grown and Isaiah was past sixty, he still harbored a fierce lust for Amanda and an unbridled sense of entitlement. One morning, a great-granddaughter was authoritatively informed, he confronted Amanda by the well and demanded, once again, that she sexually submit to him. Isaiah may have believed that Amanda, as a Negro woman (a hewer of wood and drawer of water), had no right of refusal, though slavery was a decade past. And she must have realized that neither the law nor kin could protect her. As the ancient prophet Isaiah had once declared: "There is none to guide her among all the sons whom she hath brought forth." When Amanda Cribbs tried to repulse the lecherous and enraged Isaiah Day, he reportedly cudgeled her with a heavy wooden bucket and crushed her skull. Unrepentant, unpunished, and comfortably ensconced with his second wife, Isaiah died in 1879 and—despite his undeniably documented extramarital excursions and Amanda Cribbs's violent demise—was buried alongside others of Liberty County's most honored citizens, while Amanda had been relegated to an unmarked grave.[13] Isaiah's widow as well as his white and mulatto offspring remained in the same small town, clutching their harrowing but unspoken and unresolved common legacy.

Aaron Day, Sr.—Amanda and Isaiah's eldest—married by 1870, but he and his wife Silvanna had no children. A few miles south of Dayton, Aaron began accumulating property, including livestock that he branded with the converged "AR" registered to the "heirs of Amanda Day."[14] One-quarter of Liberty County's farmers were nonwhite (African Americans, Mexicans, Chinese), and like others of them, Aaron built his fences "horse-high, hog-tight, and bull-strong," paid his poll taxes, and became a Texas citizen and voter. After Silvanna died, he wed an eighteen-year-old named Flora Spaight, who was a member of a propertied local family, descended, she had heard, from "Molaglaskans"—Negroes brought as slaves to the United States from the island of Madagascar.[15] Flora Spaight Day's kin would remember her as a diligent, ambitious, but ungenerous woman. By 1890, Aaron and Flora owned fifty rural acres, several lots in Dayton itself, a buggy, twenty head of cattle, seven horses and mules, and they had amassed assets of more than a thousand dollars. Despite a frightening bout with malaria, their children survived: Ethel, born in 1889, Aaron Junior, two years later, and Alfred in 1899.[16]

Aaron Junior and his sister and brother grew up on the farm, while their uncle Henderson Day, who owned an adjacent ranch, and his three sons all worked as cowboys. By early in the new century, several related families of Days ("Papa" Isaiah's descendants, whom census takers categorized as mulattoes), had homes nearby. Willingly or not, a number of Texas Negroes "mixed their blood" with Anglos, Frenchmen, *chicanos,* and Native Americans, and the folk song *The Yellow Rose of Texas* immortalized a woman of similar complexion and ancestry.[17]

The Days were frugal and hardworking. The children pitched in with chores, and Aaron Junior sometimes had to wear his sister's hand-me-down high-button shoes. Cold weather was rare in Liberty County, but he long remembered those few frigid mornings when they had melted snow for water. Young Aaron enjoyed a vigorous outdoor life, attended the Baptist church, respected his elders and women, and heeded his parents' edicts about acquiring an education. The children grew up with a powerful awareness of being "the Days of Dayton." They were Americans and Negroes, of course, but also, very distinctively, Texans.[18]

The Civil War had a belated finale in their state. The last battle had been fought there more than a month after Robert E. Lee had surrendered in Virginia, and not until June 19, 1865, did the Union's General Gordon Granger sail into Galveston harbor and deliver the mandate that declared all Texas Negroes free. "This involves an absolute equality of rights of property between masters and slaves," Granger cautioned the disgruntled Rebels.

"One mornin' Papa Day calls all us to de house and reads de freedom papers," a former slave recalled. "De gov'ment don't need to tell you you is free, 'cause you been free all you days," Captain Isaiah Day had told them on that occasion, adding, "If you wants to stay you can and if you wants to go, you can. But if you go, lots of white folks ain't gwine treat you like I does." Though they cherished their belated emancipation, Isaiah's former slaves, and others like them who continued to farm the land belonging to Anglos who once had owned them, discovered the harsh truth of his counsel, and another white man who rode through the county remarked on a wretched " 'free-nigger patch,' with demoralized log-huts" along-side the Trinity River.[19] "Papa" Day's paradoxical spasms of benevolence and fury must have created perplexing choices for his often propertyless former bondsmen as county residents entered the postwar era and (adhering to classic directives from the Old Testament's Isaiah) beat their swords into plowshares and spears into pruning hooks.

July 4 was the country's Independence Day, Negroes in places such as Norfolk, Virginia, commemorated the Emancipation Proclamation on January 1, and August 1 marked slavery's termination in the British West Indies. Similarly, June 19th—"Juneteenth"—when General Granger had made his pronouncement in 1865, became the date on which black Texans thereafter celebrated their freedom. In towns where Negro domestic servants refused to work, some white husbands even instituted an out-to-dinner night for their sulky spouses, who had no one to cook for them.[20]

African Americans in Dayton and Liberty observed Juneteenth much as did others throughout the state. "The colored people have looked forward to 'the 19th' with fond anticipation," the Liberty County *Vindicator* reported in 1893, asking, "who with a spark of patriotism cannot . . . say they are right in remembering and celebrating the day that unshackled them and made them free?" "[The] sound of the bass and kettle drum was heard at the rendezvous near the river," the article continued, appending an account of "recitations, tableaux, etc. by the Baptist school children." "Everything passed off peaceably," the local newspaper concluded. "The 19th of June was just a second Christmas," a onetime southeast Texas slave recalled, and the revelry included brass bands and speeches, hoedowns, rodeos, and bounteous spreads featuring fried fish, mouth-watering barbecue, and much more. It truly was a day for eating "high on the hog."[21]

On Juneteenth (and other festive and commonplace occasions), food, its preparation, and its rituals were very significant for black Texans, including the Days, and for the most part, meat meant pork. Those who had been raised in slavery ate "everything but the squeal," from "streak-o'-lean" bacon, to ribs, trotters, hogshead cheese, chitlins and other innards, and they passed on such gustatory legacies to their offspring. The thrifty Flora Day fixed those traditional vittles and many others.[22]

A favorite yarn concerned the young Texan whose sweetheart wanted venison. "You see dat deer 'bout five miles down de road wid his tail turnt to us?" his honey asked, "Ah wants dat deer for mah dinner . . . but Ah doesn't wan' 'im shot in de body." Her beau grabbed "his double-barrel shot-gun, puts hit up to his shoulder, points hit at de deer, den outruns de bullet an' turns de deer 'roun' so his haid'd be in front when de bullet done rech him." Boys such as Aaron Junior learned to run like jackrabbits, ride tall in the saddle, and shoot the eyes off grasshoppers—or hunt deer, squirrels, and wild birds for family meals.[23]

Negroes in rural Texas enjoyed pigs' feet with peas and rice, and believed that "iffen you'd have dat on New Year's Day you have good luck all de year." They were "raised on greens, pork and potlikker, 'taters and ash cake." Those denizens of the New South roasted corn or ground it into meal, with "flint" kernels boiled in lye water until the skins dropped off, then dried and pulverized for grits. Flora Day prepared light-as-air biscuits from flour, milk, "grease," and baking powder. They became one of her signature treats and occupied a higher rung on the bread ladder than humble corn pone or hush puppies. Mustang grapes, figs, and melons grown by the Days and others were always favorites, and Texans boasted that their produce was superior to that raised anywhere else. "Wow, that's a big watermelon over there. Must be about fifteen feet in diameter," one visiting city slicker exclaimed. His black Texas friend looked puzzled, paused, then asked, "Y'all talkin' about that cucumber?"[24]

Aaron Day, Sr., was a successful farmer. His extended family provided a nucleus for Dayton's small, middle-class "colored" community, and the nearby town of Ames included a similarly well-situated colony of French-speaking Negro Creoles from Louisiana. By 1910, Aaron Senior had become a U.S. Mail rider as well; his wife Flora managed their capacious, two-story boardinghouse, where she served memorable meals; and their daughter Ethel taught school.[25]

The Days were among their community's more economically secure Negroes, but Flora and Ethel did not see themselves as mere
domestic adjuncts to Aaron Senior or "at home," as did the majority of local women of all backgrounds. Some black women worked
outside the house because of economic necessity, and few of them
had much choice but to become servants or farm laborers. Many
white men, on the other hand, resented any evidence of their wives'
independence. "Our hens are putting on airs," a column in the *Vindicator* protested during the Populist era; "they wear spurs, have
combs, and strut around like the rooster. . . . We'd rather have . . .
more eggs and less style."[26] But Aaron Day, Sr., respected his industrious spouse and well-educated daughter, and shunned that
sort of patriarchal crowing.

Despite pockets of stark opposition among Anglos, from the
early postbellum years onward, Liberty County always made some
education available for its "colored" children, and in the early
twentieth century, Aaron Senior (as much a civic leader in his region as any other man of his race) served quite a spell as the Negro
representative on the local school board.[27] Nonetheless, he and
Flora must have realized that the county would not provide their
daughter and sons with the education they needed to succeed in the
world. Ethel had left Dayton for Prairie View Agricultural, Mechanical, and Normal (A., M. & N.) College in 1904, and two years
later the Days prepared to send fifteen-year-old Aaron Junior to
join her.

That was also the summer of a dreadful racial incident in
Texas. In July 1906, despite complaints from black troops about
the pervasive discrimination they faced in the Deep South, the army
dispatched a unit of Negro soldiers from Nebraska to a fort in the
city of Brownsville, near the mouth of the Rio Grande, three hundred miles down the sultry Gulf Coast from Galveston.

Brownsville's Anglo inhabitants embraced Jim Crow. Shops,
parks, and eateries denied entry to members of the newly arrived
"colored" battalion, and the very presence of those "reliable men
and very quiet soldiers, very inoffensive in their manner" (as one of
their officers described them) riled the local whites. Tensions escalated when one Anglo resident clobbered a uniformed Negro with

a gun butt and another booted a drunken black soldier into the river. White army officers saw nothing unusual or untoward in such incidents, and admitted that for Brownsville's citizens to pistol-whip, kick, or otherwise abuse blacks (or Mexican Americans) was simply in the natural order of things.

The sores festered and finally erupted near the fort on August 14, but precisely what happened that evening was never clarified. Anglo witnesses, however, claimed that a band of unidentified Negro soldiers deserted their posts, swarmed all over town, then fired a hail of bullets into a store where they previously had been badly treated. One white man died and several others were injured. Military police quickly rounded up a group of African American soldiers, but learned nothing from the men, who refused to confess or implicate their colleagues. Investigators could not determine who might have been involved, and had no evidence to support any courts-martial. But the army's frustrated inspector general maintained that *all* of the Negro soldiers stationed there were culpable, and had entered into a conspiracy of silence to protect the criminals among them, who supposedly had murdered and maimed innocent white citizens in Brownsville.

As commander-in-chief, President Theodore Roosevelt promptly accepted the army's recommendations and dishonorably discharged (and barred from all future military or other government service) almost every man in the suspected companies. Roosevelt, however, strategically delayed that harsh announcement until after the November 1906 congressional elections and sidestepped any threat to the traditional allegiance of Negro voters to his Republican Party. But soon thereafter, he publicly excoriated the suspect Brownsville soldiers, calling them "bloody butchers [who] ought to be hung." The only reason they were not executed, he added, was "because I couldn't find out which ones did the shooting."

With predictable restraint, Booker Washington responded that "the race is not so much resentful or angry, perhaps, as it feels disappointed." That was his strongest ever reproach of Roosevelt—his patron. But other Negroes who took great pride in their men's military service were outraged and far more outspoken, with Boston's Monroe Trotter attacking Roosevelt's "monstrous breach of equity." Most African Americans viewed the nasty fiasco that welled up in Texas as further testimony to their continuing impotence in, perhaps, an inevitably hostile country.[28]

An investigation instigated by Senator Joseph Foraker (a political rival of President Roosevelt), who maintained that such severe retribution never should have been imposed without due process, seemed to prove that the black soldiers' "conspiracy" more likely was a conspiracy among Brownsville's white citizens in an attempt to rid their town of Negro troops. Nonetheless, the Senate in its entirety disagreed, and upheld the president's dismissals. After Roosevelt left the White House in 1909, 14 of the 167 dishonorably discharged soldiers were quietly reinstated. In 1972, when only one of them survived, President Richard Nixon (prompted by a resolution sponsored by the dogged African American Representative Augustus Hawkins) addressed the probability of prejudgment at Brownsville, denounced the arguments supporting indiscriminate mass punishment, and directed the army to rectify its sixty-six-year-old injustice.[29] That official penitence was a lifetime ahead, but the debacle seriously muddied the region's racial waters as Aaron Day, Jr., headed off to school in 1906.

Prairie View A., M. & N. was located about fifty miles due west of Liberty County, situated atop a gentle rise in the plains where the grounds petered out into undulating waves of amber and green grasslands that stretched to the edges of the Texas sky. During Reconstruction, a seminary for white girls called Alta Vista had occupied what, a decade later, would become the heart of a new campus for Negroes.[30]

That college, established in 1879, became the state's foremost school for blacks. As a land-grant institution and a subordinate adjunct to (all-white) Texas A. & M., Prairie View qualified for supplemental funds under provisions of the federal Morrill Acts. It focused on teacher training and prepared three-quarters of the state's Negro educators. But like Hampton and Tuskegee, the famous "colored" institutes that it emulated, Prairie View really was more a trade and high school than a college.

Enrollment hovered around nine hundred during Aaron's student years. The YW and YMCA were active, with Bible study and weekly chapel attendance mandatory, grace sung before all meals, and *Stand Up for Jesus* everyone's favorite hymn. Young men wore uniforms of "serviceable blue material [and] brown campaign hats similar to those worn by the United States Army." The school had fifteen brick or wooden academic buildings and thirty residential cottages, and its sixteen hundred-plus acres made it the "second largest physical plant of any Negro institution in the country." Principal E. L. Blackshear, a disciple of Booker T. Washington who maintained that the "life of constant labor in the fields made of the ex-African savage a sane, healthful, virile, cheerful and useful laboring class," led the thirty-person, all-Negro administration and faculty. Most were Texas born, raised, and educated, but several of them previously had been associated with Tuskegee Institute, Oberlin College, and even Harvard University. One, Annie Evans, had attended the University of Chicago.[31]

Aaron Day, Jr.'s leadership potential and competence in the sciences soon became apparent, and following his 1910 graduation the school hired him as a chemistry instructor. But Aaron and his family also believed that he could benefit from further education. In those years, the University of Chicago cast out a wide net in the south-central states seeking candidates for its summertime teacher training programs, yet its president authorized his Texas recruiting agent to "get rid of anyone who may be obnoxious to you" (meaning nonwhites) and acknowledged his reluctance to admit blacks. Nonetheless, the new Charles Smiley scholarships could be granted to "poor, but promising, Negro students," and Rosenwald fellowships lured occasional African Americans to the world-class university that had a Nobel laureate on its faculty and excelled in scientific research. So for the summers of 1911 and 1912, then the full academic year 1913–14, Aaron made the trek from rural Texas to the distant shores of Lake Michigan.[32]

Those may have been lonely times for Aaron as Chicago's congested vertical cityscape and ocean-sized lake supplanted his familiar prairies. The "City of the Big Shoulders" had more residents than Texas, including forty thousand-plus Negroes, most of them migrants from the South. The Galveston-born world heavyweight boxing champion Jack Johnson had become Chicago's most famous black resident, and his Cabaret de Champion its most popular nightclub. In defiance of customary practice, it catered to patrons of both races, and Johnson himself conspicuously and extravagantly courted white women (underaged ones at that), then had to flee the country in 1913 to avoid legal prosecution.[33]

During those years, Negro University of Chicago students (who could not live in dormitories) were very few, and "colored" faculty there were nonexistent. Among the handful of Negroes who preceded Aaron Day were Prairie View's Annie Evans and the neophyte historian Carter Woodson, who went on to earn his Ph.D. at Harvard. Though Aaron never received a degree at the university (probably due to financial shortages and not academic deficiencies), he compiled a fully respectable record.[34]

During and after his Chicago sojourns, Aaron Day, Jr., maintained his affiliation with Prairie View. He matured into a "really good-looking fellow" with a mahogany complexion, square jaw, militarily erect carriage, and curly black hair. He courted the Houston-born Ethel Scott (an attractive young woman known as a "stylish dresser"), a home economics teacher at the school, whose brother Emmett had been Booker T. Washington's inestimable aide at Tuskegee Institute. In October 1917, soon after the United States entered the Great War, Secretary of War Newton Baker—yielding to pressure from the black community and influential whites—appointed Emmett Scott as his special assistant for Negro affairs. As an early initiative, Scott championed a Student Army Training Corps (SATC) at Prairie View, and made soldiers from Texas one of his central concerns.[35]

A few months earlier, because of antagonisms generated by recent U.S. Army incursions into Mexico, President Woodrow Wilson had perceived a clear need to fortify his country's military presence in Texas. Information included in a curious, intercepted cable from German to Mexican officials purportedly projected a hostile postwar treaty that might return parts of the Southwest to Mexico. That missive further compounded the tensions. So to beef up the borderlands' defenses, the army relocated portions of the black Twenty-fourth Infantry to a camp near Houston. Following the United States' April declaration of war on Germany, however, twenty-five of its sergeants had been transferred north to start training as commissioned officers, leaving the unit with a dearth of mature Negro leadership.[36]

By Texas standards, Houston's racial climate might have seemed benign, but galling Jim Crow laws nonetheless segregated the city. Negroes had to sit "behind the screen" on streetcars, drink from water cans designated "colored," and tolerate white Houstonians (especially hostile police) calling them "niggers." Those conditions outraged the soldiers, who claimed that they were "treated as dogs," and as members of the U.S. Army deserved greater respect. When a rash black private tried to restrain a white policeman who was assaulting a Negro woman, the interfering soldier was pistol-whipped and arrested, as was a corporal with the military police who went to inquire about his man's welfare. Law enforcement officials soon released the two soldiers, but the African American troops were hardly assuaged, and his ignominious treatment especially infuriated the young corporal.[37]

On August 23, a number of soldiers, prodded by their angry corporal and lacking the prudent leadership that their recently departed top sergeants would have provided, armed themselves and set out on a two-hour rampage that killed sixteen white people and wounded twelve others, including several policemen. Five of the mutinous Negroes also died in the fray.[38]

The army brought charges of murder and mutiny against 156 black men. A mass court-martial (the largest murder trial in United States history) was convened in San Antonio, and it quickly condemned thirteen soldiers to be hanged. Five men were acquitted, with the remainder confined to long terms at hard labor. Surveillance of the supposedly insurrectionary African American community in Texas became so intense that Aaron Day, Jr.'s sister Ethel had a close friend who was "arrested for . . . seditious writ[ings]" because she corresponded with several of the condemned soldiers. Their executions were covertly carried out on December 22, 1917, only three days after the convictions, and three months *before* the sentences were appealed or the trials even procedurally reviewed. Later proceedings doomed six more soldiers who would die on the gallows nine months later.[39]

The policeman whose maltreatment of Negroes had precipitated the mutiny was not restrained. Late in 1917, he killed two black people while supposedly making arrests, was indicted and tried, but a white jury acquitted him. One Anglo-Houstonian drawled: "It costs twenty-five dollars to kill a buzzard [but only] five dollars to kill a nigger."[40] The turmoil erupting out of that city combined with seventy lynchings in the country that year—at least half a dozen occurred within a hundred miles of Aaron Day, Jr.'s southeast Texas home and school—generated a volatile racial climate as Day and multitudes of other Negroes prepared to join the United States Army to help make the world safe for democracy.[41]

"The great World War had been in progress about three years when because of the constant and repeated infringements upon our rights to travel upon the high seas," a black physician named William Holmes Dyer wrote in his diary, "the United States became involved, therein casting her lot to-gether with the Allies, against the ever offending German Nation." Dr. Dyer, known as Billie, hailed from Lincoln, Illinois, and in July 1917 he became his hometown's first Negro to enlist in the army.[42]

That spring, the NAACP's white chairman, Joel Spingarn, had spearheaded efforts to have Negroes like Dyer and Day included in the army's officer corps, despite the fact that fifteen training camps already had geared up, none of which knowingly accepted African Americans. To generate support for his plan and to insure ample volunteers, Spingarn had composed an open letter to the country's well-educated black men. "There is now . . . an opportunity possible for you . . . to become leaders and officers instead of followers and privates," he had written. That epistle stimulated creation of the Central Committee of Negro College Men (CCNCM), which began spreading word about those new opportunities throughout the middle-class African American community.

The peacetime army had very few Negro commissioned officers, raising questions as to how, when, and where new black candidates might be trained. Most white southerners (and lots of Yankees) opposed having any "colored" officers, while many blacks resisted the idea of a camp designated for their race alone, maintaining that it was one more example of Jim Crowism, and would make their men look like second-rate citizens and officers. But moderate voices prevailed, with W. E. B. Du Bois and others successfully arguing that circumstances dictated looking past the segregated facilities in an effort to bring the nation together and train Negro officers who could lead Negro troops into battle.[43]

The army grudgingly yielded to the calls for black officers, but instituted extremely limiting provisos as to their use. Negro candidates would comprise only two percent of total officer trainees (compared to thirteen percent for black draftees), and less than half of those candidates would ever be commissioned. None of the new African American officers could exceed the rank of captain, and finally, those who did acquire commissions knew that they might be demoted or dismissed under any possible ruses.[44]

Once the camp's existence had been reluctantly agreed to, its location needed to be decided. A training site for "colored" officers ideally would be situated in an area with minimal race prejudice, distanced from both hostile white and dynamic black communities. After much haggling, Secretary of War Baker settled on Iowa's Fort Des Moines. The military chose that locale because it was rural, not southern, and nearby Des Moines (the state capital) had a small, "respectable" Negro population that maintained good relations with the majority. The army selected 1,250 men for training. About 250 would be pulled from the ranks of existing black noncommissioned officers (like those recruited from the dishonored Twenty-fourth Infantry), with the remainder culled from the civilian community's "better element."

The CCNCM contacted thousands of men through its nationwide network of Negro colleges and fraternities. "Dear Brother:" its recruitment call began, trumpeting news of the projected Reserve Officers' Training Camp. "Realize what this means. . . . Over due recognition at last. . . . We must succeed," it continued, then concluded, "Look to the future, brother, the vision is glorious!" Applications from professionals such as Dr. Billie Dyer and Aaron Day, Jr., poured in, and training at Fort Des Moines began in June 1917.[45]

Aaron Day was a splendid officer's candidate. His frontier life had toughened his body and made him an adept equestrian and marksman. The army rated his health "excellent," deemed his posture "erect," and eyesight and hearing "perfect." Aaron's academic training had prepared him for the upcoming intellectual and administrative challenges, while classroom work had honed his ability to deal with young people. Trainees would be reimbursed for their travel to Des Moines ($25.55 in Aaron's case) and received room, board, and other expenses, but otherwise were not paid.[46]

The army knew that it needed to make the most of its human resources, but whites opposed integrating their boys with black soldiers, and at least as strongly resisted the establishment of an "elite" body of Negro officers. The white-owned and -operated Liberty *Vindicator* reported the enlistments and departures of a number of local Negroes, but never conceded that Aaron Day, Jr., one of the county's best-known "colored boys," was heading off to Iowa to become an officer.[47] No matter how able, well-educated and intelligent, dynamic or gentlemanly a black man might be, race stigmatized him, and he remained an unwelcome outsider in the United States Army, and especially its officer corps. The experience of Lieutenant Colonel Charles Young spoke to that harsh reality.

Since the Spanish-American War, Young (a West Point graduate) had been known as one of the country's most skillful and inspiring officers, and his assignments had taken him to the Philippines, the Caribbean, and Liberia. As the United States prepared to enter the war in Europe, the army placed him in command of the Tenth Cavalry. Resistance to Young escalated because of concerns that he might be assigned to a position in which he could command white troops. Some white junior officers had refused to salute their few African American superiors, and fears of further confrontations generated increasing bias against "colored" officers. The European crisis might even see Young promoted to the unprecedented and "inappropriate" rank of general. The military dealt with those dilemmas by placing him on inactive status on trumped-up grounds of failing health. To refute that medical determination, Young rode on horseback from Ohio to Washington, D.C. Despite that testament to his fitness, the army denied his requests to return to active service. The decision aroused anger, protests, and profound disappointment in the black community, but Charles Young's ultimate reactivation (with the rank of full colonel) would not take place until a week before the war's end.⁴⁸

In addition to the controversy surrounding Colonel Young, many Negroes resented the military's refusal to admit them except under segregated conditions. A recent Harvard Law School graduate of Portuguese-African parentage, for one, was "outraged" when the army assigned him to a "colored" company, because, like so many other Americans, he considered himself a patriotic immigrant volunteer, not a black person. An unknown number of similarly light-skinned Negroes opted to pass for white to serve their country under less distasteful circumstances.⁴⁹

Joseph Abernethy, a colleague of Aaron Day, Jr., at Prairie View, also volunteered and trained at Fort Des Moines, where he received a commission as a second lieutenant. Most other loyal Texans similarly pitched in, but even at their school, support for the war was not unanimous. A student named C. L. Dellums registered with the Selective Service, which pressured him to join Prairie View's SATC. Dellums, however, ultimately thwarted the draft board's best efforts by insisting that his *only* choice of service would be with the new Army Air Corps—that accepted no blacks at all. In his magazine, *The Messenger,* A. Philip Randolph, a young African American Socialist, commented that while men of his race had little sympathy for Germany, many "would rather fight to make Georgia safe for the Negro," an opinion echoed by the fledgling historian Carter Woodson.⁵⁰

The "colored" officers' training camp at Fort Des Moines filled up with hundreds of educators, businessmen, and lawyers. Discipline was rigid and the regimen demanding, with sixteen hours per day of physical drills and classroom work. In most instances, white officers conducted the program according to the same standards that applied elsewhere to candidates of their own race, but in Iowa they included almost no specialty training.

Despite the candidates' exemplary behavior, a number of Iowans protested their presence. A Chinese restaurant owner was one who denied them service. "No servee black men; me lose all bliziness," he reportedly grumbled. Nonetheless, the YM and YWCAs welcomed them, and many civilians took the trainees into their hearts, homes, and churches. "Here was the best blood of the Nation in that great school of the Soldier, fitting themselves to become leaders of Men in the Army of our Nation," Billie Dyer asserted. The young men formed a baseball league, held parades and band concerts, and local children never tired of emulating "their dusky brethren in khaki." "No member of the camp can walk through the town without a dozen small darkies trailing worshipfully at his heels," the *Literary Digest* reported.[51]

Visitors included Tuskegee Institute's R. R. Moton. Most of the men applauded his presence, but the future Lieutenant W. N. Colson (a cocky Harvard graduate) labeled Moton the "high priest of Negro servility," excoriated his "disgraceful, clownish and asinine address" at Fort Des Moines, and characterized it as "an exhortation for Negroes to keep in their places."[52]

The camp's white commander, Colonel Charles Ballou, forewarned the officer candidates that their success required "strong bodies, keen intelligence, absolute obedience to orders, unflagging industry, exemplary conduct, and character of the highest order." As a rule, his men satisfied him, and he claimed that "the boys are far more obedient and much less difficult to handle than a similar body of white men. . . . We have the making of a large number of good officers." The puzzlingly inconsistent Ballou later complained, however, that his whole division "was made the dumping ground for discards, both white and black."[53]

At the last minute, the War Department postponed the original September graduation date because it had not yet formulated a scheme to incorporate the new Negro officers into active service. One candidate, Anselmo Krigger, recently had "Americanized" the spelling of his name, because (reflecting the jingoistic temper of the times) he thought that the original Kruger sounded too Germanic. Like many others, however, Krigger washed out of the program. In that case, white officials maintained, "he was too temperamental."[54] The army brass continued to challenge the camp's advisability and raised doubts as to whether black men ever would be commissioned. The recent Houston riot also had terrified whites and jeopardized the activation of any African American troops at all. Negro candidates resented implications that they were traitorous, untrustworthy, or incapable of completing the training within the scheduled period of time, and at that juncture a few simply packed up and left, convinced that the army never intended to commission them.[55]

During the additional month, however, the War Department finalized plans for a 92nd Division that was authorized to have about 625 Negro and 150 white officers. On October 15, 1917, the Fort Des Moines program graduated and commissioned just about enough of the original candidates (533 first and second lieutenants and 106 captains) who performed in exemplary fashion to satisfy the divisional requirements.

With the exception of a few well-educated, well-disciplined, and very hardy former civilians like Aaron Day, the new captains (called "the old men") previously had been regular army noncoms, and were selected for the highest rank granted at Fort Des Moines on the basis of long military experience. Lieutenant Colson protested the army's favoritism in granting captaincies only to those men whom he considered the most obsequious, and scoffed that "[Captain] Adam E. Patterson won a commission by singing plantation songs." The military later demoted or ousted many such men who had received less than adequate instruction and directed harsh retribution at that small band of Negro captains who, often arbitrarily, were declared unfit for their duties as company commanders.[56]

An overlapping training cycle at Des Moines addressed the nation's need for Negro medical officers. Seventy-five "colored" men, including Billie Dyer, were commissioned as military doctors and dentists a month after the initial class finished. The army commissioned other African Americans who trained elsewhere, but they never approached the numbers that went through Fort Des Moines. Ultimately, thirteen hundred became officers during the World War and served exclusively with the two black divisions: the 92nd and the always incomplete, provisional 93rd.[57]

General John "Black Jack" Pershing later complained that the army recruited and trained the 92nd's Negro commissioned officers too hastily, and they therefore did not have the required skills, experience, or competence. Other white officers predetermined that the division's "colored" leaders would not (must not) succeed, and those expectations sometimes were fulfilled. The NAACP's canny W. E. B. Du Bois knew that the whole unit had been established over bitter protests from army brass, and he argued that Negro officers lacked both adequate preparation and able white leadership. "Is it possible," he sharply queried, that "the War Department wish this division to be a failure?"[58]

When Captain Aaron Day, Jr., completed training in October, the military dispatched him to Camp Funston (annexed to Fort Riley) in northeast Kansas. A month later, Lieutenant William Dyer joined him. They were among 44 Negro commissioned officers who went from Des Moines to Funston. In time, that base had 8,300 "colored drafted soldiers," but the army always maintained what it considered a "safe ratio" of at least two whites for each black man. Once there, Day started receiving his captain's pay of two hundred dollars per month, less seven dollars for "war insurance."[59]

For half a century, the oft-praised Negro frontier units had been called Buffalo Soldiers. Whether they were stationed at Funston or dispersed among any of six other cantonments scattered throughout the country, men with the 92nd Division all displayed the distinctive olive-banded buffalo patch on their uniforms.

Aaron Day, Jr., received his captain's commission (with only ten Negro majors and two colonels ultimately outranking him), and took command of Company B in the 92nd Division's 317th Ammunition Train. Ironically, just more than a half century earlier, Aaron's white grandfather Isaiah Day also had become a captain, but he had fought with the secessionist Confederacy, championing states rights and maintaining what he considered his God-given right to enslave others—including his own mulatto children.

The 317th Ammunition Train had 1,333 officers and men, seven companies, and was divided into a horse battalion and a motorized battalion. Aaron Day, Jr.'s company was motorized. Training at "Camp Function," as some soldiers called it, included topography and map reading; lectures and hands-on instruction concerning the care of vehicles, horses, and pack mules, weaponry and ammunition. Also, their manual iterated, "Commanders will instruct their companies in military courtesy." Some officers, however, were not up to those tasks because they lacked the experience and background or had received inadequate training themselves.[60]

Lieutenant William Dyer described Camp Funston as a "desol[ate], forsaken looking place . . . in a valley surrounded on every side by rolling foot-hills and as far as the eye could reach, newly constructed wooden barracks." It was the largest temporary army post ever developed in the United States, with fourteen hundred new buildings, including barracks for fifty thousand men and tents for many more. A month after Dyer arrived, the military command attached him to the 317th Ammunition Train, where he became Captain Day's physician for Company B. The 317th was one of a few units in which almost all of the commissioned officers were Negroes.

Aaron Day's interval at Funston was hardly without incident. In late 1916, Day's fellow University of Chicago attendee Carter Woodson had tried unsuccessfully to enlist Day as a sales agent, and had mailed him an unsolicited carton of books (Woodson's own *Education of the Negro Prior to 1861*) that Day promptly relegated to a Prairie View storage facility. On December 6, 1917, Woodson wrote Secretary of War Newton Baker a dyspeptic letter concerning what he called Captain Day's "debts." "Knowing that you do not encourage dishonesty on the part of men who have been chosen to lead the World War," Woodson declared, "I am directing your attention to this delinquency." "Anything which you may do to enable me to recover this amount due . . . $33.33," he concluded, "will be very much appreciated." A colleague confirmed Woodson's notoriously "insulting" correspondence, conceding that he "put more acid and sting into a letter than any man I ever knew."[61]

The country needed African American officers, but the army often went out of its way to remove them. All Negroes of any sophistication whatsoever understood that their successful tenure in the military hung by the slenderest of threads. The astute but petulant Carter Woodson surely would have known that accusations of financial impropriety such as those which he put forth easily could have scuttled Captain Aaron Day's future.

That, however, did not happen. Emmett Scott, the secretary of war's special assistant for Negro affairs whose sister Ethel was one of Aaron's sweethearts, probably diverted or made light of Woodson's epistle, and Day acted promptly as well. He wrote the War Department, swearing: "I am not now nor ever have been indebted to writer . . . of letter, neither have I acted as his agent for said books," and he concurrently beseeched a friend at Prairie View to return the unordered books to Woodson posthaste. Despite Woodson's attack, with its implicit threat to his commission, Day's army career survived. Carrie Bond was visiting various encampments on behalf of the Circle for Negro War Relief at that time, and she may have met with and offered guidance to Captain Day as he grappled with Woodson's puzzling but consistent irascibility.[62]

"The draft boards of Kansas, Mo., Colorado, Arizona and Texas were sending us men by the hundreds," Lieutenant Dyer wrote about his own months at Funston. "We labored diligently . . . caring for the sick and seeking out those unfit for the Military Service," he added. But disaster threatened the Ammunition Train during that frigid January and February when, Dyer stated, "an epidemic of Cerebro-Spinal Meningitis broke out." "The disease spread like wild fire" and throughout the winter medics sprayed "the noses and throats twice daily of all officers and enlisted men with antiseptic solutions." As the meningococcal outbreak subsided, a worse plague imperiled them. The very first diagnostic confirmation of the influenza pandemic that would sweep the world was made in early March 1918 right there at Camp Funston, where 233 soldiers succumbed to pounding headaches, body aches, and "knock-me-down fever," often followed by pneumonia.[63]

The "colored" YWCA opened a Hostess House at Funston to help keep "the woman problem . . . to a minimum," yet that did not avert several disasters. One crisis arose on March 16, when the division's judge advocate informed Captain Aaron Day, Jr., that Sergeant Charles McClendon, from Day's company, "killed his wife at ten o'clock last night, and is in prison." Day wrote McClendon explaining why his case had been referred to civil and not military authorities, and detailing his few continuing army benefits. "If there is anything that you want me as your company Commander to officially do for you, why let me know," Day added. "I am really sorry to hear of your misfortune," he concluded, "Don't fail to write me for any information." Within a month, McClendon had been tried, convicted, discharged, and incarcerated, but Captain Day did not forsake his man. He advised the penitentiary warden that McLendon had "soldiered hard and showed himself to be a deserving Noncommissioned officer," and added his sincere hopes that the sergeant's "deportment and work will be of such nature that will cut short his sentence."[64]

One of the war's most controversial racial incidents also unfolded that spring at Funston. Kansas law did not sanction segregated public facilities, but one black soldier complained that the "men of the 92d . . . are barred [from the] amusement zone in the white section of the camp," while a noncommissioned officer challenged a white civilian who denied him entry to a movie theater in a nearby town.[65] In response, on March 28, under the newly promoted General Ballou's direction, Lieutenant Colonel Allen Greer issued the statement that "no useful purpose is served by such acts as will cause the 'color question' to be raised." "To avoid such conflicts," the bulletin continued, "the Division Commander has repeatedly urged that all colored members of his command, and especially the officers . . . should refrain from going where their presence will be resented." Every Negro, it added, must place "the general good above his personal pleasure and convenience." The sergeant in question, the memo claimed, "is guilty of the greater wrong in doing *anything*, no matter how *legally* correct, that will provoke race animosity." "The success of the Division . . . is dependent upon the good will of the public," that directive concluded: "White men made the Division, and they can break it just as easily if it becomes a trouble maker."[66] In the eyes of Funston's white commanders, any African American soldier who exercised his legal rights became "a trouble maker." That order outraged "colored" troops, officers, and the entire black community. The NAACP called the army's actions "unjust, humiliating, and inexpedient," and demanded General Ballou's transfer. Negro soldiers had considered him one of their most empathetic white officers. If that was how Ballou supported them, what might they encounter elsewhere?[67]

In fact, that ignominious affront to African Americans in Kansas did not compare to what black soldiers in the Deep South experienced. They faced malevolence everywhere. A sergeant named Noble Sissle, for one, was buying a newspaper in a South Carolina hotel lobby when the proprietor attacked him from behind, knocking off his hat. "Do you realize you are abusing a United States soldier and that is a government hat you knocked to the floor?" Sissle protested. But urged on by raucous cohorts, the white man cursed Sergeant Sissle and booted him out the door.[68]

Even more dire circumstances often befell Negro civilians. On June 4, 1918, Anglos lynched a black woman and her six children in a Texas town not far from Dayton and Prairie View because one of her boys allegedly had threatened a white man.[69] Just two days after that atrocity, as the 317th completed its cursory stateside training, Lieutenant Dyer reported, "the order came for the trains of the 92nd Division . . . to proceed to Camp Upton, Long Island, N.Y. preparatory to embarkation overseas."

Dyer and Day's unit was but one small cog in the 92nd, which was the army's only division that had been totally fragmented throughout its training, and therefore had no chance to develop cohesion or esprit de corps. On June 7, Lieutenant Dyer reported, "the organizations began leaving and train after train pulled out." "We reached Camp Upton in about three days," he continued (both Carrie Bond and the YWCA's Lugenia Hope may have crossed paths with Captain Day at that juncture), and "remained there from the 11th June to the 13th when we were hurried to the embarkation port of Hoboken, New Jersey, and put aboard the steamship Covington." From then on, the army considered its men "at war." It increased Day's base pay by half, and added one hundred or more dollars per month in supplementary combat allotments.[70]

In mid-June, the *Covington,* a "magnificent old German passenger Vessel of the Hamburg-American line," weighed anchor. Including "the soldiers aboard enrout for Europe," the *Covington,* on which both Negro and white servicemen sailed to France, "had a personnel of 5000." "Staterooms were equipped with every modern convenience, [and] the lower compartments which the enlisted men occupied [were] clean and well ventilated," Lieutenant Dyer observed.

"It was beautiful," he declared, "as we steamed [down] the Hudson amid the cheers of civilians on shore and on ferries as we passed." "The returning cheers of our soldiers," however, "were only semi-enthusiastic, for in each breast was that impulse half of anxiety, half of dread as we pulled away from those native shores." "We passed that most honored, most noble of all monuments the 'Statue of Liberty,' " Dyer recalled, and "waved a passing farewell" until Long Island's hazy dunes "faded from our sight and we were at sea."

Their odyssey, however, was fraught with anxiety. "Germany by this time having declared the whole Atlantic Ocean a War Zone, no lights were allowed about the ship after sun-down," Lieutenant Dyer wrote. The *Covington* sailed amid a "convoy of nine transports, two battle cruisers, [and] a half-dozen torpedo boat destroyers which searched the water all about us for submarines." For the most part, Dyer added, as the flotilla followed the limpid Gulf Stream northeastward, "the sea was . . . calm and beautiful, [but] each day the men busy themselves in watching for the ever-expected periscopes of a submarine," as well as "porpoises that were constantly jumping up and racing with the ships."

Impending attacks by U-boats, however, were not the only issues that plagued Lieutenant Dyer and Captain Day. "From the very start," Dyer continued, "there was that feeling of prejudice, . . . for among the first orders issued were those barring Colored Officers from the same toilets as the whites, also barring them from the barber shop and denying [them] . . . use of the ship's Gymnasium." One dining room was set aside as "a recreation room and smoking room by white officers," with another for "colored" officers. Soldiers with the 317th composed a catchy ragtime song that they titled *When Sambo Goes to War,* as Jim Crow set off to sea with the AEF.[71]

Late in June, Lieutenant Dyer's journal revealed, "we spied several hydroplanes flying above us and our hearts were filled with delight for we knew that land was near." They soon spotted a "lone light-house off the coast of Brest, followed in a few hours by the dim grey shore of France." For most American soldiers, including Captain Aaron Day, Jr., that was their first sight of an unknown continent, and their profound (though temporary) relief when they safely disembarked on June 27 was well grounded. Only four days later, one of the fearsome *Unterseeboote* that it had eluded on its way east across the Atlantic torpedoed and sank the *Covington* as it carried a full shipload of German prisoners of war on its return voyage to the United States.[72]

The AEF units in France whose exploits were most closely followed and celebrated were the combat troops, to which only ten percent of the 400,000 black U.S. soldiers were assigned. On the other hand, Services of Supply labor battalions—stevedores, road builders, grave diggers—where three of every four Negroes served, were the least prestigious, yet those men did much of the war's filthiest, toughest work. In terms of status, combat support units such as ammunition trains occupied an intermediary position. Despite those differing assignments, many white Americans categorically disparaged all black soldiers with the AEF, yet a few others sometimes lauded them. A stateside newspaper claimed that the exploits of the 92nd "call for special recognition," and one self-amused journalist asked, "Is there no way of getting a cargo of watermelons over there?"[73]

Lieutenant Dyer and his colleagues found a country depleted by war, and sought to befriend the beleaguered French. "The women young and old all wore black and seemed to be in the deepest mourning," Dyer said, "and many little children poorly clad were running along the roadside begging us for pennies." Those *gamins* followed members of the 317th Ammunition Train all around Brest. One day, Dyer visited a park, and "soon they were sitting upon my knees and pointing to my eyes, nose, and ears, trying to teach me the French words." Captain Day, in fact, knew some French from his college years, and more from long association with the community of mulatto Creoles who lived near his home in Dayton, Texas.

From Brest, the 317th's Company B moved on to St. Laômir. The newly arrived officers were domiciled there in unoccupied houses where local women "would come over and sing for us and try to teach us their latest country dances." "The people soon fell in love with us," Dyer wrote, "many of them visiting the camp daily, the French girls and our boys strolling about to-gether." "What pleased us most," Dyer added, was that "there was no thought of prejudice, for with them there was <u>No Color Line</u>."

The U.S. Army brass abhorred the relationships that Negro soldiers established with the French, but what a pleasant change that camaraderie must have been for a Texan such as Captain Day who had grown up in the world's supposed bastion of democracy and equality where he had been denied the friendship of white women. White American officers ineffectually demanded that black soldiers must have no contact at all with the *mesdemoiselles* whom they sternly cautioned about Negroes' "unbridled sexuality." AEF headquarters disseminated scurrilous literature "explaining . . . that to show ['colored' officers] social courtesies not only would be dangerous, but . . . would be an insult to the American people." "The French people . . . had been told that [blacks] were incapable of becoming officers and leading their own people," an African American woman in France reported. Americans of both races also did not know that whites and blacks had fought side by side in the Foreign Legion for years, and the French Army had two revered Negro generals, four colonels, and a slew of other officers.[74]

Members of the 92nd Division went with AEF field artillery units for specialized instruction at Bourbonnes-les-Bains, La Cortine, and Montmorrillon, as well as St. Laômir. At those AEF training facilities, however, Negro officers were insulted, "confined to certain streets, . . . forbidden to attend entertainments," and had to wait for all white soldiers (regardless of rank) to be seated before they were allowed to enter classrooms.[75]

On July 22, the Ammunition Train's Companies B and C received orders to leave St. Laômir by rail bound for Marseille, "for the purpose of getting ammunition trucks . . . to be driven overland to the Western Front." Captain Day, Lieutenants Abernethy (Day's Prairie View colleague), Dyer, and ten other officers embarked on that "splendid trip to the Mediterranean, and greatest sea-port in the World."[76] "The enlisted men were put in box-cars," Dyer added, but "we officers were furnished first-class passenger coaches."

African American officers never had enjoyed such choice accommodations in their own country's segregated South.

Wartime France stirred those Yanks: "Vegetation was in bloom with the beautiful country of rolling hills & villages, woods & pastures; fields . . . with women and children and old men tending them." "Ox-teams were on every farm, sheep, goats or cattle on every hill-side," Dyer observed, "but no horses or young men were

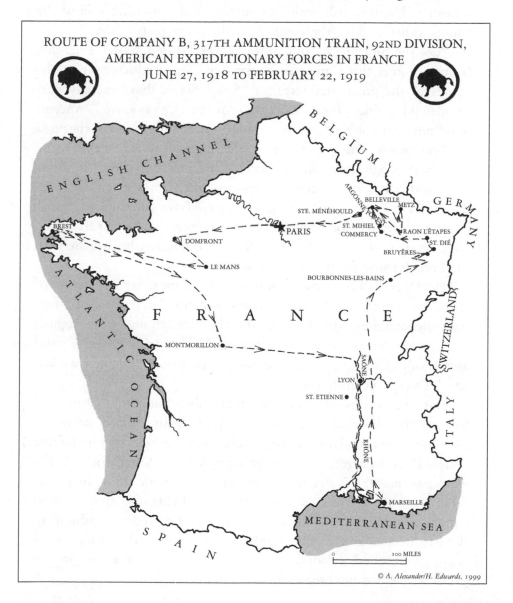

ROUTE OF COMPANY B, 317TH AMMUNITION TRAIN, 92ND DIVISION, AMERICAN EXPEDITIONARY FORCES IN FRANCE JUNE 27, 1918 TO FEBRUARY 22, 1919

© A. Alexander/H. Edwards, 1999

seen, these all being in service on the Western Front." They also saw shackled Germans along the roadsides, "each dressed in a uniform with large white letters stamped on the back of their coats, P.G."—*prisonnier de guerre.*

The ammo train continued on to Lyon, where the Saône joined the Rhône, which Dyer (and probably Day as well) judged "about the size of the Chicago River." The river and railroad tracks then meandered southward, with "mountains high on either side of the Rhone valley making the country all the more picturesque."

"On the morning of July 26th," Dyer exulted, "after emerging from a tunnel three miles in length we came suddenly upon the shores of the great Mediterranean Sea." Soon, they reached war-swollen Marseille: "the most cosmopolitan city on earth." Ancient buildings and cobbled streets jammed with donkey carts charmed the Americans, but the fact that "the population . . . seems to be one great conglomeration of races" most pleased them. "It seems that God just transplanted a sample of his people from all kingdoms of the earth in this strange old city," Dyer commented, noticing the Algerian soldiers, "many of whom were black as tar." They were among more than 600,000 Negro colonials who fought with the French throughout the Great War.[77]

Dr. Dyer also concerned himself with the morality and health of *les Marseillaises* (and his own troops) because "sixty-thousand registered prostitutes is the boast of the city." "Each night," he sighed, "beautiful women are seen soliciting the sale of their virtue . . . and as a result of this, venereal diseases are prevalent." "It is a wicked city," Dyer reluctantly conceded.

But the Yanks relished the atmosphere at the *bistros* and learned that *bouillabaisse* was just Mediterranean fish stew and *pieds de cochons* plain old pigs' feet. They drank very palatable wines, Dyer reported, because the French had warned them: " 'Do leau pas bon!!' (Water is no good.)" Everyone they met was "friendly and regarded us curiously, we being the first colored American officers they had ever seen. . . . Our soldiers bathe[d] in the Mediterranean that they might boast of same when they return home [and] found welcome in the best hotels, cafés, theaters, in fact every where, for the French have no prejudice."

The convivial respite at Marseille ended abruptly, however, when members of Company B learned that their promised vehicles were unavailable. They reversed course, reembarked, and as they traveled north by rail to rendezvous with the Ammunition Train's other companies and the rest of the 92nd Division, they neared the combat zone. The countryside became "less beautiful, the fields less well attended and the population much less dense than in southern France." They armed themselves and went on by truck. "From this time on," a grim Lieutenant Dyer observed, "I knew that it was up to me 'to live or die, to survive or perish,' so buckling my pistol on my side, I started on my mad hunt for the Germans."

Dyer's precautions were well warranted. At the next stop in Bruyères, he said, "we saw our first German aero-planes . . . and at nights often heard terrific bombardments . . . we were fast approaching that awful Western Front." Bruyères, they learned, though not a large town, had become a hive of wartime activity because it was a critical railroad exchange where French and American troops and supplies transferred on their way to the front.

The reunited 317th continued north toward "Raon L'Étape [where] the roads were packed with convoys of our division," said Dyer. "While marching to the front," Corporal Lloyd Blair later wrote, Captain Day's "Co. B was singing Church songs, [but his own] Co. A Broke it up By Singing Cheer, Cheer, The gang all here."[78] "Infantry men marching this distance of forty miles were strewn all along the road having fallen out from fatigue," Lieutenant Dyer added, and "and in the woods were graves of the brave French soldiers who in 1914 had met the German assault." "I was thirsty for that man who dared to represent the Kaiser," he vowed.

Late one night, the 317th Ammunition Train reached Raon L'Étape, which the Germans had decimated in 1914. "[In] this town clothed in death-like stillness and spelling desolation and destruction everywhere," their trucks pulled into an alley where the exhausted Day and Dyer lay down together "on a cold, cold stone in front of a building, using the door step for a pillow." The next morning, "a German aero-plane soared high above us and, although shot at constantly by our anti-aircraft guns, persisted in staying to get such information concerning our movement as he could." Fortunately, Captain Day located more secure billets for his men, because the Boche *Fokkers* dropped four bombs that detonated right where they had slept a few hours earlier.

"Pine groves contained barbed wire entanglements so thick that travel through same was impossible," Dyer lamented, since his unit had not been properly supplied with wire cutters. The ammo train endured heavy air bombardments, watched "German observation baloons high up in the air," and cheered as they saw "a great flame of fire where one moment before the baloon had been soaring." Nonetheless, when Dyer observed mass burials of fallen German soldiers, he mourned, "I could not but have a feeling of sympathy, for they were some Mother's boys."

At Raon L'Étape, their unit "suppl[ied] ammunition of all calibre to infantries 365th, 366th, 367th, 368th [black AEF units] and the French Artillery which was operating with us." "Each evening," Dyer reported, "details were loaded on the trucks and proceeded by darkest and most dangerous routes to some lonely forsaken woods where ammunition had been hidden & from there would haul the required kinds to the infantry or artillery." "The boys had many narrow escapes," he added, and "crawl[ed] in shell holes or a crack of any kind for safety from the Boche artillery." "It was no time for fulishness. It was a matter of life or death," wrote Company A's Corporal Blair, adding, "Live or die, I must do my best for my love ones & my Country." Captain Day and the other "old men"—brass whistles at hand so that they could be heard above the cacophony—provided solid, steady leadership and pulled their youngsters through without any loss of life, though the unit suffered numerous minor casualties.[79]

On September 22 the Train left Raon L'Étape, pressing on "through most desolate and forsaken country and were put off in a lonely, filthy, muddy woods very close to the front . . . in the Argonne Forest." "No accommodations whatever were here," Lieutenant Dyer recorded, "not even water to drink . . . and mud over shoe tops everywhere." There, wrote Dyer, "I heard the most terrific bombardment of the War. It began on the evening of Sept. 25th and kept up for thirty-six hours without a stop." "The old woods . . . trembled as if by earth quake, the flashes of the cannons lighted up the inside of our tents and our ears were deafened," he added. "As I lay on my bunk and listened to that furious battle just a few miles distant I thought, how fortunate am I, e'en though close, not to be in that conflict for I knew men were dying by the thousands." Confronted the next day with death's stench, gruesome visage, and hollow silence, Day and Dyer looked on as "the dead were brought back on trucks, piled in like cordwood and dripping blood from head to foot."

Their convoy delivered armaments of all sorts to the front lines, and the next day, "the following bulletin from 92nd Division Head-quarters dated Sept. 26th 1918 was issued. 'Negro soldiers will be used to handle the Mustard gas cases because the Negro is less sus-ceptible than the whites.' " "Why is the Negro less susceptible?" Dyer angrily demanded. "No one can answer." In fact, almost seven hundred black soldiers suffered the grievous effects of mus-tard gas during their months in France.[80]

That September, the influenza pandemic spread out from port cities such as Brest and afflicted a total of 37,000 Yankee soldiers in France. Medics diagnosed 16,000 new cases during a single week, and the AEF suffered 9,000 flu-related deaths between September and November 1918. Some of the men, numbed by such miseries and disgusted with seemingly endemic bureaucratic fiascoes, quipped that AEF stood for "Ass End Forward," while others wryly opted for "After England Failed."[81]

On September 30, the 368th Infantry Regiment, supplied by the 317th Ammunition Train, was ordered to attack a hazardous strip of land north of St. Dié. One company performed admirably in that encounter, but two others succumbed to enemy pressure. In re-sponse, the army swiftly relieved thirty Negro commissioned offi-cers with the 368th of their commands. Five were court-martialed and convicted, with one sentenced to life imprisonment and four to death. The army placed full blame for the military setbacks on the black officers, with no mention of their inadequate training, poor strategic planning by white superiors, or the endemic lack of maps, wire cutters, grenades, and other crucial supplies. Units like the 369th Regiment excelled in combat and received kudos from the French, but many American critics categorically concluded that "colored" officers were incapable of leading troops into battle. "The negro as an officer is a failure," a white colonel bluntly asserted, "and this applies to all classes . . . whether from the Regular Army or from Officers' Training Camp."[82]

The Germans, however, called members of the 92nd Division *blutlustige Schwarzemänner* (bloodthirsty black men—"we were ferocious," the 366th's Simon Haley later told his son Alex), and disseminated crafty propaganda in an attempt to capitalize on the rampant abuses that they knew those soldiers encountered. Boche planes littered their campsites·with leaflets. "Hello boys, what are you doing over here?" they began: "Do you enjoy the same rights as white people do in America, the land of freedom and Democracy, or are you rather treated over there as second class citizens?" The pamphlets asked Negroes why they fought for Uncle Sam when they had been "made the tool of the egoistic and rapacious rich." "To carry a gun in this service is not an honor, but a shame," the seductive broadsides concluded: "Throw it away and come over to the German lines. You will find friends who will help you." Black Yanks with the 92nd Division surely could have used some "friends," but as much as any other AEF soldiers, they considered themselves—and served as—loyal Americans, and there were no significant desertions.[83]

On October 1, the ammo train arrived in Ste. Ménéhould, and Lieutenant Dyer and Captain Day shared a garret where "we could hear plainly the Artillery fire . . . and the explosions of German shells." Throughout the night, Lieutenant Dyer admitted, he was "scared stiff and expecting to be blown to atoms at any moment." The next day, they "overlook[ed] the Great Forrest in which a battle was raging and . . . big guns were belching out their death notes from all hills round about." A vast cemetery was situated just two hundred yards from their billets. "Six-thousand French soldiers and one American woman, a Y.M.C.A worker, occupied this city of the dead," Dyer wrote. "The crosses on their graves," he added, were inscribed: "Repose ici Soldat Francis Mort pour la Tarre."

The new technology and powerful armaments—machine guns, potent "Jack Johnson" shells, flamethrowers, mustard gas, armored tanks, airplanes and bombs—made obsolete most traditional strategies and weapons of war.[84] Acknowledging those lethal innovations, Lieutenant James Europe and his all-black "Hell Fighters" band of the 369th Infantry Regiment captured their exploits with a ragtime beat. In October 1918, Lieutenant Europe composed a song from his hospital bed as he was recuperating (although the army deemed Negroes "less susceptible") from a gas attack. With Sergeant Noble Sissle singing the lead, it evoked the pride and fears of soldiers who endured the horrors of war in the words of a Negro officer who hissed and whispered sharp commands as he led his men into the fray: "Fall in line / All right, boys, now take it slow. / Are you ready? Steady! / Very good, Eddie, / Over the top, let's go! / Quiet, lie it, else you start a riot, / Keep your proper distance, follow 'long. / Obey my orders and you won't go wrong."

When Lieutenant Europe's band performed that number, the chorus featured his musicians replicating (with their voices, stomping feet, and instruments) the staccato throb of machine-gun fire, the buzz and hiss of grenades, and ear-shattering mortar explosions.

> *There's a minnenwerfer coming—Look out! (bang!)*
> *Hear that roar (bang!). There's one more (bang!) . . .*
> *Don't start bombin' with those hand grenades (rat-a-tat-tat!)*
> *There's a machine gun! Holy spades!*
> *Alert! Gas! Put on your mask.*
> *Adjust it correctly, hurry up fast.*
> *Drop! There's a rocket from the Boche barrage!*
> *Down! Hug the ground, close as you can.*
> *Don't stand! Creep and crawl. Follow me, that's all.*[85]

"While stationed at Saint Menehould" that fearsome October of 1918, Lieutenant Dyer reported, "the Ammunition Train was busy night and day supplying our infantry and the French Artillery who were in terrible daily conflict." And as Captain Day and his troops slogged through perilous northeast France, his would-be nemesis Carter Woodson (safe on the home front) sought financial support for a proposed definitive history of Negroes with the AEF.[86]

Leaving Ste. Ménéhould, Captain Day's company "passed through the Ste. Mihiel sector where last July, the Germans had attempted their terrible and supposedly final drive and where the Americans met them and turned them back," Lieutenant Dyer wrote. "In many of the towns through which we passed," he added, "not one house was standing whole, . . . not a woman or child to be seen, and the towns were occupied by French (Senegalese) or Americans."

Not far from St. Mihiel, Henry Ossawa Tanner worked with a cadre of convalescent soldiers. Tanner, a virtuoso painter, was a light-skinned Negro who had left the United States for France years earlier when he married a white woman, so that they would not be harassed. Still, he confessed, "Deep in my heart, I love America." Though too old for active duty, he wanted to help his country's war efforts, and negotiated an assignment to the Red Cross as a lieutenant in the AEF's Farm Service Bureau. During the war, his team raised vegetables on vacant lands around military hospitals. Tanner, however, clearly did not reveal his full racial identity that October of 1918 when he attended a "rather gay dinner" where a scornful but prophetic "Capt. R——," said concerning the company he commanded, "We will have to kill several of those niggers . . . before we will be able to get them back in their place." Tanner rarely was outspoken, preferring to let his art eloquently speak for him, and one of the works he painted that autumn showed a uniformed Negro serving with the AEF standing outside, wistfully staring into a cheerful Red Cross canteen where warm, comfortable white soldiers received rations and sympathetic attention from white female volunteers.[87]

Passing the town of Commercy in a blinding downpour, the equally unwelcome men of the 317th Train's motorized battalion could not stop, but had to drive on through the inky night of October 27, with Dyer perched out "on an open truck helping the driver watch the road to prevent running over an embankment, which would probably have meant death." Near dawn, the soaked, weary unit reached the "dreary little village" of Belleville, where, Dyer stated, "the Ammunition Train was put to work . . . supplying our infantries and Artillery." The troops that they supplied in those weeks "made an envious record and were termed by French authorities the best Artillery . . . in that area."

"During the whole month of October," reported Dyer, who, like many Yanks, sensed that the war's end was imminent, "we labored on, hearing much talk of peace, and were very anxious for the final drive which would end forever Autocracy and give Democracy the right to reign." On November 8, Colonel Allen Greer prepared an encouraging memo for his Negro officers asserting that "the enemy . . . regards the 92nd Division as an uncomfortable neighbor, and intends to avoid close relations in the future." He also requested that "unit commanders will promptly submit reports of all specially meritorious actions of officers or enlisted men, in order that the same may be appropriately recognized."[88]

A year later, in his history (assisted by Carter Woodson) of Negroes in the great war, Emmett Scott added, "In this last battle . . . the non-combatant units [including] the 317th Ammunition Train under the command of a colored major, Maj. Milton T. Dean, . . . must not be overlooked." "Distributing the many tons of ammunition along the route of the advance and moving it up to the American combatants in this final drive," Scott continued, "was a big task but it was well done by a colored ammunition train."[89]

The black soldiers at Belleville, however, would not see the war's long-awaited conclusion before they experienced yet another sobering episode. The very day of Greer's memo, "a colored boy who had been convicted of rape in August, was hanged or lynched in an open field not far from my infirmary," wrote Lieutenant Dyer. "The execution was a military order," he added, "but so openly and poorly carried out that it was rightly termed a lynching."[90]

That hanging must have evoked dismal memories of home for Day and his cohorts. Men in the 92nd often were casually accused of rape, and the 317th's Corporal Blair complained that his white officers exhibited far "to much Pregesty." Colonel Greer, who (exaggeratedly) reported thirty sexual attacks, labeled the 92nd the "rapist division," and scoffed that the men "have, in fact, been dangerous to no one except themselves and women." Reckless accusations abounded, but just five of the 200,000 92nd Division soldiers ultimately were convicted of assault with intent to rape, and only one convicted of rape itself. Greer charged that "colored officers neither control nor care to control the men, [because] they themselves have been engaged largely in the pursuit of French women." But what Greer would not acknowledge was that the 92nd's single convicted rapist (whose execution Day and Dyer observed) had served with a unit commanded by white commissioned officers.[91]

The morning after that hanging, the 317th Ammunition Train, along with many other units, embarked on "the final drive towards Metz." "While the terrific drive was still going on," said Lieutenant Dyer, "the first official news reached us that Germany had signed the Armistice." At the designated eleventh hour of the eleventh day of the eleventh month of 1918, guns mercifully fell silent along the Western Front, while, Dyer added, "bells rang, whistles blew, men, women and children shouted for joy at the ending of the World's greatest conflict and the winning of the right." A few miles south, an exuberant sergeant with Lieutenant Jim Europe's unit remembered that "the sun was shining and we were marching and the band was playing and everybody's head high and we were all proud to be Americans, proud to be black."[92]

In recognition of their service, many Negro soldiers, like those with Lieutenant Europe's 369th Infantry Regiment, received medals from the grateful French (some black AEF units had been attached to the French army because the United States did not consider the men able or brave enough for combat duty) and, more reluctantly, from their own country. Such, however, was not the case with the conscientious and effective, but unacclaimed and undecorated, 317th Ammunition Train. Concerning the contributions of his regiment (the 369th) and many other blacks to the war effort, Sergeant Noble Sissle wrote: "Every Hun son of a gun / We mowed them down at Verdun / We stacked them in the fields of Lorraine / And every time they tried to come / We slaughtered them at the Somme / So to hell with Germany."[93]

African American soldiers and officers had been cherished and lauded by the French, but their own superiors exhibited mixed responses to them. A week after the armistice, at the direction of General Charles Ballou (the 92nd's commander), Colonel Greer dispatched a memo to his "colored" officers. "His work is done and will endure," but, Greer warned, "the results have not always been brilliant, and many times were discouraging." Nonetheless, he continued, "a well organized, well disciplined, and well trained colored Division has been created and commanded by him to include the last shot of the great war."[94]

Shortly after the armistice, Tuskegee Institute's R. R. Moton went to France at the War Department's behest. He made a special point of visiting the 317th Ammunition Train because of its achievements and high percentage of black officers. "The record you have made in this war, of faithfulness, bravery and loyalty," he told them on December 16, "deepened my faith in you as men and as soldiers, as well as in my race and country." "You will go back to America heroes, as you really are," Moton added. He further urged the men to find work and "settle down," but cautioned, "I hope no one will do anything to spoil the magnificent record you have made in war." Moton's repeated pleas for restraint and perseverance so enraged a few black soldiers in another unit that they reportedly hatched a barely thwarted plot to assassinate him.[95]

A couple of days later, Day's company "was ordered to hike thirty kilometers . . . to entrain for a rest camp preparatory to sailing for home." At the end of that trek, they located their billets in a field hospital "covered with tar paper with dirt floors and no heating apparatus of any kind." "Poor Algerian soldiers who knew nothing of sanitation and were dirty, ragged and half starved" occupied the facility, Dyer recalled, and the North Africans' condition in that "horrid" place made the weary African Americans grateful for a few material blessings.

Finally, they hooked up with the evacuation railroad cars, on which officers and enlisted men were crammed "into one little compartment . . . unable to stretch out even at night." "The old coach leaked, which to-gether with the cold added to our misery," Dyer wrote as they bypassed Paris. On December 24, 1918, without stars to guide them, the grimy, chilled, and unheralded Negro sojourners detrained near midnight at the old town of Domfront.

As Aaron Day sought quarters for his bone-tired pilgrims, Lieutenant Dyer respectfully watched Domfront's devout Catholic women "coming back from Church . . . that Christmas morning in the rain and snow, and while I stood there shivering with cold, the truth of a text came to me, 'Foxes have holes and the fowls of the air have nests, but the son of Man hath no where to lay his head.' " "Finally," Dyer continued, "through persistent efforts of our Captain [Day], our building was located and we moved in."

"The narrow and tortuous streets, the gabled houses whose stories are supported by pillars and arcades constructed of marble, give [Domfront] an aspect of a city of the Middle Ages," observed Dyer. On the first peaceful yuletide that Europe had known for five years, he added, "the people . . . showed us the greatest hospitality." The ammo train's commissioned officers (thirty-one Negroes and three white men) posed in the courtyard of the lace-curtained Vieux Manoir de Chaponnais for a local photographer named Giraud. The exhausted Americans were erect, their tan uniforms immaculately pressed, boots spit-polished and crossed-cannon brass insignia gleaming on their collars. Though most had on their "fore-and-aft" overseas caps, Captain Aaron Day, wearing his "saucer," stood at the upper left, with Lieutenant William Dyer in the center of the second row. The recently promoted Milton Dean, one of the army's finest officers and one of its handful of Negro majors, sat in front. Monsieur Giraud preserved the occasion, developed his prints, and mounted Captain Day's copy of the 1918 Christmas portrait on a cardboard mat bordered with ornate depictions of the ancient artifacts of war, featuring the ever-resonant words "*HONNEUR*" and "*PATRIE*."[96]

Following the armistice, the army denied most Negro officers the opportunities it granted whites of the same ranks to enroll in courses at European universities. Nor were they permitted to march in the huge Allied victory parade in Paris, although the black and brown colonial soldiers who fought with French and British forces appeared prominently. But military bands such as Lieutenant Jim Europe's played throughout the liberated country and introduced *le jazz* to France, launching a love affair that could not be quelled. The mournful blues and exuberant ragtime, with their deep-seated African roots, had given birth to jazz, which black Americans inspiringly nurtured. That magnetic, improvisational music had welled up from the Delta, ratcheted north along the Mississippi, over-flowed its banks and levees, spread throughout the country, then jubilantly leapfrogged the ocean during the Great War when African American soldiers first were called "Jazz Boes." "Jim [Europe] and I have P[aris] by the balls in a bigger way than anyone you know," Sergeant Noble Sissle exulted.[97]

Amid that torrid romance, W. E. B. Du Bois, editor of *Crisis* and a godfather of the Circle for Negro War Relief, had landed in Brest on December 9. He acquired a pass to meet with Negro soldiers, started collecting material for a proposed magnum opus to be titled "The Wounded World," and formulated plans for a Pan-African Congress that might shape debate on the future of colonialism after the Great War. "This war is an End, and also a Beginning," Du Bois wrote, "Never again will darker people of the world occupy just the place they have before." A valued companion during his ventures that winter in France was Ida Gibbs Hunt, the college-educated daughter of one Negro diplomat and the wife of another. The multilingual Ida Hunt resided in St. Étienne (between interludes at her home in Washington, D.C.) in central France with her husband William Henry Hunt, the U.S. consul general in that city, who often served as a valued wartime liaison to top-ranking French military and civilian officials.[98]

Du Bois's perambulations brought him to Domfront in January, and "officers of the Ammunition Train . . . met him at the leading café in the town where we drank and told him of our experiences," Dyer reported. Dyer, Day, and others "called on [Du Bois] for a speech." Unlike R. R. Moton, however, the more controversial Du Bois "had to decline, saying that he was under strict censorship and could not make any addresses but . . . would have plenty to say when he returned to the United States."

Combat bonuses ceased around that time, the ammo train's officers were returned to their prewar pay levels, and the Spanish flu that he so often had treated when it struck others caught up with Lieutenant Dyer.[99] After a week-long hospitalization, he recovered in time to head on with his unit to the "delousing station" at Le Mans where the men stripped off their infested uniforms, then, Dyer wrote, "entered a large well heated room with showers, plenty of soap and disinfectants." "When the bath was over they filed into adjoining rooms where new supplies of clothing was issued them and when they finally emerged from the building," he added, "they were wearing a complete new outfit." Reuniformed and "cootie"-free, they relocated to new quarters, awaiting orders "to go to the port of Embarkation."

Early in February, the men of the Ammunition Train (officers included, "for the purposes of maintaining better discipline") boarded packed boxcars. Despite their discomfort, "all night and practically all of the next day we traveled, the boys yelling and cheering at the French people and receiving their greetings in return," said Dyer. They finally reached Brest, where "the raw wind off the Ocean penetrat[ed] to the marrow," and the weeks there were miserable "due to poor sanitary conditions, the rain & mud, overcrowding & badly prepared food." Addie Hunton, one of a very few Negro women with the AEF, reported that at least fifty thousand "colored" soldiers passed through that port.[100]

On February 21, 1919, the ammo train received orders to "march to the docks for embarkation early next morning." The day started with a three o'clock reveille, and by six A.M. all columns were underway. "How silent they marched along," Dyer observed, "without a song or a cheer from any of them, it reminded me more of a funeral procession than a group of soldiers, light hearted and happy at their journey home." Their silence, however, hardly was voluntary, "for we would gladly have sung and cheered but Military Orders had been issued . . . that if any disorder existed in the ranks, or if the packs were not uniformly rolled, guns & shoes polished, or if in any way we made an unfavorable appearance, we would be sent back to camp and detained indefinitely." "The order was obeyed to the letter," Dyer reported, and as the muted soldiers filed down toward the harbor, they sighted the RMS *Aquitania* anchored about a mile at sea. As soon as the men assembled near the docks, Dyer added, "we began loading onto small barges and were carried out to the magnificent ship." Others were not so fortunate. After one company of Negro troops completely loaded the vessel on which they were scheduled to depart, a white officer issued orders that he absolutely would not sail with a shipload of black men, and the despondent soldiers had to return to their encampment.[101]

On February 22, however, the ocean liner promising the 317th's deliverance prepared to start west across the Atlantic, and the men bid France a bittersweet *à bientôt*. "The Aquitania," wrote Lieutenant Dyer, "is an immense passenger ship nine hundred and seven feet long and so spacious that it reminded me of a modern Hotel floating on the water." It had accommodations for four thousand passengers and a thousand in crew. Dyer settled into his stateroom and "was in the bath tub about 4:20 P.M. [when] I realized that we had put out to sea." Negro officers with the 317th had their own separate dining table, where "British waiters in full dress suits" served them "sumptuous" meals—despite Dyer's attack of *mal de mer*. His nausea soon abated, and though "the ocean was very rough, . . . the Aquitania was so large that the waves did not make any appreciable difference as she ploughed on leaving in her path a mass of seething foam."

Dr. Dyer attended to both military and civilian passengers stricken with influenza. One patient even died. Compared to the grim voyage eight months earlier, however, the return was festive: "The ship was brilliantly illuminated and every thing was gay." In February 1919, the homeward-bound Captain Aaron Day traversed the Atlantic for a second time, under circumstances quite unlike those once endured by his shackled "Molaglaskan" ancestors, who also had been transported westward and somehow survived the egregious Middle Passage more than a century before. The 366th Infantry band—all of them, similarly, the descendants of America's slaves—"gave concerts quite to the delight of the passengers." Then on February 28, 1919, Dyer exulted, "we spied the shores of the U.S.A." "As we pulled into New York harbor," he wrote, "delegations aboard small vessels came out to meet us, cheering and waving as we passed." "About 9:25 A.M.," the joyous Lieutenant Dyer recounted, "[we] again put our feet on American soil."

From the Hoboken docks, the returnees were transported to Long Island's Camp Upton, where a cameraman photographed the 116 men and 3 commissioned officers of "Company B: 317th Ammunition Train, A.E.F., Capt. Aaron Day, Jr. Commanding." The proud Yanks stood or sat in front of bleak jerry-built shacks. Many carried their "thirty-ought-six"-calibre Remington-Enfield rifles, and more than a dozen displayed chevron wound stripes above their left cuffs. "JUST BACK FROM FRANCE," reads the caption, and Captain Day (uniformed, solemn, and every inch the steadfast and responsible leader) appeared with his men, front and center.[102]

On March 5, while they remained at Upton, "M. T. Dean, Major, . . . Commanding" distributed a warm, circular letter. "Before the hour itself arrives that I shall shake your many hands and bid you God speed and an au revoir," said Dean:

> I wish to express . . . my appreciation of the . . . service rendered the Government at home and before the enemy across the seas . . . by each officer and enlisted man of the 317th Ammunition Train, 92nd Division; and also to testify to the excellent qualities of young manhood achieved by you during this period, November 1, 1917, to March 4, 1919, eight months of which time was spent in active service in France.

Major Dean lauded his men's "intelligence, attention to duty, unselfishness, sobriety, excellent character, modesty, [and] enviable record of no general courts-martial, either among the enlisted or commissioned personnel." "Every task required of you," he continued, "no matter where, when or how, . . . night or day, behind the lines, or before the enemy under his murderous shell fire, you have nobly responded and efficiently executed the required orders." "I feel assured," he optimistically added, that "such efficiency, dependability, conscientious performance of duty . . . will carry into your civil pursuits and there [you will] overcome, as you did here, the myriad of obstacles which lie before each man." "Do not let us forget," Dean concluded, "those brave souls which the toll of war demanded we lay to rest amid the sacred spirits and in the soil of that land of Liberte, Egalite and Fraternite, from which we have just returned."[103]

No courts-martial or inefficiency charges marred the 317th Ammunition Train's record with the AEF. As for the 92nd Division in its entirety, perhaps the black officers and men performed better than anyone should have expected. Nonetheless, the shortcomings of a few poorly trained, poorly led, poorly equipped units unjustly stamped the entire division a failure. Concerted efforts by the biased, hidebound white army brass meant that the division that had started with eighty-two percent black commissioned officers ended up with only fifty-eight percent. Unlike most white soldiers, the men of the 92nd did not experience an unequivocally joyful welcome home. Many believed they had been humiliated, and branded cowards or misfits.[104]

Amid such controversies, the army honorably discharged Captain Aaron Day, Jr., from active duty (Camp Zachary Taylor, Kentucky, was the 317th's central demobilization point, but Day was separated on March 17, 1919, at Camp Bowie, Texas) and sent him and his men along their separate ways.[105] He soon obtained a commission with the army reserves, but that March ended almost two frustrating, challenging, perilous yet perhaps rewarding years for Captain Day, serving his country at home and abroad.

What many Americans called the War to End All Wars was over, democracy presumably had prevailed, and Aaron returned to the Lone Star State. The Liberty *Vindicator* exhorted local citizens to buy Victory Bonds, calling such purchases a "real test of Americanism," and the town acquired a "captured German cannon, which we can set up upon our court house square." Residents organized a county-wide barbecue featuring a speech by one white man about his "experience as an over-seas soldier," while the paper saluted another boy who "died with his face to the enemy." The Red Cross assured his grieving parents that "such an account . . . cannot fail to cause you the greatest pride and joy in his manner of meeting death." The *Vindicator* recognized a few "colored" privates but could not bring itself even to acknowledge Captain Aaron Day, Jr. (a grandson of Dayton's founding father and the former slave whom he reportedly had slain four decades earlier), who had been Liberty County's ranking AEF officer.[106]

As soldiers returned home throughout that first year of peace, lynchings in the United States increased. At least ten victims were uniformed black veterans who were "lynched for the usual"— meaning suspicion of rape. A southern senator warned that the "French-women-ruined negro soldiers [must] understand that they are under surveillance." On two occasions, white men (with no provocation) assaulted Negroes in Dayton and Liberty. Zealots attacked a white NAACP "troublemaker" in Austin, Texas, and the deadly, racially provoked riots in nearby Longview resembled those in major cities such as Chicago and the nation's capital.[107] Those ugly incidents exposed the roiling anger of whites at a time when African Americans who had put their lives on the line in defense of their country expected (even demanded) to be treated as citizens and equals back home.

Two years earlier, Du Bois had urged Negro Americans to "Close Ranks" as his country entered the Great War, but in spring 1919 he proclaimed: "Make Way for Democracy! We saved it in France, and by the Great Jehovah, we will save it in America, or know the reason why."[108] Race leaders began talking about the "New Negro," and many black veterans and civilians had lost their innocence and illusions, acquired new gumption, new pride, and a greater sense of self-awareness and race consciousness than they had known in 1917. "What does the Negro want?" an essayist asked rhetorically in September 1919: "He wants every right and privilege guaranteed to every American citizen by the Declaration of Independence and the Constitution of the United States."[109]

The serious and mature Carrie Bond whom Aaron Day, Jr., had encountered through the Circle for Negro War Relief graduated from Radcliffe College and moved to New York City shortly after he arrived home from France, and by the time Aaron returned to teach chemistry again at Prairie View that tumultuous autumn of 1919, his school had a new principal. The SATC still flourished on campus and "opened a new opportunity for service to young Negroes as commissioned officers in the Army," another Prairie View professor reported.[110] Like many other men just back from the war, Aaron might have felt the yen to settle down that had been voiced by former Sergeant Noble Sissle and the late Lieutenant Jim Europe, who had survived the war—but not the peace:

Hello, dearie!
Yes, yes—this is me!
Just landed at the pier
And found the telephone
We've been parted for a year
Thank God at last I'm home!
Haven't time to talk a lot . . .
I've only time to say:
   I have come back home to you, my honey true.
   Wedding bells in Juney June,
   And all will tell by their tuney tune
   That vict'ry's won, the war is over,
   The whole wide world is wreathed in clover![111]

Aaron may have wooed Carrie Bond with telephone calls, cables, or letters expressing similar sentiments, and those two war-seasoned, war-weary individuals were no longer as far apart as they once had seemed. Both of them came from well-established families and belonged to the country's small, scattered community of the educated Negro upper-middle class. After his rural Texas beginnings, Aaron had honed his intellect at the University of Chicago. Two years in the military, including eight months in France and in battle, had sobered and sophisticated him.

From shortly after her 1919 graduation on into the next year, Carrie remained in New York employed by the national YWCA. She then took time off (not in "Juney June" but late in February) and traveled to Texas to reunite with Captain Day.

Carrie Bond must have known that she had not been the only woman in Aaron's life. In addition to Ethel Scott, at least one other former sweetheart believed that he would marry her after the war. Aaron Day, Jr., was known as "quite a lady's man"; nonetheless, he deeply respected and cared for his Carrie.[112] Similarly, he had not been the only person who pursued her. An eligible gentleman from Montclair, New Jersey, courted Carrie Bond after the war. He was a widower named Harrison Tate, an engaging postal service employee whose late wife Laura had been one of the founders of

Montclair's YWCA. Harrison Tate had admired Carrie from the period when she served as the YW's director in his hometown. During the 1918 influenza pandemic that took the lives of half a million Americans and ten million people worldwide, Laura Tate and her brother, tragically, had both died on the same day. A year later, however, Carrie Bond did not see herself as the woman to console Harrison Tate and take him as her life's companion, or to "tame the lion," as she wryly referred to her ardent suitor.[113]

One of Aaron Day's colleagues owned a new Ford, but roads around their country school were so abysmal that Captain Day probably had to board a Jim Crow railroad coach in nearby Hempstead, because Prairie View had no depot—or restaurant, hotel, or proper church. He traveled down to Houston, where, on March 1, 1920, Rev. C. K. Brown of the Trinity Methodist Episcopal Church married Aaron Day, Jr., to Miss Caroline Lucile Stewart Bond.[114]

After the Civil War, Trinity had become Houston's first independent Negro church when the white congregation bequeathed to the former slaves who always had worshiped there the modest frame structure right behind their own. Black parishioners loaded up and carted the old building to another site ("the most valuable piece of real estate owned by any [Negro] denomination or society in the State, if not the entire South," a local account claimed) in an area called Freedmantown. They enlarged the existing edifice, and "new" Trinity, with its Gothic-arched windows, intricate wooden carvings, and lofty turrets, became the "mother of other Methodist Episcopal churches in the city," and the "silk stocking" house of worship frequented by many successful Negro Houstonians. Carrie cherished her stepfather's Episcopal Church, but absent that "elite" denomination's local availability, she would have settled for nothing less than "colored" Houston's most esteemed substitute as the site for her nuptials.[115]

The uncommon pattern of Carrie and Aaron's marriage began that March as it would continue, with a brief time spent together followed by a far longer period apart. Their mutual affection was solid and deep, but over the ensuing twenty-eight years, separations exceeded their time together. Shortly after the wedding, Carrie Bond Day returned to her YWCA work in New York and spent a considerable interval at the residence of W. E. B. and Nina Du Bois. She finally rejoined her husband for a visit to Washington, D.C., and from there, the capital city's "colored" newspaper reported in late July, "Captain and Mrs. Aaron Day, Jr. returned to their home in Dayton, Tex. after having been the honored guests of [Carrie's parents] Mr. and Mrs. J. P. Bond."[116] Carrie secured a job for the 1920–21 school year as dean of women at Paul Quinn College, an AME institution founded in 1881 and located in Waco.

Paul Quinn's student body barely topped three hundred, while the all-black faculty, led by Principal J. K. Williams, numbered only fifteen. It was known more for the bounteous agricultural production that helped keep the school financially afloat than for its academics. Nonetheless, Paul Quinn trained a number of Negro teachers and was "regarded by the best people of Waco . . . as a potent factor in the uplift of the race."[117] Aaron Day, meanwhile, remained 125 miles to the southeast at Prairie View.

The next fall, Carrie negotiated a transfer to Aaron's school, where she headed the English Department. The following year, she may have acquired a teaching position at her alma mater (Atlanta University) first, or, perhaps Aaron, who had proven himself a leader during the Great War, initiated their move to Georgia when he decided that he was dissatisfied in academia, where no black college could adequately remunerate him. The prestige attached to his rare captaincy in the U.S. Army gave him a few more occupational opportunities, and his father-in-law J. Percy Bond provided the contacts Aaron needed to obtain a job in the world of Negro insurance.[118] In autumn 1922, as he and Carrie headed east to Atlanta, Aaron left behind the unquiet spirits of Captain Isaiah Day, Amanda Cribbs, and his mother's often-evoked "Molaglaskan" forebears; nurturing parents, a sister and brother, peripheral relatives; and thirty-one years of contradictory experience in and around Liberty County and Prairie View, Texas.

CAPITAL TIMES:
"A PARADISE *of* PARADOXES"

Gran, am I not American? . . .
In your veins is a mixed tide:
Irish, English, Dutch, beside
Just a little touch of the Jew,
to teach ancient pain to you.
Granpa . . . showed me how alone
this America has grown,
Fairest champion of Truth the world has known;
How the people of all lands
Have fared forth from many strands.
Black, brown, palest-faced sons and daughters,
Dared the Seven Seas threatening waters. . . .
That is what it means to be
Of America, the free.
Thanks, dear Gran. My, it certainly feels good
To know I'm that—American!

JESSIE FAUSET, *The Brownies' Book,* 1920

CAPTAIN AARON DAY, JR., and Carrie Stewart Bond served
their country wisely and well during the Great War, while her stepfather Percy had joined thousands of African Americans, propelled
from the Deep South by racial hostility and adverse economic conditions, who streamed into the nation's capital. The *Bee,* the journalistic voice of "colored" Washington, reported in July 1916 that
"Mr. J. Percy Bond of Alabama is expected . . . to take up the work
of establishing a Standard Life Insurance [branch] in this city." By

the time Percy opened Standard's new offices in the 1100 block of U Street, Northwest—the city's premier corridor for Negro commerce—his company was profitable, expanding, and basking in its success.[1]

Despite a continuing influx of black people, the capital's demographic changes did not compare to those in many northern and midwestern urban centers. From 1910 to 1920 (especially during the war years when it briefly topped half a million), Washington's population mushroomed from 330,000 to 440,000 as Negroes increased from fewer than 95,000 to nearly 110,000, but their share of the total actually dropped a bit. Their percentage in the District of Columbia remained greater than in any other of the country's largest cities, but no tidal waves of black rural southerners engulfed the preestablished "colored" population, and white people had little valid reason to fear submersion in a newly blackened metropolis.[2]

Recounting her roughly concurrent arrival at Washington's Union Station, a Negro newcomer exclaimed: "When you looked up at the ceiling, you knew you were North! . . . the ceiling so tall and beautiful with gold all over it. I just knew that gold was going to fall into my hands!" But it never did, and "North" was only relative, because in many ways the nation's capital remained a southern town. Like Percy Bond, that woman walked outside onto "streets wide, wide, wide." The wedding-cake capitol dome shimmered ahead as she exited the depot, but soon, she glumly added, "things started to not look as nice as you saw more colored people." Percy had moved to Washington seeking an improved quality of life for his family, as well as "more colored people" who needed and could afford to buy insurance policies. Still, his "gold" might prove even harder to glean than that which lavishly gilded the station's coffered ceiling.[3]

Percy's wife Georgia and the younger children, Wenonah and Jack, followed a few months later, while Carrie became a frequent visitor to her family's new hometown, where she already knew some and soon befriended others among the city's bevy of Negro intellectuals. The community of which the Bonds became a part, however, remained (according to *Crisis* magazine) a "Secret City,"

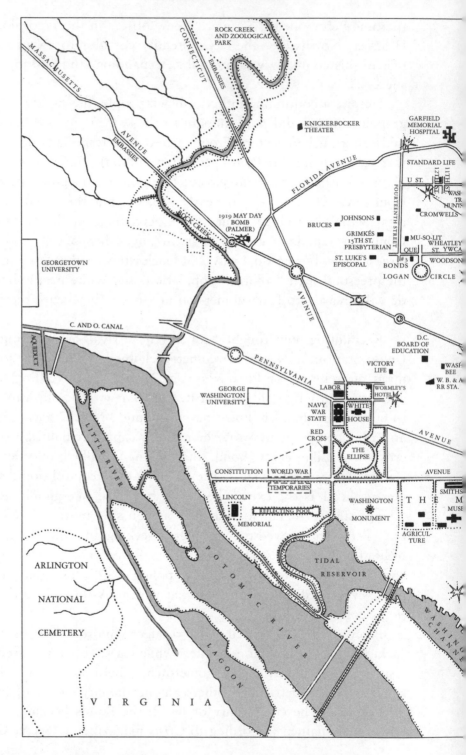

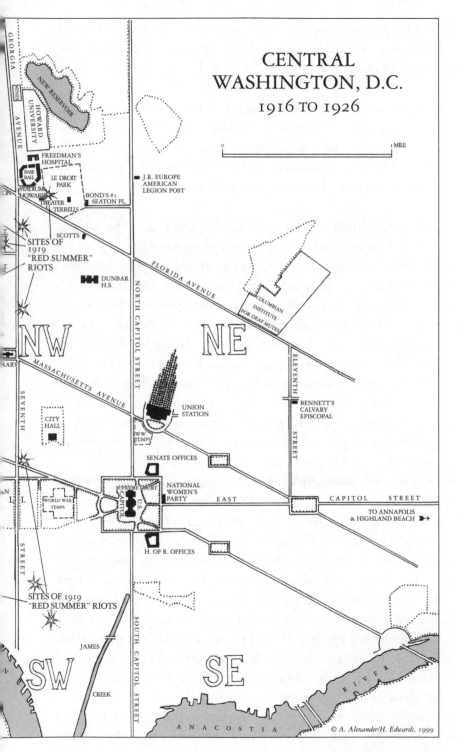

little known to residents of the white metropolis that surrounded but declined to embrace it.[4] Their terra incognita, an observant "colored" Washingtonian explained, included:

> hundreds of men in the professions, a growing number in large business enterprises, prosperous banks, insurance companies, newspaper and printing establishments, theaters, real estate, drug stores, etc., a large and cultured intellectual class and a great mass of laboring people, the bone and sinew of any state.

"Our people are grouped in . . . organizations and clubs," he added, "some for social service, others for self improvement."[5]

The Bonds' first house in the nation's capital (on Seaton Place, in a neighborhood near Howard University called Le Droit Park) had been confiscated from some German nationals as the United States entered the Great War. Eleven-year-old Wenonah was relieved that they had secured such a pleasant domicile in the war-clogged city. She also, however, felt profound conflicts, knowing that another family, perhaps much like her own, had been ousted from their residence because they were German-born aliens, and the federal government—yielding to the virulence of "spy fever"—had deprived them of rights and property when, almost overnight, they became seditious "Krauts," and "the enemy."[6]

Wartime house hunting in Washington was arduous for anyone, but homes available to African Americans already had been limited by statutes barring them from many of the nicer neighborhoods. That was true even for distinguished, well-to-do Negroes such as federal judge Robert Terrell and his wife Mary (an acquaintance of Georgia Bond from her Tuskegee years and women's club activities, as well as one of Carrie's Delta Sigma Theta sorority sisters), who had faced continuing rebuffs in their own search for a new home—for which they ultimately had to pay a good deal more than the listed price. On that occasion, Mary Church Terrell observed that "African blood is truly a luxury in the United States for which those who show or acknowledge it pay dearly."[7]

For Georgia Bond, the light-complexioned Terrells, and others like them, their "drop of African blood" seemed to symbolize the irrationality of racial discrimination, but it also became a badge of pride and identity that bound the Negro "elite" to others of their socially and legally defined race. The J. Percy Bonds encountered racial barriers as well as they shuttled from Seaton Place to Thirteenth Street before settling into a gracious four-story brick home at 1316 Que Street, Northwest (a "good" address, around the corner from Logan Circle's splendid mansions), that satisfied Georgia's lofty expectations.[8]

The nation was shuffling down the road to war as the Bonds arrived in Washington. In 1917, the War Department appointed Tuskegee Institute's Emmett Scott as a special assistant to the secretary, while the Department of Labor placed George Haynes, cofounder of the National Urban League, in a position of responsibility as head of a new Division of Negro Economics. Haynes's wife Elizabeth became a dollar-a-year employee and contributed to the first federal survey of black female workers.[9] As white men left old jobs and moved on to critical wartime occupations, employment opportunities sometimes opened up for Negroes (as well as women) that netted them higher wages than they had earned in peacetime. Despite increasingly inflexible barriers of discrimination in the public sector under President Woodrow Wilson's leadership, many African Americans thought that the war ultimately might prove beneficial to the race. Fighting for the United States, they believed (as they had believed during the Civil and Spanish-American Wars), surely would earn their white fellow citizens' respect.

Blacks, as well as a small cadre of white men, had tried to convince Wilson to reverse his segregationist course. His resolve only stiffened, however, when delegations led by Boston's Monroe Trotter demanded that the president treat African Americans more equitably. But such protests had to be tempered, because Negroes wanted and needed to take advantage of any possible government employment. "We are not supposed to complain," a frustrated Washingtonian wrote, "and the white community calls us 'radical' and even 'crazy' when we call attention to this fundamental injustice to the future citizens of the nation." During the Wilson years, the few government appointments that traditionally had been set aside for black people dwindled, and they knew that (with rare exceptions) race would keep them pinned down in the lowest grades of federal service. By the time their country entered the war, members of the capital city's "colored" upper class also understood that their economically sufficient lives and social standing within the segregated community would and should not separate them from their less well-situated brethren. As a rule, Washington's Negro Four Hundred, as some observers called them, did not want to be closely associated with the black lower class (any more than elite whites wanted to be associated with the riffraff of their race), but they were quick to defend the race as a whole, and race pride became a significant motivational factor in their lives.[10]

Washington's Howard University was Negro America's academic capstone and had a greater enrollment than all other historically black colleges combined. In spring 1917, black fraternities recruited men for the country's officers corps and Howard supplied three hundred candidates from its own students, graduates, and faculty. Several returned from the "colored" officers' training camp at Fort Des Moines, Iowa, to instruct the Student Army Training Corps (SATC), culled from seventy schools nationwide. Howard's coeds knit socks, scarves, and sweaters that they dispatched to American soldiers and sailors, often through the auspices of the Circle for Negro War Relief—led in the District of Columbia by the poet Georgia Douglas Johnson and in its New York headquarters by Carrie Bond. The young women drilled under cadet officers and formed an auxiliary branch (because white units refused to accept African American volunteers) of the Red Cross. During the Christmas holidays that year, Howard's SATC companies, accompanied by a marching band and a chorus of those college girls, proudly uniformed in khaki, sang *Victory* on the White House ellipse.[11]

When the United States declared war, two thousand "colored" Washingtonians gathered to protest "Discrimination in the Army and Navy," the *Bee* reported, but patriotic Negroes who joined a preparedness parade were "Jim Crowed with a vengeance," and then encountered the War Department's ignominious segregation orders. The initially projected exclusion of African American officers had deeply concerned them. "The South fear[s] that colored officers will outclass many a southern gentleman," the *Bee* protested.

"If white soldiers [are] inclined to be supercilious," it predicted, "the time will come when they will be mighty glad for the company of colored troops on the firing line." In response to complaints about blacks' supposedly limited capabilities and dubious loyalty, the paper angrily responded that it could not "recall one leader of American Negroes whose pacifism had led him into activities hostile or hampering to the government [or] one Negro arrested for sedition, treason, plotting sabotage." Even in the face of Wilson's racial bias, the *Bee* argued that in the nation's time of need, the president trusted the Negro man. "He is the only American the President of the United States will permit to prepare his meals," the paper contended in December 1917, adding (in an inadvertently humorous phrase that might have astonished the Wilsons) that it was only the black man whom "that noble and gracious lady in the White House will permit to dress her."[12]

The District of Columbia became increasingly segregated under Wilson's stewardship. The president already had phased out Negroes from many of their traditional appointments and long-standing civil service jobs. Further to divide the races, he ordered screens placed in government offices, where he also instituted newly separate "white" and "colored" toilets and lunchrooms. A saddened and bitter Washingtonian observed:

> There is not a theater, restaurant, or other place of public accommodation where a colored man or woman can go, and even in the government restaurants segregation or exclusion is attempted while equality in the civil service, a reasonable number of Federal appointments, and a decent respect for manly complaint against social wrongs are unthinkable.[13]

For the first time in a Washington courtroom, black people heard themselves called "darkies," and the *Bee* howled when the U.S. Senate restaurant (one of the few local eateries that had not followed a Jim Crow policy in the past) refused to serve Negroes.

The black community's newspaper voiced futile complaints that "the land cannot become safe for democracy unless our women are on the same basis with other women," and vigorously applauded an address by Eva Bowles, Carrie Bond's YWCA colleague, who spoke about "colored" women's centrality to the war efforts. An irate headline further charged, "Incompetent White War Workers Appointed in Preference to Competent Colored Girls."[14]

In that era, Washington's "colored" upper class, with the Terrells in the vanguard, embraced a number of Howard University's faculty and administrators, but when the trustees chose a new president in 1918, they brought in yet another white man, the Reverend J. Stanley Durkee. Among Howard's Negro leaders were Deans Kelly Miller and Lucy Slowe, the cantankerous Carter G. Woodson (for a few years), and Emmett Scott, who became the school's secretary-treasurer after he left the War Department in 1919. Another was Alain Locke, a Harvard Ph.D. like Woodson, Philosophy Department chair, and the nation's best-known black academic, who led the intellectual vanguard. Locke's 1925 anthology, *The New Negro*, would include the work of prodigies like Zora Neale Hurston, Langston Hughes, and E. Franklin Frazier.[15]

Even before the war's end, the Bonds also had been welcomed by the District's Negro elite. Intellectual, social, economic, civic, and (limited) political leadership shaped that circle, which, in addition to valid indicators of merit, was established and maintained according to distinct patterns of who knew, or was related to, whom. One acute observer saw it as a "most conscious community of American Negroes: The poets, the intellectuals, the scholars of . . . Howard University, the bureaucrats with government jobs." "They were aware of their ghetto," he added, "and their awareness corroded their instinctual relation with the Negro peasant . . . of the South."[16] Percy's training and occupation, dedication and respectability, New England roots and Episcopalianism, combined with Georgia's charms, pale complexion, and Fisk background, made the Bonds welcome in Washington's "colored" upper class, and from both Boston and Tuskegee, they already were well acquainted with some members of that group.

Those old friends included the likes of the Hyde Park–rooted Grimké family. Reverend Francis Grimké, a harsh critic of his nation's wartime discrimination, led the Fifteenth Street Presbyterian Church, a spiritual and social center for the "colored elite," while

Archibald headed the local NAACP and became vice president of the national organization.[17] Carrie Bond—Day, as of 1920—had been a Radcliffe schoolmate of Eva Dykes and Mary Gibson. And Dykes and Gibson, like Archie Grimké's daughter Angelina, taught at Paul Laurence Dunbar High School, the mecca of Negro public education. The Bonds knew Robert and Mary Terrell, the Emmett Scotts and Roscoe Bruces (the two latter families from Tuskegee Institute) as well. Since 1907, Roscoe Bruce had been Washington, D.C.'s assistant superintendent of schools for Negroes.

Percy Bond, along with Professor Alain Locke and twelve others, was elected to membership in Washington's esteemed Mu-So-Lit (*mu*sical, *so*cial, *lite*rary) Club in January 1918, an occasion when Emmett Scott addressed the group. Men such as Roscoe Bruce, W. E. B. Du Bois, and Archibald Grimké spoke at other meetings, and over the ensuing years the membership expanded to two hundred. Percy soon joined the Board of Governors, and in October 1919 that body convened at his home to discuss policies, programs, and purchases. "Mr. Bond invited the committee to sit at a most appetizing repast and continue the business of the evening," the minutes reported, and before leaving, the officers unanimously proffered a warm "round of thanks to Mr. and Mrs. Bond for the enjoyable evening spent at their residence."[18]

That all-male, almost exclusively Republican group, established in 1909, was unique among Negro organizations in that shortly after Percy joined, it bought a three-story clubhouse a block from the Bonds' home. The building included music, billiard, and dining rooms (the latter "furnished in beautiful mahogany and a large silver and china service"), a library, meeting hall for the Board of Governors, plus overnight accommodations for a caretaker and guests. The club's annual Lincoln-Douglass birthday celebrations and charity balls ranked well among "colored" Washington's social highlights. It hosted convocations of the intellectually elite American Negro Academy, lobbied for improved recreational facilities for the race, and advanced and supported the NAACP. It also encouraged unity within the upper class by welcoming as members (who already included the likes of Judge Robert Terrell and Frederick Douglass's progeny) men from many professions, different generations, longtime residents, and newcomers like Percy Bond. The *Bee* admitted that some people viewed the Mu-So-Lit and other such clubs as "idling halls for smokers and game players, as refuge for the near frivolous." But to the contrary, the paper insisted, "the greatest clearing house for great business deals is the American clubhouse." "No social agency," it concluded, "is more helpful, more beneficial and more necessary than a club of real gentlemen." That was the Mu-So-Lit's unblemished, patrician, and decidedly success-enhancing reputation.[19]

The Bonds attended Reverend F. I. A. Bennett's Calvary Episcopal Chapel in northeast Washington. They crossed town (though the larger St. Luke's Episcopal Church, "col'd.," was much nearer their home) to affiliate themselves with Bennett. His chapel "became a beacon light for the community, with its congregation always working for moral and social improvement." He presided over church rituals, accepted only the "finest of everything for the House of God," his successor insisted, and brought notably high standards to his services.[20]

Reverend Bennett, a Howard graduate, had launched Calvary in 1901. In 1909, it moved to a strikingly simple and handsome new brick edifice (that Bennett helped to design and even construct) at Eleventh and G Streets, Northeast. His ardent parishioners produced plays, started a kindergarten, and operated a public library branch to stimulate their literary interests. Aided by a supporter from the nearby Columbian Institute for Deaf Mutes (Gallaudet College), Bennett even initiated services for the hearing impaired. During the World War, a Department of Agriculture employee held classes in food conservation, and soon thereafter the elders commissioned and installed the majestic carving of an eagle (symbolizing universal dissemination of the gospel), dedicated to members of the congregation who recently had served their country in battle.[21]

The community esteemed Reverend Bennett, and his appointment in 1924 as one of the few Negro members on the District's Board of Education further enhanced his status, and Calvary's as well. On that occasion, Washington's *Evening Star* editorialized that "for a quarter of a century he has devoted his energies toward the crystallization of the higher forms of individual and community

life." It characterized F. I. A. Bennett as "a fluent speaker, an indefatigable worker [who] will demonstrate what can be done by one
who has no friends to reward and no enemies to punish."[22]

Elizabeth Bennett, the minister's daughter, was a great pal and
schoolmate of Wenonah Bond. The Bonds and Reverend Bennett,
his wife Zelie, and their two children often had dinner after Sunday
services ("there's always enough chicken to go around," Zelie Bennett promised), much as the Bonds had shared that meal with their
white pastor and his family in Selma. With eight of their own congregations in the capital city, however, a diocesan-wide "gentlemen's agreement" meant that dedicated Negro Episcopalians like
Percy Bond did not join, and rarely even attended, "white"
churches, where they would not have been welcomed socially or allowed to involve themselves in governance. The District's pulpits
provided superb platforms for eloquent spokesmen like Bennett and
the Presbyterian Reverend Francis Grimké, but by 1920, members
of Washington's Negro Four Hundred more often sought out secular arenas for their social reform inititives.[23]

Even during the melancholy (for African Americans) Wilson
years, the District's public transportation was nonsegregated, as
were libraries, museums, and a few other facilities; but schools,
restaurants, hospitals, hotels, and theaters were strictly Jim Crow.
One rare event from which Negroes had not been excluded or separated was the annual Easter Monday egg-rolling contest on the
White House lawn. For several hours, children of all classes, races,
and nationalities mingled, "all beaten up . . . in a social omelette
[while] eggs of every color are rolled back and forth," stated an enthusiastic account. "There are just as many shades, if not as many
colors, of skin as of egg shell," it concluded. Those eight Mondays
during his two terms in office seemed to comprise the entirety of
Woodrow Wilson's reluctant acquiescence to a minimally desegre-
gated capital city.[24]

Department stores accepted black people's money and trade,
but never allowed them to try on clothes, use rest rooms, or have a
drink, sandwich, or ice cream at their lunch counters. In response
to those rebuffs, and convinced of the potential for profit, Ware's
Department Store, owned and operated by African Americans,

opened in 1916 in a centrally located commercial district—yet some women among the fastidious Negro elite considered its facilities and merchandise second-rate.[25]

The specter of black suffrage had helped to kill early home rule, and since passage of the 1870s' Organic Acts, everyone in the District of Columbia had endured the disgrace of being denied any representation in Congress, even the right to cast ballots for president. Congressional committees, plus three presidentially appointed (white male) commissioners governed the city. In the world's greatest democracy, its handsome capital's residents enjoyed fewer citizenship rights than Americans who lived anyplace else in the country, while the darker-skinned minority faced the added insults of segregation. Through the war years, Washington had been spared lynchings and the Ku Klux Klan, but otherwise its Negroes were subject to most of the same degrading manifestations of discrimination imposed elsewhere in the South.

They nonetheless never abandoned hope, and, one man claimed, "long for the return of the Negro to the halls of congress where he belongs." Meanwhile, the capital city's leading white newspaper scolded local "colored" leaders for their continuing struggles to get "the ballot, . . . admission to theaters and restaurants, . . . public parks and other prerogatives," instead of benignly supporting vocational training schools for the race, like the Deep South's numerous and thriving "new Tuskegees."[26]

"At this very hour the ghost of slave power is stalking about seeking to perpetuate the aged master-and-slave scheme of society," a canny black man wrote, adding, "the more cultured and ambitious the Negro, the greater is the delight in humiliating him, and in forestalling his power." "Cultured and ambitious" people like the Bonds may have faced the brunt of those systemic and personal humiliations, but they also had some resources to help them circumvent and survive the worst assaults.[27]

Percy and Georgia Bond, like many other African Americans, deemed Washington's undemocratic trade-offs worthwhile, and one resident astutely characterized their city as "a paradise of paradoxes." Clearly, education (from the elementary level up to and including Howard University), though segregated, was the best available south of the Mason-Dixon line, if not anywhere in the country. Dean Kelly Miller confirmed that "Howard University and the public schools together center about the city of Washington the cream of the intelligentsia of the Negro race."[28]

The District also offered Negroes substantial business, social, and cultural opportunities. By the era of the Great War, the local NAACP, under Archibald Grimké's leadership, had become the largest branch in the country, and the J. Percy Bonds always belonged. In a town often splintered into disparate African American factions, "school teachers whom you would not believe cared for anything but pleasure, society women, [and] young men," the *Bee* reported, united in the NAACP's ongoing efforts to resist segregation and better their common lot.[29]

"Before this terrible war . . . we had grown tired of being told for many decades to be 'patient' a while longer," the *Bee* editorialized in 1919, adding, "We expect, with our returning colored heroes . . . the same kind of democracy which we were called upon to help establish in alien lands." But officials banned black soldiers from the capital's welcome-home parade, and they had to form separate units of the new patriotic fellowship, the American Legion. That year, some of Washington's five thousand African American war veterans named their Post No. 5 to commemorate the acclaimed District native Lieutenant James Reese Europe. A reluctant President Wilson met with Negro leaders, praised black soldiers' wartime patriotism, but cautioned the group against impatience. One White House visitor, however, responded: "I fear, Mr. President, before the negroes of this country again will submit to many of the injustices which we have suffered . . . the white man will have to kill more of them than the combined number of soldiers that were slain in the great world war."[30]

Some white men may have sought to make that a mission in a notably tumultuous year. The first postwar May Day brought threats of anarchy and a rash of "dynamite bombs" posted to the secretary of labor, the postmaster general, a Supreme Court justice, and other government leaders. A powerful explosive also gutted the home of Attorney General Mitchell Palmer, a sworn enemy of all "Reds," who lived less than a mile from the Bonds.[31]

As Washington's volatile summer of 1919 simmered, a couple of highly publicized sexual attacks roused whites to a contagious frenzy that soon focused on the Negro community in its entirety. The NAACP warned that "inflammatory headlines and sensational news stories" brought a perilous instability to the city, while a host of idle and cocky white servicemen meandered around Washington and contributed to the pervasive malaise.

One mid-July day, two black men snatched an umbrella from a white woman who fled screaming, then on Saturday the nineteenth the city exploded. Some white soldiers had gone to the city's heavily black Southwest quadrant to buy moonshine, had been scammed with a bottle of tea, then returned with their buddies bent on revenge. "Men in Uniform Attack Negroes," the next day's headlines read. The District's leading newspaper interpreted the resultant violence "as a climax to the assaults on white women." "A band of more than a hundred [white] soldiers, sailors and marines last night invaded the Southwest and beat several colored people," it continued, and "the race riot swept over Washington." The worst disturbances engulfed Southwest, but spread to Twelfth and U Streets, Ninth from P to R, Fourteenth and Florida, and Seventh and Pennsylvania Avenue, Northwest.[32]

Howard University's Carter Woodson was headed home via the latter thoroughfare, when, he later testified, "there ran by me a Negro yelling for mercy . . . pursued by hundreds of soldiers." He soon encountered another frenzied mob that "had caught a Negro and deliberately held him as one would a beef for slaughter, and when they had conveniently adjusted him for lynching they shot him." Woodson cowered in a doorway fully expecting to be lynched himself.

Savage outbursts erupted near the White House, central library, blocks from Percy Bond's residence and work, his children's school, and Howard. "If it had not been for the good work of police . . . who kept the large mobs from contact, the city would have been a shambles," the police chief boasted. Negroes in the District did not agree that the police acted either efficiently or equitably. Forty people altogether may have died, and eyewitnesses of both races confirmed that white men had initiated the riots, but only eight of the more than a hundred persons arrested during that time of troubles belonged to the majority race.[33]

A number of African Americans believed that acquiescence to such broad-gauged attacks was not an acceptable response. They armed themselves, fought back, even killed a few white marauders. "Colored" sharpshooters manned the roof of the Howard Theater while carloads of armed men cruised along Seventh Street. In a Sunday sermon, the Reverend Francis Grimké quoted a black woman who exclaimed that the "riot gave me a thrill that comes once in a lifetime." "The pent-up humiliation, grief and horror of a lifetime," she declared, "was being stripped from me." Many community leaders thought that their outrage had been properly expressed and duly heard, and convinced themselves that widespread, successful assaults on Jim Crow soon would be a possibility.[34]

The *Bee* stressed different aspects of the disturbances than those emphasized by the white press. "Innocent Colored Citizens Attacked . . . Pulled from Street Cars," its headlines read. One trolley rider barely escaped his rabid pursuers, who cried out, "Lynch him!" while a conductor drew a revolver and fired at him. "[A] crowd of white men attacked a black man on a bicycle," reported the *Bee*, and a Negro sniper took a bullet in the hip when police raided her house—but not before she had shot a white detective. It also related the account of a "colored young woman . . . caught in a white neighborhood by four white men." "She was forced to undress," the *Bee* continued, "and compelled to walk out of the neighborhood in a nude condition." "Not a police officer . . . could be found," that shameful story concluded. Only timely summer downpours combined with an intervention by U.S. Marines and mounted cavalry quelled the riots after four days.[35]

From his new position at Howard University, Emmett Scott issued a statement asserting that although white servicemen had started the riots, "white and colored citizens freely counseling together in the interest of law and order" negotiated an end to the disturbances. Proponents of the "New Negro" movement saw the community's aggressive responses to the assaults as indicative of a sea change in race relations. From New York, the NAACP's president claimed that Washington's African Americans had acted properly "in defense of their lives and homes," instead of retreating when faced with unprovoked attacks. The aftermath of those disruptions and white people's supposed shame concerning their roles, he overoptimistically prophesied, would "mark a turning point in the psychology of the whole nation regarding the Negro problem."[36] During the ensuing weeks, the NAACP and the *Bee* jointly exhorted Negro citizens that racial solidarity remained essential.

Following the District's riots (a key chapter in what the NAACP's James Weldon Johnson labeled the "Red Summer," his imagery evoking both the freely spilled blood and a burgeoning paranoia over perceived threats of anarchy and Bolshevism), the Labor Department's George Haynes analyzed the melees that disrupted and wounded many American cities—especially Washington. He acknowledged that the city's pervasive absence of interaction between the races created a distrustful, unstable ambience, then cited the negative contributions of reckless journalism. On the heels of the Great War, Haynes further held that the black man wanted and expected new respect: "His safety demands that he protect himself and his home." And, Haynes claimed, "everywhere one can hear [whites'] expressions of disgust at the expensive clothes of successful Negroes, their owning automobiles, etc." Many white Americans, he argued, would tolerate nothing but an indigent, docile, subservient "colored" populace. Finally, as a result of its role in the recent war, Haynes asserted, the United States had become a major world power and thereby came "face to face with the problem of dealing with the darker peoples of Asia, Africa, Central and South America." Those peoples, he insisted, would judge this country by the way it treated its own oppressed, dark-complexioned minorities. Issues concerning American Negroes (especially in the nation's capital) had acquired a global import, Haynes concluded, and no longer were strictly local or domestic issues.[37]

That same year, Washington's "colored" community slogged through a controversy that threatened the tenure of Percy Bond's old colleague Roscoe Bruce as assistant superintendent of education. The *Bee* labeled it "the Bruce imbroglio." The press and Bruce's subordinates often accused him of favoritism, inefficiency, even arrogance, and in 1915 he and several female teachers had been involved in a minor auto accident, marked by "excessive hilarity among a party of joy riders." The more serious 1919 scandal, however, erupted when local residents learned that a scientist from the Netherlands named Herman Moens (introduced to the District by W. E. B. Du Bois, the *Bee* charged, and recommended to Bruce by the Dutch embassy) had snapped nude photographs of Negro schoolchildren, ostensibly on the grounds of gathering anthropometric data. The notorious Dutch anthropologist also, reportedly, took "indecent" liberties with a black teacher. Those incidents generated protests in the streets and deep schisms within the school board, with the majority grudgingly supporting Bruce and labeling the stories about Moens "gross exaggerations"—although District police did bring criminal charges against him. The Negro community found itself deeply divided, with the *Bee* claiming that the ugly debacle summoned up Bruce's prior "moral delinquencies" as well as what it considered endemic decadence among the "upper tens." Many white people saw the whole brouhaha, especially the vociferous public demonstrations by black parents, as evidence of the emotionality, puerile behavior, and lack of probity supposedly characteristic of the darker race.[38]

Those opprobrious Caucasians would have been stunned to have heard Harvard's (thoroughly reputable) anthropologist Earnest Hooton elucidating select New England audiences on the subject of "elite" Negro Washingtonians' sophisticated culture—about which the District's white majority knew (or cared) almost nothing. Hooton had learned a good deal about that "colored" upper class through his familiarity with Carrie Bond and her research, and he became further informed as one of the few white scholars whom Carter Woodson solicited to serve as an advisor to his Washington-based Association for the Study of Negro Life and History and its offshoot publication, the *Journal of Negro History*.[39]

But like the Washingtonian who said about the 1919 riots, "I've always tried to stay away from those things," the Bonds aimed to avoid turmoil and controversy such as that generated by "the Bruce imbroglio." And Georgia, in her ongoing endeavors to maintain a position among Washington's "better element," persuaded Percy to purchase a building lot in the Anne Arundel County, Maryland, vacation community on Chesapeake Bay known as Highland Beach. Some decades earlier, the family of the nineteenth-century titan Frederick Douglass had been denied food and service at the local Bay Ridge Inn, but Negro landowners named Brashear who lived nearby warmly welcomed them. Frederick's sons (veterans of the Fifty-fourth Massachusetts Infantry in the Civil War) purchased forty-four acres from the Brashears, then started building a house and making lots available to create an idyllic sanctuary of common culture and security. They wanted to develop an enclave where family and friends could spend precious vacation time without fear of embarrassment or rejection based on race.[40]

The Douglasses had designed and erected their cottage, Twin Oaks, with a turret facing the water. That aerie was to have been the aging Frederick's retreat "so that I, as a free man, could look across the Bay to the Eastern shore where I was born a slave," he reportedly stated. But the great abolitionist died shortly before his family completed that summer home in 1896.[41]

In addition to the Douglasses, early residents included the Terrells as well as the Wormleys, proprietors of Washington's elegant Wormley Hotel (catering to a white clientele), where the Hayes Compromise had been signed in 1877, bringing down the curtain on Reconstruction. They and a few others of their ilk began to populate Highland Beach during the century's first decades, but by the time the Bonds occupied their new cottage in 1921, homeowning families still numbered fewer than fifteen.

Patrons at Bowen's (later Flagg's) Cottage and Ware's Hotel, however, augmented their numbers. Those facilities "at the exclusive colony near Annapolis" had opened as guest houses around the turn of the century when Highland Beach was already attracting visitors like Booker T. Washington, W. E. B. Du Bois, novelist Charles Chesnutt, and Alice and Paul Laurence Dunbar. Dunbar had characterized the beach crowd as "such a gathering of this race as few outside of our own great family circle have ever seen." Later, the Emmett Scotts, Mary McLeod Bethune, and the widowed Margaret Washington often stopped by. During the mid-1920s, the Wares "altered and improved" their hotel. "A whole floor has been added," explained the Washington *Tribune* (which replaced the defunct *Bee* in 1922), providing "a total of seventy-five rooms." Highland Beach boys waited tables for Mrs. Ware—who was a splendid cook. Her "new dining room provides an excellent view of the bay," the *Tribune*'s report continued. "Two in room, with board" cost patrons "$15.00 per week, each, [with] children under 12 years, half price." In reference to those rates, Mary Terrell noted with guarded approval that "the expenses are such as to maintain a superior atmosphere."[42]

Highland Beach's early "colored" community occupied the north side of a spit of land between Black Walnut and Oyster Creeks, with five hundred feet of sandy beachfront on Chesapeake Bay. The founding families named their new roads for notable African Americans—Douglass, Washington, Reconstruction's Governor P. B. S. Pinchback, and several others—reflecting the respect with which residents held their heritage and honored leaders.

On occasion, the *Tribune*'s society column noted that "Mrs. Bond, with her daughter and son Jack, are at their summer home at Highland Beach," while Carrie Bond Day confided to a friend, "There is a group of white people who absolutely do not believe that we have such a group as live [there]."[43] "Here, some of the flower of the social flock of Washington . . . take their summer outings in pretty little cottages which they themselves own," Mary Terrell added. "In this beautiful country spot on the Chesapeake Bay," she concluded, "the beach is perfect."[44]

The Bonds, especially Georgia and her teenagers, enjoyed their bungalow throughout the summer, while Carrie often joined them. Aaron Day, Jr., however, felt ill at ease at his in-laws' houses in Washington and Highland Beach, and preferred to return to his family in Dayton, Texas, or he went off to summer reserve officers' training camps to fulfill the obligations of his army commission.[45]

For several weeks, Wenonah Bond with her friends Julia Dulaney, Doris Ridgely, and Hortense Mims also attended the YWCA's Camp Li-ho-co-wo a mile down the road. They boated, swam, hiked, and presented plays, and diligent Wenonah earned as her honor badge "The Lamp: Symbol of Service and Spirit."[46]

Several more families decided that, like the Bonds, they all (not just the girls) could better enjoy the holidays if they built cottages. "No Man's Land"—a phrase taken from the recent war—designated the undeveloped strip between Highland Beach and the adjoining property once owned by whites. The Mimses and Ridgelys joined other new "colored" residents on the peninsula's south side, called Venice Beach. By 1921, Highland Beach had its own postmistress. The next year, the *Tribune* reported, it became "the first community of colored citizens to be given a charter by the state of Maryland," and elected as mayor Frederick Douglass's grandson Haley, a Dunbar High School teacher. Residents did all that they could to keep their enclave "free from the dangers, evils and burdens" that might have resulted "from its becoming an open public resort." Mary Terrell, Dunbar's Anna Julia Cooper, four in the Wormley family, five Douglasses, and "Mr. and Mrs. Percy Bond"—men and women who could not vote in Washington, D.C.—numbered among Highland Beach's early homeowning electorate.[47]

The Bonds' single-story, pitch-roofed cottage typified the simple Highland Beach style. Its consummate feature was a screened porch (the Douglasses called theirs a verandah) seven feet wide that encircled the bungalow and constituted most of the living area, while several snug bedchambers surrounded an indoor common room. Like their neighbors, the Bonds pumped water from a well, had neither gas nor electricity, cooked on a wood-burning stove on the back porch, and squatted in an outhouse that was slaked with lime daily and emptied every Saturday.[48]

Bucolic Julys stripped Highland Beach's residents of urban time-clock and school-bell fetters as they yielded to the primal rhythms of sun, moon, stars, and tides. Dawn splashed their tidal bay with liquid gold or mauve. On idle afternoons, beachgoers and boaters watched the sun-striped and foam-laced waters that looked like the puckered fabric of gentlemen's blue seersucker summer suits. Muffling fog banks often shrouded the beach, leaden August storm clouds hurtled in from the west, and raindrops pelted craters in the sand. After the throbbing thundersqualls sprinted eastward, silent rainbows waded into the bay. Queen Anne's lace, goldenrod, black-eyed Susans, and tiger lilies (begging to be picked) fringed the corrugated dirt roads. Wenonah captured fireflies in glass jars to make flickering magic lanterns, while kerosene lamps glimmered on darkened porches. The heady perfume of pine, honeysuckle, wood smoke, and brine melted into a sensual nocturnal fugue with ripples of laughter, ukulele thrums, wind-up gramophone tunes, buoy bells, and the whispers of dancing feet that drifted across the peninsula. Summertime's gleeful children spied Harriet Tubman's Drinking Gourd that pointed the way to Douglass's North Star, as their wishing comets pierced the fathomless, black-sapphire skies.

Georgia Bond never held a job in Washington, so she was able to vacation at the beach through the whole season, as congenial young people tumbled in and out of her cottage. Whatever adults were around tended to the next generation. Pinafored tots fluttered after pale cabbage butterflies, while mothers and aunts (in traditional gingham frocks or the new women's slacks made respectable during the recent war) looked on. Thigh-length bathing dresses were the older girls' costumes de rigueur, and they preserved blissful memories and silvery images of their waterside larks with Kodak Brownie reflex cameras. Creamy skin toasted to honey; caramel deepened to chocolate. Sunburned noses and shoulders, mosquito bites (citronella was essential), and salt- and sand-snarled hair usually seemed their most pressing concerns.

Nonetheless, because neither her mother—who read, sunned, waded, and played bridge—nor her indulged light-skinned brother Jack lifted a hand around the house, Wenonah's routine included what she considered onerous doses of laundry, cleaning, and cooking. Once, when her school chums Hilda and Otwiner Smith were houseguests, Wenonah (with her tan complexion) dramatically protested: "In this family, Jack is the white prince and I am the black slave!"[49] Even in a caring clan such as the Bonds', sibling rivalry, combined with the appearance of favoritism based on both sex and skin color, sometimes made unwelcome intrusions.

Most summer weekends, hardworking Percy left Washington and drove out to join Georgia and the children. At Highland Beach, he could gaze down the Chesapeake and savor his progress and good fortune. One hundred fifty miles south, but a lifetime away, he had been born; his mother had grown up a slave in the Lower

Virginia Tidewater, raising white folks' crops; and his immigrant, seaman father, who had sailed the treacherous Atlantic with the tides and stars, had recuperated from a near-fatal gunshot wound at a Portsmouth naval hospital during the Civil War.

Few (but increasing numbers of) women drove cars in the 1920s, and one resourceful Highland Beach mother took a course in auto-mechanics so that she could cope if her vehicle broke down. Mary Terrell sometimes motored to the beach with friends like the Bonds, but her husband had grown up in the country, disliked rural life, and vowed not to leave the city. Accompanied by her daughters, guests, pets, or a housemaid, therefore, Mary Terrell often drove herself east to "the nearest salt water summer resort to Washington," the *Tribune* explained, "38 miles via [the] new Defense Highway."[50] Homeowners or visitors who had no automobiles traveled by train. *Tribune* advertisements directed them to Washington's Twelfth Street depot for reliable "electric car service over the W. B. & A. [Washington, Baltimore & Annapolis] line; get off at West Street Station, Annapolis." The clattering spurline trolley to Bay Ridge, an arduous hike, an accommodating friend with a roadster, or a long taxi ride south to Highland Beach comprised the journey's final leg.[51]

A few years earlier, Frederick Douglass's granddaughter had died of typhoid fever when Highland Beach's well water became contaminated, so residents remained cautious about everything they drank and ate. The iceman brought fresh milk and bread in addition to weighty blocks of his foremost commodity, which summer residents loaded into wooden ice chests on their shaded porches. A local farmer with his horse-drawn wagon stopped by hawking chickens, corn, watermelons, and peaches, but most cottage dwellers raised their own tomatoes, onions, squash, and peas. "Boating, fishing and crabbing are the order of the day," Mary Terrell explained, "together with an occasional dance, to which a few of the sweltering friends of Washington are invited." No church services filled their secular July and August Sundays. Some homeowners went down earlier, but Independence Day's lemonade, hard-boiled eggs, wieners, bonfires, sparklers, and patriotic observances marked summer's official kickoff at the beach.[52]

During the 1920s, however, two incidents cast a pall over usually paradisial Highland Beach. In 1923, just a week after her daughter's elegant wedding (where Georgia Bond had served as a hostess), Mary Terrell, "accompanied by her maid and bull dog," the *Tribune* wryly reported, was injured when a telephone company truck rammed into her automobile as she headed down to the shore to enjoy a festive Fourth of July. The impact shattered Terrell's kneecap, and after emergency treatment in Annapolis, she was moved to Washington's Garfield Memorial Hospital.[53]

Garfield's staff recognized the light-skinned Terrell as a Negro (albeit the District's most renowned and elegant "colored" woman) and denied her the private room she requested. Instead of transferring to Howard's Freedmen's Hospital at Howard University, however, she elected to remain at Garfield, although "the girl at the desk" told concerned visitors that they had a patient named "Mary" Terrell, but no "Mrs." Terrell, tartly explaining that "no colored person was ever 'Miss,' 'Mrs.' or 'Mr.' at the Garfield Hospital." That haughty iteration of segregation's ignominies outraged the *Tribune*, but it simultaneously complained that "Mrs. Terrell bears out the oft-repeated statement that it is our educated and most refined Negroes who always throw their patronage to the other race." The newspaper fired still more darts at Terrell when she retained a cadre of white lawyers to pursue her suit against the telephone company for damages incurred in the car crash.[54]

A second unfortunate event occurred over the Labor Day weekend two years later. Henry Lincoln Johnson (the poet Georgia Douglas Johnson's husband, who had long held a responsible government post, served as legal counsel to Standard Life Insurance Company, and belonged among the Bonds' circle of friends) suffered what proved to be a fatal stroke while enjoying "one last plunge in the salt water" at Highland Beach. Bayside life was sweet and carefree, but that tragedy must have dampened the season-ending festivities that included a tennis tournament at the court by the Wormleys' house—the men sporting white linen Wimbledon trousers—a "lawn fête" at the Douglasses' grove, dances, and a "marshmallow roast on the beach by the younger set."[55]

In contrast to their respites at rustic Highland Beach, in Washington, D.C., the Bonds dwelt in a large, gracious brick home. The furnace, kitchen, and a formal dining room comprised its lower level. The family set their table with starched linen napery, napkin rings, "an array of silver," and amber goblets for every meal, which the housekeeper Nettie (a "neat little person" with prematurely gray hair) prepared on her polished gas range. Nettie shopped daily at the grocery store around the corner, and conscientiously cleaned the entire house—bottom to top. The main floor included a parlor with sliding mahogany doors that opened onto the living room, graced with "beautiful crystal chandeliers" and a cozy gas fireplace. A flight of steps led from the shaded back porch down to the garden, the garage, and an outside coal shed.[56]

Jack Bond was charming and handsome, and he remained his mother's favored and indulged baby-child. When Georgia, whom he still provocatively called "Darly," asked him to help wash the dishes, he tossed dirty plates out the kitchen window instead. She even tried to bake for him, though her inept efforts produced only scorched cakes that crumbled on the plate. A prolific grape arbor graced the Bonds' back yard. But instead of making the jelly herself that Jack and Percy loved, Georgia gave a neighbor sugar, pectin, preserving jars, paraffin, and the right to pick and eat all the fruit she wanted in exchange for providing Georgia with enough preserves to satisfy her "boys."[57]

In the Bonds' home, the two stories above the parlor level each had a bathroom, plus one small and two larger bedchambers. "That's where the girl stayed," Wenonah recalled seven decades later as she pointed to a top-floor window at the back of her family's onetime Que Street residence. When asked if the Bonds might have been living beyond their means, since they had an automobile, summer cottage, and live-in servant, one of Wenonah's longtime friends responded: "We all did!" Despite that claim (which *did* apply to a number of their small but relatively privileged circle), most of Washington's Negroes did *not* own cars and second homes, or employ full-time maids.[58]

As in the Bonds' house, however, one servant remembered that she, too, had "lived in a room in the attic." "The first thing they done was take me to 'my place,'" recalled another black woman

who came to Washington from the rural South in the early twentieth century. Their work was exhausting and endless. "Do this, do
that, run here, run there, and when you get through—do this!" an
unhappy "girl" protested, "You got no peace living-in." Those female migrants quickly concluded that the demands, and especially
the social standing of one's employer, determined what was (or was
not) a worthy position, and some domestics refused to work for
others of their race. Georgia's friend Mary Terrell confessed her
unequivocal rejection by a Negro laundress who bluntly stated:
"Lady, I can't work for you; I'm in society myself."[59]

For many servants in Washington, whether (in most instances)
whites or (less often) other Negroes employed them, their work
lives seemed to reverberate with dreary echoes of a still recallable
plantation hierarchy. Some such working-class women viewed the
governance of households as elaborate stage productions that female employers—like Mrs. J. Percy Bond—meticulously directed.
The genteel supervision of their domiciles and domestic workers legitimized their lives and was the only real power that many of those
more affluent women had. One of Wenonah's childhood friends
confirmed that the Bonds' home undeniably was Georgia's personal
domain.[60]

Because another Negro woman relieved her of the burdens of
housework, Georgia could satisfy her own expectations of being a
lady and fully participating in Washington's "colored" society. She
had energy and time to enjoy her family; entertain community leaders such as the men from the Mu-So-Lit Club; do needlework and
paint china; read poetry, biographies, and journals like *Crisis,* and
attend meetings of the Booklovers Club—a group of civic-minded
women that also was a favorite of her friends Mary Terrell and Ida
Hunt. Georgia joined the Women's International League for Peace
and Freedom (a predominantly white organization for which Terrell and Hunt recruited a few friends from their social set), remained tangentially associated with the National Association of
Colored Women, volunteered at the Phillis Wheatley YWCA, and
played cards every week with Terrell and other devotees. Mary
Terrell wrote in her diary that for a gathering of their Matrons'
Whist Club she served chicken croquettes (one of Georgia's fa-

vorites), peas, and for dessert, "cut oranges into baskets and filled them with Orange Chocolate." Terrell worked diligently on behalf of suffrage, education, and other reforms affecting Negroes and women. Three decades later, when she was in her late eighties, she also became a key facilitator in Washington's desegregation efforts. Georgia Bond, on the other hand, was a less consequential person, but an admiring male contemporary wrote about such women:

> To attend any social function is to see a marvel in self-culture, for we see women of various colors . . . the equal in physical beauty, refinement of conduct, grace in manner and dress, and exquisite social charm of the highest bred Anglo-Saxon woman anywhere in the world.[61]

Within their homes, the lives of Washington's "colored elite" often resembled those of their white counterparts. But outside the protective walls of Georgia's residence and beyond her circle of similarly positioned friends, the capital city remained insultingly segregated. Georgia, however, did not let that unpleasant reality deter her. She had little tolerance for Jim Crow's exclusionary practices, her ivory complexion allowed her to go where she chose, and she dared white people to thwart her. When challenged about the identity of the meticulously groomed, tan-skinned children whom she often escorted to her city's choicest but racially restricted activities, she imperiously swept aside bureaucratic barriers. Georgia informed maladroit, working-class white guards or clerks that the youngsters were "of foreign extraction," and with her mannerly wards in tow, breezed through previously barred gates with minimal interference.[62]

For others of similar appearance and status, "passing" might be permanent, transitional, situational, even accidental. It was sometimes a necessity, often a game, but always a challenge and a risk. Associates of those who chose to (and reasonably could) pass, rarely exposed their colleagues. Darker-skinned friends or relatives might be critical or envious, but they nonetheless believed that, ultimately, they had all outfoxed the white folks.

Some of Wenonah Bond's light-skinned schoolmates would stand in theater lines conspicuously chatting in French or Spanish.

If box office attendants tried to deny them entry, with great hauteur (and affected accents), the audacious young people announced that they "would have to take it up with the embassy." On many occasions, insecure ticket sellers, anxious to avoid a diplomatic incident, reluctantly admitted them. At least one observer called those sly maneuvers "passing on the basis of exoticism." Upper-class American Negroes who could afford such luxuries bristled at the humiliating paradox when employees at such "whites-only" facilities in the District sought to bar them, yet welcomed Latin Americans, Asians, and swarthy southern Europeans.[63]

Several Washington theaters hired Negro "spotters" to ferret out and "bounce" impostors who might be undetectable to whites, but knowing the economic realities of the times, few in the black community condemned those men for earning a living that way. Wenonah's classmates Doris Ridgely and Carolyn Evans yearned to see a well-received new motion picture one wintry afternoon in December 1922 and, unbeknownst to their parents, went over to the segregated Knickerbocker Theater, one of the city's premier movie houses. Their pale skin and brown curls usually made the girls racially unidentifiable, but a black custodian recognized them. They took in the whole matinee, however, because he chose not to blow their cover and send them home in shame, but he did telephone their parents to warn them that he knew that the two had "misrepresented themselves." Word of the girls' unauthorized escapade and subsequent detection rapidly spread among their families' close circle of friends.[64]

The more significant news that the theater's roof caved in under the weight of two feet of snow later that evening and killed almost one hundred moviegoing Washingtonians (apparently all of them "legitimately" white), however, overshadowed the trivial brouhaha over the passing incident.[65] It was the city's single deadliest tragedy—but one that spared the Negro community, thanks to the ironies of segregation. "No Colored Killed When Roof Falls," trumpeted the *Tribune*'s headline, while it also reported that a black nurse who had tried to gain admission that night had been brusquely turned away. The newspaper further noted that a rescue crew from the District's only "colored" fire station promptly arrived on the scene, while several Negroes in the private sector were among the first "to reach the unfortunate people, pinned like rats in a trap." For hours, those Samaritans worked cooperatively on the salvage mission in the wet, numbing cold, but they were denied any nourishment or even hot coffee "although all the whites who engaged in the rescue work were served," said the *Tribune*. It was "a winter you would never forget," a longtime Washingtonian remembered more than seven decades later.[66]

Segregation sometimes denied the Bonds access to much of white Washington, but the beguiling, murky universe of lower-class black people was almost equally foreign to them. Among the Negro Four Hundred, only a few, like Governor P. B. S. Pinchback's renegade grandson Jean Toomer (a Dunbar High School graduate), voluntarily traversed some of the seamier stretches of "Seventh Street . . . a bastard of Prohibition and the War." Toomer portrayed that neighborhood as "a crude-boned, soft-skinned wedge of nigger life breathing its loafer air, jazz songs and love." There, he observed "Bootleggers in silken shirts / Ballooned, zooming Cadillacs, / Whizzing . . . down the street-car tracks," and discovered forbidden charms in the "life of nigger alleys, of pool rooms and . . . near-beer saloons."[67]

Georgia Bond (and others like her) tried to ignore that netherworld, but in segregated Washington she made every effort to enrich her life, even if it meant "passing" at cinemas like the Knickerbocker Theater or even leaving behind her dark-skinned husband. In many instances, however, such subterfuges were not necessary in New York City's Harlem, which became the primary home to the Negro Renaissance of the 1920s. Nonetheless, the nation's capital was a close creative second, where both "high" (classical music, theater, literature) and "low" (bawdy dances, dance hall songs, blues and jazz) culture emerged and thrived.

Edward Kennedy Ellington wrote his first sassy tunes, *Soda Fountain Rag, Bitches Ball,* and *What You Gonna Do When the Bed Breaks Down?* in Washington, his hometown, where in 1918 he formed a swinging combo called Duke's Serenaders. " 'Negro music,' 'American syncopation,' [or] 'ragtime' . . . is here to stay; for it has already caught the ear of the people the world over," the "colored" composer J. Rosamond Johnson had written in 1909. Scott Joplin's death a decade later officially marked the ragtime era's demise, but African American musicians already had given birth to its richly complex offspring they called jazz. Even prior to the war, the country had gone wild over "animalistic" Negro dances like the fox trot, grizzly bear, camel walk, and bunny hop, legitimized and sanitized for white society by Irene and Vernon Castle and their favorite bandleader, the District's own James Reese Europe.[68]

Despite demurrers from Langston Hughes, who became a major voice in the Negro Renaissance, the arts and letters of all sorts flourished in Washington. Hughes's family ties (one eponymous antecedent was John Mercer Langston, an educator, diplomat, and congressman from Virginia in the late 1800s) gave him easy entrée into the city's "colored" bourgeoisie. He nonetheless hated the "pseudo culture, . . . slavish devotion to Nordic standards, . . . detachment from the Negro masses and . . . vast sense of importance to themselves" that he claimed characterized that faction in Washington. He often griped that the Negro upper class showed "little concern for poets or playwrights."[69]

Howard University was the country's major institutional locus of African American intellect and culture, but the city's preeminent informal literary enclave flourished at the S Street Northwest home of Georgia Douglas Johnson, whom many called the "foremost woman poet of the race." Johnson held salons in the mid 1920s that many Negro essayists, playwrights, and other poets living in or visiting Washington attended, and her group became known as the Saturday Nighters. She mothered them, nourished their creativity, and her bountiful table sated their physical hunger and thirst as they read from their new work, and gabbed and gossiped late into the night about writing and writers. "If dull ones come, [Johnson] weeds them out," one regular acutely observed.[70]

Members of that engaging crowd defined themselves by their creative product, but knew that jobs and social standing required that they scrupulously preserve the appearance of respectability. Nonetheless, an unspoken secret was that some of Johnson's gifted guests were homosexual or bisexual. By necessity, theirs became a doubly covert "Secret City." Alain Locke, who had a known weakness for his male students, and Langston Hughes, who fondly described the sailors he could "touch and know and be friends with," were among those whose talents made them welcome at the salon so long as their ambiguous erotic preferences and practices remained discreet. Other regulars were Mary Burrill (sister of Clara Burrill Bruce and beloved of Howard's Dean Lucy Slowe) and Angelina Grimké whom Percy Bond first had known from their childhoods in Hyde Park. Grimké's poetically reconstructed adolescent amours with a female schoolmate stayed prudently unpublished and her sexuality had been repressed by an obedient acquiescence to her family's lofty and puritanical behavioral expectations. Participants from out of town included empathetic white literati like H. G. Wells and Edna St. Vincent Millay, Negro New Yorkers such as W. E. B. Du Bois, James Weldon Johnson, Countee Cullen, Locke's suave friend Eric Walrond, and Wilmington's Alice Dunbar-Nelson—who had romances with Emmett Scott as well as several women.[71]

Most white people held distorted and exaggerated views of all African Americans' sexuality, and anything that threatened to mar the veneer of gentility for the District's Negro bourgeoisie had to be concealed, even at Georgia Douglas Johnson's otherwise freewheeling salons. Carrie Bond Day became one of Johnson's dear friends. "I cannot let my only poetess in the group escape," Carrie gently cajoled Johnson about participating in her own ongoing anthropological research. She also knew others, like her talented Radcliffe schoolmate Marita Bonner, in the District's premier literary circle, of which—though she resided and worked in Atlanta—Carrie remained a transient member.[72]

A number of people in Washington's creative vanguard (such as Johnson, Grimké, Burrill, and Locke) stayed in the nation's capital, tied to work, homes, and friends. Others (Ellington, Hughes, Toomer, Zora Neale Hurston, and James Reese Europe, among them) left, seeking greener pastures and broader opportunities for artistic expression in more open-minded New York City.

In the Bonds' community during that era, baseball fans like Robert and Mary Terrell attended professional contests at nearby

Griffith Stadium, where Negro and white spectators usually were not segregated in the stands, stood in the same ticket and food lines, and rooted wildly for their common team.[73] Baseball remained Percy Bond's favorite sport, and Washington's (all-white) Senators dominated the mid-1920s much as had his old hometown Boston teams a decade earlier. In 1924, the Senators—then known as the Nationals, or Nats—clinched the pennant, then won the World Series over the New York Giants in a critical seventh game, as the tolerant "colored" *Daily American* cheered: "Long live King Baseball, the only monarch who recognizes no color line." The contest's goat, whose error let the District's boys of summer wave in the winning run, was the same long-in-the-tooth Hank Gowdy who had triggered the Boston Braves' series victory a decade earlier. The capital city's team won the pennant again the next year, but lost to the plucky Pittsburgh Pirates in another epic Series that went the full seven games.[74]

Howard University's baseball team participated in contests such as that when its boosters madly cheered the 1925 extra-inning game in which the mighty Bison downed the University of Japan all-stars that already had handily outclassed college teams from Harvard and Yale. The Thanksgiving Day Howard-Lincoln football matches (played at the neighboring Griffith Stadium) also became celebrated events. Those prestigious Negro schools maintained a heated rivalry, and myriad spectators (students, faculty, alumni, and outsiders) traveled to Washington from as far as a thousand miles away. "The occasion afforded a scene which, so far as our group is concerned, could not be duplicated anywhere else in the world," the *Howard University Record* reported.[75]

In addition to sports, Howard sponsored popular concerts and theater performances. Its choir was equally likely to perform a Handel oratorio or one by the recently deceased Anglo-African composer Samuel Coleridge-Taylor. The Ira Aldridge Club and Howard University Players (its work lauded by W. E. B. Du Bois as "one of the significant achievements of the race for the year 1922") performed often and well. *Shuffle Along,* Eubie Blake and Noble Sissle's spiffy musical revue that would launch the career of an audacious young woman named Josephine Baker, reached the Broadway stage only after its Washington debut.[76] Carrie Bond Day often attended productions such as those in the District of Columbia, and directed plays herself at Atlanta University.

In the realm of juvenile culture, *The Brownies' Book,* a monthly publication sponsored by W. E. B. Du Bois, encouraged Negro youngsters ("Children of the Sun") to prize their heritage. It first appeared in January 1920 as a harbinger of the Harlem Renaissance. Du Bois had expressed grave concerns that young people of his race "unconsciously get the impression that the Negro has little chance to be good, great, heroic or beautiful," and his new magazine taught "Universal Love and Brotherhood for all little folk— black and brown and yellow and white." It inspired African American youths to see themselves as components of and contributors to an admirable and historic international community, and *The Brownies' Book* stood in contrast to the best-selling American children's monthly, *St. Nicholas,* which at the same time featured poems like "Ten Little Niggers."[77]

The first issue included a letter from thirteen-year-old Wenonah Bond to her sister Carrie's mentor and her mother's erstwhile Fisk schoolmate. "Dear Dr. Du Bois:" she wrote, "Our *Crisis* came a few days ago, and I was very glad to see the advertisement for *The Brownies' Book.* I had just been talking to mother about giving me a subscription to some children's magazine and was delighted to know that we shall soon have one of our very own." "I want to be one of the first subscribers," Wenonah added.[78]

Her "very own" magazine told of real-life heroes like Paul Cuffe, Toussaint L'Ouverture, Samuel Coleridge-Taylor, Alexandre Dumas, and Harriet Tubman, and featured news stories, fiction, and poetry graced by elegant illustrations. *The Brownies' Book* motivated Wenonah with a profile of Sojourner Truth titled "A Pioneer Suffragette," and an August 1920 article praised Negroes who had defended democracy in France. "We're especially proud of our girl patriots—for girls do have such a weary time trying to prove they have brains, and can be inspired and have ambitions," it insisted. The following month, it published Carrie Bond Day's story, "Big Round Date and Little Bean," featuring her cinnamon-skinned protagonists and loving evocations of African foodways and culture. The magazine told young readers about this country's pending, restrictive immigration laws, and the "three thousand Negroes . . . led by Marcus Garvey [who] have held a month's convention in New York City and made a demand for 'Africa for the Africans.' " It also reported that during the 1920 presidential campaign, it was "charged that President [Warren] Harding had colored blood." Despite that rumor, it added, "he received the largest popular vote ever given to an American President." *The Brownies' Book* warned that the Ku Klux Klan had staged a revival as a "protest against colored people and Catholics and Jews," while another report noted that "two Italians have been sentenced to death for murder." "Many people think they are not guilty but that they were sentenced because they had radical views of government," it continued. That item concerned the contentious Nicola Sacco–Bartolomeo Vanzetti trial in Dedham, Massachusetts (just down the road from the home of Percy Bond's youth, where most of his family still lived), that stimulated the country's paranoia about anarchy and alien-imported Bolshevism.[79]

Wenonah remained devoted to *The Brownies' Book*. Its contributors included Colonel Charles Young, Georgia Douglas Johnson, Langston Hughes, W. E. B. Du Bois's daughter Yolande, as well as the white anthropologist Elsie Clews Parsons, while the November 1920 issue featured Jessie Fauset's sparkling fiction. A double portrait captioned "Billy and Rosemary" illustrated her Thanksgiving story, "Turkey Drumsticks," but it was really a photo of Wenonah and Jack Bond. Through her mother and sister, Wenonah had always revered Dr. Du Bois. She adored his magazine, sold subscriptions, penned letters to the editor, even sent in personal photos, and mourned when *The Brownies' Book* folded after only two years—but what splendid years they had been![80]

The Bonds strongly encouraged reading in particular and education in general, and both Wenonah and Jack (who, at best, maintained a tenuous truce with one another) attended Paul Laurence Dunbar High School—the jewel in the crown of Negro public schools. In the 1920s, Dunbar also provided a superior academic grounding to people such as the future Judge William Hastie, scientist Dr. Charles Drew, and Robert Weaver, who, four decades later, became his nation's first African American cabinet secretary. Despite limited professional and economic opportunities for the race in its entirety, Dunbar's graduates maintained high hopes for their own prospects.

Guided by their parents, offspring of the Bonds' social and professional colleagues in Washington prepared to pursue careers suited to the realities of segregated life, and most young women planned to become teachers. Hilda and Otwiner Smith's mother advised her daughters that they had only two occupational options: to teach, or to do domestic work. "Even if you worked in the White House," she warned them, "you'd still be a maid." They and their girlfriends dutifully went on to college, and most ultimately did teach, because education (though segregated in the District) remained a field with many opportunities—as well as many barriers—for Negroes. Washington's African American community still greatly esteemed its teachers, who earned almost as much as whites.[81]

Dunbar's faculty (until 1918 all women who taught in the city's public schools had to be single, and long thereafter that bias and restriction frequently persisted) included Anna Julia Cooper, Radcliffe's Eva Dykes, Smith College's Otelia Cromwell, and Mary Burrill who taught English, as did Angelina Grimké. Others had graduated from institutions such as Harvard, Yale, Amherst, and the University of Michigan. They suffused their students with information about the advantages that those colleges might offer, and instilled in young people like Wenonah and Jack Bond a love of learning, a sense of duty, racial pride, and knowledge of black history and culture. Dunbar's curriculum was unparalleled in other schools for Negroes, and was on a par with that offered by most of the country's finest (virtually all-white) preparatory academies.[82]

Lacking other career opportunities because of both race and sex discrimination, four of Dunbar's female teachers held, or were earning, Ph.D. degrees in the mid-1920s. Mary Gibson, another Radcliffe graduate from Carrie's era, taught French, while Mary Europe, sister of the recently deceased bandleader James Reese Europe, was the music instructor who brought remarkable Negro performers to her school. Major Milton Dean (Captain Aaron Day's superior in the 317th Ammunition Train) headed the cadet corps, then moved on to Howard University in the same capacity. Were it not for the country's endemic racism and the District's southern orientation and lack of political representation, cadets from Dunbar would have made splendid candidates for West Point and Annapolis. One Negro from New York received a nomination to the Naval Academy in 1922, the *Tribune* reported, but added that none of the three men of his race who had preceded him "stayed more than a year because of their treatment."[83]

Photographs of Wenonah Bond's Dunbar classmates in 1924 show 225 solemn, meticulously groomed graduates with an infinite range of skin tones, undermining the persistent rumor that their school denied entry to dark-complexioned students. One contemporary labeled those charges "ridiculous."[84] Nonetheless, paler-skinned girls and boys were more prevalent at Dunbar than among Washington's African American population in its entirety. Parental guidance, pressure, and expectations, plus a heritage of economic, social, and educational advantage contributed to a legacy of privilege that often served to link continuing academic success and class status with lighter skin and straighter hair.

In 1922, Wenonah and her closest school chums formed a club called the Mignonettes. They were short and tall, their complexions ranged from ivory to mahogany, and their hair from frizzy beige, to chestnut ripples, to black ringlets. Some (Hilda and Otwiner Smith) were blood sisters, others (the Dulaney, Ridgely, and Evans girls) were cousins, while still others were unrelated to anyone else in the group. Nonetheless, the Mignonettes became sisters under the skin. The club—whose members would share each others' triumphs and tragedies for three-quarters of a century—had but two rules: meetings were held only on Fridays, and no one would steal another's boyfriend. Each Mignonette had a nickname derived from her initials: Julia Dogan Dulaney was "Jumpy Dumpy Dog," Carolyn Beatrice Evans was "Catty Batty Eel," and they called Wenonah Stewart Bond, "Willie Silly Billy."[85]

During Wenonah's Dunbar years, in addition to the Scotts, Bruces, Johnsons, Terrells, and their Highland Beach neighbors, her family's friends included William and Ida Hunt—he a U.S. Consular Service officer, she a writer, onetime teacher, keen internationalist, Du Bois's colleague at the 1919 Pan-African Congress in Paris and cochair for the 1923 London conference. For years, the Hunts divided their time between Washington and Europe. In 1922, the visiting Ida Hunt lectured District of Columbia students about "The Women of France," and the Booklovers Club (Georgia Bond and her daughter Carrie both became members) was her favorite diversion. Ida Hunt had no children, and she invited Wenonah, who called her "uzzer muzzer" (other mother), to return and live with her at the American consulate in St. Étienne, France. Wenonah studied French, yearned to travel, and could envision herself a citizen of the world. Georgia Bond, however, adamantly refused, initiating a testy intergenerational feud when she insisted that she could (or would) not let her venturesome teenaged daughter leave the country with the Hunts.[86]

Nonetheless, Wenonah remained close to her parents, and internalized the values (obedience, respectability, hard work) that her elders stressed. Driven by her mother's insistence that she acquire the skills and grace that proper young ladies should have, Wenonah took piano and dancing lessons. Because segregation kept them from trying on shoes at shops in Washington—and because their parents would settle for nothing but the best—each fall Wenonah and her friends traipsed up the hill to Howard University's campus, where a representative from an outlet for ballet garb stood each one on a parchment sheet and traced around her feet to determine the precise size and configuration for her new slippers. The shoes then were custom-ordered from New York City and soon arrived by mail back in Washington.[87]

In addition to attending ballet classes, on Saturdays, Wenonah Bond and her minister's daughter Elizabeth Bennett roller-skated to the central Carnegie Library, the site of a lynching during the 1919 riots but still one of the city's few unsegregated public facilities. Nonetheless, a Washington man accurately complained, "in our city library there is not a single colored employee, and the librarian . . . told me plainly . . . that he would employ no colored person there except in the capacity of charwoman."[88]

Wenonah initiated a similar ritual with her friend Doris Ridgely. Every year on George Washington's birthday, the pair skated across town, through Rock Creek Park, past the zoo, over to the embassies along Connecticut and Massachusetts Avenues. When they arrived at a predetermined destination, they sat down to rest on the stone steps. Guards asked the teenagers if they wanted or needed anything, but Wenonah simply had to know (though Europe recently had been denied her and still remained a dream) that from the nation's capital she could reach out to touch the world.[89]

As they edged toward adulthood, girls like Wenonah Bond looked up to the women in their social firmament (including leaders of the National Association of Colored Women [NACW] led by Carrie Bond's YWCA colleague Addie Hunton) who confronted issues of politics, sex, color, and caste. Irate NACW members gathered in Washington to protest the proposed erection of a statue honoring the "Faithful Colored Mammies of the South." They also met with Alice Paul, head of the National Women's Party (NWP) in 1921, and reiterated their determination to be included in the country's newly expanded franchise, because a headline in Washington's black newspaper had warned: "Fear Colored Women May Vote."[90] The Nineteenth Amendment's ratification the previous year, however, had been a pyrrhic victory for all women in the nation's capital, where regardless of gender or race, no one could vote.

Nonetheless, the NWP established its headquarters in Washington, and the installation of a portrait statue of three white suffragists in the capitol rotunda (though male members of Congress swiftly relocated that marble tribute to the basement) highlighted its 1921 convention. Black women, however, received short shrift from the NWP. They had no representation whatsoever at the statue's dedication, while one white feminist admitted that "all doubtful subjects like birth control and the rights of Negro women were hushed up." An article in the *Nation* observed that those women had minimal conference delegates, were denied the floor during seminars, even barred from riding elevators. Alice Paul also rescinded a prominent Negro woman's invitation to speak, on the

grounds that she represented an organization (the NAACP) that focused on race, not sex. Addie Hunton commented that "Miss Paul,
I fear, is not a bit interested in the question of suffrage as it relates
to the colored women." "Although thoroughly hostile to the delegation," Hunton continued, "[Paul] said it was the most intelligent
group of women who ever attacked her." Over Paul's protests,
"colored" delegates brought to the NWP's convention floor their
provocative resolution stating:

> We cannot . . . believe that you will permit this Amendment [the
> Nineteenth] to be so distorted in its interpretation that it shall lose
> its power and effectiveness. Five million women in the United
> States can not be denied their rights without all the women of the
> United States feeling the effect of that denial. No women are free
> until all women are free.[91]

The next year (on hallowed Decoration Day) Tuskegee Institute's principal "[R. R.] Moton was chosen to speak at the dedication of the Lincoln Memorial, and rough marines were stationed in
the audience to force colored people into Jim Crow seats at the
point of the bayonet," the *Tribune* reported. Its headline read,
"Near Fight Erupts as Citizens Are Jim Crowed." Some of Washington's leading "colored" residents had received invitations marked
"Platform Seats." They were heading to their reserved places when
marines "swore at them," then shoved and rerouted them toward a
segregated section across a road from the favored white guests.
After he spoke, Moton allowed himself to be ushered to a Jim
Crow seat, but the Emmett Scotts and a handful of others promptly
left the observance honoring the Great Emancipator rather than endure such humiliation. Despite the shabby treatment given to "distinguished" Negroes, "ordinary" African Americans, much like
their plebeian white counterparts, stood and eagerly watched the
ceremony wherever they could elbow in.[92]

A few months earlier, the *Bee* (ever critical of Roscoe Bruce's
tenure as assistant superintendent of education typified by the
Moens scandal and rumors of sexual favors he demanded of novice
teachers) had reported that Bruce had asked for and been granted a

leave of absence. That leave, it said, was presumed "to mean his virtual severance." His wife, Clara Burrill Bruce, soon took her children off to Massachusetts, where she became law review editor and a star scholar at Boston University Law School. The Bruces never officially separated, but thereafter, Clara returned to the District only intermittently. Roscoe's tarnished reputation also threatened to undermine the tenure of Clara's sister Mary Burrill at Dunbar High School, but Mary's intimate relationship with Howard's Dean Lucy Slowe may have imperiled her job security as well. Even after Roscoe's fall from grace, however, Percy Bond did not forsake his old friend. On several occasions, the *Tribune* reported, he visited the Bruces' Maryland poultry farm as Roscoe's guest.[93]

Percy soon became embroiled in his own spat with that paper's editors. As a promotional gimmick, Standard Life distributed a calendar featuring the birthdates of Jefferson Davis and several other Confederates. The *Tribune* excoriated the company, the calendar, and its exclusion of Negro leaders. As "agency supervisor of the Standard Life Insurance Company, . . . Mr. J. P. Bond" responded. He lamely explained that the secessionists' birthdays only "inform[ed] our friends and policy-holders in the South of the legal holidays, upon which all banks are closed." Percy Bond bristled at any suggestion that Standard should emulate the "White Ice Cream Company [which] distributed Negro Historical Pictures," claiming that such advertising had only been "forced upon them [by a] progressive Negro business man." Standard, Percy added, "is purely a Negro Organization working for, employing, and interested in everything that pertains to Negro development, and . . . would do nothing to neglect or reflect on the race."[94]

A follow-up *Tribune* editorial argued that white-controlled southern banks could give out their own calendars if they wished. Neither Percy nor other leaders at Standard, it asserted, had the "sagacity and persistence and business acumen" to see that it would be " 'good business' to print and distribute Negro historical pictures." What worked for a white-owned ice cream company could "be just as good if not better business for the Standard Life." Percy professed to support black businesses, the *Tribune* added, but as the "representative of this great Negro commercial enterprise, [Bond] cannot say that we would know it by his patronage of . . . colored enterprises in Washington." "Racial solidarity is the slogan of The Tribune," it crowed, "and insurance companies of the race . . . should foster that example by example as well as in theory." "We know a company by its representatives," the editorial concluded, "and their actions are contrary to their professions—since 'actions speak louder than words.' " Percy came off sounding like a doltish Uncle Tom as that debacle grew into an ugly squabble that he must have wished had never surfaced.[95]

A number of people in Washington's Negro upper class hoped that President Harding might soften segregation's barriers, which had stiffened under Woodrow Wilson, and they had wholeheartedly celebrated his 1921 inaugural. During the campaign, his detractors had circulated pseudoscientific propaganda designed to show that "Warren Gamaliel Harding is not a white man . . . he is a mestizo." If that were true, like many men and women in the District's Negro upper class, Harding possessed a telling "drop of African blood." Despite the rumored "touch of the tar brush," and even though he maintained in his inaugural address that African Americans' "sacrifice in blood on the battle-fields of the Republic has entitled them to all freedom and opportunity, all sympathy and aid that the American spirit of fairness and justice demands," Harding failed them. A group of Negroes went to his White House to discuss policy issues, but the president claimed that they came seeking patronage. He griped that they were "very hard to please. . . . If they could have half of the Cabinet, seventy-five percent of the Bureau Chiefs, . . . [and] two-thirds of the Diplomatic appointments perhaps there would be a measure of contentment temporarily, but I do not think it would long abide." In fact, neither Harding's administration nor any that preceded it had ever included a black cabinet member or "Bureau Chief," and only the rare midlevel diplomatic official, such as William Henry Hunt in France. Within months, the *Bee* angrily reported: "Harding Official Segregates Rock Creek Park."[96]

Scandalous personal and financial improprieties during Harding's tenure humiliated the president and the country alike. He died in office, and Calvin Coolidge succeeded him. Percy Bond would have been pleased that his home state's Republican former governor had attained the presidency, but the habitually acerbic *Tribune* made its editorial position known in September 1924 with a cartoon that it (probably unfairly) captioned "Keep Kool with Koolidge." It wickedly parodied Coolidge's campaign slogan, and evoked the enduring specter of the Ku Klux Klan.[97]

Wenonah graduated from Dunbar that year and departed for Atlanta University. Members of the Mignonettes (most of whom were headed to Howard or the city's "colored" Miner Teachers College since local "white" schools such as Georgetown, George Washington, and American Universities were denied them) went down to Union Station with their friend, stood on the platform, and wept as she boarded her train. Wenonah was going to join Carrie Bond Day, who would assume the responsibility of parenting her younger sister. Wenonah had wanted to attend Massachusetts' renowned but pricey Smith College, and was headed south for financial reasons, but also because Georgia Bond believed that her younger daughter needed to absorb the genteel manners, style, and expectations of a southern lady.[98]

The Bond family offered love, fostered strong moral values, provided a shield against segregation's harshness, and helped prepare Wenonah to continue her education and shoulder what she considered her obligations to help uplift the race. Dunbar's yearbook revealed that she planned to become a "social service worker." She missed her parents during the ensuing years, and Percy and Georgia occasionally ventured south to visit their two daughters— one a college professor, the other a college student.

In 1925, thirty thousand masked, robed Ku Klux Klansmen arrived and congregated at Union Station, then marched along the District's noblest thoroughfare, Pennsylvania Avenue, and down the Mall. A ceremony at the Washington Monument (though local authorities denied the Klan permission to burn a cross) climaxed the procession. Much of the white press treated it as a national celebration, but the capital's black newspaper ranted, blessed the thunderstorm that rained on the KKK's parade, and ridiculed the single Negro participant who meekly drove a carriage bearing three costumed white women portraying the "Lost Confederacy."⁹⁹ The Bonds, along with the city's entire "colored" population, must have been horrified, but that event, despite its symbolic import, only minimally affected their lives.

The following year (as the Supreme Court upheld the legality of the District's covenants that prevented Negroes from buying homes in white neighborhoods), Carter Woodson inaugurated the observance of Negro History Week. Howard's President J. Stanley Durkee also resigned, and the Board of Trustees convened for the purpose of "looking toward the election of a successor." Their major agenda item was: "Should the new President be white or colored?" Durkee had engaged in bitter disputes with many of his school's African American leaders, but a startling new disclosure revealed that while he was Howard's president, Durkee concurrently held another position. He headed the "Curry School of Expression in Boston from which Negroes are excluded," a report divulged. That racial exclusion at Curry was a recent development, however, because it was the same institution at which Adrienne Herndon, Carrie Bond's teacher and inspiration at Atlanta University, had studied around the turn of the century. "Upon motion," an ensuing trustees' meeting resolved, "it was voted that Dr. Mordecai W. Johnson . . . shall take office as President of the University, effective September 1, 1926." For the first time, Howard University had a Negro at the helm.¹⁰⁰

Percy Bond continued to work in Washington for Atlanta, Georgia's Standard Life Insurance Company, bruited in 1924 by the esteemed *Forbes* financial magazine as "The Largest Negro Commercial Enterprise in the World." White companies hired persons of Percy's race only as menials and strictly limited their policies covering Negroes, whom they unvaryingly considered poor insurance risks. Ironically, that denial of coverage allowed black-owned insurance companies to flourish in the century's early decades. *Forbes* estimated Standard's assets at $2,400,000 "with $30,000,000 insurance in force." Those amounts, claimed the magazine, comprised one-third of "the total volume of business done annually by Negro enterprises in the United States." Standard operated in "thirteen states

Right: Wenonah, Georgia, and Jack Bond in Selma, Alabama, 1913. *Below:* Wenonah and Jack Bond in 1915. This photograph also appeared in a story in W.E.B. Du Bois's young people's magazine, *The Brownies' Book*, in 1920, captioned "Billy and Rosemary."

Left: Carrie and Wenonah Bond at Lena Bond and David Chesnut's wedding in Hyde Park, 1908. *Right:* J. Percy Bond and an employee in front of his haberdashery in Birmingham, Alabama, 1911. The writing on the postcard is from Georgia Bond to a nephew. *(All photos collection of the author)*

Top left: Carrie Stewart Bond, Wenonah Bond, and an unidentified friend at Carrie's Atlanta University graduation in 1912. *(Collection of Elizabeth Alexander)*
Top right: Earnest Hooton, ca. 1926. Carrie Bond's anthropology professor at Radcliffe College wrote glowingly about her work on interracial families. His interest may have been partially stimulated by his own racially ambiguous appearance. *(Harvard University Archives)*

Above: Adrienne Herndon, actress and teacher, ca. 1900, when she first met Carrie and Georgia Stewart in Boston. She became Carrie's mentor and friend at Atlanta University, where Carrie ultimately took her place as a teacher of drama and elocution. *(Day Collection, Peabody Museum, Harvard University, and the Herndon Home, Atlanta) Left:* Carrie Bond *(second row, second from left)* with YWCA friends and associates, including her mentors, Addie Hunton and Eva Bowles *(to the immediate left and right of Carrie)*, in Brooklyn, 1915. *(YWCA of the U.S.A. Archives, courtesy of Ralph Carlson)*

Officers of the 317th Ammunition Train, 92nd Division, AEF, during the Christmas season in Domfront, France, 1918. (*Top row, far left*) Captain Aaron Day, Jr.; (*second row, fifth from right*) Lieutenant William Holmes Dyer; (*front row, third from left*) Lieutenant Colonel Milton Dean. (*Photograph by Giraud, collection of Bernard Day*)

In Memory of A Great Leader

The late Lieut. James Reese (Jim) Europe

Born in Mobile, Ala., 1880   Died in Boston May 9th, 1919

Published by E. Townsend Welcome   Copyright Underwood-Underwood

Left: Lieutenant James Reese Europe, a renowned musician, served with the 369th Regiment of the AEF, introduced jazz to France, then was killed by a member of his famous "Hellfighters" band in Boston in 1919. (*Moorland Spingarn Research Center, Howard University*) *Below:* Members of Company B, 317th Ammunition Train, at Camp Upton, Long Island. Captain Day (*front row, center*) married Carrie Bond a year later. (*Photograph by Hughes and Estabrook, collection of Bernard Day*)

JUST BACK FROM FRANCE
COMPANY B. 317TH AMMUNITION TRAIN A.E.F.
CAPT. AARON DAY JR. COMMANDING.
FEB. 28, 1919

Left: Carter G. Woodson, a graduate of the University of Chicago and Harvard, almost scuttled Captain Day's military career. He helped Emmett Scott write *Scott's Official History of the Negro in the World War* and started the Association for the Study of Negro Life and History in Washington, D.C. *(Day Collection, Peabody Museum, Harvard University)*

Above right: W. E. B. Du Bois was Carrie Bond's academic mentor and inspiration at Atlanta University, guided her to Radcliffe College, and remained her good friend. *(Day Collection, Peabody Museum, Harvard University) Above left:* William Henry Hunt, a friend of the Bond family, was U.S. Consul General in St. Etienne, France. He appears here *(far left)* with French officials during World War I. *(Day Collection, Peabody Museum, Harvard University) Right:* Georgia Douglas Johnson, 1926. A friend of Carrie Bond Day in Washington, D.C., she convened that city's premier circle of African American writers during the Harlem Renaissance years.*(Johnson Collection, Moorland Spingarn Research Center, Howard University)*

Top left: Wenonah Bond *(front row, far left)* with members of her Dunbar High School club, the Mignonettes, 1922. *(Collection of the author)* *Center:* Wenonah and an unidentified companion on the beach at Highland Beach, 1922. *(Collection of the author)* *Bottom left:* Mary Church Terrell, a noted civic and social leader in Washington, D.C., and a friend of the Bond family, around the time when she met Georgia Stewart at Tuskegee Institute. *(Terrell Collection, Moorland Spingarn Research Center, Howard University)*

Top right: Alice Dunbar-Nelson, a controversial colleague of Carrie Bond Day, was a lecturer, writer, and leader of the Circle for Negro War Relief. *(Moorland Spingarn Research Center, Howard University)* *Bottom right:* A'Lelia Walker Robinson, a supporter of Carrie Bond Day in the Circle for Negro War Relief and a leading Harlem Renaissance hostess, 1926. *(Walker Collection of A'Lelia Bundles)*

Top left: Wenonah Bond and Ida Gibbs Hunt, under the grapevine at the Bonds' home in Washington, D.C., 1920. Ida and William Hunt wanted Wenonah to return with them to St. Etienne, France. *(Collection of the author)*

Right: Wenonah with her friend (and future sister-in-law) Myra Logan, alongside Carrie Bond Day's cottage at Atlanta University, 1926. *(Collection of the author) Bottom:* Carrie's production of Richard Sheridan's *The Rivals* at Atlanta University, featuring her sister, Wenonah *(seated, center)*. *(The Herndon Home, Atlanta)*

Above: Betty Bond on the occasion of her confirmation at the Church of the Good Shepherd in Dedham, Massachusetts, 1915. *Right:* Bob Bond, ca. 1935, in his old U.S. Navy uniform.

Center: Frankie and Evelyn Bond and an unidentified friend, 1926.

Bottom: Bob Bond surrounded by his merchandise, standing near his store alongside Mother Brook and across from Fairview Cemetery in Hyde Park, Massachusetts. *(All photos collection of the author)*

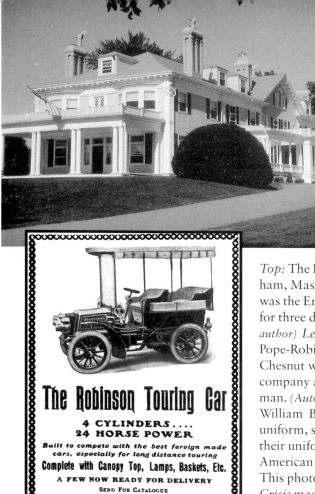

Top: The Endicott estate in Dedham, Massachusetts. David Chesnut was the Endicott family's chauffeur for three decades. *(Collection of the author) Left:* Advertisement for Pope-Robinson cars, 1903. David Chesnut worked for the Hyde Park company as a mechanic and salesman. *(Automotive Quarterly) Bottom:* William B. Gould in his GAR uniform, surrounded by his sons in their uniforms from the Spanish-American War and World War I. This photograph also appeared in *Crisis* magazine in 1917. *(Collection of William B. Gould, IV, and Black Civil War Sailors Project, Howard University)*

including the District of Columbia." "Altogether," the article continued, it "has 2,500 people—all colored—on its payroll."[101]

Forbes's story lauded "the financial genius of Heman Perry [Standard's president], the commercial Booker Washington." Perry, *Forbes* added, was "building up a gigantic commercial institution whose very spirit is already beginning to revolutionize conditions for the Negro." He received an annual salary of $75,000, and his personal worth was estimated at $8,000,000.[102]

Those plaudits, however, stunned the Georgia insurance industry's regulators, who apparently were appalled that a Negro should enjoy such success. Investigators scoured the corporate records, concluded that Heman Perry's economic kingdom was dangerously undercapitalized, and his house of cards began to tremble. A clique of well-meaning white philanthropists offered to bail him out, but the race-proud Perry refused their help; then a small circle of black leaders tried to raise the needed money, but could not do so. Perry had to accept a short-term loan from a white-owned insurance company with fifty-one percent of Standard's stock put up as collateral. When he failed to meet his financial obligations in a timely fashion, that company assumed control. The *Tribune*'s headline blared: "Standard Life Lost to the Race / White Company Takes It Over for Less Than $175,000." Standard had to be substantively restructured, and Percy Bond (like many other company executives) forfeited his equity investments.[103]

Soon, however, Percy acquired a position as "supervisor of [the] Eastern Division" for the Chicago-based Victory Life Insurance Company, a newer and considerably smaller operation that Negroes still owned and operated. The fickle *Tribune*, which had been so critical of him three years earlier, praised Victory Life's "Mr. J. Percy Bond [as] one of the best-informed insurance men of our race, [with] a nation-wide reputation as a progressive business man." In 1926, Percy hosted the local visit of his company's president, who assured Washingtonians that he was optimistic about the future of the Negro insurance industry "despite several untoward happenings in recent years with other companies less fortunately situated than Victory."[104]

In 1997, Rupert Clark, a stalwart in Washington's insurance industry for more than seven decades, recalled from his earliest years in the city that every African American in his field "looked up to Percy Bond . . . respected and revered him." "When we spoke of insurance, we spoke of Mr. Bond," asserted Clark, a black Panamanian who came to the United States in 1921 seeking the same opportunities as did so many European immigrants.[105]

Standard Life Insurance Company's collapse probably upset the "respected" and "revered" Percy Bond even more than the District's glum political and racial circumstances in the mid-1920s, but he kept up a stoic facade and continued his civic activities. He and Georgia maintained their social standing, and joined the small, select group (including Mary Church Terrell, Anna Julia Cooper, and Georgia Douglas Johnson) attending a chic "Literary Tea" late in 1926 that honored W. E. B. Du Bois, who held forth about his "Trip Through Russia and the Russian Theater." With other audiences, however, Du Bois boldly proclaimed that if what he had seen and heard "in Russia is Bolshevism, I am a Bolshevik."[106]

Their setbacks did not force the Bonds to give up their automobile or Georgia's servant, nor did Wenonah have to drop out of college. But even as Percy Bond received pre-Christmas tidings from Hyde Park about the abrupt decline in his eighty-year-old mother's physical condition, he had to consider selling the Highland Beach cottage to one of his Mu-So-Lit Club colleagues. As Percy's own health incrementally began to degenerate, the Bonds' accustomed way of life started to unravel.[107]

ALL *the* WORLD'S *a* STAGE

*More and more the art of the Negro actor will seek its materials
in the rich soil of Negro life, and not in the threadbare tradition
of the Caucasian stage. . . . The deliberate turning back for dramatic
material to the ancestral sources of African life and tradition is a
very significant symptom.*

ALAIN LOCKE, in *Theatre Arts Monthly*, 1926

"SOUTH OF THE North, yet North of the South, lies the City of a
Hundred Hills, peering out from the shadows of the past into the
promise of the future," W. E. B. Du Bois had written in 1903 about
Atlanta, the place he then called home. Almost two decades later,
his former student Carrie secured a coveted appointment at Atlanta
University, and late in 1922 its alumni bulletin announced that
"Mrs. Caroline Bond Day has returned to her Alma Mater as a
teacher of Expression." "We are fortunate in getting a teacher of
such unusual ability and training as she," it added, "one who
knows what a high mark in dramatics and expression . . . was set
by Mrs. Adrienne Herndon." In addition to classroom work, Carrie would direct the college's theater productions, following in the
footsteps of Herndon, her deceased, but still revered mentor.[1]

Under the aegis of his father-in-law J. Percy Bond, and bolstered by a solid education at Prairie View and the University of
Chicago, two years as an army captain and ten of college teaching
experience, Aaron Day, Jr., left academia in 1922 to take a more remunerative job at Standard Life Insurance Company's Atlanta

headquarters. The Houston-born Heman Perry, Standard's president and a fellow southeast Texan, may have found in Captain Day both a common spirit and an uncommonly desirable recruit.

Perry and others of Atlanta's entrepreneurial Negroes played major roles as insurance companies anchored the city's flourishing black business community. While Perry headed Standard, Alonzo Herndon (Adrienne's widower) ably guided Atlanta Life. "The amazing metamorphosis that is taking place at 180 Auburn [Standard's headquarters], the Wall Street of Atlanta's 'Black Belt,' " dazzled Eric Walrond, the reporter from New York who profiled Perry's company for *Forbes* financial magazine.[2]

Eric Walrond was much more than a one-time correspondent for *Forbes*. He was a handsome, urbane young man of British Caribbean birth and education. Walrond flirted with Marcus Garvey's Pan-Africanism, became an editor and writer with the National Urban League's magazine *Opportunity,* and soon would author one of the Harlem Renaissance's most acclaimed anthologies, *Tropic Death,* which explored themes and issues ranging from migration and cultural disorientation to racial exclusion or assimilation.[3]

Walrond encountered "men and women from Harvard, Yale, Oxford, Cornell, Fisk, Columbia, Amherst, Pennsylvania, Carnegie Institute of Technology, Chicago [probably Aaron Day], Ohio State, . . . Wisconsin, Michigan," and other elite schools among Standard's employees in Georgia, though one of Atlanta's white corporate lawyers seemed amazed that "these people are no longer serfs." Walrond wrote that he "felt like one in a trance" as he "entered the $152,000 office building of the Standard Life," with its furnishings and equipment valued at an additional $100,000.[4]

In addition to Standard, Heman Perry's commercial ventures included several banks, laundries, real estate, trucking, and construction businesses. His building enterprise, "whose payroll alone amount[ed] to $11,000 weekly, [employed] Negro architects, engineers, brick masons, carpenters, etc." *Forbes* noted that Perry "is spoken of variously as a dreamer, a wizard; . . . ten years ahead of his ablest associates, twenty years ahead of the average person, and fifty years ahead of the South." He also was rumored to be personally "insured for $1,000,000."[5]

The men who "direct[ed] the affairs of Standard Life and its subsidiary companies," wrote Eric Walrond, were "keen, alert, hardheaded," and he described Standard Life Insurance Company's vice president W. H. King as a "self-made man." The savvy King assured the reporter that "Mr. Forbes' 'Men Who Are Making America' . . . has been my prayer book," then added, "I never dreamed of living to see the time when a colored man would be sent down here to get a story for 'Forbes Magazine.' " Perry's lieutenants, who arrived as green outsiders, secured their social status by "marrying up" into the established Negro elite, as Atlanta's new money successfully merged with its old, respected families.[6]

Auburn Avenue, adjacent to the city's finest "colored" residential neighborhood, was home to a plethora of businesses that formed an apparently solid economic base for the African American community. That bustling strip featured the black-owned Atlanta *Independent*'s news bureau, funeral homes, restaurants and hotels, banks, florists, grocers, fraternal organizations, the YMCA and YWCA, and a branch of the National Urban League. By 1922, five Negro insurance companies had offices on "Sweet Auburn."[7]

Forbes's reporter Walrond noted that "the colored population of Atlanta is 75,000." He boasted that "it is, however, the most *literate* kind of population, for Atlanta is a sort of breeding place for Negro schools and colleges . . . the home of Morehouse College, Atlanta University, Morris Brown, Clark, and Spelman Seminary." By comparison, the cynical New Yorker scoffed, "Harlem . . . is shaming in its backwardness."[8]

Like Fisk and Howard, Atlanta University (often called AU) and the city's other "colored" colleges had developed a sizable clientele among the Negro "better" classes, many of whom could not afford, or did not want their children to face discrimination at, predominantly white schools. But they chose as alternatives only the best, academically oriented, historically black colleges, where their offspring could study alongside others of similar backgrounds, and young women would meet the "right" young men to marry. AU still had a white president—the aging New Englander Myron Winslow Adams—but increasing numbers of its teachers and administrators were African Americans.[9]

One well-established Negro instructor was George Towns, Carrie's neighbor, onetime teacher, and the professor of English and pedagogy with whom she worked on student oratory. Carrie also gravitated to Towns because he was a friend of Du Bois and a Harvard graduate (the only black man in the class of 1900), who, one critic claimed, had "more of the Yankee brogue in his speech than a downright Easterner." Towns, whose credo was "the ballot is the right preservative of all rights," also was renowned at the Negro colleges because he always rode his bicycle around Atlanta rather than submit to segregated seating on streetcars.[10]

E. Franklin Frazier (the Howard- and Clark University–trained sociologist whom members of the group that Du Bois designated the Talented Tenth would label a traitor three decades later when he wrote his contentious treatise *Black Bourgeoisie*) was a newcomer. Frazier arrived in 1922 to accept an appointment heading AU's new school of social work. He observed and lavishly praised Negroes' entrepreneurial endeavors, especially admired the successes of Standard and Atlanta Life Insurance Companies, but also cautioned that his new city "has gone her way in her mad pursuit of wealth." "Today," Frazier continued, "some think of Atlanta . . . as the home of the present Ku Klux Klan," and indeed, that racist cabal recently had been revivified in nearby Stone Mountain, Georgia, but, he conceded, "it is not as active in Atlanta as in places where Negroes enjoy a greater share of freedom."[11]

Frazier also complained that "White Atlanta knows nothing of Black Atlanta, except through Negro servants and criminals." "The *Constitution* [the city's leading white-owned newspaper] continues to insult Negroes by refusing to print Mr. and Mrs. or Miss before their names," he asserted, and "by picturing [them] as 'contented darkies,' criminals and clowns." Concerning the legal system, he protested, "a civilized man cast among cannibals would have a better chance of justice than a Negro in an Atlanta court."[12] Few blacks could vote, but Frazier based his hope for future racial progress on the fact that "the Atlanta Branch of the National Association for the Advancement of Colored People is attempting to regain its former place of honor." He also cited his new hometown as "headquarters of the Committee on Interracial Co-Operation," which, he continued, "is endeavoring to get the South to provide the same educational and health facilities and protection of the law for Negroes as for other citizens."[13]

Frazier boasted that "Atlanta is the colored educational center of the South" and described his world as one of "college-crowned hills looking down upon White Atlanta scrambling in the market places for gold." He applauded whites (who still outnumbered black educators in the college division) like the university's President Adams and Professor Edgar Webster, who "has 'kept the faith' through all its years of struggle for Negro manhood." Atlanta's colleges, Frazier added, demonstrated that "Negroes have reached a high cultural development, but this does not mean that White Atlanta has shown [them] any more respect." The city's African American intellectuals had achieved a great deal, he believed, but had not yet "buil[t] up a community of scholars, who, through contact and mutual criticism, would be as productive as other scholars." "[They] should give to Atlanta a richer and deeper community life," he insisted.[14]

He harshly chastised members of his race whose "social life . . . revolves around the churches." "[They] go to church all day Sundays," Frazier complained, then "on week days, they seek as a stimulus for their drab lives the puerile movies." In the same vein, George Towns's ardent, college-age daughter Grace advocated boycotting the city's movie houses with their "Nigger Heaven" balconies. In the school magazine, she declared: "Self-pride and self-respect are far more valuable than the admission of inferiority by going up high to see a 15-cent show."[15]

During E. Franklin Frazier's years at AU, his school changed substantially. It started phasing out the venerable Preparatory Division when the city's Booker T. Washington High School opened— largely staffed by AU's graduates. The university also added not only the School of Social Work, but a business program, and evening and summer sessions. The first joint classes between coed Atlanta University, all-male Morehouse (formerly Atlanta Baptist) College, and all-female Spelman Seminary began at that time as well, and pointed toward a formal affiliation.[16]

John Hope, who would lead that new consortium a few years

later, was Morehouse's president, while his wife Lugenia, who had worked with Carrie during the Great War, directed a volunteer organization that addressed black Atlanta's moral, educational, and public health concerns. Lugenia Hope spoke for many Negroes when she protested that "the white woman, . . . thinks of the servant in her home because that is the only colored woman she knows." "How many . . . white women of the South know about our educational institutions?" Lugenia asked on behalf of her race, sex, and class. Lugenia and John Hope, E. Franklin and Marie Frazier, George and Nellie Towns, Morehouse's director of music Kemper Harreld and his wife Claudia, the Heman Perrys, the W. H. Kings, and others of their ilk comprised Carrie and Aaron Day's social, intellectual, and professional circles in Atlanta.[17]

The Days' status, however, was based far more on education, culture, manners and mores ("family and character," one Atlanta matron confided) than on money.[18] But if they enjoyed public success during the mid-1920s, they also established unusual and fluctuating private lives. For two years, Carrie resided in an AU girls' dormitory, while Aaron maintained separate "bachelor" quarters nearby. But at other times, Carrie confirmed that "my husband and I are living on the campus." In that period, her most congenial abode, overflowing with books and magazines like her favorite *Theatre News Monthly,* was the Bumstead Cottage (named for and originally the residence of AU's second president), a charming, gabled and vine-covered, two-unit transplanted New England house where Adrienne and Alonzo Herndon had once resided. It stood next door to the neoclassic Herndon mansion and across the street from the Townses' home. Aaron traveled extensively on business, but Carrie entertained friends like the Townses and the Harrelds, whom she engaged in scintillating Sunday evening discourses about politics, the theater, and anthropology.[19] With their attachments to the intellectual elite through Carrie's university work, and the entrepreneurial establishment courtesy of Aaron's ascending rank in Standard Life, the Days were well hitched to Negro Atlanta's upper class.

Those were their circumstances in fall 1924 when Carrie's sister matriculated at Atlanta University and came more fully under her aegis. Carrie was delighted, felt profoundly maternal, and soon wrote a friend: "Wenonah . . . is a very conscientious child and a great joy and comfort to me since I have none of my own." Her eager scholars, plus a beloved younger sister, provided Carrie with ample opportunities for parenting.[20]

Wenonah Bond, however, never became the compliant student her mother might have hoped for at that respected but conservative southern school. In the postwar years, AU still tried to enforce what one observer characterized as a "code of conduct . . . as high-minded as it was narrow." It banned unchaperoned courting, drinking and smoking, and maintained a dated dress code. "To promote the interests of true democracy, to discourage extravagance and cultivate habits of reasonable economy," its catalogue insisted, the college required girls to wear "cotton and wool. Preferably white and navy, and natural color pongee." It forbade "extremes in styles," even insisting that "shoes with French heels cannot be worn."[21]

Young people such as Wenonah chafed at such stylistic and behavioral strictures. She became an editor of the AU student magazine, the *Scroll,* where she complained (among other things) about the library. "It is a physical impossibility to do the required . . . readings under the existing circumstances," Wenonah wrote. "Book hogs," she declaimed, refused to relinquish reserved assignments, while students stomped around conversing loudly with nary a thought to others. She bristled at her school's rigid parietal rules. "If the library is the only place 'sufficiently chaperoned' for us to have social contacts between men and women," she protested, "why do we not ask for more?" "Things about which there are regulations, we grumble over among ourselves, and never think of talking them over [with] the executives, and yet we resent it when we are treated like children," Wenonah concluded. But in a less confrontational tone, she made certain that her colleagues were fully informed about eligibility, applications, and terms for student loans.[22]

She made great friends, and two of them became lifetime comrades. Grace Towns, whom Wenonah described as "a gay, witty creature, but always intellectually curious," was the daughter of Carrie's AU colleague George Towns. Willowy, blue-eyed Myra

Logan, who also served as an editor of the *Scroll,* was the youngest sister of Carrie's old pal Ruth Logan Roberts and daughter of the Bond family's onetime Tuskegee Institute associates Warren and the late Adella Logan. Myra ultimately became an accomplished surgeon, while four decades later, following passage of the 1965 Voting Rights Act, Atlantans elected Grace Towns Hamilton as the first female African American member of any Deep South state legislature. Until 1926, when Wenonah, Myra, and Grace roomed together, Grace lived at her family's home across from Carrie's cottage.[23]

Myra spoke out as bluntly as did Wenonah and Grace. She protested that "the [student] council has not worked hard enough . . . it has not put any thought into its plans." As a "cure" for life's "drab, colorless moments," however, Myra—a gifted pianist and actress—also challenged her classmates to "enjoy a bit of poetry, a lovely picture, a few measures of melody."[24]

Carrie's work in theater brought her accolades, and she cast Wenonah and Myra in several productions. In 1924, the school magazine stated that "the class in Elocution under Mrs. Carrie Bond Day gave two especially good one-act plays." On another occasion, the journal applauded her as "directress" of *The Slave with Two Faces.* "The audience was thrilled," it added, and "everyone was sorry to leave when the time of departure came." The *Scroll* also singled out "the acting of Miss [Myra] Logan . . . [as] especially commendable." When Carrie's AU college troupe presented Richard Sheridan's comedy *The Rivals,* the magazine enthused that her "untiring efforts are met with great results."[25]

The university's dedicated and senior-most white professor, Edgar Webster, recently had commissioned a portrait of Frederick Douglass for his school. Then in 1925, Thomas Jefferson Flanagan, class lyricist and artist, donated to AU the fine likeness in oils that he had painted of Webster. Flanagan also submitted an outstanding entry to the *Constitution*'s annual art contest, but when the newspaper discovered his race, it removed his work from the general competition, stripped him of his previously announced prize, and granted him a "special" award.[26]

The college library was expanding (the Cambridge, Massachusetts, educator Maria Baldwin, one of Carrie's colleagues in the Circle for Negro War Relief, willed it all of her books), and Atlanta University fostered the visual, performing, and literary arts in its role as a vital outpost of the 1920s' Harlem Renaissance. As a bit player in that burgeoning, race-based creative explosion, in addition to directing and teaching, Carrie wrote for the NAACP's *Crisis* and the National Urban League's *Opportunity.* For some pieces, she reconfigured traditional African folklore, while her article in *Crisis,* "What Shall We Play?" (illustrated with a photo from one of her AU Shakespearean productions), detailed dramas and comedies well suited to Negro theater groups like the student thespians whom she directed. Pulling material from sources such as *Theatre Arts Monthly,* she identified plays that included roles she deemed especially suitable for what she characterized as her "bouquet race." Carrie hardly ignored the classics, but primarily recommended works that were "free from royalties, not necessarily expensive, entirely within the grasp of amateurs, and . . . allow some parts for persons of mixed blood and of purely Negroid types."[27]

She divided them into three groups. The first included "allegories, moralities, and adapted fairy tales." A second cluster featured "Plays of Different Nationalities," with one-acters set in the Near and Far East, North Africa, and the world of Native Americans. "Among the modern sketches" (her final category) Carrie recommended works by Russian, Spanish, and many Asian playwrights. "With their latent histrionic ability," Carrie continued, "our younger group is going to develop a splendid technic by producing the better type of plays." "The time is not far off," she optimistically predicted, "when there will be a great demand for good Negro actors and actresses."[28]

Though unmentioned in that article, Carrie also read plays by members of Georgia Douglas Johnson's Washington, D.C., writers' circle. Johnson herself wrote *Little Blue Pigeon,* the story of a mother who had to pass for white so that she could keep a job and support her child.[29] *Crisis* published Alice Dunbar-Nelson's "*Mine Eyes Have Seen,*" a play about the Great War, in which a young draftee demanded: "Must I go and fight for the nation that let my father's murder [by white men] go unpunished?" His sister's exhortation that "we do need you, but your country needs you more" began to persuade him otherwise. "Above that," she continued, "your race is calling you to carry on its good name." Carrie promptly penned a laudatory letter to Dunbar-Nelson in which she pronounced the new work "splendid."[30]

Dunbar High School's Mary Burrill wrote *"Aftermath"* for the Socialist magazine the *Liberator*. It dealt with a Negro war hero who returned from battle to learn that his father had been lynched. Another Burrill play, *"They That Sit in Darkness,"* appearing in *Birth Control Review*, recounted the story of a poor black woman who had been denied access to contraceptives and endured numerous debilitating pregnancies. "You are punishing yourself by having children year after year," a visiting nurse warned, but the woman died as the result of her fatally weakened heart. Carrie, with her own rheumatic condition, may have read it and sworn that she absolutely would not share such a fate.[31]

Angelina Grimké (also a Dunbar teacher) wrote and staged a play titled *Rachel,* in which the protagonist vowed never to bear children because of the ignominies her race endured and that any of her potential daughters or sons presumably would face as well. Like her heroine, Grimké too had resolved neither to marry nor have children. Both Burrill's *"They That Sit in Darkness"* and Grimké's *Rachel* held white society largely responsible for making pregnancy, childbearing and -rearing so potentially hazardous for "colored" women. Those two plays by members of Georgia Douglas Johnson's (and Carrie Bond Day's) cadre of female colleagues also tacitly gave "colored" women license to reject having children and to control the circumstances and consequences of their sexuality. They challenged traditional notions that childless women were unfeminine, incomplete, unfulfilled, or only existed for or achieved satisfaction through procreation.[32]

Marita Bonner, one of Carrie's Radcliffe contemporaries, moved to Washington in 1924, where she, too, penetrated Georgia Douglas Johnson's literary domain. Soon thereafter, Bonner completed her first play, *The Purple Flower,* a lyrical allegory that placed the racial conflicts and stress that all African Americans experienced into a universal context.[33]

Howard University's Alain Locke published two articles concerning Negroes' involvement with the American theater in Carrie's preferred, well-perused journal, *Theater Arts Monthly*. He praised Angelina Grimké and W. E. B. Du Bois as "noteworthy" Negro playwrights, and cheered the appearance of new black theater groups in New York and Washington. "One of the main reactions of Negro drama must and will be the breaking down of those false stereotypes in terms of which the world still sees us," Locke asserted. He also insisted that "drama should stimulate the group life culturally," encouraged "development of a thoroughly racial drama," and urged gifted Negro authors and actors to "achieve creative independence."[34]

Like her counterparts in Washington, D.C., Carrie Bond Day continued her own writing. "The Pink Hat" appeared in *Opportunity* and won a third prize in the National Urban League's 1926 short story competition. The League honored all of its annual literary winners with a gala dinner, replete with luminaries of the Negro Renaissance and dignitaries of both races in the "gold-mirrored dining room" of one of New York City's most elegant restaurants. Other awardees (in various categories) during the mid-1920s included Georgia Douglas Johnson, Countee Cullen, Langston Hughes, Marita Bonner, E. Franklin Frazier, Eric Walrond, and Boston's Dorothy West.[35]

"The Pink Hat" was a minimally fictionalized account chronicling the changes that temporarily altered the life of Carrie's protagonist (a thinly veiled depiction of Carrie herself) when her racially ambiguous appearance caused her to be mistaken for a white woman. "This hat has become to me a symbol," she wrote. "It is at once my magic carpet, my enchanted cloak, my Aladdin's lamp." The "rough, straw hat" that hid her "frizzy hair smoothed by the Marcel" and reflected a rosy glow onto her skin became a vehicle for her metamorphosis. When first she wore it, Carrie explained, a "gentleman of obvious rank arose and offered me a seat" on the streetcar. Next, a "lad jumped to rescue my gloves [then] a policeman helped me across the street." She was stunned when a "salesgirl sweetly drawled, 'Miss or Mrs.?'" Minus the hat, whites addressed her with a first name only, "for you see this is south of the Mason and Dixon line, and I am a Negro woman of mixed blood unaccustomed to these respectable prefixes." She "encountered a new girl" at another store "who was the essence of courtesy." When that salesclerk asked, "But where do you teach?" Carrie's protagonist answered truthfully, giving the name of a local college for African Americans. "Well—I felt sorry for her," the narrator continued. "She had blundered. She had been chatting familiarly, almost intimately, with a Negro," Carrie concluded about the naive white woman who had lost her footing on the muddy slope of southern racial protocol.

After those first heady experiences, she admitted, "I deliberately set out to deceive. Now, I decided, I would enjoy all that had previously been impossible." "So thus disguised," she continued, "I enjoyed everything from the attentions of an expert chiropodist, to grand opera, . . . I could be comforted with a hot drink at the same soda-fountain where ordinarily I should have been hissed at." "I could pull my hat down a bit and buy a ticket to see my favorite movie star," she added. That rarefied universe inhabited by white women became irresistible. "I could . . . have the decent comfort of ladies' rest rooms," Carrie wrote, "have my shoes fitted in the best shops, and be shown the best values in all of the stores—not the common styles 'which all the darkies buy.' " The transformational hat "transported [her] into the midst of a local art exhibit, to enjoy the freshness of George Inness . . . to see white-folk enjoying [works by the expatriate Negro painter Henry] Tanner—really nice, likable folk too, when they don't know one." Carrie rediscovered gratifying diversions as she escaped the day-to-day indignities inflicted on all Negroes in the American South. Ultimately, she attended a gala Christmas concert but found that she "could not enjoy this without compunction . . . for there was not a dark face . . . among all of those thousands of people, and my two hundred bright-eyed youngsters should have been there."[36]

Then, however, the fragile bubble burst. "One does have . . . down here, subconscious pictures of hooded figures and burning crosses," Carrie admitted, and as she was "hurrying out to avoid the crowd," she stumbled and broke an ankle. She was taken home and put to "bed with my family—a colored family—and in a colored section of town." She hoped to try osteopathy, but when a once gracious white practitioner learned where she resided and taught, he reneged, saying, "No . . . it is against the rules of the osteopathic association to serve Negroes." When her own physician "talked bone-surgery," a companion (a "dear, loyal daughter of New England") suggested Christian Science, adding, "They will give you absent treatments, and when you are better we will go down." Carrie, in her surrogate's voice, regretted snapping back in anger: "Where, to the back door?" for she truly had not intended to wound her well-intentioned white friend.

The ankle mended, she wrote, "and mirabile dictu! . . . My spirit had knit together as well as my bones." Carrie was pleased "to be well again and back at [her] desk." "My brown boys and girls have become reservoirs of interest," she said, proudly adding, "One is attending Radcliffe this year." She rediscovered Chaucer, "dug out forgotten romances to be read aloud, [and ordered] seed catalogues for spring." Savoring those pleasures, Carrie (through her heroine) cast aside any residual desire once again to don her alchemic bonnet and pass for white. "Who'd want a hat?" her narrative nonchalantly concluded.[37]

Carrie's story raised the controversial issue of passing that intrigued so many writers of the Harlem Renaissance who grappled with the inanities surrounding the social and legal constructions of race. Many light-skinned Negroes toyed with the notion but rejected it as a way of life. Yet those who did pass (selecting race as they might a costume—or a rose-colored chapeau—to put on or take off in order to perform differing societal roles) sometimes served as bridges across a deep racial divide. They became cultural transmitters: carriers of whiteness into the Negro community and occasional conduits to or interpreters of blackness to the majority. Yet Carrie found many of Atlanta's light-skinned Negro elite reluctant to discuss either passing or their white ancestry. They considered it part of an ugly history and a distasteful present that they would as soon forget.[38]

Carrie's job, marriage, poor health, and limited finances combined to postpone her academic ambitions, but she still hoped to complete her Du Bois–inspired studies on racial admixtures—including the import of passing. Some of her relatives passed at will, and, considered in toto, they illustrated all of the diverse physical traits seen in what Carrie would call "Negro-White Families in the United States." She faithfully described herself in "The Pink Hat." "I look like hundreds of other colored women . . . slightly heavy featured, with frizzy brown hair," she wrote; "the ruddy pigment of Scotch-Irish ancestry is my inheritance, and it is this which shows through my yellow skin."[39]

Carrie Bond Day ultimately decided not to pass. She had reinforced her racial identity and hobbled American citizenship through her work on behalf of Negro soldiers during the recent war and through her passion for suffrage, and also embraced diverse familial roles as a daughter, sister, and wife. She considered herself a good Christian and a member of the African American social and intellectual elite. She became a theater director, teacher, scholar, and writer who revealed a strong allegiance to her black cultural heritage through some captivating African folktales. Embracing a multiracial world vision, she equally esteemed the artistry of painters like the expatriate African American Henry Tanner and the Anglo-American George Inness. She read and produced plays by England's William Shakespeare, Russia's Anton Chekhov, and India's Rabindranath Tagore, as well as her friend Alice Dunbar-Nelson.[40] At the same time, however, Carrie tried to pull shut a semiopaque curtain of respectability and deception to obscure her sexual identity.

If women who establish primary emotional and romantic attachments with others of their sex, whether or not they engage in intimate genital relations, can (and should) be considered lesbians, then aspects and details of Carrie's life indicate that customary late-twentieth-century categorizations suggest placing her among the Sapphic sisterhood. She probably did not choose to identify herself that way, but the patterns and rhythms of her life, clues provided by her work, and sustained observation by several people who knew her well, combine to hint at her unorthodox, and possibly homosexual, preferences.[41]

As for revealing particulars from Carrie's history, her adolescent affection for Adrienne Herndon seemed singularly intense, and in that same impressionable period she probably shunned a "normal" interest in boys. While she was in her twenties, like many white women who have been identified as lesbians or bisexuals, Carrie immersed herself in close circles of unmarried female reformers through social service work. She also had resolved to attend Radcliffe, a women's college, and live in all-female residences. And for her generation's tastes and practices, she remained single too long and married too late. She pursued a male-dominated scientific field, and that countered prevailing sexual stereotypes of women as intuitive and guided by emotion, and men as avatars of the intellect. Her interest in anthropology easily could have been considered symptomatic of a "mannish" woman.

Almost immediately after they wed in 1920, Carrie left Aaron in Texas, and they scarcely were together again until she went to teach at Prairie View eighteen months later. When they moved to Atlanta, their separations continued, as Aaron Day, who radiated virility and was known as "a ladies' man," traveled with Standard Life Insurance Company for extended stretches.[42] Those absences offered both of the Days opportunities for extramarital liaisons. Any of Aaron's possible extracurricular romances did not generate Carrie's erotic preferences, but they might explain his lack of concern about the marriage's apparent absence of a sexual component. They maintained separate abodes for several years when Carrie took up residence in a girls' dormitory at AU. By late 1926, she was preparing to move back to Boston—again without Aaron—to pursue graduate study at Harvard. Any or all of those separations, however, might be interpreted alternately as simply pragmatic, or unusually progressive for the times. The Days were a rare couple who did not subordinate Carrie's education, career, and diverse interests to those of her husband. The fact that she never became pregnant reflected appropriate medical concerns about her rheumatic heart, but also suggests that she may have used that infirmity as an excuse to abstain from sexual intercourse, because throughout their married life, even when they shared a home, Carrie and Aaron virtually never shared a bedroom.[43]

One of Carrie's Washington friends and correspondents, Dunbar High School's Otelia Cromwell, frankly admitted: "I closed my door on matrimony," a decision common to many mutual acquaintances.[44] Female professionals who made that choice because of work—their missions, their callings—established a single status unencumbered by men. Some women in that faction fostered exclusive and intimate female alliances, while others, like Carrie (despite the ways that her marriage may have played out behind closed doors), ultimately chose to marry.

Otelia Cromwell and her sisters shared a gracious home (where Georgia, Carrie, and Wenonah often went for tea) and probably suppressed their romantic yearnings as, together, they embraced spinsterhood. But that was not the case with others of Carrie's circle in the nation's capital, where she spent so much time with her family. The Bonds' friend Georgia Douglas Johnson convened Washington's foremost literary salon, which attracted a brilliant coterie of writers, including the reputed homosexuals Alain Locke, Countee Cullen, Langston Hughes—perhaps even Eric Walrond.[45] Dunbar's Angelina Grimké, Mary Burrill, and her companion and housemate, Howard's Dean Lucy Slowe, also belonged to that clique. They, too, seem to have preferred and sought out physical intimacy with same-sex partners. Carrie's associate and correspondent Alice Dunbar-Nelson lived in Wilmington, Delaware, but she often visited the District, where she attended Johnson's soirées. Dunbar-Nelson wed three times, yet intermittently took male and female lovers as well. Rumors of lesbianism also circulated about Dunbar's Mary Gibson (although she, too, eventually married but was childless) and Eva Dykes, both of whom remained close friends following their Radcliffe College years, which overlapped Carrie's.

Within her institution, Dean Slowe committed herself to creating a secure, discreet milieu for Howard's women, and it is hard to believe that a school such as Atlanta University did not develop an analogous circle. Like a number of female couples at the elite (and almost all-white) Seven Sisters colleges, some black female academics similarly formed intimate, supportive relationships with members of their own sex in lieu of, or in addition to, conventional but predictably restrictive marriages.

Another of Carrie's acquaintances in New York during World

War I was A'Lelia Walker Robinson, whom elitist Harlemites derided as the "dekink heiress" because, they snickered, her wealth derived from products that straightened Negroes' hair. She nonetheless became one of the Harlem Renaissance's favorite hostesses. A'Lelia wed several times, but she, too, may have used marriage as a facade to conceal her own variant preferences, like those displayed at her gala, freewheeling, lesbian-friendly salons that attracted swanky socialites and entertainers of both races to her Hudson River estate and Harlem residences. She collected fabulous costumes, jewelry, and motorcars, and surrounded herself with a retinue of servants and a multinational, interracial entourage of handsome, exquisitely decked-out women and notably effete men.[46] The Renaissance (defined by race and so seductive for Negro intellectuals like Carrie Bond Day throughout the country) blatantly defied traditional, "all-American" cultural norms. In New York its participants—and curious onlookers—usually embraced, or at least condoned, such avant-garde activities and deportment.

That tolerance, however, scarcely extended to cities such as Washington, Atlanta, and Boston, where members of the Talented Tenth maintained their creativity, whispered about those among them who did not conform, and only reluctantly stomached the unorthodox behavior flaunted in Harlem. Wherever and whatever their erotic preferences, "elite" Negro women tried to counter the degrading stereotypes of themselves as wanton and promiscuous, and to do so, sometimes sought to repress their sexuality altogether.[47]

Carrie and many other upper-class Negroes usually shrank from identifying with women whose behavior suggested or evoked sexual "primitivism." In 1925, Jo Baker sailed for Europe (she knew she was free, she said, when she saw the Statue of Liberty sink below the horizon) with *La Revue Nègre*. In Paris, she jiggled her bare breasts, draped ostrich feathers or rubber bananas around her gorgeous "African" rump, performed *La Danse Sauvage,* and became France's favorite exotic, erotic fantasy.[48] Harlem's bawdiest performers included Gertrude "Ma" Rainey, who wrote *Prove It on Me Blues,* with its suggestive lyrics: "Went out last night, / With a crowd of my friends, / They musta bin womens, / Cause I don't

like no men." Another, Gladys Bentley, as hefty as a man, performed in a white tuxedo and top hat, and enjoyed flagrant affairs
with members of her own sex. Atlanta and Washington were straitlaced, but exhilarating Harlem (Eric Walrond, for one, complained
that it had become "a white man's house of assignation") maintained its reputation as a place where Negroes and thrill-seeking
whites looking for a walk on the wild side went seeking wanton
sexual adventures. Those variant influences, even if somewhat geographically removed, all contributed to Carrie's diverse cultural
ambience.[49]

Many Negro intellectuals, labeled the "Niggerati" by sassy Zora
Neale Hurston, shied away from the music spawned in sundry
cathouses and gin mills, so Carrie swayed sedately to the rhythms
of the times but kept a safe distance from most of the more "common" manifestations of African American culture.[50] Nor did she
write (or at least she left no record of) any explicitly Sapphic plays,
essays, or poems. Her earliest narrative from her Tuskegee years,
however, featured an impassioned attachment between two girls.[51]
In her autobiographical story "The Pink Hat," Carrie faithfully described herself, confirmed her "heroine's" marital status, but gave
it only passing mention, perhaps suggesting that her own matrimonial bonds were ancillary.

None of Carrie's literary imagery was as revealing or erotic as
that of a few women in her circle, such as Angelina Grimké ("I may
never press / My lips on thine in mute caress / E'en touch the hem
of thy pure dress,") or Alice Dunbar-Nelson, who evocatively wrote
about a new female amour: "I had not thought to ope that secret
room." Carrie intermittently corresponded with Dunbar-Nelson,
and one flattering missive confessed, "My students have quoted
from your little poem called 'Violets.' "[52]

Unlike her correspondence with men, Carrie's letters to some
other women were intimate and flirtatious. Writing a former student, she regretted that "I couldn't offer the attractions here in Atlanta which Chicago had for you," then coyly queried, "Now what
are those attractions?" She complimented another, "You and some
other young ladies were such beautiful belles in Washington . . . society," and to a third she admitted, "I never cease to miss you."[53]

Nonetheless, those tender scribblings provide no real proof of lesbian romance or physical intimacy.

But perhaps Carrie's familiarity with Shakespeare provided theatrical parallels to her veiled sexuality. Might she have masqueraded as Viola/Cesario and expected or hoped to be wooed by a comely Olivia? What escapades might she have stimulated to replicate the Bard's gender transmogrifications and evocations of transvestism exemplified by Orlando's sylvan romps with the elusive Rosalind (as Ganymede)? Or could Carrie, like Lady Macbeth, have yearned to cry out, "Come, you spirits . . . unsex me," or have pictured herself as an androgynous Ariel? A 1925 article in *Theatre Arts Monthly,* "The Women in Shakespeare's Plays," assessed some similarly gendered dramatic ambiguities. In the theater, lights, a scrim, nuanced gesture or language, costume or makeup, could always transform age, ethnicity, race—or sex.[54]

The recurrent patterns of Carrie's life, a few of her writings, and the cast of lesbians, gays, and bisexuals who crossed her stage, combine to hint at her anomalous sexuality. Moreover, some of her colleagues and relatives firmly believed that Carrie's physical displays of affection for several women friends surpassed "normal" compassionate expressions of sisterhood—yet others take exception to such interpretations.[55]

Might Carrie's teacher Adrienne Herndon (though she married one of Atlanta's Negro entrepreneurs and became a mother) have caressed her adolescent protégée and initiated Carrie into a penumbral world of love between women? Then could Carrie, a few years later, have done the same with one or more of her own students? Did her abrupt withdrawal from college dances suggest an early (and then abiding) distaste for physical contact with the opposite sex? Or had she shared covert embraces with her lovely friend who appeared in their tender 1912 graduation photograph from AU? And might elusive rumors of "deviant" behavior even have deterred that school's dean from endorsing Carrie Bond's admission to Radcliffe College three years later?

How easy or difficult would it have been for Carrie to proceed from sharing an apartment with a companion of her own sex to sharing a boudoir, to sharing a bed? She had opportunities to establish a "Boston marriage" in all-female residences while she studied at Radcliffe before and after the World War. Might she have developed deeply intimate friendships with associates or schoolmates there, an "Adamless Eden," where some of her contemporaries, though circumspect, were less guarded about their sexual preferences?[56]

How far could it have been from companionably trying on a girlfriend's new frock to removing it? How simple to progress from chaste kisses on the cheek to lingering ones on the lips, or breasts? From entwined fingers to entangled limbs? When life's harshness and dissonances demanded a shoulder to weep on, did choice or desire steer Carrie toward more ardent embraces with someone who had a downy cheek instead of a bristly jowl and a yielding body that almost replicated her own? Did post-Victorian prudishness and a well-reinforced predilection to uphold the external manifestations of respectability that so often consumed the Negro upper class mean that she suppressed her sexuality, or did verve, curiosity, and passion inspire her to explore different modes of expression and more adventuresome amorous possibilities?

Carrie had a fling with passing for white but rejected it as a permanent mode of living. On the other hand, she may have concealed her erotic preferences from most associates to "pass" as a "normal" woman, because even sophisticates like her mentor Du Bois sometimes succumbed to homophobia. Marriage furnished Carrie and Aaron with an opaque cloak that helped to deflect probing inquiries. It could have allowed them space to conduct their intimate behavior in nontraditional ways, and provided a secure base and the solid camaraderie that was important to both of them. For Aaron, Carrie epitomized the essence of wit and wisdom, elegance, style, and kindness, while he was her constant friend, her oak, her provider. Even an unconsummated marital partnership provided a cocoon of respectability so crucial to upper-class Negroes who, because of white America's perverted perceptions, were vulnerable to criticism and censure concerning their sexuality. Fear of scandal, humiliation, and loss of social and financial status obsessed them. Among the Talented Tenth, sex of any sort had to remain discreet, often was repressed, frowned upon even as a topic of conversation.

The 1920s' "New Negroes" expressed their racial pride and struggled to alter white America's archaic visions of race, much as "New Women" challenged traditional standards of femininity. Those women—often castigated as feminists—who had aided their country in war, smoked, drank, drove autos, pursued careers, voted, and utilized birth control methods often became renegade "flappers" who flung up their coltish legs to the Charleston's contagious pulse, sheared womanly tresses into boyish bobs, wore bosom-flattening chemises and mannish trousers. Some traditionalists linked such iconoclastic behavior and "cross-dressing" to lesbianism, while much of the decade's "New Music," especially the blues, featured coarse, "unladylike" lyrics that shattered traditional erotic taboos and mirrored black women's (often harsh, sometimes variant) sexuality.[57]

In those years, the prevalent medical, intellectual, and psychological theories advanced by Sigmund Freud promoted the widespread belief that adult lesbianism was a manifestation of childhood trauma or a symptom of profound mental disorder, and as such, needed "curing." As a woman for whom the Bible remained a font of inspiration and solace, Carrie also would have recalled traditional interpretations of scriptural tirades concerning female pariahs who distorted "the natural use into that which is against nature," and Old Testament castigations of women's sodomy as "harlotry." Nonetheless, a more lenient and open-minded source— her favorite, William Shakespeare—could have reassured her through an informed reading of *The Merchant of Venice* that "the devil can cite Scriptures for his purpose."[58]

In her earlier work at Radcliffe and then at Atlanta University, Carrie envisioned and created for herself a cross-cultural, interracial, multinational world. She knew that in her United States, rigid lines between the races were legally and socially constructed—not genetic, fixed, or preordained. In Carrie's life, and in her scientific work venue of physical anthropology, "Negro" and "Caucasian" were not dichotomous polar opposites, but amorphous and unresolved categories that skimmed along a multihued spectrum where passing became one means of blurring the borders. But could she have imagined that the boundaries between female and male were comparably porous and equally artificial? She embraced "women's interests" through literature, theater, and art, and "men's interests" through her pursuit of anthropological science. Carrie Bond Day married for a lifetime, but neither assumed a traditional spousal role nor set aside her love of women.

In Carrie's family, as in any other, establishing a sexual identity was crucial. But any facet of identity assumes added import when the majority perceives its expression as abnormal, despicable, even dangerous. In a predominantly Anglo-American society, whiteness remained the norm and scarcely required acknowledgment. If race was undeclared, whiteness was (and is) presumed, and esteemed. Similarly, if sexual orientation went unmentioned, heterosexuality was assumed, and lesbians usually have been judged an aberrant minority who did and do generate hostility from the "normal" majority. For Carrie Bond Day, revealing or concealing her "deviant" sexuality perhaps became a deliberate, even a political, act. Her apparent need to hide that portion of her inner self, and not any prurient erotic fixation, continues to make her sexual orientation significant.

No conclusive evidence, however, firmly pins down Carrie's sexual preferences, and that void epitomizes the often willful concealment of that aspect of Negro women's (especially "elite" Negro women's) lives. Rather than being characterized as frigid, asexual, bisexual, or homosexual, labeled bulldaggers, dykes, queers, or hermaphrodites, perhaps they should be allowed to categorize and reveal themselves—or not. Current political determinations, judgments, or labels probably should not be imposed on the practices, conventions, manners, and mores of the early twentieth century, and Carrie had neither the time nor inclination to embroider her sleeve with a scarlet L.[59]

Her Radcliffe schoolmate Marita Bonner addressed other complexities associated with "Being Young—a Woman—and Colored." In a 1925 *Crisis* essay, Bonner admitted that she and many educated women (like Carrie) "know what you want life to give you: A career as fixed and as calmly brilliant as the North Star." About the frequently iterated responsibilities they bore as members of the more privileged class, she wrote, "All your life you have heard of the debt you owe 'Your People' because you have managed to have the things they have not." She, and others of her background and generation, wanted "a husband you can look up to without looking down on yourself." Bonner pondered why so many people saw "a colored woman only as a gross collection of desires," affirming that the rampant sensuality attributed to Negroes remained an onerous stereotype. In an ever-shifting world, Bonner added, "old ideas, old fundamentals seem worm-eaten, out-grown, worthless, bitter, fit for the scrap-heap of Wisdom." Sometimes, she wrote, "you long to explode and hurt everything white, but you know that you cannot live with a chip on your shoulder." "Being a woman," Bonner continued, "you must sit quietly . . . with a smile ever so slight, . . . so that Life will flow into and not by you." Two decades earlier in *The Souls of Black Folk,* W. E. B. Du Bois had contemplated and analyzed his own "two-ness," as "an American and a Negro." Marita Bonner added a third (while Carrie Bond Day may have appended a fourth) element to that sticky amalgam for herself, and other well-educated African American women.[60]

Carrie loved her work, but also confessed: "Teaching is an exhausting profession unless there are wells to draw from, and the soil of my world seems hard and dry." She bemoaned the fact that "starvation of body or soul sometimes breeds criminals," yet added about her life's continuing satisfactions: "a job, young minds and souls to touch, . . . some books, a child, a garden, Spring!" As a dedicated academic, Carrie embraced the words of her onetime teacher, Du Bois. "The Wings of Atalanta are the coming universities of the South," he had written, adding, "They alone can bear the maiden past the temptation of golden fruit."[61]

Wenonah Bond may have begun to deal with similar promises and frustrations. She followed in Carrie's footsteps and joined her friends Grace Towns and Myra Logan, both of whom also worked with the YWCA. Grace relentlessly prodded that group to desegregate its youth conferences, and she was elected the Student Division's vice president as the YW became the first national organization to embark on such a "radical" racial course. Wenonah, Myra, and Grace believed that interracial activities provided "a beacon light for young women in the South and a spearhead for social change." "We are getting used to meeting with each other," Grace stated, then asked: "How can friendship grow without contact?"[62]

In contrast to her sister, Wenonah had beaus aplenty. Like many American girls in the Jazz Age she "vamped" and smooched, cut her hair, painted her lips, shortened her skirts, teetered on French heels, puffed cigarettes with Myra, Grace, and Carrie, even drank a little speakeasy gin—all in covert disregard of the university's regulations.[63] Like others among the young African American intelligentsia who cavorted to the beat and spirit of the Harlem Renaissance, Wenonah considered herself both a "New Negro" and a "New Woman." She and her girlfriends joined in as the whole country (black, white, and all shades between) ignored the horizon's ominous economic clouds. They rolled down their hose, cranked up the gramophone, and rolled up the rugs. With happy feet and arms and legs akimbo, they pranced and swiveled to the Charleston, the lindy hop, and the black bottom, as they shim-sham-shimmied the evenings away.[64] Building on the impetus generated by the 1920s Negro musical revues like *Runnin' Wild*, their schoolmate Thomas Jefferson Flanagan wrote:

> *Sweet li'l' maid tha's trippin' thro' the ring;*
> *Honey, can you "Charleston"?*
> *When the whistle blows and the man says: "swing,"*
> *Sweet, you want to "Charleston." . . .*
> *Hands on shoulders and heel to heel,*
> *Then, toes to toes and a sort of reel,*
> *Then a wild step and a sort of a kneel,*
> *That's the way to "Charleston."*[65]

During their Christmas holiday in 1926, Wenonah went north with her roommate to visit Myra Logan's eldest sister Ruth in New York City. Ruth and her husband Dr. E. P. Roberts lived in an elegant Harlem town house that was becoming a noted political and intellectual salon. There, Wenonah first spied their youngest brother Arthur—a lanky, curly-haired freshman at Massachusetts's

Williams College—perched atop a ladder in Ruth's kitchen, painting the ceiling. He was, Wenonah later admitted, "the most beautiful boy I'd ever seen." She fell in love with the city that ultimately became her home, and with Arthur Courtney (named for Samuel Courtney, his parents' Tuskegee friend and Georgia and Carrie Stewart Bond's onetime landlord in Boston) Logan, whom she married a decade later.[66]

Those, however, were dark days for Standard Life Insurance Company. Aaron Day, Jr., worked out of Atlanta, but also traveled extensively before settling in as assistant agency director. Negro insurance salesmen like Aaron faced endemic discrimination in trains and hotels, were even chased out of towns they visited. Nonetheless, one reported, "we stayed out there, . . . got a lot of enjoyment out of it [and] met a whole lot of fine people."[67]

As a harbinger of the Great Depression that soon would sweep the country, conditions were worsening in the black business community by the mid-1920s. At first, Standard's president Heman Perry basked in the glow of the publicity generated by Eric Walrond's laudatory *Forbes* article about his company, but he soon came to rue the spotlight that had focused on him. Some Negro business leaders alleged that a white cabal brought him down. Others saw Perry's decline and Standard's collapse as skirmishes in a satanic war that the Ku Klux Klan waged on black men. They claimed that the Klan intended "not only to intimidate the Negro with the rope and the torch, but also to strike at the foundation of his economic strength." They knew about, and feared the implications of, the 1921 terrorism in Tulsa that had annihilated that city's prosperous Negro business sector, killed hundreds, and left thousands homeless. After Georgia's Insurance Department officially ruled Standard "impaired," a number of its employees around the country (like Percy Bond and Aaron Day) sought work elsewhere.[68]

Standard's collapse reverberated in black communities throughout the nation. A setback of that enormity undermined the confidence of African Americans in a variety of entrepreneurial efforts. "I do not rejoice at their downfall, but I prayed for them and grieved with them," observed Alonzo Herndon, president of Standard's foremost competitor, Atlanta Life Insurance Company.

Morehouse College president John Hope, one of the team of influential Negroes who tried to salvage Standard, added that "a dozen white insurance companies might go by the boards and hardly cause a ripple," but, he insisted, "such is not the case with us."[69]

As for Carrie Bond Day, her health had always been delicate. She confided to a friend that in 1925 she had a "severe attack of inflammatory rheumatism . . . which left me a little lame." Nonetheless, as the following year drew to a close, she learned that Harvard University (prompted by Professor Earnest Hooton, who expressed his concern that Carrie was in "poor health and funds were exhausted") had granted her a graduate fellowship so that she might continue her anthropological work.[70] Back to Boston, her favorite city! She could vote; she no longer would have to step to the back of a streetcar or be denied entry to an art gallery, theater, or tea room. She really could study again!

"Many are called but few are chosen for such choice vocations," Georgia Douglas Johnson applauded, while Carrie confided to Nina Du Bois that Aaron "agreed to my going since he expects to be on the road most of the time . . . himself." Agreeably or not, Aaron Day accepted the fact that his wife's new Massachusetts sojourn would be one more inevitable episode in a continuing series of separations. Despite their platonic alliance, Carrie took pride in her husband, who went to work for National Benefit Life Insurance Company after Standard's collapse, and was advancing impressively in the corporate world of Negro insurance. One correspondent shared his view that "Mr. Day . . . is already demonstrating his ability as a leader of men," while Carrie informed another friend that she and Aaron were "still talking about that African trip."[71]

Late in 1926, Wenonah initiated her own plan to leave Atlanta. Industrial schools like Tuskegee Institute flourished in that era, but quality liberal arts colleges for the race such as AU (which defiantly maintained its integrated faculty and dining facilities in the face of Jim Crow laws and endemic disapproval among whites) struggled along in poverty. When the university's board of directors demanded E. Franklin Frazier's resignation that autumn because of his foolhardy "impatience with the niceties of interracial diplomacy," the divided campus seethed as he reluctantly agreed to leave at the end of the academic year. Wenonah, Myra, and Grace could not have ignored that heated debate.

The December issue of *Crisis* carried a photo of a group of costumed Atlanta University students (with Wenonah in the foreground) who performed in the play *Milestones* "under the supervision of Mrs. Caroline Bond Day." The three roommates blithely partied, but diligent study also paid off when they earned academic honors. Grace Towns and Myra Logan would both graduate the following June, and Wenonah hardly wanted to be left behind, so she arranged to head north to continue her education at Boston University. Once there, she would be situated only a few miles from Carrie, as well as her father's family in Hyde Park.[72]

Back in Washington, Percy Bond may have tried to conceal his economic reverses from the younger generation, but Carrie, Wenonah, and even young Jack must have known all about Standard Life Insurance Company's collapse. And they surely heard that their barely known paternal grandmother, Emma Thomas Bond, died in Massachusetts that bittersweet Christmas season.

"Well, 1926 farewell!" Carrie Bond Day's pal Alice Dunbar-Nelson wrote in her diary; "You've been a cruel year in some respects, and yet you could have been infinitely worse."[73] The Bond sisters, Carrie and Wenonah, might well have agreed.

. V .

THE WIDOW'S MIGHT

FURTHER HYDE PARK CHRONICLES,

1905–1926

Reverse: Osie and Frankie Bond (*top*); Betty and Evelyn Bond (*below*), ca. 1933.

· 1 6 ·

PURGATORY:
THE POISONED TREE

There's more to his terrible plight:
His pupils won't close in the light
 His heart is cavorting,
 His wife is aborting,
And he squints through his gun-barrel sight.

He's been treated in every known way,
But his spirochetes grow day by day;
 He's developed paresis,
 Has long talks with Jesus,
And thinks he's the Queen of the May.

Early-twentieth-century doggerel used to teach Boston
medical students about syphilis

"MANY YEARS AGO," the GAR's foremost Negro leader, James Wolff, wrote in 1904, "the Hon. Frederick Douglass said to me: 'Washington, sir, is the heaven of the colored man!' " "It is, . . . with due respect to you," Wolff had contradicted the grand old man, "a political hell." "But Boston . . . gives us everything the white man has," Wolff continued; "schools are open to our children, political suffrage is ours freely, and we have about everything we could desire." "You cannot compare Washington with Boston," James Wolff staunchly contended, "Never!"[1]

But Washington or Boston (where most of the Bond family remained) as heaven, purgatory, or hell largely depended on the eyes and circumstances of the beholder. "Industrially, the situation has some drawbacks," even Hub City boosters like Wolff agreed. "I fear that the attitude toward us in the stores and factories is not as liberal as in other respects," he admitted, and "it may be that the unions are antagonistic." Though neither law nor practice kept black men such as Bob Bond from voting, James Wolff also rued the perturbing political situation for their race in Massachusetts. "Our people are given no recognition by the parties," he sadly admitted; "[they] do not think it necessary to go out of their way to get the colored vote."[2]

Many of Boston's Negro residents understood that in terms of racial amity, "the honeymoon was over" after 1900, and they had entered a new epoch of interracial friction and political impotence. The city (in fact, the whole state) had no black elected officials and few government appointees in those years, although a Negro lawyer was appointed assistant U.S. attorney in 1920 to handle immigration cases. Most of his duties concerned European aliens, but Massachusetts's increasing numbers of black and brown immigrants from the British Caribbean also fell under his jurisdiction.[3]

The Bonds' old friend Isaac Mullen was a native New Englander who had served with the navy for six years, including the entire Civil War, when he ended up in Portsmouth, Virginia. He then had moved to Boston, where he held a minor government post and operated a printing shop. Bostonians of both races admired Mullen, and a journalist observed that "he occupied a position of importance in civil life . . . and was a fine orator, proud and distinguished looking." A white man, however, inherited Mullen's appointment, and Mullen fell on hard times. By 1907, he was aging, ill, and lived alone, supported by a navy pension. His wife passed away that year, while their only son had died in childhood.[4]

Despite Boston's paucity of politically influential Negroes, James Wolff—another former Civil War sailor—retained his luster and clout, and in 1910 became the first of his race to deliver the city's official Fourth of July oration. Dedham's Louis Brandeis, the first Jew granted that honor, would speak five years later. "Colored" Bostonians basked in Wolff's reflected glory on that occasion—the same date when they cheered on one of their idols, the black heavyweight champion boxer Jack Johnson. But crowds of white men also gathered, listening in dismay as public announcers read from a ticker tape, blow-by-blow accounts of the contest between Johnson and Jim Jeffries, the former champ (called "The Great White Hope") who had been recruited for a comeback bid to wrest the title from the cocky Negro. But neither Wolff's speech nor Johnson's ferocious knockout victory generated Independence Day melees in Boston, as that racially charged bout did in other American cities. In the wake of those disturbances, the United States Congress enacted new statutes forbidding the interstate transport of any prizefight films on the grounds that showing a black boxer defeating a white one could incite race riots.[5]

After John Bond, Sr., died, Emma and the rest of her family (with the exception of her son Percy) remained in Hyde Park, residing, as always, in the 1800 block of River Street. People in her hometown and throughout the state chose sides in the contentious 1912 textile strike (organized by the Industrial Workers of the World) in nearby Lawrence, involving laborers of fourteen nationalities. But greater interest focused on debates over local issues such as "A Zoo for Hyde Park" and tragic episodes like that which generated the Hyde Park *Gazette*'s front-page headline "Italian Shoots Brother-in-Law in Readville."[6]

The previous year, the all-male electorate of both Hyde Park (its population exceeded fifteen thousand but its African Americans had decreased to only eighty-seven) and Boston had voted two-to-one to annex the Bonds' predominantly working-class suburb to the country's fourth-largest city, which James Wolff characterized as "the paradise of the Negro." "Hyde Park has voted in favor of annexation to Boston," the *Gazette*'s lead story proclaimed. That territorial appendage (it would be Boston's very last), nonetheless, generated deep political conflicts and carried hefty religious baggage as well. "The Protestant churches were against joining Boston. The Catholic Church was for it. And Hyde Park was predominantly Catholic," one resident recalled. His town's entrepreneurs promoted merger in the interests of what they called "greater goals for Hyde Park." "Now We Are Ward 26," the local newspaper crowed in January 1912.[7]

Blacks from the South (known as "homies") and immigrants from the British Caribbean (called "monkey chasers" or "black

Jews," who considered themselves subjects of the king and often congregated in their own autonomous institutions) pressed into recently expanded Boston. By 1910, the city included thirteen thousand Negroes, and a decade later their numbers had increased to sixteen thousand. A bit of that growth came with annexation, but most resulted from the continuing West Indian and southern influx. A sociologist who wrote about Boston in 1914 contended that men and women who had grown up in the Black Belt were "accustomed to regard the color line as a fact rather than a grievance." "Their most immediate and vital concern is to earn a living," he added; "they have therefore accepted the gospel of salvation through work."[8]

Negroes did work hard, but at least one minister disagreed about their racial outlook. He claimed that Boston's dark-skinned newcomers had "been quick to detect discrimination due to race prejudice, and have not been backward about making a noise." Many longtime "colored" Bostonians considered themselves educationally and culturally superior to the rural southern- and island-born interlopers. "Present conditions have led the public to think of colored people as a race," the pastor warned, "rather than to forget the accident of race descent and to think only of the individual." "As long as such a state . . . exists," he added, "the best colored man must share . . . the odium against his race which is provoked by the lower type." "The self-respecting colored man," he concluded, "refrains from even the slightest appearance of intrusion upon those whom he believes despise his blood." "Self-respecting" people like the Bonds tried to avoid associating with Negroes of "the lower type," and differences of class, skin color and race (the United States' most defining fault lines), regional and even national origin, all hindered cohesiveness in Boston's diverse "colored" community.[9]

Some of the city's African Americans kept to themselves in the early 1900s, but many others "intruded" in different ways and venues. Most of Boston's baseball fans were first- and second-generation European immigrants, but Fenway Park and Braves Field did not turn away Negro patrons, although restaurants and hotels increasingly denied them accommodations. The men who controlled professional baseball enforced their mandate that the city's major league players (and others throughout the country) were and would remain exclusively white. They even countered their own best interests by denying opportunities to brilliant athletes like the onetime Tuskegeean and Harvard graduate William Clarence Matthews, whom the Braves' player-manager had wanted to add to his roster in 1905. Matthews had promised that if given a chance in Boston "I will show them that a colored boy can play better than lots of white men and he will be orderly on the field." He had protested: "I think it is an outrage that colored men are discriminated against in the big leagues." "What a shame it is that black men are barred forever from participating in the national game," Matthews added; "I should think that Americans should rise up in revolt against such a condition." Such eloquence, however, fell on deaf ears. "Americans" did not revolt against segregation, and Boston would not overcome its racial restrictions in professional baseball until 1959—a dozen years after the major leagues began lowering the color bar elsewhere.[10]

Boston's all-black semipro nines were neither as skilled nor as renowned as those in other United States cities with larger or more concentrated Negro populations. Nonetheless, local squads like the Colored Giants challenged Anglo-American or ethnic teams such as those representing the Hyde Park Athletic Association before crowds that often reached several thousand.[11]

Race and ethnicity remained significant factors in the sports-obsessed country, and the onset of the city's reign as the nation's major league baseball capital coincided with Woodrow Wilson's presidential election in 1912, a year when the Red Sox (formerly the Stockings) clinched the World Series. The upstart National League Braves' Series sweep in 1914 reinforced Boston's supremacy on the diamond, then the Sox were victorious again in 1915 and 1916.[12]

The Series debut the latter year of a beefy but talented twenty-three-game-winning pitcher whom his fans and teammates called "the Bambino" provided Bostonians with thrills to end all. George Herman Ruth yielded one run in the second game's first inning at Fenway Park, then hurled a string of thirteen scoreless innings, the last six hitless, until his team rewarded him with a winning score in the fourteenth. In 1918, Babe Ruth pitched his Red Sox to yet another pennant. The uniquely early September Series that fall when America's young men, ballplayers included, prepared to march off to war, climaxed that glorious season. Boston's fans could not have known that it presaged the end of their golden era, as well as a brief but significant disillusionment with the whole sport that would follow the 1919 White Sox (excoriated in the press as the "Black Sox") scandal, when members of that Chicago team succumbed to gamblers' bribes and threw the World Series. Nonetheless, for several years, Ruth held sway as Boston's idol and even dined at the home of Mayor James Michael Curley. But when the churlish young pitcher blurted out, "That's a lot of bullshit, Mr. Mayor," the (at least superficially) prudish Curley rose, pointed to the door, and sternly ordered; "You are to leave this house immediately." Soon thereafter, Ruth vacated the Hub City altogether.[13]

Curley had been born, had grown up, and had worked after school delivering groceries—even to the Bonds' Hyde Park—in mostly Irish-American Roxbury. He became a ward politician who was convicted and incarcerated on corruption charges, serving time in 1904 at the same Charles Street jail as had Monroe Trotter following his clash with Booker T. Washington the previous year. But, quickly forgiven by his constituents, Curley soon again rose to power. His cronies' threats to expose the lubricious relationship between Boston's Mayor John "Honey Fitz" Fitzgerald and a cigarette girl called "Toodles" hastened Curley's political ascent as Fitzgerald reluctantly withdrew from the 1914 mayoral race. That year, "A whiskey glass and Toodles' ass made a horse's ass out of Honey Fitz" became the city's favorite underground ditty. A diverse coalition, including much of the city's usually Republican "colored" electorate as well as Hyde Park voters (men such as Bob Bond) in their first election as part of Boston proper, supported James Michael Curley and elected him mayor. For a while, Curley encouraged alliances between Boston's Irish and its black working class against the old Yankee "codfish aristocracy."[14]

That period also occasioned the harshest confrontation to date between a Negro and any American president. The Boston *Guardian*'s Hyde Park–raised Monroe Trotter led a delegation to the White House to protest President Wilson's heightened, federally mandated segregation. "Have you a 'new freedom' for white Americans and a new slavery for your Afro-American fellow citizens?" Trotter demanded. Trembling with fury, the president retorted, "You are the only American citizen who has ever come into this office . . . [and] talked to me in a tone with a background of passion." "Mr. President," the *Guardian*'s contentious editor interjected, "my whole desire is to let you know the truth we know. . . . We are not wards." Concerning Trotter's verbal skirmish, a decade later another black Boston journalist would maintain that "Massachusetts has produced the only citizen, white or colored, who has dared walk into the White House and call a President a ding-dong liar."[15]

Trotter's credo was "Segregation for colored is a real permanent damning degradation in the U.S.A.—Fight it!" and in 1915, he remained a notable gadfly in Boston.[16] That same year, the great boxer Jack Johnson, in exile with his young white wife and hounded by accusations that he had violated the Mann Act (criminalizing the transportation of a woman across state lines for immoral purposes), supposedly took a dive in a championship fight against yet another "white hope" in Havana, Cuba. Johnson claimed that he threw the contest because federal authorities had promised—untruthfully, it turned out—to drop charges against him if he did so and thereby relinquished the coveted heavyweight crown, and he desperately wanted to return to his homeland. As Jack Johnson's saga unraveled, Trotter worked with Boston's NAACP to protest showings of D. W. Griffith's notorious, cinematically innovative movie, *The Birth of a Nation.*

At first, Trotter hoped for—even expected—success, since nine years earlier he had persuaded Mayor Fitzgerald to shut down Thomas Dixon's stage drama *The Clansman,* from which the new motion picture was adapted. Like that play, *Birth of a Nation* portrayed rapacious black bucks during Reconstruction as the defilers of white women (such as the movie's young star, Lillian Gish, called "America's sweetheart"), and glorified "The Fiery Cross of the Ku Klux Klan" and its white-robed night riders as the saviors of Anglo-American southern civilization. Griffith cast a few Negro actors in his film, but for most of the "colored" roles (he employed a staggering five thousand extras), black greasepaint and woolly wigs transformed whites into grotesque, clownish, or frightening "jigaboos." Lynchings increased that year, with a number of racial incidents seemingly linked to the epic's screenings.[17]

Nonetheless, Negroes and other NAACP supporters (Boston's branch was the oldest and remained the largest in the country until 1918, when Washington's surpassed it) who advocated banning that movie had a tough case to make. It was historically inaccurate and slandered blacks, but champions of the First Amendment claimed that such faults hardly justified suppression in a city that was often ridiculed for its censorious blue laws. "Banned in Boston" became synonymous with the repression of free speech, and Mayor Curley heavy-handedly stifled erotic references or innuendo in print or on the stage, even disallowing artistic performances such as those of the interpretative dancer Isadora Duncan, because she liked to perform bare-legged. In keeping with widespread local acquiescence to such censorship, Trotter and the NAACP argued that *The Birth of a Nation*'s theme of black men's lust for white women was indeed pornographic.[18]

Tactics became hotly contested. Trotter threatened Curley that renewed support from Negro voters in 1918 depended on how he responded concerning the movie. "Where is . . . lovable Jim Curley, whom we coloured people supported for the mayoralty?" Trotter asked, adding, "If this was an attack on the Irish race he would find a way pretty quick to stop it." But Curley refused to act. Boston's police billy-clubbed and arrested Trotter and other Negroes during a scrap that erupted as they bought tickets and picketed the film. "[At] the first objectionable scene," one participant recalled, "the colored audience rose as one [and] splattered the screen with rotting vegetables." "If there is any lynching in Boston, Mayor Curley will be responsible," the resolute Trotter insisted.[19]

As soon as he was released, Trotter organized and spoke at a rally attended by fifteen hundred protesters. The following day, he addressed another group that marched on the statehouse, singing *Nearer My God to Thee* as it passed near Boston's oldest African American neighborhood, often called "Nigger Hill." The NAACP rallied behind proposed new state legislation intended to suppress lewdness more than racism, but it also forbade "any show or entertainment which tends to excite racial or religious prejudice or tends to a breach of the public peace."[20]

Most of Boston's white-owned newspapers opposed the bill on constitutional grounds and supported unlimited access to the film that one journal lauded as "patriotic" and representative of "true Americanism." President Wilson underscored that ardor when he declared: "It is like writing history with lightning. And my only regret is that it is all so terribly true." A rabbi analogized that although he abhorred the character of Shylock, he never would seek to ban Shakespeare's plays. "The Negroes have made splendid progress in the last fifty years," he continued, "but the large majority of them are still children, and this statement is proven by their action in Boston." Advocates of the legislation nonetheless packed the same AME Zion church where Trotter had clashed with Booker Washington a dozen years earlier. The controversial bill passed and the governor signed it into law. The new censorship panel promptly received a petition with more than six thousand signatures asking it to shut down *The Birth of a Nation*—but it refused to do so. Despite continued demonstrations led by the African American community, the hateful though riveting motion picture ("silent," but accompanied by melodramatic, heart-pounding organ music) enjoyed an unprecedented run in Boston and continued showing to packed houses throughout the country.[21]

Whether or not they directly involved themselves in protesting that movie, members of the Bond family would have been well aware of the controversies that swirled around the onetime Hyde Park resident Monroe Trotter, who, true to his promise, successfully activated black voters to oppose Mayor Curley's 1918 reelection bid. A group of loyal ethnic Democrats, however, rallied in his support right across the street from the Bonds' homes "at Roger J. Flaherty's shop, 1850 River St.," but Curley (at least temporarily) was thwarted in his mayoral campaign.[22]

Boston's African Americans unsuccessfully opposed *The Birth of a Nation* in 1915 (although their city did ban a return engagement five years later); nonetheless, they had other motion pictures to patronize and stars to idolize. Mack Sennett's *Bathing Beauties,* Theda

Bara as Cleopatra, Elmo Lincoln as Tarzan of the Apes, and suave Rudolph Valentino as the Sheik dazzled America's audiences. The Negro filmmaker Oscar Micheaux produced his first "race" movies in 1919 (but could not achieve effective distribution), while D. W. Griffith's less controversial eight-reel epics like *Hearts of the World,* and other anti-German war propaganda films such as *The Kaiser: The Beast of Berlin,* enjoyed successful runs at Hyde Park's Cleary and Everett Square cinemas.[23]

Trotter's interactions with President Wilson had led him to oppose the World War. After it ended, the Department of State denied him a passport, so Trotter assumed an alias and made his way to France by working in a ship's galley with the express intent of representing African Americans' interests at the 1919 Versailles Peace Conference. Trotter failed to gain entry to those deliberations, but he wrote articles for the French press about the dire circumstances that his race still faced in the United States. He excoriated his white countrymen, yet remained aloof from Marcus Garvey and Pan-Africanism, stressing instead Negroes' inherent Americanism. "The colored people here, some of whose very distant relatives were natives of Africa, are Americans, not Africans," he contended in tart response to a scathing editorial in the Boston *Transcript* that inexplicably castigated black Americans for failing to "civilize" Liberia.[24]

The Trotters had left Hyde Park, but J. Robert (Bob) Bond, Jr., stayed on River Street, where the family owned two residences within spitting distance of one another. Bob and his wife Osie lived in one, while Emma and her daughter Lena Bond Chesnut's new family (Lena married David Chesnut in 1908 and bore her sons in 1910 and 1912) remained in the same old clapboard house where Emma, John, and Percy first had moved in 1874. Following the birth of her daughter Elizabeth (Betty) in 1902, and several miscarriages, Osie Grimes Bond had two more girls: Evelyn Augusta, born in 1907, and Frances Mary (called Frankie) in 1909. In their early years, Betty, Evelyn, and Frankie Bond attended Hyde Park's Damon Grammar School on nearby Readville Street, as had their father Bob, their uncle Percy, and aunts Lena and Tooty.[25]

Because Bob Bond had contracted syphilis in 1899, however,

heavy clouds shadowed his family. He seems to have infected Osie early on during sexual intercourse, and apparently received no treatment for his own chronic condition at least until 1914.[26]

Nonetheless, Bob and Osie plugged along. They purchased properties at several sites on Hyde Park's River Street, in nearby Dedham and Milton, and as far away as Boston's northern suburbs of Everett and Malden, where a number of middle-class Negroes were moving. Bob worked as a waiter, a chauffeur, and then started and ran a secondhand furniture store. He also maintained storage facilities (barns, he called them) for the sometimes fabulous, sometimes shabby merchandise that he often piled in disorderly hillocks on his waterside lot. Despite that appearance of chaos, he became a shrewd businessman who kept his small van meticulously polished, and painted "John R. Bond / Antiques" on its doors in neat gilt letters.[27] Behind his home and store coursed, not the river that the street's name promised, but the historic canal known as Mother Brook and its illusively placid millpond. Just across those waterways, the bucolic hillside cemetery where John R. Bond, Sr., had been interred overlooked the family homes and Bob's businesses.

In addition to trading in "antiques" (he attended estate sales and snatched wads of bills from the overstuffed drawstring tobacco pouch always tied to his belt to buy wholesale lots of treasures or junk), the entrepreneurial Bob Bond took advantage of his site and its potential for riverine activities. He built a dock, bought several rowboats and canoes, and Hyde Park's residents patronized his commercial operations throughout the summer as they rented skiffs to row, paddle, fish from, or daydream in. Emma preferred to remain ashore, but her daughters Lena and Tooty loved the water, and with their sons and Bob Bond's girls they boated and angled on the canal behind the family home.

Bob was also a fine skater. He often competed in wintertime ice hockey games, and entertained Hyde Park's youngsters with his figure-eights and twining grapevines on frozen Mother Brook. The *Transcript* (published in neighboring Dedham), however, warned parents: "Watch out for your children when [the] Mill Pond is frozen over. Have them skate near the shore. Tell them when it is safe." Other Hyde Park residents, fearing the waterway's treachery, chose to ice-skate with less anxiety on the town's flooded baseball diamond.[28]

Bob and Osie Bond (at least officially) continued living together in a tall, frame "double house" with a mansard roof and an ample wraparound porch. It was large enough that they had sufficient space for themselves and even could rent out an apartment. One family who dwelt there temporarily was named McCraw. They had arrived in Boston only recently, but several members of their clan originally had known Osie Grimes Bond from Virginia. While they resided with the Bonds in 1916, the McCraws had a baby whom they named Elaine. They almost became part of the Bond family.[29]

Like their mother Osie, Bob Bond's younger daughters Evelyn and Frankie were very light skinned, with wavy brown hair, and were, Elaine McCraw admitted decades later, "as pretty as movie stars."[30] But the girls' ways of dealing with their deceptive looks as they were growing up generated profound familial tensions. Despite the presence of their father and other brown-skinned kin nearby in mostly white Hyde Park, Osie Bond's conflicted daughters (who had absorbed the all-American message that Negroes were inherently inferior and bore the stamp of Cain) really wanted to be white. Their loving grandmother had cradled her creamy-complexioned granddaughters in her coffee-colored arms, their silky locks contrasting with her frizzy gray upsweep, but as the girls matured, they began to distance themselves from Emma. Betty, who was Bob and Osie's oldest daughter, on the other hand, became so demented that she had to be intermittently institutionalized, and several observers believed that much of her envy and vitriol stemmed from the fact that she was slightly darker skinned than her younger siblings.[31]

Betty also had serious academic problems at Hyde Park High School. She received D's, E's, and F's, had to make up courses in summer sessions, and finally graduated in 1922, at the age of nineteen, without distinction of any sort. In the yearbook (inauspiciously named *The Black and Blue*), classmates cracked tired jokes about being seen as yokels by "wise student[s] from an in-town school." "If Hyde Park is such a wonderful place," a smart-aleck Bostonian taunted, "what do they call potatoes out there?" A local humorist retorted, "They don't call them—they dig them!" Betty's graduation featured student orations that debated seemingly eternal questions such as "The Immigration Problem" and "Shall We Have Another War?"[32]

Evelyn (Bob and Osie's second daughter) followed Betty to high school, where her scholastic deficiencies even exceeded those of her older sister. In 1922, she failed all of her courses and dropped out. Her radiant looks clearly did not surmount her academic short-comings. Evelyn was a "social butterfly" who loved movies, pretty clothes, talking on the telephone, skating and sledding, parties, ice cream, her parents and sister Frankie, and their fluffy white dog named Prince. She was superficial and somewhat laconic, but she did not quit school altogether. One of Hyde Park's old-timers re-called that in their working-class community "more than half the kids that graduated from grammar school didn't go on to high school. They went to work." But Evelyn took a year off, not to take a job, but apparently because she had to navigate through some sort of mental or emotional crisis, and she finally acquired a high school diploma when she was twenty years old.[33]

Like her older sister Betty, Evelyn ultimately suffered a break-down so profound that she, too, had to be hospitalized, while the youngest, Frankie, sometimes exhibited such bizarre behavior (on at least one occasion she ran through the streets naked) that a shrewd acquaintance characterized her condition as "dementia," and remarked that if she were not institutionalized "she should have been." Yet her very average schoolwork outclassed that of her older sisters, and Bob Bond always believed that his last—his fa-vorite—child would become the most capable woman in his family. He resolutely declared that "my . . . daughter [Frankie] will take care of her mother and sisters if necessary."[34]

In his odd, insouciant, "loud talking" way, Bob was deeply re-ligious, and as his disabilities intensified, he lamented: "[I] cannot even go to church." He may have feared the torturous verity of the biblical prophesy, "Ye shall know them by their fruits . . . every good tree bringeth forth good fruit, but a corrupt tree bringeth forth evil fruit," but he nonetheless remained a loyal member of Dedham's Episcopal Church of the Good Shepherd, where his family had been parishioners since the 1870s. His daughters (following John Bond, Sr.'s Anglican traditions) were christened and confirmed there, as were Lena Bond Chesnut's sons. For years, Lena herself played the organ and ran Good Shepherd's Sunday school nursery program. William Gould's family also stayed active at that church, but the Goulds, Bonds, and Chesnuts were virtually its only "colored" parishioners.[35]

Among Hyde Park's newer African American residents, Elijah and Edith Glover and their children joined the almost all-white—and distinctly upper-class—Episcopal Christ Church on River Street. Most "colored" Bostonians maintained their traditional affiliations with Baptist or Methodist denominations, but by the 1920s, nearby Roxbury supported two new Negro Episcopal churches, one of which ministered to that neighborhood's increasing numbers of British West Indian immigrants. With its onetime predominantly Irish-American residents briskly relocating to South Boston, Charlestown, or leaving town entirely, Roxbury was on its way to becoming the city's most concentrated black community.[36]

Despite their church affiliations and other solid links to family, community, and country, Bob and Osie's marriage became increasingly strained. But they were mutually devoted to their daughters and linked to one another by complex financial affairs. They remained in Hyde Park, often lived separately, but never divorced.

Bob Bond stubbornly resisted conforming to Boston's staid ways, as his eccentricities escalated. The onetime sailor smoked heavily, sometimes drank to excess, and dressed as if he envisioned himself a buccaneer, toting a pearl-handled revolver, sporting colorful head wraps and vests, and five or six gold and diamond rings on his fingers. Bob could be fun-loving, witty, and generous to his daughters and to Boston's neediest citizens. He "would do anything" for his mother and sisters, and his devotion to his favorite nephew and namesake, Bob Chesnut, was lasting and noteworthy. But he also became deeply depressed, and frequently exploded in towering paroxysms of rage. Those thunderbursts rained terror even on family and friends.[37]

Similar fluctuations of mood or act often accompanied neurosyphilis, and physicians at the Boston Psychopathic Hospital saw men with that condition who were profoundly "cranky, . . . [began] shouting, whistling and slamming doors." One patient experienced "marked delusions of grandeur, [and] periods of excitement with peremptory insistence on obedience to his wishes." Bob sometimes bellowed at his beloved daughters, complained as did other syphilitics that he was "broke or nearly so," although he had several businesses and ample real estate holdings. Like another man who mourned "I am all gone; I am good for nothing . . . I can't write or talk," Bob became disheartened and increasingly antisocial by 1920. He could not sleep at night but suffered from daytime narcolepsy. His physicians confirmed that his "irregular pupils with sudden somnolent attacks are suggestive of cerebro-spinal syphilis." He worked hard but fitfully, often cooked for himself alone (slapping choice steaks into a filthy skillet and searing them atop a grimy kerosene stove), and intermittently drifted into deep sleep on a cot in his congested, disorderly store. Many syphilitics, like Bob, were notably "quick-tempered," displaying symptoms "characteristic of manic-depressive psychosis." A Boston diagnostician argued in 1917 that it was often "impossible on purely clinical grounds . . . to tell the depression of neuro-syphilis from the depression of manic-depressive psychosis."[38]

The staff of the psychopathic hospital employed six standard diagnostic procedures to evaluate neurosyphilitics: "The W. R. [Wassermann Reaction] on blood serum and spinal fluid, cell count, globulin test, albumin test, [and] gold sol test." Similarly, Bob Bond wrote that nurses at the Chelsea naval facility where he received treatment in the 1910s and 1920s "took a Back Bone Puntcure [a spinal puncture] to see what ailed me."[39]

Few of Bob's medical records survive, but the local mental hospital medicated its syphilitic patients with salvarsan compounds, mercury, iodides, arsenic, and antimony. Doctors there administered those medications "by mouth, intramuscular injections, intravenous, spinal intradural, cerebral subdural and intraventricular [means]." Most patients received "doses of salvarsan, twice a week, aided by mercury and potassium iodide." Following brief, intensive courses of therapy, the reports asserted, a successful convalescent might "run for several years without further trouble, both with and without treatment."[40]

One of Bob Bond's most agonizing symptoms was his rectal distress, and many other Bostonians suffering from syphilis similarly experienced "sphincter disturbances." Bob underwent surgery in 1914, 1917, and twice in 1921 in attempts to ameliorate the damage to his rectum incurred during his hitch in the navy, but he nonetheless became increasingly agitated, incontinent, and otherwise physically impaired. In 1922, under provisions of a new veterans' disability act, he applied for and soon began receiving a partial military pension. Bob's records from those years confirm that "claimant . . . is incapacitated in the performance of manual labor to a degree of one tenth and is entitled to twelve dollars per month."[41]

One of the Boston Psychopathic Hospital's physicians asked rhetorically: "What is the relation of neuropathic heredity to neurosyphilis?" a question that appropriately might have been raised about Bob Bond's wife and children. Their individual and collective idiosyncracies closely resembled the variant syphilitic symptoms frequently observed at that institution.[42]

Boston physicians encountered many instances when they could not "conclude from the . . . look of a neurosyphilitic's family that the normal looking members are not syphilitic," and Bob Bond's wife Osie and their troubled girls certainly looked "normal" and (for some years) seemed physically sound. "Considering the prevalence of syphilis, it is rather to be wondered that more such cases of 'innocent' infection do not occur in children," the doctors concluded, and insisted that the "family should not be forgotten in diagnosis and treatment."[43] But Osie, Betty, Evelyn, and Frankie probably were forgotten—at least at first—when Bob commenced his treatment at the navy medical facility.

Many female neurosyphilitics, Boston's specialists insisted, became "irritable and untidy . . . often unreasonable." One such woman (not unlike Osie) reported a notable "lack of energy [and] neglected her housework." Even after decades in Boston, and though she still intermittently managed to dress appropriately, Osie Grimes Bond often displayed what neighbors and relatives considered extremely odd behavior. Old-line Negro New Englanders said she looked like "poor white trash," or they called her a "Virginia hillbilly."[44] During Prohibition, like some of the folks in rural Orange County, Virginia, where she had grown up, Osie fermented bootleg spirits that she served to her teenagers and their friends— but she chose not to cook. When one of the McCraws paid a social call at the Bond house, where the family had boarded a few years earlier, Osie proudly showed her visitor the eggs she was incubating and chicks she was hatching in her otherwise idle oven. Acquaintances remembered Osie as a wretched homemaker, but that domestic insufficiency was probably another indicator of her neurosyphilitic disorientation. For years, she maintained a tenuous grasp on respectability and normalcy, but by the early 1930s, like her daughters, she, too, would have to be briefly institutionalized.[45]

Clinicians warned that "the wives of syphilitics are frequently infected without being aware of it. In such cases, they receive no treatment and consequently have a larger chance of developing neurosyphilis." That almost certainly was true of Osie Bond, who probably transmitted the disease to her girls in utero. In those years, Boston doctors diagnosed a daughter of syphilitics like Bob and Osie whose "retention of school knowledge was poor" and who suffered a "loss of capacity as to mental work." The Bond women's peculiarities and mental lapses most likely were based, at least in part, in neurological problems generated by syphilis.[46]

Hospital data also indicated that "abortions, miscarriages and stillbirths occur . . . in 18%" of syphilitic women. Sterility and the inability to carry a pregnancy to full term are others of the disease's chameleonlike symptoms, and Osie almost certainly miscarried several times. Frankie and Evelyn both married, and Evelyn (but neither of her sisters) conceived at least once. But she did not give birth, losing the pregnancy either through deliberate abortion or spontaneous miscarriage.[47] The Bond sisters had lived with the specter of syphilis, and it seems likely that they never wanted to chance conveying their affliction to another generation.

Perhaps more important than Bob's own escalating infirmities, the knowledge that he had disgraced his family and been responsible for his daughters' loathsome inheritance must have embittered him and intensified his quixotic behavior. While he was at sea in the navy in 1899, a priapic bully had assaulted him and left him with an enduring syphilitic legacy. As Bob had been terrorized, he sporadically terrorized others. Manifestations of his "shameful" disease estranged him from a number of old friends and family members, especially his staid and respectable older brother Percy.[48] The syphilis that Bob inadvertently had transmitted to his three girls caused them physical and mental anguish, but its vicious, quirkish symptoms also meant that they would never bear children. Betty, Evelyn, and Frankie Bond would be the last of their line.

In the 1880s, Emma Bond's onetime neighbor Dr. Rebecca Lee Crumpler had claimed that she could "trace the cause of insanity to the pernicious custom of rubbing the gums of infants." Crumpler had advocated isolation "in a cool, quiet room" and "bromides of potassium" for what she called "the alarming symptoms of brain fever," much like those that Emma must have observed in her second son, daughter-in-law, and granddaughters decades later. "The hair should be shaved," Crumpler had insisted, and "cloths wrung out of warm water . . . kept continually over the scalp."[49] As the Bonds' in-house family health care provider, Emma may have retained similar traditional beliefs and recommended such therapies for Bob, Osie, Betty, Evelyn and Frankie, and what she might have seen as their "insanity," or ongoing manifestations of "brain fever."

In addition to their episodic mental lapses and disorientation, the fact that they looked white befuddled Evelyn and Frankie's lives and raised again the knotty question of "passing." A cynical Boston journalist observed the phenomenon of "passing for white" in his city at that time. "Suffice it to say that there are hundreds of 'Portuguese' who were once just plain . . . Mary Browns," he wrote, and " 'Armenians,' 'Greeks' and a few 'Italians' who came to this great center of culture and liberty from Shoe Button, Mississippi; Hop Toad, Georgia; and Corn Pone, Arkansas." "Most of the colored folk . . . settle here with every intention of remaining loyal to their smaller percentage of black blood," he believed, but "after being constantly mistaken for 'white,' come finally to resent the imputation that they are anything else." Dorothy West, a Boston contemporary of Frankie and Evelyn Bond, wryly observed about a girl who must have looked much like them, that "her very fair skin and chestnut hair singled her out, accorded her a special treatment [and] pointed out to her how preferable was the status of whites, since even a near-white was made an idol."[50] That was just the situation that the pretty Bond sisters encountered.

During the school year in ethnically diverse Hyde Park, many classmates and neighbors thought that Evelyn and Frankie were Italian, and the girls simply let those assumptions stand. Years later, one of their white former schoolmates revealed her wonder at and ignorance of the vagaries of miscegenation when she asked: "Did you know they had a black grandmother?"[51]

In the summertime, however, Betty, Evelyn, and Frankie Bond journeyed (not to Shoe Button, Hop Toad, or Corn Pone, but) to Barboursville, a remote Orange County, Virginia, town named for the state's onetime Governor James Barbour. That county, nestled in the Piedmont belt, twenty-five miles from the Blue Ridge Mountains, was the site of the Civil War's brutal Battle of the Wilderness. It was also the ancestral home of their mother Osie Grimes, and of presidents James Madison and Zachary Taylor as well.

Approaching Barboursville from the east via train or auto, the first glimpse of the misty, forested slopes of the fabled mountains that readily absorbed tinges of the azure sky awed returning natives and new arrivals alike. The Charlottesville & Rapidan Railroad (with a whistle stop at Barboursville's depot) and the modest heights of the Southwest Mountains bisected the county. Small but vigorous creeks, such as the Blue, Wilderness, and Negro Head Runs (so named, it was said, because whites once had displayed by that stream the head of an errant slave who had been drawn and quartered as a warning to other potential miscreants), fed into the Rapidan or Pamunkey Rivers. They bordered Orange County, then splashed through the Appalachian foothills down toward Chesapeake Bay.[52] Three-quarters of a century later, one of Barboursville's oldest male citizens still remembered with scarcely concealed delight the annual 1920s' sojourns of those beautiful, light-skinned city slickers, the Bond girls from Boston who traveled to Orange County to visit Osie's relatives at the Grimes family's property up off the old Ridge Road.[53]

Osie Grimes Bond's father Daniel was a farmer who had six pretty daughters, each one, a relative observed, "as white as snow." Daniel Grimes's forebears included leading white citizens (the Revolution's Benjamin Grymes and the Civil War's Dr. W. S. Grymes may have been among them) as well as some of their slaves. In the late-antebellum years the county had been home to more than six thousand enslaved Negroes. The white Grymeses once had owned local gold mines, and Daniel reportedly had a cache of gold nuggets buried someplace on his hundred-acre farm.[54]

The Grymeses' onetime slaves proclaimed their independence after emancipation when they changed the spelling of the name, replacing their former masters' distinctive *y* with a new *i*. Local men from Virginia's First Families, however, continued to enjoy illicit sexual relations with the county's "colored girls," as they bleached the genetic pool, but officials concurrently hanged several of the county's wayward Negroes for "ravishing white women." Yet no matter how pale their skin, most people named Grimes (with an *i*) were "black" in Orange County. To clarify any racial confusion and to thwart "passing," the Commonwealth of Virginia had enacted legislation in 1910 that specifically "defined as Negro" anyone with "one-sixteenth or more Negro blood." A few Grimeses remained in Barboursville, but by that time all of Daniel's pretty snowflakes, save one, had drifted out of the blue-green Virginia hills to Philadelphia, New York, and Boston.[55]

Osie had joined (and had married Bob Bond at) Boston's Ebenezer Baptist Church, but her daughters cleaved to their father's Episcopalianism. Nonetheless, the Bond girls' annual Barboursville visits coincided with the fourth-Sunday-in-August "Big Meetings" at the Blue Run Baptist Church. Blue Run Baptist's founding as a white church dated back to 1769, but members of the Negro community purchased it right after the Civil War. It maintained its roots in rural religious fundamentalism, yet also took its social obligations seriously and had erected an agricultural and community center on the property by 1900. The Grimes family had always belonged and worshiped there (although the county's few "colored" Episcopalians also formed congregations from time to time), and

Osie and her sisters probably had attended the tiny nearby "School House #7 (Col.)."[56]

Early on those August homecoming mornings, women walked down from the nearby hills toting on their heads heavy baskets filled with unrevealed delights, while dusty pickups, surries, and farm wagons crammed with food-laden trunks began to line up along the road by the church. Big Meeting Sundays were always daylong affairs, and the first call to worship started by ten.

Farmers laced up their oxfords and donned their best suits. Wives gussied up in mail-order dresses as their daughters teetered on new high heels. But visitors especially wanted to demonstrate their success and show off their city ways, city clothes, and city cars.[57] Bostonians like Betty, Evelyn, and Frankie would have been thoroughly scrutinized, admired, and envied as they made their conspicuous appearances at Barboursville's Blue Run Baptist Church, their pale, pretty faces enhanced with lipstick, powder, and rouge, and wearing pale silk stockings, French-heeled pumps, voile frocks, even stylish new hats created by their Aunt Lena.

The Baptist church's shouts, hand clapping, and foot tapping sharply contrasted with the inflexible Anglo-Saxon hymns and staid rituals at the Bonds' working-class Episcopal home parish in Dedham. "Praise God," Blue Run's preacher might call out, evoking his congregation's joyful responses: "Preach it, Brother," and "Thank you, Jesus!" The "Amen corner," a source of ecstatic outpourings from true believers, was located down near the pulpit. As the old pipe organ warmed up, robed choir members glided and two-stepped down the aisle, caroling out old favorites like *Wheel in a Wheel, My Soul Is a Witness for My Lord,* and *When Peace Like a River Pervadeth My Soul.* Every year on that memorable August Sunday, the congregation welcomed returnees, dipped and celebrated the newborn and reborn, mourned the deceased, fervently prayed for those who were ill or had strayed from the paths of righteousness, and testified to their own eternal faith. The church depended on donations it received that day, and Blue Run Baptist's preacher passed the collection plate twice if he spied more affluent members who had returned from the city.[58]

After a three-hour morning service, the preacher, deacons, choir, and worshipers burst through the doors in anticipation of the generous midday repast. They unbuttoned collars, loosened shoe-laces, shed hats, jackets, and robes. Cotton cloths were spread on plank tables in deep pools of shade, ice blocks unsheathed, fires kindled, and the fragrant baskets, boxes, and trunks that had ar-rived earlier in the day unpacked under the trees.

Everything grown in the garden, raised on the farm, or shot in the woods turned up at Big Meeting church dinners, including a pig or two, slow-barbecued overnight—always men's work—glazed hams, pork chitlins, and mustard, turnip, kale, or collard greens simmered down with ham hocks. It was hog heaven! "Hogs . . . had a special fascination for the negroes," Orange County's white his-torian had written in 1907, charging that the "colored" people much preferred to steal than raise them. There was also ample Brunswick stew, fried chicken, candied yams, watermelon rind and chow-chow pickles, potato and egg salads, corn pudding and corn bread (even moonshine corn liquor doled out behind the farm wag-ons), lemonade, iced tea, clabber milk, spiced pears, peach ice cream, strawberry-rhubarb pie, apple fritters, angel and devil's food cakes. After the feast, the sated assembly, instead of allowing them-selves blissfully to doze off, went back inside for more impassioned singing, prayers, and "hallelujahs." That whole summer day evoked profound feelings of contentment, recalled one participant, "like a spring of cool water in a weary land."[59]

Osie's sister Elizabeth Grimes lived right next to Blue Run Bap-tist, and Betty, Evelyn, and Frankie Bond passed their summer sojourns at her house.[60] That remote Virginia community could hardly have been less like Highland Beach, the Chesapeake Bay re-treat enjoyed by Washington's Negro "elite," including the J. Percy Bonds, who did not invite their somewhat disreputable relatives to join them there. Barboursville was familiar, but drab and unexcit-ing for the Bond girls, with no neighborhood movies, dance parties, boat rides, or trolleys to downtown Boston, and only softball, cro-quet, church services, and languid porch swings for diversion.

Boston's Hyde Park was the Bond girls' home most of the year, however, and in 1925, Eugene F. Gordon, an African American journalist who (quite uniquely) edited the women's pages of the white-owned and -operated *Daily Post,* tried to untangle the shifting relationships between the city, its Negroes, and its immigrants. He argued that Massachusetts "ranks . . . sixth in population, and first in the practice of those humanitarian principles upon which the foundation of these United States allegedly stands." "To say, however, that Massachusetts is the Utopia of the other forty-seven varieties of oppressed," he continued, "is to tamper with the sacred truth." Gordon asserted that two centuries after the first Negro captives had been brought from Africa to Boston, members of another ethnic group started arriving en masse: "an arrogant, domineering, boasting fellow [who] couldn't see why 'the niggers' should have it all." "That newcomer," he said, "was the Irishman."[61]

Gordon confirmed that Massachusetts had "fewer Irishmen than Canadians, and fewer Negroes than either Irishmen or Canadians; yet, the Irish today in this Commonwealth are the most dominant group in politics." By the early twentieth century, Boston's political power had shifted from the old Protestant Yankee elite to Irish Catholic newcomers, and from Republicans to Democrats. Irish Americans dominated the city's politics, but they and African Americans remained at the bottom of the economic heap. Nonetheless, Gordon added, "next to the Irish, [the Negro] makes more noise with the mouth than all other racial groups combined." Yet many employers refused to hire black people, and newspaper classifieds often read "No Irish Need Apply." Dorothy West, one of Massachusetts's gifts to the Harlem Renaissance, recalled meeting an "entrenched Bostonian" who admitted her own prejudices and haughtily said of the Irish immigrants: "They did not come here in chains or by special invitation. So I disdain any responsibility for them and reserve the right to reject them." "I have decided to rent my house to colored," she concluded.[62]

A few members of those dichotomous groups tried to find common interests and join in common causes, yet Boston's Negro leaders more often hoped and tried to emulate the white Brahmin establishment. Nonetheless, Monroe Trotter cited Ireland's revolutionary struggle with England as a model for black activism, and (unlike most members of his race but like the Boston Irish) he usually voted Democratic. Trotter's conciliatory, collaborative efforts, however, amounted to little more than tilting at windmills, because the city's African Americans and Irish Americans often found themselves squabbling over the same, meager crumbs.[63]

Debates over race and ethnicity raged in the early twentieth century, while Hyde Park had large numbers of Irish and Italian Catholics and its ethnic population continued to diversify. By 1907, the town had included enough Jews to maintain a synagogue, and eight years later the *Gazette* announced the "first dancing party of the Hyde Park Young Zionists." Poles, Germans, and Swedes also proliferated. In 1909, however, the *Colored American* magazine had reported that "The Naturalization Bureau of the Department of Commerce and Labor . . . has just declared that Turks, Armenians and Syrians and other Asiatics may not become American citizens." "They are not," that article continued, " 'free white persons' as mentioned in the law. Neither are they of African blood." "New definitions must be made as to who is white and who is black," the journal urged. But like their counterparts elsewhere in the country, white Bostonians (of all stripes) often held that Negroes, uniquely, were irredeemably "different" and inferior. Any Europeans could learn English, modify their dress and demeanor, and eventually be assimilated into the Caucasian mainstream, but people of African ancestry, the majority firmly believed, no matter how long they had been in residence, no matter what their education or social and economic status, never would be fully "Americanized."[64]

Eugene Gordon rued the decline from Boston's "glorious" past, when men such as Crispus Attucks and Peter Salem fought during the Revolution, "not as Negroes, but as Americans." Other early residents (like the patriotic, African-born poet Phillis Wheatley, abolitionist David Walker, and the black Masons' founder Prince Hall) who contributed their ideas and voices, he argued, helped to "establish this Commonwealth as the land of the free and the home of the brave colored man." Before 1900, Gordon recalled, his race had representatives "in the State Legislature, in city councils, on boards of aldermen, . . . and politicians, who knew the game of politics as well as their opponents." What Gordon viewed as the abandonment of their forebears' aggressive dedication to citizenship undergirded his criticism of his fellow black Bostonians by the 1920s. "The colored man of Massachusetts has more freedom than material possessions, more rights than initiative, more mouth than a desire to work," he concluded.[65]

Assessing Boston's demographic shifts, Gordon added, "the Irish have driven the Yankee from South and East Boston, the Italians have banished him from the North End . . . the Jews have crowded him from the West End . . . and the colored folk long ago saw to it that if the Yankee did not mind too much he might get out of the South End." Dorothy West, whose father was one of the city's new, hardworking West Indian–born "monkey chasers," cynically watched those fluctuating racial tides during her youth and commented that Boston's well-established Negroes "viewed their southern brothers with alarm, and scattered all over the city and its suburbs to escape this plague of their own locusts."[66]

Eugene Gordon observed that the old, Anglo-American New Englander still "hangs on along Beacon Street and Commonwealth Avenue and certain sections of the West End, while in recent years, considerable numbers have migrated to the suburbs." Those descendants of the first white settlers, Gordon asserted, had become "almost as unknown as some rare New England fauna, and almost as sacred in their exclusiveness as the grasshoppers on Faneuil Hall." "This Yankee," he generalized, "does not know the Negro and the Negro does not know him."[67]

But that was not the case for Hyde Park's few "colored" residents like the Bonds, because their town (before and after its annexation to Boston) had few Negroes, and retained a good number of its "old Yankees." Southern European immigrants continued their abundant incursions at least until the restrictive Immigration Act of 1924, which became law largely as a result of rigorous governmental lobbying by organizations such as the Boston-based Immigration Restriction League—mostly comprised of the Brahmin elite—many of whom considered everyone who was not of "good" northern European stock to be genetically inferior.[68]

But wherever they lived, Gordon continued, true-blue New Englanders had decided "that the white folk of Massachusetts have done their share for the colored folk, and that now it is time the colored folk helped themselves." He rued what he saw as a tragic apathy among his city's blacks. "Too much 'freedom' has made [the Negro] indolent; why should a free man work like a slave?" he asked. "He talks when he should act; he spends when he should save; he thinks in terms of 'race' when he should think in terms of nationality," the crotchety Eugene Gordon concluded.[69]

Many others, however, differed, and members of the Bond family worked diligently (yet hardly like slaves) and sometimes obfuscated their race. But they always thought in terms of nation. "If anyone coughed," Bob Bond's nephew recalled, his hometown "used it as an excuse to have a parade." The Bonds and Chesnuts decked their houses with the (by then forty-eight) Stars and Stripes. On the evening of July 3, all of them enjoyed the town's bonfires, and the next day marched in parades and watched fireworks. Bob Bond proudly joined in Hyde Park's patriotic celebrations. Long after his own wretched experience at sea and the "splendid little war" in the Caribbean with its ugly coda in the Philippines, he still loved his country so profoundly that he sometimes donned his turn-of-the-century U.S. Navy uniform, impishly grinned at the camera, and raised his hand in a snappy salute.[70]

With the exception of her son Percy and his wife Georgia's nuclear family in Washington, D.C., Emma Thomas Bond remained deeply immersed in her children's and grandchildren's lives in the 1920s. Bob was her only son in Boston, and she resided contentedly just down the street from his home and businesses with her daughter Lena, Lena's husband, and their boys. The main pleasures and responsibilities of caring for Emma lay with them.

NIGHTS WHEN *the* MUSIC STOPPED

———

[I would] fight for the better education to give chance to any other peoples, not the white people but the black and the others, because they believe and know they are mens like the rest. . . . You already knew that we were radicals, that we were underdogs, that we were the enemy of the institution. . . . I am suffering because I am a radical, and indeed I am radical; I have suffered because I was an Italian, and indeed I am Italian. . . . I am so convinced to be right that if . . . I could be reborn two other times, I would live again to do what I have done already.

BARTOLOMEO VANZETTI, Dedham, Massachusetts, 1921

IN THE 1890s, a couple named Chesnut moved from Stoneham, Massachusetts, to Milton, a town adjoining Hyde Park. One of their sons, David (born in 1874), finished Milton's high school and a few years later found a mechanic's job at the Hyde Park enterprise which manufactured the sumptuous but little-known new Robinson automobiles. By the early 1900s, that jaunty, well-mannered young man was routinely bicycling down River Street to the Bonds' house after work, sitting and harmonizing around their piano with a congenial circle of friends, and courting Lena Bond.[1]

Hyde Park's John T. Robinson Company had made card-cutting and box-making machinery since 1867, but in 1899, like many small factories nationwide and even locally (the Lenox Company, for one, was situated right in Hyde Park), it converted to an automobile shop. Its first "light gasolene machine" was the Bramwell-Robinson Sociable, a tiller-steered three-wheeler powered by a horizontal three-horsepower, single-cylinder engine. Bramwell-Robinson progressed from those original "tricycles" to make 1,800-pound two-seaters with aluminum steering wheels rimmed in burnished mahogany, sidelamps, bulb horns, mudguards, and water-cooled two-cylinder engines set behind the seats. The models displayed at the American Automobile Club's first exposition at New York's Madison Square Garden in November 1900 sold for $1,500, and a laudatory column in *The Horseless Age* described them as "self-lubricating and water cooled," with oil-tight crank cases, electric ignitions, and pneumatic tires.[2]

As the number of registered, four-wheeled, gasoline-powered vehicles in the country surged past fourteen thousand, the Pope brothers' partnership with Robinson succeeded that of Mr. Bramwell, and Pope-Robinsons soon ranked among New England's premier autos. Rear-entrance tonneaus powered by chain-driven, four-cylinder T-head engines comprised the top of the line. In 1901, the company built a $3,000 touring car that could maintain an awesome thirty miles per hour, and J. T. Robinson competed in five-mile races at the nearby Brookline Country Club, where he won two of three heats.

That same September, his company entered its newest model in a five-hundred-mile marathon from New York City to Buffalo. Despite continuing downpours and muddy, rutted roads, Robinson's roadster (the only entry that carried a driver plus three passengers—all dressed in yellow oilskin slickers and goggles—over the entire route) progressed well. But as the vehicles were warming up for the final leg, the organizers abruptly terminated the competition when they received word of President William McKinley's assassination in Buffalo by a crazed Polish-American anarchist named Leon Czolgosz, who ranted that McKinley "was the enemy of . . . the good working people." Despite the race's suspension prompted by that catastrophe, Robinson's automobile had achieved the sixth-best average miles per hour and earned its "First Class Certificate"—while the state of New York moved swiftly and electrocuted Czolgosz the next month.[3]

By 1902, J. T. Robinson's luxurious cars weighed 2,750 pounds and cost $3,500. A contemporary article praised him as "the first in America to build four cylinder engines; the first to build a tonneau body; the first to build a high priced car; the first to introduce the new Chaise Top." "Most people," boasted one gleeful Pope-Robinson owner and enthusiast, "think it is a 60 horsepower Mercedes!" The most elegant model appeared in 1903. At 3,000 pounds, it was "a large, green-colored touring car with cover and yellow wheels . . . four cylinders, 24-horse power engine with three speeds and reverse." That vehicle, with its "attractive brass-trimmed metal bonnet," a catalogue description added, seated "five passengers and sells for $5,000." Robinson's autos all featured lustrous, hand-buffed leather upholstery, "acetylene lamps with mirror lens reflectors mounted on the side of the car, [and] mahogany tool boxes." The company did nothing but fine custom work, making only about one hundred automobiles altogether between 1899 and 1904, and it never proposed to provide transportation for the working-class Americans whom Henry Ford so effectively would court with his new Model-T's.[4]

But the five short years that the Robinsons of Hyde Park (sequentially with Bramwell and the Popes) devoted to auto manufacture were stellar ones, as carmakers plus a few ingenious tinkerers like the men who built the gas-fueled Harley-Davidson two-wheelers called motorcycles proliferated around the country. But in November 1904, J. T. Robinson died. His son did not have the cunning or moxie needed to continue in the competitive and rapidly evolving automobile industry, and he refocused on the company's original endeavors fabricating box-making machinery. The next month, a *Motor Age* report announced that "the Buick Motor Co. of Flint, Mich., was admitted to membership [in the Association of Licensed Automobile Manufacturers] after having presented satisfactory proof that it had purchased the Pope-Robinson Co. of Hyde Park, Mass." That was the company for which David Chesnut worked diligently in the early 1900s as he heeded the time-proven advice given to many Negroes around Boston and throughout the country that "a colored man . . . must always be superior to a white man if he wants to be that white man's equal."[5]

One afternoon in 1904, Dedham's Henry B. Endicott, a true enthusiast of the new horseless carriages who had amassed a fortune manufacturing shoes, visited the Pope-Robinson operation. Chesnut expertly demonstrated the latest model and showed off its luxury features and mechanical intricacies. Then and there, Endicott contracted to purchase the auto, and said to Chesnut, "Now that I've got this thing, won't you come and be my chauffeur and mechanic?" "How much are you making now?" he asked; "I'll top it!" So Henry Endicott acquired his Pope-Robinson touring car as well as someone to care for it, and David Chesnut acquired the job that he would hold for the next three decades as chief driver (even residing for a while in Endicott's servant quarters) for the fleet of as many as a dozen cars—including a Rolls-Royce, a Cadillac, an Isotta-Fraschini, several Packards, and a Ford runabout—that would be housed in a huge garage on the grounds of the new Endicott estate that was arising on East Street in Dedham.[6]

Curious Dedham and Hyde Park residents like the Bonds observed the construction of that magnificent residence, while news of various social events engaged them as well. Maude Trotter (Bob Bond's feisty contemporary who had gained notoriety when she supposedly stabbed a police officer with her hatpin during the anti–Booker T. Washington fracas orchestrated by her brother Monroe) married Dr. Charles Steward in 1907. The Trotter-Steward wedding, the Boston *Herald* observed, was "a quiet home function, at which only relatives and intimate friends . . . were present." Nonetheless, well-known Negro out-of-towners such as Carrie Bond's Atlanta University professor George Towns, and Robert and Mary Terrell who became Georgia and Percy Bond's friends in Washington, D.C., were among those who sent gifts, which were, the newspaper stated, "numerous, useful, rich and beautiful."[7]

At the Bonds' home the next October, Lena Bond married David Chesnut, with the Church of the Good Shepherd's venerable rector William Cheney officiating. Like Lena's late father, her groom David was a Prince Hall Mason. His brother Sam, and Lena's sister Tooty attended the couple, and one of their ushers was Tooty's new beau, Ulysses Howley. "The bride's dress was of white point de sprit, trimmed with French medallions," the Hyde Park *Gazette* reported. Lena carried a bouquet of roses (probably from her mother's garden), and her "long veil was caught up with orange blossoms." Emma Bond, the account continued, wore "gray voile with French medallion trimming, silk braid embroidery and a yoke of Irish lace." Guests arrived for the occasion from Dedham, Milton, and elsewhere in Boston's environs. Out-of-towners from Philadelphia and Washington attended, and Percy Bond, with his girls Carrie and two-year-old Wenonah, came up from Alabama. "Mr. and Mrs. Chesnut departed on the 11 P.M. train en route for New York and vicinity, and upon their return," the newspaper story concluded, the couple expected to make their residence with Emma Bond on River Street. David Chesnut also planned to return promptly to his position driving and caring for Henry Endicott's cars.[8]

Working as a private chauffeur or hack driver was a respected and relatively common occupation for diligent Negro Bostonians. It could provide them with a decent income, did not challenge the powerful unions' racial exclusions, and easily maintained the widely accepted master-servant relationship. David Chesnut's brother-in-law Bob Bond had done the same sort of work for a few years, while Hyde Park's African American newcomer Elijah Glover operated both a printing shop and a taxi service in nearby Roxbury.[9]

On his part, Henry Endicott was such a believer in the future of the whole range of gasoline-powered vehicles that he donated a sleek water pump truck and hook-and-ladder engine to his hometown, which gratefully retired its old horse-drawn wagons. Endicott had good reason to mistrust the antiquated equipment because his first residence had burned to the ground in January 1904, on an icy, frenzied night when Dedham's fire department was occupied fighting several blazes on the other side of town. But he interpreted that conflagration and his resultant loss as a divine command to design and build a no-holds-barred replacement, and the new Endicott estate soon became one of Dedham's landmarks.[10]

An Ionic-columned ballroom, elaborate plumbing installations (including a walk-in shower stall—one of the first in any private home—that sprayed inward from all directions), numerous fireplaces, wall paneling and woodwork, and parquet and marble floors embellished Endicott's house. His own cars, and the limousines that transported his many guests, circled up to the front entrance under an elegant portico. The twenty-five acres of grounds included the sparkling white twenty-room mansion, a large stable to accommodate blooded racing and carriage horses, greenhouses, manicured lawns, trees, shrubs, and a proliferation of flowers, quarters for some of the staff (of about two dozen), as well as a twelve-car garage. Wearing his visored cap, jacket, puttees, and polished boots, David Chesnut (whose own family car was an Essex) proudly tended to Henry Endicott's automotive fleet and supervised five other drivers. Over the ensuing decades, the Endicott family made the Chesnuts welcome at the Dedham estate: David and Lena's sons frolicked around the garage, and they all went on two-week (working) vacations to the Endicotts' huge North Shore summer "cottage" at Beverly Cove, where Lena and her boys blissfully sunned and swam at the beach.[11]

After her marriage, Lena stopped working in the millinery department of the chic Boston emporium where she had been employed for a decade, but continued to give piano lessons (at fifty cents each) to the neighborhood children, and created custom-made chapeaus for a select group of clients. Nor was she alone in that sort of endeavor. A River Street neighbor, Mrs. Louis Gabarino, ran the Hyde Park Hat Shop, and additional local competition, the *Gazette* reported, came from "Mrs. I. L. Andrews and Miss Anne J. Heming, [who] had their annual showings of millinery."[12]

In 1909, the bubbly and inquisitive Tooty Bond married Ulysses S. Grant Howley (named for his parents' American hero), a janitor from Cambridge. Lena Bond Chesnut gave birth to young Dave in 1910, then Bob in 1912, and Tooty Bond Howley's son Edward arrived just weeks later. Not long thereafter, Tooty lost an infant girl and Edward remained an only child. Tooty and Ulysses moved to Roxbury where they found themselves living right next door to Bob and Osie Bond's one-time renters, the McCraws.

Members of the Chesnut and Howley families also discovered that they very much enjoyed the nearby horse races.[13] The Readville racetrack, built on the site of old Camp Meigs, catered to an elegant crowd of Bostonians, and going to "the trotters" became a fashionable pastime. "Sulky racing was really a society thing in those days," reported an old Hyde Park resident, for which "the elite of Boston would come out." "They'd run special trains from

South Station, and there was a spur off the railroad so you could get right off at the track," he continued. The grandstands and clubhouse attracted up to twenty thousand patrons on major stakes days. Willowy socialites wearing stylish frocks shaded themselves with ruffled parasols when they attended events sponsored by the New England Trotting Horse Breeding Association. Clever Lena Chesnut (bandbox smart with her tailored white shirtwaist, dark skirt, straw skimmer, and walking stick) strategically befriended the guards, her son recalled. For Saturday meetings, she and Tooty would often "hang around the gate and look pretty," and after the "moneyed people with tickets" entered, the gatekeepers beckoned to them and their boys, calling: "Go on in, go on in!" The last trotters and pacers competed in 1924, but the track also began holding more controversial motorcycle races, as the rolling thunder of sleek Harley-Davidsons (powered by new V-twin engines and painted a signature gray), Indians, and their European rivals, like Germany's Daimlers, reverberated throughout Readville.[14]

During the Great War, David Chesnut's sons listened to marching songs on their gramophone and played "going off to war games," while his employer, Henry Endicott, became a dollar-a-year official in the state's domestic mobilization efforts. Bob Chesnut remembered proudly watching Endicott's gleaming Packard, with his father at the wheel and Massachusetts and United States flags fluttering atop its fenders as it navigated the streets of Hyde Park and Dedham. In his role as the Commonwealth's administrator of home production and food conservation, Endicott had his vast lawns on East Street dug up and then replanted with potatoes and cabbages to set an example for others, while the local newspaper prodded its readers to become part-time farmers as a way to support efforts of the American Expeditionary Forces (AEF). It offered a "suggested list as follows: Beans, corn, beets, carrots, peas and tomatoes." Growing those vegetables, the *Gazette* insisted, required neither much experience nor space. "We are urged to eat more potatoes which are plentiful and raised nearby," it advised Hyde Park's home-front patriots.[15]

During the summer of 1917, some Boston radicals bearing banners asking "Is This a Popular War? Why Conscription? / Who

Stole Panama? Who Crushed Hayti? / We Demand Peace!" organized a small but voluble antiwar parade, but most of the Commonwealth's residents supported their country's wartime initiatives. The *Gazette* challenged the citizenry with: "Is Hyde Park going to uphold her reputation as she did in '61 and '98 or is she going to lay down and be the butt and ridicule of the other towns and cities in the state? The Army, Navy, Marine Corps, Reserve Corps, National Guard and Home Guard need men." "The world must be made safe for democracy," it continued, "the supreme test of Nation has come." It established an Honor Roll of those who volunteered, like the Bonds' recently Americanized River Street neighbors, Antonio di Chiara, Pasquale Trocchio, and Domenico Ricco. "Thirty-five men including one colored man were sent to Camp Devens," Hyde Park's newspaper also reported. The War Camp Community Service Society (an organization affiliated with the Circle for Negro War Relief), it added, started clubs at Fort Des Moines, Iowa, and other locales, while a white Dedham man applauded the African Americans who "told me of the loyalty of their folks . . . in purchasing bonds and giving to the Red Cross." The *Gazette* urged that "Hyde Park Women Can Help by Needlework," but assumed a neutral stance when it reported: "Female Banker Tries to Enlist in Marines." Sadie Kitchen, a Boston woman, "enlisted . . . but has not yet been accepted," the article continued. "Her case has been referred to Washington for final action," it concluded.[16]

The Bonds' longtime friend, the Civil War navy veteran William Gould, posed in his GAR regalia flanked by his six sons, wearing their Spanish-American and Great War uniforms, for a photograph that appeared in *Crisis* magazine late in 1917. The three youngest Goulds (officers who trained at Fort Des Moines with Captain Aaron Day, Jr.) were preparing to serve their country in France with the AEF. At the 1918 Decoration Day celebrations, the Dedham *Transcript* stated, "Wm. B. Gould, a naval veteran of the Civil War, was given an ovation welcome." Gould informed the assembled crowd that "the big fighting machines of the now, were simply improvements of the smaller fighting ships of the then." "[His] tribute to his three boys in the service," the article continued, "was a splendid one, just such a one as an American father should pay to red-blooded sons ready to do and die for the honor of their country and flag." "I have tried to set them a good example," William Gould modestly concluded. On parade days well into the 1920s, old Mr. Gould graciously acknowledged cheering curbside crowds from the back of a red-white-and-blue festooned car, while the Bonds, Chesnuts, Glovers, and other Dedham and Hyde Park residents watched with pride, energetically waving American flags.[17]

By that time, the Chesnuts had organized their "Blue Ribbon Orchestra." The whole family gathered around the living room piano as Emma listened, hummed along, and tapped her foot, Lena tickled the ivories, and David Senior played violin—and almost anything else. His brother, "Uncle Sam," blew both a "licorice stick" and the saxophone; David Junior drummed; young Bob trumpeted; cousin Eddie Howley joined in on bass, with his father Ulysses on alto horn. Every week they held "orchestra rehearsals" and Sunday "musicales." David Senior also worked professionally with several local combos, and got choice pickup dates with visiting nationally known groups. He removed his chauffeur's uniform and boots, and transformed himself for those evening engagements with his tuxedo, dinner jacket, or white tie and tails. He became active in the musicians' union, played for private dances, weddings, and at nearby boathouses such as Moseley's-On-The-Charles in Dedham, where popular new ensembles like Duke Ellington's performed.[18]

The family band played everything from hymns and classical overtures to Sousa marches, mazurkas, schottisches, waltzes, and Christmas carols. They enjoyed Scott Joplin's *Maple Leaf Rag*, W. C. Handy's *St. Louis Blues*, Shelton Brooks's *Darktown Strutters' Ball*, Ellington's jazzy tunes, Charlestons, anything from the Broadway revue *Shuffle Along*, and favorites from the Great War like *Mademoiselle from Armentières* and *Over There*.[19]

Years later, Bob Chesnut also recalled the hoopla generated by Lieutenant James Reese Europe and the 369th U.S. Infantry Band. They had won Europeans' hearts when they performed their exuberant marches, jazz, and rags all around France. After the armistice, they took New York by storm as they boldly strode up Fifth Avenue in the city's unsurpassed welcome-home parade, and in spring 1919 they prepared to spread their captivating music throughout the United States.

That March, Europe's band, featuring Noble Sissle as star tenor soloist, launched a ten-week "victory" tour. Sissle reported that their "stirring marches, favorite overtures, and jazztime strains to the moaning blues" entranced audiences whenever they played. Those itinerant musicians journeyed from New York to Philadelphia, then headed north and became the first military band ever booked into the Boston Opera House, where they performed before cheering sold-out audiences. A western swing followed, but two months later, an exultant advertisement in the Boston *Herald* announced: "Return Visit by Popular Demand: Three Jubilee Days of Sunshine in Music [by] Lieut. 'Jim' Europe and the Famous 'Hellfighters' 369th U.S. Infantry Band."[20]

Despite the promised "sunshine in music," New England's spring weather was abysmal. Jim Europe came back to Boston on May 9 suffering with a heavy chest cold, and archaic Mechanics Hall where the "Hellfighters" would perform seemed prophetically chilled and gloomy. On a more upbeat note, Governor Calvin Coolidge invited the men to play on the state house steps the next morning and honored Lieutenant Europe by scheduling him to lay a wreath at the base of the Robert Gould Shaw–Fifty-fourth Massachusetts Infantry monument on Boston Common. Despite the less-than-ideal circumstances, an "unusually large" crowd (including the country's favorite blackface performer, Al Jolson) assembled at Mechanics Hall and jammed "the house to the rafters," Sissle recalled.[21]

Their performances featured a variety of numbers including French marches and *chansons,* "plantation melodies," a jazz medley, and a show-stopping syncopated version of Rachmaninoff's *Prelude in C Sharp Minor* that Jim Europe called his "Russian Rag." Handy's *St. Louis Blues,* followed by a dazzling snare drum duet by the so-called Percussion Twins, Herbert and Steve Wright, led into the intermission. The band closed its concerts with two of Europe and Sissle's popular wartime songs, *On Patrol in No Man's Land,* and *All of No Man's Land Is Ours.*[22]

But on the star-crossed evening of May 9, Herb Wright seemed disoriented, sullen, possibly drunk—and almost missed his first-act finale. "Lieutenant Europe, you don't treat me right," the drummer whined in his leader's dressing room during the break. He petulantly hurled down his drum and sticks and, brandishing a small pocketknife, screamed, "I'll kill anybody that takes advantage of me. Jim Europe, I'll kill you!" Europe, weakened by his bronchitis, picked up a chair for protection, then let it drop, turned aside, and muttered, "Herbert, get out of here!" "Like a panther," Wright threw himself at Europe, but then "became as calm and quiet as a child" as Noble Sissle firmly ushered him down the hall. Sissle remembered that he returned to Europe's dressing room only when another band member urgently called, "Come at once. Herbert stabbed Lieutenant Europe!" Sissle found his best friend pressing a crimson-stained towel against his throat to stanch a pulsing stream of blood.[23]

Two Boston policemen went backstage and apprehended Herb Wright. Jim Europe was fully conscious, identified his assailant, and detailed what had happened. Always the consummate professional, Europe ordered his men back on stage to finish the concert under the direction of his assistant conductor. One of the managers announced that Lieutenant Europe had been taken ill as the audience settled in to enjoy the remainder of the concert, unaware of what really had occurred. As an ambulance prepared to take him away, Europe instructed Sissle: "Don't forget to have the band down before the State House at 9 in the morning. I am going to the hospital, and I will have my wound dressed, and I will be at the Commons in the morning." Later that evening, Sissle and several others who had witnessed the assault went to the police station to provide their accounts, but while there, received a call from the hospital warning them that Europe's condition had worsened. They rushed over and were preparing to donate blood for a transfusion when, Noble Sissle recalled, an orderly "sorrowfully whispered, 'Lieutenant Europe is dead.' "[24]

The next morning, admirers and music lovers like the Chesnut family, as well as many other Bostonians who knew or cared almost nothing about the man, his patriotism, or his art, awoke to see the *Globe*'s devastating headline: "J. R. Europe, Band Leader,

Murdered." Newspapers across the country carried reports that a member of his band had killed the "King of Jazz."

Europe's body was transported to New York. A memorial cortege started in Harlem as throngs of mourners (black and white) observed the solemn procession that snaked down to midtown, where American and French soldiers, musicians, and theater folk paid their tributes. "No color line was drawn," the New York *Tribune* reported. The casket was put aboard a train to Washington, where Europe's family (including his grieving sister Mary, who taught music at Dunbar High School) lived. A second ceremony ensued in the nation's capital. Headlines from that city's *Afro-American* newspaper read, "Country Mourns Death of Great Colored Bandmaster," as Lieutenant James Reese Europe, the intrepid AEF officer who introduced France to the improvisations, riffs, and syncopated delights of African American jazz, was buried with military honors at Arlington National Cemetery.[25]

That same year, Boston's largely Irish-American police force (including Readville's patrolman, with his heavy brogue, who was a favorite of the Chesnut boys) went on a wildcat strike that stunned the city and the whole country. Soon thereafter, mobs of angry Bostonians assaulted May Day marchers, disrupted meetings, and trashed the local Socialist Party headquarters. The city's reconstituted constabulary did not arrest any of the rampaging "patriots," but did charge their radical victims with rioting and disturbing the peace. "Bolshevist agitation has been extended among the Negroes," the Boston *Herald* cautioned, adding, "The sinister influence of the I.W.W. [Industrial Workers of the World] and of bolshevism [is] clearly evident." In January 1920, local authorities arrested, shackled, and herded through the city's streets five hundred Socialists and supposedly anarchistic I.W.W. leaders.[26]

That June, Boston residents first heard news of what initially seemed to be a brutal but uncomplicated payroll robbery and double homicide in nearby South Braintree. Soon, however, the crime and its aftermath began to assume ominous implications for the Commonwealth and the whole nation. In less than a year, Dedham, Massachusetts, and its Norfolk County jail and courthouse became known worldwide, as attention focused on the felony murder trial of Nicola Sacco and Bartolomeo Vanzetti, which played out not far from the Bond and Chesnut families' residences. It was half a mile from their homes to Dedham's Oakdale Square, where River Street ended in the Church of the Good Shepherd's driveway, then less than a mile more to the stately court building near the town's tranquil New England green.[27]

One of Dedham's daughters had been a Radcliffe schoolmate of Carrie Bond. That young woman, Elizabeth Brandeis (whose father recently had been elevated to the Supreme Court over objections from critics who challenged the appointment of a Jew, whose "Oriental" mind, they argued, could not fully grasp a legal system shaped by "Occidental" principles), appraised her hometown. "Square, comfortable, white houses with 'colonial' doors lined . . . High Street," she wrote, and "two dignified white churches—meeting houses we must call them—faced each other across a green Common." "Of the inhabitants," she continued, "the greater part had lived in Dedham all their lives, and their great-grandfathers before them. . . . Dedham adhered staunchly to its dignified, if somewhat threadbare, gentility." After 1900, however, as cramped Bostonians (including a handful of Jews like the Brandeis family) pushed westward from the city, "Dedham succumbed to its miserable fate, [and] became 'suburbanized.' . . . [It] assimilated the invaders and lived on invigorated by the new blood."[28]

"But harsher fate was in store," Elizabeth Brandeis added, and "the fall came with the new sewer system." Most Dedhamites welcomed it, but "a few old fogies shook their heads and reminded the [town meeting] that our Puritan fathers had been quite satisfied to live without a sewer." Nonetheless, "the worthy citizens voted to build, and went home with a sense of achievement to tell their wives." What no one had expected was that "an influx of swarthy foreigners who wore red handkerchiefs about their necks and gesticulated excitedly while jabbering in an alien tongue" would arrive along with the construction of their new waste disposal facilities. The old Yankees realized, too late, that "in their need of cheap labor, the sewer contractors had imported into Dedham a great band of Italians."[29]

"The strangers certainly received no hearty welcome," Miss Brandeis continued: "Good ladies held their skirts close about them as they crossed the street, and shuddered at the flow of uncouth speech." But the Catholic newcomers whose popish ways somehow seemed to threaten the town's established and dominant Protestantism remained undeterred. They "liked Dedham, and there they have settled." By the end of the Great War, she added, "we [could] show you our Italian quarter, [and] the lots about the houses laid out in the neatest of vegetable gardens." "Groups of children sport about the street with an abandon unknown among restrained Yankees," Brandeis observed, while "Italian women sit on their doorsteps nursing their babies and chatting with their neighbors in the long summer twilight." One "majestic full-formed woman in blue calico," she continued, "pastures two cows on the far side of town, [and] morning and afternoon she stalks behind [them]." "Twice a day," Elizabeth Brandeis's canny essay concluded, Dedham's "white colonial houses watch her pass."[30] She distilled to its essence the old Yankee–new Italian venue where the Sacco-Vanzetti saga would unfold.

The trial started the last day of May 1921, with Worcester's Judge Webster Thayer presiding, but no Dedhamites, Italian Americans, or Negroes were chosen to serve on the jury of twelve men selected from a pool of seven hundred Norfolk County voters. One observer claimed that the town's streets were almost deserted that June, and argued that local residents dismissed the unfolding drama as just one more case concerning two obscure, ne'er-do-well Italians. But in fact, many quiet Dedham and Hyde Park citizens became increasingly distressed.[31]

The jurymen were "practically cut off from the outside world during the progress of the trial," Dedham's newspaper reported, though townspeople could hardly avoid the various participants. Reporters and members of the defense team roamed around Dedham's back streets, and strolled by the Charles River and Mother Brook. On weekends, jurors took "walks about town and automobile rides under the . . . watchful eyes of [the] Deputy Sheriff," as the Bonds, Chesnuts, and other residents went to market, the movies, and their nearby churches. The sequestered panel "spend the rest of the time and sleep in the court house," the article continued.

On the Fourth of July holiday break, the meticulously guarded, heavily escorted jury was driven eastward past Hyde Park to Braintree (where the crime had taken place), and then on through Weymouth, headed for a sportive, secluded outing at Cohasset Bay on Massachusetts's South Shore. They fished off granite rocks by the ocean's edge and contemplated the vast Atlantic that their own forebears, as well as Nicola Sacco and Bartolomeo Vanzetti, had optimistically traversed. That Independence Day as they weighed the fates of the two immigrants whose lives or deaths they commanded, the jurymen enjoyed a classic New England shore dinner of steamed clams and lobsters, corn, onions, and potatoes cooked over seaweed in huge steamer pots.[32]

Judge Thayer stated that "so long as people conduct themselves with decorum they are welcome to this courtroom to see and hear what is going on," while the Dedham *Transcript* observed that "court officials are constantly on the lookout for concealed weapons among the spectators." Every day they searched myriad observers but recovered only one revolver. Reporters from several "radical" Boston and Italian journals numbered among the throng, the local paper noted with dismay. Some of the seats reserved for spectators remained empty, but the press came out daily in full force. Security throughout the town was highly visible, as mounted state troopers circled the courthouse and police motorcycles growled up and down nearby roads. Every morning, Sacco and Vanzetti were bathed, shaved, dressed, and fed, handcuffed to one another, then each to a sheriff's deputy, and marched along Village Avenue, past the Brandeis house, where Nicola Sacco's wife and baby were staying, then up to the courthouse. They returned to the jail at lunchtime along the reverse route and repeated that exact routine on each of the trial's thirty-eight days.[33]

During the proceedings, one telling exchange occurred when the prosecutor prodded Vanzetti: "Why did you feel you were being detained for political opinions?" "Because," he answered, "I was asked if I am a Socialist, if I am I.W.W., if I am a Communist, if I am a Radical." Most Americans retained undifferentiated images of alien anarchists ranging from Leon Czolgosz, who had assassinated President McKinley, to I.W.W. leaders of the Lawrence textile workers' strike, to Boston's and Washington's postwar May Day protesters. The defendants had already been condemned as Bolsheviks who read "Socialistic" literature. Both briefly had fled the country in 1917 to avoid the draft and, like a number of their immigrant colleagues, had been threatened with deportation for violating the Selective Service Act.[34]

Felix Frankfurter, a future justice of the Supreme Court, argued shortly after the drama played out that his country's hysteria concerning all "Reds" was striking. Even before the infamous crime in South Braintree, he wrote, Sacco and Vanzetti had been targeted by the Department of Justice "as radicals to be watched, [and] they were especially obnoxious because they were draft-dodgers."[35] During his cross-examination, the district attorney asked Vanzetti, "When this country was at war, you ran away, so you would not have to fight as a soldier?" "Yes," Vanzetti admitted. Out of fears of being railroaded, both men had also lied about minor details of their activities on the day of the crime, and thus undermined their alibis and credibility. That seemed to reinforce their guilt in the eyes of the jurymen in Dedham.[36]

Frankfurter contended that "the temper of the times made it the special duty of a prosecutor and a court engaged in trying two Italian radicals before a jury of native New Englanders to keep the instruments of justice free from the infection of passion or prejudice." He (and a number of other critics) concluded, however, that "in the case of Sacco and Vanzetti no such restraints were respected."[37]

The district attorney's final words to the jury were: "Do your duty. Do it like men. Stand together, you men of Norfolk [County]." In his charge to the panel, Judge Thayer further appealed to emotion more than to logic. "Although you knew that such service would be arduous, painful, and tiresome," he told them, "you, like the true soldier, responded to that call in the spirit of supreme American loyalty." On July 14, 1921, the Norfolk County jurymen decided in only five hours and twenty-three minutes that, as true Americans, they had to return a guilty verdict. As he would many times again, Nicola Sacco cried out "*Sono innocente!*" The Dedham *Transcript*'s headline read, "Guilty of Murder in the 1st Degree Is Jury's Verdict." The newspaper earnestly editorialized: "The fact that they were men of alien birth, that they were slackers during the World War, or were affiliated with elements inimical to the best interests of our country had no influence in determining the verdict."[38]

Most Negro activists, such as W. E. B. Du Bois, seemed to pay the decision little heed (although he later opposed Sacco and Vanzetti's execution), but a few, like A. Philip Randolph in his labor-oriented, Socialist magazine the *Messenger*, expressed outrage. "The verdict was crushingly unexpected, and so far unwarranted by the evidence," Randolph railed in November 1921:

> Only a jury behaving under the influence of the insidious drug of class and race prejudice could give credence to the identifications. . . . Only a jury searching for an excuse . . . to send "alien reds" out of this best of all capitalist worlds could have swept aside the alibis of both men. . . . If Sacco and Vanzetti die, they will be paying the death penalty for their loyalty to labor.

Randolph continued his futile protests, arguing that "we workers, black and white, Jew and Gentile, native and foreign should stand behind these men. . . . They must not die."[39]

The verdict did not quench the unease in Dedham. In late October, law enforcement officers surrounded the jail where Sacco and Vanzetti remained incarcerated. They illuminated it with searchlights following rumors that some radical Italians from New York City were about to descend on their town.[40] The Department of Justice then placed undercover agents in the lockup to spy on the Italian Americans. New and persuasive exculpatory evidence unearthed by the defense team (and put forward by Randolph in the *Messenger*) did not move Judge Thayer to approve motions for a new trial, possibly because it called into question Thayer's own behavior during the original proceedings as well as his charge to the jury. "For all practical purposes," Frankfurter's critique concluded, Thayer "sat in judgment upon his own conduct."[41]

The Sacco-Vanzetti imbroglio consumed Bostonians, but other events streamed along as well. In 1920, the country had granted women the right to vote. It must have seemed too late for the aging and minimally literate Emma, but her daughters did exercise the franchise, although (unlike Emma's longtime suffragist daughter-in-law Georgia Bond and her daughters) politics never became a central issue for them.[42] Boston's men *and* women reelected James Michael Curley mayor in 1922, and in 1924 the country (including an estimated one million black voters) chose Massachusetts' governor Calvin Coolidge as its new president.

Bostonians revered the proud but contradictory legacy of Negroes at Harvard, and the university's Edward Gourdin represented the U.S.A. (and his race) when he won a silver medal in the long jump at the 1924 Olympic Games in Paris. Gourdin skipped his law school graduation to make that historic trip to France, and consequently missed the rambunctious cadre of alumni who cavorted in Ku Klux Klan robes. Members of the Chesnut family counted several Harvard men among their friends, but could not have known that their futures would be linked to Gourdin's when his daughter married Lena's second son several decades later.[43]

At the Chesnut's home in Hyde Park, Emma Bond remained the primary cook as her grandsons grew up. On Thanksgiving mornings, Dave and Bob Chesnut and Eddie Howley fought over who would take charge of her chopping board for the all-American holiday feast. They nibbled as they minced cabbage, then salted and sugared it for cole slaw. It became the family's preferred side dish for their traditional stuffed, oven-roasted turkey, surrounded by both southern yams and Irish white potatoes. As a young slave, Emma had cooked on an open hearth, but by the 1920s had a fine gas stove in her kitchen, where she fricasseed chickens and simmered celery, carrots, onions, potatoes, and ham for boiled dinners. Young Dave adored her down-home black bean soup. Boston's journalist Eugene Gordon described "the genuine Yankee, the kind with the twang like Coolidge's who eats baked beans for Saturday night's supper and apple pie for breakfast," and those dishes became favorites in the Bond-Chesnut household as well, with molasses-rich, nut-and-raisin-studded brown bread served alongside slow-baked, onion-and-salt-pork-flavored navy beans.[44]

Emma also prepared homemade ice cream, succotash, cornbread, and biscuits as she had been taught in Tidewater Virginia seven decades before, and often traded her fruits over the back fence for neighbors' fresh eggs and vegetables. She baked pies and sweet apple dumplings that Bob Chesnut loved, and after supper would say, "I'll just go to 'the store' to get dessert," as she marched downstairs to the cellar pantry where she kept shelves full of preserved crabapples, peaches, and pears that the whole family had picked together from Emma's backyard orchard throughout the summer.[45]

Eddie Howley took the trolley with his mother from Roxbury to Readville, and "ran headlong, lickety split" down the street as soon as he spied his cousins Dave and Bob Chesnut. Tooty and Eddie Howley stayed with Emma and the Chesnuts "in the country" every weekend. As the boys were growing up, their three-generational family meals incorporated African and Anglo-American influences from Emma Bond's childhood. She stirred in culinary elements from her late husband's African-English-Irish heritage, and adapted old Yankee legacies and new recipes from Hyde Park's Italian and German immigrants. Augmenting her all-American gallimaufry, Emma could have discovered that slivers of Virginia's Smithfield hams were virtually interchangeable with prosciutto; grits a first cousin to polenta; kale and collards akin to arugula; and black-eyed peas, lima, navy, or kidney beans little different from other *fagioli*. Codfish and potatoes remained ubiquitous staples all around the Atlantic rim, and for the Bond family (especially Percy), flaked, milk-soaked salt cod, plus leftover mashed potatoes mixed with minced onion and a beaten egg all shaped into plump pillows, rolled in cracker crumbs, and then fried brown and crusty in bacon fat, made irresistible breakfast cakes.[46]

One summer, the Chesnuts, the Howleys, and Emma Bond took a train to Washington to visit Percy and his family. J. Percy Bond, Bob Chesnut recalled, was "kind of pompous," and he met them at Union Station wearing white flannel trousers. The Chesnuts never forgot that trip—especially those pants. Percy's daughter Wenonah scarcely knew the Chesnuts and Howleys as she grew up, yet always remained curious about them and especially her pretty, though "flighty," cousin Frankie Bond. Percy, who had immersed himself in Washington's "colored" establishment, loved his mother and sisters, but wanted nothing to do with his somewhat disreputable brother Bob.[47]

Like their mother, aunt, and uncles before them, Lena's sons attended the Damon School, trudging over with neighbors such as the Coelho and Spinelli boys. "No one took a second look" because of race, Bob Chesnut remembered, no one had problems with immigrants, and different religions seemed "no issue" in his innocent eyes. Lena and David Senior always stressed manners, and taught their children to stay neat and clean, be careful how they dressed, and "look people straight in the eye." "Be proud of yourselves at all times," the Chesnuts insisted. "You're just as good as anyone else." Lena drew pictures and arranged family outings, while David played baseball with his sons, took them to the YMCA to swim, built crystal sets and vacuum-tube radios, and carried them on his shoulders up the steps to bed at night. Henry Endicott's son was an enthusiastic amateur musician who frequently invited Dave and Bob to the Endicott family mansion in Dedham to play in the elegant music salon, and he also sponsored the boys' lessons at Boston's New England Conservatory of Music. "My childhood was wonderful," Bob Chesnut recalled.[48]

Bob Bond's daughters were poor to indifferent students at Hyde Park High School, but young Dave Chesnut made his mark. He was in the same grade as Frankie Bond, but because Frankie tried to conceal her full racial heritage, she snubbed her more accomplished brown-skinned cousin. (Many decades later, Bob Chesnut made the gracious excuse for the Bond girls that "they probably didn't want to be bothered with us little kids.") Dave ran track with great energy and moderate success, and became a musician who gained city-wide acclaim. The school heaped praise on "Dave Chesnut and his band," and one of his few Negro contemporaries at school well remembered that stylish combo. "Whenever music is needed, he can supply it," the plaudits continued: "Dave sure knows his Bermudas when it comes to music!" Forecasting rosy futures for "our stars," the yearbook predicted that a quarter-century hence, everyone's favorite orchestra leader would be "the world-famous Dave Chesnut."[49]

The high school that Betty, Evelyn, and Frankie Bond and Dave and Bob Chesnut attended prepared them well enough in the 1920s, and some Hyde Park students (like Eleanor Bowen, one of Carrie Bond's few Negro contemporaries at Radcliffe) went on to attend the country's best colleges. But their training in Boston, supposedly the country's educational Utopia, paled in comparison to what their cousins Wenonah and Jack Bond received at Washington's segregated Dunbar High School, and certainly much of the rich heritage of Negro history and culture bypassed the Bostonians. Hyde Park's white teachers were adequate, but not on a par with the dedicated African American educators who prodded and inspired Dunbar students in those same years.

In the 1880s, the Bonds' wise neighbor Dr. Rebecca Crumpler had written, "After the turns have ceased altogether, a woman may live to a good old age, and fill many hours of usefulness," and those words aptly characterized Emma Bond's later years. She cared for the house and her beloved grandsons, and gathered medicinal leaves and roots to treat family and friends with tried-and-true botanical remedies. Emma gardened in the sanctuary around her home, with its roses, faithfully blooming dooryard lilacs and frowning purple pansies in front, and fecund fruit trees and grapevines in the rear garden that sloped down to the reedy, violet-fringed banks of Mother Brook.[50]

For thirty years, Emma had dutifully gone to the Episcopal Church of the Good Shepherd with her husband John, but after he died, she transferred her allegiance and started worshiping at Dedham's First Baptist. In the 1860s, she had attended and been married in the all-black Bute Street Baptist Church in Norfolk, Virginia. In Dedham, however, her grandson Bob Chesnut recalled, "we always felt very close to God, . . . [but] we were the only colored ones there." Nonetheless, every Sunday morning Emma put on a "high collar and long black dress," dabbed on her best perfume, picked up her Bible, took the Chesnut boys in tow, and strolled along River Street to the neighborhood Baptist church, where she soon knew everyone, and everyone knew and loved her.[51]

Emma hummed old hymns around the house, got down on her knees with Dave and Bob every night to say bedtime prayers and "talk to Mrs. Moon," and told hilarious, magical stories about gigantic fish, "baaing" goats, and "mooing" cows. She was a loving but firm mentor who skillfully mediated her grandsons' squabbles and often warned Bob, "I know what you're doing now, Robbie." Emma sewed fabric scraps into miniature quilts and mattresses to embellish the dolls' beds made from chocolate boxes that she presented to the neighborhood girls, who patently adored her. On her old sewing machine, she stitched up the frilly white aprons that she wore every day, as she spun straw into gold and made silk purses from sows' ears. "She couldn't do anything wrong," her grandsons firmly believed: "She was a genius."[52]

The timeless Old Testament directed couples like John and Emma Bond to "beget sons and daughters; and take wives for your sons, and give your daughters to husbands, that they may bear sons and daughters; that ye may be increased."[53] And it came to pass by 1926 that Emma Bond's four children had increased her line with nine grandchildren. Percy and Georgia's Caroline, Wenonah, and Jack Bond; Bob and Osie's three girls; Lena and David Chesnut's two sons; and Tooty and Ulysses Howley's one ranged in age from thirty-seven down to fourteen years. Emma remained healthy and vigorous at her River Street home in Hyde Park that she shared with the Chesnuts until late that year when she turned eighty.

"On May 12, 1926," Felix Frankfurter wrote about the Sacco-Vanzetti case, the Massachusetts Supreme Court "found 'no error' in any of the rulings of Judge Thayer," essentially discerning "no abuse of judicial discretion." But by that time, Frankfurter argued, new evidence not only pointed away from the convicted men but definitively implicated others. Nonetheless, at the year's end, Webster Thayer, who had presided over the initial judicial affair, issued a Christmas Eve edict that was remarkable, Frankfurter declared, for "discrepancies between what the record discloses and what the opinion conveys, . . . honeycombed with demonstrable errors and a spirit alien to judicial utterance." Thayer once again denied the men's motion for reconsideration. "Finding no error," he wrote, "the verdicts are to stand."[54]

In saloons, classrooms, parlors, offices and shops, on street corners and trolleys from Boston to Washington, D.C., Atlanta, and points west, Americans of all stripes (including the Chesnuts and Howleys, Bonds and Days) discussed whether the Commonwealth of Massachusetts was preparing to execute the men because they had committed murder or because they were aliens, draft-dodgers, and anarchists. The national debate hammered on, while many Italian Americans in Dedham and Hyde Park concluded that the whole judicial process of trial and repeated but fruitless appeals, most of which had played out virtually in their own back yards, had been decidedly unjust.[55]

Judge Thayer delivered his end-of-year opinion on Sacco and Vanzetti's final state appeal, and a few months later Justice Louis Brandeis would have to recuse himself from the U.S. Supreme Court's ultimate hearing because members of his family in Dedham had been so sympathetic to Nicola Sacco's wife Rosina. On Christmas morning 1926, Bartolomeo Vanzetti glumly conceded, "I know perfectly well that within four month the Massachusetts will be ready to burn me."[56] His prediction proved chillingly accurate.

The Bonds and Chesnuts, however, knew that their lives were charmed when a bolt of lightning struck their house and, as Emma watched, a fiery lightning ball rolled across the parlor floor but injured no one. Perhaps they convinced themselves that she was immortal. The Chesnuts also were looking toward the future in 1926 as Ernest Gould, a son of John Bond, Sr.'s old navy comrade, designed and had almost completed constructing a new home for them just down River Street across the Dedham town line. But a sudden stroke felled Emma shortly before the December holidays. Lena Chesnut took her mother to the doctor, and returned home to tell her sons that "grandmother was not going to be feeling well for a while." The cerebral incident left Emma weakened, with diminished muscle control on one side of her face, but otherwise young Dave and Bob found her little changed. The family celebrated a subdued Christmas, but the next evening, Emma slipped away from them. She died surrounded by her children, grandchildren, and love in the house where she had lived well for half a century. Like Liverpool's River Mersey where John Robert Bond had grown up, and the James River of Emma Thomas's childhood in Virginia, the waterway behind her home flowed toward the Atlantic.[57]

The Chesnuts draped the front door with black crepe, and the open casket remained in the living room for several days as relatives, friends, and neighbors—black, white, and of all ethnicities—paid their respects. Lena had been concerned that her boys would be devastated by Emma's death, but more than anything, they simply could not believe that their grandmother who had cooked, sewed, and washed for them, taken them to church, told them stories, been with them since birth, and always poured her soothing oils on troubled family waters really was gone. Dave and Bob Chesnut stood beside the casket and looked down at her: "[They] just wanted to talk with grandmother one last time."[58]

Emma Bond's onetime neighbor Rebecca Davis Lee Crumpler had died forty years earlier and her husband Arthur a decade later. Their remains had been interred in Fairview cemetery, as were James Trotter's, John Robert Bond, Sr.'s, and then Emma's. Boston's Frank Whiting, James Wolff, and William Gould had all passed away in recent years, and only Isaac Mullen among John Senior's old Negro comrades from the Civil War navy survived as 1926 drew to its close.[59]

An ancestral African proverb holds that when an old person dies, a library has burned to the ground. So it was with Emma Thomas Bond, who prevailed the classic four-score years. She practiced the narrator's art, but never wrote her own story or sought to preserve the tales that comprised the priceless library of her life. Emma left that task to a late-twentieth-century descendant who never had the chance to know her, but only heard tell of her mother's dimly recalled "grandmother in Boston."[60]

NOTES

HERITAGE

1. Partially contradicting this thesis concerning the endemic disavowal of BASPs' existence, Nathan Hare wrote *The Black Anglo-Saxons* (New York: Collier, 1965).

2. A 1990 study by the National Opinion Research Center found that a majority of white Americans still view black people as decidedly less patriotic, less willing to defend their country, as well as less intelligent and lazier than Caucasians.

3. Ruth Bond, widow of John Percy Bond, Jr., shared this story about her late husband and the photograph of his grandfather.

4. From the Emma Lazarus poem "The New Colossus," inscribed in 1903 on a tablet in the pedestal of the Statue of Liberty in New York's harbor.

5. Professor Jan van Sertima, the eminent historian and expert in African culture, does not think that this song has African roots. Examination by the author of slave narratives from many locales in the South finds *Keemo, Kimo* present *only* in southeast Virginia.

6. Very little has been written about black immigrants to the United States. The work of Roy Bryce-Laporte is an almost singular exception, and it primarily concerns the twentieth-century migrations of West Indians to this country. Even they have been largely ignored in the overwhelming emphasis on and literature concerning European immigrants.

7. Noel Ignatiev, *How the Irish Became White* (New York: Routledge, 1995), 41, argues that in the country's early decades it was not entirely clear who, in fact, was "white," with the Irish sometimes called "niggers turned inside out" and black people referred to as "smoked Irish."

8. The major legislation that structured policies and practices concerning citizenship during the Republic's first century was the Naturalization Act of 1790 limiting naturalization to "free white men." Black men were excluded from that original provision in 1870. The Chinese Exclusion Act of 1882 specified that na-

tionality's prohibition, and the "Gentlemen's Agreement" of 1907 shut down immigration from Japan. In 1924, "undesirable" immigrants (especially those from southern and eastern Europe) were limited to percentages established by their pre-existing presence in the population of the United States. See esp. Frank George Franklin, *The Legislative History of Naturalization in the United States* (Chicago: University of Chicago Press, 1906); and James H. Kettner, *The Development of American Citizenship, 1608–1870* (Chapel Hill: University of North Carolina Press, 1978). Though the legal record is somewhat inconclusive, into the early 1900s, women usually claimed citizenship rights only derivatively, through a father or spouse.

9. Douglas Turner Ward's controversial 1965 play, *Day of Absence,* expounds on the idea that when black Americans stayed away from work one day, white Americans could not cook, clean, or even take care of their own children, lacking their essential, servile workforce. In a less ironic vein, see Ralph Ellison's essay "What America Would Be Without Blacks" in *Going to the Territory* (New York: Random House, 1986).

10. Throughout its history, this country has seen numerous and diverse "back to Africa" movements. Some have been stimulated by white Americans trying to "solve" the "Negro problem," while others (those of Paul Cuffe in the early-nineteenth century and Marcus Garvey in the early twentieth, for example) have been generated by blacks themselves hoping to return to their "homelands."

11. My teacher and colleague Arnold Taylor first made me think about the question of when black people became Americans. James Oliver Horton, *Free People of Color: Inside the African American Community* (Washington, D.C.: Smithsonian Institution Press, 1993), 159, observes that by the mid-nineteenth century most blacks "identified themselves as Americans of African heritage rather than as Africans in America." When discussing events prior to issuance of the 1863 Emancipation Proclamation, I call people of African ancestry "slaves," or more inclusively, "blacks" or "Negroes." Some contemporary writers capitalize "black" and contend that current usage makes it the legitimate successor to "Negro." I reject that argument, because despite laudatory intent, parallelism, and a certain logic, indiscriminate capitalization often creates more problems than it solves. "We are the hyphenated people of the [African] Diaspora," wrote essayist Audre Lorde, "whose self-defined identities are . . . declarations of strength and solidarity." See Patricia Bell-Scott, ed., *Life Notes: Personal Writings by Contemporary Black Women* (New York: Norton, 1994), 410. But Lorde's hyphen now seems inappropriate. Contemporary usage rejects "Afro-American" in favor of "African American." With that revised designation, I simply choose to dispense with the hyphen. "Negro" might appear dated nowadays, yet it still seems appropriate when referring to our people during the years when we sought out and favored that term. All fashions, including linguistic ones, constantly mutate. In

1908, Ray Stannard Baker observed that "many Negroes who a few years ago called themselves 'Afro-Americans,' or 'Coloured Americans,' and who winced at the name Negro, now use Negro as the race name with pride." See Baker, *Following the Color Line: American Negro Citizenship in the Progressive Era* (New York: Doubleday, Page, 1908), 228. Henry Louis Gates, Jr., recalls his childhood when he declares that he likes " 'colored' best." See Gates, *Colored People: A Memoir* (New York: Knopf, 1994), xvi. I use "colored" only to indicate the thinking of those who used it, when they used it. "People of color," however, may better reflect the disparate composition of a nonwhite community that the country's Euro-American majority generically has relegated to a marginal status as "others." We African Americans, like members of any "tribe," sometimes refer to ourselves in terms that, when uttered by outsiders, become "fightin' words." They may reflect a self-hatred generated by centuries of abuse in a country that often has made darker skin seem an abiding badge of inferiority. Those racist and xenophobic expressions are neither bypassed nor soft-pedaled here. I use them, when called for, to underscore the often injurious intent and effect of those who enunciated them. The powers of language must not be underestimated, and definitions, leverage, and impact vary according to who uses which words in what particular contexts.

12. Fox Butterfield's *All God's Children: The Bosket Family and the American Tradition of Violence* (New York: Knopf, 1995) is a recent example of a study that emphasizes the destructive patterns of black family and community life.

13. Gail Lumet Buckley, Lena Horne's daughter, for example, has detailed her family's genesis in *The Hornes: An American Family* (New York: Knopf, 1986). The biographical and autobiographical literature about black celebrities (entertainers, athletes, men of God) is enormous. Among the relatively few works about nonpathological, unrenowned African American families are Pauli Murray, *Proud Shoes: The Story of an American Family* (New York: Harper & Row, 1956); Dorothy Spruill Redford, *Somerset Homecoming: Recovering a Lost Heritage* (New York: Doubleday, 1989); Carole Ione, *Pride of Family: Four Generations of American Women of Color* (New York: Summit, 1991); Sarah and A. Elizabeth Delaney with Amy Hill Hearth, *Having Our Say: The Delaney Sisters' First 100 Years* (New York: Kodansha, 1993); and Shirlee Taylor Haizlip, *The Sweeter the Juice: A Family Memoir in Black and White* (New York: Simon & Schuster, 1994).

1. MONGREL LIVERPOOL

1. The 1851 census estimated Liverpool's "Old Borough" population as almost 260,000. Its "Parliamentary Borough" population that same year was 376,650, excluding some 12,000 transient seamen. This information and most ge-

ographic references come from Edward Howell's 1851 map of "Liverpool with its Parliamentary and Municipal Boundaries, with Part of the River Mersey & Cheshire Coast," and Hilliar's 1848 map of the "Borough of Liverpool, with the Parliamentary Boundaries, Ecclesiastical Divisions, and a Part of the Cheshire Coast." Although London was a larger city, unlike Liverpool, it was not considered primarily a port.

2. Friedrich Engels, *The Condition of the Working Class in England* (1st English ed., 1892; reprint, Chicago: Academy Chicago, 1984), 43.

3. Elizabeth Cleghorn Gaskell, *Mary Barton: A Tale of Manchester Life* (1847; reprint London: J. M. Dent & Sons, 1911), 273. This novel also depicts various aspects of life in Liverpool in the 1840s.

4. Not until 1877 did India become the "Jewel in the Crown," and Victoria its empress.

5. Peter Fryer, *Staying Power: The History of Black People in Britain* (Atlantic Highlands, N.J.: Humanities Press, 1984), 43.

6. Norma Myers, "In Search of the Invisible: British Black Family and Community," in *Slavery and Abolition* 13, no. 3 (December 1992), citing J. Salter, *The Asiatics in England,* argues that the mid-nineteenth-century British defined Lascar sailors who served in the merchant service (usually only temporarily) quite broadly. Those "Eastern seamen" included Burmese, Malays, Bengalis, Chinese, and Siamese, as well as natives of East Africa and Arabia. These diverse peoples as well as those of African ancestry were all, in most cases, referred to as "black." Concerning Kroo (or Kru) seamen, see W. E. F. Ward, *The Royal Navy and the Slavers: The Suppression of the Atlantic Slave Trade* (New York: Pantheon Books, 1969), 102–3.

7. One discussion of the undifferentiated categorization by the British of everyone who was not white as "coloured" appears in Hiro Dilip, *Black British, White British* (London: Monthly Review Press, 1971), vii. Writing about nonwhites in Britain, I use "coloured," the preferred spelling in England.

8. Edward Scobie, *Black Britannia: A History of Blacks in Britain* (Chicago: Johnson Publishing, 1972), 120. England's racial amalgam, both in Liverpool and as a whole, is difficult to calculate because nineteenth-century British census records designate country of birth but not race.

9. W. E. B. Du Bois, *Dusk of Dawn* (New York: Harcourt Brace, 1940), 41.

10. Many Anglo-Saxon names derived from occupation (Baker, Shoemaker, Cooper, Smith) or status (Lord, Commoner, Freeman). James's name may have originated in the medieval use of "bondsman," as the equivalent of "serf," and referred to a condition of bondage. As Edmund Spenser wrote: "The thrals which there in bondage lay." Ira Berlin, "From Creole to African: Atlantic Creoles and the Origins of African-American Society in Mainland North America," *William and Mary Quarterly* 53, no. 2 (April 1996): 251–88, analyzes the metamorphoses

of black Atlantic creole cultures, including a discussion of name changes. For a fine overall discussion of blacks' transatlantic peregrinations, see W. Jeffrey Bolster, *Black Jacks: African American Seamen in the Age of Sail* (Cambridge: Harvard University Press, 1997).

11. Engels, *Working Class in England,* 123. Gaskell, *Mary Barton,* 79. Cobh is the Irish name for the port of Cork. In the antebellum United States as well as in England, the Irish were described with adjectives (apish, simian, etc.) that resembled those which described people of African ancestry. David R. Roediger, *The Wages of Whiteness: Race and the Making of the American Working Class* (New York: Verso, 1993), chap. 7, deals with the impact of the Irish famine years.

12. Roediger, *Wages of Whiteness,* 134; and Cecil Woodham-Smith, *The Great Hunger: Ireland 1845–1849* (New York: Old Town Books, 1989), 19.

13. The Hyde Park, Massachusetts, neighborhood where Eliza Kelly's son settled included immigrant families named Higgins and Murphy. Callahans and Fitzgeralds were notable among the Boston Irish.

14. Ian Law and June Henfrey, *A History of Race and Racism in Liverpool, 1660–1950* (Liverpool: Merseyside Community Relations Council, 1981), 15 and 22; Douglas A. Lorimer, *Colour, Class, and the Victorians* (Leicester: Leicester University Press, 1978), 79; and Woodham-Smith, *The Great Hunger,* 272–79. Controversies surrounding the great potato famine continue. Shortly after he took over the reins of government in May 1997, Prime Minister Tony Blair expressed regret for Britain's role in the famine. The British had controlled the land and exacerbated the situation by continuing to export Irish grain and cattle even as the poor starved. Sarah Lyall, "Past as Prologue: Blair Faults Britain in Irish Potato Blight," *New York Times,* June 3, 1997.

15. The 1772 Somerset decision is the most accepted landmark in the termination of slavery in England itself. Several similar cases followed in its wake. Norma Myers, "Servant, Sailor, Tailor, Beggarman: Black Survival in White Society 1780–1830," *Immigrants and Minorities* 12, no. 1 (March 1993): 47–74, 48–50, and 54. Throughout *Black Jacks,* Bolster addresses issues of transplanted African culture.

16. Richard J. M. Blackett, "Cracks in the Antislavery Wall: Frederick Douglass's Second Visit to Britain, 1859," unpublished paper.

17. F. N. Boney, ed., *Slave Life in Georgia: A Narrative of the Life, Sufferings, and Escape of John Brown, A Fugitive Slave* (1855; reprint, Savannah: Beehive Press, 1991), 142. Law and Henfrey, *Race and Racism in Liverpool,* 15.

18. This organization kept its full title long after slavery had ended throughout the British Empire.

19. Martin R. Delany's novel *Blake; or, The Huts of America,* first appeared in the *Anglo-American Magazine* from January to July 1859. Reprinted in Ronald T. Takaki, *Violence in the Black Imagination* (New York: Putnam, 1972), 200.

20. Benjamin Quarles, *The Negro in the Civil War* (1953; reprint, New York: Da Capo Press, 1989), 81.

21. Ibid., 18. William Wells Brown, *The American Fugitive in Europe* (1860; reprint, New York: 1969); William Craft, *Running a Thousand Miles for Freedom* (London, 1860); and Frederick Douglass, *Life and Times of Frederick Douglass* (1892; reprint, London: Collier-Macmillan, 1969). R. J. M. Blackett, *Beating against the Barriers: The Lives of Six Nineteenth-Century Americans* (Baton Rouge: Louisiana State University Press, 1986), 211. Also Lorimer, *Colour, Class, and the Victorians,* 54; and Fryer, *Staying Power,* 435.

22. See, for example, James Walvin, "British Abolitionism, 1787–1838," in Anthony Tibbles, ed., *Transatlantic Slavery: Against Human Dignity* (Liverpool: Merseyside Museums and Galleries, 1994), 91.

23. Norma Myers, "In Search of the Invisible," 163. The *Times* of London, April 4, 1857, reported Morley's election.

24. The phrase "Am I not a man and a brother" was widely quoted by abolitionists on both sides of the Atlantic. "Never during the whole time" in England, Frederick Douglass also stated, had he "met with a single word, look, or gesture which gave me the slightest reason to think that my colour was an offense to anyone"; in Lorimer, *Colour, Class, and the Victorians,* 49 and 71. See also chap. 7, "Scientific Racism and Mid-Victorian Racial Attitudes." James Walvin, *Black and White: The Negro and English Society, 1555–1945* (London: Allen Lane, Penguin Press, 1973), 189–90. Charles Darwin's theories concerning the "origin of the species" and "survival of the fittest" came into play in the development of these theories of racial superiority.

25. Lorimer, *Colour, Class, and the Victorians,* for example, argues that the attitudes of middle- and upper-class Victorians concerning race was more a question of ethnocentrism than true racial bigotry. He also notes that often in England during this period "Negrophobe warred against Negrophile," 21.

26. Since the late fifteenth century, the international slave trade had been successively dominated by the Portuguese, Spanish, and Dutch. Dilip, *Black British, White British,* x.

27. Quoted in Norma Myers, "Liverpool and the Slave Trade," unpublished paper, 17. See also Anthony Tibbles, "Oil Not Slaves: Liverpool and West Africa after 1807," in *Transatlantic Slavery.*

28. Ervin L. Jordan, Jr., *Black Confederates and Afro-Yankees in Civil War Virginia* (Charlottesville: University Press of Virginia, 1995), 245; Alfreda M. Duster, ed., *Crusade for Justice: The Autobiography of Ida B. Wells* (Chicago: University of Chicago Press, 1972), 134; and Lorimer, *Colour, Class, and the Victorians,* 72.

29. Lorimer, *Colour, Class, and the Victorians,* 15.

30. Engels, *Working Class in England,* 207; Law and Henfrey, *Race and Racism in Liverpool,* 5.

31. Woodham-Smith, *Great Hunger,* 278.

32. Ibid., 188–95.

33. Noel Ignatiev, *How the Irish Became White* (New York: Routledge, 1995), 140, claims that in 1847 one-sixth of the potential immigrants died at English points of debarkation or en route to the United States.

34. Marcus Lee Hansen, *The Atlantic Migration, 1607–1860* (New York: Harper Torchbooks, 1961), 250.

35. Ibid., viii, 119, 251, 292. Also Douglass, *Life and Times,* 232-33, 246; Law and Henfrey, *Race and Racism in Liverpool,* 25; and Lorimer, *Colour, Class, and the Victorians,* 48.

36. On her son's birth and baptismal records, Eliza Kelly called herself "Mrs. Bond." My search of English marriage records from 1833 through 1847, however, revealed no marriage between a couple with those names. Since there is no indication that Eliza and James Bond ever married, I refer to her as "Kelly."

37. Birth certificate of John Bond, from the Office of Population, Censuses and Surveys, London. Woodham-Smith, *Great Hunger,* 272–79; Merseyside Maritime Museum, Maritime Records Centre, "History of the Albert Dock"; and Tibbles, "Oil Not Slaves," 80.

38. Law and Henfrey, *Race and Racism in Liverpool,* 3; and Walvin, *Black and White,* 69. Myers, "In Search of the Invisible," 161–63, finds that few Negroes were baptized, and most of those who were received the sacrament only as adults. In her unpublished paper " 'Indelible Allegiance': Ethnicity and Nationalism in Slavery and Impressment Narratives," 4, Beth Donaldson points out links between baptism and blacks' nonslave status and raises the question of the religious as political. She cites Olaudah Equiano, who stated: "I have been baptized; and by the laws of the land, no man has a right to sell me."

39. Baptism records of St. Peter's Church, Liverpool, 1846–50.

40. Ibid. Myers, "Liverpool and the Slave Trade," 22, 26, states that John Sparling, an affluent member of Liverpool's self-made mercantile class, became a justice of the peace. The Sparlings moved out of central Merseyside Liverpool to a northwest neighborhood called Everton.

41. Norma Myers acquainted me with this lower-class nonwhite English tradition that resembled the slave ritual in the United States known as "jumping the broom." Myers, "In Search of the Invisible," 164. See, for example, Eugene Genovese, *Roll, Jordan, Roll: The World the Slaves Made* (New York: Random House, 1972), 475–81.

42. Gaskell, *Mary Barton,* 290.

43. Information from the 1841 and 1851 British Census records, Public Records Office, London. In the area around Sparling Street, about forty percent were Lancashire County born, twenty percent Irish born, fifteen percent from elsewhere in England, the rest Scottish, Welsh, other European, and miscellaneous

peoples of the empire. John Bond's 1846 birth certificate lists his parents as James and Eliza Kelly Bond, and their address as 34 Sparling Street, but the family did not live on Sparling Street either in the 1841 or 1851 census years. There were, however, other Irish-born Kellys on that street.

44. There is confusion between "Toxteth" and "Toxteth Park." The latter-designated neighborhood is newer than the former, but they lie adjacent to one another, with Toxteth Park to the south and farther from central Liverpool. When John Robert Bond was growing up in the city, Toxteth Park still consisted mostly of open spaces. Now it is a congested ghetto that is home to much of Liverpool's black population.

45. Henfrey and Law, *Race and Racism in Liverpool,* 13.

46. Fryer, *Staying Power,* 5, dates the first documented appearance of Africans in England to 1555.

47. Lorimer, *Colour, Class, and the Victorians,* 26. Myers, "In Search of the Invisible," 161, cites a similar advertisement from *Williamson's Liverpool Advertiser* in 1756, seeking: "A Negro Boy. He must be of deep black complexion, and a lively Humane disposition, with good features."

48. Fryer, *Staying Power,* 37.

49. Scobie, *Black Britannia,* 18–19. Also see Duster, ed., *Crusade for Justice,* 130. Wells's diary from 1893 reported that the intoxicated thespian cried out: "Have I come from London to be hissed by you; every brick in whose walls is cemented by the blood of slaves?"

50. Waverly Root, *Food* (New York: Simon & Schuster, 1980), 380, 383, argues that potatoes were first taken to Ireland by Francis Drake in 1586, and cultivated in Lancashire starting in 1634.

51. Myers, "In Search of the Invisible," discusses the difficulty in detailing the domestic lives of people of African ancestry in England.

52. Fryer, *Staying Power,* 5, 235; Walvin, *Black and White,* 197; and Dilip, *Black British, White British,* xi. Myers, "Liverpool and the Slave Trade," quotes a 1764 journal that cites the 20,000 figure. Fryer, however, argues for the greater accuracy of the lower numbers. It is difficult to come up with accurate figures for Britain's black population after 1771, when there was still a separate listing for slaves. Unlike United States censuses, the British census did not indicate race, although it did show place—country and/or city—of birth.

53. In 1821, the independent country of Liberia was founded, governed, and largely populated by former slaves from the United States. Its capital, Monrovia, was named for the American president James Monroe.

54. P. E. H. Hair and Roger Amstey, *Liverpool, the African Slave Trade, and Abolition* (Historical Society of Lancashire and Cheshire, 1976), 3. Myers, "Liverpool and the Slave Trade," 17; and Ward, *Royal Navy and Slavers,* 203.

55. Paul Edwards and James Walvin, *Black Personalities in the Era of the Slave Trade* (London: Macmillan, 1983), 31. Myers, "Liverpool and the Slave Trade," cites a 1788 journal which stated that there were fifty to seventy African students in Liverpool at that time.

56. Bolster, *Black Jacks,* 68, quoting Melville's *Billy Budd;* Law and Henfrey, *Race and Racism in Liverpool,* 13–14, 19; and Walvin, *Black and White,* 194.

57. Caroline Bond Day, *A Study of Some Negro-White Families in the United States* (Cambridge: Peabody Museum of Harvard University, 1932), 31–32. Liverpool's nonwhite community is probably the oldest and most established in Britain. See Stephen Small, "Racialised Relations in Liverpool: A Contemporary Anomaly," *New Community* 17, no. 4: 511–37. In addition to the sources already cited, supplemental useful works about Liverpool and race in England include: Paul Gilroy, *There Ain't No Black in the Union Jack* (London: Hutchinson Publishers, 1987); F. E. Hyde, *Liverpool and the Mersey* (Bristol: David & Charles, 1971); Folarin Shyllon, *Black People in Britain, 1555–1833* (London: Oxford University Press, 1977); James Walvin, *The Black Presence: A Documentary History of the Negro in England* (New York: Schocken, 1972); and Carlton E. Wilson, "A Hidden History: The Black Experience in Liverpool, England, 1919–1945" (Ph.D. diss., University of North Carolina at Chapel Hill, 1991).

58. Boney, ed., *Slave Life in Georgia,* 29–39. This quote bears a remarkable resemblance to Frederick Douglass's words: "I knew a ship from stem to stern, and from kelson to crosstrees," quoted in Paul Gilroy, *The Black Atlantic: Modernity and Double Consciousness* (Cambridge: Harvard University Press, 1993), xiii.

59. Lorimer, *Colour, Class, and the Victorians,* 42.

60. Blackett, "Cracks in the Antislavery Wall"; Fryer, *Staying Power,* 253, 441, 450–53. Charles Dickens saw William Henry Lane in New York City and described his dancing. See Sterling Stuckey, *Going through the Storm: The Influence of African American Art in History* (New York: Oxford University Press, 1994), 72–73. Also Eric Lott, *Love and Theft: Blackface Minstrelsy and the American Working Class* (New York: Oxford University Press, 1993). Antebellum minstrelsy in the United States evoked negative racial stereotypes and excluded most blacks from the stage, though a few, such as Virginia's "Blind Tom," performed in the slaveholding South. Nick Salvatore, *We All Got History: The Memory Books of Amos Webber* (New York: Times Books, 1996), 60. The British Order of Oddfellows (usually one word in England) was established in the early 1700s. The first United States Odd Fellows lodge was formed in 1819, but the all-white American groups separated from the European parent order in the 1840s.

61. James M. O'Toole, "Passing (in) the Fleet: Racial Identity and the Case of Captain Michael Healy, USRCS," unpublished paper shared by the author.

62. Bolster, *Black Jacks,* 218. Myers, "Servant, Sailor, Soldier, Tailor, Beggarman," 58, provides statistics showing that more than one-quarter of the identifiable black men in London in the early 1800s were employed as seamen. Percentages would have been higher for seamen and related occupations in the port city of Liverpool. Stan Hugill, *Shanties from the Seven Seas: Shipboard Work-Songs from the Great Days of Sail* (London: Routledge & Kegan Paul, 1961), xiv.

63. Walvin, *Black and White,* 198. Myers, "Servant, Sailor, Soldier, Tailor, Beggarman," 63.

64. Walvin, *Black and White,* 198. Myers, "Servant, Sailor, Soldier, Tailor, Beggarman," observes that Lascar, or other Asian seamen, were not regarded as British sailors and therefore drew lower pay and lesser rations. Law and Henfrey, *Race and Racism in Liverpool,* 15, 19–20. Most etymologists suggest that "tar" derives from "tarpaulin."

65. See especially Winthrop Jordan, *White over Black: American Attitudes Toward the Negro, 1550–1812* (New York: Norton, 1968), chap. 1, "First Impressions."

66. Fryer, *Staying Power,* 235. The quote is from William Cobbett in 1804.

67. Myers, "In Search of the Invisible," 158–60, 165.

68. Fryer, *Staying Power,* provides a thorough analysis of early British racial attitudes in chap. 7, "The Rise of English Racism." See also Myers, "In Search of the Invisible," 167; Shyllon, *Black People in Britain,* 103; and Walvin, *The Black Presence,* 72.

69. There are two competing theories on the etymology of the disparaging term "wog." One school argues that it was an acronym for "Wily Oriental Gentleman," while the other suggests that it referred to any nonwhite person in England, and probably derived from "golliwog," a grotesque caricature of a black man.

70. Small, "Racialised Relations," 513, 521–23; and Law and Henfrey, *Race and Racism in Liverpool* 4, 19, 25. William Shakespeare, *The Tragedy of Othello, The Moor of Venice,* act 1, scene 1. See Lorimer, *Colour, Class, and the Victorians,* 27. Lorimer points out that nineteenth-century British law forbade "miscegenous unions of Irish Catholics and English Protestants." The word "miscegenation" was coined in the United States around 1860, replacing the term "amalgamation." See also chap. 4.

71. Shyllon, *Black People in Britain,* 104, quote from Edward Long's "Colonial Reflections" of 1772. See also Myers, "In Search of the Invisible," 167.

72. The most skillful of the early British caricaturists and engravers was William Hogarth (1697–1764), who often included portrayals of lascivious black people in his street scenes of lower-class life, as did George Cruikshank in the early nineteenth century. See also Kim F. Hall, *Things of Darkness: Economies of Race and Gender in Early Modern England* (Ithaca: Cornell University Press, 1995).

73. Walvin, *Black and White,* 63. The Forster Education Act of 1870, however, had a greater impact.

74. New Bedford *Evening Standard,* December 6, 1862. Not only English but also New England newspapers carried articles about Liverpool's economic troubles. Engels, *Working Class in England,* provides detailed descriptions of conditions among the poor, especially in Manchester during the early 1840s.

75. My thanks to Valerie Burton at the Memorial University of Newfoundland who shared with me the 1867 Agreement and Account of Crew (#33993) for the *Pactolus,* and tracked down its ownership. Root, *Food,* 84. Gilroy explores the transoceanic intellectual exchange at length in *The Black Atlantic.*

76. Christopher T. Watts and Michael J. Watts, *My Ancestor Was a Merchant Seaman* (London: Society of Genealogists, 1986), 26. The holy-stone was a soft sandstone used to scrub a ship's decks. Bolster, *Black Jacks,* 80–83, and generally, discusses black sailors as citizens of the world and transmitters of culture. Gaskell, *Mary Barton,* 146.

77. *Times* of London, June 4, 1862, and May 14, 1863.

78. Hugill, *Shanties from the Seven Seas,* 18, 347.

79. Bolster, *Black Jacks,* 92. One of John Robert Bond's grandsons and a great-grandson were called Jack.

2. NEW BEDFORD AND THE *CAMBRIDGE*

1. John Robert Bond's citizenship papers show that he arrived in New Bedford in September 1862. The *Pactolus* was the only ship from Liverpool that arrived in New Bedford during the period in question. New Bedford *Evening Standard,* September 15 and November 1, 1862. British sailors were called "limeys" because they were given limes to eat. The citric acid in the limes prevented scurvy, which could be brought on by an inadequate shipboard diet. In 1866, the only dates for which crew records from the *Pactolus* have been discovered, the ship had a captain (and owner), first mate, one ordinary seaman, plus five able-bodied seamen aboard. Their ages ranged from twenty-two to fifty. Also, Christopher T. Watts and Michael J. Watts, *My Ancestor Was a Merchant Seaman* (London: Society of Genealogists, 1986), 26.

2. See esp. Maria Luisa Nunes, *A Portuguese Colonial in America, Belmira Nunes Lopes: The Autobiography of a Cape Verdean-American* (Pittsburgh: Latin American Library Review Press, 1982), 3–6.

3. F. N. Boney, ed., *Slave Life in Georgia: A Narrative of the Life, Sufferings, and Escape of John Brown, A Fugitive Slave* (1855; reprint, Savannah: Beehive Press, 1991), 32. Despite protests from Britain and the U.S. government, the southern coastal states began jailing black sailors who arrived in their ports even before 1830. For a thorough discussion of the South's Black Seamen's Acts, see chap. 7, "Free Sailors and the Struggle with Slavery," in W. Jeffrey Bolster, *Black*

Jacks: African American Seamen in the Age of Sail (Cambridge: Harvard University Press, 1997). See also Philip M. Hamer, "Great Britain, the United States, and the Negro Seamen's Acts," *Journal of Southern History* 1 (1935): 3–28; and Harold D. Langley, "The Negro in the Navy and Merchant Service—1789–1860," *Journal of Negro History* 52, no. 4 (October 1967): 283–84.

4. Bolster, *Black Jacks,* 186; and Herman Melville, *Moby Dick; or, The Whale* (1851; reprint, London: Penguin Classics, 1986), 162, 126. Frederick Douglass, *Life and Times of Frederick Douglass* (1885; reprint, New York: Colliers, 1972), 206, 210; Bolster, *Black Jacks,* 220; and F. N. Boney, Richard L. Hume, and Rafia Zafar, eds., *God Made Man, Man Made the Slave: The Autobiography of George Teamoh* (Macon, Ga.: Mercer University Press, 1990), 111. See also Virginia M. Adams, ed., *On the Altar of Freedom: A Black Soldier's Civil War Letters from the Front* (Amherst: University of Massachusetts Press, 1991).

5. Bolster, *Black Jacks,* 173. Sierra Leone was often a destination for free people of color from the United States.

6. Barbara Clayton and Kathleen Whitley, *Guide to New Bedford* (Montpelier, Vt.: Capital City Press, 1979), 135, 169–70; Douglass, *Life and Times,* 206; Adams, *Altar of Freedom,* xix; and James Oliver Horton, *Free People of Color: Inside the African American Community* (Washington, D.C.: Smithsonian Institution Press, 1993), 156–57.

7. Bolster, *Black Jacks,* 186, 187; Boney, Hume, and Zafar, *God Made Man,* 106; and Writers' Program, Work Projects Administration, *The Negro in Virginia* (1940; reprint, Winston-Salem, N.C.: John F. Blair, 1994), 151. There is disagreement as to whether Bayne originally came from Virginia, Maryland, or North Carolina.

8. Bolster, *Black Jacks,* 186, 187; Boney, Hume, and Zafar, *God Made Man,* 106; and Henry W. Parker, *The Despised Race* (New Bedford, Mass.: Mercury Press, 1863), 9.

9. The actual barrels for collecting whale and sperm oil were usually constructed right on the whaling ships themselves. Clayton and Whitley, *Guide to New Bedford,* 170; and Adams, *Altar of Freedom,* xxiii.

10. Bolster, *Black Jacks,* 163; and Melville, *Moby Dick,* 154.

11. *Evening Standard,* December 29, 1862, and May 9, 1863.

12. Ibid., May 22, 1863.

13. Boston *Post,* May 25, 1863. Paul Dickson, *War Slang: American Fighting Words and Phrases from the Civil War to the Gulf War* (New York: Pocket Books, 1994), 17, traces the origin of "the pond," meaning the Atlantic Ocean, from the Civil War.

14. Ibid., May 19 and 20, 1863, and *Evening Standard,* December 29, 1862, and January 13, 1863. The infamous CSS *Alabama* also had been built in Liverpool.

15. *Evening Standard,* September 18 and 26, 1862. The president had recently been granted standby authority to recruit blacks for the Union army. The first contraband regiment was organized in South Carolina during the summer of 1862, under the command of Thomas Wentworth Higginson. Their official date of muster was November 15, 1862. The First Kansas, Colored, was mustered in on January 13, 1863, then the Fifty-fourth Massachusetts began recruiting on February 9, 1863. See esp. Thomas Wentworth Higginson, *Army Life in a Black Regiment* (1869; reprint, New York: Norton, 1984), 263–64.

16. *Evening Standard,* September 18 and 29, 1862, and January 1, 3, 1863.

17. Boney, Hume, and Zafar, *God Made Man,* 109.

18. *Evening Standard,* January 24, February 14, March 7, 14, and 28, 1863; and Adams, *Altar of Freedom,* xxviii.

19. *Evening Standard,* March 7, 14, and 28, 1863. Benjamin Quarles, *The Negro in the Civil War* (1953; reprint, New York: Da Capo Press, 1989), 185; and Adams, *Altar of Freedom,* xxx. Another account specifies the spelling Nicholas Saib, who came from what is today's Mali, and credit him with only five languages. Ervin L. Jordan, *Black Confederates and Afro-Yankees in Civil War Virginia* (Charlottesville: University Press of Virginia, 1995), 272. Jordan also states, 268, that eleven percent of the men in the Fifty-fifth Massachusetts were Virginians.

20. *Evening Standard,* October 4, 1962.

21. Conversations with and information from Wenonah Bond Logan, the author's mother and the first John Robert Bond's grandchild.

22. Diary of William B. Gould. My thanks to William B. Gould IV (who also is working on a memoir) for sharing his great-grandfather's diary and allowing me to quote it. For an analysis of blacks in the Union navy who enlisted from New England ports, see Joseph P. Reidy, Roger A. Davidson, Lisa Y. King, and Yohuro R. Williams, "With a Tattoo of 'Liberty' on His Right Forearm: Toward a Social History of Black New England Sailors in the Civil War Navy," unpublished paper.

23. F. N. Boney, *Southerners All* (Macon, Ga.: Mercer University Press, 1991), 107, quotes this phrase from one of the Lincoln-Douglas debates of 1858.

24. Quarles, *The Negro in the Civil War,* 31.

25. "Sambo's Right to Be Kilt" from Joseph T. Wilson, *The Black Phalanx,* foreword by Dudley Taylor Cornish (1887; reprint, New York: Da Capo Press, 1994), 164. A slightly different version appears in a number of secondary sources, including David Roediger, *The Wages of Whiteness: Race and the Making of the American Working Class* (New York: Verso, 1993), 173.

26. Gould diary.

27. *Evening Standard,* May 16, 1863; Gould diary. *Dictionary of American Naval Fighting Ships* (Washington, D.C.: Naval History Division, 1976), 5: 143–44; and Paul H. Silverstone, *Warships of the Civil War Navies* (Annapolis, Md.:

Naval Institute Press, 1989). Photographs of the USS *Ohio*, #43860, #60677, and #92940 from the Naval Historical Center, Basic Collections, and Smithsonian Negative #81-995.

28. This observation (made from a photograph) about John Robert Bond's carriage was suggested by Carol Sawyer Bond, wife of that seaman's great-grandson, J. Percy Bond III.

29. Rendezvous reports and Bond's early service records state that he was twenty-two when he enlisted, meaning that he had been born in 1841. Census reports, pension records, and his death certificate, on the other hand, confirm that he was born in Liverpool in 1846. The record of his birth in Britain's Office of Population, Census, and Statistics shows that he was born there on May 14, 1846. Joseph P. Reidy, "Black Men in Navy Blue: The Impact of the Civil War Service on Free Men in the U.S. Navy," unpublished paper. *Evening Standard,* January 24, 1863.

30. *Evening Standard,* January to April 1863.

31. Bolster, *Black Jacks,* 80, discusses the skills required of able seamen who could steer a ship and had full knowledge of rigging and rope work: "To put a marlinspike in a man's hand and set him to work upon a piece of rigging, is considered a fair trial of his qualities as an able seaman." Cooks and stewards were petty officers, and received higher salaries of about thirty dollars per month. That greater remuneration, however, did not negate the more servile nature and perception of their work. Concerning cooks on merchant ships at this time, Bolster comments, 168, "many black men paradoxically assumed the most 'feminine' roles aboard white-dominated ships to maintain their masculine roles as respectable providers in the black community."

32. The intermediary rank of ordinary seaman, requiring three prior years of experience, lay between that of seaman and landsman. Officers' pay in the navy ranged from $5,000 per year for rear admirals down to $750 for third assistant engineers. Also, Bruce Catton, *The American Heritage Picture History of the Civil War* (New York: American Heritage Publishing Co., 1960), 170.

33. Unless otherwise cited, this and other information about the personnel and itinerary of the USS *Ohio* is found in that ship's log for 1863 in the National Archives.

34. Gould diary.

35. See esp. Langley, "Negro in the Navy and Merchant Service," 273–86.

36. Ibid. Also, according to Jordan, *Black Confederates, Afro-Yankees,* 187, at first, black men were limited to five percent of the total in the Confederate navy, and then officially banned from that branch of the service after 1863. During the desparate final months of the war, however, the Confederacy's secretary of the navy admitted that he needed more than eleven hundred additional black seamen.

37. Richard S. West, Jr., *Mr. Lincoln's Navy* (New York: Longmans, Green, 1957), 53.

38. David L. Valuska, "The Negro in the Union Navy, 1861–65" (Ph.D. diss., Lehigh University, 1973), 49.

39. USCT troops were not actually activated for several more months, but contraband slaves had been used by the Union army in support positions almost from the start of the Civil War.

40. James M. O'Toole, "Passing (in) the Fleet: Racial Identity and the Case of Captain Michael Healy, USRCS," unpublished paper shared by the author.

41. Herbert Aptheker, "The Negro in the Union Navy," *Journal of Negro History,* 1947, 178–79, estimates that 30,000 Negroes (twenty-five percent of total enlistments) served. Quarles, *Negro in the Civil War,* 229–32, accepts the figure of 29,511 as substantiated by the Naval War Records Office. More recently, David Valuska, on the other hand, counted fewer than 9,000, about eight percent. Since virtually all black men (except those who passed for white) in the Union army were relegated to separate units, they are more easily enumerated. Names and numbers of black sailors, on the other hand, must be gleaned from individual recruitment and rendezvous reports, plus ships' muster rolls, and therefore are much more difficult to find and count. The still unfinalized figures from the Black Civil War Sailors Project at Howard University will provide the most accurate estimate yet. They now count about 18,000. See also Pauli Murray, *Proud Shoes: The Story of an American Family* (New York: Harper & Row, 1956). Murray's family history includes a chapter devoted to her grandfather Robert Fitzgerald's varied military experiences in the Civil War. Fitzgerald served in the navy from July to November 1863. My thanks to Becky Livingston at the National Archives for alerting me to the Negro commissioned officer (pilot second class) named James Taliaferro (or Tolliver) who served with the Union navy.

42. William A. Gladstone, *Men of Color* (Gettysburg, Pa.: Thomas Publications, 1993). The sailors awarded the Navy Medal of Honor for their contributions during the Civil War were Aaron Anderson, Robert Blake, William H. Brown, Wilson Brown, Clement Dees, John Lawson, James Mifflin, and Joachim Pease. Earlier sources than Gladstone, however, list only four black sailors who received this recognition. In addition, William Tillman received six thousand dollars in prize money for his capture of a Confederate schooner. In 1862, Robert Smalls, a slave who worked on the sidewheel paddle steamer *Planter,* captured that ship in Charleston's harbor and, accompanied by members of his family and other contraband, made his escape when he surreptitiously bypassed the Confederate stronghold at Fort Sumter, raised a white flag, and turned over his prize to a Yankee ship in the blockade. Smalls received bounty money, became a commissioned USCT officer, and continued to work as a pilot throughout the war. See esp. Quarles, *Negro in the Civil War,* 230–32.

43. Quarles, *Negro in the Civil War,* 31, 91. See also Langley, "Negro in the Navy and Merchant Service."

44. Langley, "Negro in the Navy and Merchant Service," downplays the negative aspects of the treatment of blacks. Frederick S. Voss, *Majestic in His Wrath: A Pictorial Life of Frederick Douglass* (Washington D.C.: Smithsonian Institution Press, 1995), 59.

45. Bernard C. Nalty, *Strength for the Fight: A History of Black Americans in the Military* (New York: Free Press, 1986), 33, would seem to refute this claim. Welles did initially limit the enlistment of contrabands (but not other blacks) to the rank and pay of "boy," but the equal-pay-for-equal-rank principle seems to have operated in practice even in the initial months of the war.

46. In the Union army, black soldiers were officially permitted to bear arms and serve at all only after 1862. For several years thereafter, they received inferior pay for the same ranks. This changed only after all members of the Fifty-fourth Massachusetts, a renowned black unit, refused to accept lower pay than white soldiers. With few exceptions, African American soldiers served in segregated units under white commissioned officers (plus a handful of blacks) throughout the Civil War. In more recent years, the navy has been the most discriminatory of the United States armed services, with the fewest black officers and the fewest opportunities for minority advancement.

47. Altogether, twenty-nine units of Massachusetts soldiers trained at Readville's campgrounds.

48. One of Frederick Douglass's sons joined the Fifty-fourth Massachusetts Infantry, another joined the Fifth Massachusetts Cavalry. *We Fight for Freedom: Massachusetts, African Americans, and the Civil War* (Boston: Massachusetts Historical Society, 1993), 2. Adams, *Altar of Freedom,* 19; and *Evening Standard,* May 19, 1863.

49. Quarles, *Negro in the Civil War,* 201.

50. The exploits of the Fifty-fourth Massachusetts have been popularized in the movie *Glory.* The men began their boycott of unequal pay after they had gone south. Only in mid-1864 did the U.S. Government agree to pay all black troops at the same level as white soldiers, including reimbursement for previous pay inequities. Dudley Taylor Cornish, *The Sable Arm: Black Troops in the Union Army, 1861–1865* (1956; reprint, Lawrence: University Press of Kansas, 1987), 98; and generally, James M. McPherson, *The Negro's Civil War* (1965; reprint, New York: Ballantine Books, 1991), chap. 14, "The Struggle for Equal Pay," 197–207. See also Jim Cullen, " 'I's a Man Now': Gender and African American Men," in Catherine Clinton and Nina Silber, eds., *Divided Houses: Gender and the Civil War* (New York: Oxford University Press, 1992).

51. In Connie Slaughter, "African Americans in the Civil War," *Cultural Resources Management* (CRM) 20, special issue 19, 2, 1996, *Connections: African-American History and CRM,* U.S. Department of the Interior, National Park

Service. Douglass made this statement on July 6, 1863, at a meeting "For the Promotion of Colored Enlistment." See Nalty, *Strength for the Fight,* 46. The Confederacy used slaves in munitions factories, as laborers, as body servants, and in menial positions on a number of ships. Proposals to draft them into the military as soldiers (in exchange for their ultimate freedom) struggled through the CSA legislative bodies, but were never implemented. A militia body of New Orleans mulattoes offered their services to the Confederacy early in the conflict, but they were rejected.

52. Cornish, *Sable Arm,* 148; and Luis F. Emilio, *History of the Fifty-Fourth Regiment of Massachusetts Volunteer Infantry, 1863–1865* (Boston: Boston Book Co., 1894), 31–32; and Adams, *Altar of Freedom,* 25. Quarles, *Negro in the Civil War,* 8–13, provides a superb depiction of the Fifty-fourth's departure from Boston.

53. Unless otherwise cited, all details about the personnel and the itinerary of the USS *Cambridge* come from the ship's logs for 1863–64 in the National Archives.

54. Specifications for the USS *Cambridge,* from *Dictionary of American Naval Fighting Ships,* 2: 20; and Silverstone, *Warships of the Civil War Navies,* 88. The log of the *Cambridge* refers only to rifles. Other sources specify guns and cannons.

55. Ibid.; and Edward K. Rawson, ed., *Official Records of the Union and Confederate Navies in the War of the Rebellion,* series 2, vol. 1 (Washington, D.C.: Government Printing Office, 1899), 50.

56. West, *Mr. Lincoln's Navy,* 279.

57. Dickson, *War Slang,* 3.

58. Catton, *Pictorial History of the Civil War,* 176. Catton does not provide a source for this cartoon.

59. From the New York *Commercial Advertiser,* quoted in J. Cutler Andrews, *The North Reports the Civil War* (Pittsburgh: University of Pittsburgh Press, 1955), 223.

60. Valuska, "Negroes in the Union Navy," 74.

61. Ella Lonn, *Foreigners in the Union Army and Navy* (New York: Greenwood Press, 1969), 621–42.

62. Puerto Rico remained a Spanish colony until 1898. This information compiled from data provided by Joseph P. Reidy from the files of the Black Civil War Sailors Project.

63. Valuska, "Negroes in the Union Navy," 79. The Black Civil War Sailors Project has identified forty-three Negro seamen from the British Isles who served during the Civil War. Thirty-three were from England, seven from Ireland, three from Scotland. Unlike most African Americans in the navy, most of the foreigners already were mariners when they enlisted. At least eighteen were called mu-

lattoes, suggesting an interracial heritage similar to that of John Robert Bond. Most of the Union navy's many non-American sailors of African ancestry came from the Caribbean.

64. James M. McPherson, *Battle Cry of Freedom: The Civil War Era* (New York City: Oxford University Press, 1988), 378.

65. My thanks to Willard Gatewood for raising this important point. It was true for the Confederacy as well as for the Union.

66. My thanks to James O'Toole for sharing his manuscript "Passing: Race, Religion, and the Healy Family in America."

67. Quarles, *Negro in the Civil War,* 166. The most thorough account is contained in Iver Bernstein, *The New York City Draft Riots: Their Significance for American Society and Politics in the Age of the Civil War* (New York: Oxford University Press, 1990). Also, Noel Ignatiev, *How the Irish Became White* (New York: Routledge, 1995), 120.

68. Waves of anti-immigrationist "Native Americanism" preceded the Civil War. That bias was frequently reinforced by the anti-Catholic sentiments of the Know-Nothing, or American, Party.

69. Quarles, *Negro in the Civil War,* 238–46. Bernstein, *New York City Draft Riots;* and Roediger, *Wages of Whiteness,* 136, 150.

70. McPherson, *The Negro's Civil War,* 73–77.

71. Darlene Clark Hine, Elsa Barkley Brown, and Rosalyn Terborg-Penn, eds., *Black Women in America: An Historical Encyclopedia* (Brooklyn: Carlson Publishing, 1993), 1179. Nalty, *Strength for the Fight,* 44.

72. Nalty, *Strength for the Fight,* 38.

73. Ibid.; and Stephen B. Oates, *A Woman of Valor: Clara Barton and the Civil War* (New York: Free Press, 1994), 91, 171, 174.

74. Quarles, *Negro in the Civil War,* 18; and Nalty, *Strength for the Fight,* 38.

75. McPherson, *The Negro's Civil War,* 194–95. Although 186,000 usually has been accepted as the number of blacks who served in the Civil War, new work on the navy, plus the impossible-to-estimate number of "invisible Negroes" who "passed," however, brings the total to at least 200,000. There is some doubt as to whether black women who served with the armed forces as scouts and nurses were included in the original lower figures.

76. Margaret Mitchell's hero, Rhett Butler, in her saga *Gone with the Wind,* participated in blockade-running activities.

77. Newport had become the naval academy's wartime home. Jack Sweeterman, *The United States Naval Academy: An Illustrated History* (Annapolis, Md.: Naval Institute Press, 1979), 104–6 and 207. Sweeterman dates the first admission to the Naval Academy of several black midshipmen to the Reconstruction period, but their experiences were so traumatic that they resigned. A few others were admitted during the 1930s, but the first black man to graduate from the academy,

Wesley Brown, did so only in 1949. The numbers did not climb significantly until the 1970s. Foreigners also attended the academy from time to time. From the late 1860s until 1906, for example, a few Japanese were included in the brigade. The academy grudgingly admitted its first women in 1976, and they graduated with the class of 1980.

78. Both North and South Carolina had coastal towns called Beaufort, and both played crucial roles in the Civil War. North Carolina's is pronounced "Bow-fert," while South Carolina's is pronounced "Byew-fert."

79. Rawson, *Official Records of the Union and Confederate Navies,* 1, 9: 190, 192, 225, 231.

80. Dickson, *War Slang,* 6; Valuska, "Negroes in the Union Navy," 180. Gould diary. Jordan, *Black Confederates, Afro-Yankees,* 143, reports that on another vessel white sailors called black shipmates "God Damn nigger," "black dog," and "bitches" as they kicked and cursed them.

81. Nalty, *Strength for the Fight,* 33; Valuska, "Negroes in the Union Navy," 133. Gould diary also reports a shipboard "Minstrel Troup."

82. Valuska, "Negroes in the Union Navy," 133.

83. McPherson, *Battle Cry of Freedom,* 378.

84. B. R. Burg, *An American Seafarer in the Age of Sail: The Erotic Diaries of Philip C. Van Buskirk, 1851–1870* (New Haven: Yale University Press, 1994), xi. In great part, this study deals with homosexual life aboard navy ships.

85. Richmond C. Holcomb, *A Century with Norfolk Naval Hospital, 1830–1930* (Portsmouth, Va.: Printcraft Publishers, 1930), 309.

86. Log of the USS *Cambridge.* In Boney et al., *God Made Man,* 83, George Teamoh commented that seamen "who had retired to their hammocks were thrown from there by the netlings being cut."

87. Langley, "Negro in the Navy and Merchant Service," 281–82, details the practice and abolition of shipboard floggings; and Bernard A. Botkin, *A Civil War Treasury of Tales, Legends, and Folk Lore* (New York: Random House, 1960), 242.

88. Photograph of Capt. William Spicer, #44855, Naval Historical Center, Basic Collections.

89. Gould diary.

90. W. E. B. Du Bois, *The Suppression of the African Slave Trade* (1896; reprint, Baton Rouge: Louisiana State University Press, 1969), 185; and Rawson, *Official Records of the Union and Confederate Navies,* 1, 9: 225, 231.

91. Rawson, *Official Records of the Union and Confederate Navies,* 1, 9: 467–68; and Log of USS *Cambridge.*

92. Rawson, *Official Records of the Union and Confederate Navies,* 1, 9: 467–68; Oates, *Woman of Valor,* 82; Dickson, *War Slang,* 9; and Silverstone, *Warships of the Civil War Navies,* 88.

93. Du Bois, *Suppression of the African Slave Trade,* 185.

3. ABLE-BODIED NO MORE

1. Stephen B. Oates, *A Woman of Valor: Clara Barton and the Civil War* (New York: Free Press, 1994), 61. This Latin phrase roughly translates (despite the fact that rifles postdated Roman times) as "a rifle wound." Unless otherwise cited, information concerning Bond's period in the infirmary of the *Cambridge* comes from the Surgeon's Log of that ship for 1864, National Archives.

2. Log of the USS *Cambridge* and diary of William B. Gould. Unless otherwise cited, information about the personnel and itinerary of the *Cambridge* comes from that ship's log for 1864 National Archives.

3. Bruce Catton, *The American Heritage Picture History of the Civil War* (New York: American Heritage Publishing Co., 1996), 187. The carcass of the confederate submarine *Hunley* was discovered May 1995, two miles off shore near Charleston. The device was not blown up in the explosion, but probably popped its rivets, began leaking, and turned into "a water-filled coffin." *Washington Post,* May 12, 1995 and *New York Times,* May 14, 1995. Gould's diary noted that sailors from the *Cambridge* saw a "submarine Batry cigar shape, that is propelled by a screw and fires a gun underwater after being submerged," in Newport News, Virginia.

4. Gould diary.

5. Several accounts attest to the use of southern harbor pilots in assisting Union ships.

6. Henry L. Swint, *Dear Ones at Home: Letters from Contraband Camps* (Nashville: Vanderbilt University Press, 1966), 149.

7. Charles O. Pitts, Jr., "Hammond Hospital, Part II," *News-Times,* Morehead City–Beaufort, N.C., August 15, 1993.

8. The Civil War Letters of Private Lyman Chamberlin, February 9, 1864, Beaufort Historical Society.

9. Pitts, "Hammond Hospital, II."

10. Ibid.; and Oates, *Woman of Valor,* 10. The Union recognized the need for female nurses and organized the Sanitary Commission under the aegis of Dorothea Dix, but female nurses were paid far less than their male counterparts. Clara Barton also feared that she would be seen as a camp follower or prostitute. The first nursing schools in the United States were established in 1873.

11. Pitts, "Hammond Hospital, II."

12. None of these physicians appear in the *Dictionary of American Military Biography,* which leads to the assumption that they were civilians temporarily detailed to the army. "Annals of the Sisters of Mercy," New York City, 1846–1920. Transcribed copy provided courtesy of Fort Macon State Park. Pitts, "Hammond Hospital, Part V," September 5, 1993, and "Hammond Hospital, Part VI," September 12, 1993. Chamberlin letters, October 24, 1863.

13. "Annals of the Sisters of Mercy." Those North Carolina barrier isles are now known as the Emerald Islands.

14. Benjamin Quarles, *The Negro in the Civil War* (1953; reprint, New York: Da Capo Press, 1989), 247; and Oates, *Woman of Valor,* 376, 46. Jane E. Schultz, "Race, Gender, and the Bureaucracy: Civil War Army Nurses and the Pension Bureau," *Journal of Women's History,* forthcoming.

15. "Annals of the Sisters of Mercy."

16. Ibid.; and Chamberlin letters, July 12, 1863.

17. "Annals of the Sisters of Mercy."

18. Ibid.; and Pitts, "Hammond Hospital, Part VII," September 19, 1993.

19. "Annals of the Sisters of Mercy."

20. Chamberlin letters, July 12, 1863; and Pitts, "Hammond Hospital, Part V."

21. "Annals of the Sisters of Mercy"; and Chamberlin letters, July 12, 1863.

22. Chamberlin letters, October 24 and December 6, 1863. The use of the word "ladies" in Chamberlin's letter suggests that he was only referring to white women.

23. Oates, *Woman of Valor,* ably describes army field hospitals.

24. "Annals of the Sisters of Mercy." Pitts, "Hammond Hospital, Part VI" and "Hammond Hospital, Part VII." Chamberlin letters, November 13, 1863. Oates, *Woman of Valor,* 176, and other sources have observed that many Civil War medical facilities were segregated.

25. "Annals of the Sisters of Mercy."

26. Chamberlin letters, April 15, 1864.

27. Ibid.

28. "Annals of the Sisters of Mercy." Chamberlin letters, March 20 and June 11, 1863, July 24 and August 21, 1864. Oates, *Woman of Valor,* 254.

29. *Dictionary of American Naval Fighting Ships* (Washington, D.C.: Naval History Division), 6: 66.

30. Various accounts of Turner's brief escape differ on whether or not he hid in the Dismal Swamp. A number of escaping slaves, however, dwelt there as clandestine "maroons" for years on end.

31. Descriptions of the Naval Hospital at Portsmouth from Richmond C. Holcomb, *A Century with Norfolk Naval Hospital, 1830–1930* (Portsmouth, Va.: Printcraft Publishers, 1930); "U.S. Naval Hospital, Norfolk/Portsmouth, Virginia," an unpublished document from the Civil War shared by the Public Affairs Office, U.S. Naval Medical Center, Portsmouth, plus my own observations of the original building, which still stands.

32. Ibid. Dr. Sharp's name is variously spelled with and without a final *e.*

33. "U.S. Naval Hospital," 7 and 10.

34. Holcomb, *Century with Norfolk Naval Hospital,* 300.

35. Ibid.

36. Ibid. "U. S. Naval Hospital" also confirms the pervasiveness of "ants, bugs and other vermin," 11.

37. Holcomb, *Century with Norfolk Naval Hospital,* 300.

38. Ibid.

39. Ibid., 301.

40. *A Documented History of the First Baptist Church, Bute Street, Norfolk, Virginia, 1800–1988* (Virginia Beach, Va.: Hill's Printing Co., 1988), 7, states about Rev. Tucker: "His work was not confined to the walls of his church, nor to the members of his congregation."

41. Naval pension records of John Robert Bond, National Archives.

42. Ibid.; and Paul Dickson, *War Slang: American Fighting Words and Phrases from the Civil War to the Gulf War* (New York: Pocket Books, 1994), 4.

43. Holcomb, *Century with Norfolk Naval Hospital,* 301.

44. Isle of Wight County, Virginia, had a number of slaveholders bearing the surname Thomas. Although some slaves rejected their former owners' names during or after the Civil War, many others kept them. Isaac Thomas's name was found in the civilian employment records of Portsmouth's naval hospital, National Archives. Records of Norfolk's Freedman's Bureau Bank, at the Norfolk State University Archives, indicate that he was born in Isle of Wight County's town of Smithfield. The slave schedule of the United States Census for Isle of Wight, Virginia, in 1860 shows a black female the same age as Emma Thomas, and a black male of Isaac Thomas's age living on Jonathan and Martha Thomas's plantation in that county. In 1870, Isaac appears in the census records for neighboring Southampton County.

45. A conversation in December 1993 between the author and Elaine Mc-Craw Chesnut, widow of John Robert Bond's grandson, concerns the story of Emma Thomas bringing fruit. John Robert Bond's navy pension records describe the way that Emma Thomas Bond helped to dress and undress him.

46. John Higham, *Strangers in the Land: Patterns of American Nativism, 1860–1925* (New Brunswick, N.J.: Rutgers University Press, 1955), 13.

47. The Naturalization Act of 1790 limited naturalization to "free white men." An 1862 provision, designed to stimulate military enlistments, gave citizenship preference to foreigners who served in the United States armed forces and received honorable discharges. It reduced the years of residence required prior to eligibility for citizenship from five to two. These issues are discussed in later chapters.

48. Hospital ticket for John Robert Bond, National Archives.

4. "Turkey Buzzard Lay Me"

1. Frederick Law Olmsted, *The Cotton Kingdom* (1855; reprint, Arthur M. Schlesinger, Sr., ed., New York: Random House, 1984), 110.

2. Thomas E. Barden, ed., *Virginia Folk Legends* (Charlottesville: University of Virginia Press, 1991), 218. I appreciate the critique of this chapter by Helen Haverty King, Isle of Wight's most knowledgeable historian.

3. Betty Fussell, *I Hear America Cooking* (New York: Viking, 1986), 168.

4. Numerous sources cite this quote from Rolfe's accounts. See, for example, W. E. B. Du Bois, *Dusk of Dawn* (New York: Harcourt Brace, 1940), 263. The issue of whether the first Africans in the mainland North American colonies were considered slaves or indentured servants remains debatable. An English colony in what became coastal North Carolina predated Jamestown by several decades, but it did not survive.

5. Helen Haverty King, *Historical Notes on Isle of Wight County, Virginia* (Isle of Wight, Va.: County Board of Supervisors, 1993), 189. Early Tidewater tobacco had smaller leaves than the hybrids with which we are familiar today.

6. Fussell, *I Hear America Cooking*, 169.

7. Caroline Darden Hurt, ed., *The Smithfield Cookbook: 350 Years of Dining Traditions from Smithfield and Isle of Wight County, Virginia* (Lynchburg, Va.: Progress Printing, 1979), iv, 2–3, 156, 182.

8. King, *Isle of Wight*, chap. 18; and Henry D. Spalding, ed., *Encyclopedia of Black Folklore and Humor* (Middle Village, N.Y.: Jonathan David Publishers, 1990), 31. The Queen Victoria dialect anecdote continues: "I reckon she be mos' ready ter lef' de frone an' come hyar ter live wid us, case anyhow, oneasy lays de haid dat w'ars de crown."

9. U.S. Census for Isle of Wight County, Virginia, 1850. According to the 1870 census, yet another Emma Thomas, a white woman, lived in the region. She resided in Norfolk and was born about 1842. It has been impossible to ascertain whether there were further links between the three girls named Emma Thomas. In Wilma King, *Stolen Childhood: Slave Youth in the Nineteenth-Century South* (Bloomington: University of Indiana Press, 1995), 215–18, a list of slave children born in neighboring Nansemond County revealed no Emmas, suggesting that it was not a common name for black girls in the region.

10. Hurt, ed., *Smithfield Cookbook*, 77.

11. See especially King, *Stolen Childhood*, chap. 2, "Us Ain't Never Idle."

12. Osnaburg, its name suggesting the German city from which it first came, was the coarse, inexpensive cotton or flax fabric most often used for slaves' clothing.

13. George P. Rawick, ed., *The American Slave: A Composite Autobiography*, vol. 16, *Virginia Narratives* (Westport, Conn.: Greenwood Publishing Co., 1972), 15–20; John W. Blassingame, ed., *Slave Testimony: Two Centuries of Letters, Speeches, Interviews, and Autobiographies* (Baton Rouge: Louisiana State University Press, 1977), 170, 172; and Charles L. Perdue, Jr., Thomas E. Barden, and Robert K. Phillips, *Weevils in the Wheat: Interviews with Virginia Ex-Slaves* (Char-

lottesville: University Press of Virginia), 149. Accounts of the smallest slave children working as "scarecrows" and "fenceposts" were especially prevalent in the area around Norfolk, Virginia. All of the ensuing examples of slave life are taken from this specific region. King's *Stolen Childhood* effectively develops this thesis concerning the experiences of slave children as workers.

14. King, *Isle of Wight,* 139.

15. See esp. Edmund S. Morgan, *American Slavery, American Freedom: The Ordeal of Colonial Virginia* (New York: Norton, 1975), concerning the origins of the deliberate separation of lower-class whites from blacks.

16. Mechal Sobel, *The World They Made Together: Black and White Values in Eighteenth-Century Virginia* (Princeton: Princeton University Press, 1987), 45. According to David R. Roediger, *The Wages of Whiteness: Race and the Making of the American Working Class* (New York: Verso, 1991), 155–56, the word "miscegenation" "combined the Latin words *miscere* ('to mix') and *genus* ('race') in a neologism designed to replace the older term 'amalgamation.' It conjured up 'mongrelization' in the United States as a political issue. By racist Democratic logic, Republican policies in 1864 threatened literally to establish a 'miscegen-' nation." "Miscegenation" more specifically was defined as sexual congress with one white partner and the other (in most cases) a Negro. Some such "crimes" were prosecuted, others were not. Charges never were brought, for example, when a white man had intercourse with a black woman. Antimiscegenation laws were finally terminated in the United States only by the 1967 Supreme Court decision *Loving v. State of Virginia.* In making his ruling upholding the prohibition against interracial relations, the state trial judge in that case had asserted: "Almighty God created the races . . . and placed them on separate continents. . . . The fact that he separated the races shows that he did not intend for the races to mix." Quoted in A. Leon Higginbotham, Jr., *In the Matter of Color: Race and the American Legal Process in the Colonial Period* (New York: Oxford University Press, 1978), 42.

17. King, *Isle of Wight,* 9. See also Higginbotham's *In the Matter of Color* for a discussion of the rapid establishment of racially discriminatory laws in colonial Virginia.

18. The Supreme Court's Dred Scott decision of 1857 determined that the founding fathers had never intended that Negro Americans of any hue should enjoy the privileges of citizenship. See also Timothy Breen and Stephen Innes, *"Myne Owne Ground": Race and Freedom on Virginia's Eastern Shore, 1640–1676* (New York: Oxford University Press, 1980); and Willard Gatewood, *Free Man of Color: Augustus Hodges* (Knoxville: University of Tennessee Press, 1983), concerning the lives of free people of color in nearby Princess Anne County.

19. The Constitution insisted that fugitive "property" found any place in the country should be returned to the owners. That controversial provision was reinforced by federal law in 1850.

20. There was also a class hierarchy within the slave community based especially on age, wisdom, skills, position, or the status of one's owner. "Guinea nigger" was a derogatory phrase applied to Virginia slaves in general and in earlier times to any new arrivals from Africa. Gene-Anne Polk shared with me her family's oral history that recollects an ancestor who was brought from the Guinea coast to Isle of Wight County sometime prior to 1800. An old song from the Charles M. Wallace, Jr., Collection of Negro Music and Lyrics, Virginia State Library, includes the verse:

> *Guinea nigger glutton*
> *Eat a whole leg-o-mutton*
> *Eyes shine like a button*
> *Ain't good for nuttin'.*

Todd L. Savitt, *Medicine and Slavery: The Diseases and Health Care of Blacks in Antebellum Virginia* (Urbana: University of Illinois Press, 1978), 32, notes that forty percent of Virginia's slaves originated in this region of Africa, while others came from further south. Sobel, *World They Made Together,* 6 and 244. After 1778, Virginia statutes forbade the importation of African slaves, but the United States officially terminated the trade only in 1807, though some illegal slave importation continued. Sobel further asserts that most Virginia slaves came from the Niger Delta, Gold Coast, Senegambia, Angola, and the Bight of Biafra. In different parts of the South, planters preferred slaves from different parts of Africa. Melville J. Herskovits, *The Myth of the Negro Past* (Boston: Beacon Press, 1958), 47, gives a detailed breakdown of the African origins of Virginia slaves in the colonial era.

21. King, *Isle of Wight,* 6, 47.

22. The age of the woman believed to be Emma Thomas's mother was ascertained from Isle of Wight's 1850 and 1860 slave censuses listing Jonathan and Martha Thomas's slaves by age, sex, and color. It has not been possible to learn her name.

23. Because the law considered them property in most instances, and certainly not responsible adults, slaves could not become primary parties to a contract. Marriages were officially considered contractual arrangements. See especially Mark Tushnet, *The American Law of Slavery, 1810–1860: Considerations of Humanity and Interest* (Princeton: Princeton University Press, 1981).

24. Perdue et al., *Weevils in the Wheat,* 94.

25. Rawick, ed., *Virginia Narratives,* 12.

26. Ervin L. Jordan, Jr., *Black Confederates and Afro-Yankees in Civil War Virginia* (Charlottesville: University Press of Virginia, 1995), 170.

27. Perdue et al., *Weevils in the Wheat,* 63.

28. Rawick, ed., *Virginia Narratives,* 63. John Currie's name appears on Emma Thomas Bond's 1926 death certificate, so she clearly told her children about him. There is no evidence, however, that he played any continuing role in her life. The 1860 U.S. Census slave schedule for Lancaster County, Virginia, confirms that a male slave of appropriate age belonged to the Currie family there. The 1870 Census for that county shows a black man named John Currie with a wife and adult child. Only one other black John Currie appears in these later censuses, and he was in northern Virginia. And see Deborah Gray White, *Ar'n't I a Woman: Female Slaves in the Plantation South* (New York: Norton, 1985), 109.

29. Jordan, *Black Confederates, Afro-Yankees,* 149; and Perdue et al., *Weevils in the Wheat,* 134. Running away and other forms of resistance increased around and after 1860 as the elusive promise of emancipation seemed nearer. Nonetheless, Sobel, *World They Made Together,* 102, cites one case of an Isle of Wight man who escaped as early as 1752.

30. The 1860 Census slave schedule suggests that ten people lived in a cabin with Emma Thomas and her mother, but this is difficult to validate.

31. Sobel, *World They Made Together,* chap. 9, argues that, at least during the eighteenth century, the houses of poor whites and slaves in Virginia were quite similar, and that many shacks reflected building techniques similar to those seen in Africa.

32. John Vlach, *Back of the Big House: The Architecture of Plantation Slavery* (Chapel Hill: University of North Carolina Press, 1993), 158–60, 176, 180, calls such quarters "double-pen cabins." He shows photographs of cabins of similar configuration and construction in South Carolina.

33. Ibid., 153, from a memoir by Letitia Burwell. Isle of Wight's Four Square (sometimes Foursquare) is listed in the National Register of Historic Places. The Historic Williamsburg Foundation has surveyed the outbuildings and drawn up accurate plans. I appreciate the help of Roger and Amelia Healey, who now own Four Square, and John Vlach, who helped me understand the significance of these dependencies. King, *Isle of Wight,* 442–43.

34. Rawick, ed., *Virginia Narratives,* 44.

35. F. N. Boney, Richard L. Hume, and Rafia Zafar, *God Made Man, Man Made the Slave: The Autobiography of George Teamoh* (Macon, Ga.: Mercer University Press, 1990), 64.

36. Rawick, ed., *Virginia Narratives,* 20, 44; and F. N. Boney, ed., *Slave Life in Georgia: A Narrative of the Life, Sufferings, and Escape of John Brown, A Fugitive Slave* (1855; reprint, Savannah, Ga.: Beehive Press, 1991), 6. White, *Ar'n't I a Woman,* provides the most comprehensive study of the lives of female slaves in the antebellum South. Hurt, ed., *Smithfield Cookbook,* 198, mentions the tradition of female slaves making "horse cakes."

37. Marriage records for Isle of Wight County, 1772–1852, and U.S. Census, Isle of Wight, 1840, 1850, and 1860. I thank Prof. Raymond J. Jirran and his students Inger Dowden, Teri Gelhizer, Macwell Gillespie, Jusbyn Lockard, Sheila Morris, Jennifer Moore, Philip Ruggaber, and Glen Schaefer at Thomas Nelson Community College for their assistance in unearthing archival materials about the Thomas family in the Isle of Wight County Courthouse.

38. Thomas C. Parramore, Peter C. Stewart, and Tommy L. Bogger, *Norfolk: The First Four Centuries* (Charlottesville: University Press of Virginia, 1994), chap. 13, "The Ghosts of Julappi." Barden, ed., *Virginia Folk Legends,* 290.

39. Parramore et al., *Norfolk,* 191; and Savitt, *Medicine and Slavery,* 242–46. The forebears of many mainland slaves not only originated in Africa, but many had spent a period of "seasoning," or acclimation, on Caribbean plantations prior to being shipped to the southern United States.

40. Hurt, ed., *Smithfield Cookbook,* 140. Dr. Jonathan R. Purdue, "History of Education in Isle of Wight County," MS, Historical Society of Virginia, 1880.

41. For a fictional account of Quakers in this region, see James Michener's *Chesapeake.* Throughout the Upper South, free people of color also worked with the Underground Railway, but no evidence of these activities has surfaced concerning Isle of Wight.

42. These men appear as heads of households in the U.S. Censuses for Isle of Wight County in 1840, 1850, and 1860. The slave schedule for 1850 shows that Jonathan Thomas owned thirty-six slaves, Josiah owned eighteen, Jordan and John P. Thomas had three each, James had twelve, and William J. Thomas owned six. In nearby counties, very few persons bearing that surname were slaveholders, though both Jonathan and Josiah also owned slaves in Norfolk.

43. Isle of Wight marriage records show several marriages of Jordans to Thomases.

44. U.S. Census for Isle of Wight County, Virginia, free schedule and agricultural schedule, and for Norfolk County, free and slave schedules, all 1860. Charles Driver Jordan diary, 1857–60, MS, Virginia Historical Society. Rawick, ed., *Virginia Narratives,* 30.

45. Jordan diary. The Jonathan R. Purdue Papers, Isle of Wight County Museum, for example, record the hire of a "negro woman Jinny" on Christmas Day, 1853. Traditionally, such annual contracts began and ended at Christmas. Purdue promised to pay George W. Carroll $17 for one year of Jinny's services, and to provide "good usual clothing & a blanket."

46. From an unpublished, late 1980s flyer by L. J. Kuhnemann, who briefly owned Four Square in recent years, provided to me by the Isle of Wight Historical Museum. Segar Cofer Dashiell, *Smithfield: A Pictorial History* (Norfolk: Donning Co., n.d.), 115.

47. Elizabeth R. Varon, "Tippecanoe and the Ladies, Too: White Women and Party Politics in Antebellum Virginia," *Journal of American History* 82, no. 2 (September 1995): 494–521.

48. King, *Isle of Wight*, 153; and Jordan diary. On Stephen Douglas and the 1860 presidential campaign, see Roediger, *Wages of Whiteness*, 142–43.

49. Jordan diary.

50. Hurt, ed., *Smithfield Cookbook*, 11, 118, 126, 161, 167, 179, 189.

51. Mary Randolph, *The Virginia Housewife; or, Methodical Cook* (Mineola, N.Y.: Dover Publications, 1993), 80–84, 89. *The Virginia Housewife* was a perennial favorite in the southern states. It was first published in 1824, then reprinted and revised. The version used here came out in 1860. Randolph spent much of her married life on a James River plantation.

52. King, *Isle of Wight*, 196. It has been widely reported that Virginia "gentlemen" were notoriously heavy drinkers. Some sources argue, however, that distilled spirits were safer to drink than the South's often polluted water.

53. See esp. Barbara Jeanne Fields, *Slavery and Freedom on the Middle Ground: Maryland during the Nineteenth Century* (New Haven: Yale University Press, 1985). In the South as a whole, an estimated twenty-five percent of whites owned slaves in the late-antebellum years. Virginia's overall population was the greatest in the South. It had the greatest number, but far from the highest percentages, of slaves. By 1860, in the District of Columbia and Delaware, free people of color actually outnumbered slaves.

54. When they were emancipated, some free people of color took or kept their former owners' names, but others did not.

55. U.S. Census, Isle of Wight County, 1850. The free black laborers Lewis and Douglas Hill lived with the Jonathan E. Thomas family.

56. Luther Jackson Porter, *The Virginia Free Negro Farmer and Property Owner, 1830–1860* (Chicago: University of Chicago Libraries, 1939), 433. U.S. Census, Isle of Wight County, 1860, free and slave schedules. Also Fields, *Slavery and Freedom on the Middle Ground*. The U.S. Census, Isle of Wight County, 1840, indicates that Betsy Thomas owned twenty-one slaves, Lany Thomas had twelve, and Lucy Thomas had one. More than likely, they were considered responsible free people of color, and the control and putative ownership of relatives or friends had been turned over to them. Despite this explanation, it is unusual to find free people of color "owning" that many slaves.

57. King, *Isle of Wight*, chap. 8. David Hart, a descendant of free people of color in neighboring Surry County, has found no record of manumission papers for his antecedents. They do not appear in the county's rosters of free people of color, or in the 1850 and 1860 censuses. This situation was not unusual in the South. See, for example, Adele Logan Alexander, *Ambiguous Lives: Free Women of Color in Rural Georgia, 1789–1879* (Fayetteville: University of Arkansas Press, 1991).

58. Information from Isle of Wight and Norfolk County free and slave censuses for 1850 and 1860. Boney et al., *God Made Man,* details the lives of the Josiah Thomases, owners of George Teamoh, in Norfolk. I have not been able to ascertain how they were related to Isle of Wight's Jonathan Thomas. Ferries and stagecoaches went to and from Smithfield, but railroad lines traversed western Isle of Wight. The U.S. Census agricultural schedule indicates that Jonathan Thomas owned 1,400 acres, but county records show that he had more than 2,400 acres by 1860.

59. Parramore et al., *Norfolk,* 188–89, details life in antebellum Norfolk.

60. U.S. Censuses, Isle of Wight County, 1840, 1850, and 1860, slave schedules, 1850 and 1860, agricultural schedule, 1860.

61. Will of John Thomas, 1802, Isle of Wight County Courthouse. Fussell, *I Hear America Cooking,* 180, and King, *Stolen Childhood,* 30, 36. Proslavery southerners developed a complex philosophy to justify the "peculiar institution." Slavery, they argued, was necessary as a "school," and to Christianize the "inferior" Negroes. It was both benign and sanctioned by the Bible, they contended. They believed that slavery was economically essential to provide the South with cheap labor to produce plantation products, especially cotton, both for export and for northern mills. The Constitution, they concluded, defended property rights, including human property, and protected states rights from federal intrusion.

62. Rawick, ed., *Virginia Narratives,* 75.

63. For the significance of female slave networks on antebellum plantations, see White, *Ar'n't I a Woman.*

64. Rawick, ed., *Virginia Narratives,* 15–20, 30.

65. Savitt, *Medicine and Slavery,* esp. 171–84. The reference to "ladies" clearly means "white women." *Many Voices: An Oral History of Isle of Wight County, Virginia, 1900–1950* (n.p., 1986), 77, 183, 201, 215.

66. Writers' Program Work Projects Administration, State of Virginia, *The Negro in Virginia* (1940; reprint, Winston-Salem: John F. Blair, 1994), 32–33; and Parramore et al., *Norfolk,* 192. King, *Stolen Childhood,* xix, observes that "most Yorubas did not know their age but dated their existence by events since age without events made little sense." Dr. Merritt Cox was one of Isle of Wight County's early residents. Whether this is the same family of physicians as that of the region's fabled Dr. Phillip Cox cannot be ascertained.

67. Hurt, ed., *Smithfield Cookbook,* 151, suggests that taffy pulls or "pulled sugar" were common diversions for children in the white community as well. *Keemo, Kimo* seems to appear only in the recollections of slaves from southeastern Virginia. It is not of African origin. The author's mother, Wenonah Bond Logan, who was Emma Thomas's granddaughter, sang a similar version of this song.

68. Rawick, ed., *Virginia Narratives,* 30. Also Perdue et al., *Weevils in the Wheat,* 49. The phrase "that takes the cake" supposedly derives from cakewalk

contests. Pauline Hopkins's novel, *Contending Forces,* describes these same dances, which blacks performed in Boston around 1900.

69. Having Sundays off was more the pattern than the exception, but some masters did not even respect that common compromise. Rawick, ed., *Virginia Narratives,* 27–30.

70. Reverend Blunt performed the marriage of Jonathan Thomas and Martha Stringfield, and his church almost adjoined the Thomas plantation. Apparently, no churches led by blacks alone had been established in Isle of Wight prior to the Civil War. WPA, *Negro in Virginia,* 119. For a thorough examination of religion in this period, see Albert J. Raboteau, *Slave Religion: The "Invisible Institution" in the Antebellum South* (New York: Oxford University Press, 1978).

71. Reports of the number of white people killed by the rebellious slaves are quite specific, but different sources report widely varying numbers of black people slain during the retaliatory bloodbath. See especially Henry Irving Tragle, *The Southampton Slave Revolt of 1831* (Amherst: University of Massachusetts Press, 1971); and Herbert Aptheker, *American Negro Slave Revolts* (New York: International Publishers, 1963), chapter 12. Additional quotes from the Teamoh autobiography, Boney et al., *God Made Man,* 69.

72. Generally, see Tragle, *Southampton Slave Revolt;* and Aptheker, *Negro Slave Revolts,* chap. 12.

73. According to Genesis, Ham watched his father, Noah, who was naked, while his brothers averted their eyes. God inflicted the "curse" as punishment for Ham's lack of respect for his father.

74. Boney et al., *God Made Man,* 70. It is probably more than coincidence that like so many of the white Thomases from Isle of Wight (probably including his own master Josiah Thomas), George Teamoh and his wife give three of their children names beginning with the letter *J.*

75. King, *Stolen Childhood,* 78.

76. Boney et al., *God Made Man,* 71. Rawick, ed., *Virginia Narratives,* 11–14 and 42; and Perdue et al., *Weevils in the Wheat,* 149. Though Emma Thomas Bond was "officially" illiterate (census and other written records indicate that she did not read or write), Elaine McCraw Chesnut, the widow of one of Emma's grandsons, heard that Emma had been taught to read by members of her master's family, despite Virginia's restrictive laws. With the intentional or unwitting help of whites or as a result of their own initiatives, many slaves acquired at least a rudimentary proficiency in both reading and writing.

77. Some of Virginia's northwestern counties broke away from that state and became the Union's new state of West Virginia. The "loyal" slaveholding states of Maryland, Delaware, Missouri, and Tennessee never seceded.

78. King, *Isle of Wight,* chap. 9.

79. Rawick, ed., *Virginia Narratives*, 46–49. The fort was named for the Confederate General Benjamin Huger.

80. Parramore et al., *Norfolk*, 202, 207; and Dashiell, *Smithfield: Pictorial History*, 87–88. Freedmen and Southern Society Project (FSSP), History Department, University of Maryland, file C-3321.

81. New Bedford *Evening Standard*, November 11, 1862, and April 18 and May 30, 1863.

82. That gilded eagle is still on public display in Smithfield. Dashiell, *Smithfield: Pictorial History*, 85.

83. Jordan, *Black Confederates, Afro-Yankees*, 256; and Dashiell, *Smithfield: Pictorial History*, 88. The Healeys, Four Square's present owners, shared this story, which was told to them by one of Julius Thomas's granddaughters. FSSP, file C-3321.

84. King, *Isle of Wight*, chap. 9.

85. Ibid., 176.

86. Lee A. Wallace, ed., *Under the Stars and Bars: A History of the Surry Light Artillery* (1909; reprint, Morningside Bookshop, 1975), 117; and FSSP, file T-305. King, *Isle of Wight*, chap. 9.

87. Jordan, *Black Confederates, Afro-Yankees*, develops a controversial thesis suggesting that many black Virginians remained loyal to their masters and to the Confederacy.

88. The Healeys, who presently own Four Square, related this story of the postbellum loyal servants as told to them by one of Julius Thomas's granddaughters, Waverly Gwinn Thomas McLeod. King, *Stolen Childhood*, xix, quotes a disgruntled slaveowner who used the phrase "unruly negro girls" to describe some runaways.

89. Boney et al., *God Made Man*, 100. I have come across two other black women born in the antebellum period named America. One was Olivia America Davidson. She was born free in the North and later became Booker T. Washington's second wife. The other was Amanda America Dickson, the daughter of David Dickson (Georgia's wealthiest planter) and one of his slaves. Amanda America was indulged by David Dickson, but did not officially acquire her freedom until the end of the Civil War. See Kent Anderson Leslie, *Woman of Color, Daughter of Privilege: Amanda America Dickson, 1849–1893* (Athens: University of Georgia Press, 1995).

90. John Hart was a free person of color in Surry County, just north of Isle of Wight. He and a group of eleven other young men, all categorized "contrabands," enlisted in the Union navy at James Island in 1862. His grandson, David Hart, shared this story. The Black Civil War Union Sailor's Project at Howard University has discovered many other contrabands (as well as free men of color)

who joined the navy from this region. Former slave Mary Jane Wilson of Portsmouth reported that her father worked in the navy yards as a teamster. Rawick, ed., *Virginia Narratives,* 56 and 42. Jordan, *Black Confederates, Afro-Yankees,* 73, 177.

5 · WARTIME NORFOLK

1. Frederick Law Olmsted, *The Cotton Kingdom* (1855; reprint, Arthur M. Schlesinger, Sr., ed., New York: Random House, 1984), 111–12.

2. See Richard C. Wade, *Slavery in the Cities: The South, 1820–1860* (New York: Oxford University Press, 1964). Norfolk and Portsmouth's populations from U. S. Census, Norfolk County, 1860; and Thomas C. Parramore, with Peter C. Stewart and Tommy L. Bogger, *Norfolk: The First Four Centuries* (Charlottesville: University Press of Virginia, 1994), 182, 189.

3. Parramore et al, *Norfolk,* 171, 188, 189, 192; and Henry L. Swint, *Dear Ones at Home: Letters from Contraband Camps* (Nashville: Vanderbilt University Press, 1966), 66, 73.

4. U.S. Census, Norfolk County, 1860.

5. Although some of his data have been refuted, Wade's *Slavery in the Cities* still provides the best overall analysis of the "peculiar institution" in the South's urban centers. Wade, however, only tangentially examines Norfolk. Also, F. N. Boney, Richard L. Hume, and Rafia Zafar, eds., *God Made Man, Man Made the Slave: The Autobiography of George Teamoh* (Macon, Ga.: Mercer University Press, 1990), 6.

6. W. Jeffrey Bolster, *Black Jacks: African Americans in the Age of Sail* (Cambridge: Harvard University Press, 1997), 223.

7. Cassandra L. Newby, " 'The World Was All Before Them': A Study of the Black Community in Norfolk, 1861–1885" (Ph.D. dissertation, College of William and Mary, 1992), 276; Bolster, *Black Jacks,* 64–65. Robert Farris Thompson, *Flash of the Spirit: African and Afro-American Art and Philosophy* (New York: Random House, 1983), includes a substantive discussion about the decoration of black grave sites.

8. Ronald T. Takaki, *Violence in the Black Imagination* (New York: Putnam, 1972), 88; and Parramore et al., *Norfolk,* 157–58. The hostile environment that evolved following the abortive Nat Turner slave rebellion encouraged a few Lower Tidewater blacks to emigrate to Africa under the aegis of the ACS during the 1830s. Until the late twentieth century, most Liberian political leaders were "creoles" whose ancestors had come from the United States.

9. See Gary Collison, *Shadrach Minkins: From Fugitive Slave to Citizen* (Cambridge: Harvard University Press, 1997).

10. Boney et al., *God Made Man*, 5, 11, 96. George Teamoh's master, Josiah Thomas, also belonged to the Gosport Navy Yard's interracial workforce. Parramore et al., *Norfolk*, 226, and Writers' Program, Works Progress Administration, *The Negro in Virginia* (1940; reprint, Winston-Salem: John F. Blair, 1994), 144. Different sources dispute Bayne's original home, some suggesting Virginia, others Maryland or North Carolina. Certainly, however, he lived in Norfolk after the war. Minkins was also known by other names, especially Frederick Wilkins.

11. Martin R. Delany, "Blake; or, The Huts of America," in *Anglo-American Magazine*, April 1859, 107.

12. Ervin L. Jordan, Jr., *Black Confederates and Afro-Yankees in Civil War Virginia* (Charlottesville: University Press of Virginia, 1995), 70; Parramore et al., *Norfolk*, 183; and WPA, *Negro in Virginia*, 188–89.

13. This amount shocks me, but it is clearly indicated in the U.S. Census of 1860.

14. Jordan, *Black Confederates, Afro-Yankees*, 210, 158.

15. Parramore et al., *Norfolk*, 185. Margaret Douglass, the white teacher, had the courage and convictions to teach black children, but was hardly an integrationist, and had strong opinions about the morality of black women and their interracial sexual relations. "Southern women know that their husbands come to them reeking with pollution from the arms of their tawny mistresses," she wrote. "Father and son seek the same source of excitement and alike gratify their inhuman propensities, scarcely blushing when detected and recklessly defying every command of God and every tie of morality and human affection," she concluded; "the whole practice is plainly, unequivocally, shamelessly *beastly*." See Jordan, *Black Confederates, Afro-Yankees*, 101, 128.

16. Parramore et al., *Norfolk*, 197; Jordan, *Black Confederates, Afro-Yankees*, 158; and Newby, " 'World Was All Before Them,' " 72.

17. Parramore et al., *Norfolk*, 177.

18. *Daily Southern Argus*, Norfolk, December 5, 1849. Noel Ignatiev, *How the Irish Became White* (New York: Routledge, 1995), 33, provides a variant, cartoon version of this story from 1852, which suggested that the black man was not Irish, but rather just a mimic who replicated the newcomer's brogue. "*Patrick*, (*just landing*.) 'By my Sowl, you're black, old fellow! How long have ye been here?' / *Nigger*, (*imitating the brogue*.) 'Jist three months, my honey!' / *Pat*. 'By the powers, I'll go back to Tipperary in a jiffy! I'd not be so black as that fur all the whiskey in Roscrea!' "

19. Parramore et al., *Norfolk*, 180, 177. The Naturalization Act of 1790 was slightly amended over the antebellum years but not substantially changed until the Civil War and Reconstruction. Also Ignatiev, *How the Irish Became White*, 76.

20. John Brown and a contingent reportedly consisting of fourteen white and five black men raided the federal arsenal. Brown was tried and hanged for his

crime. Harper's Ferry was in the mountainous portion of the state (where there were few slaves) that later withdrew from Virginia, remained loyal to the Union, and then became West Virginia. Collison, *Shadrach Minkins,* 48; and Parramore et al., *Norfolk,* 197–98.

21. Parramore et al., *Norfolk,* 169.

22. Ibid., 200.

23. Jordan, *Black Confederates, Afro-Yankees,* 213.

24. Ibid., 84.

25. Ibid., 83.

26. Parramore et al., *Norfolk,* 201; and Jordan, *Black Yankees, Afro-Yankees,* 173.

27. George P. Rawick, ed., *The American Slave: A Composite Autobiography,* vol. 16, *Virginia Narratives* (Westport, Conn.: Greenwood Publishing Co., 1972), 2.

28. WPA, *Negro in Virginia,* 211–13; and Herbert G. Gutman, *The Black Family in Slavery and Freedom, 1750–1925* (New York: Random House, 1976), 412.

29. Jordan, *Black Confederates, Afro-Yankees,* 102; also, Newby, " 'World Was All Before Them,' " 83–84; and Darlene Clark Hine, Elsa Barkley Brown, and Rosalyn Terborg-Penn, eds., *Black Women in America: An Historical Encyclopedia* (Brooklyn, N.Y.: Carlson Publishing, 1993), 914.

30. Leon F. Litwack, *Been in the Storm Too Long: The Aftermath of Slavery* (New York: Random House, 1979), 495.

31. Parramore et al., *Norfolk,* 203; and Jordan, *Black Confederates, Afro-Yankees,* 285–86. Some sources, esp. G. Allen Foster, in *Ebony,* December 1977, 131–34, spell her last name "Louvestre." My thanks to James Holton for retrieving some of this material.

32. Parramore et al., *Norfolk,* 203.

33. WPA, *Negro in Virginia,* 214.

34. Ibid., 213; and Parramore et al., *Norfolk,* 193.

35. Parramore et al., *Norfolk,* 193–98, 203; and Benjamin Quarles, *The Negro in the Civil War* (1953; reprint, New York: Da Capo Press, 1989), 92. James Wolff Pension Records, National Archives. In differing accounts throughout his life, his name was alternately spelled "Wolfe."

36. Parramore et al., *Norfolk,* 197.

37. During the Civil War, both sides, but especially the Union, developed and launched a number of other ironsides, but the USS *Monitor* and the *Merrimac* (officially, the CSS *Virginia*) were far and away the most renowned.

38. *New York Times,* March 30, 1995.

39. Parramore et al., *Norfolk,* 204–5.

40. Ibid.

41. Quarles, *Negro in the Civil War,* 52; Rawick, ed., *Virginia Narratives,* 6, 8, 20, 48; and Charles L. Perdue, Jr., Thomas E. Barden, and Robert K. Phillips,

Weevils in the Wheat: Interviews with Virginia Ex-Slaves (Charlottesville: University Press of Virginia, 1976), 95, 134.

42. Perdue et al., *Weevils in the Wheat*, 69, 80.

43. During the war, Gen. Burnside's distinctive pattern of facial hair spurred many men's interest in growing and grooming their own "sideburns."

44. Parramore et al., *Norfolk*, 205.

45. The abolition of slavery in the District of Columbia was accompanied by compensation to former owners. Quarles, *Negro in the Civil War*, 146.

46. Parramore et al., *Norfolk*, 208.

47. Ibid., 207.

48. Quarles, *Negro in the Civil War*, 55. *A Documented History of the First Baptist Church, Bute Street, Norfolk, Virginia, 1800–1988* (Virginia Beach: Hill's Printing Co., 1988), 7.

49. Perdue et al., *Weevils in the Wheat*, 100; Henry L. Swint, *Dear Ones at Home: Letters from Contraband Camps* (Nashville: Vanderbilt University Press, 1966), 22, 124; and Ps. 18:2, 39 KJV.

50. *First Baptist Church, Bute Street*, 8.

51. Rawick, ed., *Virginia Narratives*, 13, 42–43, 55.

52. Newby, " 'World Was All Before Them,' " 113; Parramore et al., *Norfolk*, 214.

53. Parramore et al., *Norfolk*, 213; Swint, *Dear Ones at Home*, 68; and Tommy Bogger, "The Slave and Free Black Community in Norfolk" (Ph.D. diss., University of Virginia, 1976), 305.

54. Newby, " 'World Was All Before Them,' " 97; Parramore et al., *Norfolk*, 217; Jordan, *Black Confederates, Afro-Yankees*, 89; Perdue et al., *Weevils in the Wheat*, 5, 103; and *First Baptist Church, Bute Street*. The Fenchurch Street Methodist Church School, the Nicholas Street School, and the Norfolk Mission College were other early schools for blacks in Norfolk.

55. Dorothy Sterling, ed., *We Are Your Sisters: Black Women in the Nineteenth Century* (New York: Norton, 1984), 271–73, 277–79. Hine et al., eds., *Black Women in America*, 1104; Parramore et al., *Norfolk*, 214; and Jordan, *Black Confederates, Afro-Yankees*, 104.

56. Quarles, *Negro in the Civil War*, 164.

57. Swint, *Dear Ones at Home*, 51, is largely comprised of Lucy and Sarah Chase's wartime correspondence to and from Norfolk.

58. Newby, " 'World Was All Before Them,' " 91; Parramore et al., *Norfolk*, 213; Jordan, *Black Confederates, Afro-Yankees*, 86, 101–3, and Swint, *Dear Ones at Home*, 90, 101.

59. Quarles, *Negro in the Civil War*, 168.

60. Maryland, Delaware, Missouri, and Kentucky were slave states that did not secede from the Union. Tennessee was also exempted from the provisions of

the Emancipation Proclamation, and much of the area around New Orleans was occupied by Union armed forces during the war, and was therefore exempt as well.

61. Newby, " 'World Was All Before Them,' " 21, 40–44.

62. *New York Times,* January 4, 1863; Bogger, "Slave and Free Black Community," 304; and Jordan, *Black Confederates, Afro-Yankees,* 256.

63. Jordan, *Black Confederates, Afro-Yankees,* 177, 257–59; and Swint, *Dear Ones at Home,* 97.

64. Jordan, *Black Confederates, Afro-Yankees,* 256, 265.

65. Rawick, ed., *Virginia Narratives,* 11–14; and Perdue et al., *Weevils in the Wheat,* 5.

66. Newby, " 'World Was All Before Them,' " 69–70; and Jordan, *Black Confederates, Afro-Yankees,* 265.

67. Jordan, *Black Confederates, Afro-Yankees,* 267.

68. Parramore et al., *Norfolk,* 209–11. Unless otherwise indicated, ensuing details about this incident have been gleaned from Parramore's account.

69. Jordan, *Black Confederates, Afro-Yankees,* 282; and Newby, " 'World Was All Before Them,' " 49.

70. Log of the USS *Cambridge,* National Archives.

71. Parramore et al., *Norfolk,* 217; and Jordan, *Black Confederates, Afro-Yankees,* 268–69.

72. Black men generally could not join white Masonic orders. Following the lead of Boston's Prince Hall, they established separate lodges, and formed their own order chartered by the British Masons. See chaps. 7 and 10. Jordan, *Black Confederates, Afro-Yankees,* 257. Log of the USS *Cambridge.*

73. Newby, " 'World Was All Before Them,' " 68, 71.

74. In the nineteenth century, the word "huckster" (with etymological roots similar to "hawker") had not acquired its more contemporary negative connotations. Norfolk's hucksters (often black women) were urban peddlers—usually purveyors of agricultural and other food products. Before, during, and after the war, they were significant factors in that port city's commercial life. Jordan, *Black Confederates, Afro-Yankees,* 21.

75. Ibid., 128. I have interpreted this quote to mean: "About the nigger women, I was out the other night and saw some good, big, lusty ones, but dared not touch them for fear I might get my old thing [penis] crooked."

76. Ample documentation suggests that many black people strictly adhered to principles of "premarital" chastity, but contradictory evidence argues that although "marital" fidelity was important, the main purpose of monogamous couples was to nurture children, and only then did sexual fidelity become significant. In addition, laws that excluded slaves from legally binding conjugal relations, combined with many owners' efforts to use their female slaves as breeders dis-

couraged adherence to standards of sexual behavior that whites advocated for their own women.

77. Elaine McCraw Chesnut, widow of one of John and Emma Bond's grandsons, told this story about the couple's meeting.

78. Boney et al., *God Made Man*, 15.

79. Newby, " 'World Was All Before Them,' " 125; and W. E. B. Du Bois, *Black Reconstruction in America, 1860–1880* (1935; reprint, New York: Atheneum, 1983), 208.

80. Some white officers faulted the behavior of their new black troops, but by and large, their deportment was admirable and their bravery undisputed. WPA, *Negro in Virginia*, 223, 235; and Litwack, *Been in the Storm Too Long*, 170. *John Brown's Body* and *Glory, Hallelujah* were alternate vernacular titles for Julia Ward Howe's stirring anthem, *Battle Hymn of the Republic*.

81. Elizabeth Keckley, *Behind the Scenes; or, Thirty Years a Slave, and Four Years in the White House* (1868; reprint, New York: Oxford University Press, 1988), 166–68.

82. WPA, *Negro in Virginia*, 251.

83. Ibid., 235.

84. Bogger, "Slave and Free Black Community," 311; and Newby, " 'World Was All Before Them,' " 145–46.

85. Nick Salvatore, *We All Got History: The Memory Books of Amos Webber* (New York: Times Books, 1996), 147.

86. Jordan, *Black Confederates, Afro-Yankees*, 134. Also, Margaret Burnham, "An Impossible Marriage: Slave Law and Family Law," *Law and Inequality* 5 (July 1987): 221.

87. Information concerning Emma Thomas and John Robert Bond's marriage appears in his navy pension records, National Archives.

88. *First Baptist Church, Bute Street*, 3–11.

89. Swint, *Dear Ones at Home*, 69.

90. According to the U.S. Census, Norfolk, 1870, the Tuckers and Blyes lived in the city's Third Ward. Mrs. Blye is listed there as "Mary Bly." Later correspondence identifies her as "Martha Blye," but there seems little doubt that it is the same person. In the antebellum years, the Bute Street Baptist Church included black people named "Bly," "Blye," and "Bligh" among its members. Prof. Tommy Bogger generously shared this information.

91. The marital relationship between the Whitings and the Mullens and information about his wartime hospitalization appears in Isaac Mullen's navy pension record, National Archives.

92. In "What America Would Be Like Without Blacks," in *Going to the Territory* (New York: Random House, 1986), 111, for example, Ralph Ellison pointedly states, "One of the first epithets that many European immigrants learned

when they got off the boat was the term 'nigger'—it made them feel instantly American."

93. Antoinette G. van Zelm's unpublished paper, "Virginia Freedwomen and Former Mistresses Define Emancipation In and Beyond the Domestic Workplace," cites several instances when former mistresses attended, supervised, and attempted to control weddings of their former "servants." Immediately after the war, Norfolk-Portsmouth city directories listed no blacks simply as residents. It also excluded them from most business listings. It did, however, include black institutions such as churches and schools, with the names of their pastors, directors, etc. Blacks also were listed in local tax rolls. Some of these people opened accounts with the Freedmen's Bank in the late 1860s. Those microfilmed bank records, now in the National Archives, often included detailed personal information.

94. Bogger, "Slave and Free Black Community," 314; and Swint, *Dear Ones at Home,* 165, 169.

95. Parramore et al., *Norfolk,* 228; and Swint, *Dear Ones at Home,* 169.

96. "Address from the Colored Citizens of Norfolk, Va., to the People of the United States"; and Parramore et al., *Norfolk,* 226–27.

97. Swint, *Dear Ones at Home,* 169.

98. Ibid., 89.

6. THE HOBBLED PHOENIX

1. "Forty Acres and a Mule" is the name of Spike Lee's movie production company evoking this postbellum dream of black people, at last, having something of their own.

2. Writers' Program, Virginia Works Project Administration, *The Negro in Virginia* (1940; reprint, Winston-Salem: John F. Blair, 1994), 244; W. E. B. Du Bois, *Black Reconstruction in America 1860–1880* (1935; reprint, New York: Atheneum, 1983), 538; and see Willard B. Gatewood, *William Augustus Hodges, Free Man of Color* (Knoxville: University of Tennessee Press, 1983).

3. Du Bois, *Black Reconstruction,* 136.

4. Norfolk *Virginian,* December 29, 1865, and March 20, 1866. Records of the Freedmen's Savings & Loan Company, Norfolk. Frederick Douglass became the token Negro on the board of directors, and he took much of the blame when the Freedmen's banking system failed in 1873.

5. Thomas C. Parramore, with Peter C. Stewart and Tommy I. Bogger, *Norfolk: The First Four Centuries* (Charlottesville: University Press of Virginia, 1994), 228.

6. Ibid., 228, 230–32.

7. The Republican-controlled United States Congress refused to seat former Confederates who were elected just after the war. Provisions of the Fourteenth Amendment, which the requisite number of states ratified in 1868, insured their expulsion—though only for a few years.

8. Stephen F. Miller et al., "Between Emancipation and Enfranchisement: Law and the Political Mobilization of Black Southerners During Presidential Reconstruction, 1865–1867," *Chicago-Kent Law Review* 70, no. 3 (1995): 1069–72. F. N. Boney, Richard L. Hume, and Rafia Zafar, *God Made Man, Man Made the Slave: The Autobiography of George Teamoh* (Macon, Ga.: Mercer University Press, 1990), 19; Cassandra Newby, " 'The World Was All Before Them': A Study of the Black Community in Norfolk, Virginia, 1861–1884" (Ph.D. diss., College of William and Mary, 1992), 152–53; and Du Bois, *Black Reconstruction,* 174. Philip S. Foner and George E. Walker, eds., *Proceedings of the Black State Conventions, 1840–1865* (Philadelphia: Temple University Press, 1976), 2:257. Delegates from the Hampton Roads region to the August 1865 Convention were: Robert Bailey, Nicholas Barber, John M. Brown, John Cary, George W. Cook, William Davis, Richard Hill, Edmund F. Jones, William Keeling, William H. Kelly, Robert Ruffin, J. R. V. Thomas, George Toamoth (Teamoh), James Tyres, Edward W. Williams, Joshua (or Joseph) Wilson. Also, Parramore et al., *Norfolk,* 233.

9. Foner and Walker, eds., *Black State Conventions,* 264–67.

10. Norfolk *Virginian,* December 29, 1865.

11. WPA, *Negro in Virginia,* 263; and *Virginian,* January 2, 1866. And on June 15, 1868, for instance, the *Virginian* reported, "a negro 'society' paraded yesterday afternoon—for what purpose we don't know—with white pants, black coats and blue scarves." Also Newby, " 'World Was All Before Them,' " 160–62.

12. Parramore et al., 228.

13. *True Southerner,* January 11, 1866. Carpetbaggers were the entrepreneurial, sometimes rapacious, northerners who came south after the Civil War to take advantage of the region's desperate straits. Scalawags were southerners who abandoned the Confederate cause, worked with the Yankees, encouraged blacks to demand equal rights and especially to vote Republican. The South's "respectable" white people despised both groups.

14. In a number of locations throughout the South, newspapers published for and by the African American community sprang up shortly after the Civil War. Lack of finances and resistance from whites doomed most of them to brief lives. George Tucker, *Virginian-Pilot and the Star-Ledger,* February 19, 1989, "Ex-slave: Wilson's Career Spanned Sailor, Soldier, Editor Roles."

15. *True Southerner,* November 24, 1865.

16. Ibid.

17. Virginia Sapiro, "Women, Citizenship, and Nationality: Immigration and Naturalization Policies in the United States," *Politics and Society,* 13, no. 1 (1984): 1–26.

18. *True Southerner,* December 1865–March 1866.

19. Parramore et al., *Norfolk,* 236.

20. Ibid., 224–25.

21. Ibid.

22. Ibid.; and Freedmen and Southern Society Project (FSSP), History Department, University of Maryland, Files K-122 and A-7478.

23. Ibid.

24. Parramore et al., *Norfolk,* 226–28. Memphis and New Orleans were among those southern cities that experienced race riots at that time. FSSP, File A-7598.

25. Newby, " 'World Was All Before Them,' " 213; and FSSP, Files A-7426 and VA-3802.

26. Du Bois, *Black Reconstruction,* 538. Elizabeth Hafkin Pleck, *Black Migration and Poverty: Boston, 1865–1900* (New York: Academic Press, 1979), 25.

27. Boney et al., *God Made Man.* See esp. Rebecca (Lee) Crumpler, M.D., *A Book of Medical Discourses in Two Parts* (Boston: Cashman, Keating, 1883), 2; and Darlene Clark Hine, ed., *Black Women in America: An Historic Encyclopedia* (Brooklyn: Carlson Publishing, 1993), 290. I thank Vanessa Northington Gamble, medical historian, for sharing the "mule doctor" story.

28. Miller et al., "Between Emancipation and Enfranchisement," 1069–72; and FSSP, File A-7619.

29. FSSP, File A-7619.

30. *True Southerner,* March 29, 1866.

31. Boney et al., *God Made Man,* 18.

32. Nina Silber, "Intemperate Men, Spiteful Women, and Jefferson Davis," in Catherine Clinton and Nina Silber, eds., *Divided Houses: Gender and the Civil War* (New York: Oxford University Press, 1992), 302, 296.

33. It was a curious quirk of fate that the very first position in Washington, D.C., held by Elizabeth Keckley, the ex-slave who became Mary Todd Lincoln's modiste and confidante, was as Varina Davis's dressmaker. Varina Davis unsuccessfully importuned Keckley to remain in her employ when the southern states seceded.

34. The dates of birth for Emma and John Robert Bond's surviving children are included in his navy pension records. Caroline Bond Day, *A Study of Some Negro-White Families in the United States* (Cambridge: Peabody Museum, Harvard University, 1932), 32.

35. Norfolk *Virginian,* March 9, 1866.

36. My mother, Percy Bond's daughter, told me that this song came from her father.

37. Norfolk *Virginian,* July 3 and 6, 1868.

38. *True Southerner,* January 11, 1866.

39. Du Bois, *Black Reconstruction,* 641; and Parramore et al., *Norfolk,* 235.

40. Boney et al., *God Made Man,* 21; and FSSP, File A-10508. Norfolk *Virginian,* June 1, 1868. Parramore et al., *Norfolk,* 237, reports that in 1869 the "Colored National Labor Union" attempted to organize black dockworkers. Their efforts fell short because of continuing debate as to whether Negroes should organize together with, or separate from, whites. For the most part, the white labor movement deliberately excluded blacks.

41. FSSP, File A-10508.

42. Ibid.; and Parramore et al., *Norfolk,* 213.

43. Du Bois, *Black Reconstruction,* 541.

44. Ibid., 544.

45. U.S. Census, Norfolk, 1870. Portsmouth's tax rolls of 1866–70 show both Isaac Mullen and Frank Whiting as taxpayers. Parramore et al., *Norfolk,* 235, 238.

46. Parramore et al., *Norfolk,* 238. WPA, *Negro in Virginia,* 263, retells the story of Negro delegates to the state's 1868 Constitutional Convention who attempted to buy tickets to a Richmond theater and were sent to the upper gallery.

47. Boney et al., *God Made Man,* 20. In 1867, black voters in Norfolk outnumbered white voters 2,049 to 1,910. Parramore et al., *Norfolk,* 236–37. Virtually all Negro voters were Republicans. Over the next few years, as increasing numbers of former Rebels became "reconstructed," the balance shifted.

48. WPA, *Negro in Virginia,* 252–53; and Boney et al., *God Made Man,* 119.

49. WPA, *Negro in Virginia,* 252–53.

50. Norfolk *Virginian,* June 1, 1868; Parramore et al., *Norfolk,* 236–37; Boney et al., *God Made Man,* 20; WPA, *Negro in Virginia,* 254; and Du Bois, *Black Reconstruction,* 541.

51. Du Bois, *Black Reconstruction,* 542–43.

52. Ibid., 542; and WPA, *Negro in Virginia,* 297.

53. Newby, " 'World Was All Before Them,' " 228, 231; Du Bois, *Black Reconstruction,* 658; and Parramore et al., *Norfolk,* 236.

54. Du Bois, *Black Reconstruction,* 542–43; and WPA, *Negro in Virginia,* 255.

55. Norfolk *Virginian,* July 6, 1868. Tommy Bogger, "The Slave and Free Black Community in Norfolk" (Ph.D. diss., University of Virginia, 1976), 63.

56. Frederick Douglass, "We Are Not Yet Quite Free," speech, August 3, 1869.

57. In 1866, for example, virtually all of the black churches in Memphis were burned. Du Bois, *Black Reconstruction,* 675.

58. Parramore et al., *Norfolk,* 233. Michael Edward Hucles, "Postbellum Urban Black Economic Development: The Case of Norfolk" (Ph.D. diss., Purdue University, 1990), 140.

59. WPA, *Negro in Virginia,* 255–56.

60. Ibid. Also, Parramore et al., *Norfolk,* 237–38; and Boney et al., *God Made Man,* 21, 22.

61. Parramore et al., *Norfolk,* 238; and Du Bois, *Black Reconstruction,* 545.

62. Du Bois, *Black Reconstruction,* 546.

63. Boney et al., *God Made Man,* 1–2, 127.

64. Ibid., 1–2, 121.

65. The following chapter details one of Revels' New England lectures.

7. No Room at the Inn

1. In the 1870s, the Worcester *Evening Gazette* ran regular advertisements for the Bay State House. United States Census for Worcester, Massachusetts, 1870, and Worcester City Directories, 1870–73. It is impossible to know precisely when John, Emma, and Percy Bond came to, and ultimately left, Worcester. They certainly resided in Norfolk through 1869, and had arrived in Worcester by the summer of 1870 when the federal census was taken. The Bonds stayed there at least well into 1873, but their presence in Hyde Park could not be confirmed until early 1875.

2. Franklin P. Rice, *The Worcester Book: A Diary of Noteworthy Events in Worcester Massachusetts, from 1657 to 1883* (Worcester, Mass.: Putnam & Davis, 1884), 19.

3. Throughout 1870 and 1871, Worcester's *Evening Gazette* included a listing of arrivals at the Bay State House.

4. The Worcester City Directories, 1870–72, show the Bay State House as John Robert Bond's place of residence. The *Evening Gazette* made mention of other employees who boarded at the hotel.

5. The *Evening Gazette* (esp. December 6, 1871) reported the political activities of Ward Six's F. F. Goulding, a Republican lawyer and school board member for whom that small neighborhood enclave was apparently named.

6. U.S. Census, Worcester, 1870.

7. Ibid.

8. Roy Rosenzweig, *Eight Hours for What We Will: Workers and Leisure in an Industrial City, 1870–1920* (New York: Cambridge University Press, 1983), 11.

9. Ibid., 31, 132–33.

10. *Evening Gazette,* throughout March 1870.

11. Ibid., March 14 and May 2, 1870.

12. Debates rage over the origins of Memorial, or Decoration, Day. Some say that southern women initiated Decoration Day during the Civil War. The superintendent of schools in Reconstruction Charleston, South Carolina, organized ceremonies there in 1865 to honor the Civil War dead on both sides. The first ceremony in the North took place the next year. The first to be held on May 30 took place near Richmond, Virginia, and was organized by Major Andrew Washburn, who later moved to Hyde Park, Massachusetts. In 1868, John A. Logan, a Union general and commander-in-chief of the GAR, suggested that date as an official day to honor the dead in America's wars. Until World War I, the GAR maintained charge of Decoration (or Memorial) Day ceremonies nationwide. See Mary E. Pitts, "The Origins of Memorial Day," unpublished paper.

13. Nick Salvatore, *We All Got History: The Memory Books of Amos Webber* (New York: Times Books, 1996), 158. For an effective evaluation of the GAR, see Stuart McConnell, *Glorious Contentment: The Grand Army of the Republic, 1865–1900* (Chapel Hill: University of North Carolina Press, 1992).

14. Franklin D. Tappan, *The Passing of the Grand Army of the Republic* (Worcester, Mass.: privately published, 1939), 23–24. Salvatore, *We All Got History*, skillfully analyzes the Bassill Barker incident, 168–69, but uses the alternate spelling: Bazzel. Barker's name does not appear on a current compilation of the Sixth Cavalry roster provided by the National Park Service in 1998—but then neither does that of Amos Webber.

15. McConnell, *Glorious Contentment*, 111. The GAR officially did not discriminate according to race, but, especially in the South, local custom mandated separate posts for whites and African Americans.

16. Salvatore, *We All Got History*, 146. Pauli Murray, *Proud Shoes: The Story of an American Family* (1956; reprint, New York: Perennial Library, 1987), 135–55, details Robert Fitzgerald's experiences with the Fifth Massachusetts Cavalry.

17. Salvatore and I compiled somewhat different totals for the number of black members of the GAR's Post 10.

18. Salvatore, *We All Got History*, 163.

19. Ibid. Salvatore skillfully articulates this theme throughout and esp. 152. Also see Joseph Glatthaar, *Forged in Battle: The Civil War Alliance of Black Soldiers and White Officers* (New York: Meridian, 1990).

20. *Evening Gazette*, July 5, 1870.

21. Rosenzweig, *Eight Hours*, 71–72, 85.

22. U.S. Census, Worcester, 1870.

23. The 1870 revisions of the Naturalization Act of 1790 evolved from the aims of Reconstruction concerning citizenship and political rights for former slaves. Those revisions did not, however, lift the ban on naturalization for other nonwhite men, including Asians and Native Americans. It also did not change the law to grant women the right to become naturalized citizens.

24. Virginia Sapiro, "Women, Citizenship, and Nationality: Immigration and Naturalization Policies in the United States," *Politics and Society* 13, no. 1 (1984): 3. Sapiro states, for instance: "The Acts of 1855 and 1907 took away rights that women had under common law and thus made women's identity even more dependent."

25. Salvatore, *We All Got History*, 101. My colleagues Richard Stott and Tyler Anbinder persuasively argue that at least prior to passage of the Chinese Exclusion Act of 1882, few foreign-born (white) Europeans would have been required to provide proof of citizenship as a prerequisite to voting.

26. Elizabeth Hafkin Pleck, *Black Migration and Poverty: Boston, 1865–1900* (New York: Academic Press, 1979), 19.

27. Franklin P. Rice, ed., *The Worcester of Eighteen Hundred and Ninety Eight* (Worcester, Mass., 1899), 39; and Salvatore, *We All Got History*, 100.

28. Salvatore, *We All Got History*, 165. Schuyler Colfax served as vice president during President Grant's first term, 1869–73.

29. Salvatore, *We All Got History*, 165–66.

30. Ibid., 165–67; and Worcester *Evening Gazette,* April 14, 1870.

31. U.S. Census, Worcester, 1870; and Worcester City Directories, 1870–1873. Bond's sixty-hour workweek is an estimate based on comparable labor information. See, for example, Rosenzweig, *Eight Hours,* 39.

32. Rosenzweig, *Eight Hours,* 50, 58.

33. *Evening Gazette,* September 19, 1870. Although this impetus was especially apparent among the supposedly benevolent white members of the American Colonization Society, some black Americans who had become outraged at racial prejudice and discrimination in the United States did want to emigrate to Africa. A small but vocal minority of diverse Negro Americans supported various back-to-Africa movements from the time of the efforts of Paul Cuffe and others in the early 1800s, through Garvey in the 1920s, and up to the present time. W. E. B. Du Bois and Stokely Carmichael (later Kwame Touré) are among the better-known Negro Americans who left their homeland for Africa in the twentieth century.

34. Alexander DeConde, *Ethnicity, Race, and American Foreign Policy* (Boston: Northeastern University Press, 1992), 46.

35. Salvatore, *We All Got History*, 181–82; and "Amos Webber Thermometer Record and Diary," MS, American Steel and Wire Collection, Baker Library, Harvard University Graduate School of Business Administration.

36. Salvatore, *We All Got History*, 181–82; and *Evening Gazette,* March 3 and August 1, 1871.

37. John R. Bond was listed in Worcester's City Directory in 1870 as a fireman, and then in 1871 as a bellboy at the Bay State House. I have found no evidence suggesting racial discrimination concerning patrons at that particular hotel.

38. Rosenzweig, *Eight Hours,* 18, 13.

39. Ibid., 11, 12; and Salvatore, *We All Got History,* esp. chap. 7, "Civil Duties." Also, "Worcester: Headwaters of the Blackstone" (Worcester: Massachusetts Audubon Society Environmental Affairs Office, n.d.).

40. Rosenzweig, *Eight Hours,* 12, 24.

41. Salvatore, *We All Got History,* 155–60.

42. *Evening Gazette,* November 1 and 2, 1870, March 21, 1871. Salvatore, *We All Got History,* 156; and Rosenzweig, *Eight Hours,* 24.

43. "Worcester: Headwaters of Blackstone."

44. Albert B. Southwick, *Once-Told Tales of Worcester County* (Worcester, Mass.: Databooks, 1994), 58.

45. James O'Toole has graciously shared his manuscript, "Passing: Race, Religion, and the Healy Family in America." Eight of the Healy children reached adulthood. In addition to James and Patrick who achieved such success in the Roman Catholic church, Sherwood became rector of Boston's Cathedral of the Holy Cross, Michael was a captain in the Coast Guard, and Eugene was a charming ne'er-do-well. Martha married a white man and raised her family in Newton, Massachusetts; Josephine was a nun in Montreal's Hôtel Dieu, a nursing order; and Eliza became a superior in several of the Sisters of Notre Dame's convents.

46. James O'Toole is wrestling with the ways that the Catholic Church may have dealt with the Healy boys' "illegitimacy," since marriage between the races was forbidden in Georgia and throughout the South. Officially, the church could not ordain a child born out of wedlock, so how did it manipulate and justify the clerical careers of the Healys? I am indebted to Mark Savolis, archivist at the College of the Holy Cross, for supplying information about that school's early years.

47. Salvatore, *We All Got History,* 154.

48. *Evening Gazette,* April 8, 1874; and *All Saints' Church, Worcester, Massachusetts: A Centennial History, 1835–1935* (Worcester, Mass., 1935), 46.

49. Charles Emery Stevens, *Worcester Churches, 1719–1889* (Worcester, Mass.: Lucius Paulinus Goddard, 1890), 126; and Paula Rowse Buonomo, *Forward Through the Ages: A History of St. Matthew's Episcopal Church, 1871–1995 in the Village of South Worcester, Massachusetts* (Worcester, Mass.: n.p., 1995), 8–12. My thanks to Gail Jackins at St. Matthew's for sharing this book with me, and to George R. Frye, All Saints' archivist, who, in the parish records, uncovered John Robert Bond's attendance both at that church and at St. Matthew's. Also, Salvatore, *We All Got History,* 154; and *Evening Gazette,* September 22, 1871.

50. My thanks to Jeannette Greenwood for directing me toward the Wilson family saga, Corrine Bostic's *Go Onward and Upward* (Worcester, Mass.: Commonwealth Press, 1974), 9–10. See also Thomas Wentworth Higginson, *Army Life in a Black Regiment* (1869; reprint, New York: Norton, 1984).

51. Salvatore, *We All Got History,* 100.

52. Willard B. Gatewood, *Aristocrats of Color: The Black Elite, 1880–1920* (Bloomington: Indiana University Press, 1990), 232–34. The Vanderbilts and their ilk built their ostentatious summer "cottages" in Newport around the turn of the century.

53. Ibid.

54. *Evening Gazette,* January 4, 1872. The "redowa" was a popular nineteenth-century ballroom dance in triple time (much like a waltz) while the "varsovienne" was a mazurka—the name suggesting its origins in Warsaw, Poland.

55. For an extensive discussion of class in the African American community in New England, see Adelaide M. Cromwell, *The Other Brahmins: Boston's Black Upper Class, 1750–1950* (Fayetteville: University of Arkansas Press, 1994).

56. Salvatore, *We All Got History,* found no evidence of differentiation according to color among Worcester's Negroes, although most historians suggest that skin tone usually played at least *some* role in achieving "elite" status in the African American community. More successful African American men certainly sometimes tried to choose lighter-skinned wives. Gatewood, *Aristocrats of Color,* analyzes the qualities that characterized members of the Negro upper class.

57. Webber diary, 1: 117, May 10 and 24, 1871. The Earle family owned the Worcester *Spy* and were abolitionists and women's rights advocates. See Southwick, *Once-Told Tales,* 61.

58. *Evening Gazette,* January 11, 1872. The word "gouts" evokes not the familiar ailment, but the older English meaning, as in the Shakespearean "on thy blade and dudgeon gouts of blood." Webber diary, May 29, 1871, passim. Salvatore, *We All Got History,* 173.

59. Massachusetts Birth Records, City of Worcester, May 1872.

60. Salvatore, *We All Got History,* 194–95. According to W. E. B. Du Bois, *Black Reconstruction in America, 1860–1880* (1935; reprint, New York: Atheneum, 1983), 436, James Lynch was so incensed when white delegates to Mississippi's 1868 "Black and Tan" convention insisted that Negro delegates have the word "colored" appended by their names that he moved to amend the regulations so that the color of every delegate's hair be added as well.

61. *Evening Gazette,* November 5, 1872,

62. Webber diary, 178, April 5, 1873.

63. Ibid., 194–96, September 11 and November 5, 1873.

64. Salvatore, *We All Got History,* 183–84.

65. The English usually used the compound "Oddfellows."

66. Salvatore, *We All Got History,* 189.

67. Ibid., 188–89; and *Evening Gazette,* March 26 and 27, 1872.

68. Multiracial New Bedford was an exception to the extreme numerical dominance of Caucasians throughout Massachusetts.

69. Elaine McCraw Chesnut, the widow of one of Emma and John Bond's grandsons has been especially perceptive in evaluating the personalities of John and Emma Bond.

70. *Evening Gazette,* April 15, 1871.

71. Salvatore, *We All Got History,* 188; and *Evening Gazette,* July 8 and December 5, 1873.

72. *Evening Gazette,* April 8 and 9, 1874; and Rice, *Worcester,* 18, 42, 133.

73. Du Bois, *Black Reconstruction,* 599–600. The Freedmen's Savings & Trust Company records from the Norfolk branch show savings accounts of many Thomases, Whitings, Tuckers, and Blyes.

74. Henry L. Swint, *Dear Ones at Home: Letters from Contraband Camps* (Nashville: Vanderbilt University Press, 1966), includes several letters from the Chases to the Grimkés.

8. Citizenship and a Dutiful Son

1. At least twenty-nine units trained at Camp Meigs, including three black regiments. W. A. Stokinger, A. K. Schroeder, and Capt. A. A. Swanson, *Civil War Camps at Readville: Camp Meigs Playground and Fowl Meadow Reservation* (Boston: Reservations and Historic Sites Metropolitan District Commission, 1990), 6; and "Historic Hyde Park Salutes the New Boston," supplement to the Hyde Park *Tribune,* January 1963. Lt. James M. Trotter from the Fifty-fifth Massachusetts was interred in Hyde Park's town cemetery. Others of the soldiers were buried in neighboring Dedham.

2. Elaine McCraw Chesnut, a Bond family member and local resident, told me about the designation of their enclave as "Nigger Village."

3. Peterson Files, MSS, Hyde Park Public Library; and Norfolk County *Gazette,* April 18 and August 28, 1874.

4. *Gazette,* July 24 and September 18, 1875.

5. Peterson files. Hyde Park at times was part of Norfolk County, at times part of Suffolk County. After 1911, it became Ward 26 of the city of Boston.

6. "Historic Hyde Park Salutes the New Boston."

7. My thanks to Joseph Reidy and the Black Civil War Union Sailors Project for comparing names of black men in Hyde Park with the new computer base of all black sailors, and to John Peterson and the National Park Service for sharing lists of the Fifty-fourth and Fifty-fifth Massachusetts Infantry Regiments and the Fifth Massachusetts Cavalry, which trained at Readville. See also Stokinger et al., *Civil War Camps at Readville,* 321. Information on Weeden from Donald M. Jacobs, ed., *Courage and Conscience: Black Abolitionists in Boston* (Bloomington: Indiana University Press, 1993), 144.

8. Adelaide M. Cromwell, *The Other Brahmins: Boston's Black Upper Class, 1750–1950* (Fayetteville: University of Arkansas Press, 1994), 48. The late African American writer Ann Petry used the phrase "birthright New Englander" to describe herself.

9. The third Grimké boy, John, had little contact with his Hyde Park relatives. See Dickson D. Bruce, Jr., *Archibald Grimké: Portrait of a Black Independent* (Baton Rouge: Louisiana State University Press, 1993). On "shadow families" (as well as color consciousness), see Willard Gatewood, "Skin Color," *Encyclopedia of African-American Culture and History* (New York: Macmillan Library Reference, 1996), 5: 2444–49.

10. See Mary E. Pitts, *Theodore Dwight Weld: This Was a Man!* (Hyde Park, Mass.: Albert House Publishing, 1987), 22.

11. *Municipal Register of the Town of Hyde Park* (Hyde Park, Mass.: Press of the Norfolk County Gazette, 1876), Report of the Overseers of the Poor, 28; and *Tenth Annual Report of Receipts and Expenditures of the Town of Hyde Park for 1878*, 35.

12. Parish records, Church of the Good Shepherd. See also Electa Kane Tritsch, ed., *Building Dedham: Celebrating 350 Years of History* (Dedham, Mass.: Dedham Historical Society, 1986), 56.

13. Trotter's book was first published, by varying reports, from 1878 to 1883.

14. Warren Logan (ca. 1856–1942) was my paternal grandfather. He attended Hampton Institute from 1874 to 1877, where he sang with and managed the chorus. I assume that he accompanied the group on this New England concert tour, though the Norfolk County *Gazette* article mentions no names. Motto, senior class supper, 1877, Warren Logan folder, Hampton University Archives.

15. John Robert Bond, Navy pension records, National Archives.

16. Nancy Huges Hannan, *A Compendium of Hyde Park History in Three Volumes* (Hyde Park: Albert House Publishing, 1989), 3: 387; Robert B. Beath, *History of the Grand Army of the Republic* (New York: Bryan, Taylor, 1889), 417, 651; and Frank Rich Scrapbook #4, Hyde Park Public Library.

17. Hannan, *Compendium of Hyde Park History,* 3: 387; and Beath, *History of the GAR,* 417.

18. *Gazette,* March 15, 1879. Mary E. Pitts, "Hyde Park, Massachusetts Civil War Roundup," unpublished paper, 1992.

19. Mark Alvarez, *The Old Ball Game* (Alexandria, Va.: Redefinition Books, 1990), 94, 142.

20. U.S. Censuses, Norfolk County, Massachusetts, 1870 and 1880; Boston *Advocate,* July 3 and September 25, 1886; and John Daniels, *In Freedom's Birthplace: A Study of the Boston Negroes* (Boston: Houghton Mifflin, 1914), 461.

21. Annual Reports, Hyde Park, Massachusetts, 1875–1889.

22. Bruce, *Archibald Grimké,* chaps. 2 and 3.

23. Ibid.; and *Gazette,* July 9, 1919.

24. Beath, *History of the GAR,* 417.

25. *Gazette,* June 4, 1881, July 7, 1883, and January 6, 1883. Hannan, *Compendium of Hyde Park History,* 3: 4.

26. Frank Rich Scrapbook #4.

27. Stuart McConnell, *Glorious Contentment: The Grand Army of the Republic, 1865–1900* (Chapel Hill: University of North Carolina Press, 1992), 165.

28. Susie King Taylor, *Reminiscences of My Life in Camp* (Boston: S. K. Taylor, 1902), xii, 13; "James H. Wolff," in *Colored American* 6 (March 1903): 358–59; and *Proceedings, Grand Army of the Republic Encampment, Massachusetts Division* (Boston, 1905).

29. *Gazette,* September 5, 1874. Boston 200 Neighborhood History Series, *Black Bostonia,* 5; and Hyde Park, Annual Reports of Receipts and Expenditures, 1878–1880.

30. My thanks to Mary E. Pitts for providing information about Hobart Cable. Little has been written that even touches on voluntary immigration to the United States by people of African ancestry prior to World War I. Nonetheless, see Roy Simon Bryce-Laporte, "Black Immigrants: The Experience of Invisibility and Inequality," *Journal of Black Studies,* September 1972; Bryce-Laporte, "Black Immigrants," in Peter I. Rose, Stanley Rothman, William J. Wilson, eds., *Through Different Eyes: Black and White Perspectives on American Race Relations* (New York: Oxford University Press, 1973); and Ira De Augustine Reid, *The Negro Immigrant: His Background, Characteristics, and Social Adjustments, 1899–1937* (New York: Columbia University Press, 1939).

31. See esp. Frank George Franklin, *The Legislative History of Naturalization in the United States* (Chicago: University of Chicago Press, 1906); Thomas G. Patterson and J. Garry Clifford, *American Foreign Policy: A History to 1914* (Lexington, Mass.: D. C. Heath, 1963); and James H. Kettner, *The Development of American Civilization, 1608–1870* (Chapel Hill: University of North Carolina Press, 1970).

32. Patterson and Clifford, *American Foreign Policy,* 272–75. In 1855, the Congress decided that "every woman married . . . to a citizen of the United States should be deemed a citizen." There were few objections because women possessed no political rights, and "negro, Indian, or Chinese women" were specifically excluded.

33. Darlene Clark Hine, Wilma King, and Linda Reed, eds., *"We Specialize in the Wholly Impossible": A Reader in Black Women's History* (Brooklyn, N.Y.: Carlson Publishing, 1995), 226. Sojourner Truth was first known as Isabella Baumfree or Bomefree, then as Isabella Van Wagenen. She became an abolitionist and advocate of women's rights, and died in 1883.

34. Franklin, *Legislative History of Naturalization,* 35, 165; Patterson and Clifford, *American Foreign Policy,* 169; and Kettner, *Development of American*

Citizenship, 345. *Dred Scott v. Sandford* cites the Naturalization Act of 1790 as one justification for its decision denying citizenship rights to Negroes in 1857.

35. Kettner, *Development of American Citizenship,* 246.

36. Lawrence B. Evans, *Cases on American Constitutional Law* (Chicago: Callaghan, 1952), 476; and Lawrence M. Friedman, *A History of American Law* (New York: Simon & Schuster, 1985), 350, 507–9. The Chinese Exclusion Act determined that men from China could work in the United States for limited periods but could not bring families, settle, or expect to become citizens like so many European immigrants. Reid, *Negro Immigrant,* 32.

37. Reid, *Negro Immigrant,* 12, 26, 27, 42; and Bryce-Laporte, "Black Immigrants," in Rose et al., 47.

38. Naturalization papers of John Robert Bond, 1884, National Archives.

39. *The Hub,* August 2, 1884. Elizabeth Hafkin Pleck, *Black Migration and Poverty: Boston, 1865–1900* (New York: Academic Press, 1979). One of Pleck's major themes concerns the endemic lack of economic opportunities for blacks in the Boston area.

40. *Hub,* August 4, 1883, gives the 6,000 Negro voters figure, and September 22, 1883, names many of the black activists. Cromwell, *Other Brahmins,* 47, 49.

41. The oral history relayed to me by John Bond's granddaughter, Wenonah Bond Logan (my mother), identified him as a lamplighter in Hyde Park. "Historic Hyde Park Salutes the New Boston."

42. Nick Salvatore, *We All Got History: The Memory Books of Amos Webber* (New York: Times Books, 1996), 280–85. Boston *Advocate,* June 5, 1886.

43. *Gazette,* January 1, 1876, and August 7, 1880. Percy Bond's attendance at Bryant & Stratton is confirmed by oral history. The yearbooks of Hyde Park High School mention others who went to Bryant & Stratton. "Historic Hyde Park Salutes the New Boston."

44. Hannan, *Compendium of Hyde Park History,* 1: 69, 87, 71.

45. *Advocate,* April 4, 1885.

46. Rich Scrapbook #7; and *Gazette,* February 11, 1899.

47. *Catalogue of Fisk University,* 1885–86. This is the only place I have found mention of Georgia Fagain's middle name.

48. U.S. Census, Boston, Massachusetts, 1900; Daniels, *In Freedom's Birthplace,* 189 and 360; and Robert C. Hayden, *African-Americans in Boston: More than 350 Years* (Boston: Public Library, 1991), 48. The author's father was named Arthur Courtney Logan for Dr. Samuel Courtney, a family friend from Tuskegee. Bits of information about Courtney have come down on both the Bond and Logan sides of the family.

49. My thanks to Kenneth Hamilton for his information concerning Samuel Courtney and his relationship with Booker T. Washington and the National Negro Business League.

50. NNBL records for this early period are not complete, and Percy's involvement is only verifiable after 1906, but it seems highly unlikely, given his professional status and relationship with Samuel Courtney, that he did not first join at this time.

51. See Willard B. Gatewood, *Aristocrats of Color: The Black Elite, 1880–1920* (Bloomington: Indiana University Press, 1990); and Cromwell, *Other Brahmins*.

52. That social set in Boston is the subject of Cromwell, *Other Brahmins*.

53. Ibid., 78, 227; and Walter J. Stevens, *Chip on My Shoulder* (Boston: Meador Press, 1946), 77.

54. Caroline Bond (Day) possessed a photograph of Adrienne Herndon taken in the 1890s, leading to my belief that Georgia Stewart and Adrienne knew each other at that time.

55. Caroline Bond Day, *A Study of Some Negro-White Families in the United States* (Cambridge: Peabody Museum, Harvard University, 1932), 21.

56. See Cromwell, *Other Brahmins,* 13. A number of personal sources have confirmed that the dark-skinned Percy Bond was transfixed by Georgia's whiteness.

57. Different censuses and other varied sources suggest that Georgia was born sometime between 1869 and 1871.

58. My earliest memories of my grandmother, Georgia Fagain Stewart Bond, include her vain attempts to teach me to crochet and embroider.

59. From early memories of my grandmother, Georgia Fagain Stewart Bond, and extensive conversations with my mother (Georgia and Percy's daughter), Wenonah Bond Logan.

60. My mother told me about these gifts of used clothing. See also Deborah Gray White, *Ar'n't I a Woman: Female Slaves in the Plantation South* (New York: Norton, 1985), 143.

61. Fisk University catalogs, 1885–86, 1886–87, 1887–88.

62. W. E. B. Du Bois, *Darkwater: Voices from Within the Veil* (1920; reprint, New York: Schocken Books, 1969), 14; and Fisk University catalogs, 1886–87, 1887–88.

63. U.S. Census, Nashville, Tennessee, 1880. Caroline Bond Day's writings and correspondence make reference to her Cherokee background.

64. "Moses to Georgia" wedding ring in the possession of the author. Notes from Wenonah Bond Logan. Different sources have different dates for the death of Moses Stewart, but Georgia's letter to her sister pinpoints it as no later than early 1894.

65. A number of poetry indexes failed to reveal the source of this stanza or its author. It is also remotely possible that Georgia, with her literary pretensions, wrote it herself.

66. Some sources state that Maria Baldwin took over the principalship of the Agassiz School in 1889; others date it as 1899. I don't know whether Carrie

Stewart actually attended that school, but remember that she revered Baldwin. On Boston residents and their devotion to education, see Cromwell, *Other Brahmins,* 35.

67. U.S. Census, Boston, Massachusetts, 1900.

68. Ibid.

69. Georgia F. Stewart to Booker T. Washington, March 31, April 8, April 12, April 19, 1901, Booker T. Washington Papers, General Correspondence, Manuscript Division, Library of Congress.

70. *Colored American Magazine,* August 1901, 273–76.

71. Stewart to Washington, April 29, 1901, BTW Papers. Louis R. Harlan, *Booker T. Washington: The Wizard of Tuskegee, 1901–1915* (New York: Oxford University Press, 1983), 113.

72. Stewart to Washington, April 29, 1901.

73. Correspondence between Clara Burrill and Roscoe C. Bruce, Boxes 10-1 and 10-2, Bruce Family Papers, Manuscript Division, Moorland Spingarn Research Center, Howard University.

74. Gatewood, *Aristocrats of Color,* 37–38, 144. Blanche Kelso Bruce sat in the United States Senate from 1875 to 1881.

75. One of Roscoe Bruce's letters mentions Boston's well-known Glover family, some of whom moved to Hyde Park in 1920. One of the Glovers was an attendant in Bob Bond's 1901 wedding. Conversation with Louise Glover Hinds, April 1998.

76. *Gazette,* June 21, 1902.

77. Roscoe C. Bruce to Clara Burrill, August 17 and 25, 1902; and n.d., Bruce Papers.

78. Du Bois, *Darkwater,* includes the fable "The Princess of the Hither Isles," which, arguably, is an allegory about what Du Bois considered Booker T. Washington's tyranny.

9. WAKE OF THE *LANCASTER*

1. Nancy Hughes Hannan, *A Compendium of Hyde Park History in Three Volumes,* vol. 3 (Hyde Park, Mass.: Albert House Publishing, 1985); Norfolk County *Gazette,* July 8, 1876. George Custer is usually referred to as "General," the temporary rank he achieved during the Civil War. He was then reassigned the permanent rank of captain.

2. Parish records, Church of the Good Shepherd, Dedham, Mass.

3. *Gazette,* June 21, 1890, May 2, 1992, and June 6, 1897.

4. Gail Bederman, "Civilization, the Decline of Middle-Class Manliness, and Ida B. Wells's Antilynching Campaign (1892–94)," in Darlene Clark Hine, Wilma

King, and Linda Read, eds., *"We Specialize in the Wholly Impossible": A Reader in Black Women's History* (Brooklyn, N.Y.: Carlson Publishing, 1995), 408–9.

5. For background, see Elizabeth Hafkin Pleck, *Black Migration and Poverty: Boston, 1865–1900* (New York: Academic Press, 1979). A June 1890 reference in Hyde Park's newspaper is the latest evidence I have found of Bob Bond's formal education. From the 1880s to the 1920s, the town's population grew incrementally, but the number of its high school graduates increased many times over, reflecting the country's overall trend toward longer school attendance and diminution in child labor. *Gazette,* June 21, 1890, May 2, 1992, and June 6, 1897.

6. *Gazette,* August 1 and 8, 1896.

7. Ibid.

8. See esp. Gail Bederman, *Manliness and Civilization: A Cultural History of Gender and Race in the United States, 1880–1917* (Chicago: University of Chicago Press, 1995). Mildred I. Thompson, *Ida B. Wells-Barnett: An Exploratory Study of an American Black Woman, 1893–1930* (Brooklyn, N.Y.: Carlson Publishing, 1990), 197, 241–53; and Paula Giddings, *When and Where I Enter: The Impact of Black Women on Race and Sex in America* (New York: Morrow, 1984), 82.

9. Thompson, *Wells-Barnett,* 207, 239.

10. Ibid., 241.

11. Darwinist theories were also invoked to justify the privileged position of the upper classes and helped to rationalize the United States' acquisition of a non-white overseas empire. Thompson, *Wells-Barnett,* 410; and Alfreda M. Duster, ed., *Crusade for Justice: The Autobiography of Ida B. Wells* (Chicago: University of Chicago Press, 1972), 100–101.

12. Bederman, "Civilization," 420.

13. The Salem witch trials in the late seventeenth century might be compared to lynching. In that situation, British colonists in Massachusetts abused a number of marginalized residents, but at least maintained a semblance of legitimate judicial process.

14. The Monroe Doctrine, formulated in 1823, basically asserted that the United States would maintain civic order throughout the Western Hemisphere, European nations would attempt no further colonial expansion in that region, while the United States promised not to build an extrahemispheric empire itself.

15. Alexander DeConde, *Ethnicity, Race, and American Foreign Policy* (Boston: Northeastern University Press, 1992), 62.

16. Willard B. Gatewood, Jr., *Black Americans and the White Man's Burden, 1898–1903* (Urbana: University of Illinois Press, 1975), 26. Other sources acknowledge only twenty-two black sailors killed on the USS *Maine.* Nicholas H. Campbell, "The Negro in the Navy," *Colored American* (May–June 1903): 406–13. My thanks to Charles Brewer for showing me this article.

17. Bernard Nalty, *Strength for the Fight: A History of Black Americans in the Military* (New York: Free Press, 1986), 75.

18. Gatewood, *Black Americans and White Man's Burden,* 199, 220, 282.

19. Nalty, *Strength for the Fight,* 76; and George P. Marks III, ed., *The Black Press Views American Imperialism (1898–1900)* (New York: Arno Press, 1971), 62.

20. Gatewood, *Black Americans and White Man's Burden,* 63, 233, 25.

21. Ibid., 169, 301. Nonetheless, as had been the case in earlier decades, very few American Negroes opted to emigrate.

22. Archibald H. Grimké, *Open Letter to President McKinley by the Colored People of Massachusetts,* October 3, 1899.

23. Howard Zinn, *A People's History of the United States* (New York: Harper Perennial, 1995), 296.

24. Gatewood, *Black Americans and White Man's Burden,* 192, 210, 180, and generally chap. 8, "A Swell of Anti-imperialism"; and DeConde, *Ethnicity, Race, and American Foreign Policy,* 67, and generally, chap. 4, "Ethnic Transformation."

25. Willard B. Gatewood, *"Smoked Yankees" and the Struggle for Empire: Letters from Negro Soldiers, 1898–1902* (Fayetteville: University of Arkansas Press, 1976), 3–6, 14.

26. Gatewood, *Black Americans and White Man's Burden,* 83, 53, 201. After the brief war in Cuba, the U.S. Army mustered out the last black volunteers, at which point Lt. Charles Young and several chaplains were the only Negroes holding commissions. More on Young appears in chap. 13 herein.

27. Gatewood, *Black Americans and White Man's Burden,* 201–2, 243.

28. Ibid., 69–71, 107; and Nalty, *Strength for the Fight,* 71. Penn placed his life in danger to extinguish a blaze aboard the USS *Iowa.*

29. Nalty, *Strength for the Fight,* 72. See chap. 4 herein for a discussion of blacks' resistance to yellow fever in an earlier generation.

30. *Gazette,* November 5, 1898, and July 10, 1918.

31. Ibid., September 3 and October 1, 1898.

32. Ibid.

33. Most information concerning John Robert (Bob) Bond, Jr.'s service in the navy is included in the Veterans Administration files concerning his disability pension application, #1851454.

34. This ideology acquired its label and was epitomized by Rudyard Kipling's famous poem *The White Man's Burden* (1899). Gatewood, *Black Americans and White Man's Burden,* 181–86, analyzes the effects of that poem and its ideology, and responses from within the African American community.

35. Bob Bond pension application. Interviews with Robert Chesnut, July 1994.

36. Job 9:26 KJV.

37. The *Lancaster*'s eagle is on display at the Naval History Museum, Newport News, Virginia.

38. See chap. 6 herein.

39. The most renowned Perrys were the brothers Oliver and Matthew, but during the nineteenth century a number of other men who were more distant relatives also served as officers in the United States Navy. Log, USS *Lancaster,* 1898–1899, National Archives. My thanks to my colleague Ronald Spector for pointing out the endemic understaffing of navy ships at the turn of the century.

40. Muster Rolls, USS *Lancaster,* December 31, 1898, March 31 and June 30, 1899.

41. Insights into and specifics about Bob Bond's personality from interviews with Robert Chesnut (Bob Bond's lone surviving nephew) and Elaine McCraw Chesnut (widow of another nephew), summer 1994. Log, USS *Lancaster* 1898–1899, and Bob Bond pension application.

42. Jonathan H. Paynter, *Joining the Navy; or, Abroad with Uncle Sam* (Hartford, Conn.: American Publishing, 1895), 30.

43. Log, USS *Lancaster,* 1898–99. Frederick S. Harrod, *Manning the New Navy: The Development of a Modern Naval Enlisted Force, 1899–1940* (Westport, Conn.: Greenwood Press, 1978), 10.

44. Campbell, "Negro in the Navy."

45. Ibid.

46. Harrod, *Manning the New Navy,* 57.

47. Ibid.

48. James M. O'Toole, "Passing (in) the Fleet: Racial Identity and the Case of Captain Michael Healy, USRCS," unpublished paper, graciously shared by the author.

49. Harrod, *Manning the New Navy,* 57.

50. Campbell, "Negro in the Navy."

51. Ibid.

52. Ibid.

53. Ibid.

54. Harrod, *Manning the New Navy,* 55. Several African Americans had been appointed to the Naval Academy during Reconstruction but were so tormented that they left. The next blacks briefly attended the Academy in the 1920s and 1930s, but the first one graduated only in 1949. A Negro named James Taliaferro (or Tolliver) was commissioned during the Civil War. See chap. 2.

55. Harrod, *Manning the New Navy,* 10.

56. Log, USS *Lancaster,* 1898–99.

57. Ibid.

58. Harrod, *Manning the New Navy,* 57. Officially, the navy took on the appellation "The Great White Fleet" in 1907.

59. Letters between John Robert Bond, Sr., and Cmdr. Thomas Perry, January 31 and February 4, 1899, collection of the author. John Bond's letter is not

in the handwriting of his son Percy, or his daughter Lena (who was twenty-one by that time), so I assume that he penned it himself.

60. Gatewood, "*Smoked Yankees*," 237.

61. Capt. Thomas F. Jewell replaced Capt. Thomas Perry, then Capt. Charles M. Thomas replaced Jewell. Log, USS *Lancaster*, 1898–99.

62. *Report of the Surgeon-General, U.S. Navy to the Secretary of the Navy* (Washington, D.C.: Government Printing Office, 1898), 203.

63. Log, USS *Lancaster*, 1898–99.

64. James Duncan Gatewood, M.D., *Naval Hygiene* (Philadelphia: P. Blackiston's Sons, 1909), 45.

65. Bob Bond, pension application. W. Jeffrey Bolster, *Black Jacks: African American Seamen in the Age of Sail* (Cambridge: Harvard University Press, 1997), 92, explains that "tattoo" was a Polynesian word and the practice became common among sailors of all races after Captain James Cook's voyages to the South Pacific in 1770. Tattooing came to underscore their masculinity and emphasize seamen's occupational identity, independent of race.

66. Harrod, *Manning the New Navy*, 117, 197. Harrod finds no court-martials for sodomy prior to 1906, and no more than thirty-seven in any year up to World War II. See also Lawrence R. Murphy, *Perverts by Official Order: The Campaign Against Homosexuals by the United States Navy* (New York: Harrington Park Press, 1988), and Gatewood, M.D., *Naval Hygiene*, 41.

67. Log, USS *Lancaster*, 1898–1899. *Report of the Surgeon-General, U.S. Navy to the Secretary of the Navy* (Washington, D.C.: Government Printing Office, 1901), 123.

68. Log, USS *Lancaster*, 1898–1899.

69. *Report of the Surgeon-General* (1901), 170–73.

70. Gatewood, M.D., *Naval Hygiene*, 37–40.

71. Louis R. Harlan, *Booker T. Washington: The Wizard of Tuskegee, 1901–1915* (New York: Oxford University Press, 1983), 451; and James H. Jones, *Bad Blood: The Tuskegee Syphilis Experiment: A Tragedy of Race and Medicine* (New York: Free Press, 1981), 31, 45–46.

72. Theodore Rosebury, *Microbes and Morals: The Strange Story of Venereal Disease* (New York: Viking, 1971), 81.

73. Bolster, *Black Jacks*, 179; and Jones, *Bad Blood*, 71. U.S. Department of Health, Education, and Welfare, Public Health Service, *Syphilis: A Synopsis* (Washington, D.C.: Government Printing Office, 1968), provides a useful overview.

74. Randy Shilts, *Conduct Unbecoming: Lesbians and Gays in the U.S. Military, Vietnam to the Persian Gulf* (New York: St. Martin's Press, 1993), 5–6. Frederick Douglass, "Introduction," in Ida B. Wells, ed., *The Reason Why the Colored American Is Not in the World's Fair* (Chicago, 1892).

75. Roosevelt himself often characterized "Speak softly . . ." as a proverb of West African origin. He probably picked it up on one of the big-game-hunting safaris that he relished. Bederman, "Civilization," 409; and George Chauncey, Jr., *Gay New York: Gender, Urban Culture, and the Making of the Gay Male World, 1890–1940* (New York: Basic Books, 1994), 113.

76. George Chauncey, Jr., "Christian Brotherhood or Sexual Perversion? Homosexual Identities and the Construction of Sexual Boundaries in the World War I Era," 301, 310–11; and generally, Jeffrey Weeks, "Inverts, Perverts, and Mary-Annes: Male Prostitution and the Regulation of Homosexuality in England in the Nineteenth and Twentieth Centuries," both in Martin Duberman et al., eds., *Hidden from History: Reclaiming the Gay and Lesbian Past* (New York: New American Library, 1989).

77. Shilts, *Conduct Unbecoming,* 12. See also B. R. Burg, *An American Seafarer in the Age of Sail: The Erotic Diaries of Philip C. Van Buskirk, 1851–1870* (New Haven: Yale University Press, 1994).

78. The singing group is the Village People. Their other big hit, *YMCA,* carries similar implications about homosexual behavior in all-male surroundings. A character in the movie *Philadelphia,* about the gay life and AIDS, asks another: "Do you want to play sailor?"

79. Paynter, *Joining the Navy,* 30; and Pete Daniel and Raymond Smock, *A Talent for Detail: The Photographs of Miss Frances Benjamin Johnston, 1889–1910* (New York: Harmony Books, 1974), 64.

80. A few court-martials or dismissals for nonconsensual sodomy in the U.S. Navy were recorded earlier in the nineteenth century.

81. Bederman, "Civilization," 409.

82. Chauncey, *Gay New York,* 88, argues that this 1892 citation harks back to Shakespeare: "He's neither man nor woman; he's punk"; and Duberman et al., eds., *Hidden from History,* 295–304, 310. Bob Bond's nephew Robert Chesnut characterized his uncle as a "man's man."

83. Duberman et al., eds., *Hidden from History,* 313–16; and Chauncey, *Gay New York,* 144.

84. Rom. 1:27 KJV. In the Old Testament, Leviticus, which is consumed with uncleanness of all sorts, includes the similar but even more punitive passage: "If a man lies with a male as with a woman, both of them have committed an abomination; they shall be put to death" (20:13 KJV).

85. In the late nineteenth and early twentieth centuries, the navy hardly accepted black men as anything other than coal heavers, stewards, and mess boys, but then from the early 1920s through the early 1930s, no African Americans *at all* were allowed to enlist in the navy, even in the most menial positions.

86. Desertion for the navy as a whole was about fifteen percent in 1899 according to Harrod, *Manning the New Navy,* 117.

87. John Robert Bond to Cmdr. Chas. M. Thomas, July 1, 1899.

88. Duberman et al., eds., *Hidden from History,* 299. Proverbs, 17: 25 KJV.

89. Bob Bond pension application.

90. Ibid.; and Duberman et al., eds., *Hidden from History,* 199.

91. *Directory and Programme, Massachusetts Encampment, Grand Army of the Republic* (Boston, 1902), 121. See Louis R. Harlan, *Booker T. Washington: The Making of a Black Leader, 1856–1901* (New York: Oxford University Press, 1972), chap. 16. Evidently, the participants did not initially consider how much that engagement would roil the waters. This apparent naïveté was lampooned by the Mobile *Weekly Press,* December 24, 1901:

> *"Will you walk into my parlor*
> *And my guest this evening be?"*
> *'Twas the President inviting*
> *The distinguished "Booker T."*
> *"Oh, yes thanks your Excellency,*
> *I will take a tea and chat,*
> *For the world will scarcely notice*
> *While I rest my coat and hat."*

92. Robert C. Hayden, *Faith, Culture, and Leadership: A History of the Black Church in Boston* (Boston: Institute for Boston Studies, Boston College, 1985), 34–37. Hayden quotes from the autobiography of Ebenezer Baptist's founding minister, Reverend Peter Randolph. Hayden also reports that the name of the pastor from 1898 to 1907 was J. Leroy Montague, not Leroy T. Montague. Adelaide M. Cromwell, *The Other Brahmins: Boston's Black Upper Class, 1750–1950* (Fayetteville: University of Arkansas Press, 1994); and Willard B. Gatewood, *Aristocrats of Color: The Black Elite, 1880–1920* (Bloomington: Indiana University Press, 1990), discuss the import of religious affiliation to class status.

93. Hyde Park *Gazette* (the local paper changed its name in 1899), January 4, 1902.

94. *Gazette,* November 1, 1902.

95. Jones, *Bad Blood,* 38. Bob Bond's pension application provides evidence of his syphilis, the time of its inception, and states that he was only treated around 1915. Further discussion appear and details appear in chap. 17. My thanks to Dr. C. Carnot Evans and Dr. Vanessa Northington Gamble for their insights, critiques, and information about syphilis.

96. Elizabeth Bond birth certificate.

10. IN EMMA'S FOOTSTEPS

1. Information about Emma Thomas Bond's knowledge of herbal medicine comes from conversations with Elaine McCraw Chesnut, widow of Emma's grandson. Special thanks to my sharp-eyed daughter Elizabeth Alexander, who spotted an obscure mention that Dr. Rebecca Lee Crumpler lived for several years in Hyde Park.

2. Rebecca (Davis) Crumpler, Record of Death, Commonwealth of Massachusetts, March 9, 1895. My sincere thanks to Dr. Vanessa Northington Gamble for sharing this document.

3. *Sixteenth Annual Catalogue and Report of the New England Female Medical College* (Boston, 1864). Although this is titled the sixteenth catalogue, the first class graduated in 1854, and the school only established itself under that name in 1857. Dr. Gamble also provided me with information about Rebecca's first marriage to Mr. Lee from her death certificate.

4. *Catalogue, New England Female Medical College.* Faculty minutes, New England Female Medical College, 1864.

5. "Rebecca Lee Crumpler," in Darlene Clark Hine, ed., *Black Women in America, An Historical Encyclopedia* (Brooklyn, N.Y.: Carlson Publishing, 1993), 290–91; and Rebecca Crumpler, M.D., *A Book of Medical Discourses in Two Parts* (Boston: Cashman, Keating, 1883), 2.

6. Crumpler, *Medical Discourses,* 88.

7. Ibid.; and Boston *Sunday Globe,* July 22, 1894.

8. Crumpler, *Medical Discourses,* 4, 79. Many medical texts of the period were, indeed, directed to other physicians, but a tradition of primers for women's home medical care also appeared. Among those treatises were Fleetwood Churchill, *On the Diseases of Women, Including Those of Pregnancy and Childbirth* (Philadelphia: Blanchard & Lea, 1857); A. M. Mauriceau, *The Married Woman's Medical Compendium* (New York: A. M. Mauriceau, 1855); and Mrs. W. H. Maxwell, *A Female Physician to the Ladies of the United States* (New York, 1860). The idea that there was a "proper" and specially ordained sphere of concentration appropriate to female physicians was one shared by many of those women themselves. A discussion of this phenomenon appears in Regina Morantz, C. S. Pomerleau, and C. H. Fenichel, *In Her Own Words* (New Haven: Yale University Press, 1982).

9. Elaine McCraw Chesnut told me about Emma Thomas Bond's use of medicinal herbs. *Globe,* July 22, 1894.

10. The preferred nineteenth-century use of "botanical" can be roughly equated to the word "pharmaceutical." I have no hard evidence that Rebecca Crumpler served as Emma Bond's obstetrician, but given their common roots, interests, and residential proximity from 1880 to 1886, it is difficult to believe otherwise. The 1880 census shows "keeping house" as Rebecca Crumpler's occupation

(a census enumerator would never have seen, or known what to make of, a "colored" female physician), but Hyde Park's directories indicate that she did indeed practice medicine in that town during the early 1880s. In 1905, Frank Whiting testified as to his presence at the 1865 Norfolk marriage of John and Emma Bond, confirming the Whiting family's Boston residence.

11. Crumpler, *Medical Discourses,* 10, 11.

12. Ibid., 15–18, 96. And see, for example, Megan Seaholm, "Midwives," in Hine, ed., *Black Women in America*; Martia Graham Goodson, "Medical-Botanical Contributions of African Slave Women to American Medicine," *Western Journal of Black Studies* 11, no. 4 (1987); Beatrice Mongeau, Harvey L. Smith, and Ann C. Maney, "The 'Granny' Midwife: Changing Roles and Functions of a Folk Practitioner," *American Journal of Sociology,* March 1961; and S. A. Robinson, "A Historical Development of Midwifery in the Black Community: 1600–1940," in *Journal of Nurse-Midwifery* 29 (1984).

13. Crumpler, *Medical Discourses,* 21–32, 44, 100.

14. Ibid., 42, 3, 83.

15. Ibid., 93, 92, 97.

16. Ibid., 125, 134, 137, 142–43.

17. Ibid., 144.

18. Ibid., 58, 114.

19. Ibid., 87, 106; and *Globe,* July 22, 1894.

20. Crumpler, *Medical Discourses,* 111, 122.

21. Ibid., 116, 115, 119, 134.

22. Ibid., 112.

23. Ibid., 118.

24. Norfolk County *Gazette,* September 3, 1893, and July 2, 1898, reported drowning deaths in Mother Brook. Peterson Files, Hyde Park Public Library, acknowledge forty-nine local deaths by drowning in Mother Brook and the Neponset by 1897.

25. *Memorial Studies: The First Twenty Years of Hyde Park, Massachusetts* (Boston: L. Banta, 1888), 25.

26. Genesis 7:18, 8:7 KJV. According to the Hyde Park directory, the Crumplers left there in 1886. Whether the flood was the final determinant is uncertain. Dr. Rebecca Crumpler's home on Joy Street in Boston has been marked on the African American Freedom Trail, and indicates that she lived there prior to her sojourn in Virginia in the early 1870s. For "Nigger Hill," see Adelaide M. Cromwell, *The Other Brahmins: Boston's Black Upper Class, 1750–1950* (Fayetteville: University of Arkansas Press, 1994), 27.

27. *Gazette,* May 2, 1885, April 3, 1886, and December 7, 1889.

28. *Colored American,* August 1907, reprinting clippings from the Boston *Herald, Journal,* and *Courant,* February 1891.

29. Ibid.

30. *Gazette,* March 5, 1892. James and his wife Virginia Isaacs Trotter are buried in Hyde Park's Fairview Cemetery.

31. Cromwell, *Other Brahmins,* 63.

32. Bob Chesnut, conversations with author, July 1994. Several of Hyde Park's directories indicate that John R. Bond sold produce.

33. *Dedham Church of the Good Shepherd,* also Good Shepherd Parish Records.

34. The *Hub,* December 6, 1883; and Crumpler, *Medical Discourses,* 111, 122.

35. Chesnut conversations.

36. Ibid. "In Colored Society," Boston *Sunday Globe,* July 22, 1894, stated: "In one of the largest stores there are no less than three colored clerks."

37. *Gazette,* September 4, 1894, April 8, and July 9, 1898.

38. *Colored American,* June 1901; and Hine, ed., *Black Women in America,* 284.

39. Crumpler, *Medical Discourses,* 131.

40. Poem to Theodore D. Weld, "On His 90th Birthday," by Angelina Weld Grimké, *Gazette,* November 22, 1893. Gloria T. Hull, *Color, Sex, and Poetry: Three Women Writers of the Harlem Renaissance* (Bloomington: Indiana University Press, 1987), 111.

41. Washington quote provided by Boston's Museum of Afro-American History.

42. *Gazette,* June 4, 1898.

43. *Grand Army of the Republic, Proceedings of the Encampment, Department of Massachusetts,* 1900–1906.

44. *Proceedings of the Encampment,* 1903.

45. Ibid.

46. Ibid. A few years later, Mayor Fitzgerald, grandfather of President John Fitzgerald Kennedy, became known as "Honey Fitz."

47. Cromwell, *Other Brahmins,* 31.

48. Joseph A. Walker, Jr., *Black Square and Compass: 200 Years of Prince Hall Freemasonry* (n.p., 1979), 21, 56; and Sidney and Emma Nogrady Kaplan, *The Black Experience in the Era of the American Revolution* (Amherst: University of Massachusetts Press, 1989), 202–12.

49. Ibid., 90, 132, 136. Also, *We Fight for Freedom: Massachusetts, African Americans, and the Civil War* (Boston: Massachusetts Historical Society, 1993), 29; and *Proceedings of the Most Worshipful Prince Hall Grand Lodge, Free and Accepted Masons of Massachusetts,* 1898, 11.

50. *Proceedings,* Prince Hall Masons, 1898, 13, 26. I have not found in the U.S. Census any black person in Hyde Park named Brooks. However, the 1890 census is missing, and Brooks could have lived there for as long as from 1881 to 1899.

51. Charles H. Brooks, *The Official History and Manual of the Grand United Order of Odd Fellows in America* (1902; reprint, Freeport, N.Y.: Books for Libraries, 1971), 36, 126.

52. Dickson D. Bruce, Jr., *Archibald Grimké: Portrait of a Black Independent* (Baton Rouge: Louisiana State University Press, 1993), chap. 7.

53. U.S. Census, Norfolk County, 1900.

54. *Gazette,* August 22 and 29, 1896.

55. U.S. Census, Norfolk County, 1900.

56. Ibid. Elizabeth Hafkin Pleck, *Black Migration and Poverty: Boston, 1865–1900* (New York: Academic Press, 1979), chap. 3.

57. Walter J. Stevens, *Chip on My Shoulder* (Boston: Meador Press, 1946), 129–30.

58. Ellen Craft Dammond, Maude Trotter Craft's daughter, shared this Hyde Park story.

59. Bruce, *Archibald Grimké,* 101–3.

60. David Levering Lewis, *W. E. B. Du Bois: Biography of a Race* (New York: Henry Holt, 1993), 299–301; and Louis R. Harlan, *Booker T. Washington: The Wizard of Tuskegee, 1901–1915* (New York: Oxford University Press, 1983), 44–47.

61. Bruce, *Archibald Grimké,* 103.

62. Harlan, *Booker T. Washington,* 51.

63. W. E. Burghardt Du Bois, *Dusk of Dawn: An Essay Toward an Autobiography of a Race Concept* (New York: Harcourt, Brace, 1940), 76.

64. Dr. LaSalle D. Leffall provided information about the symptoms and treatment of rectal cancer. Homeopathy appealed to many sufferers because it advocated gentler treatments than did the harsher "heroic" medicine prevalent at the time. Frank Rich Scrapbook #4, Hyde Park Public Library, documents Sturtevant's navy duty. Thanks to Mary E. Pitts for her further information about Sturtevant. Elaine McCraw Chesnut remembered that John Bond's daughters walked with him during his final illness, and his pension records substantiate his attendance by Sturtevant. Mary (Tooty) Bond's academic records from Hyde Park High School.

65. *Gazette,* January 2, 1897.

66. Ibid., June 14, 1905. Cornelius Weeden, John Bond's good friend and fellow veteran, died in 1896.

67. Stuart McConnell, *Glorious Contentment: The Grand Army of the Republic, 1865–1900* (Chapel Hill: University of North Carolina Press, 1992), 153. Lisa Y. King's unpublished paper "Black Sailors' Blues: A Few Sketches in the Lives of African-American Union Sailors in the Post-Civil War Era" includes an excellent description of how the widows of black Civil War seamen did, or did not, obtain their late husbands' pensions.

68. John Robert Bond Navy Pension Records, U.S. Census, Norfolk County, 1900, and Hyde Park Directories, 1900–1910. Cromwell, *Other Brahmins,* 53.

69. Ps. 128:3 KJV.

70. "Tribute to Sons of Civil War Was Unveiled in 1911," in *Memory Lane,* January 21, 1937. This section was a supplement to an unidentified newspaper, and commemorated the twenty-fifth anniversary of Boston's annexation of Hyde Park. David Blight, "The Origins of Memorial Day and Historical Memory," unpublished paper.

11. ALABAMA TRILOGY

1. *Annual Catalogues, The Tuskegee Normal and Industrial Institute* (Tuskegee, Ala.: Tuskegee Institute Press, 1903–1906), 1902–3, 11.

2. Ibid.; and W. E. Burghardt Du Bois, *Dusk of Dawn: An Essay Toward an Autobiography of a Race Concept* (New York: Harcourt, Brace, 1940), 76.

3. Tuskegee Catalogues, 1902–3, 20, 21, 136; 1904–5, 10, 22, and "Minutes of Tuskegee Normal and Industrial Institute Executive Committee, 1900–1903," May and November 1902, Archives, Tuskegee Institute.

4. Roscoe C. Bruce to Clara Burrill, February 2, 1903, Box 10-1, Roscoe C. Bruce Papers, Moorland Spingarn Research Center, Howard University.

5. Ibid., n.d.

6. Burrill to Bruce, March 3, 1903, 10-1, Bruce Papers. Even with the help of archivists at the Congregational Church history center I have not been able to find any publication called *Congregational Week,* so this article has proved unretrievable.

7. *Tuskegee Student,* August 7, 1904. My thanks to J. Percy Bond III for sharing this photograph of our grandfather.

8. Josephine Bruce to Booker T. Washington, April 2, 1902, Reel 191; and Jane Clark to Booker T. Washington, April 24, 1902, Reel 194, Booker T. Washington Papers, Library of Congress.

9. For a thorough examination of Washington's personal as well as public life, see Louis R. Harlan, *Booker T. Washington: The Making of a Black Leader, 1856–1901* (New York: Oxford University Press, 1972); and *Booker T. Washington: The Wizard of Tuskegee, 1901–1915* (New York: Oxford University Press, 1983). A number of people at Tuskegee told me about such rumors concerning Adella Hunt Logan, my paternal grandmother.

10. Tuskegee, *Twenty-second Annual Catalogue,* 1902–3, 9; and *Twenty-fifth Annual Catalogue,* 1904–5, 22, 82, 88.

11. Noted from Wenonah Bond Logan.

12. The Tuskegee Woman's Club did sponsor spin-off female groups comprised of students, ministers' wives, and town women.

13. Adella and Warren Logan's youngest son was later named Arthur Courtney Logan for Boston's Dr. Samuel Courtney. Allison Davis, *Leadership, Love, and Aggression* (New York: Harcourt, Brace, Jovanovich, 1983), 3. Davis details his own father's veneration of Theodore Roosevelt and his emulation of Roosevelt's ideologies and physical persona. Warren Logan also may have deliberately nurtured his inherent resemblance to the president.

14. See Adele Logan Alexander, *Ambiguous Lives: Free Women of Color in Rural Georgia, 1789–1879* (Fayetteville: University of Arkansas Press, 1991). Mrs. Warren Logan, in D. W. Culp, ed., *Twentieth Century Negro Literature; or, A Cyclopedia of Thought on the Vital Topics Relating to the American Negro* (Atlanta: J. L. Nichols, 1902).

15. The Logans, like the Bonds, are my own family. Much of my information about them and Tuskegee has been gleaned from years of informal and unrecorded conversations.

16. Information about Logan and her woman suffrage activities appears in Adele Logan Alexander, "Adella Hunt Logan and the Tuskegee Woman's Club: Building a Foundation for Suffrage," in Mary Martha Thomas, ed., *Stepping Out of the Shadows: Alabama Women, 1819–1990* (Tuscaloosa: University of Alabama Press, 1995), 96–113; and Alexander, "Adella Hunt Logan, The Tuskegee Woman's Club, and African Americans in the Suffrage Movement," in Marjorie Spruill Wheeler, ed., *Votes for Women! The Woman Suffrage Movement in Tennessee, the South, and the Nation* (Knoxville: University of Tennessee Press, 1995), 71–104.

17. Adella Hunt Logan to Emily Howland, 1899, Emily Howland Papers, Cornell University.

18. *Tuskegee Student*, June 6, 1903, and January 30, 1904.

19. Ibid., May 21, 1904, and February 18, 1905; and Tuskegee Woman's Club Notes, 1904–7, Tuskegee Institute Archives.

20. According to NAWSA Annual Reports, the second Alabama woman to become a life member only did so a decade later.

21. Alexander, "Adella Hunt Logan" (in both Thomas and Wheeler). The most authoritative source concerning this overall topic is Rosalyn Terborg-Penn, *African American Women in the Struggle for the Vote, 1850–1920* (Bloomington: Indiana University Press, 1998).

22. Logan to Howland, December 1, 1901.

23. Notes from Wenonah Bond Logan. See Adele Logan Alexander, "How I Discovered My Grandmother, and the Truth about Black Woman and the Suffrage Movement," *Ms.*, November 1983: 29–33.

24. Adella Hunt Logan, "Woman Suffrage," *Colored American*, September 1905; and Alexander, "Adella Hunt Logan."

25. Alexander, "Adella Hunt Logan," in Wheeler, 80. Booker T. Washington, ed., *Tuskegee and Its People* (New York: Appleton, 1905), 68. My mother, Wenonah Bond Logan, told me that my two grandmothers, Georgia Stewart Bond and Adella Hunt Logan, attended woman suffrage meetings together.

26. *Tuskegee Student,* January 30, 1904.

27. Ibid.

28. An apocryphal anecdote related by my Logan relatives.

29. Linda O. McMurry, *George Washington Carver: Scientist and Symbol* (New York: Oxford University Press, 1981), 95. As late as the 1980s, old-timers at Tuskegee sometimes covertly referred to the rumors about Carver's sexuality.

30. Ibid., 131. See also Kenneth R. Manning, "Race, Science, and Identity," in Gerald Early, ed., *Lure and Loathing: Essays on Race, Identity, and the Ambivalence of Assimilation* (New York: Penguin Press, 1992). Manning convincingly argues that George Washington Carver was acceptable to whites because he "espoused the traits of humility, diligence, and manual dexterity that whites appreciated in blacks," and that Carver's work was lauded because it was "inventive, rather than scientifically creative; product-oriented, rather than pressing to new theoretical heights; and carried out in the black community with few if any intrusions into the white."

31. McMurry, *George Washington Carver,* chap. 2, "Trouble on the 'Tuskegee Plantation.' "

32. Ibid., 121.

33. Ibid., 48.

34. Conversations with Rowena Hunt Bracken, 1990. Members of the Logan and Bond families have offered this explanation.

35. William Warren Rogers et al., *Alabama: The History of a Deep South State* (Tuscaloosa: University of Alabama Press, 1994), 345.

36. I assume that J. Percy Bond, my maternal grandfather, voted in Tuskegee, Alabama, once he qualified to do so in 1904. I know that Warren Logan, my paternal grandfather did. I have a copy of the receipt he received when he paid his poll tax in 1903.

37. Werner Sollors, Caldwell Titcomb, and Thomas A. Underwood, *Blacks at Harvard: A Documentary History of African-American Experience at Harvard* (New York: New York University Press, 1993), 123. The disrespectful reference to "Dr. Dubious" is a Logan family story from Tuskegee. J. Percy Bond to Archibald Grimké, July 1, 1904, Grimké Papers, Moorland Spingarn Research Center, Howard University.

38. Notes from Wenonah Bond Logan. No corroborating information in Tuskegee's records confirms this Cotton Valley story.

39. Washington's daughter had attended Wellesley College, where Emmett Scott's daughter went a decade later. Roscoe Bruce had graduated from Harvard,

and Ruth Logan would soon head off to Oberlin's preparatory school in Ohio. *Tuskegee Student,* June 3, 1905. In an August 1996 interview, Dorothy Height stated that during a mentoring session in 1939, Caroline Stewart Bond Day, in her "broad Boston accent," explained that it was important for the novice Ms. Height to realize that she would have to deal with both the "clahsses" and the "mahsses" in Washington, D.C.'s African American community. Karl Lindholm, "William Clarence Matthews," *Harvard Magazine,* September–October 1998, 58–59.

40. Personal papers, Wenonah Bond Logan.

41. The bonbon dish is in the possession of Elizabeth Alexander.

42. No documentation exists as to whether there was any formal adoption, but certainly Carrie Stewart Bond always thought of Percy Bond as her father.

43. Larry Ragan, *True Tales of Birmingham* (Birmingham, Ala.: Birmingham Historical Society, 1993), 24; and Marvin Y. Whiting, "Landmark: Giuseppe Moretti," *Journal of the Birmingham Historical Society* 9, no. 1 (December 1985).

44. Carl V. Harris, *Political Power in Birmingham, 1871–1921* (Knoxville: University of Tennessee Press, 1977), 12, 25, 32.

45. *The Other Side: The Story of Birmingham's Black Community;* and Rev. A. D. Mayo, *The Negro Citizen in the New American Life* (n. p., 1890), 11.

46. Harris, *Political Power in Birmingham,* 35; and J. Mason Davis, conversation with author, February 1996. Will Battle, retired Ensley steel plant worker, in *Birmingfind* Calendar, 1985.

47. Harris, *Political Power in Birmingham,* 221–22.

48. Henry M. McKiven, Jr., *Iron and Steel: Class, Race, and Community in Birmingham, Alabama, 1875–1920* (Chapel Hill: University of North Carolina Press, 1995), 2, 19, 41, 171; and Davis interview.

49. *Other Side;* and *Colored American,* October 1907 and February 1908.

50. Ragan, *True Tales,* 27; and McKiven, *Iron and Steel,* 48–49, 120, 121. The original Alabama Penny Savings Bank was located next door to Bond & Co. Its better-known building constructed by Windham Brothers at 310 North Eighteenth Street, in the next block, was completed in 1913.

51. *The Survey: A Journal of Constructive Philanthropy* 27, no. 14 (January 1912).

52. Ragan, *True Tales,* 57; and Harris, *Political Power in Birmingham,* 31. Historian Leon Litwack argues that Birmingham's streetcars were segregated, with black people forced to sit in the *front.* Nonetheless, my Alabama sources all talk of riding in the back, as was the case in other jurisdictions.

53. Birmingham, City Directories, 1907–1912. J. Percy Bond's advertising postcards in the possession of the author.

54. Birmingham *Age-Herald,* June 18, 1913; and *Other Side.*

55. *Other Side;* and Davis interview.

56. Ragan, *True Tales*, 30, 50; Birmingham *Age-Herald*, June 18, 1913; Marjorie Longenecker White, "Images of Smithfield," *Journal of the Birmingham Historical Society* 9, no. 1 (December 1985); *Colored American*, May 1908; and Charles A. Brown, "W. A. Rayfield: Pioneer Black Architect of Birmingham, Ala." (Birmingham: Gray Printing Co., n.d.).

57. White, "Images of Smithfield"; Brown, "W. A. Rayfield," *Crisis*, May 1913; and Mary Martha Thomas, *The New Woman in Alabama: Social Reforms and Suffrage, 1890–1920* (Tuscaloosa: University of Alabama Press, 1992), 137.

58. Terborg-Penn, *African-American Women in the Struggle for the Vote*, details these women's involvement in the woman suffrage movement. Nonetheless, much of the Negro community remained disinterested. McKiven, *Iron and Steel*, 142.

59. Box 21, Folder 5, Herndon Papers, the Herndon Home, Atlanta, Georgia. A lead character in Herndon's 1905 play was Wah-no-nah, identified as an "Indian Girl." Carrie Bond would also have been familiar with Pauline Hopkins's historical romance, *Winona: A Tale of Negro Life in the South and Southwest*, serialized in the *Colored American* in 1902.

60. Photo of Carrie and Wenonah Bond in the collection of the author. Georgia may not have gone on that journey to Hyde Park. According to Lena Bond Chesnut's daughter-in-law, Lena did not recall ever meeting her niece, Wenonah.

61. My thanks to Ruth Bond, Jack Bond's widow, for sharing this story.

62. *Crisis*, April 1915.

63. McKiven, *Iron and Steel*, 146.

64. *Colored American*, September 1907.

65. Parish records from St. Mark's Episcopal Church. My sincere thanks to Bertrand Perry for sharing these. Rev. Charles W. Brooks to Caroline Bond Day, April 26, 1930, Box 1, Caroline Bond Day Papers, Peabody Museum, Harvard University. Davis interview; Barbara Smith, "St. Mark's Academic and Industrial School, 1892–1940," 1976, unpublished paper; and Sadie E. Beach De Vigne, "St. Mark's School, Birmingham, Alabama," *Colored American*, May 1907.

66. Told to the author July 1995 by Bertrand Perry, whose father was a pastor of St. Mark's Episcopal Church.

67. National Negro Business League, Annual Convention Proceedings, 1907–1912.

68. Birmingham *Age-Herald*, June 18, 1913.

69. NNBL Convention Proceedings, 1910, 24–25.

70. Ibid., 105.

71. Alston Fitts III to the author, April 8, 1996.

72. NNBL Convention Proceedings, 1910, 187. After he left the presidency, Theodore Roosevelt was often called "Colonel," dating back to his rank in the Spanish-American War.

73. Ibid. They were business*men*. The first significant involvement of a woman was that of Madam C. J. Walker in 1912. She made a fortune with her line of hair-care products for black women, plus her schools that trained operators to use them.

74. NNBL Convention Proceedings, 1910, 187.

75. Ibid., 193.

76. Harris, *Political Power in Birmingham,* 172.

77. Ibid., 229. Fitts to the author, October 27, 1997.

78. See Alston Fitts III, *Selma: Queen City of the Black Belt* (Selma, Ala.: Clairmont Press, 1989).

79. Fitts to the author, January 29, 1996. Notes from Wenonah Bond Logan.

80. Fitts, *Selma,* 77–80.

81. Fitts to author, October 27, 1997.

82. Ibid.

83. Notes from Wenonah Bond Logan. Selma City Directories, 1914 and 1920, show a Melton family, mentioned by Wenonah Bond Logan, living in the next block to the Bonds on Washington Street.

84. I don't know exactly when my grandmother, Georgia Stewart, painted her teacups and made her quilts, but in my early childhood, I was told that they were "very old." Georgia's foster grandson Bernard Day also remembers her quilting and crocheting.

85. Conversations with and notes from Logan. *Colored Alabamian,* April 10, 1998.

86. Selma City Directories, 1914, 1920; and Selma *Journal,* July 15, 1914.

87. Notes from Logan; and Fitts to the author, October 27, 1997.

88. Fitts to the author, February 20, 1996, and October 27, 1997; and Selma *Times,* September 4, 1900.

89. Rom. 12:11 KJV; and Selma *Advocate,* May 22, 1915.

90. My thanks to Kate Gamble, daughter-in-law of St. Paul's minister at that time, for her comments and insights, May 1997.

91. "A Brief History of St. Paul's Church."

92. Conversation with Kate Gamble, May 1997, and *Alexander's Magazine,* October 1907, 300. *Colored American,* September 1907.

93. Notes from Wenonah Bond Logan; and Kate Gamble, conversation with author. Mrs. Gamble recalled no black families who belonged to St. Paul's from the time when she joined in 1935 until 1965, amid the Civil Rights struggles, when the bishop of Alabama insisted that the church admit them for services. Even now, the church attracts Selma's white upper class and includes only one black family among its parishioners. Fitts to the author, October 27, 1997.

94. My gratitude to Alston Fitts III, who found an acknowledgment of J. Percy Bond's poll tax payment and other details about the Bonds in Selma. Kate

Gamble believes that it would be totally in character for Rev. Edward Gamble to sponsor Percy Bond as a voter and cannot imagine any other white man in Selma who would have done so at that time.

95. Rogers et al., *Alabama*, 347; and Fitts, *Selma*, 98, 101. "Grandfathering" meant that if a man's father or grandfather had been a voter prior to the Civil War, he might automatically qualify. Naturally, that loophole excluded black people. The Supreme Court heard the case of *Giles v. Harris* in 1903, but upheld an Alabama court's ruling that the new laws concerning suffrage raised political and not constitutional questions.

96. Ray Stannard Baker, *Following the Color Line: American Negro Citizenship in the Progressive Era* (New York: Doubleday, Page, 1908), 242.

97. Selma *Advocate*, May 22, 1915.

98. Selma *Journal*, November 16, 1915, and October 12, 1914. Paul Adomites, *October's Game* (Alexandria, Va.: Redefinition, 1990), 42–43, 60.

99. Selma *Journal*, July 5, 12, and 15, 1915.

100. Notes from Wenonah Bond Logan. Baker, *Following the Color Line*, 64.

101. C. C. Grayson, *Yesterday and Today: Memories of Selma and Its People* (New Orleans: Pelican Press, 1948), 133.

102. *Colored Alabamian*, April 10, 1915; Fitts, *Selma*, 114; and Fitts to the author, October 27, 1997.

103. Some of the information here is speculative and based on Tuskegee rumor and gossip. Certainly, the Logans were having marital difficulties and Adella was mentally unstable. Certainly, there was a fire at Warren Logan's office, and certainly a family meeting convened immediately thereafter, after which Adella was sent off to the Kellogg Clinic in Michigan. I cannot prove definitively that she set the fire, but strongly believe that was the case. Material in the author's possession.

104. Accounts of Adella Hunt Logan's death compiled from family stories and conversations with elderly Tuskegeeans, 1990.

105. Story told the author by several Tuskegee sources in 1990.

106. Unfortunately, I lost the newspaper clipping with the reference to this eulogy.

107. *Crisis*, August 1917, reported that a white Selma policeman who had murdered a black man "was imprisoned for one second and immediately released."

108. Fitts, *Selma*, 107–8; and Fitts to the author, April 8, 1996.

109. Notes from Wenonah Bond Logan. Len Cooper, "The Damned," *Washington Post*, June 16, 1996; and Pete Daniel, *The Shadow of Slavery: Peonage in the South, 1901–1969* (Champaign, Ill.: University of Illinois Press, 1990). Fitts to the author, April 8, 1996.

110. Notes from Wenonah Bond Logan.

111. Fitts, *Selma*, 93; and Fitts to the author, April 8, 1996, and October 27, 1997.

112. I have not found any documentation pinpointing Caroline Fagain's death, but a picture shows her in Selma around 1913, and the *Colored Alabamian* mentions her visit to the Bonds in April 1915, when she was apparently quite ill. There is no record of her visiting the Bonds in Washington, or of them visiting her after that time. She does not appear in the 1920 Alabama census.

113. Baker, *Following the Color Line,* 112.

12. CARRIE: THEORIES OF EVOLUTION

1. *Annual Catalogue, The Tuskegee Normal and Industrial Institute, 1902–1903* (Tuskegee, Ala.: Tuskegee Institute Press, 1903), 19, 20, 136.

2. *Tuskegee Student,* July 4, 1903.

3. Ibid., December 26, 1903.

4. Caroline Bond Day, "What Shall We Play?" *Crisis,* September 1925, 220–22; and *Tuskegee Student,* June 3, 1905.

5. *Tuskegee Student,* June 17, 1905.

6. At the time of its founding in the late 1860s, Atlanta University's faculty members were all white, with the first African American teachers joining them around 1880. After Reconstruction, the interracial campus life often aggravated state officials, who withdrew the university's governmental funding and threatened to close it down. And see Hubert B. Ross, "Caroline Bond Day: Pioneer Black Female Anthropologist," unpublished paper presented to the American Anthropological Association, November 1983.

7. *Catalogue of the Officers and Students of Atlanta University,* 1905–1906, 27, and 1906–1907, 22.

8. Phillips Verner Bradford and Harvey Blume, *Ota Benga: The Pygmy in the Zoo* (New York: St. Martin's Press, 1992), 259–60. See also Lee Baker and Thomas C. Patterson, eds., *Race, Racism, and the History of U. S. Anthropology,* a special issue of *Transforming Anthropology* 5, nos. 1 and 2 (1994).

9. St. Clair Drake, "Anthropology and the Black Experience," *Black Scholar* 11, no. 7 (Fall 1980): 2–31. J. H. Van Evrie, possibly "the father of racism in the United States," published *White Supremacy and Negro Subordination* in 1868. He was followed, among others, by Daniel G. Brinton, *The Basis of Social Relations: A Study in Ethnic Psychology* (New York: Putnam, 1902); and Robert Lowie, "The Inferior Races from an Anthropologist's Point of View," *New Review,* December 1913. See also Faye V. Harrison, "The Du Boisian Legacy in Anthropology," *Critique of Anthropology, Sage,* 12, no. 3 (1992): 239–60.

10. Desley Deacon, *Elsie Clews Parsons: Inventing Modern Life* (Chicago: University of Chicago Press, 1997), 97. Also see William Stanton, *The Leopard's Spots: Scientific Attitudes toward Race in America, 1815–59* (Chicago: University

of Chicago Press, 1960). Stanton discusses the earlier, very different "American School" of anthropology and ethnology that arose in the mid-nineteenth century led by Josiah Clark Nott of Alabama. Nott and his followers argued that "the races had separate origins and constituted separate species," and as such, any racial "cross-breeding" (as between a horse and an ass) should result in sterile, hybrid offspring, 65, 152.

11. Drake, "Anthropology and the Black Experience."

12. Ibid.

13. See esp. Arnold Taylor, *Travail and Triumph: Black Life and Culture in the South since the Civil War* (Westport, Conn.: Greenwood Press, 1976), 44–46; and generally, Ray Stannard Baker, *Following the Color Line: American Negro Citizenship in the Progressive Era* (New York: Doubleday, Page, 1908).

14. Atlanta Baptist College soon would be renamed Morehouse. Jacqueline Anne Rouse, *Lugenia Burns Hope: Black Southern Reformer* (Athens: University of Georgia Press, 1989), 43; and Alexa Benson Henderson, *Atlanta Life Insurance Company: Guardian of Black Economic Dignity* (Tuscaloosa: University of Alabama Press, 1990), 24. Taylor, *Travail and Triumph,* 45–46.

15. W. E. B. Du Bois, *Darkwater: Voices from Within the Veil* (1920; reprint, New York: Schocken Books, 1969), 26; Darlene Clark Hine, ed., *Black Women in America* (Brooklyn, N.Y.: Carlson Publishing, 1993), 596; Lorraine Elena Roses and Ruth Elizabeth Randolph, *Harlem Renaissance and Beyond: Literary Biographies of 100 Black Women Writers, 1900–1945* (Cambridge: Harvard University Press, 1990), 177–78; Rouse, *Lugenia Burns Hope,* 44; and Henderson, *Atlanta Life Insurance Company,* 29.

16. Clarence A. Bacote, *The Story of Atlanta University: A Century of Service, 1865–1965* (Atlanta: Atlanta University, 1969), 129.

17. Ibid., 249.

18. Ibid. The first African American Radcliffe graduate was Alberta V. Scott, class of 1898.

19. Caroline Stewart Bond's Atlanta University transcript from Radcliffe Archives.

20. Caroline Bond Day's rheumatic condition confirmed by many conversations with her sister, Wenonah Bond Logan, and her foster son, Bernard Day, June 1996. See also Caroline Bond Day, *A Study of Some Negro-White Families in the United States* (Cambridge: Harvard University, Peabody Museum, 1932).

21. *Who's Who in Colored America: A Biographical Dictionary of Notable Living Persons of Negro Descent in America* (New York: Who's Who in Colored America Corp., 1927).

22. *The Scroll,* March and April 1910. Similar relationships are documented in Carroll Smith-Rosenberg, *Disorderly Conduct: Visions of Gender in Victorian America* (New York: Oxford University Press, 1985).

23. Logan, conversations with author.

24. Photograph in the collection of Elizabeth Alexander.

25. "Alabama State University Through the Years," from that university's archives. Patricia Ann Palmieri, *In Adamless Eden: The Community of Women Faculty at Wellesley* (New Haven: Yale University Press, 1995), provides a good analytical framework for examining the lives of female academics in this period. The situation, however, differed in many ways for black women.

26. Hortense Tate, conversations with author, May and June 1997. Mrs. Tate became director of that same YWCA in the 1920s. Adrienne Lash Jones, who is writing a history of African American women in the YWCA, confirmed Tate's version of the Montclair branch's origins. Washington, D.C.'s Phillis Wheatley branch also was autonomous. Lorraine Nelson Spritzer and Jean B. Bergmark, *Grace Towns Hamilton and the Politics of Southern Change* (Athens: University of Georgia Press, 1997), 48.

27. Folder 2, Box 42a, YWCA Papers, Sophia Smith Collection, Smith College.

28. The name "Hooey" is alternately spelled without the *y*. "Testimonial Dinner Honoring Mrs. Alice Hooe Foster, November 18th, 1937"; "Afro-Americans in Montclair, New Jersey," and "Washington Street Branch," MSS, from the Montclair Historical Society; and Tate interviews.

29. "Our Town and the Old Townsmen of Montclair," MS, 1952, Montclair Historical Society; Henry Whittemore, *History of Montclair Township* (New York: Suburban Publishing, 1894), 105; and *Colored American,* May 1908, 258.

30. Folder 2, Box 42A, YWCA Papers; Caroline Bond Day to Alice Dunbar Nelson, April 27, 1927, Caroline Bond Day Papers, Peabody Museum, Harvard University. Dorothy Schneider and Carl I. Schneider, *Into the Breach: American Women Overseas in World War I* (New York: Viking, 1991), 170. Tate interview. See also Gloria T. Hull, ed., *Give Us Each Day: The Diary of Alice Dunbar-Nelson* (New York: Norton, 1984); and Gloria T. Hull, *Color, Sex, and Poetry: Three Women Writers of the Harlem Renaissance* (Bloomington: Indiana University Press, 1987). *Crisis* magazine made several references to the NAACP branch in Montclair, but the NAACP papers at the Library of Congress do not have lists of membership as far back as 1916.

31. See esp. Smith-Rosenberg, *Disorderly Conduct;* Lillian Faderman, *Surpassing the Love of Men: Romantic Friendship and Love Between Women from the Renaissance to the Present* (New York: Morrow, 1981); Martha Vicinus, *Independent Women: Work and Community for Single Women, 1850–1920* (Chicago: University of Chicago Press, 1985); and Kathryn Kish Sklar, "Hull House in the 1890s: Community of Women Reformers," *Signs,* Summer 1985, 659–77.

32. Deacon, *Parsons,* 43, 49, 77; and see Lee Virginia Chambers-Schiller, *Liberty, a Better Husband: Single Women in America: The Generations of 1780–1840* (New Haven: Yale University Press, 1984).

33. Deacon, *Parsons,* 54, 113, 118, 129.

34. "Afro-Americans in Montclair"; and Addie W. Hunton, *William Alphaeus Hunton: A Pioneer Prophet of Young Men* (1938; reprint, New York: G. K. Hall, 1997), 459. A photograph in the author's collection shows this group.

35. In addition to Radcliffe and Smith, the "Seven Sisters" were Wellesley, Mount Holyoke, Vassar, Barnard, and Bryn Mawr. Otelia Cromwell, from the class of 1900, was Smith's first Negro graduate; interview with Adelaide Cromwell, November 1997. Catherine Grigsby Mayo, "Personal Impressions of Early Montclair Residents: William Robert E. Grigsby," MS, Montclair Historical Society.

36. Deacon, *Parsons,* 17, 19.

37. Bond to Buckingham, May 16, 1916, and Buckingham to Bond, May 31, 1916, Radcliffe Archives. Louise Cook Hill, Radcliffe 1921, confirmed that Negroes could not live in the dormitories. The first Radcliffe student to do so was Johnnie Davis (Carey), who went to the school in 1926. She later became the first full-fledged Negro member of the YWCA's National Board.

38. Conversation with Louise Cook Hill, July 1995. "Radcliffe in My Life," Mary Gibson Hundley file, Radcliffe archives, Radcliffe College *Directory,* 1916–17; and Stephen Birmingham, *Certain People: America's Black Elite* (Boston: Little, Brown, 1977), 136.

39. Maria Luisa Nunes, *A Portuguese Colonial in America: Belmira Nunes Lopes. The Autobiography of a Cape Verdean-American* (Pittsburgh: Latin American Library Review Press, 1982), 75.

40. Dorothy Height especially remembers Caroline Bond Day's "broad Boston accent" from their first meeting in 1939. Conversation with Height, August 1996.

41. "Radcliffe in My Life," Hundley file.

42. In late 1994 and early 1995, I talked on the telephone with twelve white Radcliffe graduates from the classes of 1917–1922 (Althea Treadwell Allen, Gladys Ottalea Bolton, Edith Manwell Chamberlain, Jennie Hubbard Farnham, Estelle Frankfurter, Edna Ryan Gilmore, Dorothy Sumers Green, Evelyn Beard Hoffman, Eleanor Gilbert Montgomery, Elizabeth Benton Swan, Amy Brown Townsend, Gertrude Knowlton Wilson) and with Louise Cook Hill, Radcliffe 1922, who was the only surviving African American from that period, hereafter collectively designated "Interviews, 1917–22."

43. Schneider and Schneider, *Into the Breach,* 241.

44. Interviews, 1917–22, and Radcliffe *Yearbook,* 1919.

45. Rankin was the *only* member of the House of Representatives who opposed her country's entrance into World War II.

46. Interviews, 1917–22; Deacon, *Parsons,* 182; and Nell Irvin Painter, *Standing at Armageddon: The United States, 1877–1919* (New York: Norton, 1987), 303. The author declined a job as choreographer for the renowned Hasty Pudding revue in 1958 because that club still denied entry to African Americans.

47. Deacon, *Parsons,* 183.

48. Lettie Gavin, *American Women in World War I* (Niwot: University Press of Colorado), 14; and Schneider and Schneider, *Into the Breach,* unpaginated illustration.

49. Schneider and Schneider, *Into the Breach,* 4–5, 12, 14–15, 59, 267.

50. Radcliffe College *Annual Report,* 1917, 57; Schneider and Schneider, *Into the Breach,* 16, 23, 27, 240; *Radcliffe Magazine,* June 1918, 133; and Maurine Rothschild, "The Search for Frances," MS, Radcliffe College Archives. Interviews, 1917–22.

51. Gavin, *American Women in World War I,* 46, 204; and Palmieri, *In Adamless Eden,* 235–42.

52. Gavin, *American Women in World War I,* 4, 6; and Schneider and Schneider, *Into the Breach,* 16, 18. I greatly appreciate my George Washington University colleague Linda De Pauw telling me about the World War I recruiting poster.

53. Darlene Clark Hine, "The Call That Never Came," in Darlene Clark Hine, ed., *Black Women in United States History* (Brooklyn, N.Y.: Carlson Publishing, 1990), 6: 649–53.

54. Ibid., 43, 59–60. Other reports assert that a few black nurses were called to active duty in the final weeks of the war.

55. Addie W. Hunton and Kathryn M. Johnson, *Two Colored Women with the American Expeditionary Forces* (1920; reprint, New York: G. K. Hall, 1997), 171.

56. Ibid., 13, 33, 105.

57. Ibid., 178, 188, 190, 196–97, 251.

58. Hull, ed., *Give Us Each Day,* 91. Emmett Scott apparently gave Dunbar-Nelson a ring that bore an army insignia and matched one that he always wore. Hull, *Color, Sex, and Poetry,* 72, cites Carrie's March 1918 letter to Dunbar-Nelson praising her play, *"Mine Eyes Have Seen,"* that appeared in *Crisis* earlier that year.

59. Alice Dunbar-Nelson, "Negro Women in War Work," in Emmett J. Scott, *Scott's Official History of the American Negro in the World War* (Chicago: Homewood Press, 1919), 374.

60. Ibid., 375–78, 379, 390.

61. Folder 2, Box 42a, YWCA Papers; Hine, ed., *Black Women in America,* 153; Rouse, *Lugenia Burns Hope,* 95.

62. My thanks to A'Lelia Perry Bundles for sharing this information about her grandmother, A'Lelia Walker Robinson. From Madam C. J. Walker's October 8, 1918, letter to her attorney, F. B. Ransom, Bundles Papers.

63. Dunbar-Nelson, "Negro Women," 388; and Hine, "Call That Never Came," 651.

64. *Crisis,* February 1918, 201, and March 1918, 304.

65. "The Circle for Negro Relief, Inc.," annual report, 1919.

66. Dunbar-Nelson, "Negro Women," 389; and Circle for Negro War Relief letterhead, Spingarn Papers, Library of Congress.

67. "Circle" report, 3.

68. Dunbar-Nelson, "Negro Women," 395–97.

69. Ibid., 384, 389.

70. Georgia Douglas Johnson, "The Potent Hour," in Hunton and Johnson, *Two Colored Women,* 10.

71. New York City *Directory,* 1918; Day interviews; and Logan conversations.

72. Radcliffe *Directory,* 1818–19.

73. Gavin, *American Women in World War I,* xi, 15.

74. *Radcliffe Magazine,* March 1919, 67.

75. Janice Delaney, Mary Jane Lupton, and Emily Toth, *The Curse: A Cultural History of Menstruation* (Urbana: University of Illinois Press, 1976), 139.

76. *Radcliffe Magazine,* October 1918, 39.

77. Roses and Randolph, *Harlem Renaissance and Beyond,* 18; and Nunes, *Portuguese Colonial in America,* 74, 77. I cannot be sure whether Carrie Bond joined Delta Sigma Theta at this time or when she taught at Atlanta University after 1922. She later changed her affiliation to Alpha Kappa Alpha. Early African American Students Files, Radcliffe College Archives. In the author's class of 1959, four black students entered in 1955, with only three among the three hundred who graduated four years later. Werner Sollors, Caldwell Titcomb, and Thomas A. Underwood, *Blacks at Harvard: A Documentary History of African-American Experience at Harvard and Radcliffe* (New York: New York University Press, 1993), 5–6, 129.

78. CSB Radcliffe transcript. Drake, "Anthropology and the Black Experience," cites Caroline Stewart Bond as the first of her race seriously to study anthropology, and almost certainly the first to do the graduate work that she officially started at Radcliffe in 1927. A few others probably took it as an undergraduate major, but that is not documented.

79. W. E. Burghardt Du Bois, *Dusk of Dawn: An Essay Toward an Autobiography of a Race Concept* (New York: Harcourt, Brace, 1940), 61. See also Joel Williamson, *New People: Miscegenation and Mulattoes in the United States* (New York: Free Press, 1980).

80. Earnest A. Hooton, "Radcliffe Investigates Race Mixture," in *Harvard Alumni Bulletin,* April 3, 1930, 768–76. Hooton apparently did not recall that Carrie Bond had attended his introductory anthropology course two years earlier.

81. Deacon, *Parsons,* 106, 172, 264, 283.

82. Hooton, "Radcliffe Investigates."

83. Ibid. The studies to which Hooton referred would have included Edward B. Reuter, *The Mulatto in the United States: Including a Study of Mixed-Blood Races throughout the World* (Boston: Richard Badger, 1918); and Melville J. Herskovits, *The American Negro: A Study in Racial Crossing* (New York: Knopf, 1928). Ensuing works include Edwin Embree, *Brown America: The Story of a New Race* (New York: Viking Press, 1931); and Louis Wirth and Herbert Goldhamer, "The Hybrid and the Problem of Miscegenation," in Otto Klineberg, ed., *Characteristics of the American Negro* (New York: Harper & Bros., 1944); and then much later, John German Mencke, "Mulattoes and Race Mixture: American Attitudes and Images from Reconstruction to World War I" (Ph.D. diss., University of North Carolina, 1976).

84. Hooton, "Radcliffe Investigates."

85. CBD to Mordecai Johnson, May 1, 1927, Day Papers, Peabody Museum, Harvard University.

86. Hooton, "Radcliffe Investigates"; CBD to Claudia Harreld, July 7, 1934. My thanks to Josephine Harreld Love for sharing this letter.

87. Hooton, "Radcliffe Investigates"; and CBD to Mrs. J. H. King, April 4, 1920, Day Papers.

88. Hooton, "Radcliffe Investigates" Langston Hughes, *The Big Sea* (1940; reprint, New York: Hill & Wang, 1993), 296; and Herskovits (who began his work on racial crossings in 1923), *American Negro,* 39. Davenport and Love's work in *The Medical Department of the United States Army in the World War,* vol. 15, pt. 1, *Army Anthropology.*

89. Hooton, "Radcliffe Investigates." I am grateful to Paulette Curtis, Elizabeth Sandager, Sarah Demb, and everyone associated with the Day Papers at the Peabody Museum for their cooperation. The photographs and hair snippets (along with a body of correspondence and anthropometric records) that CBD assembled are catalogued and preserved in the archives at Harvard University's Peabody Museum. See also Caroline Bond Day, "Race-Crossings in the United States," *Crisis,* January 1930, 81–82, 103, in which Day mentions James H. Johnson, Jr.'s article "The Social Significance of the Intermixture of Races in the Colonial and National Period," and George Dixon's "Race Crosses," both prepared at the University of Chicago. CBD provides no citations for those works.

90. Hooton, "Radcliffe Investigates."

91. Ibid.; and CBD to King, Day Papers.

92. CBD to Mrs. N. G. Du Bois, July 26, 1927, Day Papers.

93. CBD to Kate Graves, April 29, 1930; CBD to Dr. Mordecai Johnson, May 1, 1927; Lulu Pearl Partee to CBD, April 12, 1927; and "Mama" Penney to CBD, August 23, 1927, Day Papers.

94. *Radcliffe Magazine,* November 1919, 27.

95. Caroline Bond (Day) transcript, Radcliffe College Archives.

96. Radcliffe College *Yearbook, Annual Reports,* Commencement Program, 1919, and *Fiftieth Anniversary Report,* 35.

97. *Crisis* published Carrie Bond's "A Fairy Story" in September 1918.

13. CAPTAINS' TALES

1. Liberty *Vindicator,* October 24, 1902. My thanks to Penny Clark at the Sam Houston Regional Library and Research Center for her assistance, especially in locating relevant articles in the *Vindicator,* and to Kevin Ladd for information about Dayton.

2. Miriam Paltrow, *Liberty, Liberty County, and the Atascosito District* (Austin, Tex.: Pemberton Press, 1974), 28.

3. Ibid., 27, 28, 65.

4. Debra Ann Reid, "Farmers in the New South: Race, Gender, and Class in a Rural Southeast Texas County, 1850–1900" (M.A. thesis, Baylor University, 1996), 19, 31, 58, 143. I am indebted to Reid for sharing her research and observations. "John Price's Slave Narrative," in *Texas Illustrated Magazine,* February 1998.

5. Reid, "Farmers in the New South," 31; and Paltrow, *Liberty,* passim.

6. Reid, "Farmers in the New South," 73; and "The History of Ames, Texas," Houston *Forward Times,* August 25, 1984.

7. See Herbert Molloy Mason, Jr., *Death from the Sea* (New York: Dial Press, 1972).

8. *Vindicator,* January 24, 1890; and Reid, "Farmers in the New South."

9. Isa. 44:3–4 KJV.

10. Company Officers of the State Troops in the 2nd Brigade, 224. George P. Rawick, ed., *The American Slave: A Composite Autobiography,* vol. 4, *Texas Narratives,* pt. 1 (Westport, Conn.: Greenwood Press, 1968), 254–56.

11. Caroline Bond Day, *A Study of Some Negro-White Families in the United States* (Cambridge: Harvard University, Peabody Museum, 1931), 40, names nine children (Aaron, Francis, Henderson, Theophilis, Milton, Lorena, Wilena, Leana, and Cora) of Amanda Cribbs and Isaiah Day. Lulelia Walker Harrison, Henderson Day's granddaughter, remembered her father's siblings named Nilly and Lobe, in addition to Henderson and Aaron. Lulelia Walker Harrison, conversations with author, July 1997. Reid, "Farmers in the New South," 134–35, details the will and legal entanglements of Liberty County's Fanny Crib[b]s, who must have been Amanda's mother. A Henderson Montgomery lived nearby and Fanny Cribbs left him property. The repetition of that unusual given name in the Day-Cribbs family probably is not a coincidence.

12. Rawick, ed., *American Slave,* vol. 4, *Texas Narratives,* pt. 1, 255; and Day, *Some Negro-White Families,* 40.

13. Harrison, conversations. Penny Clark provided information about Isaiah Day's gravestone, and the lack of any for Amanda Cribbs.

14. Liberty County, Texas, "Marks and Brands Records, Transcribed, 1875–1971," MS provided by Debra Reid.

15. Day, *Some Negro-White Families,* 40; and Reid, "Farmers in the New South," 57, 49. In the postcolonial era, Madagascar became the Malagasy Republic—that traditional name even more closely resembling the "Molaglaskan" nomenclature remembered in the Spaight family. Reid's notes show that Flora Spaight's father and brother owned at least 150 acres of land.

16. Harrison, conversations; and Aaron Day, Jr., "Report of Physical Examination," 1929, United States Army Records.

17. Reid, "Farmers in the New South," 114, 124, 152.

18. Ibid., 12. Penny Clark to the author, May 28, 1997; Bernard Day, conversations with author, June 1996; and discussions with Wenonah Bond Logan. South Texas lore reports a few rare snowstorms in those years.

19. Rawick, ed., *American Slave,* vol. 4, *Texas Narratives,* pt. 1, 255; and Reid, "Farmers in the New South," 145.

20. William H. Wiggins, Jr., "Juneteenth: A Red Spot Day on the Texas Calendar," in Texas Folklore Society 54, *Juneteenth Texas: Essays in African-American Folklore* (Denton: University of North Texas Press, 1996), 238; Rawick, ed., *American Slave,* vol. 4, *Texas Narratives,* pt. 1, 255, and pt. 2, 241; and Robert V. Haynes, *A Night of Violence: The Houston Riot of 1917* (Baton Rouge: Louisiana State University Press, 1976), 27.

21. *Vindicator,* June 23, 1893; Wiggins, "Juneteenth," 239–40.

22. Wenonah Bond Logan, conversations with author,

23. T. Lindsay Baker, "More Than Just 'Possum'n Taters: Texas African-American Foodways in the WPA Slave Narratives," in Texas Folklore Society, *Juneteenth Texas,* (54): 97–115; and J. Mason Brewer, *Dog Ghosts and Other Negro Folk Tales* (Austin: University of Texas Press, 1958, 1976), 54. Bernard Day conversations.

24. Baker, "'Possum'n Taters," 97–115; J. Mason Brewer, *American Negro Folklore* (Chicago: Quadrangle Books, 1968), 81; and conversations with Logan, who especially remembered Sunday meals (ham, biscuits, grits) with the Days in the 1920s.

25. Reid, "Farmers in the New South," 159; and U.S. Census, Liberty County, 1900, 1910.

26. Reid, "Farmers in the New South," 124.

27. Several other black men in Liberty County served in public office during those years. Reid, "Farmers in the New South," 155; and *Vindicator,* July 20, 1907.

28. Kenneth O'Reilly, *Nixon's Piano: Presidents and Racial Politics from Washington to Clinton* (New York: Free Press, 1995), 73.

29. Bernard C. Nalty, *Strength for the Fight: A History of Black Americans in the Military* (New York: Free Press, 1986), 90–97. The apology was finally issued by President Gerald Ford.

30. My thanks to Minniezine Taylor, archivist at Prairie View A&M University, for the bounteous information she unearthed.

31. E. B. Evans, "Down Memory Lane," MS, Prairie View A&M University Archives, 12. George Ruble Woolfolk, *Prairie View: A Study in Public Consciousness, 1878–1946* (New York: Pageant Press, 1962), 67, 75, 116, 133, 138, 146, 168, 173. *Crisis,* October 1913, 269, reported that enrollment dropped from nine hundred to six hundred because of a lack of funds. *The Prairie,* 1917; and *The Red Book: A Compendium of Social, Professional, Religious, Educational, and Industrial Interests of Houston's Colored Population* (Houston: Sotex Publishing, 1915), 179–83.

32. Marian Talbot to H. P. Judson, June 20, 1907, and Judson to Talbot, June 22, 1907, President's Papers 1889–1925, Box 24, University of Chicago Archives. Jacqueline Goggin, *Carter G. Woodson: A Life in History* (Baton Rouge: Louisiana State University Press, 1993), 19. The University of Chicago hired its first African American faculty member after World War II. Richard Storr, *Harper's University: The Beginnings; A History of the University of Chicago* (Chicago: University of Chicago Press, 1966), 110, also states that "in 1901, five students of about thirty-five hundred were Negroes." University records, however, do not list its early students by race, making it difficult to ascertain names and numbers.

33. Carl Sandburg's 1914 poem "Chicago" designated it the "city of the big shoulders." Jack Johnson, *Jack Johnson Is a Dandy: An Autobiography* (1927; reprint, New York: Chelsea House, 1969), 66–70.

34. My thanks to Dr. James Bowman for his guidance concerning black students at the University of Chicago. Kenneth R. Manning, *Black Apollo of Science: The Life of Ernest Everett Just* (New York: Oxford University Press, 1983), 56–66, details the world that Just encountered when he went to the university in 1915. Aaron Day, Jr., academic transcript, University of Chicago.

35. Conversation with Thelma Scott Bryant, May 1997. Lt. Walter Giles, who trained with Aaron Day, Jr., at Fort Des Moines, worked with Prairie View's SATC after the war.

36. Many analysts believe that the strange and notorious German-Mexican "Zimmermann telegram" was fabricated to prompt the relatively isolationist United States to enter the World War. See also Haynes, *A Night of Violence,* passim.

37. Arthur E. Barbeau and Florette Henri, *The Unknown Soldiers: African-American Troops in World War I* (New York: Da Capo Press, 1974), 26–31.

38. Different sources give slightly different numbers for members of both races killed in the riot.

39. Ethel Tears to Caroline Bond Day, September 18, 1927, Box 1, Caroline Bond Day Papers, Peabody Museum, Harvard University. Barbeau and Henri, *Unknown Soldiers*, 30. Government agents threatened the African American journalist Ida B. Wells-Barnett because she distributed buttons supporting the accused men.

40. Nalty, *Strength for the Fight*, 101–6; Haynes, *Night of Violence*, 74.

41. Barbeau and Henri, *Unknown Soldiers*, 21, and *Crisis*, February 1918, 183.

42. "War Time Diary of Dr. William Holmes Dyer," MS, Lincoln Public Library, Lincoln, Illinois. Also, William Maxwell, *Billie Dyer and Other Stories* (New York: Plume Books, 1993), 3–35.

43. Krewarsky A. Salter, " 'Sable Officers' ": African-American Military Officers, 1861–1918" (M.A. thesis, Florida State University, 1993), 89–93.

44. Barbeau and Henri, *Unknown Soldiers*, 58. The projected percentages of Negro officers remained roughly intact, but a few were ultimately promoted to the rank of major and above.

45. Salter, " 'Sable Officers,' " 96–98.

46. Payments to Officers, U.S. Army, for Capt. Aaron Day, Jr., 1917–19. Aaron Day, Jr., "Physical Examination at Place of Enlistment." My thanks to Jackie Ostrowski at the National Military Personnel Records Center for ferreting out these records.

47. *Vindicator*, June 21, 1918.

48. Barbeau and Henri, *Unknown Soldiers*, 65, 67. Salter, " 'Sable Officers,' " 104–6. Charles Young was promoted to full colonel when he was reactivated at the end of the Great War.

49. Maria Luisa Nunes, *A Portuguese Colonial in America, Belmira Nunes Lopes: The Autobiography of a Cape Verdean-American* (Pittsburgh: Latin American Library Review Press, 1982), 79. Adella and Warren Logan's son Paul apparently was one who passed for white when he went into the army in World War I.

50. Theodore Kornweibel, Jr., "Apathy and Dissent: Black America's Negative Responses to World War I," *South Atlantic Quarterly*, 322–338; and Barbeau and Henri, *Unknown Soldiers*, 12.

51. Salter, " 'Sable Officers,' " 111; *Literary Digest*, July 21, 1917.

52. Salter, " 'Sable Officers,' " 106–8. Lts. W. N. Colson and A. B. Nutt, "The Failure of the Ninety-second Division," *The Messenger*, September 1919, 22–25; and *Crisis*, October 1917, 312.

53. Salter, " 'Sable Officers,' " 108–9; Barbeau and Henri, *Unknown Soldiers*, 66.

54. Nunes, *Portuguese Colonial in America*, 64.

55. Barbeau and Henri, *Unknown Soldiers*, 60; and Salter, " 'Sable Officers,' " 112–13.

56. Barbeau and Henri, *Unknown Soldiers,* 61–62. Only four of the fifteen Negro "old men," or captains, sent to Camp Funston were not Regular Army. For the term "old men," see Paul Dickson, *War Slang: American Fighting Words and Phrases from the Civil War to the Gulf War* (New York: Pocket Books, 1994), 85.

57. Salter, " 'Sable Officers,' " 131. A number of black men were commissioned as army chaplains, and others received field commissions in France.

58. Barbeau and Henri, *Unknown Soldiers,* 69, 70.

59. Ibid., 39; Payments to Officers, Capt. Day; and *Crisis,* December 1917, 85.

60. Salter, " 'Sable Officers,' " 121. Training Schedule, Company B, 317th Ammunition Train, National Archives. World War I Research Project, Army Service Experiences Questionnaire, Cpl. Lloyd Blair, Co. A, 317th Ammunition Train, Military History Center, Carlisle, Pa.

61. August Meier and Elliott Rudwick, *Black Historians and the Historical Profession, 1915–1980* (Urbana: University of Illinois Press, 1986), 19.

62. Carter G. Woodson to Sec. of War, December 6, 1917; Aaron Day, Jr., to R. L. Isaacs, January 20, 1918; and Day to War Dept., n.d., Co. B, 317th Ammunition Train, 92nd Division, World War I Records, National Archives. Wenonah Bond Logan and Bernard Day both confirmed that Carrie Bond and Aaron Day, Jr., met during World War I. Maceo C. Dailey, Emmett Jay Scott's biographer, confirms that Scott considered men from Texas his special concern and, when needed, interceded on their behalf. See Maceo Crenshaw Dailey, Jr., "Emmett Jay Scott: The Career of a Secondary Black Leader" (Ph.D. diss., Howard University, 1983). For further details, see Dailey's upcoming biography.

63. Alfred W. Crosby, Jr., *Epidemic and Peace, 1918* (Westport, Conn.: Greenwood Press, 1976), 19.

64. Folder 12, Box 42b, YWCA Papers, Sophia Smith Collection, Smith College. In various letters, the sergeant's name is spelled McClinton and McClendon. Maj. A. M. Craven, Judge Advocate, to Captain Aaron Day, March 16, 1918; Day to Charles McClendon, March 21, 1918; Day to Warden J. K. Codding, April 16, 1918, and Day to Adjutant General of the Army, April 16, 1918, Co. B, 317th Ammunition Train.

65. Barbeau and Henri, *Unknown Soldiers,* 86.

66. Ballou/Greer memo attached to Dyer diary. The Washington *Bee* reported a few months later that the movie house owner ultimately had been charged and fined for defying Kansas law when he refused entry to the Negro soldiers,

67. Barbeau and Henri, *Unknown Soldiers,* 86–87. Emmett J. Scott, *Scott's Official History of the American Negro in the World War* (Chicago: Homewood Press, 1919), 97.

68. Reid Badger, *A Life in Ragtime: A Biography of James Reese Europe* (New York: Oxford University Press, 1995), 159.

69. *Crisis,* December 1918, 180.

70. Except where otherwise noted, descriptions of the exploits of the 317th Ammunition Train en route, in France, and on the journey home, are excerpted from the "War Time Diary of William Holmes Dyer." Payments to Officers, Capt. Day.

71. For similar examples, see Barbeau and Henri, *Unknown Soldiers*, 102. Blair Questionnaire. My thanks to A'Lelia Bundles for sharing the memo "Headquarters 366th Infantry, Aboard U.S.S. Covington, 12 June 1918," from the papers of her grandfather, Lt. Marion R. Perry, who also served with the 317th Ammunition Train.

72. An unidentified newspaper clipping from July 1, 1934, marking the sixteenth anniversary of the *Covington*'s sinking accompanies Lt. Dyer's diary.

73. Edward M. Coffman, *The War to End All Wars: The American Military Experience in World War I* (Madison: University of Wisconsin Press, 1986), 320.

74. Barbeau and Henri, *Unknown Soldiers*, 142–43; Salter, " 'Sable Officers,' " 127; and Addie W. Hunton and Kathryn M. Johnson, *Two Colored Women with the American Expeditionary Forces* (1921; reprint, New York: G. K. Hall, 1997), 185, 233.

75. Barbeau and Henri, *Unknown Soldiers*, 65; *Crisis*, June 1919, 83; and Hunton and Johnson, *Two Colored Women*, 185. St. Lâomir and La Cortine do not appear on any French maps or in any atlases that I have been able to find.

76. Three officers were white. Of the blacks, in addition to Dyer, Day, and Abernethy, Capt. Lee Hicks and Lt. John Wilson were Kansans; Lt. Harry Cox, a Missourian; and Lts. William Campbell and Wil Evans, Texans. All of those Negro officers had trained and received their commissions at Fort Des Moines.

77. Barbeau and Henri, *Unknown Soldiers*, 17.

78. Blair Questionnaire.

79. Ibid. Chevrons on the left sleeves of members of Company B, 317th Ammunition Train, indicated battle injuries.

80. W. Allen Sweeney, *History of the American Negro in the Great World War* (1919; New York: Johnson Reprint, 1970), 202. Simon Haley, who served with the 366th Infantry, was one victim of a gas attack. Alex Haley, *Roots* (Garden City, N.Y.: Doubleday, 1976), 661. Mustard gas, a vesicant, was an effective weapon for the Germans because it was heavier than air, did not rapidly disperse, and contaminated both soil and water. It mixed with any body moisture and burned the skin, eyes (causing temporary blindness), and respiratory tract. Uniforms suffused with the gas could produce the same problems in medical personnel who handled them much later.

81. Crosby, *Epidemic and Peace*, 145, 153–59. Dickson, *War Slang*, 37.

82. Salter, " 'Sable Officers,' " 134; Coffman, *War to End All Wars*, 317; and Henri Florette, *Bitter Victory: A History of Black Soldiers in World War I* (Garden City, N.Y.: Zenith Books, 1970), 107. Later, when cooler heads prevailed, the

court-martialed Negro commissioned officers were almost completely exoner-
ated.

83. Barbeau and Henri, *Unknown Soldiers,* 148–49; Sweeney, *Negro in the Great War,* 229; and Haley, *Roots,* 687.

84. "Jack Johnsons" were the German's seventeen-inch shells nicknamed for the controversial dethroned Negro heavyweight boxer, who was living in exile in Paris. That designation carried clear sexual connotations. Dickson, *War Slang,* 72.

85. *Lieut. Jim Europe's 369th U. S. Infantry "Hell Fighters" Band,* Memphis Archives CD, 1996, liner notes; and Badger, *Life in Ragtime.* I have combined and minimally revised the punctuation of these two versions of Europe's lyrics so that they make the best sense to me.

86. Goggin, *Carter G. Woodson,* 43.

87. Marcia M. Mathews, *Henry Ossawa Tanner, American Artist* (Chicago: University of Chicago Press, 1969), 176. Tanner's paintings of the World War are situated at the American Red Cross Headquarters in Washington, D.C. Barbeau and Henri, *Unknown Soldiers,* 41. June 1996 lecture by Rae Alexander-Minter at the American Red Cross History and Education Center.

88. Greer letter appended to Dyer diary.

89. "Attack on Negro Soldiers Resented" by Emmett J. Scott, June 10, 1925, Cont. 68, Spingarn Collection, Manuscript Division, Library of Congress.

90. For reports of black soldiers who were hanged, see Barbeau and Henri, *Unknown Soldiers,* 169–70.

91. Ibid., 144–45, 160; and Blair Questionnaire.

92. Badger, *Life in Ragtime,* 197.

93. Noble Sissle, "To Hell with Germany," in Robert Kimball and William Bolcom, *Reminiscing with Sissle and Blake* (New York: Viking, 1973), 70.

94. Greer memo appended to Dyer diary.

95. Robert Russa Moton, *Finding a Way Out* (1920; reprint, New York: Negro Universities Press, 1969), 263. David Levering Lewis, *W. E. B. Du Bois: Portrait of a Race, 1868–1919* (New York: Henry Holt, 1993), 700, reports that Moton met with officers of the 317th Ammunition Train on December 16, 1918. The Washington *Tribune* reported on the assassination plot March 28, 1924.

96. The photograph that M. Giraud took in Domfront was shared by Bernard Day, Aaron Day's foster son. A picture postcard of Le Vieux Manoir de Chaponnais included in Lt. Dyer's diary appears to be the same old stone house behind which the officers of the 317th Ammunition Train posed at the end of 1918. Maj. Dean trained and was commissioned as a captain at Fort Des Moines, but was promoted to major in France.

97. Barbeau and Henri, *Unknown Soldiers,* 65 and 166; Badger, *Life in Rag-time,* 192, 194; and Dickson, *War Slang,* 73.

98. Barbeau and Henri, *Unknown Soldiers,* 7. Du Bois never completed "The Wounded World," but reports of his trip through France appeared in *Crisis* in 1919. Photographs of William Hunt in the Caroline Bond Day Papers, Peabody Museum, Harvard University.

99. Du Bois reported that the army stopped paying members of the 92nd Division in January 1919. According to Capt. Day's records, that was not so in his case.

100. Hunton and Johnson, *Two Colored Women,* 8.

101. Barbeau and Henri, *Unknown Soldiers,* 170.

102. Bernard Day shared this photograph.

103. Maj. Dean's "Circular" appended to Dyer diary. One white colonel refused to endorse Dean's retention in the army after the World War, stating, "Major Dean is a very efficient officer, but for reasons which I care not to state but which are well known, I cannot recommend him." The "well known" reason almost certainly was that Dean was a Negro.

104. Barbeau and Henri, *Unknown Soldiers,* 138–39, 148.

105. "Report of Physical Examination of Officer Prior to Separation from Service in the United States Army," Capt. Aaron Day, Jr.

106. *Vindicator,* February 7, March 7, April 18, and August 19, 1919.

107. Mark R. Schneider, *Boston Confronts Jim Crow, 1890–1920* (Boston: Northeastern University Press, 1997), 156.

108. Barbeau and Henri, *Unknown Soldiers,* 177–78, 180.

109. Ibid., 188, 189.

110. Evans, "Down Memory Lane," 12–14.

111. *Europe's "Hell Fighters" Band,* liner notes.

112. Harrison, conversation.

113. My thanks to Hortense Tate for sharing this story. She ultimately married the widowed Harrison Tate and succeeded Caroline Bond Day as director of the Montclair YWCA.

114. Evans, "Down Memory Lane," 12, 17. Marriage Records 1920, Harris County, Texas.

115. Bryant, conversation with author; and *Red Book,* 21.

116. Washington *Bee,* July 10 and 31, 1920.

117. *Red Book,* 118.

118. Day, conversations.

14. Capital Times

1. Washington *Bee,* July 8, 1916; *Alexander's Magazine,* February 1924. Standard Life was chartered in 1908, but did not gear up until 1913.

2. Constance McLaughlin Green, *The Secret City: A History of Race Relations in the Nation's Capital* (Princeton: Princeton University Press, 1967), 200, 202; and Brett William Beemyn, "A Queer Capital: Lesbian, Gay, and Bisexual Life in Washington, D.C., 1890–1955" (Ph.D. diss., University of Iowa, 1977), 57. Birmingham had a higher percentage of blacks in that period but remained a considerably smaller city than Washington.

3. Elizabeth Clark-Lewis, *Living In, Living Out: African American Domestics in Washington, D.C., 1910–1940* (Washington, D.C.: Smithsonian Institution Press, 1994), 70–71.

4. Green, *Secret City*, vii–viii.

5. Neval H. Thomas, "The District of Columbia—A Paradise of Paradoxes," in Tom Lutz and Susanna Ashton, eds., *These "Colored" United States: African American Essays from the 1920s* (New Brunswick, N.J.: Rutgers University Press, 1996), 82. Thomas's essay first appeared in *The Messenger* in October 1923.

6. Wenonah Bond Logan, conversations with author. I have not found any German-sounding name among the previous residents listed in the Washington, D.C., City Directories for the houses that the Bonds lived in between 1916 and 1920. The ousted Germans, however, could have been renters, and therefore not listed, or perhaps their names were not recognizable as such. Logan, however, was very insistent about this incident. Mark Sullivan, *Our Times: America at the Birth of the Twentieth Century*, edited with new material by Dan Rather (1926; New York: Scribner, 1996), 360.

7. Green, *Secret City*, 127; Beemyn, "Queer Capital," 53.

8. Jacqueline M. Moore, "A Drop of African Blood: The Transformation of Washington's Black Elite, 1880–1920," MS; and District of Columbia City Directories, 1917–1927.

9. Darlene Clark Hine, ed., *Black Women in America: An Historical Encyclopedia* (Brooklyn, N.Y.: Carlson Publishers, 1993), 548–49.

10. Green, *Secret City*, 174; Kenneth O'Reilly, *Nixon's Piano: Presidents and Racial Politics from Washington to Clinton* (New York: Free Press, 1995), 83; Thomas, "Paradise of Paradoxes," 81; and Moore, "Drop of African Blood," 430.

11. Green, *Secret City*, 181, 183.

12. *Bee,* December 1917.

13. Thomas, "Paradise of Paradoxes," 80.

14. *Bee,* May 19, June 2, August 4, November 3, December 1, 1917, and May 25, 1918. Green, *Secret City,* 186.

15. Rayford W. Logan, *Howard University: The First Hundred Years, 1867–1967* (New York: New York University Press, 1968), 184, 208; Green, *Secret City,* 210; Beemyn, "Queer Capital," 64; and David Nicholson, "The Legacy of Howard's Literati," in *Howard Magazine,* Spring 1998. Carter Woodson served on Howard's faculty for only a few years.

16. David Levering Lewis, *When Harlem Was in Vogue* (New York: Vintage Books, 1982), 67.

17. Moore, "Drop of African Blood," 472.

18. Mu-So-Lit Papers, Moorland-Spingarn Research Center, Howard University.

19. *Bee,* January 19, 1918, February 12 and 19, 1921; Washington *Tribune,* March 18 and December 30, 1922, and February 7, 1924. Sandra Fitzpatrick and Maria R. Goodwin, *The Guide to Black Washington* (New York: Hippocrene Books, 1990), 186. Mu-So-Lit Papers, MSRC. Moore, "Drop of African Blood," 118.

20. Rev. James West, former pastor of Calvary Episcopal Church, conversation with author, October 1997; and Calvary Episcopal Church's history, *Fiftieth Anniversary, 1901–1951,* Calvary's Archives.

21. *Fiftieth Anniversary.*

22. Ibid.

23. Elizabeth Bennett Williamson, conversation with author, August 1996; and *Tribune,* May 10 and June 14, 1924. Moore, "Drop of African Blood," 137.

24. Green, *Secret City,* 161.

25. Logan, conversations. Moore, "Drop of African Blood," 305.

26. Green, *Secret City,* 162, 182; and Thomas, "Paradise of Paradoxes," 84.

27. Thomas, "Paradise of Paradoxes," 76–87.

28. Beemyn, "Queer Capital," 58.

29. *Bee,* January 11, 1919.

30. Arthur E. Barbeau and Florette Henri, *The Unknown Soldiers: African-American Troops in World War I* (New York: Da Capo Press, 1974), 188, 189; *Bee,* April 27, 1919; Federal Writers' Project, *Washington: City and Capital* (Washington, D.C.: Government Printing Office, 1937), 81. James Reese Europe was born in the Deep South, but spent his formative years in Washington, D.C.

31. Sullivan (Rather), *Our Times,* 621.

32. Moore, "Drop of African Blood," 473; *Bee,* July 26, 1919; and Michael Schaffer, "Lost Riot," *City Paper,* April 3, 1997.

33. Lewis, *When Harlem Was in Vogue,* 19.

34. That quote was first published in *Crisis.* Green, *Secret City,* 191–92; Moore, "Drop of African Blood," 475; Schaffer, "Lost Riot."

35. *Bee,* July 26, 1919; Schaffer, "Lost Riot."

36. Green, *Secret City;* and Schaffer, "Lost Riot."

37. Green, *Secret City,* 194–95.

38. *Bee,* April 6, 1919; Green, *Secret City,* 189–90, and Willard B. Gatewood, *Aristocrats of Color: The Black Elite, 1880–1920* (Bloomington: Indiana University Press, 1990), 326. The Moens incident went so far as to generate intense congressional hearings.

39. Green, *Secret City,* 189–90. Green does not cite the source for her report of Earnest Hooton discussing Washington's "colored" society in New England. She could have gleaned it from his 1930 article about Caroline Bond Day, but neither that article nor Day's book appears in her bibliography or footnotes.

40. Carroll Greene, Jr., "Summertime in the Highland Beach Tradition," *American Visions,* May–June 1986, 46–50; and Schaffer, "Lost Riot."

41. Shirlee Taylor Haizlip, "The Black Resorts," *American Legacy,* Summer 1996, 12.

42. Haizlip, "Black Resorts," 15; *Tribune,* August 11, 1923, and May 14, 1926; Moore, "Drop of African Blood," 106; Betty Francis Henderson, "A Trilogy: Reflections of Life at Highland Beach, Maryland" (1994).

43. *Bee,* June 15, 1918; and *Tribune,* July 16, 1926. Caroline Bond Day to Elizabeth Cook, March 30, 1927; and CBD to Mrs. N. J. Broughton, August 17, 1927, Box 1, Caroline Bond Day Papers, Peabody Museum, Harvard University.

44. Moore, "Drop of African Blood," 105.

45. Bernard Day, conversations with author, June 1996; and Doris Ridgely Moses, conversations with author, November 1997.

46. *Tribune,* July 15, 1921.

47. Hortense Mims Fitzgerald, conversation with author, June 1996; *Tribune,* June 24 and September 2, 1922, September 8, 1923, and July 16, 1926; Janis Johnson, "Black Beach Town: Small Population, Large Reputation," *Washington Post,* May 1, 1978; unidentified clipping, May 19, 1922, Highland Beach Archives.

48. Henderson, "Trilogy."

49. Amelia Cobb Grey, conversation with author, August 1996.

50. *Bee,* September 9, 1916; Thelma Blackwell Austin, conversation with author, July 1996.

51. *Tribune,* May 14, 1926.

52. Moore, "Drop of African Blood," 105; Henderson, "Trilogy."

53. *Tribune,* June 30 and July 4, 1923.

54. Green, *Secret City,* 192–94; *Tribune,* June 30 and July 4, 1923; and *Bee,* June 28, 1919. Thomas, "Paradise of Paradoxes," 84, raised similar protests about elite Negroes using the services of white professionals.

55. Henderson, "Trilogy"; *Tribune,* September 12, 1925, and September 8, 1923.

56. Day, conversation, June 1996.

57. Logan and Day, conversations.

58. Moses, conversation, November 1997.

59. Clark-Lewis, *Living In, Living Out,* 99, 100, 109, 113, 122, 125; and Green, *Secret City,* 160.

60. Clark-Lewis, *Living In, Living Out,* 109; and Moses, conversation.

61. William Henry Hunt Papers, Moorland-Spingarn Research Center; Logan and Day, conversations. Thomas, "Paradise of Paradoxes," 82; and Moore, "Drop of African Blood," 116.

62. Logan, conversations.

63. Moses, conversations. Eve Tyler Wilkins, conversation, December 1997, cites a family story in which a Negro woman who looked somewhat Asian had taken her seat for a performance when an usher challenged her presence and demanded to see her ticket. Feigning confusion, in an imperious tone she protested: "Tickee, tickee, always ask tickee!" prompting the frustrated employee to retreat in dismay. Similar stories in Green, *Secret City,* 207; and Moore, "Touch of African Blood," 108.

64. Moses, conversation.

65. Ibid.

66. On April 13, 1919, the *Bee* had reported the establishment of the city's first and only "all-colored fire engine company." Washington *Tribune,* February 4, 1922.

67. Jean Toomer, *Cane,* introduction by Darwin T. Turner (1923; reprint, New York: Liveright, 1975), 39, 50; Lewis, *When Harlem Was in Vogue,* 61.

68. John Edward Hasse, *Beyond Category: The Life and Genius of Duke Ellington* (New York: Simon & Schuster, 1993), 37–44; and *Colored American,* January 1909, 639.

69. Green, *Secret City,* 209.

70. Lewis, *When Harlem Was in Vogue,* 67; Gloria T. Hull, *Color, Sex, Poetry: Three Women Writers of the Harlem Renaissance* (Bloomington: Indiana University Press, 1987), 165–66, 178. Many of Georgia Douglas Johnson's papers are at the Moorland Spingarn Research Center, Howard University.

71. Lewis, *When Harlem Was in Vogue,* 81, 87, 127, 150.

72. CBD to Georgia Douglas Johnson, March 21, 1927, Day Papers. Aaron and Carrie Day moved to the District before 1930.

73. Green, *Secret City,* 215–16; and Moore, "Drop of African Blood," 113.

74. Green, *Secret City,* 202; and Paul Adomites, *October's Game* (Alexandria, Va.: Redefinition, 1990), 165–68. Other accounts argue that the fatal error that allowed the Senators (Nats) to win the Series was made by the Giants' third baseman, Fred Lindstrom. Washington *Post,* March 29, 1999.

75. Logan, *Howard University,* 215.

76. Moore, "Drop of African Blood," 261; Nellie McKay, "Black Women Playwrights and the Harlem Renaissance," in Marita Bonner file, Radcliffe College Archives; and Nicholson, "Howard's Literati."

77. See Dianne Johnson-Feelings, ed., *The Best of the Brownies' Book* (New York: Oxford University Press, 1996). My sincere thanks to Elinor DesVerney Sin-

nette for sharing her knowledge and insights, and her unique run of all issues of this magazine.

78. *Brownies' Book,* January 1920.

79. Ibid., February, 34; August, 220; September, 259–62; October, 320; and December 379, all 1920; and February, 53; April, 184; July, 207; and December, 346, all 1921.

80. Ibid., November, 1921, 342; and "Jessie Redmon Fauset," in Darlene Clark Hine, ed., *Black Women in America,* 411–16.

81. Dunbar High School *Yearbook,* 1924. Moore, "Drop of African Blood," xv, 177. Story from Amelia Cobb Gray, Hilda Smith Cobb's daughter.

82. Mary Gibson Hundley, *The Dunbar Story (1870–1955)* (New York: Vantage Press, 1965), 24, 31, 53. Austin, conversation.

83. *Tribune,* April 1, 1922; Hundley, *Dunbar Story,* 56, 135. Cooper, Dykes, Cromwell, and Georgiana Simpson were Dunbar's Ph.D.'s. The first African American graduated from the U.S. Naval Academy only in 1949.

84. Dunbar High School *Yearbook,* 1924; Dorothy Davis Lucas, conversation with author, October 1997.

85. Logan, conversations. Wenonah appropriated the middle name "Stewart" from that of her mother's first husband, in order to emulate her adored half sister Caroline Stewart Bond Day.

86. Ida Gibbs Hunt to Wenonah Bond Logan, February 1938, collection of Elizabeth Alexander; *Tribune,* May 22, 1922.

87. Logan, conversations.

88. Williamson, conversation. Thomas, "Paradise of Paradoxes," 80; and Schaffer, "Lost Riot."

89. Moses, conversations.

90. *Tribune,* February 19, 1921, February 3 and March 24, 1923; and *Bee,* June 28, 1919.

91. Paula Giddings, *When and Where I Enter: The Impact of Black Women on Race and Sex in America* (New York: Morrow, 1984), 167–69.

92. Thomas, "Paradise of Paradoxes," 85; *Tribune,* June 5, 1922.

93. Moses and Austin, conversations.

94. *Tribune,* January 6 and 13, 1923.

95. Ibid.

96. O'Reilly, *Nixon's Piano,* 96. Harding was accused both of having "colored blood" and of flagrant sexual improprieties. In the view of many Americans, those matters may have been linked. Robert C. Weaver became the country's first African American cabinet member during the administration of President Lyndon Baines Johnson. Office of Equal Employment Opportunity, Department of State, "A Chronology of Key Negro Appointments in the Department of State and the

Foreign Service, 1869–1969," unpublished document, U.S. Department of State. Up to and including the Harding years, only George H. Jackson, William Hunt, James G. Carter, William Yerby, and Carleton A. Wall, consuls in France; Richard Greener, consul at Vladivostok, Russia; Henry W. Furniss, consul in Bahia, Brazil; Jerome Peterson, Herbert Wright, and James W. Johnson, consuls in Venezuela, represented the United States in nonblack nations. The first Negro American to achieve ambassadorial rank was Edward R. Dudley, who became ambassador to Liberia in 1949. The first Negro American to achieve ambassadorial rank in a nonblack country was Clifford R. Wharton, appointed and installed as ambassador to Norway in 1961.

97. *Tribune,* September 20, 1924.

98. Dunbar *Yearbook,* 1924. Moses, conversations.

99. *Tribune,* July 6, 1925.

100. Green, *Secret City,* 204; and Logan, *Howard University,* 231–43. Carole Merritt, director of the Herndon Home (now a historic museum) in Atlanta, insists that the directors of the Curry School in Boston definitely knew that Adrienne Herndon was a Negro.

101. Eric D. Walrond, "The Largest Negro Commercial Enterprise in the World," *Forbes,* February 2, 1924, 503–5, 523, 525, 533.

102. Ibid., 505.

103. Alexa Benson Henderson, *Atlanta Life Insurance Company: Guardian of Black Economic Dignity* (Tuscaloosa: University of Alabama Press), 101–4.

104. *Tribune,* January 24, 1925, August 8, 1925, January 29 and April 23, 1926. Henderson, *Atlanta Life,* 113.

105. Rupert B. Clark, conversation with author, January 1997; and Phil McCombs, "Going Strong at 98," *Washington Post,* Style section, January 31, 1997.

106. *Tribune,* October 1, November 12, and December 17, 1926; Lewis, *When Harlem Was in Vogue,* 177.

107. Anastasia Holmes, whose in-laws bought the Bonds' Highland Beach cottage, thought that they acquired it in 1925, but '27 or '28 seems more likely.

15. ALL THE WORLD'S A STAGE

1. W. E. B. Du Bois, *The Souls of Black Folk* (1903; reprint, Chicago: McClurg, 1940), 75. *Crimson and Gray,* November 1922; Atlanta University *Bulletin and Catalogue,* 1925–26, 5.

2. Atlanta, City Directory, 1923; Eric D. Walrond, "The Largest Negro Commercial Enterprise in the World," *Forbes,* February 2, 1924, 503; and Alexa Benson Henderson, *Atlanta Life Insurance Company: Guardian of Black Economic Dignity*

(Tuscaloosa: University of Alabama Press, 1990), 45. The widowed Alonzo Herndon remarried in 1915.

3. David Levering Lewis, *When Harlem Was in Vogue* (New York: Vintage Books, 1982), 128, 164. *Tropic Death* appeared in 1925.

4. Walrond, "Largest Negro Enterprise," 503.

5. Ibid., 504. See also August Meier and David Lewis, "History of the Negro Upper Class in Atlanta, Georgia, 1890–1958," *Journal of Negro Education* 28 (Spring 1959): 128–39.

6. Walrond, "Largest Negro Enterprise," 533; Meier and Lewis, "Negro Upper Class in Atlanta," 136.

7. Henderson, *Atlanta Life,* 71, 83; Lorraine Nelson Spritzer and Jean B. Bergmark, *Grace Towns Hamilton and the Politics of Southern Change* (Athens: University of Georgia Press, 1997), 27.

8. Walrond, "Largest Negro Enterprise," 503.

9. Spritzer and Bergmark, *Grace Towns Hamilton,* 17, 20.

10. Ibid., 23, 42.

11. Clarence A. Bacote, *The Story of Atlanta University: A Century of Service, 1865–1965* (Atlanta: Atlanta University Press, 1969), 213; Spritzer and Bergmark, *Grace Towns Hamilton,* 17, 19, 20; E. Franklin Frazier, "Georgia, or the Struggle Against Impudent Inferiority" (originally published in *The Messenger,* June 1924), in Tom Lutz and Susanna Aston, eds., *These United States: African American Essays from the 1920s* (New Brunswick, N.J.: Rutgers University Press, 1996), 92–105.

12. Frazier, "Struggle Against Impudent Inferiority," 102.

13. Ibid., 103.

14. Ibid., 104; Spritzer and Bergmark, *Grace Towns Hamilton,* 40.

15. Walrond, "Largest Negro Enterprise," 104; Bacote, *Story of Atlanta University,* 246; Spritzer and Bergmark, *Grace Towns Hamilton,* 42.

16. Bacote, *Story of Atlanta University,* 169. Until 1913, Morehouse College was known as Atlanta Baptist College.

17. Folder 9, Box 40, YWCA Papers, Sophia Smith Collection, Smith College. See Jacqueline Anne Rouse, *Lugenia Burns Hope: Black Southern Reformer* (Athens: University of Georgia Press, 1989), esp. chap. 4. Myron Winslow Adams, *A History of Atlanta University* (Atlanta: Atlanta University Press, 1930), 43, 48, 49, 61, 67.

18. Meier and Lewis, "Negro Upper Class in Atlanta," 136.

19. Atlanta, City Directories, 1922–1927. Bernard Day, conversations with author, June 1996. and Aaron Day, Jr., "Report of Physical Examination," 1929, United States Army Records. Caroline Bond Day to George Bridgeforth, March 30, 1927, Caroline Bond Day Papers, Peabody Museum, Harvard University.

Josephine Harreld Love and Carole Merritt, conversations with author, April 1998.

20. CBD to Connie Percival, July 26, 1927, Day Papers.

21. Spritzer and Bergmark, *Grace Towns Hamilton,* 14; *Bulletin and Catalogue,* 1924–25, 27.

22. *Scroll,* March 1927.

23. Wenonah Bond Logan, conversations with author. Spritzer and Bergmark, *Grace Towns Hamilton,* 36, 43. Barbara Jordan was elected to the Texas legislature the same fall that Grace Towns Hamilton was elected to the Georgia legislature.

24. *Scroll,* November 1926.

25. Ibid., February and March–April 1924, March 1925, and March 1927.

26. Bacote, *Story of Atlanta University,* 219–20.

27. Caroline Bond Day, "What Shall We Play?" *Crisis,* September 1925, 221–23.

28. Ibid.

29. Federal Writers' Program, *Atlanta: A City of the Modern South* (New York: Smith & Durrell, 1942), 148. Gloria T. Hull, *Color, Sex, and Poetry: Three Women Writers of the Harlem Renaissance* (Bloomington: Indiana University Press, 1987), 173, calls *Little Blue Pigeon* one of Johnson's "now nonexistent plays" about "average Negro life."

30. "Angelina Weld Grimké," in Darlene Clark Hine, ed., *Black Women in America: An Historical Encyclopedia* (Brooklyn, N.Y.: Carlson Publishing, 1993), 504; and Hull, *Color, Sex, and Poetry,* 72.

31. Mary Burrill, *"Aftermath,"* *Liberator,* April 1919; and *"They That Sit in Darkness,"* *Birth Control Review,* 1919.

32. Hull, *Color, Sex, and Poetry,* 124. See, for example, Bettie Wyser, *The Lesbian Myth* (New York: Random House, 1974), 53.

33. Nellie McKay, "Black Women Playwrights in the Harlem Renaissance," in Marita Bonner file, Radcliffe College Archives.

34. Alain Locke, "The Negro in the American Stage," February 1926, 113–19; and "The Drama of Negro Life," *Theater Arts Monthly,* October 1926, 701–7.

35. Caroline Bond Day, "The Pink Hat," *Opportunity,* December 1926, 379–80; Lewis, *When Harlem Was in Vogue,* 113–15, 198–99.

36. Day, "Pink Hat."

37. Ibid.

38. Spritzer and Bergmark, *Grace Towns Hamilton,* xiv.

39. That diversity within the Negro "race" is the central theme of Caroline Bond Day, *A Study of Some Negro-White Families in the United States* (Cambridge: Harvard University, Peabody Museum, 1932), derived from her Radclife M.A. thesis. Day, "Pink Hat."

40. Day, "Pink Hat"; and Day, "What Shall We Play?"

41. Bernard Day and Love, conversations.

42. Ibid.

43. Ibid.

44. Correspondence from Otelia Cromwell appears in the Day Papers. Adelaide Cromwell, conversation with author, November 1997.

45. Bernard Day, conversations; and Hull, *Color, Sex, and Poetry,* 21. Reading between the lines in Lewis, *When Harlem Was in Vogue,* esp. 127, I have assumed that Walrond was bisexual.

46. Lewis, *When Harlem Was in Vogue,* 166–68.

47. Meryl Hooker, "Sisters in Harlem-town: Lesbian Identities in the Harlem Renaissance" (unpublished George Washington University paper, 1994). On sexual dissemblance, see esp. Darlene Clark Hine, "Rape and the Inner Lives of Southern Black Women: Thoughts on the Culture of Dissemblance," *Signs: Journal of Women in Culture and Society* 14, no. 4 (Summer 1989): 912–20.

48. Martina Attille, "Still," 156; and Andrea D. Barnwell, "Like the Gypsy's Daughter; or, Beyond the Potency of Josephine Baker's Eroticism," 84–89, both in Richard Powell et al., *Rhapsodies in Black: Art of the Harlem Renaissance* (Berkeley: University of California Press, 1997).

49. See Hazel Carby, " 'It Jus Be's Dat Way Sometime': The Sexual Politics of Women's Blues," *Radical America* 4 (1986). Lewis, *When Harlem Was in Vogue,* 165.

50. Lewis, *When Harlem Was in Vogue,* 98.

51. See chap. 11 herein.

52. Hull, *Color, Sex, and Poetry,* 140; Gloria T. Hull, ed., *Give Us Each Day: The Diary of Alice Dunbar-Nelson* (New York: Norton, 1984), 25; and CBD to Alice Dunbar-Nelson, April 27, 1927, Day Papers.

53. CBD to Emma Brown, September 18, 1927, CBD to Elizabeth Cook, March 30, 1927, and CBD to Lillian Cooper, April 27, 1927, Day Papers.

54. See *Macbeth, As You Like It, The Tempest,* and *Twelfth Night.* Agnes Mure MacKenzie, "The Women in Shakespeare's Plays," *Theater Arts Monthly,* May 1925.

55. Bernard Day and Love, conversations.

56. See Patricia Ann Palmieri, *In Adamless Eden: The Community of Women Faculty at Wellesley* (New Haven: Yale University Press, 1995).

57. Carby, " 'It Just Be's That Way' "; Colin Spencer, *Homosexuality in History* (New York: Harcourt Brace Jovanovich, 1995), 342–45.

58. Wyser, *Lesbian Myth,* 3, 35, 46.

59. See Hine, "Rape and Southern Black Women"; and Hull, *Color, Sex, and Poetry,* 21. For an extensive discussion of lesbians in this era, see Carroll Smith-Rosenberg, *Disorderly Conduct: Visions of Gender in Victorian America* (New York: Oxford University Press, 1985).

60. Marita O. Bonner, "On Being Young—a Woman—and Colored," *Crisis,* December 1925, 63–65; and Hull, *Color, Sex, and Poetry,* 165. See Du Bois, introduction to *Souls of Black Folk.*

61. Day, "Pink Hat"; Du Bois, *Souls of Black Folk,* 85.

62. Spritzer and Bergmark, *Grace Towns Hamilton,* 41.

63. Logan, conversations. Spritzer and Bergmark, *Grace Towns Hamilton,* 40, argue that Grace and her friends "ridiculed" the "Victorian" campus codes, but "accepted the rules and regulations as given," but I believe that they were somewhat more rebellious.

64. Spritzer and Bergmark, *Grace Towns Hamilton,* 43.

65. *Scroll,* December 1925.

66. Logan, conversations.

67. Henderson, *Atlanta Life,* 48, 50.

68. Ibid., 101–4.

69. Ibid., 100.

70. CBD to Mrs. W. A. Granger, March 21, 1927, Day Papers; and Day, *Some Negro-White Families,* foreword by Earnest A. Hooton, iii.

71. Georgia Douglas Johnson to CBD, n.d.; CBD to T. W. Boyd, June 26, 1927; Margaret Ford Hodge to CBD, October 8, 1927; CBD to Clement Richardson, April 27, 1927; and CBD to Max Yergan, August 18, 1927, Day Papers. Aaron Day then went on to North Carolina Mutual, where he enjoyed a distinguished career.

72. *Crisis,* December 1926, 88; *Bulletin and Catalogue,* 16; and Spritzer and Bergmark, *Grace Towns Hamilton,* 54. Wenonah Bond graduated from Boston University in 1928.

73. Hull, ed., *Give Us Each Day,* 161.

16. PURGATORY: THE POISONED TREE

1. *Colored American,* May 1904, 310.

2. Ibid., and Mark R. Schneider, *Boston Confronts Jim Crow, 1890–1920* (Boston: Northeastern University Press, 1997), 182.

3. Adelaide M. Cromwell, *The Other Brahmins: Boston's Black Upper Class, 1750–1950* (Fayetteville: University of Arkansas Press, 1994), 59; and Robert C. Hayden, *African Americans in Boston: More Than 350 Years* (Boston: Boston Public Library, 1991), 107.

4. Isaac Mullen, U.S. Navy Pension Records, #32105, National Archives. Walter J. Stevens, *Chip on My Shoulder* (Boston: Meador Press, 1946), 31.

5. Schneider, *Boston Confronts Jim Crow,* 6; Jack Beatty, *The Rascal King* (Reading, Mass.: Addison-Wesley, 1992), 155.

6. Hyde Park *Gazette,* February 4 and June 17, 1905. The Boston zoo ultimately was situated, not in Hyde Park, but in nearby Jamaica Plain, where Mayor James Curley lived.

7. John Daniels, *In Freedom's Birthplace: A Study of the Boston Negroes* (Boston: Houghton Mifflin, 1914), 461. Katie Keneally, ed.-in-chief, Boston 200 Neighborhood History Series, *Hyde Park* (Boston, 1976), 7, 16. *Gazette,* March 4, 1911, and January 6, 1912. In fact, most of Hyde Park became Ward 24, not 26.

8. Daniels, *In Freedom's Birthplace,* 127; and J. Anthony Lukas, *Common Ground: A Turbulent Decade in the Lives of Three American Families* (New York: Knopf, 1985), 58.

9. Cromwell, *Other Brahmins,* 13 and passim.

10. Ibid., 72; and Hayden, *African Americans in Boston,* 157. Karl Lindholm, "William Clarence Matthews," *Harvard Magazine,* September–October 1998, 58.

11. *Gazette,* June 18, 1925. Elijah "Pumpsie" Green joined the Red Sox infield in 1959.

12. Paul Adomites, *October's Game* (Alexandria, Va.: Redefinition, 1993), 10–12.

13. Beatty, *Rascal King,* 234.

14. Ibid., 136, 157, 175; and Lukas, *Common Ground,* 58.

15. Kenneth O'Reilly, *Nixon's Piano: Presidents and Racial Politics from Washington to Clinton* (New York: Free Press, 1995), 88–89; and Eugene F. Gordon, "Massachusetts: Land of the Free and Home of the Brave Colored Man," in Tom Lutz and Susanna Ashton, eds., *These "Colored" United States: African American Essays from the 1920s* (New Brunswick, N.J.: Rutgers University Press, 1996), 145–57. Gordon's article first appeared in A. Philip Randolph's journal *The Messenger,* June 1925.

16. Cromwell, *Other Brahmins,* 62.

17. Thomas Dixon's play *The Clansman* was adapted from his novel *The Leopard's Spots.* Schneider, *Boston Confronts Jim Crow,* 122, 146–52; Beatty, *Rascal King,* 179. *Chronicles of the Cinema* (New York: DK Publishing, 1995), 111, 109, 113. Not surprisingly, Griffith's previous epic, *Battle of Elderbush Gulch,* focused on Native American war parties that attacked white women who, in turn, were saved by white men.

18. Beatty, *Rascal King,* 174; and Hayden, *African Americans in Boston,* 41.

19. Beatty, *Rascal King,* 182–84; Stevens, *Chip on My Shoulder* 133; and Lukas, *Common Ground,* 58.

20. Beatty, *Rascal King,* 182–84; and Stevens, *Chip on My Shoulder,* 132–33.

21. *Chronicles of the Cinema,* 113.

22. Schneider, *Boston Confronts Jim Crow,* 122, 146–52; Beatty, *Rascal King,* 211; and *Gazette,* December 12, 1917.

23. *Chronicles of the Cinema,* 123, 128; *Gazette,* August 1, 1917, May 1 and December 4, 1918.

24. Schneider, *Boston Confronts Jim Crow,* 95.

25. Birth certificates and Hyde Park High School transcripts for Elizabeth (Betty), Evelyn, and Frances Mary (Frankie) Bond.

26. John Robert Bond, Jr., U.S. Navy Pension Records, #1448699.

27. Photographs, deeds, and wills of JRB, Jr., in possession of the author. My sincere thanks to Carolyn French, who had the vision to send me these materials a number of years ago when I had no idea of how they might be used.

28. Elaine McCraw Chesnut and Robert Chesnut, conversations with author, January 1995; and Louise Glover Hinds, conversations with author, April 1998. Dedham *Transcript,* December 24, 1926.

29. Elaine McCraw Chesnut, conversations.

30. Ibid.

31. Elaine McCraw Chesnut and Carolyn French confirm this interpretation of Betty Bond's scantly repressed fury.

32. "Graduation Exercises, Hyde Park High School Class of 1922." Hyde Park High School yearbook, *The Black and Blue,* 1923, 39.

33. Keneally et al., *Hyde Park,* 16; and Elizabeth Bond, HPHS transcript. Author's photographs.

34. JRB, Jr., will.

35. JRB, Jr., pension records; Matthew 7:16–17 KJV, Church of the Good Shepherd, parish records; and Bob Chesnut, conversations.

36. Hayden, *African-Americans in Boston,* 131–32. See also Lukas, *Common Ground,* passim.

37. Carolyn French, conversations with author, June 1996, September and November, 1998; Robert Chesnut and Elaine McCraw Chesnut, conversations. Author's photographs.

38. Elaine McCraw Chesnut, conversations; JRB, Jr., pension records. These and subsequent references to syphilis at the Boston Psychopathic Hospital are included in Elmer E. Southard and Harry C. Solomon, *Neurosyphilis: Modern Systematic Diagnosis and Treatment* (1917; reprint, New York: Arno Press, 1973), 31, 68–69, 84–85, 93, 117, 124–25, 131–33, 154–58, 202, 263, 289, 316–18, 356, 457, 471.

39. Southard and Solomon, *Neurosyphilis;* JRB, Jr., pension records.

40. Southard and Solomon, *Neurosyphilis.*

41. JRB, Jr., pension records; and Southard and Solomon, *Neurosyphilis.*

42. JRB, Jr., pension records; Betty and Frankie Bond's HPHS records; Wenonah Bond Logan, conversations with author; Margot Webb, conversations with author, June 1998; Carolyn French and Elaine McCraw Chesnut, conversations; and Southard and Solomon, *Neurosyphilis.*

43. Southard and Solomon, *Neurosyphilis.*

44. Ibid.; and Logan, Elaine McCraw Chesnut, and French, conversations.

45. Logan and Elaine McCraw Chesnut, conversations; and JRB, Jr., pension records.

46. Southard and Solomon, *Neurosyphilis.*

47. Logan and Elaine McCraw Chesnut, conversations; and Southard and Solomon, *Neurosyphilis.*

48. Logan, conversations.

49. Rebecca Lee Crumpler, M.D., *A Book of Medical Discourses in Two Parts* (Boston: Cashman, Keating, 1883), 142.

50. Gordon, "Massachusetts," 151–52; and Dorothy West, *The Living Is Easy* (1948; reprint, New York: Arno Press, 1969), 125.

51. Story related by Mary E. Pitts, who grew up in Hyde Park. These chapters never could have been completed without her assistance.

52. W. W. Scott, *History of Orange County, Virginia* (1907; reprint, Baltimore: Regional Publishing, 1974), 114, 115, 133, 169, 202.

53. Philip Long, conversation with author, July 1996.

54. French, conversations.

55. Writers' Program, Work Projects Administration, *The Negro in Virginia* (1940; reprint, Winston-Salem, N.C.: John T. Blair, 1994), 262. Scott, *Orange County,* 40, 71, 137, 166, 275. French and Webb, conversations.

56. French, conversations.

57. Ibid.

58. Ibid.; and WPA, *Negro in Virginia,* 281, 285–86, 364, 368.

59. Scott, *Orange County,* 47, 133; and WPA, *Negro in Virginia,* 289. Scott (and other reports from the white community) maintain that whites "gave" the Blue Run Baptist Church to local blacks. Carolyn French, however, found the deed that documented its sale. Conversations with Carolyn French and Charity Hunt about Big Meeting Sundays in Orange County, Virginia. And see especially Norma Jean Darden and Carole Darden, *Spoonbread and Strawberry Wine* (Garden City, N.Y.: Doubleday, 1978), passim.

60. Philip Long, conversation.

61. Gordon, "Massachusetts," 146.

62. West, *Living Is Easy,* 47.

63. Gordon, "Massachusetts," 146, 150; Schneider, *Boston Confronts Jim Crow,* 163. See esp. Cromwell, *Other Brahmins.*

64. Keneally et al., *Hyde Park,* 12; *Colored American,* November 1909, 331; and *Gazette,* July 21 and December 1, 1915, and March 7, 1917. Political polls taken in the 1990s show that a majority of white Americans not only consider African Americans inferior, but also less patriotic.

65. Schneider, *Boston Confronts Jim Crow,* 135, 158, 161.

66. West, *Living Is Easy*, 5. Some sources have argued that Dorothy West's father was a southern-born former slave, but his West Indian origins seem to have more solid grounding. Adelaide Cromwell, conversations with the author, suggests that West often gave contradictory stories about her background.

67. Gordon, "Massachusetts," 150.

68. Ibid., 146, 150; and Schneider, *Boston Confronts Jim Crow*, 21, 135.

69. Gordon, "Massachusetts," 150.

70. Robert Chesnut, conversations. When Bob Bond applied for further disability benefits in the late 1920s, the navy would not acknowledge that he was a foreign-war veteran because the fighting in Cuba had ended before he volunteered in late 1898 and he was never transferred to the Philippines as he requested. The local VFW branch, however, of which Bob Bond became a member after 1930, did not make that distinction. Author's photograph.

17. NIGHTS WHEN THE MUSIC STOPPED

1. Robert Chesnut, conversations with author, January 1995.

2. My thanks to Susann Miller for information about the Robinson cars. G. N. Georgano, *The Complete Encyclopedia of Motorcars: 1885 to the Present* (London: George Rainbird, 1968); and Edward R. Peterson, "Robinson Meets the Pope: The Cars of John Robinson," in *Automobile Quarterly*, July 1994, 32–41.

3. Peterson, "Robinson Meets the Pope," 35; David Wallechinsky and Irving Wallace, *The People's Almanac* (Garden City, N.Y.: Doubleday, 1975), 591.

4. Peterson, "Robinson Meets the Pope," 36.

5. Ibid.; and Dorothy West, *The Living Is Easy* (1948; reprint, New York: Arno Press, 1969), 127.

6. Robert Chesnut, conversations.

7. Adelaide M. Cromwell, *The Other Brahmins: Boston's Black Upper Class, 1750–1950* (Fayetteville: University of Arkansas Press, 1994), 56.

8. Hyde Park *Gazette*, October 31, 1908. Author's 1908 photo of Carrie and Wenonah in Hyde Park. Robert Chesnut, conversations.

9. Robert Chesnut, conversations; and Louise Glover Hinds, conversations with author, April 1998. Robert C. Hayden, *African Americans in Boston: More than 350 Years* (Boston: Boston Public Library, 1991), 79, notes that Henry C. Turner started a successful livery business with horses, carriages, and coachmen for hire in 1900, then gradually changed over to motorized conveyances as automobiles gained in popularity. The image of black men chauffeuring whites was reinforced and popularized in the motion picture *Driving Miss Daisy*.

10. Chesnut, conversations; and Dedham *Daily Transcript*, March 19, 1986.

11. Chesnut, conversations.

12. *Gazette,* July 12, 1916, and October 3, 1917.

13. Robert Chesnut, conversations.

14. Katie Keneally, ed.-in-chief, Boston 200 Neighborhood History Series, *Hyde Park* (Boston, 1976), 13; Robert Chesnut, conversations; and *Gazette,* October 13, 1920. Jim Lensveld, *Harley-Davidson: Factory and Custom Dream Machines* (San Diego: Thunder Bay Press, 1996), 8–9.

15. Robert Chesnut, conversations; and *Gazette,* May 2, 1917, and April 13, 1918.

16. *Gazette,* May 2, June 6, August 1, and October 3, 1917, April 3, May 1, and September 6, 1918; *Transcript* March 29, 1919.

17. Howard Zinn, *A People's History of the United States, 1492–Present,* rev. and updated ed. (New York: Harper Perennial, 1995), 361. *Transcript,* January 5 and June 1, 1918; *Crisis,* December 1917, 83. Robert Chesnut, conversations.

18. Robert Chesnut, conversations.

19. Ibid.

20. Reid Badger, *A Life in Ragtime: A Biography of James Reese Europe* (New York: Oxford University Press, 1995), 205–6, 213–19.

21. Ibid., 213–19.

22. Ibid.

23. Ibid.

24. Ibid.

25. Ibid.

26. Robert Chesnut, conversations. Sources disagree as to whether the major roundup of Boston radicals occurred in 1919 or 1920. Mark R. Schneider, *Boston Confronts Jim Crow, 1890–1920* (Boston: Northeastern University Press, 1997), 161; and Roberta Strauss Feuerlicht, *Justice Crucified: The Story of Sacco and Vanzetti* (New York: McGraw-Hill, 1977), 111–12.

27. "Church of Good Shepherd," church history, n.p., n.d.

28. Elizabeth Brandeis, "A Type of Changing New England," *Radcliffe Magazine,* February 1917, 40–42. Wallechinsky and Wallace, *People's Almanac,* 218.

29. Brandeis, "Changing New England."

30. Ibid.

31. David Felix, *Protest: Sacco-Vanzetti and the Intellectuals* (Bloomington: Indiana University Press, 1965), 66; Francis Russell, *Tragedy in Dedham: The Story of the Sacco-Vanzetti Case* (New York: McGraw-Hill, 1971), 126. Conversations with Louise Glover Hinds, May 1998.

32. Osmond K. Fraenkel, *The Sacco-Vanzetti Case* (New York: Russell & Russell, 1969), 39; Russell, *Tragedy in Dedham,* 126, 130, 137. *Transcript,* June 11, 1921.

33. *Transcript,* June 11, 18, and July 2, 1921; Russell, *Tragedy in Dedham,* 138.

34. Felix Frankfurter, "The Crime of Radicalism," in Loren Baritz, ed., *The Culture of the Twenties* (New York: Bobbs-Merrill, 1970), 108–144; and Fraenkel, *Sacco-Vanzetti Case*, 5, 10–11, 84.

35. *Transcript*, July 16, 1921.

36. Frankfurter, "Crime of Radicalism," 108–44.

37. Ibid., 124.

38. Russell, *Tragedy in Dedham*, 214; Frankfurter, "Crime of Radicalism," 126; and *Transcript*, July 16 and August 4, 1921.

39. *The Messenger,* November 1921, 284, and June 1922, 430. Du Bois's magazine for youths, *The Brownies' Book,* did mention the trial (see chap. 15), but nothing appeared in *Crisis* at the time. In 1952, Du Bois compared what he considered the miscarriage of justice in Dedham to the Rosenberg trial. My thanks to David Levering Lewis, Du Bois's biographer, for telling me about Du Bois's opposition to the Sacco-Vanzetti executions. I have seen no copies of Monroe Trotter's Boston-based newspaper, *The Guardian,* from this period.

40. Russell, *Tragedy in Dedham*, 219.

41. Ibid., 340; *The Messenger,* June 1922; and Frankfurter, "Crime of Radicalism," 131.

42. Robert Chesnut, conversations.

43. Arthur A. Ashe, Jr., *A Hard Road to Glory: A History of the African American Athlete, 1919–1945* (New York: Warner, 1988), 79–80; and Daphne Abeel, "Edward Orval Gourdin," *Harvard Magazine,* November–December 1997, 44–45.

44. Eugene F. Gordon, "Massachusetts: Land of the Free and Home of the Brave Colored Man," in Tom Lutz and Susanna Ashton, eds., *These "Colored" United States: African American Essays from the 1920s* (New Brunswick, N.J.: Rutgers University Press, 1996), 145–57.

45. Robert Chesnut, conversations.

46. Ibid.; and Wenonah Bond Logan, conversations.

47. Logan and Robert Chesnut, conversations.

48. Robert Chesnut, conversations.

49. Hyde Park High School yearbook, *The Black and Blue,* 1928, 14, 76, 87; Hinds and Robert Chesnut, conversations.

50. Rebecca Lee Crumpler, *A Book of Medical Discourses* (Boston: Cashman, Keating, 1883), 142. Hinds, conversations.

51. Robert Chesnut, conversations.

52. Ibid.

53. Jer. 29:5–6 KJV.

54. Frankfurter, "Crime of Radicalism," 134–35.

55. Hinds, conversations.

56. Russell, *Tragedy in Dedham*, 348.

57. Robert Chesnut, conversations.

58. Ibid.

59. Isaac Mullen, U.S. Navy Pension Records, #32105, National Archives. Mullen died June 5, 1930, at the Soldiers' Home in Chelsea, Massachusetts.

60. One wing of the Bonds' house where Tooty Bond Howley and her son lived at the time burned in the 1930s. Many of the family's photographs and memorabilia were lost.

ACKNOWLEDGMENTS, *and* COMING *to* CONCLUSIONS

AFTER EMMA THOMAS BOND died in 1926, her descendants led varied lives. Her daughter, Tooty Bond Howley, was a voracious reader, yet had to support herself by working as a maid. Tooty's son, Edward, a gifted musician, served his country during World War II but died a recluse at the Bond family home in Hyde Park. Lena Bond Chesnut's sons were more prosperous than their cousin. David earned a Ph.D., taught, became a corporate manager, and was happily married for many decades. Bob Chesnut, now the only surviving descendant of his generation, was a musician like his father. His wife, Betty, is the daughter of Edward Gourdin, the Harvard man who won a silver medal at the 1924 Paris Olympics.

Bob and Osie Bond and their three girls suffered continuing episodes of neurological distress, but Bob and his youngest daughter, Frankie, kept the business in Hyde Park going for many years. Betty, the oldest, who hated her tan skin and curly hair, "led a very tragic life," a relative recalled. Evelyn (in the middle) married and divorced twice, then got her wits about her enough to attend college and teach school on the West Coast where no one knew her racial background and she was no longer labeled "a Negro." After her parents' deaths Frankie also moved to California, where she "bleached her hair blond so she'd look like Jean Harlow."*

Emma and John's eldest son, my grandfather J. Percy Bond, died in 1929, only three years after his mother. Friends believed that he worked himself to death supporting his beloved wife. When the fair Georgia passed away two decades later, her children quarreled bitterly over whether her death certificate should read "Negro" or "white."

Caroline Stewart Bond Day acquired a master's degree in anthropology from Radcliffe College. She ultimately followed her husband Aaron to Durham, North Carolina, where she continued in academia to the extent that her deteriorating

* Conversation with Margot Webb.

health allowed. Aaron became an executive with North Carolina Mutual Life Insurance Company, one of the country's largest black-owned businesses. He and Carrie had no biological children, but a foster son, Bernard Day, still resides in that city.

Percy and Georgia's son, Jack, and his first wife had two children—another Jack and (yes, really) Jill. Jack (the father) served in World War II, then worked for a United Nations agency and spent his later years at a historically black college. My cousin Jack (John Percy Bond, III) and his wife, Carol, have two adult offspring. Their daughter has children of her own, and their son, Philip Sawyer Bond, reinvigorated a family tradition of patriotic maritime service with his graduation from the United States Naval Academy. Philip's great-great-grandfather, John Robert Bond, might have foreseen his descendant's interests, skills, and patriotism, but the opportunity for someone of their race to attend one of the country's prestigious service academies probably would have seemed beyond his wildest imaginings.

My mother, Wenonah Bond, finished her undergraduate studies at Boston University where she lived at the school's International House. Sometimes curious foreign students would ask her: "What are you? Japanese? Polynesian?" "No," she answered, "I am what is called an American Negro."* After several years of further education and international travel, she married Arthur Logan.

My father volunteered to serve his country in World War II, but refused to deny his Negro identity, though his complexion and features belied that reality. The U.S. Navy determined that it had no place or use for a "colored" physician with eight years of professional seniority who would have had to outrank its white junior medical officers. Wenonah continued her work with social service agencies—especially the YWCA. One Y colleague was Ellen Craft Dammond, who is descended from the escaped-slave-abolitionists William and (her namesake) Ellen Craft, who sailed to Liverpool during John Robert Bond's childhood, and also from the Trotter family of Boston. Wenonah and Ellen once said to each other: "We really should talk about our parents' early years together in Hyde Park," but they never did.†

The lives of the Bond family and those tied to them contributed to the evolution of this book, but to complete it, I also needed help from varied institutions. They include: Alabama State University Library, Baker Library at the Harvard Business School, Beaufort (North Carolina) Historical Association, Birmingham Public Library, Black Civil War Union Sailors' Project, Boston Public Library, Dedham Historical Society and Public Library, Fisk University Archives, Fort Macon (North Carolina) State Park, the George Washington University Library,

---

* Conversation with Doris Ridgely Moses.
† Conversation with Ellen Craft Dammond.

Harvard University Archives, the Herndon Home, College of the Holy Cross Archives, Hyde Park Historical Association and Public Library, Isle of Wight Historical Association and County Museum, Library of Congress, Lincoln (Illinois) Public Library, the Masons' Grand Temple Library, Massachusetts State Library, Liverpool's Merseyside Museum, Montclair Historical Society, Moorland-Spingarn Research Center at Howard University, National Archives, Naval Historical Center and Medical Library, New Bedford Public Library, Norfolk State University Archives, Peabody Museum Archives, Portsmouth Public Library, Prairie View University Library, Radcliffe College Archives, Sam Houston Regional Library, the Schomburg Library, Selma Public Library, Spinner Publications, Swem Library at the College of William and Mary, Tuskegee Institute Library and Archives, University of Chicago Archives, U.S. Naval Medical Center in Portsmouth, Washingtoniana Collection at the D.C. Public Library, and the Worcester Historical Society.

A project such as this inevitably becomes a collective effort with expertise needed in many categories. Tyler Anbinder, Eileen Boris, Cynthia Harrison, and Richard Stott provided me with excellent advice on immigration and citizenship.

On England and especially Liverpool, I received help from Valerie Burton, Jeff Kerr-Ritchie, Stephen Small, James Walvin, and Carlton Wilson. Jane Dixon, Joyce Dotson, John Fesq, George Frye, Meg Graham, and James West provided valued assistance on the Episcopal Church, while concerning the YWCA, I relied on Dorothy Height, Adrienne Lash-Jones, and Hortense Tate.

The military (both the army and navy) was an area where I needed ample assistance. I thank David Blight, Charles Brewer, Wesley A. Brown, Dennis Burroughs, Linda de Pauw, Dan Dyer, Bill Gould, Walter Hill, Lisa King, Nia Kuumba, Becky Livingstone, William Maxwell, William Miles, John W. Mountcastle, Bernard Nalty, Jackie Ostrowski, John Peterson, Krewarsky Salter, Albert Scipio, John Slonaker, Ron Spector, Richard Sumrall, Michael Winston, and Bob Wright for answering my endless questions and providing materials I needed.

When it came to the Virginia Tidewater, I welcomed the help of Tommy Bogger, F. Nash Boney, T. H. Conaway, Marion Everett, Amelia and Roger Healey, David Hart, Michael Hucles, Gene-Anne Polk, John Vlach, and Rafia Zafar.

Concerning the chapters about Boston and Hyde Park, the wisdom of John Antoniazzi, Dickson Bruce, Jr., Adelaide Cromwell, Lucy T. Cromwell, Ellen Craft Dammond, George Fry, Louise Glover Hinds, George Merry, Susann Miller, Virginia Craft Rose, Henry Scannell, Werner Sollors, Barbara Wicker, and Dorothy Zaccaria proved invaluable. More specifically, on the Radcliffe College segments, I appreciated the contributions of Althea Treadwell Allen, Gladys Ottalea Bolton, Edith Manwell Chamberlain, Jessie Hubbard Farnham, Estelle Frankfurter, Edna Ryan Gilmore, Dorothy Summers Green, Louise Cook Hill,

Evelyn Beard Hoffman, Jane Knowles, Evelyn Gilbert Montgomery, Elizabeth Benton Swan, Amy Brown Townsend, and Gertrude Knowlton Wilson.

Alabama, too, required a bevy of helpers. Among the most important were J. Mason Davis, Ann Fitt, Kate Gamble, Jean Martin, Bertrand Perry, Marjorie Longenecker White, Dan Williams, and Cynthia Wilson. My investigations on Texas brought me a whole new category of information providers. They include Penny Clark, LeRoy Frasier, Brenda Holmes, Neal Iverson, Helen Jones, Kevin Ladd, Robert Schaadt, Minniezine Taylor, and Loulee Woods.

I also depended on others to supplement my meager grasp of anthropology. Katya Gibel Azoulay, Lee Baker, Paulette Curtis, Desley Deacon, Sarah Demb, Faye Harrison, Yvonne Jones, and Elizabeth Sandager gave invaluable assistance in that area, as did Allida Black, Katherine Colman, Janice Delaney, Jan Herman, C. Carnot Evans, Amy Robinson, and Barbara Smith on questions of health, medicine, and sexuality.

When it came to Washington, D.C., and Highland Beach, I sought the expertise of Thelma Austin, Merle Moses Bowser, Inez Browne, Rupert Clark, Elizabeth Clark-Lewis, Roxana Deane, Jo Ellen El-Bashir, Hortense Fitzgerald, Sandra Fitzpatrick, Maria Goodwin, Amelia Cobb Gray, Anastasia Holmes, Leon Langhorne, Ray Langston, Dorothy Davis Lucas, Doris Ridgely Moses, Harry Robinson, and Eve Wilkins.

Those angels who lie between and fall beyond category are Rae Alexander-Minter, Millie Barbee, Ed Berkowitz, James Bowman, Millicent Brown, A'Lelia Bundles, Ralph Carlson, Bill Clement, Betty Collier-Thomas, Maceo Dailey, Karen Dalton, Cyndy Donnell, Carolyn French, Jeanette Greenwood, Tom Holloway, Jim Holton, Beth Howse, Gail Jackins, Mary Beth Jamison, W. R. Jones, Marguerite Kelly, Kent Leslie, David Levering Lewis, Phillip Long, Josephine Harreld Love, Joan Meecham, Jerry Melendrez, Carole Merritt, Daniel Meyer, Linda Miller, Carol Moseley-Braun, James O'Toole, Adell Patton, Eleanor Hamilton Payne, Charles Pitts, Ethel Read, Lorraine Elena Roses, Leslie Rowland, Mark Savolis, Frank Schubert, Beth Shepard, Janet Sims-Wood, Elinor Sinnette, Arnold Taylor, Rosalyn Terborg-Penn, Emory Tolbert, Jan van Sertima, Barbara Walker, Linda Washington, Michael Weeks, Donna Wells, and Elizabeth Williamson. Sincere apologies to any of my valued contributors whom I have overlooked because I scribbled their names onto scraps of paper that disappeared into my archival clutter.

In addition, my son-in-law Ficre Ghebreyesus became my valued photographic consultant while Hazel Edwards brought loving and meticulous magic to the maps. Elizabeth Alexander, Richard Blackett, Charles Blockson, Carol Bolsey, Bea Stith Clark, Alston Fitts III, Vanessa Gamble, Michelle Gates-Moresi, Bob Hayden, Sandy Holloway, Jim Horton, Ray Jirran, Helen Haverty King, LaSalle D. Leffall, Jr., Maggie Morton, Norma Myers, Rachel Pollin, Jean Rather, Debra

Ann Reid, Nick Salvatore, Mary Martha Thomas, and Odessa Woolfolk hold a special place in my heart because they read and advised on various pieces of my evolving manuscript. Joseph P. Reidy and Mary E. Pitts were uniquely important readers. Both slogged through long, unwieldy chapters and patiently pointed out errors of fact, nuance, and syntax as I tried to bring order out of chaos. Willard Gatewood read and critiqued every chapter, kept my spirits up with his contagious enthusiasm about the Bonds and their worlds, then insisted on reading the entire final draft. He is the book's godfather.

My literary agent and longtime friend Ron Goldfarb believed in this project from the start and guided me to Pantheon Books. Erroll McDonald, a superb editor and publisher, encouraged me, tactfully corrected my mistakes, reshaped awkward passages, and tried to pare down my verbosity—for which I am eternally grateful. He and the matchless Altie Karper and her crack team—Susan Norton, Kristen Bearse, Johanna Roebas, and Marge Anderson—efficiently and artfully steered the book to its completion.

Family members contributed as well. Elaine McCraw Chesnut—who had been born in Bob and Osie Bond's home, lived next door to Tooty Bond Howley, then married David Chesnut—welcomed me into her home and told me stories from her own childhood and memories shared by her late husband. Bob Chesnut was reluctant at first, but ultimately proved a wonderful source. Carrie and Aaron Day's foster son, Bernard, greeted me as a long-lost friend though I had not seen him in fifty years, and became a gold mine of previously unimagined information. My cousin Jack Bond, and his wife, Carol, graciously talked with me, fed me bounteously, and introduced me to Ruth Bond, my uncle's widow and a woman of great discernment, who delighted me with stories about her late husband. Thelma Scott Bryant, Betty Chesnut, Maria Corman, Billy Gilchrist, Lulelia Walker Harrison, Charity Hunt, Margot Webb, and my Lieb and Ghebreyesus in-laws are other relatives who assisted me in varied ways. I thank them one and all, but accept full responsibility for any remaining errors of fact and judgment.

But more than it owes to those kinfolk, this book has been built on memories that I retain about my grandmother Georgia Fagain Stewart Bond, who lived with my parents and me when I was a child. There also were stories from, and recollections of, my paternal aunts Myra Logan and Ruth Logan Roberts, and my maternal aunt Carrie Bond Day. Without her *Study of Some Negro-White Families in the United States,* published in 1932, my book would never have been possible.

I followed Carrie to Radcliffe College, but gleaned my most valued education decades later at Howard University, where she had taught in the years prior to my birth. Now I teach at another major university in Washington, one that black Americans could not even have attended when Wenonah and Jack Bond reached college age in this city. Most of this family saga has been composed here in our majestic, flawed, still undemocratic, but no longer *legally* segregated nation's capital, where my Bond grandparents arrived just before the Great War.

It also pleased me to work at our weekend home by Chesapeake Bay, no more than a hefty stone's throw from the all-Negro enclave at Highland Beach, where Percy and Georgia, my mother, Carrie, and Jack spent summers in the 1920s. The house is a day's sail and a hundred-and-fifty years removed from Hampton Roads, where Emma Thomas grew up a slave, and met her future husband, the "coloured" English seaman John Robert Bond, when he was hospitalized, near death during the United States' Civil War.

My late mother, in conversations, stories, letters, songs, photographs, and other memorabilia, supplied much of the material that I have attempted to evoke, unravel, understand, and reknit here. This very long book began in 1994 as a very short essay in her memory. I love, think about, and miss her still.

This effort, however, is for the living, for generations to come more than those past. Until recently, neither my husband nor I knew that John Robert Bond's English-Irish mother had been Eliza—probably Elizabeth—like our own daughter. Elizabeth and our son, Mark, great-great-grandchildren of the almost illiterate John and Emma, are caring, brilliant, and creative (excuse me, for they befog my vision and consume my heart) professors. Elizabeth's luminous poetry—which she writes in her snug New England house, much like that of the early Massachusetts Bonds—evokes her familial and cultural heritage. Mark works in national politics, teaches constitutional law, and plumbs the depths of our most precious, significant, and formative (though imperfect) American document.

The central person in my life is my love and husband of forty years, Clifford Alexander. He has sustained me splendidly throughout this venture. Over time, the Bonds became his family as well. He made this project a marvelous common journey, and his perceptive readings, occasional (and very apt) criticism, and ceaseless encouragement carried me through. Words fail me! What a trial I must have been—but he never complained.

As the work unfolded, we were blessed with grandchildren, the most perfect of gifts. It is they to whom I dedicate this book. As this tumultuous century staggers toward its close, Mark and his wife Amy's son, Jonah—his name evoking his great-great-great-grandfather Bond's seafaring life—and their daughter, Maya, though six generations, a century-and-a-half, and several surnames distance them from their original American ancestors, now have become keepers of the flame for the first citizens Bond.

And soon, according to his East African forebears' longstanding traditions, looking back and seeking his roots through seven generations, my second grandson will learn to say:

I, Solomon Kebede Ghebreyesus, am the first born of Elizabeth Alexander and of Ficre Ghebreyesus, who came to this country from Asmara, Eritrea. My mother Elizabeth is the child of Clifford and Adele Logan Alexander, and my grandmother Adele is Arthur and Wenonah Bond Logan's only daughter. Percy and Georgia Bond begot my great-grandmother Wenonah, and my great-great-grandfather Percy was the eldest son of John Robert and Emma Thomas Bond. That same John Robert Bond (who sailed to New Bedford, Massachusetts, from Liverpool, England, in 1862, so that he might help free the American slaves) was the only child of the Negro Englishman James Bond and the Irishwoman Eliza Kelly.*

This has been a chronicle of their lives.

---

* I thank the Ghebreyesus and Berhe families for sharing this beautiful Eritrean tradition.

INDEX